The Morning Chronicle's

LABOUR AND THE POOR

VOLUME IV

THE METROPOLITAN DISTRICTS

The Morning Chronicle's

LABOUR AND THE POOR

VOLUME IV

THE METROPOLITAN DISTRICTS

HENRY MAYHEW

Edited By
Rebecca Watts & Kevin Booth

Ditto Books
www.dittobooks.co.uk

First Published by Ditto Books 2020

A catalogue record for this book is available
from the British Library

ISBN 978-1-913515-04-1 (hardback)
ISBN 978-1-913515-14-0 (paperback)

Cover Image:
Smithfield Market, London
From "Illustrated London"
W. I. Bicknell & Albert Henry Payne
Published 1846
Image courtesy of The British Library

"And you see, the worst of it is this here—children's labour is of such value now in our trade that there's more brought into the business every year, so that it's really for all the world like breeding slaves."

Contents

List of Illustrations

Preface

This work attempts to be a faithful reproduction of the "Labour and the Poor" letters as printed in *The Morning Chronicle.* Only obvious typographical errors and omissions have been corrected. Variations in the spelling and hyphenation of words have largely been retained. We hope any such inconsistencies prove to be of some historical interest to the reader.

As much as possible we have tried to recreate the original layout and styling of the text and all factual tables have been reproduced as closely to the originals as possible with only minimal alterations made where necessary to improve readability.

Not all letters were titled. Where missing we have added titles to the Table of Contents to assist navigation and explanation of content. The letters themselves are as per the originals.

A handful of illustrations have been added to each volume. These did not appear in the original text but hopefully provide added interest.

R. W.
K. B.

vii

Introduction

In 1849 a leading London-based newspaper, *The Morning Chronicle*, undertook an investigation into the working and living conditions of the poor throughout England and Wales in the hope that their findings might lead to much needed change.

The reputed catalyst for their "Labour and the Poor" series was an article written by Henry Mayhew recording a journey into Bermondsey, one of the most deprived districts of London, which was printed in September 1849. Following this it was proposed that an in-depth investigation be carried out and "Special Correspondents", the investigators, were selected and distributed around the country. The first article or "Letter" appeared on the 18th of October 1849 and the series would run for almost 2 years and 222 letters.

The well-known and respected writers and journalists recruited for the task included Henry Mayhew who was assigned to the Metropolitan districts, Angus Bethune Reach to the Manufacturing districts, Alexander Mackay and Shirley Brooks to the Rural districts and Charles Mackay to investigate the cities of Birmingham and Liverpool. The author of the letters from Wales is as yet unknown.

The "Labour and the Poor" letters were extremely popular at the time, being widely read throughout the nation and even abroad. The revelations in them caused quite a stir amongst the middle and upper classes of Victorian society. *Letters to the Editor* poured in with donations for specific cases of distress that appeared in the letters and also for the general alleviation of the suffering of the poor. A special fund was set up by *The Morning Chronicle* to collect and distribute these donations.

These *Letters to the Editor* have been included in this series, predominantly in the Metropolitan district volumes whose letters elicited the majority of responses. They provide a unique window into the thoughts and sentiments of the Victorian readership as they react to the incredible accounts of misery and desperation being unveiled.

The Morning Chronicle's extraordinary and unsurpassed "Labour and the Poor" investigation provides an unparalleled insight into the people of the period, their living and working conditions, their feelings, their language, their sufferings and their struggles for survival amidst the poverty and destitution of 19th century Britain. An investigation of such magnitude had never before been attempted and the undertaking was truly of epic proportions. Its impact at the time was profound. Its historical importance today is without question.

LABOUR AND THE POOR.

THE METROPOLITAN DISTRICTS.

[FROM OUR SPECIAL CORRESPONDENT.]

ON THE WORKERS IN WOOD AND THE SUPPLY OF THE MATERIAL.

LETTER LVII.

I now return to treat of the condition and earnings of the London Artizans.

The most convenient and systematic arrangement of the several classes of handicrafts is, as I have before said, according to the materials operated upon; and, conformably with this classification, I find that there are twelve different kinds of *skilled* workmen:—1. The workers in wool, silk, cotton, and the other textile materials. 2. The workers in skin, hair, &c. 3. The workers in woollen, silk, cotton, and leather manufactures. 4. The workers in wood, ivory, &c. 5. The workers in osier, cane, reed, rush, and straw. 6. The workers in brick and stone. 7. The workers in glass and earthenware. 8. The workers in metal. 9. The workers in paper. 10. The workers at printing. 11. The workers connected with the Fine Arts (as drawing, painting, music, &c.) 12. The manufacturers of chemicals.

This, I believe, exhausts the whole of the arts and manufactures. Every kind of artisan, mechanic, or handicraftsman, therefore, is included in one or other of the above orders of skilled labourers. Of many of these I have already treated at considerable length; and I shall proceed to inquire into the condition and earnings of the others as time and occasion may serve. At present I purpose devoting a few letters to the *workers in wood.*

These form a very considerable class, and include many handicrafts which the division of labour has long rendered distinct. Among the most important are carpenters and joiners, cabinet makers, chair makers, coach makers, wheelwrights, shipbuilders, coopers, sawyers, and turners—numbering, in London alone, upwards of 40,000 operatives and 3,500 masters. The numerical strength of the whole of the metropolitan workers in wood, at the time of taking the last census, amounted to 52,262; but of these, according to the "Post-office Directory," a considerable number (nearly 5,000) are masters—so that, deducting these, and allowing at the same time for the increase of population since 1841, it may be safely said that the entire number of working men in London connected with the fashioning of timber, is upwards of 50,000.

In my next letter I shall give a statement of the number of operatives and masters connected with each of the several handicrafts appertaining to this branch of art; at present I shall confine myself to the supply of the material.

The use of an article of such general application as timber exhibits forcibly the social and industrial progress of a people. It is of even more importance to a nation than iron or coal, being one of the principal materials used in the construction of houses, furniture, ships, boats, carts, and carriages. For each of these a different kind of wood is generally used, derived mostly from a different soil. Our houses are made principally of pine, our furniture of mahogany, our ships of oak, and our carts of ash. Most of these woods are imported from abroad; for, owing to the deficiency of our home supplies, the main part of the timber used for "framing" and "finishing" the houses in which we live, or for constructing the bedsteads on which we sleep, the chairs on which we sit, and the tables at which we eat, originally grew in some far-distant forest. The ships that we sail in, and the carts in which our goods are carried, are, however, chiefly of home produce.

Concerning the several uses to which the different kinds of wood are applied, I have obtained the following account from one of the most intelligent men belonging to the trade in the metropolis. The timber which takes precedence in point of importance over all others in this maritime country is the English oak, of which our ships are principally constructed. English oak supplies the best quality of wood, Baltic oak the next, while the American oak is the poorest of all. The number of English oak logs employed in the building of a vessel of 1,000 tons burden, including all the frame and floor timbers, is 864. African oak and teak logs, to the number of 90, supply the material for the beams, and the same quality of wood is used for the shelves, water-way, keelson, &c., for which purposes 56 logs are consumed; the planking inside and out, which is also of teak and African oak, requires not less than 926 planks; the average number of planks cut from each teak or African oak log being three. To form the keel, elm is used, and six logs supply the quantity required. Of Dantzic three and four inch deals, 500 are laid down to form the decks. The masts are of teakwood, Dantzic, or red fir wood. When the mast is in three pieces, it is dowelled and hooped together. English oak logs are not now cut for planking, hence for every 1,000 ton ship nearly 1,500 logs or trees are consumed. Oak timber, in addition to the uses of ship-builders, is used largely for furniture, staves, the frame-work of machinery, and—in some parts of the country—for gates and palings. It resists decay, or the depredations of insects, longer than most other woods, and an oak cabinet, before iron and fireproof safes were known, was accounted one of the safest depositories for deeds or valuable property. When York Minster was burnt the old oaken beams of the roof which escaped destruction were found per-fectly sound. Some had grown nearly black; while others, when cut up for souvenirs, presented hardly a darker hue than that of new oak-wood. Oak, in olden times, was also largely used for the frames of pic-tures, mirrors, and for the ornamental carved work of cathedrals and churches. The bark of the oak supplies an important article for one of our manufactures—viz., leather. Sir Humphry Davy prepared a table, showing the quantity of extractive matter and tan in 100 parts of sev-eral substances used by tanners. The white inner bark of young oak gives 77 parts; and the coloured or middle bark, 19. The entire bark of the oak gives 29; that of the elm 13, and that of the common willow 11. Elm, a close-grained and long-enduring wood, is used for coffins. No other material, it is believed, is employed in London, but in the country the cheaper coffins are sometimes made of deal. Elm is also employed largely for wheelers' work. Ash supplies the material for carts, barrows, handles for tools, and oars. Beech is made into chairs, bedsteads, shoemakers' lasts and trees, saddle-trees, and for other art-icles, where a particular shape, and the retention of that shape, are de-sirable. It is also worked largely by tool-makers. Box is used by turn-ers, and (as it is the closest-grained wood of any) by wood-engravers, the best and largest blocks being brought from Turkey. Yew is little used now comparatively, but it has been made into presses, and (in some country places) into coffins. Walnut is the wood of which gun-stocks are made, and within the last few years it has come into use for articles of furniture. It is an exceedingly knotty wood, and was formerly considered so difficult to work that a walnut-tree cabinet, a century ago, was as valuable as curious. Fir and pines (deal) are the material of which scaffoldings, masts, ladders, flooring, roofing, doors, window-frames, and shop-fronts are constructed. Larch is used for buildings in the country. For the last ten years it has been in extensive demand, too, for railway sleepers. The once unproductive hills which, as well in Scotland as in Cumberland and Westmoreland, have (many of them within the present century) been covered with larch plantations, have thus supplied a cheap and plentiful kind of timber for a purpose never dreamed of when the trees were planted. The wood of the apple and pear trees is used for butter-moulds and similar purposes. Sycamore is required sometimes for cutting boards for saddlers, bootmakers, and others who use fine-edged knives, and who must have a wood on which leather or any material may be cut without the edge of the knife being turned. Lime, however, is now accounted superior for such requirements, as chesnut was once. Maple (chiefly foreign) is used for furniture, and of late has been extensively wrought into picture frames. Birch (chiefly foreign) is employed in the manufacture of furniture, and is sometimes stained or dyed so as to resemble mahogany or rosewood. Birch bark communicates the peculiar and agreeable fragrance which distinguishes Russia leather. Willow may be cut the thinnest of any wood, so as to retain strength, and it is therefore used in making sieves, as well as by some toymakers, who also use, occasionally, alder, fir, and soft woods, working them wet. Of holly the Tonbridge ware is made (articles somewhat similar have been made of cherry tree), and it is employed for "stringing;" it is often dyed, and being white and fine grained, it would be dyed more largely to resemble ebony or the costlier foreign woods, but the small size of the tree unfits it for that purpose. Of the foreign woods, mahogany furnishes the grand staple of the better description of furniture. Coach pannels and the spokes of the wheels of the best kind of work are also constructed of mahogany, the other portions of the wood-work of wheels being usually ash. Honduras mahogany is used somewhat extensively in ship-building. Lance-wood is worked into gig-shafts, and is much used for the best kind of gig whips, and for walking-sticks. Of rosewood, satinwood, and sandalwood dressing-cases, ladies' work-boxes, writing desks, tea-caddies, and similar ornamental articles of furniture are made. Cedar is occasionally used for the like purposes, and altogether in the manufacture of pencils. It is worked too into the sides of drawers, for which its pleasant odour recommends it. Ebony and lignum vitæ are used by turners, and are made into bowls, pestles, &c.

As to the quantity of timber of all kinds used in this country, it is difficult to arrive at very accurate results. "Much uncertainty," says Mr. Porter (Progress of the Nation, p. 588), "must always attend upon computations affecting the consumption of articles which, like timber, are partly furnished from our own soil, and respecting the home production of which we are without any means of calculating." It will, however, be seen from the above statement that the three principal uses to which timber is applied are the building and furnishing of houses, the construction of ships, and the making of coffins. Concerning the quantity of timber annually consumed in this manner there exist facts sufficient to enable us to arrive at a proximate conclusion. In order to do this I shall endeavour to show, first, the quantity of timber used every year in building and furnishing the houses of this country.

The number of houses in the United Kingdom at different periods can be readily obtained from the Population Returns. From these we gather the following results:—

In 1801, the number of inhabited houses in England and Wales was 1,575,923
1811 1,797,504
1821 2,088,156
1831 2,481,544
1841 2,943,939

Hence we find, that from 1801-11, the annual increase in the number of houses in England and Wales was 22,168; from 1811-21 it was 29,065; from 1821-31 it was 39,338; from 1831-41 it was 46,239; and assuming the increase during the last ten years to have been in the same ratio, we shall find that from 1841 to 1850 there have been very nearly 55,000 houses built annually throughout the kingdom, or sufficient to form one continuous row from London to Liverpool. Now it appears, from the returns obtained under the Property-tax Act, that the gross rental of the houses and other buildings in England and Wales amounted in 1842-43 to upwards of thirty-five and a half millions sterling. The number of houses at that period was (allowing for the yearly increase) 2,990,178, which would give an average rental of very nearly £12 per house. It may therefore be asserted that there are 55,000 houses of an average rental of £12, built every year throughout the kingdom. To build a £12 house in the country, I am credibly informed, rather more than three loads of timber are required for the roofing, joists, &c., and about seven loads for the flooring, staircases, doors, windows, and other parts. A load of timber, upon an average, is the produce of two trees; consequently, as there are ten loads of timber, twenty trees are used in the building of each £12 house in England and Wales; and as it has been shown that there are 55,000 such houses built every year, it follows that no less than 550,000 loads of timber, or 1,100,000 trees are annually consumed by us in this manner. Calculating, then, that each of these trees in their native woods occupied respectively the hundredth part of an acre—or in other words, stood between twenty and twenty-one feet apart—it follows that 11,000 acres of woodland must be cleared every year to supply the timber for building the houses in England and Wales. To give the reader, however, a more definite idea of the extent of ground required for this purpose alone, it may be said that, in the course of every four years, we "use up" in the construction of our new buildings a forest equal in size to the whole of the metropolis, extending from Poplar in the east to Kensington in the west, and from Stoke Newington in the north to Camberwell in the south.

But each of these houses requires to be furnished; and I find, from inquiries among the trade, that the furniture appertaining to a twelve-pound house may be said to consist on an average of thirty-six chairs, six tables, four bedsteads, four wash-hand stands, four chests of drawers, and one wardrobe or press. The quantity of timber requisite for making these articles I am informed by an experienced and intelligent tradesman is as follows:—The tables take upon an average one twelve foot deal each, and the chairs half a deal each; the bedsteads one deal each, and the wash-hand stands half that quantity; the chests of drawers two deals each, and the press the same amount. To make the whole of the furniture above enumerated, therefore, forty 12-foot deals would be required; thirty such deals make one load of timber, and a load of timber is equivalent to two trees; hence, allowing for other wooden articles of domestic use, as wash-tubs, stools, clothes-horses, &c., it may be asserted that one load and a half of timber, or three trees, are used upon an average in furnishing each house in England and Wales. There are 55,000 new houses built every year; consequently 165,000 trees are required to make the furniture for them.

The timber required every year for the construction of the new houses in the metropolis is of course considerably less than the above, but still it is so vast as to make us wonder how the supply can possibly be maintained. According to the last census, the number of houses in London in the year 1831 was 196,666; in 1841 it was 225,531. This gives an annual increase of 2,886 houses. But an official return laid before the House of Commons in the course of last year tells us that the number of houses built within the metropolitan police district since the 1st of January, 1839, is 64,058, which gives an average annual increase during the last ten years of no less than 6,405, or very nearly double what it was in the preceding decennial period. It also tells us that the number of new streets that have been formed since that time has been 1,652, which is at the rate of 165 every year, and that the gross length of those made since 1839 is no less than 200 miles—that is to say, there have been built in London during the last ten years a row of houses, with an average frontage of 16¼ feet each, as long as the ancient Watling-street, which extended direct from London to Chester. At this rate we build every year in the metropolis houses sufficient to form one continuous line to Windsor. By the returns obtained under the Property and Income Tax Acts, the total annual value of the houses in London in 1842-43 was as follows:—

	Gross Rental.
London	£1,369,515
Inns of Court	107,527
Westminster	2,176,516
Middlesex	5,579,872
	£9,233,430

At that period the number of houses in the metropolis (allowing for the annual increase) was 231,936, which gives very nearly £40 for the average annual rental per house. I am informed that a £10 house in the country is equivalent to a £30 house in London—or, in other words, that the same quantity of materials and labour is required for the construction of the one as the other. Since, then, a £30 London house needs nine loads of timber for the construction of the roof, floors, partitions, staircases, doors, window-frames, &c., it may be safely asserted that a £40 house requires twelve loads for the same purpose, and consequently that each of the metropolitan houses consumes upon an average as much wood as is the produce of 24 trees. Hence the total number of trees used every year in building the new houses in London alone will amount to 153,720; and supposing these trees to occupy the same ground as before, and to run 100 to the acre, it follows that there are 1,537 acres of woodland annually consumed in this manner; that is to say, that the trees which are used every year in building the new streets of London, are sufficient to form a forest half as large again as the city of Bath.

The timber used in the construction of the new ships that are annually launched throughout the kingdom forms, likewise, a considerable item in the annual consumption. According to the returns for the last ten years, I find that the average number of vessels built every year in this country amounts to 944, the average burden of each being 145 tons. In McCulloch's statistics of the British empire there is a statement of the number of loads of timber required for building ships of different tonnage, and according to this estimate, a ship of 161 tons will take 186 loads of timber. Hence, a ship of 145 tons burden would use 167 loads; and supposing two of such loads to be the produce of three trees, each of the ships annually built would require upon an average 250 trees for their construction; and since there are in round numbers 950 such ships built every year, it follows that there are 237,500 trees used every year in the construction of the merchant vessels of this kingdom—which is equal to a forest of 2,375 acres.

The timber annually consumed in the construction of coffins also comes to a very large amount. The average number of deaths throughout the United Kingdom every year for the last ten years has been 376,093—hence precisely that number of coffins must have been annually made. Each coffin, I am credibly informed, takes upon an average 56 feet superficial measure of one-inch elm board. An elm tree contains upon an average about 600 superficial feet of such board, so that one tree would make about 10 average-size coffins; consequently there would be 37,609 elm trees used annually in the interment of the deceased; and assuming these trees, like the rest, to run 100 to the acre, it follows that we annually consume in the burial of our dead a plantation of elms exactly equal in size to the "City of London within the walls."

We have now to inquire whence these immense supplies are derived; and this part of the subject necessarily divides itself into two branches—viz., the resources of this country, and the amount obtained from foreign lands.

Concerning the quantity and value of the timber of this island, the following is the best Information to be obtained. The principal woodland counties in England are Kent, Sussex, Surrey, Hants, Worcester, Chester, with parts of Oxford, Northampton, Berks, Leicester, Nottingham, &c. In general the western counties are better wooded than the eastern, and the southern than the northern. In some of the

southern and in the greater number of the southeastern and western counties there are large stocks of timber in hedges and in pasture
grounds, and the woods and plantations are in many places very considerable. The trees that are said to be indigenous to Great Britain are
the oak (two species), the elm (five species), the beech, the ash, the
maple, sycamore, hornbeam, lime (three species, according to Smith),
the Spanish chestnut (?), the alder, birch, poplar (four species), and
the Scotch fir. Of these the oak, beech, birch, and Scotch fir grow in
vast forests, almost to the exclusion of other trees. The finest forests
of beech are unquestionably to be seen in the southern parts of England; that tree flourishing to an extraordinary degree in the chalk and
deep clay soils of Sussex and some of the neighbouring counties. The
Scotch fir (*pinus sylvestris*) constitutes noble forests among the moun-
tainous districts of North Britain, filling the valleys, and occasionally
ascending to the height of 2,500 feet upon the hills, and exhibiting individual specimens of extraordinary size and beauty. Oak is found in
the greatest perfection in the Weald of Kent, Sussex, and Surrey. It is
also found in great excellence in hedge-rows, in Cheshire, Hereford,
Monmouth, Flint, and many other parts of England and Wales. In
1792 the Surveyor-General of the Woods and Forests reported that
there was a great and rapidly decreasing deficiency in the supply of
oak, and he concluded by recommending that 100,000 acres in the
royal forests and elsewhere should be planted with this tree. In accordance with this recommendation various enclosures have been made
at different periods since that time, and now the entire extent of the
royal forests enclosed and bearing oak is estimated at from 50,000 to
60,000 acres. The following table, extracted from the Fourth Report
of the Commissioners of Woods and Forests, (p. 27) shows the extent
of the different royal forests, as well as of the number of acres in each,
enclosed and appropriated to the growth of timber for the navy:—

Royal Forests.	Acres in each forest.	Acres enclosed for the growth of timber.
New Forest	66,942	 6,000
Dean Forest	23,015	 11,000
Alice Holt Forest	1,892	 1,892
Woolmer Forest	5,945	 1,700
Bere Forest	1,417	 1,417
Whittlewood Forest	5,424	 3,895
Salcey Forest	1,847	 1,121
Whichwood Forest	3,709	 1,841
Waltham Forest	3,278	....
Windsor Forest	4,402	 4,402
Delamere Forest	3,847	 3,847
Parkhurst Forest	900	 900
Acres 122,622		 38,015

Lands in Kent, Gloucester, Derby, Durham, &c.,
belonging to the Crown, enclosed, and planted
with oak 6,612

Enclosures thrown open, and enclosed woods of
spontaneous growth belonging to the Crown,
estimated at 7,000

Lands in New, Dean, and Woolmer Forests, that
may be planted 11,000

Total 62,627

According to the above table, the royal forests occupy altogether 122,622 acres of ground, of which not quite one-third are enclosed and appropriated to the growth of timber for the navy. This, with other Crown lands planted with oak, makes the entire space of ground devoted to the cultivation of this one tree in England, amount to upwards of 50,000 acres.

There are, however, no means of forming anything like an accurate estimate of the total quantity of woodland in England, or the value of the timber thereon. Dr. Beeke, in his "Observations on the Income-tax," says, that an estate is in general considered as having less than its proportion of growing trees of all ages, if their value do not amount to nearly two years of the clear rent. On this hypothesis, the total value of the timber in this country would be nearly £80,000,000—the gross rental of England and Wales, in 1842-43, as determined by the assessments under the Property and Income-tax Acts, being £40,176,086, the total number of acres 4,752,000, and the average rent per statute acre, 18s. 6¾d. Mr. McCulloch doubts, however, whether the supply of timber in the kingdom, at present, is so large as it was in 1800, when Dr. Beeke's tract was published. "Perhaps we should not be far from the truth," he says, "if we estimated the present value of the timber of England and Wales at from £40,000,000 to £50,000,000, and its yearly product at from £1,500,000 to £2,000,000." The annual income from woods is said to be "4 per cent. on their value, after deducting the cost of repairs."

In the General Report of Scotland (vol. ii., page 321), the total extent of woodland in that country was estimated at 913,695 English acres, of which 501,469 were natural woods, and 462,226 plantations. If this estimate may be relied on (says Mr. McCulloch), the total woodland must now considerably exceed one million acres. The largest and most valuable woods are in Perthshire, Aberdeenshire, Ross-shire, and Inverness-shire.

Respecting the quantity of foreign timber annually used in this country, there is little difficulty in arriving at a correct estimate. The returns given in the Trade and Navigation accounts furnish us with accurate calculations upon this point. The principal places from which our supplies of foreign timber are derived are British North America, and the shores of the Baltic. The timber trade of British America, the value of which at the beginning of the present century did not exceed £32,000, surpassed all others in magnitude a few years ago. It was favoured principally by the duty upon timber imported from British possessions, as compared with that brought from the Baltic and other foreign parts. The Canadian timber is obtained chiefly from the immense forests on the shores of the great interior lakes. The trees are cut down during the winter, partly by American axemen, who are peculiarly skilful; and the business is attended with great hardship, both from the work itself and the inclemency of the season. The trees, when felled, are put together into immense rafts, which often cover acres, and on them are raised small huts—the residence of the woodmen and their families. Ten or twelve square sails are set up, and the rafts are navigated to Quebec, through many dangers, in which nearly a third of them are said to be lost. Those which are brought safe to their destination are ranged along the river in front of Quebec, forming a line four or five miles in extent, till they are taken down and exported in the shape of timber, deals, and staves. In 1830, the Canada merchants estimated the capital invested in this trade at £1,250,000. The value of the timber exported in 1831 was reckoned by Mr. Bliss at £1,038,000 sterling. The Canadian timber, however, is allowed by all parties to be of very inferior quality to that of the Baltic.

Dr. William Howeison, in his account of the forest trees and timber trade of Russia, says, while speaking of the value of the forest trees to the Russians—"They furnish them with fir timber of the finest kind, possessing the most durable and dense texture, and in the most profuse abundance, with no trouble but that of cutting down." The most common species of wood in the immense tracts of forests extending over the northern parts of the Russian empire, consists, he tells us, for the most part, of the pine tribe. In some places the pine trees grow to a great height and size. The greater the intensity of the cold the firmer and more dense does the timber become. "The timbers that we took in at Memel, in my last voyage," I was told by a seaman belonging to a Baltic vessel, "were floated alongside on immense rafts; some of them came hundreds of miles down the rivers. There are vast forests there, and they'll last for centuries to come. The first that I saw I thought was more like a black cloud than anything else. The rough timber is cut in windmills, built for the purpose; and the deals are cut and squared in them. I have seen scores of windmills on the Russian coast, and in the Gulf of Finland. Some of the windmills I have seen keep twenty saws continually going." The committee of the House of Lords observe, in their first report on the foreign trade of the country, that the North American timber is more soft, less durable, and every description of it more liable to dry-rot than timber of the north of Europe. "On the whole," they say, "it is stated by one of the commissioners of his Majesty's navy—the most distinguished for practical knowledge, experience, and skill—that the timber of Canada, both oak and fir, does not possess, for the purpose of ship-building, more than half the durability of wood of the same description. The result of its application to other purposes of building," they add, "is described by timber-merchants and carpenters to be nearly similar." (p. 4.) In his evidence before the committee, Sir Robert Seppings said, "About the year 1796 there were a certain number of frigates built of the fir of the Baltic, and their average durability was about eight years. About the year 1812 there were a considerable number of frigates built, also of fir, but of the growth of North America, and their average durability was not half that time." Mr. Copland, an extensive builder and timber-merchant, also stated, in his evidence before the same committee, that "the bulk of timber imported from America is very inferior in quality to the Baltic timber, being much softer in its nature, not so durable, and particularly liable to dry-rot; indeed, it is not allowed to be used by any professional man under Government," he said; "nor is it ever used in the best buildings in London. It is only speculators that are reduced to use it, from the price of it being much lower than the Baltic timber, on account of the difference in the duty. If you were to lay two planks of American timber upon each other, they would, to a certain extent, have the dry-rot, almost invariably, in the course of a twelvemonth."

The greater part of the mahogany imported into this country comes from Honduras, where there are thick forests containing this and the logwood tree. On this coast the English have stipulated for a right to settle. They are established on the river Belise, which is navigable for 200 miles up the country. The mahogany trees are very thinly scattered through the forests, and are cut down by gangs of negroes, preceded by what is called "the finder," who mounts the tops of the highest trees, and finds out where a mahogany tree stands. The chief expense is in the conveyance of the trunks to the coast.

Before entering into a statement as to the exact quantity of foreign timber introduced into this kingdom, it is necessary that I should explain certain customs and technicalities of the trade.

The foreign timber trade is divided into two classes—hewn and sawn timber, called in the trade "timber" and "deals." By "timber" is meant that which is merely hewn and brought to this country, squared ready for use, and fit for house or ship building. This consists of American red pine, yellow pine, elm, ash, oak, and birch. The teak trade is of recent date, and seems to be an exception to this classification. Mahogany and dye woods, again, are not styled timber. The deals are sawn for the carpenters', or joiners', use. They are sawn in Canada and the other countries from which they are imported, and where immense steam-mills have been erected for that purpose. The advantage to the trader, in having this process effected abroad rather than in England, seems to be that no refuse matter forms a part of the cargo. Were the pine brought in logs, the bark and the unevenness of the tree would add greatly to the freight for what was valueless; but, being cut into different lengths, widths, and thicknesses, it admits of more compact stowage.

When the timber is sawn it has different names applied to it, according as it is cut into pieces of different lengths, widths, or thicknesses. If cut into pieces above 6 foot long and under 2½ inches thick, it is termed *battens* or *deals*, according as they are respectively under or over 7 inches wide; if cut into pieces under 6 foot long, it is called either batten ends or deal ends, according as they are under or over 7 inches in width; while, if cut into pieces of the same length and width as the deals, but under 4 inches in thickness, they are termed *planks*, and when 1½ inch thick, the right name is *boards*. A batten, then, is strictly a narrow deal; a batten end a short batten; and a deal end a short deal. A *board*, on the other hand, is merely a thin plank. Fire-wood consists of hewn timber ends, and deal ends, not more than 18 inches long, and each of these must be twice split before leaving the ship, so that it may not be converted to other uses.

The following table, showing the quantity of hardwoods and timber imported into the United Kingdom, during the last ten years, has been constructed from the Trade and Navigation Accounts.

QUANTITIES OF HARD WOODS AND TIMBER IMPORTED INTO THE UNITED KINGDOM DURING THE FOLLOWING YEARS:—

HARD WOODS.		1839.	1840.	1841.	1842.	1843.	1844.	1845.	1846.	1847.	1848.	1849.
Box wood	Tons	496	1,609	2,405	1,082	2,779	1,328	1,377	889	1,306	1,124	No returns.
Cedar (under 8-inch square)	„	3,144	2,697	1,381	819	2,722	3,340	4,631	5,593	1,671	741	..
Mahogony	„	25,859	23,115	19,502	16,938	20,284	25,622	38,350	41,689	34,009	31,668	29,021
Rosewood	„	1,738	1,585	2,491	1,115	3,262	4,337	1,196	3,417	998	1,949	No returns.
TIMBER, viz.:—												
Batten and batten ends	Gt. Hds.	20,118	19,449	19,546	8,707							
Deal and deal ends ...	„	80,647	73,669	73,866	36,042							
Masts above 6 in. and under 8 in. diameter	Numbers	17,188	17,102	15,259	5,543							
Ditto above 8 in. and under 12 in.	„	5,263	5,932	4,854	2,164							
Ditto 12 in. and upwards	„	9,308	7,264	*7,446	*3,460							
Oak planks	„	3,558	7,012	*2,577	*2,172							
Staves	Gt. Hds.	81,020	96,849	92,069	35,797							
Fir 8-inch square and upwards	Loads	623,265	692,498	654,111	231,386							
Oak	„	50,752	59,136	44,372	11,317							
Unenumerated	„	51,676	65,529	63,687	17,200							
Wainscot logs	„	2,644	2,827	1,501	1,125							
TIMBER, entered since Oct. 10, 1842, viz.:—												
Sawn or split	Loads				159,044	609,693	727,456	881,643	775,833	861,755	864,593	811,120
By tale: Battens and batten ends, boards, deals, deal ends, and planks	Gt. Hds.				195	318	246	130	77	44	110	25
Not sawn or split	Loads				220,209	767,952	757,901	1,077,084	1,249,106	1,031,067	928,741	821,594
Staves	„				17,147	57,594	73,255	86,011	79,648	62,681	54,306	79,882

*These are counted in loads.

On reference to the above table, it will be seen that the principal kinds of hardwood and timber imported into this country are mahogany, "hewn logs of fir, eight inches square and upwards," sawn deals, and deal ends. The average quantity of mahogany imported every year appears to be 30,000 tons, and that of the hewn and sawn timber between 1,500,000 and 2,000,000 loads—a load being 50 cubic feet. Of this nearly the whole is consumed in the United Kingdom, only a small proportion—not half per cent. of the whole—going out of the country.

As a ready means, however, of obtaining a concise summary of the facts detailed in the above table, I avail myself of the annual returns given in the valuable circular of Messrs. Churchill and Sim, the eminent wood-brokers (to whom I beg thus publicly to tender my thanks), especially as the reader will be enabled by this means to arrive at the relative quantities of foreign and colonial timber that have been introduced since 1844.

	Colonial Timber and Deals in Loads.	Foreign Timber and Deals in Loads.	Total Loads.
1844	941,221	544,136	1,485,357
1845	1,281,974	676,752	1,958,726
1846	1,221,096	809,024	2,030,110
1847	1,084,000	776,000	1,860,000
1848	1,102,254	701,080	1,803,334
1849	1,072,000	580,000	1,652,000

Hence it appears that the colonial timber constitutes nearly two-thirds, and the foreign about one-third, of the entire quantity imported. If we assume the whole of the timber brought into this country to represent 100, the proportions contributed by Russia, Prussia, Sweden, Norway, and British North America, which are the principal places from which our supply is derived, will be as follows:—Russia 13.2 per cent., Prussia 12.7 per cent., Sweden 6.8 per cent., Norway 5.5 per cent., of the whole, and British North America 61.8 per cent. of the entire quantity imported.

I now come to consider the value of the timber imported into this country. Concerning the worth of the supplies derived annually from abroad, the Government returns hardly enable us to come to any definite result, for they are calculated at the *official* rates of valuation which were fixed in 1696, and these have, consequently, long ceased to be any test of the *real* value of commodities.

VALUE OF THE HARD WOODS, TIMBER, DEALS, AND STAVES IMPORTED INTO GREAT BRITAIN, CALCULATED AT THE OFFICIAL RATES OF VALUATION.

Year.	Maho-gany.	Rose-wood.	Timber, sawn or split.	Timber, not sawn or split.	Staves.	Total.
	£	£	£	£	£	£
1841	223,605	33,289	145,206	772,312	65,274	1,239,686
1842	172,588	52,447	128,739	724,118	61,737	1,139,629
1843	140,098	27,222	90,511	457,364	33,157	748,352
1844	175,872	68,496	119,568	665,690	39,147	1,068,773
1845	219,416	25,115	145,539	703,286	51,380	1,144,736
1846	342,618	92,389	179,495	990,721	57,537	1,662,760
1847	352,536	71,760	158,066	1,158,862	54,689	1,795,913
1848	304,618	21,088	186,122	980,597	46,589	1,539,014
1849	292,436	41,847	183,659	851,879	38,472	1,408,293

As a guide to the *real* value of the several kinds of wood imported into this country, I shall now give an account of the prices that foreign timber and deals have obtained in the London market for the last six years. These are collected from the circulars of Messrs. Churchill and Sim, who have kindly supplied me with copies of their annual statements since the year 1844. By these means we shall be enabled to arrive at a brief history of the timber trade; which becomes especially valuable when viewed in connection with the account of the duties given below.

The Wood trade in the year 1844 commenced with larger stocks and lower prices than had been previously known; almost every article was below the cost of importation. The great feature of the season was the Swedish wood trade—the supply of fir timber thence having been larger than had ever been known, and the price below all other Baltic timber or Quebec red pine. The importations from Canada were extensive, though less considerable than in 1843. In the foreign trade, Norway deals maintained their general character, and realised a steady price throughout the year, the importation not having been excessive. The Russian trade from St. Petersburg and Archangel was rather less than in the previous year. In 1845, the importation of wood was greater than that of 1844, the ships being of heavier tonnage. From Russia, moreover, the supply was rather under the average, in consequence of the advanced cost in shipping, price, and freight. Quebec oak and elm timber rose high towards the close of the season, but ash timber was scarcely saleable. Staves from the Baltic were imported more extensively than in former years, owing to the total remission of duty. In this year, railway sleepers of Quebec pine timber were extensively imported from the colonies, chiefly on contract. In 1846 the increased importation of foreign timber in London was the chief feature of the season. From Russia the supply of deals was rather less than usual, and remunerative rates were obtained at the latter part of the year for fresh St. Petersburg and Archangel deals. The trade in Norway deals was also much reduced. The consumption of East India teak rendered it a growing trade, especially as the supply of African teak was difficult to procure. The leading feature in the foreign timber trade of 1847 was an increased supply of Dantzic fir. In 1848 abundant supplies were received from Sweden, the trade from the ports within the Baltic being the leading feature in the foreign importation of that year. The supply from Prussia was less than in the preceding year, on account of the suspension of the trade during the Danish embargo. East India teak became an established trade, the wood being much esteemed. In 1849 the importation from Canada was very large, the deals exceeding the supply of 1848; the staves being double, while the timber remained the same. The trade with Norway was small, and the sales very difficult. The Finland supply of deals and battens was larger than in 1848. East India teak was brought in freely. Quebec red pine had again to contend with "low-priced" timber from the Baltic, the import cost being too high to be realised for a single cargo. Inferior deals and battens were likewise imported on account of the restriction of the trade between Norway and France. Firewood continued to constitute a large portion of the freights from Norway; and the ports of Sweden, in the Gulf of Bothnia, increased their supply of timber to this country. On the whole, the wood trade of 1849 was carried on with loss to Canada, and without profit to New Brunswick; it was adverse to Norway in quality, to Russia in price, and favourable only to the timber of Sweden, the deals of Russia, and the staves of all countries. Such is a brief history of the foreign timber trade for the last six years.

The next part of the subject that presents itself is the amount of duty imposed upon the different kinds of timber and hard woods, as well as the revenue derived from the importation of wood. In the Trade and Navigation Accounts the different kinds of woods are divided into two classes, viz., hard woods and timber. The hard woods there enumerated, as formerly subject to duty, are boxwood, cedar, mahogany, and rosewood; while under the denomination of "timber" are given deals and deal ends, battens and batten ends, masts, staves, fir, oak, wainscot logs, &c. Since the 10th of October, 1842, the several kinds of "timber" have been differently arranged, and now they are divided into "timber or wood sawn or split," and into "timber or wood not sawn or split, or otherwise dressed, except hewn." The rates of duty levied on the hard woods were, in 1839, from 20s. to 80s. per ton, if imported from British possessions; and from 100s. to 200s., if from foreign parts. The largest amount of duty, namely, 200s., was upon rosewood. The duty upon mahogany was as high as 100s. per ton, if brought from foreign parts, and 80s. from British possessions; while that on cedar and boxwood was 10s. and 20s. from British possessions, and 50s. and 100s. from foreign parts. The duty on hard woods continued the same until the 9th of July, 1842, when it was considerably diminished; and on the 19th of March, 1845, all hard woods were allowed to be introduced into England *free*.

The rates of duty levied on "timber" were, in 1839, as follows:— For battens, according to their size, from 20s. to 40s. per 120, if imported from British possessions; and from 200s. to 400s. per 120, when imported from foreign parts. Batten ends were rated at from 7s. 6d. to 15s. per 120, from British possessions; and from 60s. to 120s. from foreign parts. For deals, the duty ranged, according to their size, from 40s. to 200s. per 120 from British possessions; and from 380s. to 880s. from foreign parts. Deal ends were charged from 15s. to 30s. per 120, if brought from British possessions; and from 120s. to 240s., if from foreign parts. The impost upon masts was, in proportion to their diameter, from 1s. 6d. to 4s. each, from British possessions; and from 8s. to 22s. from foreign parts. Oak planks, per load, were 15s., from British possessions; and 80s., from foreign parts. Staves, according to their length, from 2s. to 10s. per 120 from British possessions, and from 23s. to 96s. from foreign parts. Fir was 10s. per load, from British possessions, and 55s. per load from foreign parts; and oak the same. Wainscot logs of British produce were 12s., and of foreign 55s. per load; while other unenumerated kinds of timber were 5s., if from British possessions; and 28s., if from foreign parts. On May 15, 1840, a slight increase took place in the duties on all the above classes of timber, with the exception of staves, the shortest kind of deals, and the smaller description of masts, which were allowed to remain the same. After this, the duties continued unaltered until October 10, 1842, when an entirely different arrangement was made. Timber was then, as I before stated, divided into "sawn or split," and "*not* sawn or split." The duty on the former class was 2s. per load, if from British possessions, and 38s. if from foreign parts; while that on the latter was 1s., when imported from British possessions, and 30s. from foreign parts. The duty on staves of British produce was fixed at 2s. per load, while the foreign were 28s. The duty on battens and batten ends, per 120, was at the same time changed to 36s. 7d. British, and 256s. foreign; and that on boards, deals, deal ends, and planks, to 58s. 8d. British, and 497s. foreign. In 1843 the duty on battens and batten ends, and on boards, deals, deal ends, and planks, was slightly decreased. The duty on staves remained unaltered, as did the duty on timber coming from British possessions, whether "sawn or split," or "not sawn or split;" while that coming from foreign parts was somewhat reduced if "sawn or split," and increased if "not sawn or split." No further alteration took place (with the exception of staves under 72 inches long, which became free on the 19th of March, 1845) until April 5, 1847. Then the duty on timber sawn or split, and not sawn or split, if imported from foreign possessions, was considerably decreased. That brought from British possessions, however, remained unaltered. The duty on battens and batten ends, boards, deals, deal ends, and planks, whether from British possessions, or foreign parts, were likewise greatly reduced. Foreign staves also underwent a slight reduction per load. On the 5th of April, 1848, a further change took place; the duty on timber sawn or split was reduced to 20s. per load, if coming from foreign parts; and that on foreign timber not sawn or split to 15s. per load. The duty on timber of British produce remained unchanged, as did that upon staves coming from British possessions; while on those coming from foreign parts it was decreased to 18s. Battens and batten ends, and boards, deals, and planks, were also reduced. Upon battens and battens ends, if imported from British possessions, the impost was 18s. 6d. per load; and from foreign parts, 129s. Upon boards, deals, and planks, it was 29s. 10d., if of British growth; and 251s. 4d., if brought from foreign parts.

The duty at the present time stands thus:—Upon "timber sawn or split" it is 2s. per load, if brought from British possessions; and 20s. per load, if from other parts. Upon battens and batten-ends, boards, deals, deal-ends, and planks, the impost is the same, while timber not sawn or split is charged at the rate of 1s. per load British, and 15s. foreign. Staves of all kinds are free.

The net revenue derived from the receipt of the duties above enumerated has been as follows:—

Year.	Hard Woods.	Timber.	Total.
1839	£63,144	£1,540,200	£1,603,344
1840	60,966	1,662,770	1,723,736
1841	55,712	1,438,331	1,494,043
1842	18,783	917,601*	936,384
1843	15,447	643,980	659,427
1844	16,969	901,078	918,047
1845	2,540†	1,431,737	1,434,277
1846	Free.	1,109,060	1,109,060
1847	...	974,299	974,299
1848	...	721,659	721,659

* The duty was altered on the 10th October of this year: the duty collected before that date in the same year was 706,803*l.*, and after it 210,798*l.*

† The duty was taken off hard woods on the 19th March in this year.

The next point that it becomes necessary to ascertain, in order to take a comprehensive view of all the parties engaged in the wood trade, is the number of hands engaged in bringing the foreign timber to this country. This is easily ascertained from the Government reports.

The following table, which has been constructed from the official returns, shows the number and the average tonnage and crew of the vessels that entered the ports of the United Kingdom from the different countries whence our foreign timber and deals are derived.

TABLE, EXHIBITING THE NUMBER AND AVERAGE TONNAGE OF VESSELS (BRITISH AND FOREIGN) TRADING FROM THE BALTIC AND BRITISH NORTH AMERICAN COLONIES THAT ENTERED THE PORTS OF THE UNITED KINGDOM IN 1848.

	BRITISH.			FOREIGN.		
	Ships.	Average Tonnage.	Average crew.	Ships.	Average Tonnage.	Average crew.
British North American Colonies	2,279	389	14	—	—	—
Russia	2,274	214	9	228	267	15
Prussia	1,343	150	6	671	193	8
Sweden	136	134	6	539	183	8
Norway	34	58	6	928	153	8

But the whole of these vessels do not bring wood cargoes only. The proportions of those coming from the several countries above mentioned, I am informed, by Mr. Taylor, of the West India Dock, may be estimated as follows:—Of the Russian and Prussian vessels, two-thirds are laden with timber; of the Swedish vessels only one-third, while the whole of the ships coming from Norway and British North America seldom or never bring any other cargo. Hence the number of seamen—British and foreign—engaged in the carrying of timber to this country may be said to be as follows:—Employed in the North American timber trade, 31,906 British seamen; in the trade from Russia, 13,644 British seamen, and 2,880 foreigners; in that from Prussia, 5,376 British, and 3,584 foreigners; in that from Sweden, 270 British and 1,440 foreigners; and in that from Norway, 204 British seamen, and 7,424 foreigners. From this, then, it would appear that the timber trade of the Baltic and the British North American colonies gives employment to no less than 51,400 British seamen, and 15,328 foreigners, or, in all, to 66,728 mariners.

Besides the seamen engaged in "carrying" the foreign timber, there are the labourers employed at the several ports and docks throughout the kingdom to discharge the cargoes of the timber ships, and the raftmen and porters to sort, pile, and stow. This class may fairly be estimated at some few thousands. The men who are engaged in the working or fashioning of the wood itself constitute a very large portion of the community, and one of the most intelligent and respectable classes among the artisans. Of these the carpenters and joiners are by far the most numerous. In Great Britain they amount to nearly 180,000 individuals. In 1841 their number was 162,977; and, allowing them to have increased at the rate of 10 per cent. since that period, their precise number at present would be 179,274. The cabinet-makers, at the time of taking the last census, were, in round numbers, 30,000; the sawyers, 29,500; the wheelwrights, 26,000; the shipbuilders, ship-carpenters, and shipwrights, 20,500; the coopers, 18,000; the coach-makers, 12,500; the turners, 7,000; and the chair-makers, 5,000; and over and above these there were upwards of 30,000 individuals engaged in other descriptions of wood work, such as patten and clog making, boat and barge building, block, mast, and oar making, lath rending and making, bobbin making, &c. &c. These altogether give a sum total of nearly 330,000 individuals; so that, allowing for the increase of population since 1841, it may be safely stated that the workers in wood throughout Great Britain at the present time are at least 350,000 in number; and, adding to these the 50,000 seamen engaged in the foreign timber trade, as well as the dock labourers and porters connected therewith, we arrive at the conclusion that there are at present in Great Britain between four and five hundred thousand working men, or nearly one fortieth part of the entire population, connected with the wood trade of this country. This agrees in a great measure with the opinions of the operatives themselves, who estimate their body at half a million strong.

The above is as comprehensive a view of the timber trade of this country generally as it is possible to give in this brief space. Concerning the trade of the metropolis in particular, it is my intention to be more explicit. But this I must reserve for my next letter.

LABOUR AND THE POOR.

◆

THE METROPOLITAN DISTRICTS.

[FROM OUR SPECIAL CORRESPONDENT.]

OF THE LABOURERS AT THE TIMBER DOCKS.

LETTER LVIII.

In my last Letter I gave an account of the supply and consumption of timber throughout the country generally. In the present I shall confine myself to the importations into London, and I shall speak more especially of the condition of the labourers connected with the foreign and colonial timber trade.

The quantity of colonial and foreign timber that has been brought into the Port of London since the year 1843 has been as follows:

Imported into London.	1844.	1845.	1846.
Colonial Deals and Battens (in pieces)	2,025,000	2,349,000	2,355,000
Foreign ditto (in ditto) ..	2,130,000	2,290,000	1,242,000
Total pieces	4,155,000	4,639,000	3,597,000
Colonial Timber (in loads)	57,200	55,800	53,600
Foreign ditto (in ditto)	58,200	68,100	86,000
Total loads	115,400	123,900	139,600
	1847.	1848.	1849.
Colonial Deals and Battens (in pieces)	3,339,000	2,740,000	2,722,000
Foreign ditto (in ditto) ..	1,996,000	2,044,000	1,903,000
Total pieces	5,335,000	4,784,000	4,625,000
Colonial Timber (in loads)	49,600	38,300	38,600
Foreign ditto (in ditto) ..	79,100	69,000	61,400
Total loads	128,700	107,300	100,000

The consumption of the metropolis has been little less than the quantity imported. In the six years above enumerated, the total importation of foreign and colonial deals and battens was 27,135,000 pieces, of which 26,695,573 were consumed in London; and the total importation of foreign and colonial timber was 714,900 loads, of which 644,224 were consumed. This gives an average annual importation of 4,522,500 deals and battens, of which only 73,238 have been sent out of the country every year. Of timber, the average annual importation was 119,150 loads, and the average annual exportation only 11,779 loads.

The number of wood-laden ships that have entered the Port of London since 1840, together with the countries whence they came, is given below. By this we shall perceive that our trade with Norway in this respect has sunk to exactly one-half of what it was ten years back; while that with Sweden and Finland has been very nearly doubled in the same time. The timber ships from the Prussian ports have increased little less than one-third, while those from Russia have decreased in the same proportion. The trade with Quebec and Montreal also appears to be much greater than it was in 1840; though, compared with 1841, there has been a considerable falling off; that of New Brunswick and Nova Scotia remains very nearly the same as it was at the beginning of the decennial period. Altogether the great change appears to have been the decline of the Norwegian and Russian timber trade, and the increase of that with Sweden and Prussia. It is also worthy of notice that, notwithstanding the increase of population, the number of wood-laden ships entering the Port of London every year has not materially increased within the last ten years.

THE NUMBER OF CARGOES OF TIMBER, DEALS, AND BATTENS IMPORTED INTO LONDON IN THE FOLLOWING YEARS:—

	1840	1841	1842	1843	1844	1845	1846	1847	1848	1849
Christiana and Sannesund	49	50	47	27	36	27	22	32	39	23
Other Ports of Norway	52	43	38	36	49	39	17	28	25	27
Gothenburg	61	64	49	59	59	66	30	67	55	41
Swedish Ports and Finland	85	84	85	102	90	149	103	101	138	154
Russian Ports	181	108	130	119	163	115	146	91	113	134
Prussian Ports	70	70	52	104	143	124	109	167	108	100
Quebec and Montreal	168	224	188	230	206	206	166	216	179	195
New Brunswick and Nova Scotia	104	97	62	134	90	102	127	145	108	105
Sierra Leone, Moulmein, &c.	16	20	29	31	5	10	20	21	13	20
	786	760	681	842	841	838	740	868	778	799

The next step in our inquiry is what becomes of the 800 "wood-laden" ships that annually enter the Port of London? Whither do they go to be unladen—to what docks or places of "special security" are they consigned to be discharged, and to have their cargoes delivered or bonded?

For this purpose there are five docks, three of which lie on the Surrey side of the river. These three are the Commercial Docks, the Grand Surrey Canal Dock, and the East Country Dock, and they are almost contiguous to each other—the Surrey Canal Dock lying immediately alongside the Commercial, and the East Country at the upper end of it. They are situated in, and indeed occupy nearly the whole of, that small cape of land which is formed by the bending of the river between the Pool and Limehouse Reach. The docks on the Middlesex side of the river, which are used for the reception and unlading of timber ships, are the West India and the "Regent's Dock," or the entrance to the Regent's Canal.

The number of wood-laden ships that have entered the three principal docks for the last ten years is given below. I am informed by Mr. Jones, of the Commercial Docks, that for every ship above 100 tons, six men are required to sort and pile away. Rafting from ships of the above burden requires one or two men daily, according to circumstances.

THE NUMBER OF WOOD-LADEN SHIPS WHICH ENTERED THE DIFFERENT DOCKS UNDERMENTIONED, IN THE FOLLOWING YEARS:—

Year.	West India Docks.		Commercial Docks.		Grand Surrey Docks.	
	Vessels	Tons.	Vessels	Tons.	Vessels	Tons.
1840	155	62,024	211	65,809	135	40,447
1841	201	82,196	215	70,438	114	34,594
1842	136	54,931	250	87,124	100	29,596
1843	169	71,211	368	121,846	108	31,299
1844	121	53,581	480	142,223	173	48,896
1845	149	70,514	424	137,047	155	43,211
1846	182	88,308	351	111,189	195	50,908
1847	228	124,114	423	143,966	226	62,433
1848	138	76,650	412	132,406	195	53,423
1849	138	67,860	410	136,329	212	58,780
Total	1,617	751,389	3,544	1,148,377	1,613	453,587
Average number of ships per year, and their average tonnage . . .	161	464	354	324	161	281

The foreign and colonial timber trade is, then, confined to five of the seven docks belonging to the port of London. Of these five, three—the Commercial, the Grand Surrey Canal, and the East Country—are situate on the Surrey side of the river, occupying altogether an area of 172½ acres, of which 100½ are water, and 72 land, and offering accommodation and protection for no less than 678 vessels. Here the principal part of the timber and deal trade is carried on—the Commercial receiving the greatest number of wood-laden vessels—perhaps greater than any other dock in the world. These, together with that portion of the West India Dock which is devoted to the same purpose, make the entire extent of the timber docks attached to the port of London about 250 acres, of which upwards of 140 are water—a space sufficient to give berths to no less than 940 ships.

I now come to speak of the condition and earnings of the labourers connected with the "timber" and "hard wood" trade. Of these it appears there are 1,030 men casually employed at all the timber docks, of whom only 132 obtain work all the year round. How the 900 casual "deal porters" and "rafters" live during the six months of the year that the "slack season" usually lasts in the timber trade, is another of the great mysteries of London life. As not a sixpence of their earnings is saved in the "brisk season," their fate in the winter is to suffer privations and afflictions which they only know.

I shall begin with the state of the Dock labourers employed at the Furniture and Hard Wood Trade. This trade is confined mainly, if not solely, to the West India Dock.

Concerning this branch of the wood trade, I give below the statement of a man who has worked at it for many years, and in doing so I wish to draw attention to the latter part of the narrative, as a proof of what I have repeatedly asserted respecting the regard exhibited by the authorities of the West India Dock, and in particular by Mr. Knight, the superintendent, for the welfare of all the men, whether directly or even *indirectly* employed by them.

This *indirect* employment of workmen, however, is the great bane of the industrious classes. Whether the middleman goes by the name of sweater, chamber-master, lumper, or contractor, it is this trading operative who is the great means of reducing the wages of his fellow-working men. To make a profit out of the employment of his brother operatives he must obtain a lower-class labour. He cares nothing about the quality of the work, so long as the workman can get through it somehow, and will labour at a cheaper rate. Hence it becomes a *business* with him to hunt out the lowest grades of working-men—the drunken, the dishonest, the idle, the vagabond, and the unskilful—because these, being unable to obtain employment at the regular wages of the sober, honest, industrious, and skilful portion of the trade, he can obtain their labour at a lower rate than what is usually paid. "Boy labour or thief labour," said a middleman on a large scale, as I showed in a former letter, "what do I care, so long as I can get my work done cheap?" I have already shown that the wives of the sweaters not only parade the streets of London on the look-out for youths raw from the country, but that they make periodical trips to the poorest provinces of Ireland, in order to obtain workmen at the lowest possible rate. I have shown, moreover, that foreigners are annually imported from the Continent for the same purpose, and that among the chamber-masters in the shoe trade, the child market at Bethnal-green, as well as the workhouses, are continually ransacked for the means of obtaining a cheaper kind of labour. All my investigations go to prove that it is chiefly by means of this middleman system that the wages of the working men are reduced. This contractor—this trading operative—uses the most degraded of the class as a means of underselling the worthy and skilful labourers, and of ultimately dragging the better down to the abasement of the worst. If *men* cannot subsist on lower prices, then he takes apprentices, or hires children; or if workmen of character and worth refuse to work at less than the ordinary rate, then he seeks out the moral refuse of the trade—those whom none else will employ; or else he flies to the workhouse and the gaol to find labour meet for his purpose. Backed by this cheap and refuse labour, he offers his work at lower prices, and so keeps on reducing and reducing the wages of his brethren, until all sink in poverty, wretchedness, and vice. I am, therefore, the more anxious to impress upon the minds of those gentlemen who are actuated by a sincere regard for the interest and comforts of the men in their employ the evils of such a system; for, however great may be the saving of trouble effected by it, yet, unless it be strictly watched (as I must confess it is at the West India and Commercial Docks), it can only be maintained by the employment of a cheaper and worse-class labourer, and therefore must result in the degradation of the workmen. I have said thus much because I find this contract system the general practice at all the wood docks, and because I am convinced that the gentlemen to whom the management of those docks is entrusted— Mr. Knight, Mr. Jones, and Mr. Cannan—have the welfare of the men in their employ sincerely at heart. Of the evils of *lumping*, or discharging wood ships by *contract*, I have already treated at considerable length. Under that system, it will be remembered, I showed that the contractor, who is commonly a publican, makes his profit not by cheapening the labourer, but by intoxicating him. Like the contractor for ballast, he gets his money out of the drunkenness of the workmen, and by this means is enabled to undersell the dock proprietors—or, in other words, to discharge the wood-laden ships at a less rate than they could possibly afford to do by the fair and honourable employment of their men. Of the effects of this system—the drunkenness of the men—the starvation of the wives—the squalor and ignorance of the children—the wretchedness and desolation of the homes—I have already treated at some length; and it will be seen at the end of the present letter, that in those docks where the supervision that is maintained at the West India and Commercial is not kept up, the labourers are reduced to almost the same state of poverty and destitution.

But to return. A man living in a small room, in a poor neighbourhood, but in a tidy apartment, and with a well-kept little garden at the back, gave me the following account of his earnings and labour in the *Mahogany Department of the West India Docks:*—

"I have worked in the West India Docks for eleven years, and for the last half of that time in the mahogany part of the wood-yard. Before that, I was eleven years in the merchant service as able seaman. But I got married, and thought I could do better in the docks, for, after all, what is £18 a year, supposing I had the luck to be at sea for nine months every year, at £2 a month? What is £18 a-year, sir, to keep a wife and family on, as well as a man himself, when he's ashore? At the West India Dock we unload the mahogany, or logwood, or fancy woods, from the ships, and pile them wherever they're ordered. We work in gangs of six or seven, with a master at the head of the gang. The logs are got out of the hold with a purchase and a jigger, and heaved ashore by a crane on to a truck, and we drag the truck to the place to stow the timber. In the wood-yards a machine lifts the timber up, by us men turning handles to work the machine, and puts it into its place in the warehouse. We are paid 2s. 6d. a day, working from eight to four. If only employed for four hours—and we're not set to work for less than four hours—we have 1s. 4d. If I could get 2s. 6d. a day all the year through I'd be a happy man, but I can't. Me, and such as me, earns 10s., 11s., or as far as 15s. a week when we are wanted. But, take the year through, I make between 9s. and 10s. a week. Out of that I have to keep a wife and four children.

I've lost one child, and my wife can get little or nothing most times to do with her needle, and if she does get work, what can she make at five farthings or three-halfpence a shirt for the slop-shops? My eldest child, however, does make 1s. or 1s. 6d. a week. I live on bread and butter, with a drop of beer now and then, six days out of the seven. On Sundays we has mostly a shilling's worth of meat—bullock's head generally. Sometimes our work is very hard with heavy lifting. A weakly man's no use, and I've wondered how I have the strength I have on bread and butter. We are all paid in the dock, and there's nobody allowed to get the men to drink or to traffic with them anyhow, but in a fair regular way. There's plenty hang about every day, who would work a day's work for 2s. There's a good many Irish. I don't know that there's any foreigners, without it be on the sugar-side. Sometimes 100 men are employed in our part of the business. To-day there was from 40 to 50 at work, and 100 more was to be had if they'd been wanted. Jobs often come in in a lump—all at once or none at all; very often with the wind. We run backwards and forwards to the sugar-side or the Surrey Dock as we expect to be wanted. We don't know what the foremen of the gangs get, but the company won't allow them to underpay us, and I've nothing to complain about either of them or the company, though we're bad off. The foreman can pick his men. Many of us has to go to the parish. Once I earned only 3s. in three weeks. Our best time is from June or July, continuing on for two, three, four, or five months as happens. We live half the year, and starve the t'other. There's very few teetotallers among us. Men want beer if they live on bread and butter. There's many, I know, lives on a meal a day, and that's bread and butter. There's no drunkards among our men. We're mostly married men with families. Most poor men is married, I think. Poor as I am, a wife and family's something to cling to, like."

I now come to the Timber and Deal trade. The labourers connected with this portion of the trade are rafters or raftsmen, and deal or stave porters; these are either "permanently" or "casually" employed. I shall give an account of each, as well as of the system pursued at each of the docks—beginning with the Commercial, because it does the most extensive business in this branch of the wood trade; and here let me acknowledge the obligations I am under to Mr. Jones, the intelligent and courteous superintendent, for much valuable information.

The Working Lumpers, as I before explained, are the labourers employed to discharge all wood-laden vessels except foreign ships, which are discharged by their own crews. The vessels unladen by the lumpers are discharged sometimes in the dock, and sometimes (when too heavily laden) in the river. The cargoes of wood-laden vessels are termed either landed or rafted goods. The landed goods are deals, battens, sleepers, wainscot logs, and, indeed, all but hewn timber, which is "rafted." When a vessel is unladen in the river, the landed goods are discharged by lumpers, who also load the lighters; whereas, in dock, the lumpers discharge them into the company's barges, which are loaded by them as well. With smaller vessels, however, which occasionally go alongside, the lumpers discharge directly to the shore, where the "goods" are received by the company's porters. The lumpers never work upon shore. Of the porters working on shore, there are two kinds, viz., deal and stave porters, whose duty it is to receive the landed goods, and to pile and sort them, either along the quay or in the bonding ground, if duty has to be paid upon them.

The hewn timber or rafted goods the lumpers thrust through the port-hole into the water; and there the raftman receives them, puts them into lengths and sizes, and then arranges them in floats—there being 18 pieces to a float. If the ship is discharged in the river, the rafter floats the timber to the docks, and then to the "ponds" of the company. If however, the ship is discharged in dock, then the raftman floats the timber only from the main dock to the ponds.

The Rafters are all freemen, for otherwise they could not work on the river. They must have served seven years to a waterman, and they are obliged to pay 3s. a year to the Watermen's Company for their license. There are 16 or 17 rafters (all preferable men) employed by the Commercial Dock Company, and in busy times there are occasionally as many as 40 casual rafters, or "pokers" as they are called (from their poking about the docks for a job). These casual men are not capable of "rafting a ship," nor are they free watermen. They are only employed to float the timber from the ship up to the ponds and stow it, or to attend to deliveries. The skill of the rafter lies in gauging and sorting the timber according to size, quality, and ownership, and making it up into floats. It is only an experienced rafter who can tell the different sizes, qualities, and owners of the timber. This the "pokers," or casual rafters, are unable to do. The "pokers," again, cannot float the timber from the river to the ponds. This is owing to two reasons—1. They are not allowed to do so, on account of not being free watermen; and 2. They are unable to do so from the difficulty of navigation. The pokers work exclusively in the docks. Neither the rafters nor pokers work under contractors; but the deal and stave porters invariably do.

The following statement of a rafter at the Commercial Dock, I had from a prudent, well-behaved, sober man. He was in company with another man, employed in the same capacity at the same docks, and they both belonged to the better class of labouring men:—

"I am a rafter at the Commercial Dock. I have been working at that dock for the last six years in the same capacity, and before that I was rafter at the Surrey Dock for between five and six years. I served my apprenticeship to a waterman. I was bound when I was sixteen. We are not allowed to work till we have served two years. In my apprenticeship I was continually engaged in timber towing, lightering, and at times sculling, but that I did only when the other business was slack. After my time was out I went lightering, and about a dozen years after that I took to rafting. I had been a rafter at the Surrey Canal before then—while I was in my apprenticeship, indeed. I had 18s. a week when I first commenced rafting at the Surrey Canal; but that, of course, all went to my master. I was with the Surrey Canal about two years as rafter; and then I joined another party, at 30s. a week, in the same capacity. This party rented a wharf of the Surrey Canal Company, and I still worked in the Dock. There I worked longer time—four hours longer. The wages would have been as good at the Surrey Canal at outside work as they were with the second party I joined. The next place that I went to as rafter was the Commercial Dock, where I am now, and have been for the last six years. I am paid by the week. When I work at the dock I have £1 1s. a week; and when I am rafting short-hour ships (*i.e.*, ships at which we work only from eight till four), I get 4s. per day. When I am working long-hour ships (*i.e.*, ships at which the working lasts from six till six), I get 5s. a day. The other rafters employed by the company are paid the same. Our wages have remained the same ever since I have been in the business. All the other men have been lowered—such as carpenters, labourers, watchmen, deal-porters, and the like; but we are not constant men, or else I dare say ours would have been reduced too. They have lowered the wages of the old hands, who have been there for years, 1s. a week. Formerly they had £1 1s., now they get £1. The men are dissatisfied. The wages of the casual dock labourers have been reduced a great deal more than those of the constant men. Three months ago they all had 18s. a week, and now the highest wages paid to the casual labourers is 15s. The reason why the wages of the rafters have not been lowered is,

I take it, because we are freemen, and there are not so many to be had who could supply our places. Not one out of a hundred lightermen and watermen are able to raft. We are only employed at certain times of the year. Our busy time begins at July, and ends in October. We are fully employed about four months in the year, and get, during that time, from £1 1s. to 30s. a week, or say 25s. upon an average. The rest of our time we fills up as we can. Some of the rafters has boats, and they look out for a job at sculling, but that's poor enough now." "Ah! very poor work, indeed," said an old weather-beaten man, who was present, and had had 40 years' experience at the business. "When I first joined it, it was in the war time," he added, "and then I was scarcely a day idle, and now I can't get work for better than half my time." "For the other eight months," continued the other man, "I should think the rafters upon an average make 5s. a week. Some of them has boats, and some gets a job at timber towing, but some (and that's the greatest number) has nothing at all to turn their hands to excepting the casual dock labour—that is, anything they can chance to get hold of. I don't think those who depend upon the casual labour of the docks, after the fall-season is over (the fall-ships are the last that come), make 5s. a week, take one man with another. I should say, more likely their weekly earnings is about 4s. There are about sixteen rafters at the Commercial Docks, and only one single man among the number. They none of them save any money during the busy season. They are in debt when the brisk time comes, and it takes them all the summer to get clear, which perhaps they does by the time the fall-ships have done, and then of course they begin going on in the old strain again. A rafter's life is merely getting into debt and getting clear of it—that is it—and that is a great part of the life of all the labourers along-shore."

He then produced the following accounts of his earnings for the last year:—

Week	£	s	d		Week	£	s	d	
1st week	£1	1	0		38th „	1	5	0	
2d „	1	8	0	(a)	39th „	1	0	6	
3d „	1	4	0		40th „	1	4	0	
4th „	1	5	6		41st „	1	10	0	
5th „	0	0	0		42d „	1	4	0	
6th „	1	1	0		43d „	1	10	0	
7th „	0	0	0		44th „	1	14	0	
8th „	1	1	0		45th „	1	5	6	
9th „	0	0	0		46th „	1	10	0	
10th „	1	1	0		47th „	0	5	0	
11th „	0	4	0	(b)	48th „	1	10	0	
12th „	1	1	0		49th „	1	10	0	
13th „	0	4	0	(c)	50th „	1	10	0	
14th „	0	17	6	„	51st „	1	7	0	
15th „	0	0	0		52d „	1	1	0	
16th „	0	0	0				1850.		
17th „	1	1	0		1st week	1	10	0	
18th „	0	10	0	(d)	2d „	0	10	6	
19th „	1	4	0		3d „	1	1	0	
20th „	0	17	6	(e)	4th „	0	12	6	
21st „	0	13	0	„	5th „	2	10	6	(i)
22d „	0	7	0	„	6th „	1	1	0	„
23d „	1	1	0		7th „	1	7	0	„
24th „	0	10	0	(f)	8th „	1	8	0	„
25th „	0	2	6	„	9th „	0	19	0	„
26th „	0	4	0	„	10th „	1	1	0	(j)
27th „	0	1	0	„	11th „	0	3	0	(k)
28th „	1	1	0	(g)	12th „	0	18	0	(l)
29th „	1	4	0		13th „	0	10	0	(m)
30th „	1	3	0		14th „	0	0	0	„
31st „	1	1	0		15th „	1	0	0	„
32d „	1	6	0		16th „	0	12	0	„
33d „	1	3	0		17th „	1	1	0	„
34th „	1	1	0		18th „	1	5	0	(n)
35th „	0	14	0		19th „	1	0	0	„
36th „	1	7	0		20th „	0	0	0	„
37th „	2	0	0	(h)					

(a) Outside work.   (b) Jobbing.   (c) Jobbing.
(d) Jobbing.   (e) Jobbing.   (f) Jobbing.
(g) Busy time begins. (h) Working Sunday and nights.
(i) Contract job on river.   (j) Dock work.
(k) Jobbing.   (l) Dock work. (m) Jobbing.
(n) Dock work.

This gives an average, for the seventy-two weeks above cited, of 18s. 6¼d. per week. "Where I get £1," the man continued, after I had copied his accounts, "many don't get 5s. I know many friends on the river, and I get a number of odd jobs which others can't. In the last six years my earnings have been much about the same. But others, I am sure, don't make half what I do. I have earned £1 8s. when I know they have been walking about and not earned a penny. In busy times as many as forty 'pokers' are employed, sometimes for as many as five weeks in the year. They get 3s. 6d. a day, from six to six. After they are out of work they do as best they can. It's impossible to tell how one-half of them live. Half their time they are starving. The wives of the rafters go some of them charing, some are glovemakers, and others dressmakers. None that I know of do slop-work."

I now come to the deal and stave porters. First, as to those employed at the Commercial Docks.

From a man who has an excellent character given of him by his employers I had the following account:—

"At our dock," he said, "timber and corn are the principal articles, but they are distinct branches, and have distinct labourers. I am in the deal part. When a foreign timber ship comes into the dock, the timber is heaved out of the port-hole by the crew themselves. The deal ships, too, are sometimes unloaded by the foreigners themselves, but not often; three or four out of a dozen may. Ours is very dangerous work. We pile the deals sometimes 90 deals high—higher at the busiest time—and we walk along planks with no hold, carrying the deals in our hands, and only our firm tread and our eye to depend upon. We work in foggy weather, and never stop for a fog; at least we haven't for eight or nine years, to my knowledge. In that sort of weather accidents are frequent. Last year there was, I believe, about 35 falls, but no deaths. If it's a bad accident the deal porters give 6d. a piece on a Saturday night, to help the man that's had it. There's no fund for sickness. We work in gangs of five usually, sometimes more. We are paid for carrying 100 of 12 feet deals, 1s. 9d.; 14 feet, 2s. 2d.; 20 and 21 feet, 3s.; 22 feet, 3s. 8d.; and from 24 to 27 feet, 4s. 3d. That's at piecework. We used to have 3d. per 100 more for every sort, but it was reduced three or four months back, or more, may be. In a general way we're paid nothing extra for having to carry the deals beyond an average distance, except for what we call 'long runs;' that's as far, or about as far as the dock extends from the place we start to carry the deals from. One week with another, the year through, we make from 12s. to 15s.—the 15s. by men that have the preference when work is slack. We're busiest from July to Christmas. I'm the head of a gang or team of five, and I am only paid as they are; but I have the preference if work is slack, and so have the men in my team.

Five men must work at the Commercial, or none at all. We are paid in the dock at the contractor's-office (there are three contractors), at four o'clock every Saturday evening. Drinking is kept down in our dock, and with my contractor drunkards are discharged. The men are all satisfied but for the lowering of their wages. No doubt they can get labour cheaper still; there's so many idlers about. A dozen years back or so they did pay us in a public-house. Our deal porters are generally sober men. The beermen only come into the dock twice a day—ten in the morning and half-past three in the afternoon—and the men never exceed a pint at a time."

An older man in the same employ said:—

"I've known deal-portering for twenty years back, and then, at the Commercial Dock, men was paid in a public-house, and there was a good deal of drunkenness. The men weren't compelled to drink, but was expected to. In that point it's far better now. When I was first a deal porter I could make half as much more as I do now. I don't complain of anybody about the dock; it an't their fault; but I do complain uncommon about the times; there's so little work, and so many to snap at it."

From a *stave porter* at the same dock I had the following account:—

"We are paid by the piece, and the price varies according to size—from 1s. 6d. to 10s. the 1,000. Quebec staves, 6 feet long by 2 inches thick, and a few inches broad, are 10s. the 1,000, and other sizes are paid in the same proportion, down to 1s. 6d. We pack the bigger staves about our shoulders, resting one stave on another, more like a Jack-in-the-Green than anything else, as our heads comes out in the middle of 'em. Of the biggest, five is a good load, and we pack all sizes alike, folding our arms to hold the smaller staves better. Take it altogether, we make at stave work what the deal porters do at their work; and, indeed, we are deal porters when staves isn't in. There's most staves comes to the Surrey Canal Dock."

A man who had worked at the West India Dock as a *deal porter* informed me that the prices paid were the same as were paid by the Commercial and East Country Dock Companies before the reduction, but the supply of labour was uncertain and irregular—chiefly at the spring and fall, and in British American ships. As many as 100 men, however, my informant stated, had been so employed at this dock, making from 15s. to 25s. per week, or as much as 30s. on occasions, and without the drawback of any compulsory or "expected" drinking. Such, as far as I could learn, is the condition of the labourers employed at these timber docks, where the "drinking system" and the payment of men in public-houses are not allowed. Concerning the state of the men employed at the other docks, where the public-house system still continues, I had the following details:—

A deal porter at the Surrey Canal Dock stated—

"I have worked a good many years in the Surrey Dock. There were four contractors at the Surrey Canal, but now there's one, and he pays the publican, where we gets our beer, all that's owing to us deal porters, and the publican pays us every Saturday night. I can't say that we are compelled to take beer—certainly not when at our work in the dock; but we're 'expected' to take it when we're waiting. I can't say either that we are discharged if we don't drink; but if we don't we are kept waiting late on a Saturday night on an excuse of the publican's having no change, or something like that; and we feel that somehow or other, if we don't drink, we'll be left in the background. Why don't the superintendent see us paid in the dock? He pays the company's labourers in the dock—they're corn-turners and rafters—and they are paid early, too. We now have 4s. 4d. a day of from eight to four, and 5s. 8d. from six to six. It used to be, till four months back I think, 4s. 10d. and 6s. 4d. In slack times, say six months in the year, we earns from 10s. to 12s. a week; in the brisk times, 30s., and sometimes more, but 30s. is about the average. We are all paid at the public-house. We gathers from after five or so every Saturday night. We are kept now and then till twelve, and after twelve, and it has been Sunday morning before we've got paid. There is more money spent, in course, up to twelve than up to ten. To get away at half-past nine is very early. I should say that half our earnings, except in our best weeks, goes to the publican for drink—more than half oft enough; if it's a bad week all our earnings, or more. When it waxes late, the wives, who've very likely been without Saturday's dinner or tea, will go to the publican's for their husbands, and they'll get to scold very likely, and then they'll get beaten very likely. We are chiefly married men with families. Pretty well all the deal porters at the dock are drunkards; so there's misery enough for their families. The publican gives credit two following weeks, and encourages drinking in course, but he does it quietly. He'll advance any man at work 1s. a night in money, besides trusting him for drink. I don't know how many we are—I should say from 50 to 200. In old age or accident, in course, we comes on the parish."

Other men whom I saw corroborated this statement, and some of their wives expressed great indignation at the system pursued in paying the labourers. None of them objected to their husbands having four pints of beer when actually at their work in the dock; it was against the publican's temptations on Saturday and other nights that they bitterly inveighed.

At the earnest entreaty of a deal porter's wife, I called on Saturday evening at the public-house where the men were waiting to be paid. I walked into the tap-room as if I had called casually, and I was then unknown to all the deal porters. The tap-room I found small, dark, dirty, and ill-ventilated. What with the tobacco-smoke and the heat of the weather, the room was most disagreeably close and hot. As well as I could count—for, though it was a bright summer's evening, the smoke and gloom rendered it somewhat difficult—there were twenty-four men in this tap-room, which is fitted up in boxes, and the number completely filled the apartment. In the adjoining room, where was a small bar, there were some six or eight more deal porters, lounging about. These numbers, however, fluctuated, for men kept coming in and going out; but all the time I was there thirty men might be stationary in the two hot, dirty, little rooms. They were strong-looking men enough, and all sun-burnt; but amongst them were some with pinched features and white lips. There they sat, each man with his beer before him. There was not the slightest hilarity among them; there was not the least semblance of a convivial Saturday night's gathering. The majority sat in silence. Some dozed—others drank or sipped at their pint measures, as if they must do it, or to while away the time. These deal porters were generally dressed in corduroy, fustian, or strong coarse blue woollen jackets, with trowsers of similar material, open big woollen waistcoats, and with coloured cotton handkerchiefs rolled round some thick substance in the way of a stock, and tied loosely round their necks over a striped cotton or coarse linen shirt. All had rough bristly beards, intimating that their shaving was confined to the Sunday mornings. With respect to the system pursued at this dock in the payment of the deal porters, it is right that I should state that I heard from many deal porters praises of the superintendent, though certainly not of the contractor or the publican. I am glad to be able to state, however, that it is the determination of the company to attempt—and that, indeed, they are now attempting—the abolition of the system of public-house payment. Mr. McCannan, the superintendent of these docks, to whom

I am indebted for many favours and courtesies, informs me that an arrangement was once made for the payment of the deal porters in "an old box" (a sort of wooden office) within the dock; but the impatience and struggling of the men who had to wait a little while for their week's earnings almost demolished the frail timbers of the old box, and the attempt was abandoned. Within the dock the supply of beer is now limited to three times a day, with a "vend" of half-a-pint a man each visit.

A middle-aged man, sun-burnt, and with much of the look of a seaman, gave me an account of his labour as a *deal porter at the East Country Dock.* His room—and he, with his wife and children, had but one—was very sparely furnished, the principal article being a large clean bed. He complained that his poverty compelled him to live in the neighbourhood of some low lodging-houses, which caused all sorts of bad characters to resort to the locality, while cries of "murder" were not uncommon in the night:—

"I have been a deal porter," he said, "nearly 20 years, and for the last few years I have worked at the East Country Dock. Sometimes we work single-handed, sometimes in gangs of two, three, or four. The distance the deals have to be carried has a good deal to do with it, as to the number of the gang. We're paid nothing extra for distance. Mr. —— contracts with the Dock Company to do all the deal portering. There are three gangs regularly employed, each with a master, or foreman, or ganger over them. They have always the preference. If three ships were to unlade on one day, there would be one for each gang, and when more hands are wanted the men of the regular gangs are put over deal porters, such as me, who are not regularly employed, but on the look-out for piece work or a day's work. We reckon when that happens that the ganger's men have 9s. for our 4s. We are paid at a public-house. The house belongs to the company. We pay 4d. a pot for our beer, and we're expected to drink not less than four pints a day. We're not obligated, you understand, sir, but we're expected to drink this; and if we don't do as we're expected, why we're not wanted next time, that's all. But we're only expected to take our regular beer when work's brisk. We're not encouraged to run into debt for drink, and work it out. Indeed, if a man be 1s. or 1s. 6d. in debt to the publican, he can't get credit for a bit of bread and cheese, or a drink of beer. We have good beer, but sometimes we'd rather be without it. But we can't work without some. Many deal porters I know are terrible drunkards. We are paid the same as at the Commercial Dock, and were reduced about the same time. If I had a regular week's work now, and no stop, I could make 26s.—less by 8d. a day, or 4s. a week, for beer. We're not expected to drink any gin. Before wages came down I could have made 30s. Our beer money is stopped out of our earnings by the masters, and paid to the publican. It's very seldom, indeed, we get a regular week's work, and take it the year through I don't clear 12s. a week. To-day there was only sixteen men at work, but sometimes there's eighty. From June to Christmas is the best time. Sometimes we may wait three or four days for a job. The regular pay for the Custom-house hours, from eight to four, is 4s. a day to a deal porter, but there's plenty to do it for what they can catch. Lots of Irish, sir. They'll work for anything, and is underselling all of us, because an Englishman and his family can't live like them. In the winter my family and me starved on 4s. or 5s. a week, but I kept clear of the parish, though plenty of us have to come on the parish. Much in pawn, sir? I have so. Look at my place—it *was* a nice place once. Most of what you may call the regular hands has been brought up as deal porters. I don't know how many you may call regular at our dock; it varies—working and waiting for a turn; but we've no regular turn at work; there's 100 perhaps, or near about it. Ours is very hard and very dangerous work. Last year one man was killed by a fall, and two had broken legs, and two broken thighs, but it was an easy year for accidents. There is no fund to help or to bury us; only the parish. In a bad case we're carried to the Dreadnought, or some hospital. We are all of us dissatisfied. I wish I could have 2s. 6d. a day for regular work, and I'd live twenty years longer than I shall now, with nothing to do one day, and tearing my soul out with slaving work at others."

The result of all my inquiries shows that the deal porters in no wise exaggerated the hardness or the danger of their labour. I saw them at work, walking along planks—some sloping from an elevated pile of timber to one somewhat more elevated, the plank vibrating as two men, carrying a deal, trod slowly, and in measure, along it; and so they proceed from one pile to another, beginning perhaps from the barge, until the deals have been duly deposited. From a distance, when only the diminished thickness of the plank is visible, they appear to be walking on a mere stick. The space so traversed is generally short, but the mode of conveyance seems rude and primitive.

In the foregoing narratives frequent mention has been made of the casual labourers at the timber docks, and I now proceed to give some short account of the condition and earnings of this most wretched class. On the platform surrounding the Commercial Dock basins are a number of men whom I heard described as "idlers," "pokers," and "casual labourers." These men are waiting "in hopes of a job," which they rarely obtain until all the known hands have been set to work before them. The casual labourers confine themselves to no particular dock, but resort to the one which they account the most likely to want hands; and some even of the more regularly employed deal porters change their docks occasionally for the same reason. These changes of locality puzzle the regular deal porters in their estimation of the number of hands in their calling at the respective docks. On my visits the casual labourers were less numerous than usual, as the summer is the season when such persons consider that they have "the best chance" in the country. But I saw groups of ten or twenty waiting about the docks—some standing alone, and some straggling in twos or threes as they waited, all looking dull and listless. These men, thus wearisomely waiting, could not be called ragged, for they wore mostly strong canvas or fustian suits—large, and seemingly often-washed, jackets predominating; and rents and tatters are far less common in such attire than in woollen cloth garments. From a man dressed in a large coarse canvas jacket, with worn corduroy trowsers, and very heavy and very brown laced leather boots, I had the following statement, in a somewhat provincial tone:—

"My father was a small farmer in Dorsetshire. I was middling educated, and may thank the parson for it. I can read the Bible, and spell most of the names there. I was left destitute, and I had to shift for myself; that's nine year ago, I think. I've hungered, and I've ordered my bottle of wine since, sir. I got the wine when railways was all the go, and I was a navvy; but I didn't like wine drinking; I drank it just for the fun of the thing—or, mayhap, because gentlemen drunk it. The port was like rather rough beer, but stronger, certainly. Sherry I only had once or twice, and liked good old ale better. I shifted my quarters every now and then till between two and three years ago, and then I tried my hand in London. At first Mr. —— (a second cousin of my father he was) helped me now and then, and he gave me odd jobs at portering for himself, as he was a grocer, and he got me odd jobs from other people besides. When I was a navvy I should at the best time have had my 50s. a week and more, if it hadn't been for the tommy shops. And I've had my 15s. in portering in London for my cousin, but sometimes I came down to 10s.—and sometimes to 5s. My cousin died sudden, and I was very hard up after that. I made nothing at portering some weeks. I had no one to help me; and in the spring of last year—and very cold it often was—I've walked after ten, eleven, or twelve at night, many a mile to lie down and sleep in any bye-place. I never stole, but have been hard tempted. I've thought of drowning myself and of hanging myself; but somehow a penny or two came in to stop that. Perhaps I didn't seriously intend it. I begged sometimes of an evening. I stayed at lodging-houses—for one can't sleep out in bad weather—till I heard from one lodger that he took his turn at the Commercial Docks. He worked at timber, or corn, or any-thing; and so I went—about the cholera time last year—and waited, and run from one dock to another, because I was new, and hadn't a chance like the old hands. I've had 14s. a week sometimes, and many's the week I've had 3s., and more's the week I've had nothing at all. They've said 'I don't know you.' I've lived on penny loaves—one or two a day—when there was no work; and then I've begged. I don't know what the other people waiting at any of the docks got. I didn't talk to them much, and they didn't talk much to me."

LABOUR AND THE POOR.

THE METROPOLITAN DISTRICTS.

[FROM OUR SPECIAL CORRESPONDENT.]

OF THE LONDON SAWYERS.

LETTER LIX.

The London Sawyers, though not a numerous body, still require full consideration, as belonging to a trade which has been extensively superseded by machinery.

According to the last census the number of sawyers in Great Britain in 1841 was 29,593; of these 23,360 resided in England, 4,550 in Scotland, 1,508 in Wales, and the remaining 175 in the British Isles. About one-tenth part of the whole of the sawyers in Great Britain were then located in the metropolis, the number in London being 2,978, of whom only 186 were under twenty years of age. Strange to say, one of the sawyers above twenty was a *female!* At the time of taking the previous census the number of the Metropolitan Sawyers above twenty years of age was 2,180; so that, from 1831 to 1841, the London trade had increased 612. Since then, however, I am informed that the number has declined nearly one half. The number of steam saw-mills in the metropolis, in 1841, was 15; at the present moment, they are 68, including those for cutting veneers as well as timber and deals.

The increase and decrease in the number of sawyers in the different parts of the country is a curious and important point to ascertain. By calculations, made from the Government Returns of 1831 and 1841, I find that the greatest addition to the number of sawyers took place in Lanark, where the population, between 1831 and 1841, increased 48 per cent., and the sawyers no less than 230 per cent.—thus making an increase of 182 per cent. over and above that of the population. The next county in rotation is Sutherland, where the sawyers have increased 156 per cent. beyond the population. After this comes Pembroke, showing an increase of 121 per cent.; Radnor and Cardigan, 100 per cent. each; the North Riding of Yorkshire, 87 per cent.; Inverness, 82; Berwick, 76; Renfrew, 75; and Cornwall, 73 per cent. above that of the population. In all of these counties, however, the population increased considerably; whereas in Dumfries, where the population decreased 1 per cent., the number of sawyers at the same time increased as much as 111 per cent., so that the total increase was equal to 112 per cent.

The great decrease in the number of sawyers seems to have occurred in the following counties. That which shows the greatest diminution of all is Linlithgow, where the population increased 44 per cent., whilst the sawyers decreased 33 per cent. After this comes Caithness; here the sawyers decreased 63 per cent. and the population increased 1 per cent. At Clackmannan the population increased 31 per cent., while the number of sawyers was augmented only 3 per cent.

In Aberdeen, Peebles, and Perth, there was an actual decrease, in each county respectively, of 7, 14, and 18 per cent., on the number of sawyers in 1841, compared with the number in 1831. Whether a comparative increase in the wages of the sawyers took place between 1831 and 1841, in those counties where the hands decreased—or whether there was a corresponding fall in the prices that the men obtained for their work in counties where the sawyers increased—I have no means of determining. Supposing the amount of work to be done to have remained the same, it is clear that, according to the law of "supply and demand," a rise or fall in the wages inversely proportional to the decrease or increase of the hands would have been the necessary result.

England, upon the whole, shows an increase of sawyers to the amount of 23 per cent. above that of the population; Wales, 44 per cent.; and Scotland, 25 per cent. Great Britain altogether gives an increase of 24 per cent.; a decrease in the wages of the sawyers, throughout the country, therefore, should have occurred to an equal extent.

Of sawyers there are four kinds—viz., the hardwood and timber sawyers, the cooper's stave, and the shipwright sawyers. The hardwood sawyers are generally employed in cutting mahogany, rosewood, and all kinds of foreign fancy woods. This work demands the greatest skill in sawing. It requires special nicety in cutting, because the timber is more valuable, and a "bungler" might be the cause of great loss to his employer. A hardwood sawyer can generally turn his hand to timber sawing, but the timber sawyers are seldom able to accomplish the cutting of hard woods. Timber sawyers are mostly engaged in cutting for carpenters and builders. The work of the cooper's stave sawyers consists principally in cutting "doublets" out of the foreign wood. The shipwright sawyers cut the "futtocks" and planks for ships. *Timber sawing*, by manual labour, has been unchanged within the recollection of the oldest man in the trade. One elderly man assured me that his grandfather, a sawyer, had told him that the work was always the same in his day. Two men work in a pit, which is generally 6 feet deep, and 4 feet 6 inches wide. These two men are termed the topman and pitman, according as they work *above* or *in* the pit. The pits are of two kinds, "scaffold" and "sunk" pits; the scaffold pit being raised from the ground, and almost always constructed of timber, while the sunk pit is dug into the earth. The men saw the trunks of trees, as well as the deals brought from the Baltic or Canada, when it is necessary to reduce them in thickness. Nearly all the English trees are roughly sawn in the woods where they are felled. Oaks felled in the Royal forests for building are sawn within the forest itself, a pit being dug as contiguous as possible to the fallen trees. The tree is lopped of its branches, and hewn; or, in other words, shaped or roughly squared with the axe for the readier work of the sawyers. Some of the timber hewers, however, are sufficiently skilful to chop the trees almost as smoothly as if it were planed. Oak is always "rended" (stripped of its bark), for tanning purposes. In some country places it is not an unfrequent thing for sawyers to sink a pit close by the building being erected, and then to saw the timber required for the frame-work of the house. In London, however, at present, this is seldom or never done. The general rule is, that "timber" is sawn at the yards, either by the steam machinery of the merchant, or by the manual labour of the sawyers in his employ. For ship timbers, the entire oak is generally sawn, for one oak is sometimes used for one of the curvilinear planks of the "futtocks" (the part above the keel). Ship timber sawing is confined to the ship-builders' yards; machinery is seldom employed for sawing the timber used by ship or barge builders, which is generally sawn curved. For planking, and the "straight cuts" in ship building, however, machinery is used. Sometimes two whole oaks are merely squared for the "beams" of the deck. For coopers' work, the timber (oak) comes in "staves" from the Baltic or America, and runs from 2 ft. to 9 ft. long, with an average of 6 inches wide and 3 inches thick. The thickness of the stave is sawn through to the substance required. "Doublets" (of which I have given an account from a cooper's stave-sawyer) are the most difficult parts of the stave-sawyer's work.

The straight sawn staves, which may be done by machinery, are used for milk and other pails, brewers' vats, and for cabinet work, such as drawer bottoms, &c. The staves are "hewn" abroad, and generally out of the trunks of the inferior trees (rarely out of the branches), and hewn to the sizes most convenient for stowage. The process observed by the shipwrights' or coopers' sawyers is the same as that of the timber and hardwood sawyers; it is all carried on in pits. These four classes of the trades, with the exception of the cooper's stave sawyers, are greatly reduced in numbers. It is generally considered in the trade that there are not half as many sawyers at present as there were five and twenty years ago. Formerly there used to be a great many shipwright sawyers along the banks of the Thames, but now, I am informed, the greater part of the yards are shut up, and many of the sawyers and shipwrights have emigrated to America. The year after the strike in 1833 there were 1,500 sawyers on the books of the union, exclusive of the cooper, staves, and shipwright sawyers; and now there are not more than 320 members belonging to the three district societies. The great decrease in the numbers of the trade is owing to the introduction of machinery. The first steam saw-mill set up in the neighbourhood of London was established at Battersea, about the year 1806 or 1807. It was erected principally for the cutting of veneers, and the trade, though aware that it could not fail to take the work from them, still believed that it never could do so to the extent that it has. "We knew," says my informant, "that the mills could cut the veneers better and thinner than what we could, and more in an inch, which is a great object of course in valuable woods, but still we never expected that steam power would be applied to the cutting of timber and deals. Since that time the mills have gone on increasing gradually, year after year, until now there are twenty regularly at work between Stangate and London-bridge, and no less than sixty-eight altogether, scattered throughout the metropolis."

The trade society of sawyers is divided into six districts. The first of these is the West London, which extends from Back-hill, near Hatton-garden, to Brentford; the second, or City District, reaches from Back-hill to St. George's-in-the-East; while the third, or Surrey District, runs from Dock-head, Bermondsey, to Westminster. These three belong to the general or timber and hardwood sawyers. The fourth district is in connection with the coopers' stave sawyers, and extends from Southwark-bridge to the Commercial Docks on the one side of the river, and to Limehouse on the other. The districts frequented by the shipwright-sawyers are Limehouse and Rotherhithe. Each class (excepting the shipwright-sawyers) has a trade society; and the following table shows the number of members belonging to each society, as well as the "non-society men" in each district, together with the total number and the aggregate total of the London operative sawyers generally:—

	Society Men.	Non-society Men.	Total Society and Non-society Men in each District.
West London District	60	140	200
City District	150	275	425
Surrey District	20	300	320
Total General Sawyers	230	715	945
Southwark, or Cooper's Stave Sawyers	60	40	100
Limehouse	..	450	450
Rotherhithe	..	100	100
Total Shipwright Sawyers	60	590	650
Aggregate Total of Society and Non-society Men	290	1,305	1,595

The houses of call at which the different societies meet have nothing whatever to do with the obtaining of employment for the men (as in the tailors' trade), but are simply places of meeting to discuss the affairs of the trade. The mode adopted by men wishing to obtain employment is making inquiry at the different yards. Concerning "benefits," or sums given in cases of affliction or distress, there are a few such provisions in connection with the trade societies, though they have no *provident funds*, such as the superannuation and vocation funds of other trades. The way in which assistance is rendered to the sick, and to the widow of a member of the trade societies, is by voluntary subscriptions, obtained either by petition or raffle—from 30s. to £3 being the sum usually collected in this manner, while, in the case of death, £5 is sometimes obtained in the city. The shipwright sawyers have a benefit society, called "The Good Samaritan," to render assistance to each other, in case of accident or death. Here the weekly contributions are 3d., and the "benefits" received from £1 to £10.

The weekly contributions paid by the members of the trade societies, are 2d. in the West London and City districts, and 3d. in the

Surrey and Southwark. The chief part of the money thus obtained is devoted to "trade purposes," and the remainder to philanthropic objects. These "trade purposes" consist principally of means adopted to uphold the wages of the trade—and the philanthropic objects, in the payment of small sums to the aged and infirm members, as well as those suffering from accidents. The tramps belonging to country societies are relieved by some of the London bodies. They are usually furnished with a card of the society to which they belong, and duplicates of these cards are kept at one or other of the London district houses. The operative sawyers of the metropolis are in correspondence with almost all the societies throughout the country, and the country societies are likewise in correspondence with each other, especially those in the north of England, where the greatest number of sawyers are located.

A tramp, upon arriving in town and producing the card of his society at one of the London houses of call, receives from the metropolitan society the sum of 5s. The country societies usually give from 1s. to 2s. to tramps, and in some cases a supper and a bed. The object of this relief to tramps is to assist a man in getting employment in another town, and the donations are given only to those parties who subscribe to some recognized society throughout the kingdom. Once a year an account of the money thus dispensed to tramps is taken; the delegates of the different country societies meeting annually in the north of England for that purpose. In the case of London, however, the districts meet in "central committee," and then make out a statement of the sum which has been disbursed by them throughout the year; this they forward to the different societies in the country. Of late years the London operative sawyers, I am informed, have been greatly opposed to any active resistance to their employers. The last strike among them took place in the years 1833 and 1834, and since that time they have generally sought to remedy any difference between them and their masters by more conciliatory measures. As an instance of this, I was furnished with copies of some circulars that had been sent round to the leading timber merchants on the occasion of the last disagreement. The tone of these was courteous and manly—neither cringing nor insulting—and spoke volumes for the intellectual and moral advance of the class since the days when Richardson's mill was destroyed by them.

The majority of the London sawyers, I am informed by some of the most intelligent and experienced members of the trade, are countrymen. They are generally the sons of village carpenters or wheel-wrights, though some have been "bred and born" in the trade, as they say. As a body of men they are essentially unpolitical. I could not hear of one Chartist among them; and, although suffering greatly from machinery, I found few with what may be called violent or even strong opinions upon the subject. They spoke of the destruction of Richardson's Saw-mill as one of the follies and barbarisms of past days, and were quite alive to the importance of machinery as a means of producing wealth in a community. They also felt satisfied that it was quite out of their power to stop the progress of it. As a body of men I found them especially peaceable, and apparently of very simple and kindly dispositions. They are not what can be called an educated class, but those whom I saw were certainly distinguished for their nat-ural good sense. They are usually believed to be of intemperate habits, and I am informed that in the palmy days of the trade there was good reason for the belief. But since then work has declined, and they have become much more sober. There are many teetotallers now among them; it is supposed that about one in ten has taken the pledge, and one in twenty kept it. The cause of the intemperance of the sawyers, say my informants, was their extremely hard labour, and the thirst pro-duced by their great exertion. Moreover, it was the custom of their employers, until within the last 15 years, to pay the men in public-houses. Since then, however, the sawyers have received their wages at the counting-houses of the timber merchants; and this, in con-nection with the general advance of intelligence among the body, has gone far to diminish the intemperance of the trade. The coffee-shops, again, I am assured, have added greatly to the sobriety of the operative sawyers. The large reduction which has taken place in the earnings of the sawyers has not been attended with any serious alteration in their habits. As a general rule, neither their wives nor their children "go out to work;" and since the decline of their trade no marked change in this respect has occurred. The majority of the men are certainly beyond the middle age—many that I saw were between sixty and sev-enty years. Cooper's stave-sawyers, however, are younger men. This is accounted for by the fact that since the decline of the trade of the "general sawyers," very few fresh hands have been brought into the trade, while many of the younger men have emigrated or sought some other employment—whereas the old men have been not only loath to leave to the country, but unable to turn their hand to a new business. The coopers' stave-sawyers, however, have considerably increased in number, owing to the difficulty of machinery to effect their work; hence, many of the other sawyers have taken to this branch. A large number of the general sawyers have been compelled to seek parish relief. Within the Lambeth workhouse alone, I am informed, there are as many as sixteen sawyers, besides others, in the receipt of out-door relief. Formerly there was in connection with each district society a fund for assisting the aged and infirm, but within the last fifteen years this has been done away with; and, as before stated, there are neither benefit nor superannuation funds belonging to two of the trade societies at the present day. The Surrey District Society, however, has recently started a "philanthropic fund" in connection with its trade society. As a rule, however, the men and their families are wholly unprovided for, either in case of sickness, old age, accident, or death, so that in the event of any affliction coming upon them, the parish alone is their refuge. From all I can gather, it appears that the general sawyers have declined in numbers at least two-fifths, and that only one-third of those now remaining can obtain full employment; another third have about three or four days' work in the week, and the other third but one day or two, and often none at all. The slack season with the general and coopers' stave-sawyers commences about a month before, and continues till a month after, Christmas. With the shipwright sawyers, however, the winter is the busiest time.

I shall now give an account of the earnings and condition of each of the different classes of sawyers above described, beginning with those engaged in the cutting of timber and hard wood. After which I purpose describing some of the principal steam saw-mills in London, and showing the amount of manual labour that they have superseded. To this I shall append a statement of two of the most intelligent men in the trade concerning the effect of machinery upon the working classes generally. In doing this I trust I need not remind the reader that the opinions there expressed are those of the *working men* themselves, who have been allowed to state their sentiments, because, suffering severely from machinery, it was considered to be but fair to express their thoughts and feelings upon this subject. It is right I should add, that I have found not one man in the trade opposed to machinery, in the abstract. The main objection of the operatives appears to be, that machinery benefits the capitalist, at the expense of the working man.

From "a pair" of deal or general sawyers, whom I found at their work, I had the following statement. The "pitman" said—

"I have been above thirty years a sawyer and a pitman; that is, the sawyer who works in the pit. We work in pairs—the topman and the pitman. The topman's part is the most difficult certainly, as he directs the saw to do her work (we always call the saw a *she*) according to the line. Every piece of timber is lined (chalked). When I first knew the trade things was much better. Me and my mate could earn between us then, £4 10s. a week easy. Top and pit men is paid alike, and has always been so. Now it is with great difficulty that we can make £3 a week the pair on us; and when we earn £3, we receive only £2 15s., for 1d. out of every shilling is deducted. The employer stops the 1d.; it's called 'pence,' for the finding of tools, all of which the master now provides for us." [Another man gave me a full account of this "pence," and calculated the amount of profit made by it.] "That wasn't the case till machinery got into full operation, twenty years ago, or somewhere thereabout." "I believe" (said the other man, the top sawyer), "the first steam saw-mill was started at the foot of Westminster-bridge by a man named Smart, thirty-five years ago, or so. We thought nothing about that then. Smart sawed deals. Master got harder and harder upon us. Our last strike was in the first year of the cholera, in 1833 I believe. We are paid for a twelve-foot deal 3¼d. a cut. Other deals are paid at the same rate. They do it cheapest at saw-mills, but not the best for working purposes, as carpenters can't 'bring it up' so well; that is, it's not so well adapted for work, because the machinery can't humour the grain. You see, sir, machinery is a ruining of all of us. Where there was 200 pair of sawyers there's not 50 now. We struck to keep up the prices of that day, which was 3½d. a cut in our yard, but the masters got so many hands in from the country and other cheap ways, even if the fellows knew nothing about a saw before, that we was obliged to give way. Ours is very hard work; the general hours is from six to seven. The year through the utmost we average a man is 25s. a week when the pence is paid. We are obligated to drink beer to keep our strength up, and that to from 6d. to 10d. worth a day; but there's no compulsion in any way as to beer. Some drink more than 10d. worth in a day, but that's more than sufficient. Our men can't afford to be what you may call drunkards (but p'r'aps one can't call them exactly sober men). The lazy fellows somehow—and I don't know how—do manage to get drunk pretty often. The wood we saw now is cut much greener than it used to be, and is worse to manage. We get English wood as it falls—oak, ash, elm, beech, and sycamore—them's the principal; and we have to trim it, knock the knots off and the bark off, but the oak comes to us stripped. For trimming the wood we're poorly paid. For ash, elm, beech, and all trees we have 6s. per 100 feet; the masters agree it's worth 1s. more. A man couldn't make 20s. a week at that, and the 'pence' to be stopped out of it. I've been a top man for more than thirty years—I should say about thirty-five. Top and pit sawyers very seldom change places, only for a make-shift. The top-man, though it's the most difficult part, gets no more than the pit man, not a morsel, and he has to keep the saw in order, and he's answerable for all work to the master. The easiest wood of all to saw is American pine; it gives to the saw easiest. English timber (elm, beech, and sycamore) is the hardest. Oak's another thing; it's difficult to get it ready to fit it for sawing, but not harder to saw than elm. With a log of mahogany the topman must humour the saw so as to cut to the master's orders, and masters are very exacting. If we vexes 'em, they puts us on spruce deals, which are the hardest deals to cut. We can't make above 2s. 6d. a man a day of it, and they keep us at it as long as they think fit. In spruce deals we have to cut what the saw-mills can't well cut; they can cut it, certainly, but they charge higher; for there's only one cut (two boards) in a spruce fir, and it takes them as much time to cut one cut as to cut ten. I've known, in 1821, when George IV. was crowned, 80 pairs of men in two sawpits, where now there isn't a single one. The pits, all of them I think, is coming to a close, and the business is going to the dogs, or the saw-mills, for it's all one. Many sawyers is now glad to go in for labourers to saw-yards, for piling and placing the timber, at 3s. or 4s. a day—perhaps only with two days' work a week—because they can't get employment at sawing. One of our saws—they run from five to seven feet—will cost £1 for five feet, and on to 30s. for seven feet, without the frame, which may cost 10s. The weight of a 7-foot saw is from 60 to 70 lbs., for two men to pull up and down all day, at the rate of, say ten strokes, or seventy feet, a minute, or 4,200 feet an hour; and that's, as you say, 42,000 feet in a day of ten hours—so that we lift upwards of half-a-hundred weight nearly eight miles high in our day's work. The resistance of the saw—as it pulls like so many hooks coming down and catching—is not an easy calculation. A scientific man—it's ten years ago, I think—calculated, and reckoned that each down stroke (for the up stroke is only a lift up of the saw, like) was equal to lifting 86 lb. My opinion is, and I judge by experience and by lifting weights, that he was right; others think so, too. I don't know what he calculated it for." [The man then, at my request, went into another calculation as to weight, of course with my assistance with the figures.] "A force of 86 lbs. is required for each down stroke: 10 in a minute is a force of 430 lbs. put out by each man every minute, and that's a power of 25,800 lbs. an hour. In a day of ten hours, the whole amount of power is equal to 258,000 lbs., or more than 18,428 stone; and divide that by 8, and that'll show how many hundred weights— more than 2,303, or upwards of 115 tons a day. The strength's put out equal by the two sawyers, top and pit, generally; and it ought to be always, when each man does his part properly, and like a workman. Provisions has been cheap for some time, and that's a great thing for working men. If we says a word about better pay, or the grievance of the 'pence,' masters stops our mouths with machinery. A 'pair' of sawyers will do three dozen cuts of 12 feet deals a day, or four dozen of battens. A 'cut' is nine inches through in a deal and seven in a batten. The saw may go ahead half an inch a stroke as near as may be. Sawyers is generally healthy men and not short-lived."

From another Deal Sawyer, who had made it his more particular inquiry, I had the following information concerning the "*pence*" alluded to in the preceding statement:—

"Putting on the pence," he said, "was one of the sort of things masters have recourse to when they don't want to seem to reduce men's wages right out. They do it by side-winds. The pence is a great saving to the masters. A good saw, which may cost 20s. at the outside, will last eight months. Suppose a pair of sawyers earn £3 a week between them less the pence (which is a penny out of every shilling), that's 5s. stopped for the saw. And suppose in a yard in regular work, and in a pretty brisk time, they work six months, or 26 weeks, at the same rate, the master then has received £6 10s. for what cost him 20s., and that's a profit of £5 10s. The saw will then last two months longer, which is £2 more profit, or £7 10s. in all. To be sure, there's the frame, which may cost, at the utmost, 10s., but one frame, unless there's an accident, will serve for four or five saws. If you reckon, besides this, 1s. a week for files and other costs of tools (though it's not 1s.), the master's clear profit out of the pence will be £5 15s., or say £5 10s. out of each saw, or 200 per cent. Now, suppose eight frames are kept on the way, as may be the case in some few yards still, then the master will clear £60 in all by the 'pence.' It does not matter as regards the master's profits on the pence, in the long run, whether work be slack or brisk, for when it's slack his saws last all the longer, only he doesn't turn over his £5 10s. profit so quick—that's all."

A tall hale-looking man, with an appearance of great respectability, gave me the following account of Ship-timber Sawing:—

"I have been a sawyer of ship timbers these forty years. I worked a few years in the country, and then I came to London. When I first worked in London we were paid 5s. a day, but we now work by the piece, except on a few things. Piece work came to be the regular system 24 or 25 years ago. We are paid the same prices for our labour as I've ever known, but there's not work enough for us, that's where the times are worse. We—that is the pair of us—are paid for sawing English oak, 7s. for 100 feet. We work topmen and pitmen, as in other pits, and are paid each man alike. Sometimes, by agreement, the topman has 1s. or 2s. extra, on account of having the saw to keep in order. We are paid the same price for Memel oak, but that's little used; it's chiefly English that we has to cut, and we've the same price for Quebec oak, and foreign elm, and for teak. There's a good deal of teak cut now. Africa (African oak) is so hard that we have 10s. 6d. per 100 ft. for it. For Dantzic and Quebec firs, such as are used for the planking of ships, we get 4s. 6d. We cut the oak used for building 1,000 ton ships in first, second, and third 'futtocks;' that's for the outward sides of the vessel, such as meet the water over the keel. First futtocks are cut 14 inches thick, and as long of course as the tree runs. Second futtocks are 12 inches thick, and thirds 11 inches. For smaller tonnages the futtocks are cut less thick in proportion, down to six inches, which is the thinnest cut, and is used for building small schooners. The 'floor' bottom of a ship of 1,000 tons is cut 15 inches thick, and for smaller craft in the same way down to six. I now reckon 40s. a man an excellent week's work, but it's not often we make that, for there's more than six months in the year very bad, when oft enough we'll not make half-a-crown a day; so the average for the year now runs between 15s. and 40s., or something less, a week. We have no 'pence' to pay, as in some saw-yards, but we have to find our own tools. Our saws are 6½ to 7 feet long. An average one will cost 19s., but the price varies according to the breadth, and that varies from one to eleven inches, though we use narrow saws most. A saw will last us twelve months, as a general calculation, when it's used three days a week. We sometimes saw circular blocks, just the shape of a wooden trencher, for ship-building, and then we are paid by the day, 5s. and 6s. Machinery ruins the saw trade; and now they've come to saw circular, for shipbuilders' use, by steam machinery, worse luck. As yet there's only one steam-mill for ship-timber sawing, besides the

Government one at Woolwich. For little masters in the general trade the steam-mills are an accommodation, as credit's given them, and men, of course, must have their Saturday nights. Accidents are very frequent among us. We have no sick fund, but I belong to a general benefit society, as do some others. The men drink a good deal; our work is hard, and four pints of beer a day is a moderate allowance. We are not paid at a public-house, and have no grievances of that sort to complain of, nor any grievances that I know of; for we're fairly treated between master and man. We are slack now. There's many ships brought here ready built, from America mostly. They don't last so long as English-built ships, and have often to be refastened; but if a merchant can insure what does he care? The teak we are now sawing runs 20ft. to 50ft. long. The English oak goes from 20ft. to 70ft. There's nothing like good English oak, sir—nothing."

A man whom I found residing with his wife and children in a little place of apparently two rooms made the following statement as to cooper's stave sawing. He lived, with many others of the same class, in one of very many alleys that run from the river side, behind the site of what was once the Globe Theatre, to Guildford-street, Southwark. The alleys are built with the utmost economy of space; some of them are almost too narrow for the passage of a horse. I saw nothing, however, to call filth. Abutting on one of the narrowest of these alleys are high dark wooden palings, from behind which come the smell and lowing of cows, a circumstance rather in contrast with the thick packing of human habitations on all sides:—

"I have been twenty years a cooper's stave sawyer," he said. "We use different saws to those of the deal sawyers. They are smaller in the teeth, and only four feet long. A saw and frame will weigh 50 lb. on an average, and I reckon that we pull 60 lbs. weight every stroke. We make 50 strokes a minute up and down. I'm sure of it. We work very quick. That's 200 feet a minute, or 4,000 yards an hour—about 2¼ miles. We are top-sawyers and pitmen. Both are paid alike, though the topman has the hardest work. When I first knew the business times was much better. I could then earn £2 a week, and my mate the same, comfortably, the year through. Now we can each of us earn 25s. on an average the year through. We are paid by the piece. For 6-foot Dantzic or Memel straight cut staves 1s. 7d. per dozen cuts is paid us. We may have one or two cuts in each stave. For Quebec staves of the same length, or even if not quite so long, 1s. 8d.; Quebec hogsheads, 1s. 4d. They run about five feet; Dantzic hogsheads, about 4 feet, 1s.

2d.; brandy pipes, about 5 feet, 1s. 4d.; barrel straight cuts (for beer barrels), between 3 and 4 feet, 1s.; if we cut them into 'doublets'—and in doublets it's easier work for the cooper, for we thin the stave for his purpose—we have 2d. a dozen extra. The master gets more profit by it, but we have only 2d. a dozen, and other sizes in proportion, up to 4d. These are the principal staves; the others are for vinegar kilderkins and small barrels (9 or 18 gallons), and paid in proportion. We work two or three different sorts of timber, but all of them oak; all foreign, Baltic or American. We saw the staves from the timber as it's brought by the ships; it's cleaved (cleft), or chopped, to our purpose abroad. In the winter of '47-8 we were on strike sixteen weeks, but only me and two mates stood out for that time. They reduced us in the doublets 6d., from 1s. 11d. for the long staves to 1s. 5d., and for straight cuts to 1s. 4d., while others were reduced in the same proportion. We formed a committee among ourselves and got our prices back again, however. We did it in a month, after forming a society, though some stave-yards didn't manage it for six or nine months. The masters gave way when they got busy. Our masters can get their staves sawn cheaper at a steam-mill by 6d. a dozen the bigger ones, the straight cuts; but the machine can't make all the turns wanted in the stave—thank God for that. For straight cuts they are working us out. We haven't many straight cuts now to what we had; less by the working sawyer from 10s. to 15s. a week wages. Some masters—mine's one—don't like to send their staves to steam-mills for straight cuts, for if the timber for the staves be crooked we can cut them to more advantage to the master than the steam-mills can. We take our money in the counting-house. I have been paid, in another employ, at a public-house, and we were obliged to take our beer from there every day, but when we formed our committee we put a stop to all that bad system. It was time, for some of us had to go home with nothing on a Saturday night. Sawing is very hard work, and requires four pints of beer a day to support a man, but many drink a great deal more. The public-house system made men drunkards—I'm sure it did, sir. I confine myself to four pints, which is enough for me. I know of no teetotallers among us. Accidents are common with sawyers. I've fallen many times, and have been cut all to pieces, so to say, by the saw." [He showed me some scars on his arms.] "We have a sick fund. Take sawyers altogether, they're fond of a drop, but I don't think them rougher than other people when they're in liquor. We are nearly all married men with families. Families seems a sort of gift to poor men, instead of to rich ones. I have known sawyers working at 70 years old, hard work as it is. We live as long as other people, I think. We pay no 'pence,' but have to find our own saws. A saw may cost from 7s. to 10s., and the frame 5s., when a new frame is wanted. A frame will last five or six saws. A saw will last us about five or six months in average use."

Another man, in the same calling, gave me information confirming all the preceding, and said further:—

"The timber sawn by coopers' stave sawyers is sawn as it's brought in from foreign parts, and it's brought in all the different lengths, and breadths, and thicknesses that are required for coopering. I'm of opinion that stave-sawyers are safe from being put to one side, for a good while, anyhow, by steam, in sawing 'doublets.' The timber runs irregular like, and is crooked sometimes. It's chiefly 'cleaved,' as we call it (cleft), with a hatchet, or whatever tools they have in those foreign parts. Out of the centre of one of these staves we saw a portion of wood, beginning almost at a point, and spreading out gradually to 'the bouge,' that's the centre, where the *bulge* is the greatest. Then, when the *bouge* is reached, we saw along the other part of the wood, just in the same round inclining form as in the first part of the work. The inner part cut this way, which is like a quarter of an orange flattened out, is used by coopers for the heads of barrels, the two *equal* sides that are sawn from off the middle parts are the *doublets*, which are in this way ready hollowed and curved in the inner part, for cooper's work. Steam won't easy do that, sir."

The first steam-mill for the sawing of planks was established (as is mentioned in the statement of a sawyer previously given) about thirty-six years ago, by Mr. Smart, near Westminster-bridge. For perhaps twenty years before that period horses had been employed to supersede men's labour. The principle on which these horse-mills were constructed was not dissimilar to that now in use in the steam saw-mills. The horses then did the work of the engine now—working nine saws at once, but with perhaps only half the motive power of steam as regards velocity. About forty-five years ago a party of sawyers one night walked abruptly into the largest of these horse saw-mills—that of Mr. Richardson, of Limehouse—and with sledge-hammers and crow-bars utterly demolished the whole apparatus, which was the work of but a few minutes. The men did not carry a single fragment away with them after the work of demolition had been done, and they studiously abstained from any other act of violence, and even from any act or words of insult. Their plea was, that these horse-mills would bring them and their families to the parish, by making beasts do the work of men, and that they had a right to protect themselves the best way they could, as no man, they said, merely for his own profit, had any right to inflict ruin upon a large body. So I was assured, and such feelings were at that period not uncommon among the ruder class of labourers. These horse-mills were but little remunerative, and Mr. Richardson did not think it worth his while to replace his machinery. It lay scattered about his yard until within 20 or 30 years ago. Another horse-mill, that of Mr. Lett, was demolished in the same way, not long after, by a party of sawyers; and the other proprietors of such places—there were perhaps about six in all—either discontinued the use of horses through fear, or the working of their mills became less remunerative, and they were gradually done away with. I had these particulars from a very intelligent man, now engaged in the sawing business. They were beyond his own recollection; but he had often heard his father, who passed a long life in the capacity of a sawyer, relate the circumstances. My informant was not altogether positive as to dates—he gave them to the best of his recollection. Yet, without this precipitate violence, horse saw-mills would have been discontinued, "for a very sufficient reason," said my informant, "because they didn't pay, I feel pretty well satisfied. Horses, you see, sir, must eat their oats of a night, or whether they are at work or not, but steam consumes coals only when at work."

Steam saw-mills continued to be gradually established throughout the metropolis until they now number 68—six at least of the proprietors being also timber merchants. These mills average three "frames" each, a frame holding nine saws. In case all the means of these mills were called into operation at one time, 1,755 saws would be at work. Of these the straight saws make 160 "revolutions," as each up or down motion of the saw is technically called, in a minute, the "revolution" being four feet in length. The circular saws, for cutting deals and timber, describe a diameter of from 18 to 36 inches, 18 inches being the most frequent size, perhaps comprising seven-eighths of the circular saws in the London mills. The "circulars" may number one-tenth of the straight saws, and these "circulars" perform 1,800 revolutions in a minute. Of the space thus traversed I have given some curious particulars from an experienced man. Another gentleman, himself the conductor of a steam saw-mill—and I have to thank him also for other valuable and curious information—took pains, at my request, to calculate the number of sawyers superseded by the application of steam power. These, from the best data, he gives as 750 "pairs," or 1,500 men.

In the course of my inquiries I visited a steam saw-mill. It is situate close upon the river, being, indeed, a wharf as well as a mill. Over head is a lofty roof of thin light-coloured timber, through which the light came with a pleasant yellow hue. A timber frontage, in some parts of the nature of a casement, looks on the river. When the machinery was not at work all was pleasant and quiet, but when eighteen saws were in full operation—that number being employed on my visit—there was anything but quiet. The usual noise of a steam-engine had the addition of the grinding sound of the saws, jumping, as it would seem to any one ignorant of the agency employed, up and down most rapidly—while at intervals, through all this combination of sounds, was heard the ripple of the Thames dashing close up to the river front of the mill, for it was then high water, and a strong breeze was blowing. The steam-engine occupies one corner of the premises, and is partly detached. The wheels and machinery by which the mill is worked are beneath the timber flooring of the yard, the main shaft occupying the centre. The frame is simply nine upright saws, each four feet in length, moving up and down as the timber is sawn, and at a distance from each other, according to the substance the plank is to be sawn. When the machinery is set a-going, the plank, by means familiar to engineers, is made to adjust itself to the action of the saws, being gradually advanced as each cut has been executed. A frame-worker attends to the due adjustment of the timber, however, as well as to the renewal of the saws when the teeth have become blunted by the rapid and severe friction. The machinery, when viewed at work under the flooring through the trap-doors, presents a very curious appearance. The imperfect light throws many of the wheels into the gloom, the brighter parts flashing to the eye, while the reverberation conveys the notion of extended space and far multiplied machinery.

Two engines, each of 10-horse power—and fewer are never fixed in any mill—cost from £650 to £800; about £700 being perhaps the most usual expense. These engines consume a ton of coals in a day of twelve hours, and a quart of machine oil.

Some further particulars concerning *steam saw-mills* I give in the words of a well-informed and observant man long familiar with their working:—

"I have been several years—I can't say precisely how many— acquainted with all the parts of the labour required in a steam saw-mill. I am now a foreman. For the management of two engines, each of 10-horse power, or one of 20, there are, besides the foreman, who overlooks the business generally, five men employed—an engine-driver, a saw-sharpener, two frame-workers, and a labourer. The business of the engine-driver and the saw-sharpener everybody can understand; the frame-worker attends to the frames, replacing the saws when it's necessary, and looking to the deals being in a proper position, and all connected with the frames; and the labourer piles the deals when sawn, and does all the 'odd jobs.' He is paid from 3s. to 4s. a day, and the others from 5s. to 6s. The steam-mill saws go from 8 to 10 'runs'—9 inches is a run—through 12 feet spruce deals, before they require sharpening; through some deals the saw will go more runs. The best and quickest sharpeners, by far, are men who have been used to work as topmen in sawpits; they are better than cutlers. The men's saws, in the pits, require sharpening rather oftener than steam-mill saws. Their saws have teeth—called 'space'—⅝ or ¾ inches apart. Steam-mill saws are closer-toothed, and cut finer, and therefore cleaner. The steam saws are made of inferior steel to those of the pit sawyers; they cost about 5s. a piece. It takes a quarter of an hour to replace the nine saws in a frame when they become blunted. One saw will last six months. Our saw sharpener does nothing else. The topman uses half-round files for his sharpening; the steam-mill saw sharpeners use round files. In our steam-mills we can't cut staves for coopers; that is, we can cut them straight, of course, but not in doublets, which is the main trade. We can't so well cut elm, oak, or ash, as the sawyers. Indeed, we can only outdo the sawyers altogether in deals; but they're more used for general purposes than all other woods put together—far more. Timber merchants who have their own steam-mills have, for some things, to employ sawyers still. We cut deals at 2s. 6d. a dozen, which, by men's labour, costs 3s. 6d. A twenty-horse power engine will do the work of thirty 'pairs' of sawyers—that's sixty men—in a day, in sawing deals, but only deals. Our saws penetrate one-eighth of an inch each 'revolution.' The pit-sawyers' penetrate from a quarter to half an inch, according to the quality of the deals. They have more 'holt' (grasp or purchase) on their saws, and so can work them deeper into the wood. A pair of sawyers would most likely beat one saw worked by steam. Our saw would go twice as quick as theirs, but their cuts would go twice as far as ours. Owing to the 'holt,' the pit sawdust is much coarser than ours. One of our frames will make from 3 to 4 sacks of sawdust in a day; almost twice as much as a pair of sawyers will make in a week. A sack, which is generally sold at 6d., is 4 bushels. Some saw-mills—ours every now and then—can't dispose of their dust quick enough, and have to burn it. It's chiefly sold to 'dust' public-house tap-rooms, and those sort of places. Of all the single consumers, no doubt Astley's is the greatest. Doll-stuffers use it too, but a single sack will stuff a famous lot of dolls. Very few saw-mills, if any, can be said to be paying. But there's the capital sunk in the machinery, and a small return is better than its standing idle. The work is irregular, and many take long credit. Small orders, too, though they must be done, are anything but a profit. A frame makes ten cuts as easy as one. A circular saw, worked by steam, performs 1,800 revolutions in a minute. Take the usual diameter of 18 inches, and, of course, the saw describes a circumference of 54 inches, or one yard and a half, and does it 1,800 times. So that in a minute one mile and a half is done, with 60 yards to spare; and, not reckoning the 60 yards at all, but supposing there was no stop in the working, 90 miles an hour, which, at no more than 10 hours in a day, is 900 miles. The straight saws perform 160 revolutions, each of 4 feet, in a minute, which gives 213 yards a minute, or within 15 yards of 7¼ miles an hour. Reckon 1,000 of these saws going just now, and that's performing a distance (not minding the fifteen yards) of 7,250 miles an hour. Or, if all the saws were going (1,755), of 12,223¾ miles an hour. Of course, that's supposing there is no stop. The penetration through the timber under these circumstances would be between 22 and 23 miles, at an eighth of an inch each cut."

Concerning the operation of the steam saw-mills upon the working men, I had the following statement from two picked men: they were general sawyers. One, who was 55 years old, had been 40 years in the trade; and the other, who was 49, had had 35 years' experience in it. "I can recollect," said the younger, "when I could save more money in a week than I can now earn in the same time. Ah! then, if a man was a goodish sawyer, and out of work, he would have twenty or thirty people after him. Often, when I've been going along London streets, with my saw on my back, a timber-merchant or a cabinet maker would hail me, and cry, 'Halloa, ho, do you want any work, my man?' and often they gave a sum of money for a good sawyer to come and work for them." The elder man said, "My father was a sawyer, and often I've heard him say that the trade was better in his younger days than even it was in mine. He used to speak of what it was seventy year ago; the wages weren't better in his younger days than they were in mine, but the work was—there was fewer hands, you see. I have heard him say that him and his mate has earned one pound a day. He became a timber merchant afterwards, and he's told me that he'd paid a pair of sawyers that he had in his employ £24 in the month. They were veneer sawyers, and that was the finest and best paid work in the trade—now that's *all* gone from us. There an't one regular veneer sawyer left in the trade. All veneers are cut at present by machinery. Thirty years ago, when London wasn't half so big, there was three times as many sawyers as there are now, and one pair in every ten out of these used to cut veneers. In every timber yard the 'first pair' was generally employed cutting veneers. In the neighbourhood where I live, the sawyers are not half so many as they were. At R——'s yard, where they used to keep nine pair, they hasn't more than three, and yet the work's increased to that extent that it would keep twenty saws going where only nine was employed before. At S——'s there used to be nineteen pairs of sawyers constantly at work, and now there's not employment for one pair. I think I have heard my father say that there was as many as 3,000 pairs in the metropolis. Why, not more than twenty year ago one master sawyer used to have as many as five apprentices. In the year '26 it was about as good a time for sawyers as ever it was—there was a good demand for men, and good wages." "I can remember it better," said the oldest of the two; "but, never mind, that's the last time that the trade's been what you may call good. It began to decline between '26 and '27—just about Fauntleroy's bankruptcy. I remember the saw mills began to get more general from that period. I can't recollect when the horse saw-mills was fust put up. Several cabinet-makers used to have hand-mills of their own, which consisted of circular saws in a bench, and worked by a couple of labourers. One of the horse-mills—I remember it was over about Pedler's-acre—was said to kill a horse a day. The first steam-mill that was set up was at Battersea. It was a Frenchman (Brunel) that took out the patent for cutting veneers by steam—that's above forty year ago. The steam-mill had been up two or three years when I first came to London, and that was in 1810. I recollect seeing some shortly after I got to town. They was cut more true than any sawyer could do them, but not half as well as they are done now. The first that was done was eight in the inch, and now they can cut 14, as thin as a wafer, and that's impossible for the best sawyer in the world to do. I have cut as many as eight in the inch myself, but then the wood was very shallow—

eight or nine inches deep. The general run of veneers cut by hand was about six in the inch. It wasn't until some five or six years after the first steam saw-mill for veneers was set up that one was erected for deals, and some time after that they were used to cut timber. About 1827, they began to get general, and as fast as the saw-mills have been starting up so we have been going down. We only have the rough work, and what the saw-mills can't or won't do. We get chiefly 'one cuts' to do, because the saw-mills can't do that kind of work so well as we can. A sawyer formerly took apprentices." "I was an apprentice for seven years," said the younger man. "And I worked along with my father," said the other. "It was a rule in our trade that the eldest son was entitled to his father's business. Now I don't see a sawyer in London who has an apprentice. Formerly we would allow no man to work at our trade unless he had been apprenticed or articled for three years; now it's open to any man, and yet none that I know of come into it. Many that I am acquainted with have left it, and many more would be glad to get away from it. I was one of the enumerators at the taking of the last census in the district in which I now live, and now I think there are not more than half as many sawyers as what there were then; the old hands die off, and no young ones fill up their places. Some few sawyers perhaps put their boys to the trade because they haven't the means to apprentice them to anything else, and the boy, you see, by working with his father, will bring in something at the end of the week. All that the two earns then goes to one home. I know many sawyers that have emigrated, and among them have been some of the best workmen, and some of the most intelligent. The trade, we think, will keep dwindling and dwindling every year; but machinery, we think, will never be able to take it all from us. I haven't been at work not a day this week. Sometimes we are worked to death, and sometimes we are picking our fingers. At the beginning of the week we are often obligated to have extra hands, and at the end of the week we are standing still, may be. There may be some few in large firms who may have constant work; but the most of our trade is idle more than half their time. It puzzles me how they live, some of them. Twenty-six years ago, my average wages was 35s. a week all the year round. Now I should say that this last year my wages hasn't been above 18s. a week all the year through. I don't think the average wages of our trade, take the good with the bad, are above £1, and formerly it was full double that. Why, twenty years ago we used to have a trade dinner every year, somewhere out of town, and to go up to the tavern—wherever it was—in grand purcession, with bands of music and flags flying (we had a union jack that cost forty odd pound then), and the dinner for the whole of the districts used to come to near upon 50 guineas. After all this I leaves you to judge what our opinion is about machinery. Of course we looks upon it as a curse. We have no chance to compete with a machine; it isn't taxed, you see, as we are. I look upon machinery as an injury to society generally, because if it drives the hands out of our trade they must go into some other, so that working men is continually pressing one upon another. If machinery can cut the wood cheaper than we can, it's a gain to the timber merchant, he is enabled to reduce the price, and so some part of society may be a gainer by it, but we think society loses more than it gets. Supposing a machine to do the work of 100 pair of sawyers, then of course it throws 200 men out of employ; and these 200 men have families, and they are all benefited by the employment of the working man's labour. But in the case of machinery only one man is benefited" [this I found to be the common opinion of the operatives]; "the money all goes to him and the others are left to starve, or else for society to support, either as paupers or felons, so that society, in the present state of things, after all, loses more than it gains. We see that as science advances the comfort of the working man declines. We believe machinery to be a blessing if rightly managed. It only works for one class at present, but the time *will* come when it *will* work for all parties." [The carpenters, it will be seen in my next letter, hold the same opinion.] "Let machinery go on increasing as it does, and there will come a time when the labour of the many will be entirely done away with; and then what will society gain when it has to keep the whole of the labouring classes? We can see machinery improving every day, so that there is less work for the people and more paupers. Our bread is being taken out of our mouths, and our children left to starve. I am quite satisfied that those who have nothing but their labour to depend upon get up every morning less independent than they went to bed. The many long heads that are scheming how to deprive men of their work is quite sufficient to bring that about. It's no use emigrating either. Let a working man go where he will, machinery pursues him. In America it's worse for sawyers, if possible, than here. There the sawing is all done by water-mills, and wood is so plentiful and so cheap that if they spoil a bit, it ain't no matter. Working-men is much disheartened at the increase of machinery, when they're a standing at the corner of streets idle and starving and see carts coming out of the yard filled with planks that they ought to have had. You see, sir, when some are injured by any alteration, they gets compensation; but here is our trade cut up altogether, and what compensation do we get? We are left to starve without the least care. I have paid 1s. 10d. for a quartern loaf before now, and I could get it much easier than I can now. When I get up in the morning, I don't know whether I shall be able to earn a 6d. before nightfall. I have been at work ever since I was eight years old, and I'm a pretty good example of what the working man has to look for; and what's the good of it all? Even the machines, some of them, can't hardly raise the price of the coals to get their fire up. When they first set up they had 6d. a foot for cutting veneers, and now they have only 1d. Machinery's very powerful, sir, but competition is much stronger."

The Morning Chronicle, Monday, July 8, 1850.

CASE OF REAL CHARITY.

TO THE EDITOR OF THE MORNING CHRONICLE.

SIR—By desire of J. N., Esq., of Oxford-square, I beg to enclose you a cheque for 2*l.*, in furtherance of the object stated in a letter signed S. A. R., dated 2d July, from the University Club, which appeared in your valuable paper.

Your most obedient servant,

Mincing-lane, July 6.   C. M.

The above refers to a donation called forth by the following letter, which, for the sake of a very deserving family, we take this opportunity of repeating:—

TO THE EDITOR OF THE MORNING CHRONICLE.

Sir—As you are the conductor of the organ of the Press which originated and set in motion the system of female emigration, now proceeding under the auspices of Mr. Sidney Herbert's excellent society, it has struck me that I cannot do better than appeal to you, in order, if possible, to obtain some help towards sending out to Australia a poor woman and her son, the two daughters of the former having already been approved as candidates for emigration at the expense of the society. My object is to keep together a poor, an affectionate, and a most deserving family, who have suffered bitterly in this country, but who entertain the most sanguine hopes of their future prospects if permitted to exercise their united industry in a land where there is abundant labour and abundant food for all.

I have already applied to your chief clerk, Mr. Jones, upon the subject. That gentleman has made the strictest inquiry into the case, and he will bear me out in stating that he found the family in a state of actual and literal starvation—that they possess an excellent character—that the mother is the widow of a respectable ship captain, who has seen better days, and is in every respect a person superior to her actual station in life; and that, with the exception of a small pittance, altogether about 5*l.* per annum, received from the Trinity House and the Merchant Seamen's fund, the family have been entirely supported by the labour, at needle-work, of the female members of it—the son having been for some time in bad health.

Lately, however, the supply of work failed, and everything which could be pawned—furniture, dress, and bedding—was gone when Mr. Jones paid a visit to the scene of distress.

The widow can raise, by giving up the pensions I mentioned, about 15*l*., which will pay for the passage of her son and herself. About 10*l*. is still required for articles of necessary outfit, and for the redemption of clothes now in pawn. If this sum can be raised, an act of real, and, because real, useful charity will have been accomplished, and a poor family preserved from a separation which is greatly dreaded by them all.

Mr. Jones will, I am sure, be happy to give the most explicit information as to the details of the case.

I remain, &c. &c.

Alpha.

LABOUR AND THE POOR.

THE METROPOLITAN DISTRICTS.

[FROM OUR SPECIAL CORRESPONDENT.]

OF THE LONDON CARPENTERS AND JOINERS.

LETTER LX.

The number of carpenters and joiners in Great Britain at the time of taking the last census, in 1841, amounted to 162,977. Of this number 128,000 were resident in England, 24,000 in Scotland, 8,000 in Wales, and 2,000 in the British Isles. There are no means of ascertaining the entire number of carpenters and joiners in the kingdom at any previous period, because the census of 1831 (which was the first that took any account of the occupations of the people) gave only the number of handicraftsmen and labourers who were 20 years of age and upwards. If, however, we compare the number of carpenters and joiners of that age who were resident in the different counties in 1831 with those located in the same places ten years afterwards, we shall arrive at many curious results; for by such means we shall be enabled to see how this particular craft has increased or declined in particular parts of the country—and then, by ascertaining the rate of wages in those districts, we shall at the same time learn how far the weekly income of the workman has been influenced by the principle of supply and demand. I regret that, at present, I have no means of making the comparison as regards the wages of the carpenters at the two decennial periods; still, to know the rate of increase in a particular craft is of the utmost importance in all questions of social economy, and I have therefore been at considerable pains in arriving at the following results.

The greatest increase among the carpenters—in comparison with the increase of population—took place in Carnarvonshire, where the trade was augmented no less than 223 per cent. more than the general population of that county. The next greatest increase occurred in Renfrewshire, where the number in the trade rose to 151 per cent. above that of the population; and the next in Merionethshire, in

which county the increase was 107 per cent. above the people generally. Then came Lanarkshire, where the carpenters increased 97 per
cent.; in Durham, 60 per cent.; Bute, 53 per cent.; and Radnorshire,
47 per cent.; while in Yorkshire the increase of carpenters was 46 per
cent. *above* the increase of the population. The following counties
show, on the whole, an increase of carpenters, but in a *less* degree
than the population:—Linlithgow shows an increase from 1831-41,
but in the ratio of 22 per cent. less than that of the population. The
population of Sussex increased 14 per cent., whilst the number of carpenters remained nearly the same. The increase of the carpenters in
Cardiganshire was 8 per cent. below that of the population. Rutland
7 per cent., Breconshire 6 per cent., Dumbarton 4 per cent., Warwick
2 per cent., and Norfolk 1 per cent.

An actual decrease of the carpenters occurred in the following
counties:—In Caithness the population increased 1 per cent., whilst
the carpenters decreased 14 per cent., making a difference on the
whole of 15 per cent. In Elgin the population was augmented 2 per
cent., while the number of carpenters diminished 9 per cent., making
a total decrease of 11 per cent. In Roxburgh the population increased
10 per cent., but the carpenters decreased 8 per cent., or 18 per cent.
on the whole. At Kinross, Peebles, and Perth both the population
and the carpenters have decreased, though the carpenters in a greater
degree than the population. The increase of carpenters over and above
the increase of the population in the three divisions of Great Britain
is as follows:—

> England, increase of carpenters, 14 per cent.
> Scotland, ditto 20   „
> Wales, ditto 37   „

The increase of the carpenters in the metropolis has been less than the
population, and stands thus:—Increase of population, 32 per cent.;
carpenters, 28 per cent.; so that the London carpenters increased at
the rate of 4 per cent. less than the general London population.

I refrain from drawing any conclusions as to the increase or decrease in the rate of wages in the counties above-mentioned, because
I am without any authentic facts for so doing; and I therefore leave
it to others, who are in a position to make the comparison, to show
how the weekly income of the carpenters in the several counties above
enumerated has been affected by the increase or decrease of their numbers.

It is with the carpenters and joiners of the metropolis that I have specially to deal. These, as I said before, numbered in 1841 as many as 18,321 individuals, of whom 16,965 were males, and 83 females, of 20 years of age and upwards—and 1,273 males below that age. But among the 18,000 individuals given in the census of 1841, both masters and working men are included, so that to arrive at a correct estimate as to the number of operatives in the metropolis we must take the number of London carpenters who are in business for themselves (and these, according to the "Post-office Directory," are 1,239), and deducting them from the 18,321 individuals cited in the census, we shall come to the conclusion that there were somewhere about 17,000 operative carpenters resident in the metropolis nine years ago; and, presuming the trade to have increased since that period at the same rate as it did in the ten years previous, it follows that there are at this present time upwards of 20,000 operative carpenters in London.

Numerically considered then, the carpenters rank amongst the most important of the working classes of the metropolis. The domestic servants, the labourers, the boot and shoe makers, the tailors, the dressmakers, and the clerks, alone take precedence of them in this respect.

About three-fourths or four-fifths of the carpenters working in the metropolis, I am informed, are from the country; for it is only within the last fifteen or twenty years that the London masters have taken apprentices. Before that time apprentices were taken—with but a few exceptions—only in the City, and those who served their time there did so solely with the view of "taking up their freedom" afterwards. Large masters in London would not then be troubled with lads, though small jobbing masters generally took one or two. Now, however, there is scarcely a master in London but what has some youths in his employ, and many of the large builders have as many lads and "improvers" as they have men, while some of them have even more. All these are used as a means of reducing the cost of men's labour. "When I first came to town, twenty years ago" (said one of the carpenters whom I saw), "I never knew a lad to be employed in any of the large firms in which I worked." As a proof of this, he told me, he never worked at that time but with one "Cockney," that is to say with a person who had been regularly brought up to the carpenter's business in London. Twenty years ago it was usual for the country carpenters to come up to London immediately after having served their apprenticeship; some did this to better their condition, the wages in town being double what they were in the west of England, and some came up to improve themselves in the business and then to return. At that time one-third at least of the number that came to London would go back into the country to settle after two or three years' practice in town. At the present time, however, it is estimated that not one in twelve who come to town from the country ever return. A great number of country carpenters are still attracted to London under the belief that the wages here maintain their former rate. When they arrive in the metropolis they find out to their cost that they can obtain employment only among the speculative builders and petty masters, where but two-thirds of the regular wages of the trade are given; and when once they take to this kind of work, it becomes impossible for them, unless very prudent indeed, ever to get away from it. This, I am informed, is one of the principal reasons of the over population of the London trade—for the work in the metropolis is now sufficient to give employment only to two-thirds of the hands. Another cause of the trade being over stocked is the reduction of wages that has taken place among those working for the speculative builders and petty masters, for I have before shown that the necessary consequences of under-pay is over-work—that is to say, if the wages of the "non-society" carpenters and joiners have been reduced one-third, then each man will endeavour to do one-third more work in his struggle to obtain the same amount of income as he previously did. Again, it will be found that a new race of employers has sprung up in the metropolis of late years, who are known among the trade as "strapping masters," from the fact of their forcing the men to do double as much work in a day as was formerly expected of them. Hence it is clear, that though the London carpenters have increased 4 per cent. less than the general population of the metropolis, still each of the operatives has been compelled of late years, either by the strapping masters, or a reduction of wages, to get through twice or three times as much work as formerly, and thus the trade has become as overstocked by each hand doing double work, as it would have been if the hands themselves had been doubled.

The carpenters and joiners that work for the low speculating builders are, generally speaking, quite a different class of men to those who are in "society." As a rule, to which, of course, there are many exceptions, they are men of dissipated habits. What little they get I am assured is spent in beer or gin, and they have seldom a second suit to their backs. They are generally to be seen on a Sunday lounging about the suburbs of London with their working clothes on, and their rules sticking from their side pockets—the only difference in their attire being, perhaps, that they have a clean shirt and a clean pair of shoes.

The great majority of the hands that work for the speculating builders are young men who have come up from the country, hoping to better their condition. About one-fourth of those who work for the speculative builders are, it is said, men of depraved and intemperate habits, and have scarcely a tool amongst them. The better class of workmen would rather part with the clothes off their backs and the beds from under them, than make away with their tools; so that it is only in cases of the most abject distress that a skilful joiner seeks to raise money upon the implements of his trade. When this is the case, I am told, it is usual for the operatives in "society" to club together, and lend a person so circumstanced, some one tool and some another, until a sufficient "kit" is raised for him to go to work with.

The majority of carpenters who are settled in London are married men with families, and mostly live in lodgings; many of the working men, however, are householders, paying as much as £70 per year rent, and letting off apartments, so as to be wholly or nearly rent free. In London there are several of what may be termed colonies of working carpenters. A great many reside in Lambeth, a large number in Marylebone, in the vicinity of Lisson-grove, and a considerable proportion are to be found in Westminster. This is to be accounted for by the fact that several of the principal firms are established in these quarters. The carpenters who live in lodgings mostly occupy a floor unfurnished, and pay from five to seven shillings rent; but men with large families generally contrive to be householders, from the fact that children are usually objected to in respectable lodgings, so that they must either live in some low neighbourhood or else pay an exorbitant rent for their residences in a better district. The more respectable portion of the carpenters and joiners "will not allow" their wives to do any other work than attend to their domestic and family duties, though some few of the wives of the better class of workmen take in washing or keep small "general shops." The children of the carpenters are mostly well brought up, the fathers educating them to the best of their ability. They are generally sent to day schools. The cause of the carpenters being so anxious about the education of their children lies in the fact that they themselves find the necessity of a knowledge of arithmetic, geometry, and drawing in the different branches of their business. Many of the more skilful carpenters, I am informed, are excellent draughtsmen, and well versed in the higher branches of mathematics. A working carpenter seldom sees his children except on a Sunday, for on the week day he leaves home early in the morning, before they are up, and returns from his work after they are in bed. Carpenters often work miles away from their homes, and seldom or never take a meal in their own houses, except on a Sunday. Either they carry their provisions with them to the shop, or else they resort to the coffee-shops, public-houses, and eating-houses for their meals. In the more respectable firms where they are employed, a "labourer" is kept to boil water for them, and fetch them any necessaries they may require, and the meals are generally taken at the "bench end," under which a cupboard is fitted up for them to keep their provisions in. In those shops where the glue is heated by steam the men will sometimes bring a dumpling or pudding and potatoes with them in the morning, and cook these in a glue-pot which they keep for the purpose. In firms where the glue is dissolved by means of hot plates small tins are provided, on which they cook their steaks, rashers of bacon, red herrings, or anything else that they may desire. These arrangements, I am informed, are of great convenience to the men, and in those shops where such things are not allowed they are mostly driven to the public-houses for their food. The men speak very highly indeed of both the Cubitts, in whose establishments the arrangements are especially conducive to the comforts as well as the intellectual improvement of the men. [I shall give an account of these in my next letter.] In some shops as many as from 200 to 300 men are employed, and one of my informants, who worked in as large a shop as any in London, says that among the 300 benchmen employed at his master's, there were not more than six drunkards, and these men were held in general disrepute among their fellow-workmen. Before the men leave their work in the large shops, it is usual for them to change their working clothes for others which they keep in a little cupboard under their bench. Their appearance in the street is as respectable as that of any tradesman.

Such is an account of the social condition of the London carpenters and joiners, gleaned from my own investigation, as well as from information supplied to me by the most intelligent and truthful of the operatives. I shall give a description of the several branches of the trade.

The term carpenter, I am told, is applicable to any one who cuts, fashions, and joins timber for building. Those who do the work of houses are house carpenters, while those who build ships are ship carpenters. Correctly speaking, however, the framer of a building is the *carpenter* and the finisher the *joiner*: nor, as I learn from the most intelligent of the workmen, can there be an interchange of the labour of these two branches without an inferior degree of skill in the execution of the work being the consequence. "In my opinion," said one experienced carpenter to me, "to have the trade right well done carpenters should never be put to joiners' work, nor joiners to carpenters'. When a man's been long at carpentering, if he's put to joinering he's often too rough and rapid; and a joiner, in the same way, is too fine and finicking-like for carpenters' work. Some men will tell you that they can do one kind of work as well as another; and so they may if they're only middling hands; but the best carpenter is always cleverest and quickest at his own branch, and the best joiner at his."

The carpenter makes and fixes the roof of a building, the skeleton parts of the floors before the boards are laid, and the wood-work for partitions. He prepares and fixes the "girders," which are the large beams that form the main support of the floors; the "binding joists," which are the smaller beams connected with the girders, and on which the floor-boards are laid (by the joiner); and in large houses he also constructs the "ceiling joists," which are a series of still smaller beams, to which the laths for carrying the plaster of the ceiling are attached— indeed, he does all the ponderous part of the wood-work appertaining to a building.

The joiner is generally termed—in contradistinction to the carpenter, who mostly works at the building, and seldom uses a plane—a "shop-hand" or "benchman," from the fact of most of his work being prepared in the shop, and executed at the bench. Should the carpenter require to smooth the surface of a piece of timber, he rigs up a bench on the premises, on two barrels, as he best can. This, however, is by no means an ordinary occurrence, the rule in the trade being that all which the plane passes over is joiners' work. Joinery is, consequently, of a more finished description, and more subdivided than mere carpentry, though the spirit of competition is fast trenching upon these subdivisions, and thereby upon that peculiar fineness of skill which the confining men to one class of work secures. In large establishments, where the division of labour is still maintained, different hands are employed on the staircases, the window-frames and sashes, the doors, the shutters, the flooring and skirting (for which inferior workmen are usually employed); while the other portions, such as the cupboards, are disposed of in any way most convenient to the master.

A Benchman

In the best descriptions of joiners' work a very high degree of skill is displayed. Let any one look at the delicacy of a window-frame, and then recollect that it is so adjusted by the skill of the workman as to be able to bear a heavy degree of pressure and to resist a great degree of violence, and yet to be light and elegant in its structure. "By keeping men to a particular sort of work," I was told by one of themselves, "it is done finer, firmer, and quicker. For instance, for such exact work as window-sash making a different 'kit' of tools is used to that for other kinds of work, and men kept to such work are readier and handier at it, so that time is gained and fewer mistakes made." In a large shop where many hands are employed the joiners' work is prepared and fitted together, ready for fixing, in the shop; frequently it is even painted there. The workmen engaged in this manner are termed *preparers*, and when their work is completed the *fixers* adjust or "fix" it on the building; and thus, again, a more perfect workmanship is attained. "With small masters," said a fixer to me, "the same joiner as prepares the work fixes it also. Large houses prefer having different hands for these departments, as the work is better and readier done that way, and the men are kept in the shop instead of every one running away out to fix each article as he makes it. In this manner a great deal of time would be lost. Again, the 'benchman,' or man who works in the shop, has always his chest of tools ready by his side; whereas the fixer requires nothing but a basket, which he takes with him to the job. The duty of a fixer is to put up the sashes, frames, shutters, doors (sometimes the staircases), skirtings, cupboards, recesses, architraves, and mouldings, and lay the floors. The preparers are generally the better workmen."

In a large establishment of the best order the joiners' work is first given out to a surveyor—generally one in the master builder's employ. These surveyors are also called "clerks of the works." In one establishment alone there are about 200 surveyors, clerks, and foremen. The architect is usually independent of these. The business of the surveyor is to take the architect's plans, make drawings in detail from them, and give specifications of the cost of the respective parts. His experience, aided by references to the books of the firm, enables him to do this. A plan is made for every story, and the surveyor has to see that all the architect's provisions for the form and elevation of the building are carried out as regards the joiners' work. The surveyor or foreman also "lays out" the carpenters' work, and gives instructions, plans, and details to guide the carpenter in its execution. In small establishments the master "lays out" both the carpenters' and joiners' work himself.

The trade, commercially speaking, divides itself, like all others of the present day, into two distinct branches, viz., the "honourable" and "dishonourable" masters—that is to say, those who have a regard for the welfare and comforts of their men, and those who care only for themselves and seek to grow rich by underselling their fellow-tradesmen, as well as by under-paying the workmen in their employ. As regards skill, these two branches of course divide themselves again into the substantial and the slop trade. The men belonging to the "honourable" part of the trade are mostly paid by the day—the wages being 5s. for ten hours' work (or sixpence per hour), from six to six, with the allowance of an hour for dinner, and half-an-hour each for breakfast and tea. Sometimes the better class of workmen are paid by the piece, and then the prices are regulated by some trade book, as Skyring's, Carpenter's, and others. Generally the operatives object to piece work. Such a mode of payment, they say, induces a man to "scamp" his work; that is, to devote less time and labour to the skilful execution of it than he would were he paid by the day. Again, they urge, that when a man is paid by the piece there is no necessity for the work being done under the eye of the master or his foreman. So long as it is completed to the satisfaction of the employer, it is no matter where or by whom it is executed. Hence the journeyman is at liberty to hire whoever he pleases to help him with it, or even to do it for him, and as this assistance is sure to be paid for by him at a less rate than he himself receives, the system of piece-work thus becomes one of the prime causes of the reduction of wages, while the operative is ultimately transformed by it into the middleman or "sweater," living on the toil and degradation of his fellow working men. The evil effects of this system have been already fully set forth in these letters while treating of the operative tailors of London; and it will be seen, when I come to treat of the speculative builders, that the same system among the carpenters and joiners seems to be attended with the same pernicious results. There it will be found that all the regulations which are observed to ensure skilled labour are utterly disregarded; the work is scamped and the operative is underpaid, and he not only loses thereby his self-respect and self-reliance, but sinks into drunkenness and demoralisation. The workman is, moreover, made the means of carrying out the system which results in his own degradation. The houses of "building lawyers" or "speculating builders" are let to a general contractor; he sub-lets the work, mostly by the piece, to others, who are usually journeymen, and these sub-contracting journeymen sub-let again to others even lower than themselves. By this process men gradually become mere machines, and lose all the moral and intellectual characteristics which distinguish the skilled artisan. Some masters reduce the wages of their workmen, not by smaller payments, but by exacting a greater quantity of work. They compel those in their employ to "scamp" it—that is, to crowd into ten hours, work which fairly requires for its skilful execution fifteen, or even twenty hours; so that the master obtains an amount of work which has been heretofore recognised as sufficient for a day and a half, or even two days, in one day; or, in other words, he gets 7s. 6d. or 10s. worth of work for the 5s. which he pays for the day's labour, while the skill of the operative is deteriorated, with the usual deplorable consequences.

Of the carpenters and joiners now in London 1,770, or about one-tenth of the entire number, are "in society." Their houses of call are almost invariably held in public-houses. The objects of these societies are twofold—the upholding of the wages of their trade, and rendering assistance to the aged, disabled, or unemployed of their own body. The members meet periodically at their respective houses of call and contribute such a sum per week (varying from 1½d. to 4d.) as is deemed necessary under the circumstances of the trade and the society. Some of the societies are managed by a check steward and three committee men; others have two auditors instead; others again a president, secretary, steward, check steward, and committee men. The officers are all paid from the funds of the society. As regards the initiation of a new member, he is proposed at one meeting, and, if considered eligible, he is admitted on the following meeting night. The expulsion of a member from society is for the following offences:—If he works under the standard rate of wages; if he goes into the country to work for his employer without having his expenses paid; and (where the society is opposed to the short-hour system) if he works short hours.

The houses of call at which these "societies" are held constitute the labour market (so to speak) of the trade. Each house of call is provided with a book, in which the unemployed members' names are inscribed in rotation, and the secretary attends twice a day to call over the names of those enrolled, and to receive notice from any other member who may be out of work. If a master wants a hand he sends to the house of call, and the first in rotation has the right of engagement. If he do not accept it his name is placed last on the list, and the next in rotation has the opportunity in like manner to accept or refuse the engagement. Now, however, it has become almost a general rule for men to call upon the masters or their foremen to solicit work. Besides what may be called the commercial objects of the society, such as upholding a fair rate of wages, there are others of a philanthropic and provident nature. In some cases they have vacation or winter funds, and in others mutual loan funds and building societies. For loss of tools by fire, security is given, from £5 to the whole amount, and by theft to half those sums. Where they have a winter fund, the unemployed members receive from 10s. to 12s. per week, but these winter funds are now giving way to loan societies and mutual building societies among the working men. Some of these loan societies charge 5 per cent. for moneys advanced upon personal security; others lend it out without the payment of interest, to be refunded by instalments when the borrower gets into employment again. The mutual building societies afford partial employment to members out of work, averaging from three days to a week, according to the number of applicants. These three last mentioned arrangements are provided for from the overplus money of the society, and require no extra contribution. There is one society, which has connected with it a Joint Stock Building Company, and is registered according to Act of Parliament—the whole of the members being connected with it. They contribute 1s. per month, for £5 shares, with the privilege of working out the whole amount of their share. Their unemployed members are "taken on" for a week, at £1 per week, in rotation, until the whole of those who are out of work get their turn, and then "go out and in" in rotation. If a man do not pay his contribution to his trade society for four months, he receives notice from the Secretary, and if he neglects payment for two months after such notice he is liable to be expelled, but extreme rigour is seldom exercised on this head. "Tramps" have not been relieved from the society's funds since the great union in 1834. The men are now generally opposed to strikes. The only thing approximating thereunto is "the short hour system." When trade is falling off, a master, not wishing to discharge his hands, proposes to the men to work so many hours less. In some societies this is not allowed, and their members, under such circumstances, are requested to "come out," and on doing so they receive from 12s. to 15s. a week till other work be obtained. Other societies permit the short-hour system. There are no superannuation funds. One of the secretaries informed me that the constant attendance of the men at their houses of call, which are, as I have said, nearly all public-houses, produced the pernicious effects to be expected; and I would here venture to impress upon the more intelligent members of the trade who are anxious for the social and moral improvement of their fellow workmen the advantage of holding their meetings at some other place.

Concerning trade societies in general, one of the most intelligent working men that I have yet met with made these observations to me:—

"The public generally suppose that combinations of working men are a great evil, because they see only one side of the question. Their impressions are that trade societies are instituted *only* to obtain an increase of wages, and that they are necessarily connected with strikes. One of the objects of our 'societies' is certainly to prevent the extortions of the capitalist upon the working men, by maintaining the present rate of wages; but this is only one of their objects. Another object of our combinations is to support the aged, and the sick, and the unemployed. To show you, sir, how the public are benefited by these institutions, I will make a calculation as to the number of men who are kept from the workhouse by such means. Now, supposing there are 100 different trades in London, and that each of these trades have 10 societies in connection with them, then we have 1,000 different trade societies, dispersed throughout the Metropolis. A fair average as to the members belonging to each of these societies would be 100, and that would make a total of 100,000 individuals contributing to, and entitled to receive benefits in case of need from such institutions. I think not more than two per cent. of this number ever put by a sixpence out of their earnings as a fund against sickness, accident, or old age; but, to be safe, let us say 5 per cent., or 5,000 out of the 100,000, and then we should have 95,000 working men in London, who, in case of their being unable to work, would have to come upon the parish for relief. In the society to which I belong, and which has 450 members appertaining to it, we paid upwards of £600 to men out of work in the winter. We supported on an average 80 men who were unemployed for 13 weeks, and gave them 12s. a week each. Two-thirds of this number had nothing else to depend upon. But say that each of the trade societies in the metropolis distributes only £100 among 100 men, in the winter (ours, I have told you, gave £600 to 450 while out of employment), and twice that amount among the aged or disabled every year, and this is a very low estimate; and then we have just upon £300,000 per annum given by the working-classes towards the support of their own poor, so that I don't think these trade combinations are quite so injurious to society as capitalists generally imagine. If they do uphold the rate of wages, at least this improved rate is used as a means of benefiting not only their own class, but the public, by keeping down the poor-rates generally."

I shall now proceed to give the statements of the men employed at the several branches of the "honourable" trade, reserving for my next letter a description of the causes and effects of the cheap or slop trade in connection with the carpenters' business. The following information I received from a highly respectable journeyman carpenter working for the best shops at the best prices:—

"I have known the London trade between twenty and thirty years. I came up from Lancashire, where I served an apprenticeship. I have worked all that time entirely at carpentering. No doubt I am a pure carpenter, as you call it, never having worked at anything else. Before I got married, eighteen years ago, I tried to make some odds and ends of furniture for myself, but I couldn't manage them at all to please myself, except in the frame of a bedstead, so I got a cabinet maker to finish my chairs and tables for me." [My informant then described the nature of the carpenter's work, and expressed an opinion that to have it executed in the first style a workman should do nothing else.] "I have always had 5s. a day, and in busy times and long days have made 33s. and 35s. a week, by working over time. I have always been able to keep my family, my wife and two children, comfortably, and without my wife's having to do anything but the house-work and washing. One of my children is now a nurse-maid in a gentleman's family, and the other is about old enough to go and learn some trade. Certainly, I shan't put him to my own trade, for, though I get on well enough in it, it's different for new hands, for scamping masters get more hold every day. There's very few masters in my line will take apprentices; but I could set him on as the son of a journeyman. If I'd come to London now, instead of when I did, I might have got work quite as readily perhaps—for I didn't get it within a month when I did come; but then I was among friends; but I should have had to work for inferior wages, and scamping spoils a man's craft. He's not much fit for first-rate work after that. I am better off now than ever I was, because I earn the same, and all my expenses, except rent, are lower. I have a trifle in the savings bank. But then, you'll understand, sir, I'm a sort of exception, because I've had regular work, twelve months in the year, for these ten or twelve years, and never less than nine months before that. I know several men who have been forced to scamp it—good hands, too—but driven to it to keep their families. What can a man do? 21s. a week is better than nothing. I am a society man, and always have been. I consider mine skilled labour, no doubt of it. To put together, and fit, and adjust, and then fix, the roof of a mansion so that it cannot warp or shrink—for if it does the rain's sure to come in through the slates—must be skilled labour, or I don't know what is. Sometimes we make the roof, or rather the parts of it, in the shop, and cart it to the building to fix. We principally work at the building, however. There's no rule; it all depends upon weather and convenience. The foremen generally know on what work to put the men so as best to suit, but in no shop I've been in has there been a fixed and regular division of the carpenters into one set as roofers, and another for the other work. Our work is more dangerous than the joiners, as we have to work more on scaffolding, and to mount ladders; but I can't say that accidents are frequent among us. If there's an accident at a building by a fall, it's mostly the labourers. I'm satisfied that the carpenters on the best sort of work are as well conducted and as intelligent as any class of mechanics. With scamping masters character is no recommendation, or very little. A very good hand I know was some-time out of work, and applied to a scamping master, and said, 'Mr. —— would vouch for his being a good workman and a sober man.' 'D—n your soberness,' was answered to him, 'what do I care for that? What I want is plenty of work done.' Men get not to care for their character when they come to be knocked about by such masters. I myself know three men, at least, that were sober and respectable when in good work: they're scamping it now, and drink all they can get. One of them's a married man, and his wife has to go out washing, and his family's in rags. We find our own tools, and a first-rate kit of carpenter's tools, with duplicates and everything proper, may cost new, and at first hand, on to £30; but perhaps not very many have more than £15 worth, and some have to get on as well as they can with from £5 to £10 worth, or less than £5; but then, of course, they must keep renewing them. It's generally all up with a carpenter if he's popped his tools, and has to get them from his uncle's when he wants them. If they are in heavy, he hardly ever gets a fair start with them all again. I never knew one do it, and I have known very industrious men forced to pledge almost all their kit. We use saws a good deal, and sharpening them is a great cost to us. Wear and tear of tools I reckon at well on to 2s. a week. That's for six days' regular work. In the winter there's mostly a slack, as building, of course, ain't so freely carried on in heavy rain, and frost and snow, and dark short days. Some carpenters have nine months of it, and not a few either have six months' work of it in a year; others just what they can catch."

A very intelligent man gave me the following information as *to the best description of joiners' work:*—

"I have been twelve years a journeyman joiner in London. I consider a joiner a man who works in a building, and usually at a bench, at everything the plane goes over, such as doors, windows, sashes and frames, closets, skirting, flooring; but that's generally sawn and planed at the mills, and we merely lay it—in fact, the joiner is the preparer, fixer, and finisher of a building. The other work is the carpenter's, such as the roof, &c. I have been ten years in one shop, in the honourable trade, where we have as good wages and as good usage as in any shop, and where between 400 and 500 hands in all branches are employed. The wages paid us are 5s. a day for ten hours, from six in the morning to half-past five. Half an hour is allowed for breakfast, an hour for dinner, and half an hour for tea, but that is generally waived, and so we leave work at half-past five. For over-hours we are paid at the same rate, 6d. an hour, unless it be after ten at night, when we have 9d. an hour. On Sunday double time is allowed— that is, 1s. an hour, as is the case in repairing Somerset-house, the Admiralty, and other Government offices, where Sunday labour is resorted to not to interrupt business. I never knew any man to object to work on a Sunday. I would not if I felt it to be a matter of necessity. If it was not a necessity I would object. In our firm over-hours are not frequent, but in some few shops the men now work until eight o'clock. The trade is greatly opposed to over-time, because it keeps many men out of employment, but sometimes it is unavoidable. We prepare the doors, &c., which we make in the workshops (I speak of large and honourable firms), and then take them to the building to be fixed. In each workshop there is a foreman, whose business it is to see that the work is properly done. In a very busy time in our firm he has an assistant, and does not work himself. He overlooks all the men, whether forty-six benches, as in our shop, which is a double shop, or in an establishment where there may be only eight or ten; but smaller masters, or jobbing or speculative builders, frequently act as their own foremen, having sometimes 'a leading hand,' who works like the other men, but may have 2s. a week extra. He 'sets out' the work, and works himself when not so employed. We have no control—I mean our society has none—over the number of apprentices, or rather boys or youths a master chooses to take. Some take an unconscionable number. At ———'s they had to every one man five or six boys or youths, not apprenticed, but learning the trade. That firm's knocked in the head now, but the same system prevails, though not so extensively. In our shop we have only one apprentice and three other boys (one is my son). We never think now, though it was the case, of requiring seven years' apprenticeship for admission into our society. The men's sons had always an exemption from this rule. One of the great evils of the trade, as regards working joiners, is the system of the masters having 'improvers.' These are young men, generally out of their time, who want 'improvement' in their business, and who often come recommended from the country, where the master joiners have many customers; or they are connected with friends of the master, and so are put on. These 'improvers' are paid from 18s. to 24s. a week, of course superseding experienced hands at the regular wages. 'Improvers' are very seldom worth the money they receive; indeed, their object is to learn their business perfectly. The foreman don't trust them with the finest and nicest sort of work, such as the frame, the sash, and the staircase, unless he sees they have great capabilities; so that after all, seven-eighths of them don't 'improve' much, but the public don't know good work from bad, and in consequence it appears cheap; and so wages get dragged down, and good hands are superseded. We seldom in our firm work by contract, but it's coming on; it's forced on the master—but then our work is very superior. Competition is ruining fine work, what you may call skilled labour, for there's not the time allowed to do it. Now, for a contract for a large building, honourable masters, treating and paying their men fairly, will take it say at £20,000. Another firm will undertake it at £14,000 or £15,000 (just look at the *Builder* about that). To make up the difference, they must use—the cheap contractors must—inferior timber, put together anyway, inferior and under-paid workmen, 'improvers,' and boys. The clerk of the works sees to the safety of the building; some are easy, and pretty easily managed; others are very strict. All Government work is done by contract, and at the lowest rates—slop wages generally. The Woods and Forests allow 28s. a week, and if an 'honourable' master gets the job he has to pay 30s., as society men won't work under. The new Houses of Parliament are, however, an exception to this rule. The best hands are in society. I have regular work, and have nothing to complain of that way; but for all that I would like to leave the country, for there's worse times coming."

From another joiner, to whom I was referred as one of the most intelligent men in the trade, I had the following statement:—

"I have known the London trade for twenty-one years. When I first knew the trade wages were the same as they are now, 5s. a day. Indeed, older men have told me that there has been no change in the rate of our wages for between thirty and forty years. About sixteen or eighteen years ago 5s. 6d. a day was gained generally throughout the trade—at least from all the principal employers; but then the advance was acquired through a strike, which did more harm than good by creating ill-feeling between masters and men, and from the time lost and the expenses incurred in completing the strike. The 5s. 6d. a day didn't continue, as well as I can recollect, above a twelvemonth, not generally, though some few hands kept it longer, but masters kept giving new hands 5s. a day, and so got rid of the 5s. 6d. gradually. The strike was more, or as much, from party spirit as from a real regard for the interests of the journeymen's trade. Before the strike the very superior hands could command 6s. a day, but that's not the case now. Twenty-one years ago it wasn't so easy or so cheap to get to London as it is now, and men came then really for improvement, and went back to their own country places; now they come here and stick here longer than they used to do, especially the west of England men. Wages are lower in Somersetshire, Devon, and Dorset, than in any other part of England. As you go north wages are better. The joiners' wages in those three counties are only 14s. or 15s. a week— it's an extraordinary man who gets 16s. there. They're handy men, many of them, when they come to London. There are so many apprentices taken in those counties, who, when out of their time, *must* find another market for their labour. When they come to London they don't undersell, unless occasionally, the regular hands, and respectable masters don't expect it. 5s. a day is a very low rate of wages, when the expense of tools is considered. Ours is one of the worst paid trades in the universe. My tools now would cost me £30 replacing, and no man in a respectable shop can get on with tools less in value than from £20 to £30. The masters find us no tools but extra moulding planes. The wear and tear of our tools is not less than 1s. 6d. a week cost to the workman, and from the loss of chisels and gouges, as well as from their wearing out, and from the expense of saw sharpening. For saws you must find your own files, and sharpen them yourself, or pay 4d. for the mere filing of a saw; 6d. if there is anything more required. Our saws require sharpening twice a week on the average. Lead pencils now cost 8d. a dozen, such as twenty years since cost 2s. A pencil may last two months, so it's little matter.

I average wear and tear, &c., of tools, at 1s. 6d. a week. I reckon that ten months' work is the year's average of employment, take the trade throughout London. Some have only four months in the year, and it's incredible how they live. There was a time, within these ten years say, when masters would keep a good man on at some inconvenience to themselves, but that's not the case now. Some shops are fairly besieged every Monday morning by men seeking work. It's within the last ten years that the great falling off in our trade has occurred, and it gets worse and worse. This is owing, I am convinced, to the increase of population, and of workmen, and to the decrease of men's labour, through greater use of machinery. Building now is generally a matter of speculation more than a matter of fair and regular trade, and so men seek to get it done in the cheapest instead of the best way. Our book of prices, Skyring's, and he's low enough for doors, gives 10s. 6d. for making a two-inch double-moulded door, but some 'scamping masters,' as we call the slop-masters, give only 5s., so that a man to make his 5s. a day at those prices must do double work, and for longer hours, at a rate that's killing him, or make the door in a very inferior way. I have known men work hard from six in the morning to nine at night, and in winter find their own candles, and not make 5s., or only 5s., then. That's the case now at Notting-hill, but that part is not the worst. Haverstock-hill and by the Brecknock Arms, Camden-town, is now amongst the worst parts of London. St. John's-wood was very bad, but building there's about over now. Some of those houses fetch low prices if they have to be sold a *second time*, the skirtings and doors and other work being so shrunk; but that's an after consideration, for at the time they're run up, the men who build them only look to sell them *once*. Machinery was first brought into competition with us in flooring boards. At first they were only planed by machinery, and the edges cut. I first heard of this planing 21 years ago. The next step was to grove (groove) and tongue the flooring. Formerly, grooves and tongues were made by hand. The joiners thought nothing at first of the planing of these boards by machinery, as only a certain class were put upon sash planing—it was beneath their dignity generally, and I have known men leave a shop rather than do it. Joiners' work is noisy, and they can't talk when carrying it on, and that may account for joiners not being such politicians or thinkers as shoemakers or tailors. The next introduction of machinery, as regards our trade, was the preparation of mouldings for doors, architraves, cornices, and base mouldings; base mouldings are the ornamental tops of the plinth or skirting. Wainscotting is coming into vogue again in some of the better sort of houses—a good deal so of late years, and especially in those in the Gothic style; but machinery affects that less, if anything, than in the general trade. It's almost purely joiners' work. In the trade wainscotting is called 'dadoing.' These are the principal things in which machinery has affected our trade, unless it be in hothouses, the roofs of which are frequently moulded by machinery, which can work ten mouldings where a workman can do one; but it's only the capitalists, the great masters, that are paid by employing the moulding machinery—it won't pay the others. These introductions have injured our trade, because only one-fifth of the workmen are now required in those particular branches. But in one instance machinery has done us good. Mr. ——, invented a very ingenious process for cutting tracing in the Gothic wood-work for churches and chapels. This introduced a taste for these things and a demand for wood carving, and this has been a benefit to the trade. The machine, too, cannot work the tracing right up to the point of a mitre, so that the joiner's work, though apparently superseded by the invention, has actually been increased by it, through the greater demand. But that's a mere trifle to the extent of work and the number of men supplanted by machinery. As the matter is at present carried on, at least one-sixth of the labour of working joiners through London is superseded in this way. It's not the mills that do all this mischief, for in Mr. ——'s, the great builder's premises, one-half of the labour is performed by his own machinery. It's not certain, however, that in our business machinery is so very profitable to the master as in a cotton factory. Machinery, besides, never does such work as moulding so perfectly as we can do it. We often have to trim and refit such mouldings."

An experienced man gave me the following statement concerning greenhouse work:—

"I have known the hot-house building, and similar branches of the trade—often called 'decorating'—for three or four years, and before that I was a joiner. There is no difference, I have ascertained, in a horticultural joiner's trade, as regards wages, for the last twenty or thirty years. The wages are the same as the joiners', and the same hours. Our work, for gardens, is more a matter of taste than house work, in which certain plans are laid down and must be observed. In hothouses the chief distinctive work is the framing, as the sashes are pure joiners' work. We make also cucumber-frames, summer-houses, conservatories, greenhouses, forcing-houses, lattice and trellice work for the training of climbing plants, and for ornamental purposes—in short, everything connected with gardens. Within these few years, say seven years, there has been a great increase in the demand for this kind of work, especially in greenhouses and conservatories. Not one-tenth of the men employed in this kind of work have been apprenticed to it solely; they are mostly joiners, for men when out of work must turn their hands to anything. Machinery affects our trade, in the preparation of sash bars, which contain the glass. They are chiefly 'stuck,' made by machinery. We can't compete with it. They charge 7s. to 8s. per 100 feet run for bars, finding the material, and having all ready prepared for use. The material, the timber, will cost two-thirds of that sum, and the labour would be, on an average, 3s. 6d. Our work, however, is considerably truer than their's. We can work with our tools to a great nicety, and that can't be done by the machine. None of their mouldings are perfectly regular. If the timber be crooked, the machine works it crooked to the timber, but we don't. Nearly all the mouldings for cucumber boxes and for general purposes are prepared by machinery. The manual labour so superseded is in my opinion one-fifth; and that drives men to undertake any job, and to go in as day workmen, and then look out for another job. Ours is chiefly outdoor work, and is very uncertain, as we can't 'fix' in wet weather. Within seven years iron and metal (composition) roofs, for hothouses and conservatories, have come into rather general use, having a lighter appearance than wood. Perhaps, however, there are nearly twice as many wood as iron or metal roofs made. Metal roofs (they're generally all called so) are fixtures usually. Another system of ventilation is pursued in them, either by a general ventilator at the top of the roof, which is the commonest way, or by perforated glass, the panes then overlapping one another, with an interval between to admit the air. In the wood work, we have sliding frames for ventilation, the upper frame being pulled down over the bottom sash, which is a fixture, the top being then left open for the admission of the air. I have been engaged in constructing hot-houses for nursery grounds and gentlemen's gardens both, from 100 to 150 feet long, for all purposes. The nurserymen have generally the larger hot-houses. There is a sort of mania for them now, and more especially since the improved system of heating by hot water came in, within these five or six years. A large-sized boiler, 24 inches diameter, is calculated to heat 1,000 feet run. If for a pinery, this heat is from underneath, in pipes fixed in brick archways, and is forced upwards. If for grapes, the hot-water pipes are laid on the ground, and the same for flowers. Only for pines, or fruits of any kind are the pipes laid underground. The heat may be regulated; it may be concentrated in one part, or may be diffused through a hot-house or any adjacent buildings by means of stop valves, which can be opened or shut at pleasure. This process is better for ripening fruit than sunshine, as it is more regular. We have no society, and I don't know the number in the trade. Our average employment for regular hands is not more than eight or nine months in the year; for those nine months the wages are 30s. in the week. Many, however, get only employment at this work two or three months in the year, and then they look out for any kind of wood work. I know of none regularly doing horticultural work cheaper, but there is slop work got up for the trade, and that can only be done by parties taking less than the regular wages; and that's almost always by inferior workmen. A good hand can get his wages. Slop masters palm off inferior work as the best, and in the long run they'll drag us all down to bad work and bad wages. It's influencing us now. Masters say, 'I can get this done at this or that low rate,' and I have to drive on to meet their views. Masters are beaten oft enough by the slop-masters, and bad men are ruining good ones. Few persons are judges of work. Only to-day a gentleman called wanting a hot-house to be built; he said he could get it done, when the price was named to him, at so much less at ——'s. He was told that one great job which had been done at this cheap slop house had all to be re-done. A great part of the bad work is brought in by slop-masters, but the public themselves, even gentlemen, go about asking prices and cheapening tradesmen in my line, who, to meet the times, must put in, and do put in, inferior materials and use machine labour, even when it's not suitable at all. Gentlemen will offer from £1 to £8 less than a fair price for a hot-house. I have known one who wanted a green-house, call at our place, and state that he could get the fixing done cheaper than we could. He offered for the wood work what was the cost of the material alone. 'There's the duty off timber,' said he, 'and the duty off glass.' He was told that wages were the same, and he replied, 'Well, then, you should reduce them too.' (Hothouses are lower since the duty was taken off glass.) He was then told that to work at his price either the timber-merchant or the working man must be robbed. He replied, 'I'll call to-morrow and tempt you with another guinea, and show you the money, and then I know you'll take it.' He is a man worth £20,000 a year and more, and left his carriage at a distance to pass as a humbler man."

From a sash-maker, one of the best hands, I received the subjoined narrative:—

"I have worked at sash-making ten years, regular. I have done very little else all that time. For nine years I was solely employed at making sashes. In most of the large shops they let the sash-work now to what is termed a task-master, and then he employs his own hands. This is done in many shops where the best prices are paid. The sash-maker in a shop is a party who makes nothing else but the sashes and frames. I have been in London 25 years; sash-making was not a distinct branch of the trade then—it is only since there has been so much contract work, and the master-builders, large and small, have taken to letting the different parts of a house out to different hands, that separate men have been employed for sash-making. By giving the different parts out to different hands, the work, I think, is done in half the time, because a man has all his tools ready and set, and in general work a great deal of time is lost in shifting from one kind of work to another. The tools require to be altered for each class of work. When a man is always doing one job, he can do it almost without noticing his tools. The sash-maker, to whom the work is let, is never paid by the day, but always by the piece; the price is so much per foot for the different kinds of sashes. Common 2-inch or 1½-inch sashes, are about 4½d. per foot (either 'scribed' or 'mitred'); the better kind of deal sashes (which run about 2½ inches) are 6d. the foot. These are the prices in good shops—they may be a halfpenny more or less in different places. The party to whom the sashes are let at these prices is called the taskmaster; and he seldom does anything himself except setting the work out and superintending. The work itself is done by men whom he employs, and these he always pays by the day. The task-master in good shops generally gives 5s. a day, and I knew one hand who had as much as 6s., but this was an exception rather than the rule. Usually the taskmasters try to cut the workman down as much as possible. Frequently they will give only 28s. a week in the best shops. The taskmaster generally works in the shop of the employer the same as the men, and the employer seldom troubles his head about what he gives those who work under him. A taskmaster will generally have from three to five, and sometimes as many as twenty hands at work for him. The taskmaster will often make 5s. out of the labour of each of the regular sash-makers that he employs under him. I have known one taskmaster to make as much as £10 a week out of ten men that he had working for him. We, of course, could measure the work as well as he could, and calculate what he got out of our labour. The taskmaster system is a very bad one for the working men, or, indeed, any system is bad where one working man is put to make money out of his fellows, for he must either employ cheap or very ready hands to get anything out of the job. It either leads to strapping—that is to making men work unusually hard—or else to making them work at unusually low prices. This is one of the reasons why a man cannot find work directly he turns the middle-age. Nothing but young strapping hands will do for the taskmasters. The cause of this hurry and scurry, and scramble, and scamping of work, and reducing of wages, is the contract system. First of all, gentlemen and others will have the work done as cheap as possible—the lowest estimate has the preference in contract work. Then masters go to work cutting under one another, just to get the job; and after that why, of course, they must make it up out of the men's muscles and bones. Before this contract system there was no such thing as letting and sub-letting of work, and one journeyman living and preying upon another. When I first came to town, such a thing as piece-work was hardly known, and if a man got a job that way, he was pretty well ousted from society for it—but now piece-work is as common as day-work; so much so, that the usual question among journeymen is whether they have the job by the day or piece. Piece-work is the worst of all things to be introduced into a trade. It has been the great evil, and will be the downfall of our trade; for directly men are paid by the piece, then of course they can employ others to assist them at lower wages than the regular pay, and then begins all kinds of scheming, strapping, and ultimately, starving of the men."

In my next letter I purpose entering more fully into the effects of the contract system.

The Morning Chronicle, Thursday, July 11, 1850.

We have to acknowledge the receipt of a Post-office order for 1*l.*, from Mrs. F., of Elstree, Herts, for the poor widow who desires to emigrate in the company of her children.

We have also to acknowledge the receipt of 3s. 7d., from some children in America, for the "Young Mud-lark."

The Morning Chronicle, Friday, July 12, 1850.

LABOUR AND POOR FUND.

On the 15th of January last we published an abstract of the "Labour and Poor Fund" account up to that date, accompanied with an explanatory statement, showing the various modes in which we had endeavoured to give effect to the benevolent intentions of the donors. During the interval which has since elapsed, large additional sums were transmitted to us, which, together with the balance then remaining in our possession, have been expended in a similar manner—with the exception of a small amount still on hand, subscribed for the relief of particular cases of distress, and held by us for the future use of the parties designated by the contributors. The account being thus virtually closed, we now lay before our readers a final statement of the entire receipts and disbursements of the Fund, brought down to the 31st day of last month:—

Dr.
Total amount of sums received £869 0 8
  Cr.
   By Disbursements:—
Blankets and sundry articles of
  clothing £73 4 8
Bread 49 2 6
Coals 9 12 11
Relief given in cash, or advanced
  on loan (the latter item being
  under 20*l.*) 721 15 3   853 15 4

Balance in hand and belonging to special cases .. £15 5 4

With reference to the general plan which has been pursued in the distribution of the Fund, and to the precautions that have been adopted with a view to prevent imposition, we have no material addition to make to the statement which we published on a former occasion. But several points to which we then briefly adverted may be deemed of sufficient interest to merit further elucidation; and we therefore subjoin the following letter, from Mr. Jones, the chief clerk in our publishing office, who kindly undertook at the outset the very onerous and arduous task of personally managing the distribution of the Fund, and who has spared neither time nor labour in his exertions to perform thoroughly the trust committed to him.

"TO THE EDITOR OF THE MORNING CHRONICLE.

"SIR—In endeavouring to lay before you a detailed statement respecting the distribution of the large funds which, during the last six months, have been confided to my disposal, I am reminded of many harrowing scenes of distress, of which even the bare recollection brings sadness into my heart. While it afforded me much happiness to be made the instrument of giving bread to the hungry and clothing to the naked, the duty which I had to perform was in many respects as painful as it was responsible; but I discharged it to the best of my ability.

"I now proceed to explain the plan upon which I set out in the distribution of the funds. With reference to the disposal of donations not expressly intended for the benefit of particular individuals, the first step taken was to provide bread and coals for the relief of distressed and deserving persons known to your Special Correspondents. The articles thus procured were distributed by means of tickets, and some few of the earlier cases were at the same time relieved with small sums of money. Next came the special cases, of which accounts had been given in *The Morning Chronicle*, in the letters of your Correspondents; and these, having been again investigated, were assisted in proportion to the immediate necessities of the parties, out of the moneys that had been received for their individual use. As the fund for general distribution increased, I laid it out partly in the purchase of blankets, flannel, calico, and sundry articles of clothing; partly in redeeming articles of wearing apparel that were in pawn; and also in wiping off, here and there, an old rent score.

"After publicity had been fully given to the existence of the Fund, letters began to pour in upon me, containing applications for relief, or recommendations by third parties of individuals who were in distress; and, day after day, for several weeks, I was obliged, during the morning, to take my seat in a private room, in order to see the applicants and hear their various tales of sorrow. This, however, I found to be so great an inconvenience, that I subsequently appointed for the purpose two days in each week, and more recently but one (the Monday) which practice I continued for several weeks—the number of applicants on these occasions averaging from 60 to 70 individuals.

"Many of these came at my own request, being persons whom I had visited at their homes, and who, I had reason to believe, were fit objects of the charity. To many of these I felt justified in affording assistance during several successive weeks, in consequence of the applicants being totally destitute of employment, or otherwise unavoidably disabled from supporting themselves. Some of those persons must have perished, or have become inmates of a workhouse, had they not been thus relieved; and among them were individuals who had been well brought up, and who had at one time been far removed from requiring the aid of charity. It was truly a painful duty, and one that was most depressing to my own mind, to have to investigate the diversified cases of distress which thus came under my notice; and the roll of letters in my possession contain narratives of human misery which could scarcely be credited by those not personally acquainted with the pinching necessities of the poor and the unfortunate.

"I now beg to state some particulars with reference to the cases that have been relieved, which will, I trust, be interesting and satisfactory to the generous contributors to the fund. I begin with the special cases, or those to which public attention was called by the prominence given to them in the letters of your Special Correspondents. These amount to upwards of 60, and the sums subscribed for the relief and benefit of the individuals, whose wants were thus made known, have varied from 5s. to between 20*l.* and 30*l.*; and in one case—viz., that of the 'Velvet Embosser'—the amount was upwards of 30*l.* In many instances, there is every reason to believe, that much real and lasting good has been effected. I may mention, for example, the case of the 'Chickweed Seller' and his family, one of the most deplorable instances of destitution that ever came under my observation. A visit to their present abode, and half an hour's conversation with the old man and woman, would prove to their kind benefactors a source of unspeakable satisfaction. Nor has a less happy change been effected in the circumstances of the 'Daughter of an Officer,' who has repeatedly expressed to me the utmost gratitude towards the authors of the timely and effectual aid which has been extended to her. In more than one instance where the illness or infirmities of the father had cut off from the family the means of subsistence previously derived from his labours—as in the cases of the 'Poor Sick Tailor,' the 'Poor Coal-whipper,' and the 'Poor Old Couple'—the utmost benefit has resulted from the assistance afforded by the fund. In the last-mentioned case many comforts were administered to the old man, in his dying hours, to which both he and his suffering wife had for a long period been utter strangers. His remains were conveyed decently to the tomb, and the expenses of his funeral were defrayed out of the fund. Another mode in which the special fund was applied was in sending out the parties as emigrants to Australia. This course was pursued in the cases of the 'Velvet Embosser,'—the 'Young Woman of 22,'—the 'Farm Labourer,'—and the 'Navvy;' each of them having been provided with a sufficient, and, in the case of the two women, an excellent outfit for the voyage. I may also name the case of the 'Artilleryman's Wife' as one in which a deserving individual has been removed from a scene of wretchedness (the Refuge for the Destitute), where she had, from no fault of her own, been compelled to seek a temporary shelter, and has been once more raised to a position of comfort and respectability. By means of the sums subscribed for her relief she was placed on board the ship Medora, bound for Halifax, in order to join her husband, who had left England with his regiment to be stationed there.

"Such are some of the most prominent of the special cases, a reference to which will show the very great amount of good which has been accomplished by means of the Fund. The remainder of the moneys entrusted to my disposal was distributed among a large number, amounting to nearly 300, of casual recipients. Of these some 40 or 50 came only under the observation of your Metropolitan Correspondent at the Refuge for the Destitute or elsewhere, and they received trifling sums through his hands. The other and larger portion of the above were relieved at this office, in sums varying from 2s. 6d. up to (in some few instances) several pounds. As I have already stated, the testing of the genuineness of these latter cases devolved upon myself. For the purpose of guarding against deception, I required, in the first instance, a note from some respectable party to whom I could afterwards apply for a confirmation of the truth of the applicants' statement; and I likewise generally visited the latter at their abodes. I may add that, in many instances (50 or 60 in all) the Fund has been employed for the benefit of children. These have in some cases been fitted for situations; in others they have been furnished with the clothing requisite to enable them to attend school.

"Various are the conditions in life included in the above-mentioned class of casual recipients. Among them were many widows gaining a wretched livelihood by needlework, and some of these had large families entirely dependent upon their exertions. Several of them worked for army clothiers; and there were also persons of all ages who were employed at other kinds of needlework. Tailors, coal-whippers, and ballast-heavers, were likewise among the participants in the various descriptions of relief afforded by the Fund.

"The cases that call for more especial notice are those of Mrs. M—— and her sister and three children, N—— the shoemaker, and the 'Young Thief,' besides some four or five females—including, with their families, about seventeen persons—all of whom had been suffering from severe distress. For several weeks consecutively temporary assistance was given to these individuals, preparatory to their leaving (by their own particular wish) this country for Australia, except in the case of N——, who sailed for the United States. And I must here mention that it was owing to the generous exertions of Lord D——, who raised for the purpose the sum of 30*l.*, that N—— was enabled to emigrate. The other cases came under the sole charge of the Female Emigration Committee.

"As you are aware, many persons who had previously been living in concubinage have, through the instrumentality of this charity, been wedded to each other. The marriage fees of sixteen couples were provided for by special contributions; and those of the remainder were paid out of the general fund. Of these there were fifteen couples, making a total of thirty-one. A list of the names, &c., of these parties accompanies this letter; and I must not omit to state that the letters of acknowledgment which I have received from many of these persons express the liveliest gratitude for a benefaction which has been the means of restoring their self-respect, and of reclaiming them to the duties and the observances of religion. I also hand you the books in which the accounts have been kept. Of these the 'Labour and Poor Fund Ledger' is, as you will observe, the one most important for purposes of reference, since it not only shows the sums received and paid on behalf of each individual case, but likewise contains a brief statement respecting the character and circumstances of the party benefited. I have likewise another book, containing the signatures of the recipients.

"I have only to add, in conclusion, that should any further information be required by any contributor to the Fund, I shall at any time be happy to show the books and vouchers in my possession, on application being made at this office.

"I remain, sir, your most obedient servant,

"D. JONES.

"*The Morning Chronicle* Office, July 10."

We cannot take leave of this subject without once more expressing, to the numerous contributors to the Fund, our conviction that their kind-hearted and generous efforts have been productive of the full amount of benefit which they contemplated. Whilst, in all cases in which assistance has been given, timely relief has been afforded to severe and urgent distress, in many instances lasting moral good has been accomplished, and the helpless and hopeless victims of penury have been raised to a position of comfort and self-supporting industry. Our only occasion for regret has been that the limited means at our disposal have not enabled us to effect much more. Let us add, in conclusion, that it will ever be to us a source of lively satisfaction that this Journal has been the medium through which—by an entirely unexpected consequence of inquiries undertaken for the purpose of throwing light on the general condition of the labouring poor—large numbers of deserving individuals have been temporarily or permanently benefited, and another signal proof has been afforded of the warmth and earnestness of those social sympathies which, in this country, unite class with class, and which never fail to respond to the calls of suffering humanity. For the satisfaction of those who may desire to know the spirit in which these benefactions have been received, we subjoin the following letters, taken almost at random from a vast mass of similar documents:—

SIR—I have thought my cool manner of thanking you for the money last Wednesday must have appeared strange. Had you seen my full heart then you would not censure me. The last time I was in the Strand was the night mentioned in my statement—the past came with such force on my mind I dared not say much. I little thought then, when homeless, friendless, starving, clotheless, and despised by all, there were such warm hearts at *The Chronicle Office*. May the God of the Magdalene bless you and Mr. Mayhew with His richest blessing. With regard to the money, I will like you to know how I have used it. The first 30s. came most fortunately nine months ago. My brother asked me to lend him, or borrow him, a sovereign—he had become answerable for a bill, and could not pay, for want of that sum. He told me they had threatened him with prison. I borrowed the money, now he will not pay me. I have had to pay it. Thus went 1*l.* 10s. for board and lodging while out of place; 10s. I have kept for a few clothes; 1*l.* in the savings bank for my poor boy. I have sent you my address.—May I be permitted sir, to remain, your humble and grateful servant,

J. A.

Sɪʀ—I now take the liberty of addressing a few lines to you, not that writing to you will convey an adequate idea of the gratitude which myself and wife feel, and indeed are bound to express to you, for your disinterested exertions in behalf of my family, in connection with Labour and the Poor. My case was noticed in your paper on Thursday, 14th February, and I shall feel thankful if you will be kind enough to return the sincere thanks and heartfelt gratitude of myself and family for the timely and needful assistance which I received from the public, as sent for "the poor shoemaker who wished to emigrate."

I have likewise to tender my grateful thanks to the gentlemen of *The Morning Chronicle* for the assistance my family received, during the winter months, from the funds placed at their disposal. Should God spare us to arrive safe at our destined port we shall not be unmindful of past benefits received at the hands of Lord D——, and all parties in connection with *The Morning Chronicle.*

As my position in life has been good, previous to meeting with the gentleman of *The Morning Chronicle*, I trust I shall be excused if I sign the name familiar to all who have rendered me assistance, and, in conclusion, I remain, sir, yours ever grateful,

THE POOR SHOEMAKER WHO WISHED TO EMIGRATE.

T.
E. } N.

Ship Victoria, Captain Johnson.
Portsmouth, April 23, 1850.

———

Sɪʀ—I must confess I am perfectly ashamed that I have not before this written to you to thank you for the very great kindness you have done me; but, after your calling upon me, a circumstance quite as unexpected as your visit took place—that of being sent to to take a situation, which I gladly accepted, although at a very little remuneration, therefore my time is not mine. I leave my home at half-past seven in the morning, and do not return until eight in the evening; being weary, I am glad to get to bed. There is, therefore, only Sunday left me, and that I am glad of for rest. I am a music collector, and it is my duty to do all for my employers, and indeed I wish I could do more than I do, as the music trade, like all others, is far from being good. I do not know who to thank, further than Mr. Mayhew and Mr. Jones; but should there be any one else, and there must be, I would wish those gentlemen to say all and everything. Words cannot express my gratitude; and could I see any one personally, I could then explain what I find unable by letter. Mr. Jones informed me there was something more for me, since I received the 6*l.* 10s., and I have called, and received the sum of twenty shillings, as I could not, from my little wages, get boots, &c., having only one lodger, and being compelled to live a little better, being so much upon my feet, walking about. I am very thankful that my health is much better since I have had more exercise, and I do hope that when the spring comes, and having less expenses—as fire and candles—I shall do yet better; but I have many pensioners upon me, which I must not name, fearing you may say I am foolish. I believe there is yet a little more left in your hands for me, from your information. Should that be the case, pray keep it until such time as I may require no more in this world. Should there be sufficient to bury me respectably, I thank you and all kindly. Should there not be so much, sell my little home, and if I have time I will tell you other things respecting my family. I do hope you will not look upon this as cant, a thing I detest above all others. I do it to show a grateful heart, and I would much rather do it to those who have been my benefactors than by letter; but a long time has now elapsed since you first found me, and I am perfectly in ignorance yet of any others than those I have seen. I see Miss H—— very often, and I am fearful she is doing but little good. I should like to see some person respecting her. I am very sorry for her; but I fear she requires more than it is possible for her to have.

Please to make what use of my letter you may, and say everything to my benefactors of gratitude your heart can dictate. And allow me to conclude, your ever grateful and most humble servant,

D. B., The Eccentric Man.

This I wrote some time since, but I could not form resolution to send my letter in such a hurry.

D. B.

———————

Sir—I must confess I scarce know how to express my gratitude to you as I could wish in these few lines; you who have been kinder to me than my nearest relations. While they have looked upon me with coldness and disdain, you have lent a kind hand, and have taken me from the misery which must sooner or later have ended in transportation, or it may be something worse, for I do not know how far I may have gone but for yours and Mr. Mayhew's kindness; but I thank God it is all over with me now. I am going to a country where I hope I shall be able to get an honest living, and not be branded as a thief.

I am getting on very well at present, sir. I like my shipmates very well; they are very agreeable men. The only annoyance I have are the rats, who keep continually running over me, and one had the cheek to walk over my face, as if he wanted to take a full view of me, but they are harmless, they don't bite. The best comrade I should like at night now is a good cat who would settle a few of them.

I am sorry B—— is not with me. I should very much like he was, as we might both stop together when we got to Sydney. I hope, sir, you will be kind enough to send me, if you cannot come to Gravesend, a written character, as I should very much like to have one to show in Sydney in case I got a situation.

I shall write to you when I arrive safe, and shall let you know all the particulars. I shall ever think of your kindness to me: it is too much to be easily forgotten. I shall endeavour for the future part of my life to get an honest living. I shall endeavour to work for my living, and if ever I have any money to spare I shall come back and have the pleasure of spending it in Old England, though, indeed, to do it justice, I ought to have no great regard for it; but the first place I shall go to is *The Morning Chronicle*, where I have derived the greatest benefit. I hope your girls will get on well. I hope that they will study what is for their benefit.

I must conclude with expressing my warmest gratitude for your great kindness to me, hoping that you and Mr. Mayhew may be the means of saving many like me from misery and wretchedness. I bless God that I ever went to you. I had no hope when I went. I had been six times in prison already, and I next expected transportation, but ye have rescued me. I should like what you have done for me to be made public, as it may be the means of helping others equally distressed; but I must conclude with my deepest gratitude to you for your kindness to me, and shall ever remain so; and may God bless you and Mr. Mayhew, and all your relations and friends, is the earnest prayer of yours gratefully,

G. C.

————

Sɪʀ—Having been one of the recipients of your generous bounty of the sum of 1*l.* 5s., five shillings of which have been paid for my marriage fees, how to express my thankfulness to you, sir, is a difficult task, and I will tell you why, as nigh as I can tell. We had been living together fourteen years. We have three children; and many times when I have looked at my children, knowing how we were living together, made me feel miserable, and often drove me to the public-house. Then I'd come home drunk, and we were sure to get into a row. There was not a week passed but what we had rows. I'd used to be very fond of skittles. I've played many a time from eight o'clock in the morning till the publican has turned us out. We never went out of our own accord. Many a time it made her miserable, and she has had to walk the streets all night. Several nights she's done it, sir, and the children they'd have flied five miles off if they could. I never thought of being married—I'd sooner spend the money in beer and porter; but your gift has been the means of making me feel and think differently. I feel I ought to have lived differently to what I have done. Two days after we were married Mr. J—— gave us a Bible. I am trying to read and write. I love my wife. I feel I have been a bad man to her, and a bad father to my children. I attended church thrice in the fourteen years. I went there for what I could get. Once I got two pounds of mutton and a quartern loaf; the second time I got a quartern loaf and a half hundred of coals; and the third time I got a jacketing because I was not married, and if the door had been open I should have run away. But since I have been married I read my book. I feel I am an altered man, and, if it please the Lord, I intend to keep so. I attend a place of worship regularly since I have been married. I intend to train my family in the same way as I train myself, and if I follow what the books say, and what Mr. J—— advises me to do, I shall not fear going wrong to the end of my life. I am so happy since I have got married, and by being with Mr. J—— I have seen so many poor creatures, that I am determined to do what I can towards helping another couple to be married. I have found the pound to be a great benefit to me, and I return you, sir, my sincere thanks for it. I could not have believed, if I had not experienced it, that twenty-five shillings could have made a family as your kind gift has made us. God bless the gentleman that gave it! I cannot express my thanks as I could wish, but I thank you all, and remain,

Your humble and thankful servant,

T. S.

LABOUR AND THE POOR.

THE METROPOLITAN DISTRICTS.

[FROM OUR SPECIAL CORRESPONDENT.]

LETTER LXI.

In my last communication I said that the carpenter's trade divided itself, like many others of the present day, into two distinct branches, viz., the "honourable" and the "dishonourable" masters—that is to say, those who have a regard for the welfare and comforts of their men, and those who care only for themselves, and seek to grow rich by underpaying the workmen in their employ.

I then treated at some length of the "honourable" part of the trade, and I now come in due order to set forth the condition and earnings of the operatives belonging to the "dishonourable" portion of it.

The journeymen in connection with the "honourable" trade amount, as I before stated, to 1,770, so that by far the greater number, or no less than 18,230 of the working carpenters and joiners in the metropolis belong to what is called the "dishonourable" class—that is to say, nearly 2,000 of the London journeymen are "society men," and object to work for less than the recognized wages of the trade, while upwards of 18,000 are unconnected with any of the trade societies, and the majority of them labour for little more than half the regular rate of pay. The "dishonourable" portion of the trade includes many varieties of workmen. In the first place, there are the class called "improvers," or inexperienced hands, who, having learnt their business in the country, come up to town to perfect themselves in the higher branches of the trade, and, while they are so improving themselves, consent to take less wages than the more experienced and skilful operative. These, it will be seen, now constitute a considerable portion of the London trade, and are largely employed by those "enterprising" firms who seek to extend their business merely by underselling their neighbours. Secondly, there are the countrymen, who without any especial view to improvement in their craft, flock to London, from the badly paid parts of the country, in the hope of obtaining higher wages in the metropolis, and who, on their arrival in town, willingly accept a less rate of pay than the superior handicraftsmen. Thirdly, there are what are called the "strapping-shops"—that is to say, establishments where an undue quantity of work is expected from a journeyman in the course of the day. Such shops, though not directly making use of cheap labour (for the wages paid in them are generally of the highest rate), still, by exacting more work, may of course be said, in strictness, to encourage the system now becoming general, of less pay and inferior skill. These strapping establishments sometimes go by the name of "scamping shops," on account of the time allowed for the manufacture of the different articles not being sufficient to admit of good workmanship.

These appear to be the three principal means by which several even of the more honourable firms are now seeking to reduce the "standard rate of wages." The means employed by the dishonourable tradesman are the contract and sub-contract system, adopted by what are called the "speculative builders." It is this contract work, it will be seen, that constitutes the great evil of the carpenters' trade, as well as of many other trades at the present time; and as in those crafts, so in this, we find that the lower the wages are reduced the greater becomes the number of trading operatives or middlemen. For it is when workmen find the difficulty of living by their labour increased that they take to scheming and trading upon the labour of their fellow-operatives. In the slop trade, where the pay is the worst, these creatures abound the most; and so in the carpenters' trade, where the wages are the lowest—as among the speculative builders—there the system of contracting and sub-contracting is found in full force. I shall now proceed to set forth the effects of each of these several causes of low wages *seriatim*—beginning with the means used by the more honourable masters, and concluding with an account of the practices pursued by the speculative builders. First, of the "*strapping*" system. Concerning this I received the following extraordinary account from a man after his heavy day's labour; and never in all my experience have I seen so sad an instance of overwork. The poor fellow was so fatigued that he could hardly rest in his seat. As he spoke he sighed deeply and heavily, and appeared almost spirit-broken with excessive labour:—

"I work at what is called a strapping shop," he said, "and have worked at nothing else for these many years past in London. I call 'strapping,' doing as much work as a human being or a horse possibly can in a day, and that without any hanging upon the collar, but with the foreman's eyes constantly fixed upon you, from six o'clock in the morning to six o'clock at night. The shop in which I work is for all the world like a prison—the silent system is as strictly carried out there as in a model gaol. If a man was to ask any common question of his neighbour, except it was connected with his trade, he would be discharged there and then. If a journeyman makes the least mistake, he is packed off just the same. A man working at such places is almost always in fear; for the most trifling things he's thrown out of work in an instant. And then the quantity of work that one is forced to get through is positively awful; if he can't do a plenty of it, he don't stop long where I am. No one would think it was possible to get so much out of blood and bones. No slaves work like we do. At some of the strapping shops the foreman keeps continually walking about with his eyes on all the men at once. At others the foreman is perched high up, so that he can have the whole of the men under his eye together. I suppose since I knew the trade that a man does four times the work that he did formerly. I know a man that's done four pairs of sashes in a day, and one is considered to be a good day's labour. What's worse than all, the men are everyone striving one against the other. Each is trying to get through the work quicker than his neighbours. Four or five men are set the same job so that they may be all pitted against one another, and then away they go every one striving his hardest for fear that the others should get finished first. They are all tearing along from the first thing in the morning to the last at night, as hard as they can go, and when the time comes to knock off they are ready to drop. I was hours after I got home last night before I could get a wink of sleep; the soles of my feet were on fire, and my arms ached to that degree that I could hardly lift my hand to my head. Often, too, when we get up of a morning, we are more tired than we went to bed, for we can't sleep many a night; but we mustn't let our employers know it, or else they'd be certain we couldn't do enough for them, and we'd get the sack. So, tired as we may be, we are obliged to look lively somehow or other at the shop of a morning. If we're not beside our bench the very moment the bell's done ringing, our time's docked—they won't give us a single minute out of the hour. If I was working for a fair master, I should do nearly one-third less work than I am now forced to get through, and sometimes a half less; and even to manage that much, I shouldn't be idle a second of my time. It's quite a mystery to me how they do contrive to get so much work out of the men. But they are very clever people. They know how to have the most out of a man, better than any one in the world. They are all picked men in the shop—regular 'strappers,' and no mistake. The most of them are five foot ten, and fine broad shouldered, strong backed fellows too— if they weren't they would not have them. Bless you, they make no words with the men, they sack them if they're not strong enough to do all they want; and they can pretty soon tell, the very first shaving a man strikes in the shop, what a chap is made of. Some men are done up at such work—quite old men and gray with spectacles on, by the time they are forty. I have seen fine strong men, of six-and-thirty, come in there and be bent double in two or three years. They are most all countrymen at the strapping shops. If they see a great strapping fellow who they think has got some stuff about him that will come out, they will give him a job directly. We are used for all the world like cab or omnibus horses. Directly they've had all the work out of us we are turned off, and I am sure after my day's work is over, my feelings must be very much the same as one of the London cab horses. As for Sunday, it is *literally* a day of rest with us, for the greater part of us lays a bed all day, and even that will hardly take the aches and pains out of our bones and muscles. When I'm done and flung by, of course I must starve."

After this the reader can readily imagine that "the old hands" have but little chance of employment in a trade where the strapping system is coming into vogue. Concerning the treatment of the elderly work-men, a well-looking man, cleanly, but poorly dressed, gave me the following account:

"I served my apprenticeship in the country as a carpenter, but have been 49 years in London this July. I am now 79. I have worked all the 49 years in London, except six months. Of course I can't work now as well as I could. I was obliged about five years ago to wear spectacles, as my eyesight wasn't as good. I could do the rougher work of carpentering as well as some years before, but then I can't lift heavy weights up aloft as I could. In most shops the moment a man puts the glasses on it's over with him. It wasn't so when I first knew London. Masters then said, 'Let me have an old man, one who knows something.' Now it's, 'Let me have a young man, I must have a strong fellow, an old one won't do.' One master discharged two men when he saw them at work in glasses, though the foreman told him they worked as well with them, and as well every way as ever they did, but it was all no use; they went. I used to wear glasses in one employ, and others did the same, and the foreman was a good man to the men as well as to the master; and if the master was coming, he used to sing out 'Take those sashes out of the way,' and so we had time to whip off our glasses, and the master didn't know we were forced to use them; but when he did find it out, by coming into the shop unawares, he discharged two men. I now work at jobbing and repairing in buildings. It's no use my going to ask for work of any master, for if I hadn't my glasses on he'd see from my appearance I was old, and must wear them, and wouldn't hear of giving an old man a job. One master said to me, 'Pooh, you won't do—you were born too soon.' The fact is, they want strong young fellows from the country, that they can sweat plenty of work out of, and these country hands will go to work for 21s. a week, so that the master has a double pull—more work out of him and less to pay for it. The work's inferior, but they don't look much after the quality of the work now. The old men have only the workhouse left. Few of us have saved money. We can't, with families to bring up, on 30s. a week. I know many old men that were in their day good workmen, now in the workhouse. I know six that's now in Marylebone workhouse that I've worked along with myself. I belong to a benefit club, or there would be nothing but the workhouse for me if I lost my jobbing. Old age coming on men in my way is a very great affliction. We try to hide our want of great strength and good sight as long as we can. I did it for two or three years, but it was found out at last, and I had to go. I average about 12s. a week at jobbing; work's so uncertain, or I could make more."

Another old man corroborated this. He had written out a statement of what he thought his grievances, and called upon me with it. It is as follows:—"Old carpenters are generally despised by master-builders; the failure of sight and wearing of spectacles is almost a death-blow to many a good old tradesman. And in many cases, masters will not give an elderly man employment at any price; the consequence is, that many have been compelled to go to the parish for relief, or into the workhouse. Employers instruct their foremen to deny a job to men above a certain age. When employers and clerks in their office are compelled to wear spectacles, it is considered with them an honourable badge; but to the poor workman it is a sudden death—he is no longer employed." "That's what I've experienced myself, sir," he added. "I was an apprentice in Bath, and have been 36 years in London. I am now 63, and strong and able to do a good day's work; but the answer always is, if I ask for work, 'You're too old.' I hadn't worn glasses many months before I was discharged from a place I'd been in a long time. We can't be employed at any price. The society rules allow us to work at reduced wages on account of our age. I job about among my friends, but I'm always in debt, for I have a sickly wife to keep and a sick daughter. Some weeks I make 20s., but many weeks I get not a stroke of work, and don't average altogether 12s. a week. There's not a farthing that's to be got by elderly men in general from masters that's had their youth and strength out of them. I'm in no benefit club. I was in two, but both failed. In case I was sick there's nothing but the parish for me and my family. I can't do work enough for a scamping master, or I might get on for one."

I now come to treat of the system pursued by the speculating builders of the metropolis. Of all the slop-trades that I have yet examined there appear to be greater evils connected with cheap building than with any other. It will be seen that from this the public derive *no benefit whatsoever*—house rent not even being reduced by it, while the journeymen are ground down to the same state of misery and degradation as in all other trades where the slop system flourishes. Of the 18,000 men working for the dishonourable portion of the building trade, it should be remembered that not one belongs to a society, and consequently they have no resource but the parish in case of sickness, accident, or old age. Consequently, as one of the more intelligent journeymen said to me, it is the master alone who, by reducing the wages of the workmen, is benefited, for though the house is built cheaper, the public have not only to pay the same rent, but to support the workmen out of the poor-rates. Moreover, it is by means of this system that the better, the more skilful, and more provident portion of the trade are being dragged down to the same wretched abasement as the unskilful and improvident workmen. In order, however, that I might not be misled by the journeymen, I thought it my duty to call upon some master-builders of the "honourable trade"—gentlemen of high character—as well as upon architects of equally high standing. I found the same opinion entertained by them all as to the ruinous effects of the kind of competition existing in their trade to a master who strives to be just to his customers and fair to his men. This competition, I was assured, was the worst in the contracts for building churches, chapels, and public institutions generally. "Honesty is now almost impossible among us," said one master-builder. "It *is* impossible in cheap contract work, for the competition puts all honourable trade out of the field; high character, and good material, and the best workmanship are of no avail. Capitalists can command any low-priced, by letting and subletting, and all by the piece. Most of these speculating and contracting people think only how to make money; or they must raise money to stop a gap (a bill perhaps to be met), and they grasp at any offer of an advance of money on account of a building to be erected. Their proceedings are an encouragement to every kind of dishonesty. They fail continually, and they drag good men down with them." Strong as these opinions are, I heard them fully confirmed by men who could not be mistaken in the matter. "Advertise for contract work," said another gentleman, "and you'll soon have a dozen applicants at all sorts of prices; and all tradesmen like myself, who calculate for a contract at a rate to pay the regular wages, and not to leave either the timber-merchant or anybody else in the lurch, and to yield us the smallest possible per centage for our risk and outlay, are regarded as a pack of extortionate men."

The system of contract-work was known forty years ago, or earlier, among the tradesmen employed in the erection of houses of the best class, but it was known as an exception rather than as an established system. It was long before that, however, not unfrequent as regards the erection of public buildings. A customer would then obtain "estimates" of the probable cost from well-known firms, and so ascertain the lowest price at which a private house could be erected. Thirty years back this system had gained a strong hold on all building capitalists, and it has gone on increasing within these 10 or 12, or more years. No mansion is built otherwise than by contract, except in the rare instance of an old connection of an old firm. The introduction of stuccos, cements, &c., within these 25 years, has further encouraged the contract system, by supplying a low-priced exterior for our houses—while the introduction of cheap paper, and of cheaper wood-work, by means of machinery, supplied the materials of a cheap interior; and a tradesman of little skill or probity can speculate in a building where he is not called upon to make heavy outlays for superior stone or timber, and can employ under-paid labour.

Respectable builders, I am informed, have often to submit to the most degrading terms in sending in their offers of contracts—terms which seem to presuppose every mode of knavery on the builder's part. One of the things in which competition is most ruinous, is, I am assured, in "contracting" for the new windows and embellishments, and the "alterations and improvements," required by competitive tradesmen, who are, at the same time, complaining of the unfair competition to which their particular trade is subject.

The employers of builders on contract have not, however, always escaped loss, and heavy loss, by grasping at a low-priced offer. The dry rot is mouldering away many a house built within these ten years, where the situation is damp. To guard against this pest, a master in the "honourable" trade would have built on a body of concrete—a thing never thought of by a scamping master. "Unless," said one architect to me, "some check be given to this dishonest system, the honourable masters must be dragged down towards the level of the others, and the best artisans must sink with them. The low-priced builders of the worst class cannot possibly do their work in any way but by cheating the tradesman and robbing the artisan."

Such are the opinions of the honourable masters in connection with the building trade, as to the ruinous effects of the slop or contract system. I shall now subjoin the statements, first, of the foremen, and lastly, of the workmen in connection with this part of the trade:—

"I am a foreman to a speculating builder. My employer is not in a very large way: he has about ten carpenters and joiners. He does not let the work, he employs all the men by the day. The highest wages he gives is 28s. a week; this sum he pays to three of his men. He gives 24s. to three others; and two more have £1 a week. Besides these he employs two apprentices. To the oldest of these he gives 15s. a week, and to the youngest 6s. The men who have 28s. are superior hands—such men as at either of the C——'s would get their 6s. a day. The 24s. men are good skilful carpenters, fairly worth 30s.; and those in the receipt of £1 are young men fresh from the country—principally from Devonshire. The wages in the west of England are from 12s. to 15s., and these low wages send a lot of lads to town every year, in the hope of bettering their condition. They mostly obtain work among the speculating builders. I suppose there are more carpenters in London from Devonshire and Cornwall than from any other counties in England. At least half of the carpenters and joiners employed by the speculating builders here are lads fresh up from the country. Apprentices are not employed by the speculators as a rule. Most of the speculators have no fixed shops. Their work is carried on chiefly in, what we term, camp shops—that is in sheds erected in the field where the buildings are going on, and that's one reason why apprentices are not generally taken by speculating builders. The speculators find plenty of cheap labour among the country lads. A hand fresh up from the

West of England can't get employment at the best of shops, unless he's got some friends, and so, after walking all London, he generally is driven to look for a job among the speculators at low wages. What few good hands are employed by the speculators are kept only to look after the countrymen. As a rule, I think young hands are mostly preferred, because there is more work in them. It is one of the chief evils of the carpenter's trade that as soon as a man turns of forty masters won't keep him on. The master whom I work for pays much better prices than most of the speculators. The average wages of the inferior hands employed in building is about 15s.; that is, I think, one-half of the hands don't receive more than that, and the other about 24s. But day-pay is the exception with the speculators. The way in which the work is done is mostly by letting and sub-letting. The masters usually prefer to let work, because it takes all the trouble off their hands. They know what they are to get for the job, and of course they let it as much under that figure as they possibly can, all of which is clear gain without the least trouble. How the work is done, or by whom, it's no matter to them, so long as they can make what they want out of the job, and have no bother about it. Some of our largest builders are taking to this plan, and a party who used to have one of the largest shops in London has within the last three years discharged all the men in his employ (he had 200 at least), and has now merely an office, and none but clerks and accountants in his pay. He has taken to letting his work out instead of doing it at home. The parties to whom the work is let by the speculating builders are generally working men, and these men in their turn look out for other working men, who will take the job cheaper than they will, and so I leave you, sir, and the public to judge what the party who really executes the work gets for his labour, and what is the quality of work that he is likely to put into it. The speculating builder generally employs an overlooker to see that the work is done sufficiently well to pass the surveyor. That's all he cares about. Whether it's done by thieves, or drunkards, or boys, it's no matter to him. The overlooker, of course, sees after the first party to whom the work is let, and this party in his turn looks after the several hands that he has sub-let it to. The first man who agrees to the job takes it in the lump, and he again lets it to others in the piece. I have known instances of its having been let again a third time, but this is not usual. The party who takes the job in the lump from the speculator usually employs a foreman, whose duty it is to give out the materials, and to make working drawings. The men to whom it is sub-let only find labour, while the 'lumper,' or first contractor, agrees for both labour and materials. It is usual in contract work, for the first party who takes the job to be bound in a large sum for the due and faithful performance of his contract. He then in his turn finds out a sub-contractor, who is mostly a small builder, who will also bind himself that the work shall be properly executed, and there the binding ceases—those parties to whom the job is afterwards let, or sub-let, employing foremen or overlookers to see that their contract is carried out. The first contractor has scarcely any trouble whatsoever; he merely engages a gentleman, who rides about in a gig, to see that what is done is likely to pass muster. The sub-contractor has a little more trouble; and so it goes on as it gets down and down. Of course I need not tell you that the first contractor, who does the *least* of all, gets the *most* of all; while the poor wretch of a working man, who positively executes the job, is obliged to slave away every hour night after night to get a bare living out of it; and this is the contract system. The public are fleeced by it to an extent that builders alone can know. Work is scamped in such a way that the houses are not safe to live in. Our name for them in the trade is 'bird cages,' and really nine-tenths of the houses built now-a-days are very little stronger. Again, the houses built by the speculators are almost all damp. There is no concrete ever placed at the foundation to make them dry and prevent them from sinking. Further, they are all badly drained. Many of the walls of the houses built by the speculators are much less in thickness than the Building Act requires. I'll tell you how this is done. In a third-rate house the wall should be, according to the Act, two bricks thick at least, and in a second-rate house, two bricks and a half. The speculators build up the third-rates a brick and-a-half thick, and the second-rates only two bricks, and behind this they run up another half brick, so that they can throw that part down immediately after the surveyor has inspected it. Many of the chimney breasts too, are filled up with rubbish, instead of being solid brickwork. The surveyor is frequently hand in hand with the speculator, and can't for the life of him discover any of these defects—but you know there's none so blind as those that *won't* see. And yet, notwithstanding all this trick-ery and swindling, and starving of the workmen, rents in the suburbs do not come down. Who, then, are the gainers by it all? Certainly not the public, for all they get are damp, ill-drained, and unsafe houses, at the same prices as they formerly paid for sound, wholesome, and dry ones. And most certainly the working men gain nothing by it.

And what is even worse than all is that the better class of masters are obliged to compete with the worse, and to resort to the same means to keep up with the times, so that if things go on much longer the better class of mechanics must pass away altogether."

Concerning ground rents, I had the following account from one well acquainted with the tricks of the speculators:—

"The party for whom I am foreman has just taken a large estate, and he contemplates making some thousands of pounds by means of the improved ground rents alone. There are several with him in the speculation, and this is the way in which such affairs are generally managed. A large plot of ground (six or seven meadows, may be) somewhere in the suburbs is selected by the speculators as likely to be an eligible spot for building—that is to say, they think that a few squares, villas, and terraces about that part would be likely to let as soon as run up. Then the speculators go to the freeholder or his solicitor, and offer to take the ground of him on a ninety-nine years' lease at a rent of about £50 a-year per acre, and may be they take as many as fifty acres at this rate. At the same time they make a proviso that the rent shall not commence until either so many houses are built, or perhaps before a twelvemonth has elapsed. If they didn't do this the enormous rent most likely would swallow them up before they had half got through their job. Well, may be, they erect half or two-thirds of the number of houses that they have stipulated to do before paying rent. These are what we term 'call-birds,' and are done to decoy others to build on the ground. For this purpose a street is frequently cut, the ground turned up on each side, just to show the plan, and the corner house, and three others, perhaps, are built just to let the public see the style of thing that it's going to be. Occasionally a church is begun, for this is found to be a great attraction in a new neighbourhood. Well, when things are sufficiently ripe this way, and the field has been well mapped out into plots, a board is stuck up, advertising 'THIS GROUND TO BE LET, ON BUILDING LEASES.' Several small builders then apply to take a portion of it, sufficient for two or three houses, may be, for which they agree to pay about five guineas a year (they generally make it *guineas* these gentlemen) for the ground-rent of each house. And when the parties who originally took the meadows on lease have got a sufficient number of these plots let off, and the small builders have run up a few of the carcases, they advertise that 'a sale of well-secured rents will take place at the Mart on such a day.' Ground-rents, you must know, are considered to be one of the safest of all investments now-a-days; for if they are not paid, the ground landlord, you see, has the power of seizing the houses; so gentlemen with money are glad to lay it out this way, and there's a more ready sale for ground-rents than for anything else in the building line. There's sure to be a strong competition for them, let the sale be whenever it will. Well, let us see now how the case stands. There are fifty acres taken on lease at £50 an acre a year, and that is £2,500 per annum. Upon each of these fifty acres fifty houses can be erected (including villas and streets, taking one with the other upon an average). The ground-rent of each of these houses is (at the least) £5, and this gives for the 2,500 houses that are built upon the whole of the fifty acres £12,500 per annum. Hence you see there is a clear net profit of £10,000 a year made by the transaction. This is not at all an extraordinary case in building speculations."

The subjoined supplies information concerning some other tricks of the speculators:—

"For the last fifteen months I have been at work on the estate. You had better not say what estate, or I shall be known. My master was a bankrupt some time back. Since his bankruptcy, he has started in business again. His friends have taken him by the hand, and a speculating builder has no need of any capital. The agents and lawyers find whatever cash is required to pay the workmen, on the Saturday night, and the builder makes a smash of it for the materials—as a matter of course. I'll tell you, sir, how this dodge is worked. A party of gentlemen who wishes to put their money into some building speculation that seems to promise well, agrees with a builder to find him all the cash to pay the workmen with, provided he will make himself answerable for the material, and for this they agree to give him a share in the profits if the spec turns out well. If, however, it should turn out bad, he is to be the party to go into the *Gazette*, for whatever may be owing. Of course everything is kept snug and secret among 'em, and if the builder goes to pieces, and doesn't let out who was his backers, why, directly he gets his certificate, they don't mind starting him again on the same terms. This is one of the ways in which building is carried on at the present time, on a large scale. The master I'm a speaking of never gives a carpenter or joiner, if they are at day work for him, less than five shillings a day; he takes it out of the timber merchant and brickmaker, instead of the journeymen."

As regards "Improvers," I had the subjoined information from a very intelligent and trustworthy man:—

"I am a joiner, receiving the regular wages. I am familiar with all the systems carried on as regards 'improvers.' These improvers are frequently the sons of carpenters and joiners, who have been instructed by their parents, and then seek to complete their knowledge of the business without going through a course of apprenticeship. Or they are often the sons of tradesmen in the country, who come to town for the name of the thing, and that they may put on their signs— 'So and So, from Messrs. ——, London.' A certain class of young men have been apprenticed, but not being perfect in their business, also go as improvers. The wages of improvers vary greatly—from 10s. to 23s. or 24s. a week. They generally have some interest to get into a shop. They know some friend of the master, or something of that kind. Then there can be no doubt that there are such things as *bonuses* to foremen. No doubt the introduction of these improvers is detrimental to the well-doing of the journeymen, who are driven, especially if they are past their prime, to work for lower wages. Masters don't like old men at all. Many masters are partial to improvers, and keep them on when they discharge journeymen. In the scamping (slop) shops, masters best like strong hearty young fellows from the country as improvers—men they can get plenty of work out of. Scamping masters soon discharge their improvers if they lose any of their strength and capability of hard work. Few improvers are kept on, as improvers, after they are twenty-five. Their ages run generally from sixteen to twenty-four. I have never known an improver become a journeyman in the shop in which he worked as an improver. Masters seem to distrust them. In speculating builders' employ there are generally more improvers than journeymen—thrice as many more. Speculating builders keep on only as few as possible journeymen, and those just to keep the work in decent order. Improvers can't be trusted by themselves. With some speculating builders the improver works by the piece, and is then ground down very low in price. A man of 22 will then not make above half wages, 15s., and work more than the regular hours to do that. Improvers find their own tools, the same as journeymen. I believe that twenty years ago there was not such a thing as a scamping master in London. Ten years ago one in ten might be scamping masters, and now quite one-third are so. Take masters altogether at 1,300, and 430 of them are scamping masters. Some of them are in a very large way, and employ occasionally 200 hands; and altogether I fancy they rank, as to the number of hands, with the honourable trade. I think the system gets worse and worse.

Mr. ———, one of the best builders in London, is now obliged to give way to competition, and get up a more scamping sort of work, instead of the fine and beautiful work that he used to supply."

The next point to be noticed is the system of letting and subletting the work. From an experienced carpenter and his son, also an experienced man in his trade, I had the following account:—

"I may say," said the father, "I have been seventy-five years in the carpentering trade, for that's my age, and I was born in the business. I worked nearly fifty years in Somersetshire, chiefly as a journeyman. Forty years ago the wages were 3s. a day in Taunton—that was the highest wages for the best men. When I left, five years since, it was a good man who got 2s. 6d.; many got 2s. a day. The decrease took place about thirty or thirty-five years back, when the competition and cheap estimates for contract work began. I remember the time, because a man came from Wellington and undertook some work which no tradesman in Taunton would undertake—the building of a market-house, which was put up to competition by the trustees. Immediately after that wages fell, for cheap contract work spread all over the neighbourhood. The man from Wellington cut down the wages directly; many worked for him at 2s. a day. Trade was dull then. It went on continually on the low system, and continues on that system still. The men that the market-house contractor employed were mostly inferior labourers, and he got them cheap. Of course it's the cheaper and worse labourers that first force the superior workmen to come down. Contracts have reduced good men as regards wages to the level of bad men, and good men must scamp it, for scamping is the rule now. I came to London five years ago to join my family, who were settled here. My family were then at work on a contract for a lawyer." "I knew nothing of the lawyer," said the son of my first informant, "but I saw a notice up that the carcases of six houses were to be finished, and made fit for inhabitants, and tenders were to be sent in; the lowest bidder of course to be accepted. The solicitor, that my brother and I had the contract from, was the agent of the ground landlord, who was anxious to have buildings erected on his property. The ground landlord had advertised that the land would be let on building leases, and that advances would be made, according to the usual dodge—for dodge it is, sir. A builder was soon found, one with little or no money, for money in such cases is no matter—that's an every-day affair. He agreed to erect six houses, and £250 was to be advanced for each house, something more than half as much as would be required to complete each of them. The builder got the carcases up, and then the agent put the stopper on him, and seized the houses for the ground landlord. Each house, in the manner it was left by the builder, when he was stopped, had full £300 expended on it of *somebody's* money, and materials. For this the builder became bankrupt and he was sent to prison. The houses were then advertised for sale and sold, the agent buying them, and just for the amount advanced— £1,500. So that after full £1,800 had been expended on the houses the agent got them for £300 less. The wages paid to the men employed on the building were as low as contract work usually is, and some carpenters there earned only 2s. 6d. a day of twelve hours. The work was let—brick-work, smith's-work, and all—and at a very low rate. Had fair living wages been paid to all employed the value of the six carcases would have been at least £2,400; so that the lawyer, you see, gains £900 by this mode of management. These are the parties who thrive by the contract system. The public gains nothing, for the house is not let for a farthing less rent than if built on a fair wages system; but the owner or his people may get 15 or 16 per cent. for their money. There is the same system now being carried on, and to a very great extent, all over the same neighbourhood. Some as good mechanics as ever took a tool in hand work from four in the morning till eight or nine at night, and earn only 4s. a day. Before the contract system it was 5s. a day of ten hours. Now on this contract system men grow rich on the degradation and suffering of the working man, and on the swindling of the timber merchant, the iron merchant, and the other tradesmen out of the materials. Nineteen out of every twenty speculating builders become bankrupts." [I may add, that in the bankrupt lists of last year, 51 are returned as builders; the largest number in any trade, except drapers and victuallers.] "So that," continued my informant, "notwithstanding all the money that these speculating builders wring out of the men, they keep failing every day. The agent I've been speaking of stuck boards up over the neighbourhood, stating that the finishing of the carcases, as I've said, was to be let to the lowest bidder, on certain terms; advances were to be made on the surveyor's report, among other conditions. I knew, if a low figure wasn't sent in, it was no use trying for the job, so my brother and I bid for the work at the lowest possible sum. We reckoned on our own labour being serviceable, as we could do so much among ourselves, and save the expense of a foreman and such like. We hoped to make something, too, out of the extras, that is for extra work not included in the specification, for the specification is never correct. Men now bid very low in hopes of making their profit in this way. My father, my brother, and myself, didn't realize more than 4s. a day, working on an average 13 hours. If we'd been employed by a contractor, who took it at the rate we did, our wages couldn't have been more than 3s. a day, and that was the reason of our bidding for it. The journeymen in that neighbourhood now get 3s. a day, all the work being let and sub-let. A journeyman will undertake work to pay himself 4s. a day, and will hire men under him at 3s.—or even less—14s. or 15s. a week. One man takes the windows, another the skirtings, another the doors, another the dwarf and high cupboards, another the stairs, another the mouldings, another the boxing shutters for the windows, and another the floors. The average price for labour in contract work windows is 6s. an opening for 25 feet, and according to Skyring's prices (which are low) the charge would be 10s. Doors, double moulded, are paid 2s. 6d. on an average, and they ought to be 5s.; of course, they must be scamped. On this work I must make two doors a day, while one properly made is a good long day's job. Some of these doors don't last above ten years. Staircases are done at £3 a six-roomed house; it ought to be from £5 to £5 10s. For boxing shutters £1 4s. is the price, instead of from £2 10s. to £3. It's a fortnight's work to do it well; it's 40 feet work, a fair price (Skyring's) being 1s. 4½d. a foot. At Nottinghill, twelve years ago, I had £2 10s. for this same work. Floors, on contract, are 2s. 6d. a square, though that's above the average, and they are honestly worth 5s.; Skyring gives 6s. 6d. Skirtings, which they take by the house, are 15s., and ought to be £2 10s. Mouldings, which are taken by the hundred feet sticking (working) are 1s. 6d. the hundred, running measure, the regular price being 4s. 2d. The dwarf and high cupboards are a shameful price by contract—2s. 6d. each, with shelves, folding doors, hanging, and everything complete. These prices are what I know of by my own experience; but when there's a further sub-letting by a journeyman contracting under the contractor, and so getting hands at the lowest possible rates, they are even less than I have specified. Contracting altogether is a bad system; it's carried on for the benefit of a few at the cost of the working men, and out of their sweat, and at the cost too of respectable tradesmen many a time. Government contracts are carried on just the same way. I myself have worked at the Post-office, and the man next me had only 18s. a week. Since the present contractor has had it, only 12s. is paid; so you can see what it must all lead to. I reckon that there are from

18,000 to 20,000 working men in my trade in London; and I believe that full two-thirds of them work at under wages. One half of the two-thirds will get 4s. a day, and the other third 2s. 6d. In London, as you have stated, sir, no doubt there are 6,405 houses built every year; and at least 6,000 of them are built by contract work, and speculating and scamping builders. All in the suburbs are. These would average (reckon the new houses erected to be chiefly in the suburbs) from £30 to £35 a year rent. One carpenter could frame and finish two such houses a year. That would give employment at the cheap built houses to 3,000 men. These houses are raised on the reduction of the working men's wages, and that reduction, as they now get 20s. where they did get 30s., makes the loss to each working man as much as 10s. a week, or £25 a year, and that amounts in all to £75,000 per annum, which somebody or other gets out of the journeymen carpenters alone. That *somebody* is not the public—that's very clear, for rents are as high if not higher, and since the majority of speculating builders become bankrupts, it's clear that the ground landlords, their solicitors and agents, are the only men benefited by the system. The effect of this reduction on the working men is, as I said, very bad indeed. Respectable masters, who would be fair and honest, are so cut down by competition, that they would almost as soon be without trade as with it. The consequence is, half of the men are unemployed, and when employed get not much more than half wages. If people only knew how the 200 miles of streets that have been built in London in the last ten years had been run up—through what sufferings to the working man and his family—they wouldn't think it quite so grand a thing."

Of the effects of the sub-contracting system an old man gave me the following statement:—

"I have known the trade forty years as a general hand, doing both carpenter's and joiner's work. Things are wonderfully altered since I first knew it. Thirty-five or forty years ago there was no cutting under, and no small masters taking work at prices that wouldn't pay them, and getting it out of the men. Lately I have been working at staircasing, and in houses run up by speculating builders. A journeyman like myself has taken my present work at 18s. a story for staircasing. Each story to this house will have 13 steps. A fair price would be £2, or £2 2s. The man who undertakes it at 18s., gives me 4s. a day of ten hours, from six to six. He employs old men—too old for first-rate work—and boys, and anybody that he can get cheap, and they 'scamp' the work as much as they possibly can. The work ain't fit to be seen, but anything will do for speculating builders, so as they have it done cheap, and plenty of it. He gives a youth of 17 only 6s. a week—1s. a day. He finds his own tools, and so do I, and so do we all; and reckon this boy spends 1s. a week on his tools, he has 5s. a week left for his labour, and he's a handy chap, too. My employer has one old man, and he makes four-pannel square doors, 2 feet 6 inches by 8 feet 6 inches, at 1s. 6d. the door. The regular charge by Skyring's prices, at 5d. a foot, and that for 16 feet, would be 6s. 8d. Of such men and boys he usually employs from 6 to 20. He has built 100 houses, I dare say, by this system of engaging the sort of hands I tell you of, and paying them as I've said. He drives these boys and men like niggers; his son acts as foreman, and sees that they cram 18 hours work into 12; if they don't they're discharged. One man 'stuck' (worked) 400 feet of moulding in a day (10 hours), and he got discharged for not doing more. According to the price-book, it would be 16s. 8d.—the charge being a halfpenny a foot, and his pay was 4s. a day for doing 16s. 8d. worth of work. The master expected 500 feet for 4s. I don't work for the same man, but for one who has taken the stairs of him. He has taken twelve houses of the sort. The speculating builder prefers to let all he can. The work's then let and sublet again. He's now got a man planing flooring-boards. He don't get them done at the mills, and I'll tell you what he gives the man. There's 6 'square' to be done; a 'square' is 100 feet; ¾-inch, white deal, edges shot; and though the proper price is 5s. 6d. a square, or 33s. altogether, he gives only 10s. for 6 square, or 20d. a square; that's for planing, shooting, and laying. A young man does it; he's only 30, and he can't earn more than 2s. a day; but what's a man to do when he's had his hands in his pockets out of work for two or three weeks, with a wife and two children? A man's then obligated to do it. These are the sort of men such as my employer always gets hold of. If I was paid fairly for my work it would come to 7s. a day from the quantity. I should get discharged if I didn't do that quantity of work, and at a moment's notice. When one's on by day there's no notice wanted—you must leave that night. The man who's taken the work I'm now upon was out a long time, and he was obligated to take it to get a crust, and so must put on men worse off than he is. If the staircase was sub-let to me, or such a man as me, I might get 12s. in the room of the 18s. Houses run up this way don't let for one farthing cheaper; they look well outside and a gentleman wouldn't know it was all badly done. It's like a rogue with a good suit of clothes on his back, the house is. These houses won't stand long, some are built without mortar; the builders get the lime that tanners have done with in their trade and make that do; all the nature's out of it; it's no more good than mud, only it's white. The cheapest timber is used, American spruce, and that's certain to fill the place with bugs; it always does. The men that work in such buildings are never society men, and are generally given to drink, and can't get work any where else. When I was a young man I had 5s. and 5s. 6d. a day. For the last four years I have had only 4s. a day, and often not more than 3s. I'm now 60. I couldn't get work at the regular prices, and I was obliged to go to a speculating builder or starve. They know all about that. The number of men working low like me has increased greatly in these five years. Many hands come from the country, too, 'specially from the west of England, where wages are 15s. to 18s., so that lots of hands can be had at almost any price in London. To-day an Irish carpenter offered to go to work at 4s. a week rather than starve. Some speculating builders take numbers of apprentices. I've worked for one who had three apprentices and one good hand. This cheap sort of work will ruin the trade altogether if a stop's not put to it. Every year it gets worse and worse, and in time there'll be no good workmen left, as everybody will be forced to scamp it. In many places they won't employ a man turned forty, for fear he can't do work enough. They like strong country fellows. When I first knew the trade there were no contracts. They've been the ruin of the trade among men and masters, who've been cutting one against another for twenty years now. No gentleman will set the most respectable builder in London to work now-a-days without a contract, it's come to such a pitch. Before contracts came into use all in the trade was well off— masters and men. Masters did their work honestly and fairly, and men were comfortable in their homes, and had their good meat dinners on a Sunday, and lived well generally. Now three-fourths of the men are starving, if you could know all, and none of them are contented. If bread and meat weren't reasonable, men couldn't live at all. Our wives had no need to work formerly, except doing their house work; they could mind their homes and their families then properly. Now they must strive and strive, and earn only 4d. or 5d. a day at needlework, and often see their children starving for all that. I know whole families who have to work now, when formerly only the father had to work, and the children are barefoot all the week. Many of our wives go out charing or washing, or they're put to making soldiers' coats. We all do four times the work we once did, families and all, and yet we don't get one-fourth the money for it that we once did. I don't make more than 10s. a week, the year through. My daughter, who is a shoebinder, makes 6d. a day."

In my next Letter I purpose describing the different kinds of machinery employed in the building trade—such as the planing, moulding, and morticing machines. I shall likewise give an account of the establishment of Mr. Thomas Cubitt, at Thames-bank, Pimlico, so that the public may have an opportunity of contrasting the present treatment of the operatives by the worse class of masters with that of the better.

LABOUR AND THE POOR.

THE METROPOLITAN DISTRICTS.

[FROM OUR SPECIAL CORRESPONDENT.]

OF THE MOULDING, PLANING, AND VENEERING MILLS.

Letter LXII.

In the present letter I shall conclude my inquiry into the condition of the London carpenters and joiners, with a description of the several applications of machinery to the purposes of their trade. These appear to consist of moulding mills, planing mills, mortising mills, and saw benches for cutting grooves, tennons, and rabbets. To estimate the quantity of manual labour superseded by these means is a very difficult calculation, and only admits of a rough approximation. I have, however, endeavoured to obtain the best information on this point, and the statement here given is, I am convinced, rather below than above the actual amount.

I shall begin with the moulding mills.

One of the most delicate applications of steam to wood work, as regards precision, nicety, and celerity, is seen in the preparation of mouldings. At the mill I visited, and over which I was obligingly shown by the manager, mouldings are prepared for the use of the joiner in house building, as well as for the upholsterer and the carver and gilder. A moulding steam-mill was first established in Paddington somewhat less than ten years ago. There had been many attempts previously, which failed of attaining full success. The one I allude to is the largest in the world. The premises in which it is carried on are of great extent, and the constant recurrence of timber, as you walk along, up stairs or down, in doors or out—of timber as it is received from lighters in the Thames (on the banks of which the premises are built), and then piled for use, or in its last stage of preparation—gives the visitor a better impression than any other place I have seen of the vastness of the timber trade of London. The establishment is erected for all the purposes of sawing, planing, and cutting wood (except veneers) by steam; but as I have already—in my letter on the Sawyers—given an account of the other processes, I shall here confine myself to the moulding mills. Any kind of wood can be formed into mouldings; but yellow pine is generally used. This pine is kept four or five years drying before it is fit for use. The wood to be "moulded"—a word which is not expressive of the process, for all is done by cutting—is prepared of the width and substance required. It is then rubbed smooth with glass paper—boys being employed at this work. When ready, it is placed into a frame by a lad, and the machinery is set to work. This consists of a multiplicity of wheels, cutters, &c., working so rapidly, that the motion of some of them is almost imperceptible, while a shower of little chips of wood—the size of peas or beans, but angular, and larger or smaller, according to the pattern worked—is thrown upon the stander-by. The peculiar construction of the machinery, which cuts the timber into a moulding; the modes of changing it so as to cut the wood to any pattern—some patterns being very elaborate as to curves and outlines, and to the depth of 12 inches—cannot be properly described without the aid of engravings. The moulding is completed in one operation. The boy "keeps feeding the machine," by putting the timber to the frame, and with the usual unconscious look of lads employed in labour the nature and importance of which they know and care nothing about. All is quiet, regular, and orderly. By "quiet," I must be understood as speaking of the demeanour of the people at work, for quiet, in the sense of noiselessness, is unknown in such places. The clatter of wheels, the grinding sound of saws, and the chip-chip of the moulding engines render conversation difficult. The persons employed, however, by a peculiar pitch of their voices, aided by gestures, seemed to make each other readily understand any order or communication. The machinery prepares the moulding complete; it is formed to the pattern—whatever curves or elevation that pattern may comprise. The moulding is also "under-cut;" that is, planed smooth—knots in the wood being no obstacle, on the under or flat side of the wood as "moulded"—and all is executed at one process. Whatever be the pattern, the machine will cut, at an average, twelve feet in a minute. A simple form thus prepared would occupy a skilled and quick mechanic one quarter of an hour. Four steam moulding machines are constantly at work at the establishment I saw, and thus they "mould" 48 feet or 16 yards a minute, 960 yards an hour, and 9,600 yards in a day of 10 hours. Ten hours is a low average, for though time is somewhat lost in changing cutters and such like, the mill is sometimes kept going from six in the morning until ten at night. The day's work is thus about 5½ miles, or 33 miles length of moulding in a week; and reckoning 50 weeks to the year, 1,650 miles in the year are "moulded" in one mill. This is the only mill which "undercuts" the mouldings, and does all by one process. The other mills may do altogether little more than half as much, and that gives, in all, 2,475 miles. For the moulding machines 5 men, overlookers and directors generally, and 15 boys, are employed. The men earn from 36s. to 40s. a week, the boys 7s. to 15s., according to age and trustworthiness. The mere errand, jobbing boy, has 4s. a week. A new moulding engine, to cut to the depth of 18 inches, is in course of erection. I may mention here also a new system of steam sawing—a simpler system, and the only one now in operation—which I saw at this mill. A steam engine is placed *above* a frame of saws, the frame containing 48 or any lower number of saws, while the piston of the engine works the saws without the intervention of further machinery.

The next kind of mills that demand our attention are those for planing by steam.

Planing mills for general work have been established in London within these twelve years; the first was Mr. Jackson's, of Pimlico. Prior to that, the process was known, and some of the masters had somewhat similar machinery to that now in use, but worked by hand instead of steam. The introduction of steam planing machines, I am informed on the best authority, was suggested by the uses of a machine in operation some thirty-five years ago, for the cutting of wood into scaleboard. It was thus cut smooth into thin planks, and was used for making hat and bonnet boxes, salve boxes, and the like; and until about fourteen years since, this scaleboard paid 21s. per cwt. duty, as it was a substitute for paper or pasteboard. Very wet timber would then frequently entail a dead loss on account of its weighing heavily. The planing machine is now worked by a steam-engine in the usual way. A shaft from the main shaft works one drum, and that one drum works alike the "endless chain," two saws for edging boards, two spindles for ploughing and tonguing, and two adzes for "thicknessing" the board, or reducing it to one perfect uniformity as regards thickness. The planing irons, two being generally used, are fixtures. The deal to be planed is placed on an iron frame thoroughly smooth and level; and when the board is thus placed upon it and fitted firmly, it is drawn rapidly along by the endless chain, which is impelled by the engines, and so the board is passed under the planing irons. The other processes that I have mentioned, viz., the edging, &c., go on when required, simultaneously with the planings, and at the same frame. Two shavings are in this way planed off the surface of the board, one rough and one fine. The wood thus planed must not exceed 11 inches in thickness. The shavings are useless, and sometimes have to be burnt in considerable quantities, that they may be got rid of. The wood so planed is entirely for the purposes of flooring, and I am informed that a joiner could not plane it so truly—if as smoothly—as the mill; for it is not easy to give, merely by the eye and the touch, a precisely uniform thickness of substance to every portion of the deal or plank. The machine effects this uniformity with infallible precision. The one that I saw planes 450 deals or planks, of the usual length of a plank, in a day. To plane them finely and in the best fashion of workmanship, a good hand would not do more than twenty such planks. Long practice might, however, I was told, enable a joiner to plane thirty in a day, if not in the very best style. Take the average at twenty-five, and the planing machine performs the work of eighteen men. There are, I am told, about eight such public planing machines in London; planing among them eight times 450 deals or planks in a day, or performing the work of 116 men in planing. This, of course, is independent of any planing machines which are private or Government property. The planing process is managed by two men, the frame-man and his assistant; the engine, of course, requires the usual amount of attention on the part of the engineer, &c. The highest amount paid to the workmen at the mill I visited was 8s. a day. The frame-men have 5s. a day, but they usually make seven days in the week, owing to the mill being frequently worked over-time. The labourers have 21s. a week. The cost of mill planing runs gradually as regards intermediate sizes, from 1s. 6d. and 2s., respectively, for 6-feet deals and planks, to 5s. 1d. and 7s. for 21-feet deals and planks.

I moreover witnessed the working of a rack timber bench for cutting logs of timber, by steam application, into scantlings and joists of all descriptions for building purposes. This machine can cut any log not exceeding two feet in depth and of any length. It accomplishes in five minutes as much labour as would occupy a pair of sawyers two hours. It will cut thirty loads of timber a day. There are five or six such machines in London, but they are not in constant working, the demand for such labour varying greatly.

Besides the machinery for planing and making mouldings, steam machinery is generally used, on the larger builders' premises, for sawing deals and timber both for flooring and roofing in the carpenters' department. In the joiners' branch there are steam machines for cutting tennons for doors, sashes, and whatever is framed together; also for ploughing, rabbeting, and indeed grooving generally. "In our shop," said one of my informants, "a machine makes any sized tennon by a single motion passed over two saws. That, of all machines, does most harm to the efficient joiners; it will do thirty men's work. We have only this machine and the steam saw. I reckon that twenty-five such machines are kept going in London, and so 750 men's labour is done away with. In one house I know of there is a morticing machine by steam, which will do twelve men's work. I know only of one in London."

In the course of my inquiries I paid a visit to the establishment here alluded to, and was not more surprised at the completeness of all its mechanical arrangements than I was delighted at the regard and consideration exhibited for the comfort and well-being of the men. There science was not only taken advantage of for the performance of the most skilful operations in connection with almost every branch of the art of building, but likewise to promote the health of all the men employed on the premises. There were steam-mills for cutting marble and for polishing it—mills for grinding the lime and cement by steam—steam-mills again for sawing the timber, and steam-mills for grooving, rabbeting, mortising, and making tennons—lathes driven by machinery, for turning wood and iron—drilling and punching machines—all worked in the same manner. But I purpose treating more fully upon this subject at a future time, and especially, upon the consideration shown for the well-being of the men, displayed in this most admirable establishment. I was informed by one of the gentlemen at the head of it that the application of machinery to building purposes generally could not but produce a great revolution in the carpenters' trade. Another gentleman thought that they had, by such means, displaced full 25 per cent. of manual labour within the last few years.

I shall now proceed to give an account of a veneer-mill.

The manufacture of veneers, now exclusively made by means of steam-machinery, is among the most curious applications of steam power to mechanical contrivances. About 38 years ago, Sir Isambert, then Mr. Brunel, turned his attention to the preparation of a process by which the sawing of wood might be facilitated by means of the steam-engine. The invention of the machinery, and its adaptation to the working of the steam-engine, as now in use, was Mr. Brunel's; and the first steam-mill for the sawing of deals was that of Mr. Smart, as I have already stated in my account of the sawyers. Mr. Brunel patented his discovery, and sold licenses to those who chose to invest their money in the establishment of the steam-mills. In the course of his experiments to improve the process for the sawing of logs of timber, he thought of applying it to the production of veneers, which, before his discovery, were sawn in the usual manner in the pits, but were rudely, as well as expensively, produced; the failures of the sawyers in the production of a perfect veneer being frequent. For two years Mr. Brunel, at considerable cost, carried on his experiments, but only with approximations to success. The saws he first used were straight, and were formed of "a solid plate" of one piece of steel. They were very fine; and from the heat produced by the friction of the timber, they soon became useless; for in working they "lengthened" and "buckled," and so lost their accuracy of performance. ("Buckling" is a technical term expressive of the blistering or puckering of the steel.) "It buckled sometimes," said my informant, who was at the time I speak of with Mr. Brunel, "like the frill of a shirt." On one occasion, when watching the working of his saws, Mr. Brunel took a file, and as if struck by a sudden thought, "nicked" the saws in the parts where they "buckled." The machinery was then set a-going, and the saws worked truly, without hitching or irregularity. It then occurred to Mr. Brunel (who was himself surprised, my intelligent informant assured me, at the effect of his simple remedy for the buckling) that saws formed of distinct pieces of steel would be better than those formed of solid plates, and this—when he had given more attention to the subject—led him to apply segment saws, of a circular form, to effect his purpose. These saws were then formed, as they are at present, of different segments of steel, by which any "buckling" or deviation from the nicest accuracy is thoroughly obviated. The first application of the segment and circular saw convinced Mr. Brunel that his discovery was perfected—a conviction which has been justified by a long tried result, for up to the present day no improvement, and indeed no alteration, has been introduced into his process, as regards the use of these saws. The first steam-mill established for the sawing of veneers was at Battersea, thirty-four or thirty-five years ago, and was the property of Mr. Brunel and his partners. This mill is still in full operation.

The veneer saw mill that I visited is the largest in the world, and in its beautiful and scientific arrangements presents a most striking example of the perfection by which the hardest as well as the softest timber can be made available for veneering purposes; a nicety and a perfection utterly unattainable by manual labour or skill. The ground occupied by the buildings covers about six acres, and is situated on the bank of a canal, up which the timber is usually conveyed. Dark and dirty looking logs, some of them of vast size, lie scattered or piled about; but among these, only distinguished by a practised eye, are the most costly and rare of all the foreign woods used in the manufacture of our richest furniture, none but the choicest timber being collected for the formation of veneers. The stateliest trees that some months back graced the forests of St. Domingo, Brazil, or Honduras, lie there until their trunks can be sawn into multiplied divisions, some of them as thin as paper. The principal woods used for veneering are the mahoganies—Spanish, Honduras, or African. The Honduras mahogany is in the most extensive use. Here, too, may be seen satin wood, Amboyna, the many varieties of rosewood, zebra-wood, ebony, tulip-wood, coromandel, bird's-eye maple, cedar, sandal-wood, and king-wood; besides our native oaks, yews, elms, ashes, birches, walnuts, and sycamores—these woods having of late come into much more frequent use as veneers.

Nor is it the costlier woods alone that are prepared in this great establishment. Deals are consumed in great quantities, and for perhaps the cheapest of all commodities which science has given to general use—the formation of lucifer-matches. The matches, however, are made by a different process from that used to prepare veneers, as I shall presently show.

The wood to be sawn into veneers is first carried into the "adzing-room," where men chip the surface with axes, or level it with planes, so as to remove any grit or dirt which might impede the action of the saw. The logs so adzed are then fixed by an application of Scotch glue to a wooden frame with transverse battens, so as to be held fixedly when subjected to the action of the saw. Scotch glue is used in preference to all others. It may not be so strong as marine glue, but marine glue is not affected by water, and for the business purposes of this mill the glue must be capable of being removed by washing, as the part to which it has been applied must be cleansed.

The timber to be sawn is then taken to the saw-room, a large well-lighted apartment, 120 feet long, 90 wide, and of proportionate height. In this room are eight circular saws, from 7 to 17 feet in diameter. There are 11 such saws in use altogether in the mill; the teeth of the 17 feet saw are five to the inch, and the rest in proportion. In the saw-room, on the occasion of my visit, there was a very agreeable odour, reminding one strongly of the perfume of a library, where the books are bound in Russia leather. Some of the woods give out a strong aroma when sawn. Among these, the rosewoods and ebony are the most pungent and titilating, the dust causing strangers to sneeze, even if they are inured to snuff-taking. The sandal and tulip woods also emit a pleasant fragrance, while the cedar, contrary to the popular notion, is not especially agreeable to the sense when being sawn—indeed, a veneer sawyer told me, that once on sawing some wet, and not very sound cedar, the smell given out was so strong and unpleasant, from the liberation of the volatile oils, that the men had to run out and "drink spirits to fortify themselves against its effects."

The timber, affixed to its frame, is placed on an iron beam, and adjusted to the exact approximation to the saw. The saw is then set rapidly revolving, and a sawyer, assisted by a boy, follows the timber as the machinery carries it along, subject to the fine and dividing edge of the saw; he keeps the teeth of the saw clear from the dust, as far as he can, and closely watches, and in some sort directs, the precise adjustment of the timber to the saw, until the veneer is completed. On my visit a large rosewood tree was being sawn, and the veneers looked like huge, dull "watered" ribbons. The strong glowing colours are afterwards brought out by varnish.

The object of my present letter does not entail upon me the necessity of describing the minutiæ of the beautiful machinery, so exquisitely adjusted in this mill. I may mention, however, that a person unused to such sights will find the "saw-room" an imposing spectacle when the saws are all going. The clatter of the steam-engine below— the rapid running of broad belts of leather connecting the various parts of the machinery—the peculiar sound of the saw-wheel as it whirls round rapidly, and as rapidly severs the timber—and the close attention and almost unbroken silence of the men at work, with the peculiar atmosphere caused by the work, present certainly a combination only known to great cities and to modern times.

To the courtesy of the proprietor, who was obliging enough to give instructions that every possible information and facility of inquiry should be afforded me, I am indebted for the following account of the extent of his business in the week preceding my visit (as regards the production of veneers). Nine saws were thus employed. The numbers 1, 2, &c., indicate the saws; the second series of figures the logs, trunks of trees, or planks sawn; and the third range of figures the number of feet sawn for veneering:—

No. 1	30	4,813
2	24	3,936
3	13	2,332
4	17	7,640
5	12	4,898
6	53	8,269
7	16	8,216
8	12	10,043
9	6	938
	183	51,085

This number, however, is below the average, which may be fairly taken at 200 logs, &c., a week, forming 60,000 feet long of veneers, averaging 10 inches wide. The mill cannot be said to work more than 50 weeks in the year, and that gives a length of 3,000,000 feet or 1,000,000 yards, which is upwards of 568 miles. For this purpose between 3,000 and 4,000 trees are yearly used. The segments of the worn out saws in this mill—now piled up in heaps—would measure in a row 13 miles. I may add that more than once a log of mahogany of the value of £500 has been cut at this mill.

The machinery *can* cut 15 veneers in the inch, though 11 and 12 to the inch is the usual demand. The sawyers can saw but little more than 6 on the average to the inch. The charge at the mill is 1d. a foot for sawing veneers; thirty years ago it was 6d. Each veneer is now canvassed at each end to prevent its splitting; and throughout the establishment are large rooms, heated by steam, for the drying of the veneers or of the timber to be sawn. The extent to which veneering is carried on in London may be estimated by computing 28 saws at work, doing the same, or nearly the same, amount of work as those I have spoken of.

Among the other performances of this mill, I have spoken of the preparation of timber for lucifer matches. For the making of these matches the best America yellow pine is used. It is first sawn into blocks as wide as the tree, or rather plank, will allow, averaging perhaps 12 inches. These blocks are 3 inches thick and 5 and 5¼ in. wide. Five of such blocks are placed on a "feeding bench," and, when the machinery is put into operation, they are subject to the incision of from 45 to 60 cutters, lancet-shaped, which cut into the timber; it is then "slit" to the thickness of a match by the operation of a knife fitted into the machine; but so rapidly is the process carried on, that to the eye the slitting and cutting seem simultaneous. The five blocks are divided into match-wood in 116 strokes of the machine, and the machine performs 122 strokes in a minute or less; so that 16,000 double, or 32,000 single, matches are thus made in that time. Two other machines perform the same quantity of work as the great one I have described. The matches, when cut, slide from the machine into another room underneath, where girls are employed in tying them up into bundles, first fitting them into parcels, which hold six dozen boxes, each box containing 50 splints. In one day 30 hogsheads of matches were sent from the mill to one man in Bristol, each hogshead containing 500 bundles, or 54,000,000 matches in all. In this mill the average of matches thus made is 156,000 gross of boxes a year, each box containing 50 splints—altogether 60 millions of matches. For the manufacture of this quantity 400 cubic feet of timber are used in a week, averaging eight trees, or 400 large trees a year for lucifer matches, only in one mill. My informant thinks that three times the number is so made throughout the country.

In this mill are also rooms for the bending of timber for coach-builders' purposes, for the chopping of dye-woods, logwood, fustic, Campeachy, Nicaraguay, &c., into small particles, for the formation of ship blocks, and for the splitting of wood for lucifer-match boxes.

The veneer-mill sawyers are paid 5s., 6s., and 7s. a-day; but for that payment the saw is "taxed" to perform 5,000 feet in a week, and for all beyond that the veneer mill-sawyer receives 7s. per 1,000 feet—his average the year through is £2 15s. a week. There is no society among these men, and their number in London—where there are eight mills with twenty-eight saws—does not exceed 40. The labourers at the veneer mills are paid 3s. and 3s. 6d. a day, and the men who pile the timber, known in the trade as "gangers," earn 6s., 7s., and 8s. a day. These gangers, however, are a very small body, only four being employed at the great mill in question. In packing and tying the matches twenty girls are usually employed.

To this it is but fair that I should append the statement of one of the most intelligent of the operative carpenters, concerning the influence of machinery upon his trade. I wish it, however, to be distinctly understood that the opinions expressed below are those of the working men, and they are given here merely in order that the public should be made acquainted with them:—

"The opinion of the journeymen generally is, that machinery cannot but make the trade worse and worse every year. The public, I know, generally believe it to be the greatest of blessings to have work done as cheap as possible, and as machinery does work cheaper than human beings, of course it is looked upon as a great benefit to society. The reason why the work can be done cheaper by machinery is, because a steam-engine only wants coals, and we require victuals—besides, masters can keep their steam-engines working night and day, and human beings *must* rest. The longer a master can keep his machinery going, the oftener, of course, he turns his capital over. You see directly they get a large quantity of machinery together, so as to keep it going continually, they will work at any price. I'm certain if they was tied to time as we are, we could beat them in our trade, for there's only particular parts that they can do effectually, and the great portion of these is the most laborious. To produce work as cheap as possible is certainly a great benefit to all those who have money to buy with; but to the working classes—that is to those who have no money but what they earn by their labour—machinery cannot but be a curse, since the object of it is to displace the very labour by which they live. Of course the capitalist gets ultimately a greater amount of profit by machinery, because he does more work with it, and so increases the returns on his capital, even though he sells at a less rate; it's by small profits and quick returns that all the fortunes are made in trade. But, only let us have machinery carried out to its full extent and then we shall soon know whether it is really a blessing or a curse to society as at present constituted. No working man that ever I heard but did not admit that machinery might be a benefit in another state of things, but that at present it must do an inconceivable amount of harm. If carried out to its full extent, of course it would displace human labour *altogether* (except the few children that would be required to tend upon it, and the few makers of it)—and when *all* labour is displaced, what is to become of the working men? But there is another point connected with machinery that also requires to be attended to. Suppose, I say, that *all* human labour is done away by it, and the working men are turned into paupers and criminals, then what I want to know is, who are to be the customers of the capitalists? The capitalists themselves, we should remember, spend little or none (comparatively speaking) of the money *they* get; for, of course, it is the object of every capitalist to save all he can, and so increase the bulk of money out of which he makes his profits. The working men, however, spend *all* they receive—it's true a small amount is put into the savings bank, but that's a mere drop in the ocean; and so the working classes constitute the great proportion of the customers of the country. The lower their wages are reduced of course the less they have to spend, and when they are entirely superseded by machinery, of course they'll have nothing at all to spend, and then, I ask again, who are to be the capitalists' customers?"

Such then are the opinions of the journeymen generally as to the effects of machinery upon them. That the difficulty of obtaining work has increased among the carpenters considerably of late years, all whom I have seen, both masters and men, agree. This is attributed by many to the increase of machinery, and by many to the introduction of the "strapping" system described in my last letter, by which each man is now compelled to do four times the work that he was once expected to execute; and that this must necessarily tend greatly to overstock the trade with hands there cannot be the least doubt. However, be the cause what it may, the following statement is given as an instance of the difficulty the men find in obtaining employment:—

"I am a jobbing carpenter, and in very great distress. All my tools are gone—sold or pawned. I have no means of living but by parish relief, and picking up what I can in little odd jobs along the water side. Sometimes I get a job at painting, glazing, or whitewashing, now that I have lost my own work; sometimes I get a day's work at the London or St. Katharine Docks—anywhere I can get anything to do. And when I can't find any other employment I go to the workhouse yard and get a job there at wheeling the barrows and breaking stones. Sometimes I go to the yard four days in the week, sometimes only one day, and sometimes the whole of the week, according as I can get work. At the workhouse yard I get 1s. 6d. when I'm paid by the day; and when I'm at work on the stones I get 2d. a bushel for all I break, and the most I can do is six bushel in a day. Some men does 9 and 10 bushel, but then they're stronger men than me. I have got a wife and three children to keep out of my earnings, such as they are. My wife does nothing. She has a young child six months old to take care on, so it all lays on my hands. My eldest is a boy of 13 years. He got a place at a glass polisher's, and gets 5s. a week. He lives with his uncle. I've only the two others to look to. On Saturday my wife has a loaf and a shilling given to her from the parish, and that, with the shilling

I earn at the yard, is all we has to keep and pay rent for the four of us, from Saturday till Monday. We can't go to work at the yard till Tuesday morning, for on Mondays we has the day to look after a job at some other place. Taking one week with another, I reckon I get, with parish allowance and all, from 5s. to 6s., and out of that I pays 1s. 6d. a week rent for one room—a first floor back, in an alley. It's my own things that's in it, and I'm obliged to scrape up 2d. and 3d. at a time to raise the rent, and give it 'em at the end of the week. I reckon we has generally from 4s. to 4s. 6d. a week at the outside to live upon—all the four. Sometimes it arn't that, for I go down to the docks to look after some work, and lose my day. We live upon bread and butter and coffee or tea, and maybe we manage sometimes to have a herring or two; and if we do have a taste of meat, why it's a bit of bacon—twopennyworth—which I buys instead of butter. Perhaps, if I've been very lucky in the week, I picks up a pound of bits at 4d. on the Saturday night, and we makes a hash on it, with a few taturs, for Sunday. My wife does the washing at home, and the things is dried in the room we live and sleep in. In the winter we all of us goes into the house (the union), because we can't afford to pay for firing outside. I leaves my things, such as they are, with my brother-in-law. To people like myself the cheapening of food has been the greatest of good. I don't know who brought it about, but I'm sure whoever it was, he has blessings for it. It was said that the bread was to be brought down to 4d. a loaf, but it's never been less than 5d. round about us. It's mostly bread that keeps us alive. Sometimes we has a pennyworth of taturs, but that's not our usual food. Half-a-quartern loaf will last us to the next day, and when I goes to work I puts a bit of bread in my hat, and that's my dinner, and all I have until night, when I go home and get a cup of tea. We have a halfpenny candle of an evening and a quarter of a pound of soap on a Saturday. My wife buys 14 lbs. of coals for 2d. about twice a week, and that serves for boiling our kettle and such like. That's how we live. This is the way I reckon that our money goes every week:—

	s.	d.	
Rent	1	6	per week.
Half-quartern loaf a day	1	3	„
Half a quartern of butter a day	0	8¾	„
Pennyworth of coffee or tea a day	0	7	„
One quartern of fourpenny sugar a day	0	7	„
One halfpenny candle a night	0	3½	„
Half-pound of soap a week	0	2	„
Fourteen pounds of coals twice a week	0	4	„
Four-halfpenny bundles of wood a week	0	2	„
	5	7¼	„

Yes, that's just about what it costs me, and if I manages to get a few pence more, why we buys a Dutch plaice (if they're in), and fries it for dinner, or else two or three fresh herrings, or may be, as a great treat, a pound of bits for the Sunday. I dare say there's hundreds in London lives like us, but I'm sure there's no one lives harder. There isn't much room for extravagance in five and sixpence a week among three and an infant—is there? The reason of my being in the state that I am is because I never belonged to no society, nor no clubs nor nothing. I never could have belonged to our regular trade society, because I never was brought up regular to the business. My father was a carpenter, and I used to work for him. He never apprenticed me, nor gave me no education, nor didn't teach me how to do the better kind of joiner's work. I can do the rough work, but sashes and frames is beyond me. When father was alive I had plenty of employment. He was a journeyman. I can't exactly call him a small master. He used mostly to take contracts on his own hands, to finish small houses and shop fronts, and then him and me used to do them together. Sometimes, may be, we'd have another hand on with us, that is, if the job was in a hurry. Father was a Yorkshireman, and I was born in Yorkshire too. He came to London with me and mother and settled here when I was six years old. I did very well till father's death. He used to keep me and give me 10s. a week. He's been dead now 12 years or better. I was 36 when he died. After his death I did pretty tidy for a short time. I got married about twelve months after that. I used to get a good bit of jobbing then from my father's connection. I took contracts, too, but somehow I used to lose a good deal by them, I was obliged to take them so cheap. I seldom got above £1, and often only 15s. a week for my labour. After that I went to work for the speculating builders about the suburbs, and then I used to pick up £1 a week as long as it lasted. There is no society nor benefit club for the men as work for the cheap builders; so if they are sick, or out of employment, why the parish must keep them, and that's the way with all the cheap masters as I know on. They screws the men down to the lowest, and leaves them when ill to go to the house for relief. Then there's no allowance for the unemployed who don't belong to society, as there is when they do, so that when a man who works for the cheap builders can't get no employment—and there's hundreds that way in London every winter—why, they're obligated to starve, and make away with their tools. When that's done, it's all up with a man—he can't never get to work again. I might have had several jobs if I'd had my tools, but they're gone, and so I'm obligated to break stones. It's a twelvemonth since I lost 'em all. I was seized with the cholera in the hot weather last year. In course as I didn't belong to any benefit club why I couldn't get no allowance, so I parted with my things one by one, and last of all with my tools, and when I got well I couldn't find nothing for me to do. I went about and about till I pretty well wore the shoes off my feet, looking for work and trying to keep out of the workhouse as long as I could, but when the winter came, I was forced to get an order to go in—I couldn't hold out no longer. We had made away with everything—blankets off the bed, shirts and petticoats off our backs, and, last of all, the brokers was put in for eight or nine weeks' rent that I owed, and so we made the best of our way to 'the house,' and stopped in it about five months. I've striven every way to work for my living, but all to no good. Since my tools have gone, I haven't tried only one thing, but many. I've worked at the docks. I've made up stools, and tables, and clothes horses, at a shopmate's of mine, who used to let me go and work at his place, and I've hawked 'em about at the brokers, but they wanted 'em so cheap that there was no living at all to be made out of them. I think the main cause of my being as I am is, because the cheap masters gives men such low wages as they can't afford to subscribe to any benefit club out of them, and so they're left to come upon the parish directly they're took ill, or thrown out of work; and another of the reasons is, because all the hands is now obligated to do double as much work as they formerly used; the consequence is, that one-half of the workmen can't get nothing to do. The men is obligated to work fourteen days to the week at the strapping shops, so where's the use of such as me hoping to get any employment. Then just look here, sir, it's not only me and my wife that's made paupers on, but my two children as well. In course, they'll be brought up in the house as paupers, and the last, you may say, has been regularly born and bred to it. I don't think I shall ever get out of the house again when I goes into it next winter, as I know I must. I'm a broken down man, sir. Work is so uncertain that I'm tired of looking for it. Work for the cheap masters as hard as a man will, he's sure to come to the workhouse at last."

It now only remains for me to exhibit the relative criminality of the carpenters, as compared with that of other trades. For this purpose the metropolitan police returns have been examined with considerable care, and, in order that as general a result as possible might be come to on this point, an average has been struck for a series of ten years, and the annual number of offenders thus obtained divided into the estimated number of individuals belonging to the craft. The same plan has been adopted with all the other trades cited below, while a similar calculation has been made as to the criminality of the entire population of London. By this means we shall be enabled to discover not only the proportion of the population to one offender belonging to any particular occupation, but also to contrast this with the relative amount of crime in other avocations, and moreover to compare the whole with the average criminality of the entire population of the metropolis. A few of the principal results thus obtained are given in the subjoined table, where those trades that have already been investigated, and some others, are placed in juxtaposition, so that the reader may perceive the tendency of each class to commit any of the crimes there specified:—

TABLE SHOWING THE NUMBER OF EACH CLASS (MALES OF ALL AGES) TO ONE OFFENDER, OF THE UNDERMENTIONED TRADES TAKEN INTO CUSTODY BY THE METROPOLITAN POLICE, BEING AN AVERAGE FOR TEN YEARS, FROM 1840-49.

	Sawyers.	Carpenters.	*Turners, &c.	Tailors.	Shoemakers.	Carvers and Guilders.
Murder	1 in 15,020	1 in 22,846	1 in 38,630	1 in 99,495	1 in 61,152	..
Manslaughter	..	„ 60,923	„ 77,260	„ 39,798	„ 40,768	..
Rape	„ 15,020	„ 7,029	„ 77,260	„ 33,165	„ 27,178	..
Assaults (common)	„ 133	„ 127	„ 868	„ 154	„ 205	1 in 80
Larceny (simple)	„ 182	„ 130	„ 757	„ 181	„ 169	„ 198
Wilful damage	„ 625	„ 356	„ 3,219	„ 527	„ 655	„ 383
Coin (counterfeit) uttering, &c.	„ 1,365	„ 862	„ 8,584	„ 861	„ 944	„ 1,568
Drunkenness	„ 63	„ 59	„ 580	„ 63	„ 91	„ 89
Vagrants	„ 143	„ 250	„ 1,030	„ 338	„ 498	„ 297
Offences against the person	„ 80	„ 70	„ 518	„ 91	„ 119	„ 60
—— against property with vio-lence	„ 2,002	„ 1,646	„ 9,657	„ 2,518	„ 2,184	„ 2,875
—— without violence	„ 100	„ 66	„ 380	„ 84	„ 84	„ 61
Malicious offences against property	„ 600	„ 354	„ 3,219	„ 525	„ 648	„ 375
Forgery and offences against the currency	„ 1,201	„ 794	„ 7,726	„ 771	„ 864	„ 1,326
Offences not included in the above classes	„ 25	„ 24	„ 167	„ 25	„ 33	„ 26
Total	„ 15	„ 13	„ 90	„ 15	„ 18	„ 14

*This class includes cabinet-makers and upholsterers.

TABLE SHOWING THE NUMBER OF EACH CLASS (MALES OF ALL AGES) TO ONE OFFENDER, OF THE UNDERMENTIONED TRADES TAKEN INTO CUSTODY BY THE METROPOLITAN POLICE, BEING AN AVERAGE FOR TEN YEARS, FROM 1840-49.

	Coachmakers.	Weavers.	Sailors.	Labourers.	All Classes.
Murder	1 in 43,980	1 in 3,711	1 in 6,242	1 in 11,030	1 in 39,818
Manslaughter	„ 14,660	..	„ 10,701	„ 5,042	„ 20,878
Rape	„ 43,980	„ 7,422	„ 12,485	„ 5,090	„ 18,337
Assaults (common)	„ 181	„ 82	„ 59	„ 45	„ 125
Larceny (simple)	„ 448	„ 81	„ 60	„ 32	„ 130
Wilful damage	„ 934	„ 340	„ 138	„ 56	„ 286
Coin (counterfeit) uttering, &c. ..	„ 1,999	„ 562	„ 1,040	„ 347	„ 974
Drunkenness	„ 106	„ 75	„ 13	„ 31	„ 81
Vagrants	„ 862	„ 55	„ 71	„ 44	„ 163
Offences against the person	„ 127	„ 58	„ 37	„ 23	„ 76
—— against property with vio-lence	„ 5,497	„ 773	„ 1,208	„ 588	„ 2,308
—— without violence	„ 227	„ 39	„ 34	„ 14	„ 56
Malicious offences against property	„ 934	„ 337	„ 137	„ 55	„ 282
Forgery and offences against the currency	„ 1,832	„ 545	„ 823	„ 330	„ 896
Offences not included in the above classes	„ 55	„ 17	„ 6	„ 7	„ 23
Total	„ 31	„ 9	„ 4	„ 3	„ 12

The following conclusions may be drawn from the foregoing table. Of all the trades or occupations above-cited the weavers are the most addicted to murder, for they appear to have 1 murderer in every 3,711 of their body. Those who seem to be the least given to this crime—as far as my investigation has already gone—are the tailors, who have only one murderer in 99,495 of their craft. The average of all classes for murder is 1 in every 39,818 individuals. The carpenters stand a little above the ordinary rate in this respect, there being 1 murderer in every 22,846 of their body. With regard to manslaughter, the labourers stand first on the list, and the turners, &c., last. The carpenters are considerably below the average on this point, there being only 1 homicide among them in every 60,793 of the class, whilst the average for *all* classes is 1 criminal in 30,878. As to rape, we find the labourers, again, the most criminal, and the turners, &c., again the least so. In this respect, however, the carpenters are greatly above the average, the number of criminals among them being 1 in 7,029; whilst the average is 1 in 18,337. In assaults, too, the labourers are at the top of the list, whilst turners, &c., still show the least of all. For assaults the carpenters are a trifle below the average, the ratio of all classes being 1 in 125; whilst the carpenters show 1 in 127. These are the principal of the offences against the person; concerning this class of offences generally the greatest amount of crime exists amongst the labourers, and the least amongst the turners, &c. The average stands thus: one criminal in every 76 individuals, while the carpenters number one in every 70 of their craft. For the crime of simple larceny we find the labourers still at the top of the tree, and the turners, &c., again the least criminal of all classes. The carpenters in this case are neither above nor below the average. The other offences against property without violence show the labourers to be still the most criminal, and the turners, &c., the least. The average is 1 in 56, and the carpenters 1 in 66, which is a trifle below it. We next come to wilful damage, and still find the labourers in the most criminal position, whilst the turners are again the least criminal in this respect. The average stands at 1 in 286; and the carpenters appear in this instance to be less criminal than the ordinary run of the people, they being 1 in 356. For the whole of the malicious offences against property the labourers still keep their position, and the turners, &c., theirs. The carpenters rank below the average in this respect, showing 1 criminal in every 354 of their craft, the ordinary rates being 1 in 282. For uttering counterfeit coin we find the labourers still the most criminal, and the turners, &c., the least. The carpenters in this case are somewhat above the average in crime. With regard to forgery and the whole of the offences against the currency, the labourers still hold the same rank; whilst the turners, &c., again show the least criminality. Next comes the vice of drunkenness, in which the sailors take the lead, showing 1 in every 13 of their number. The least drunkenness exists amongst the turners, &c., there being only 1 drunkard in 580 of their body. The carpenters in this case are considerably above the average, viz., 1 in 59; whilst the average stands at 1 in 81. The labourers are still prominent in vagrancy; whilst the turners appear the least vagrant of all classes. For all other crimes not included in the foregoing, the sailors stand the highest, being one in six, and the turners, &c., the lowest, being 1 in 167. The carpenters are a trifle below the average. Upon the whole the labourers appear to produce more criminals than any other classes, there being amongst them 1 offender in every 3 individuals, and the turners, &c., the least criminal, they having only one offender in every 90 of their class. The carpenters are slightly below the average, showing 1 in 13; whilst the average gives for all classes of crimes 1 offender in every 12 individuals. A general summary of the foregoing may be thus concisely expressed. The carpenters rank above the average of all other classes in the following offences:—Murder, rape, coining, and drunkenness; whilst as regards manslaughter, larceny, wilful damage, and vagrancy, they are more or less below the ordinary ratio of the entire population of London. The labourers appear to be the most criminal of all classes, and the turners the least so; whilst the sailors have the greatest tendency to drunkenness, and the weavers to murder.

LABOUR AND THE POOR.

◆

THE METROPOLITAN DISTRICTS.

[FROM OUR SPECIAL CORRESPONDENT.]

OF THE FURNITURE WORKERS.

Letter LXIII.

Having now set forth the earnings and condition of the Wood-workers who are engaged in the construction of our houses, I shall treat of those who are engaged in the furnishing of them.

Cabinet-making is the one generic term applied to the manufacture of every description of furniture. Upholstery is, however, a distinct art or handicraft, dealing with different materials. The cabinet-maker is a pure wood-worker; and that, perhaps, of the very highest order. Being generally engaged upon the most expensive woods, his work is required to be of the most finished and tasty description. The art is constantly calling forth a very high exercise of skill, ingenuity, and invention. It is a trade which perhaps, more intimately than any other, is mixed up with the fine arts. Marqueterie is mosaic work in wood; as wood-carving, in its higher branches, is sculpture in wood. The upholsterers, who confine themselves to their own proper branch, are the fitters-up of curtains and their hangings, either for beds or windows; they are also the stuffers of the chair and sofa cushions, and the makers of carpets and of beds; that is to say, they are the tradesmen who, in the language of the craft, "do the soft work"—or in other words, all connected with the cabinet-maker's art in which woven materials are the staple.

The cabinet-maker's trade of the best class, where society-men are employed, is now divided into the *General* and *Fancy* Cabinet-makers. There are also the *Chair-makers* and the *Bedstead-makers*. The General Cabinet hand makes every description of furniture apart from chairs or bedsteads. "A general hand," I was told by an intelligent workman, "must be able to make everything, from the smallest comb-tray to the largest bookcase. If he can't do whatever he's put to, he must go." He is usually kept, however, to the manufacture of the larger articles of furniture—as tables, drawers, chiffoniers, sideboards, wardrobes, and the like.

The Fancy Cabinet-maker, on the other hand, manufactures all the lighter or more portable articles of the trade, and such as scarcely come under the head of furniture. In the language of the craft he is a "small worker," and makes ladies work-boxes and tables, tea-caddies, portable desks, dressing cases, card, glove, gun, and pistol cases, cribbage-boards, and such like.

The Chairmaker constructs every description of chairs and sofas, but only the frame-work: the finishing, when stuffed backs or cushions, or stuffing of any kind, is required, is the department of the upholsterer.

The Bedstead-maker is employed in the making of bedsteads; but his work is considered less skilled than that of the other branches, as the woodcarver or the turner's art is that called upon for the formation of the handsome pillars of a bedstead of the best order.

To estimate the numerical strength of the cabinet-makers as a distinct body is impossible, for unfortunately the census of 1841 lumps them with the upholsterers (who are a totally different class of workmen, operating upon different materials) because their arts happen to be *locally* associated. The two *trades* are certainly conjoined in commerce, but the two *arts* are essentially distinct; that is to say, the employers are master upholsterers as well as cabinet-makers, but the operatives themselves seldom or never follow both occupations. The circumstances which govern the classification of trades are totally different from those regulating the division of work. In trade the convenience of the purchaser is mainly studied, the sale or manufacture of such articles being associated as are usually required together. Hence the master coachmaker is frequently a harness manufacturer as well, for the purchaser of the one generally stands in need of the other. The painter and house decorator not only follows the trade of the glazier, but of the plumber, too, because these arts are one and all connected with the "doing up" of houses. For the same reason the builder combines the business of the plasterer with that of the bricklayer, and not unfrequently that of the carpenter and joiner in addition. In all of these businesses, however, a distinct set of workmen are required, according as the materials operated upon are different; for, as I before showed, it is the nature of the materials that regulates the character of the work.

The cabinet-makers *and* upholsterers then, at the time of taking the last census, numbered altogether in Great Britain as many as 30,712; of these, 25,000 and odd were resident in England, 4,000 in Scotland, 650 in Wales, and 350 in the British Isles. Besides these, there were the chair-makers, who amounted throughout Great Britain to 5,123; of whom upwards of 4,800 belonged to England, and 218 to Scotland. The bedstead-makers in Great Britain were 396, and they were wholly located in England; so that, adding together these three classes, we arrive at the conclusion that there were in 1841 as many as 36,231 cabinet-makers, upholsterers, chair-makers, and bedstead-makers dispersed throughout Great Britain, and that upwards of 30,000, or five-sixths, of these resided in England.

The number of cabinet-makers and upholsterers located in the metropolis at the time of taking the last census was 6,956. The London chair-makers were 1,325, and the bedstead-makers 296: making altogether as many as 8,577 belonging to the different branches of the London trade. According to the "Post-office Directory" no less than 1,008 of these were masters in business for themselves, so that it may be said that in 1841 the London operative cabinet-makers amounted to 7,500 and odd. Such are the Government returns of 1841; and on comparing them with those of 1831, we arrive at the following curious results as to the increase or decrease of the trade in the different counties during that time:—

The greatest increase of cabinet makers from 1831-41 occurred in the county of Sutherland, where it amounted to as much as 272 per cent. above the increase of the population. In Inverness, and in Orkney and Shetland, the increase was 130 per cent.; in Roxburgh, 110 per cent.; in Huntingdonshire, 70 per cent.; in Bedfordshire, 62 per cent.; in Flintshire, 55 per cent.; in Banff, 54 per cent.; in York city and county, 35 per cent.; and in Buckinghamshire, 32 per cent. above the increase of the population. The greatest decrease, on the other hand, took place in Anglesey, where the number of the cabinet-makers, in comparison with the population, declined no less than 98 per cent. in the ten years. In Renfrew the decrease was 95 per cent.; in Linlithgow, 86 per cent.; in Derbyshire, 73 per cent.; in Cheshire and Cumberland, each 68 per cent.; in Merioneth, 67 per cent.; in Caithness, 66 per cent.; in the West Riding of Yorkshire, 62 per cent.; in Durham, 61 per cent.; and in Bute, 60 per cent. below that of the population. In England generally the cabinet-makers and upholsterers, twenty years of age and upwards, in comparison with the population of that age, decreased from 1831-41 as much as 22 per cent. In Wales there was also a decrease of 11 per cent., while in Scotland there was a still greater decrease—the number of cabinet-makers and upholsterers located there having diminished as much as 33 per cent. in the same space of time. The total for Great Britain shows a decrease in the cabinet makers and upholsterers, of 20 years and upwards, of 4 per cent.; and an increase in the population of the same age of 20 per cent., thus making, in comparison with the increase of the population, a total decrease of as much as 24 per cent. In the metropolis, with which we are here more particularly concerned, the decrease was 1 per cent.—whilst the population, above 20 years, increased as much as 32 per cent., making a decline in the numbers of this class (in comparison with the rest of the population) to the amount of 33 per cent.

The next question that naturally presents itself is, how has this reduction of the number of hands throughout the country affected the trade? According to the law of supply and demand, the decrease of workmen should have given rise to a proportionate increase in the wages, provided there was no corresponding diminution in the quantity of work to be done. As to the effect produced by the decrease of the hands upon the weekly income of the workmen in the provinces, I have no means of arriving at any accurate conclusions. Concerning the metropolis, however, I am differently situated, and to the kindness and consideration of the West-end branch of the General Cabinet-Makers' Society, I stand indebted for much important information. Of course the diminution in the number of workmen between 1831 and 1841 is a fact from which few or no deductions can be drawn, unless we can likewise arrive at some equally authentic facts concerning the increase or decrease of work during the same period. With a view, therefore, of obtaining the best information on this point, I applied to the Cabinet-makers' Society for an account of the number of their unemployed members for a series of years, as well as the number of days they had been out of employment, and the sum the society had paid them during that time. The committee immediately gave directions that I should be furnished with all the information I needed, and the secretary devoted himself for several days to the compilation of a tabular statement, in which the wished-for facts were given for every quarter of a year since 1834. This table, however, being much too long to print here, I have taken the average of the four quarters of each year, and the following is the result:—

	Number of Members.	Number of Unemployed.	Days Un-employed.	Paid to Unemployed.
1831	342	—	—	—
1832	290	—	—	—
1833	318	—	—	—
1834	371	40	632	£60 18 8½
1835	435	41	748	67 7 8¾
1836	506	40	566	53 10 1¾
1837	527	90	1,675	156 6 10½
1838	513	82	2,025	185 13 3
1839	518	61	1,321	120 13 11½
1840	504	77	1,873	170 15 7
Average from 1834–1840...	482	62	1,368	£125 14 7

	Number of Members.	Number of Unemployed.	Days Un-employed.	Paid to Unemployed.
1841	516	102	2,958	£278 3 7¾
1842	464	110	3,482	367 10 10¾
1843	412	85	2,066	216 19 11¼
1844	419	43	934	84 17 5½
1845	460	26	383	35 12 9½
1846	546	47	878	86 18 6¼
1847	506	98	2,901	256 14 8
1848	413	125	4,201	387 13 4½
1849	340	98	2,204	204 13 5½
Average from 1840–1849...	452	81	1,158	£213 4 11½

A superficial glance at this account will not enable us to come to any conclusion with regard to the state of the trade of the cabinet-makers in the different years above mentioned. In order to do this, we must find out the ratio of the employment to the non-employment of the members of the society; for the number of the unemployed is of no value *per se*. Nor is the number of members out of work alone sufficient for this purpose, for, unless we know the number of days that they were collectively unoccupied in each quarter, the true ratio of the employment to the non-employment cannot be obtained. Again, the sum paid to the unemployed members during any particular quarter is no criterion, unless we ascertain the amount that the employed members would collectively earn in the same time. It is the ratio between these several facts that will alone enable us to arrive at any definite result with regard to the state of the trade. To show the reader at a glance, therefore, the proportion that these facts bear to each other, I have in the first column of the following table given the per centage of the ratio of the days unemployed to those employed. This has been arrived at by finding first the number of days that the whole of the members in the society would have worked in the quarter, provided they had had full employment, and then calculating the proportion between that amount and the aggregate number of days unemployed. In the second column of the same table, I have likewise shown the ratio of the loss to the society by the non-employment of some of its members in comparison with its gains by the employment of the others. This I have ascertained by estimating the value of the unemployed days at the regular wages of the trade, and adding this sum to the amount paid to the members out of work, and then finding the proportion that this sum bears to the amount that the whole of the members would have earned had they been fully employed.

	Ratio of days un- employed to those employed.	Ratio of loss by non- employment to gains by employment.
1834	... 2·1 per cent.	... 2·9 per cent.
1835	... 2·2 ,,	... 2·9 ,,
1836	... 1·4 ,,	... 1·9 ,,
1837	... 4·0 ,,	... 5·5 ,,
1838	... 5·0 ,,	... 6·8 ,,
1839	... 3·2 ,,	... 4·3 ,,
1840	... 4·7 ,,	... 6·3 ,,
1841	... 7·1 ,,	... 9·9 ,,
1842	... 9·4 ,,	... 13·2 ,,
1843	... 6·4 ,,	... 8·9 ,,
1844	... 2·8 ,,	... 3·8 ,,
1845	... 1·0 ,,	... 1·4 ,,
1846	... 2·0 ,,	... 2·8 ,,
1847	... 7·3 ,,	... 9·7 ,,
1848	... 13·4 ,,	... 17·5 ,,
1849	... 8·3 ,,	... 11·2 ,,

A glance at the above table will show us that the ratio of loss by non-employment rises and falls in the same manner, though not precisely to the same extent, as the ratio of days unemployed.

We are now in a position to ascertain in what proportion the wages of a trade rise and fall, according as the hands and the work decrease or increase. It may however be said, that since the society-men of a trade never work for less than an established rate of pay, the earnings of its members cannot be influenced by any such means. This, however, we shall find, is far from the fact; for though it may be true individually, still collectively it is untrue. Even a moment's reflection is sufficient to assure us that if a body of men contribute a certain sum in the quarter to the support of their unemployed members, it is the same as if their wages had been reduced precisely that sum. If their collective earnings amounted in the year to £40,000, and out of that they gave £250 per quarter to the maintenance of those members who might be out of work, of course their gross income must be reduced one-fortieth. Whether they receive the £40,000 in full and pay the thousand pounds out of it afterwards, or whether they receive collectively £1,000 less for their labour, the result is the same—their aggregate earnings or wages have fallen from £40,000 to £39,000—the burden is only removed from one shoulder to the other; the pressure, it is true, may not be felt so severely by shifting it, but still there it is, not one atom the lighter, though more easily borne. We can, then, by comparing the ratio of the loss to the society by non-employment to its gains by employment, at one period with that existing at another, obtain an accurate account of the increase or decrease in the earnings of the trade at any given time. By doing the same with the ratio of the unemployed days to those employed, we can likewise ascertain the increase or decrease of work for the same period—while a comparison of the number of workmen belonging to the society in different years will further give us the increase or decrease of the workmen. We have thus a means of demonstrating whether the wages of a trade really depend on the quantity of work to be done and the number of hands to do it.

	Increase or decrease of hands.	Increase or decrease of work.	Increase or decrease of wages.
1835	+ 17·2 per cent.	- 0·1 per cent.	0·0 per cent.
1836	+ 16·3 „	+ 0·8 „	+ 1·0 „
1837	+ 4·1 „	- 2·6 „	- 3·6 „
1838	- 2·6 „	- 1·0 „	- 1·3 „
1839	+ 0·9 „	+ 1·8 „	+ 2·5 „
1840	- 2·7 „	- 1·5 „	- 2·0 „
1841	+ 2·3 „	- 2·4 „	- 3·6 „
1842	- 10·0 „	- 2·3 „	- 3·3 „
1843	- 11·2 „	+ 3·0 „	+ 4·3 „
1844	+ 1·7 „	+ 3·6 „	+ 5·1 „
1845	+ 9·7 „	+ 1·8 „	+ 2·4 „
1846	+ 18·6 „	- 1·0 „	- 1·4 „
1847	- 7·3 „	- 5·3 „	- 6·9 „
1848	- 18·3 „	- 6·1 „	- 7·8 „
1849	- 17·6 „	+ 5·1 „	+ 6·3 „

By the above table we perceive that in the year 1835 there were 17 per cent. more hands, and one-tenth per cent. less work than in 1834, and yet the earnings remained the same in that year as in the previous one. In 1836 the hands increased 16 per cent., and the work only 8-10ths per cent., but still the gains rose 1 per cent. In 1842 the hands decreased 10.0 per cent., and the work only 2 per cent., and yet the earnings fell 3 per cent. In 1849, however, the number of workmen declined no less than 17½ per cent., while the quantity of work rose 5 per cent.; the consequence was, that the gains of the members were upwards of 6 per cent. more than they were in the year before. Such facts as these show us that the principle of supply and demand, though undeniably true in general, still is not sufficient to account for all the fluctuations of wages. This will be even more evident when I come to treat of the Slop Cabinet Trade, for then I shall show that notwithstanding the number of cabinet-makers in the metropolis, compared with the rest of the population, decreased no less than 32 *per cent.!* between 1831 and 1841, still the wages of the non-society men (whose earnings are regulated solely by competition) have fallen as much as 400 per cent.—and this while the amount of work done has increased rather than decreased. The cause of this extraordinary decline will be found to be due chiefly to the rapid spread of what are called "Garret Masters"—a class of petty "trade-working-masters," who are precisely equivalent to the Chamber Masters among the boot and shoe makers, and to whom we found the decline of the wages in that trade were mainly attributable. This, indeed, appears to be the great evil likewise of the turner's trade, where, while hands have decreased, and work increased, wages have also fallen almost to the same extent as in the cabinet trade, and that from precisely the same reason, viz.—the increase of the "Small Masters," who are continually underselling each other.

In the present Letter, however, I purpose confining myself to the "honourable" part of the general cabinet-makers' trade. I shall first give a description of the work executed by the cabinet-makers, and then state the regulations of the trade. After which I propose speaking of the social condition of the men generally employed in it, and concluding with the statements of some of the best-informed members of the craft.

The general Cabinet hands make the following articles, on which they are principally employed:—*Pembroke Tables*, which are square-cornered, with a wide "bed" (surface), and two small flaps. They are generally of solid mahogany. *Loo Tables*, which are generally round, though a few are oblong. The making of these tables in the best style is accounted one of the highest branches of the cabinet-maker's art. The carving alone of one of the most beautiful ever made, for the Army and Navy Club, cost, I am assured, £40. Loo tables are generally veneered; rosewood, maple, and mahogany being the most frequent materials. The *Dining Table* has a narrow bed, with two long "flaps." The "extensible" dining table has telescope slides. Dining tables are all solid. The *Card Table* turns on a frame, and folds over into half the space. There are also "library," "sofa," "occasional," and other tables, which I need not describe. For the furniture of drawing rooms oak is now a fashionable wood: the small tables in recesses, or for the display of any bust or ornament, are now often made of this material. Fine English oak for such a purpose is far costlier than mahogany. *Chairs* are the most changeable in their fashion of all the furniture formed by the cabinet-maker. The Louis Quatorze style has now come again into fashion—a style which I am informed is always alternating, for, after some very opposite mode in style and form has been established for a limited period, "it works round again to the Louis Quatorze." Nearly all chairs are "worked solid," except that the "splat," or top of the back, is sometimes veneered. Of dining-room chairs I need not speak. Drawing-room chairs are of rosewood, maple, or walnut, and are, in the present fashion (of which alone I speak), covered with rich silk tabaret, or elaborate needlework. The bedroom chairs are of polished or stained birch; sometimes they are japanned, with cane-work or osier bottoms. The chairmaker is, moreover, the artisan employed in the making of sofas. These are known as cabriole, couch, and tête-à-tête. The tête-à-tête is the form of the letter S, and is adapted for two persons only, who occupy the respective bends. *Sideboards* are most frequently made of mahogany, solid or veneered, but in most cases solid. Oak, however, is now the fashionable material for a sideboard, and is elaborately carved. *Cabinets* also are now made, as in the old times, of oak and walnut. For a lady's apartment rosewood is often the material used for a cabinet. *Cheffoniers* are of rosewood or mahogany, solid or veneered. *Drawers* and *Wardrobes* are of the wood which is considered most *en suite* with the other furniture, and with the general decoration of the chamber. *Book-case* making of the best quality is accounted a highly skilled portion of the cabinet-maker's productions. One at the Carlton Club, for its beauty of proportion, and strength as well as delicacy of workmanship, is pronounced by the trade, I heard in several quarters, a perfect masterpiece. It extends 90 feet. The surface is mahogany, veneered; the interior is the finest deal.

In most large establishments the work is begun and completed on the premises; general cabinet-makers, chair-makers, bedstead-makers, upholsterers, wood carvers, French polishers, and sawyers, all being employed there.

The mode of workmanship pursued by cabinet-makers is very remarkable, as showing a dependance on the skill of the individual workman unknown, perhaps, in any other trade. The best workman among the tailors in a large establishment has but to exert his skill to put together the materials which have been cut to the nicest proportions before they are placed in his hands. So it is with the boot-maker. With the cabinet-maker, however, it is different. The foreman gives him a sketch of the article he has to make, and points out the material in the yard or the ware-room which is to be used in its construction. The journeyman then measures, saws, and cuts the wood to the shape required, and is expected to do so with the greatest economy of stuff, and so to cut it that the best portion of the wood shall occupy the most prominent part of the furniture, and any defective part be placed where it is least visible, or, in the language of the trade, "he must put the best side to London." The journeyman cuts out every portion; not only the front of the article, but every shelf required for the interior, and the minutest partitions or drawers. He then takes the material to his bench in the workshop, and puts it together without any subdivision of labour. The journeymen will assist one another in any elaborate article which is being made by piecework, but this is an arrangement merely among themselves. The master requires every workman to be able to complete whatever article he is told to make. In a large establishment, at a very busy time (and in some establishments at all times), a foreman, called a chalk foreman, is employed to mark or cut out, in order to facilitate the business; but the method I have described is that usually observed.

The cabinet-makers find all their own tools, a complete set of which is worth from £30 to £40. They all work on the master's premises, which, in establishments where many men are employed, are, with a few exceptions, spacious and well-ventilated rooms, open to the skylighted roof. Valuable timber is generally placed along the joists of the workshop, and there it remains a due time for "seasoning." When the men are at work there is seldom much conversation, as each man's attention is given to his own especial task, while the noise of the saw, the plane, or the hammer, is another impediment to conversation. Politics, beyond the mere news of the day, are, I am assured by experienced parties, little discussed in these workshops. I am told, also, that the cabinet-makers, as a body, care little about such matters.

The operative cabinet-makers of the best class are, to speak generally, men possessed of a very high degree of intelligence. I must be understood to be here speaking of the best paid. Of the poor artisans of the East-end I have a different tale to tell. I was told by a cabinet-maker—and, judging by my own observations, with perfect correctness—that of all classes of mechanics the cabinet-makers have the most comfortable abodes. The same thing may be said also, if in a less degree, of the joiners and carpenters; and the reason is obvious—a steady workman occupies his leisure in making articles for his own use. Perhaps there are not many stronger contrasts than one I have remarked in the course of my present inquiry—that between the abode of the workman in a good West-end establishment, and the garret or cellar of the toiler for a "slaughter-house" at the East-end. In the one you have the warm, red glow of polished mahogany furniture; a clean carpet covers the floor; a few engravings in neat frames hang against the papered wall; and book-shelves or a bookcase have their appropriate furniture. Very white and bright-coloured pot ornaments, with sometimes a few roses in a small vase, are reflected in the mirror over the mantelshelf. The East-end cabinet-maker's room has *one* piece of furniture, which is generally the principal—the workman's bench. The walls are bare, and sometimes the half-black plaster is crumbling from them; all is dark and dingy, and of furniture there is very little, and that, it must be borne in mind, when the occupant is a furniture-maker. A drawer-maker whom I saw in Bethnal-green had never been able to afford a chest of drawers for his own use; "besides," he added, "what do I want with drawers? I've nothing to put in them." What is meant by a "slaughter-house" will be seen in my account of the non-society cabinet-makers in Spitalfields and the adjacent districts. The same establishments in the West-end are generally described as "linendrapers;" they are indeed the drapers who sell every description of furniture and upholstery, but the workmen from whom they receive their goods are the "East-enders." These "linendrapers," and indeed all masters who employ non-society men, are known in the trade as "black" masters. "He's nothing but a black," is a sentence expressive of supreme contempt in a cabinet-maker's mouth.

"Within my recollection," said an intelligent cabinet-maker, "there was much drinking, very much drinking, among cabinet-makers. This was fifteen years back. Now I'm satisfied that at least seven-eighths of all who are in society are sober and temperate men. Indeed, good masters won't have tipplers now-a-days." According to the Metropolitan Police returns, the cabinet-makers and the turners are two of the least criminal of all the artizans; I speak not of any one year, but from an average taken for the last ten.

The great majority of the cabinet-makers are married men, and were described to me by the best informed parties as generally domestic men, living, whenever it was possible, near their workshops, and going home to every meal. They are not much of play-goers, a Christmas pantomime or any holiday spectacle being exceptions, especially where there is a family. "I don't know a card-player," said a man who had every means of knowing, "amongst us. I think you'll find more cabinet-makers than any other trade members of mechanics' institutes and literary institutions, and attenders at lectures." Some journeymen cabinet-makers have saved money, and I found them all speak highly of the advantages they, as well as their masters, derive from their trade society. The majority of the cabinet-makers in London are countrymen. There are some very good workmen from Scotland. One who has been an apprentice to a good London master is, however, considered to rank with the very highest as a skilled workman.

In the honourable trade bonuses to foremen, and "improvers," and "contracts," and "sub-letting," among the journeymen, are at present unknown. "I don't know," it was said to me, "that we have any great grievances to complain of except one—and that's the East-end." I find, however, that the "strapping system," known in this trade as the "cut and run" work, is becoming very general among the trade working masters—while many of the more respectable shops are beginning to give out their work by the "lump," instead of the "piece." To the non-existence of contracts, however, there is one exception—in the cabinet work of a great pianoforte and musical instrument maker. There the letting and sub-letting is carried on through the several grades, to the complete or comparative impoverishment of a great majority of the workmen, and the enriching of a few contractors.

The cabinet-maker's trade is generally learned by apprenticeship, and the apprentices to superior masters are often the sons of tradesmen, and are well-educated lads. There is no limit to the number a master may take, but the great firms in the honourable trade take very few, while the masters not in the honourable trade will, I am informed, take very many (one has eleven), and even put run-away apprentices to work. "They go for one thing, sir," a cabinet-maker said to me, "to get things done for half-price; it's little matter how." A journeyman can have his own son apprenticed to him, but only one at a time.

The payment of the journeyman cabinet-maker is, both by the piece and by the week, 32s. a week, being the minimum allowed by the rules of the society as the remuneration for a week's labour, or six days of ten hours each. The prices by piece are regulated by a book, which is really a remarkable production. It is a thick quarto volume, containing some 600 pages. Under the respective heads the piece-work price of every article of furniture is specified; and immediately after what is called the "start" price, or the price for the plain article, follows an elaborate enumeration of extras, according as the article may be ordered to be ornamented in any particular manner. There are also engravings of all the principal articles in the trade, which further facilitate the clear understanding of all the regulations contained in the work. The date of this book of prices is 1811, and the wages of the society men have been unchanged since then. The preparation of this ample and minute statement of prices occupied a committee of masters and of journeymen between two and three years. The committee were paid for their loss of time from the masters' and the journeymen's funds respectively; and what with these payments, what with the expense of attending the meetings and consultations, the making and remaking of models, the cost of printing and engravings, the cabinet-makers' book of prices was not compiled, I am assured, at a less cost than from £4,000 to £5,000.

The trade societies in connection with this branch of art, are those of the cabinet, chair, and bedstead makers. They are divided into three districts, viz., West-end, Middle, and East-end. These districts contain five societies—one at the West-end, another in the centre of the metropolis, and the others at the East-end. Three of these societies are in connection with the cabinet makers' trade; the remaining two belong to the bedstead-makers and the chair-makers. The following table shows the number of men in connection with each society, together with the non-society men appertaining to each branch:—

	Society Men.	Non-So-ciety Men.	Total of So-ciety and non-Society.
West-end General Cabinet-makers	300	1,400	1,700
East-end ditto	140	1,000	1,140
Fancy Cabinet-makers ...	47	500	547
Chair-makers	130	1,428	1,558
Bedstead-makers	25	238	263
	642	4,566	5,208

Thus we perceive that the society men constitute not quite one-seventh part of the trade, from which it should be remembered that the upholsterers are here excluded.

These several societies, as is usually the case, have for their object the upholding of the standard rate of wages, and providing such assistance to their members as has been found to best suit the peculiar circumstances in which the workman is placed. They are mostly officered by a secretary, president, and committee, who are differently paid, according to the importance of the body and the nature of the duties required, while the payments of the members partake of the same variable character. The West-end cabinet-makers meet weekly, and pay 6d. per week as their regular trade contribution, and the members who are unemployed obtain for a given time 10s. per week from the funds, and when on strike 16s. There is also a payment for the insurance of tools, for which 1s. 6d. is paid every quarter. The West-end General Cabinet-Makers' Society have paid no less than £11,000 to the unemployed members within the last sixteen years, which is at the rate of very nearly £700 a year. They have also expended in the insurance of tools, since 1836, £1,758, and have received during that time £708 for loss of them by fire.

The members of the East-end body differ from those at the West-end in their rate of pay. They receive 30s. instead of 32s. per week, and when on piece-work they are paid by the job, or in the "lump;" that is to say, a given labour-value is put upon the entire article, whereas the West-end workman receives an additional price for everything which can be considered as coming under the denomination of an "extra." In the East-end, the members likewise meet weekly, but pay the less contribution of 4d. The unemployed members get 8s. per week, and when on strike 15s. The tools of the members are also insured by the society, but at a less rate than in the West-end.

The contributions of the fancy cabinet-makers are lower than in either of the foregoing instances, being but 3d. per week. They in like manner meet weekly. The assistance received by the unemployed, however, is mainly dependent on the state of the society's funds, 2s. per week being the lowest amount to be granted and 6s. the highest. They also have a legitimate weekly wage of 30s.; but this at present is very rarely to be obtained. The generality of this class work in their own homes, and take out the work in the "lump," the custom of paying for extras in the fancy cabinet trade being virtually extinct.

The chair-maker's weekly contribution is 6d., the same as that of the West-end cabinet maker; he gets, also, 10s. a week when unemployed; while, in cases of strike, the pay is as high as £1 per week for four weeks, and 16s. for another four weeks. Their standard wages are 32s. per week, while their piece work is regulated by their book of prices, with every description of extra or additional work carefully specified. Like the general cabinet makers, they prefer this mode of employment to being paid by the week. An insurance is also taken out by this society for the tools of the members.

The bedstead-makers only meet once a month, and pay their contributions by the month, which is 1s. 4d. When employed by the week they get 32s.; but they receive 5s. 6d. per day when sent out to a gentleman's house, to do such repairing (including cleaning) as may be required in their line of trade. This society also insures the tools of members, at the optional values of £12, £18, or £25, the latter sum being the highest. No payments have been made by this body either to the unemployed, or to parties on strike, for so long a time now that the custom in these cases has fallen into total disuse.

As a general rule the members of all the above societies are opposed to strikes, preferring the system of arbitration.

There is no superannuation or sick fund in connection with any of these societies. When the societies of cabinet-makers first commenced, the houses of call were established upon the same principle as the tailors'—that is to say, as the labour market of the trade; but now it is oftener the case that a man calls upon the master or his foreman, instead of receiving a call from the society house. Sometimes a man gets recommended to a master or foreman by a brother workman, and so obtains employment. The non-society men call upon the masters and ask for work.

Tramps are not encouraged, as these societies have no correspondence with the country societies. If, perchance, a tramp should call at a shop, he may get a few halfpence, but that is all. The brisk season continues during the spring and summer, and the autumn and winter months are the slack period of the trade. The following table shows the average ratio of non-employment at different seasons from 1834 to 1849. It will here be seen that the periods of greatest slackness are the first and last quarters, and the period of the greatest briskness the second quarter of the year:—

TABLE SHOWING THE AVERAGE RATIO OF DAYS UNEMPLOYED TO THOSE EMPLOYED IN EACH QUARTER OF THE UNDERMENTIONED YEARS.

	August, 1st Quarter.	August, 2d Quarter.	August, 3d Quarter.	August, 4th Quarter.
1834–40....	4·5 per cent.	3·0 per cent.	3·9 per cent.	3·8 per cent.
1840–49....	8·3 „	4·6 „	6·0 „	6·2 „
1834–49....	6·9 „	3·9 „	5·1 „	5·1 „

A good-looking man, who spoke with a hardly perceptible Scotch accent, gave me the following account of his experience as a *general cabinet-maker* of the best class. His room was one of the sort I have described in my preliminary remarks:—

"I am a native of ——, in Scotland," he said, "and have been in London a dozen years or so. My mother was left a widow when I was very young, and supported herself and me as a laundress. She got me the very best schooling she could, and a cabinet-maker without some education is a very poor creature. I got to be apprenticed to Mr. ——, who took me because he knew my father. I got on very well with him, and lived at home with my mother. When I had been five years or so at the business I went with my master to Lord ——'s, a few miles off, to do some work, and among other things we had to unpack some furniture that had come from London, and to see that it wasn't injured. My lord came in when we had unpacked a beautiful rosewood loo table, and said to my master, 'you can't make a table like that.' 'I think I can, my lord,' said my master, and he got an order for one, and set me to make it as I had seen the London table, but he overlooked me, and it gave great satisfaction, and that first made me think of coming to London, as it gave me confidence in my work. I had only occasional employment from my master when I was out of my time, and as my mother was then dead I started off for London before I got through my bit of money. I walked to Carlisle and was getting very tired of the road, and very footsore. What a lot of thoughts pass through a countryman's mind when he's first walking up to London! At Carlisle

I had about a month's work, or better, as an order had just come in to Mr. —— from a gentleman who was going to be married, and the furniture was wanted in a hurry. I gave satisfaction there and that encouraged me. I walked to London all the way, coming by Leeds and Sheffield, and Leicester, and the great towns, where I thought there was the best chance for a job. I didn't get one, though. In my opinion, sir, there ought to be a sort of lodging-house for mechanics and poor people travelling on their honest business. You must either go to a little public-house to sleep, and it's very seldom you can get a bed there under 6d., and many places ask 9d. and 1s.—or you may go to a common lodging-house for travellers, as they call it, and it would sicken a dog. Then, in a public-house, you can't sit by the fire on a wet or cold night without drinking something, whether you require or can afford it or not. I knew nobody in London except two or three seafaring people, and them I couldn't find. I went from place to place for three weeks, asking for work. I wasn't a society man then. At last I called at Mr. ——'s, and met with the master himself. He asked me where I'd worked last, and I said at Mr. ——'s, of ——, and Mr. ——'s, of Carlisle. 'Very respectable men,' said he, 'I haven't a doubt of it, but I never heard their names before.' And he then asked me some more questions, and called his foreman and said, 'R——, we want hands; I think you might put on this young man; just try him.' So I was put on, and was there four or five years. I had many little things to learn in London ways, to enable a man to get on a little faster with his work, and I will say that I've asked many a good London hand for his opinion, and have had it given to me as a man should give it. I do the same myself now. A good workman needn't be afraid: he won't be hurt. I work by the piece. I have been very fortunate, never having been out of work more than a month or six weeks at a time—but that's great good fortune. These are my earnings for the last eight weeks. I've only lately begun to keep accounts, all at piece-work, and a busy time:—32s. 2d., 41s. 3d., 40s. 1d., 36s., 29s. 6d., 28s., 35s. 10d., 35s. 9d. An average of near 35s. is it? Well, no doubt I make that all the year round. I can keep a wife and child comfortably. I wouldn't hear of my wife working for a slop tailor. I'd rather live on bread and water myself than see it. Slop means slavery. In my opinion, if the black masters, or the slaughtermen, as they call them at the other end, didn't keep men always going, or didn't force them to keep them always going, they'd be troubled to get hands. But when men are always struggling for a living, they have no time to think or talk, and so they submit, and, indeed, their wives and families make them submit."

A young man, well spoken, and well dressed, gave me the following account as to the earnings of a chair-maker of the better class:—

"I was brought up as a general hand in the country, in Yorkshire, and in country towns a cabinet-maker makes everything in his own line, and sometimes does a little joiner's work. I came right away to London, between eight and nine years ago, as soon as I was out of my time. My master had seven apprentices, and didn't employ any journeymen. His was a 'cutting' shop, but he made very capital furniture, when he had a fair price. I have heard the old men in the trade say that when they were young, 40 or 50 years back, a cabinet-maker wanting work used to try York, or Leeds, or Sheffield, or Manchester, or Liverpool, before he thought of London; but now we all make for London. If a man asks for work at a country master's now, the first question generally is, 'Have you worked in London?' I was two months out of work in London, and then got on for a very good man who fitted up offices in the best style; such as for banks and insurance offices—that's cabinet-maker's work; but it's often done by joiners. We consider that they encroach on our department there. I was at this work about a year, making better than 30s. of a week, and then was out of work seven weeks. I knew a man who worked for a 'linendraper' just started in the tally system, in Westminster; and I went to make a few chairs along with him, just not to be idle. I worked a week alongside of him, and he hawked my chairs on the Saturday with his. For that week's hard work I got 7s. 3d. clear, and my chairs were abused by the tally-man as if they weren't good enough for his rubbishing place. But after he'd growled out his fault-finding, he said 'You may bring the same next week, if you like, at 1s. the half dozen less.' I made a resolution just then and there that I'd starve before I'd touch a piece of slaughter-house stuff again; and I haven't—but then I was a single man, and am still. If I'd had a family, I suppose I must have 'slaughter-housed' on. They couldn't have waited. By pawning my watch I raised 25s., and that kept me going for three weeks, until I got work at a good shop. I had joined the society before, and have been pretty lucky in keeping work ever since. I haven't kept any particular account, but I know I make about 34s. every week. I make nothing but chairs and sofa frames; chiefly drawing-room chairs. I can do best at them, and have been a chairman these four or five years. I'm afraid the linendrapers will pull down the good masters, and down with them must go the good men."

Bedstead making is, as I have stated, a distinct branch of the cabinet-maker's business. It is, however, generally carried on in the same premises as the other branches, but in some establishments bedsteads are the principal manufacture. The bedstead-maker has not to cut out his material in the same way as the cabinet-maker, as the posts are fashioned by the turner or the wood-carver ready for his purpose, and the other portions of his work are prepared by the sawyers in the sizes he requires. He is the putter together of the article, in every part, except the insertion of the sacking bottom, which is the work of the porter.

From a well-informed man, a member of "society," I had the following statement, which embodies information (which I found fully corroborated) of the social condition of the men, and the fashions of the trade. I am informed that in the society of bedstead-makers there is not one unmarried man.

"When I first knew the business, 40 years ago, I could earn at bedstead making, by hard work, 50s. or 60s. I have heard men brag in a public-house that they could make more than 60s., and masters got to hear of it, and there was great dissatisfaction. We always work by piece, and did so when I was an apprentice in London. The prices paid to society men are, on the whole, the same as in 1811. We all find our own tools, and a good kit is worth £30. I consider the bedstead-makers an intelligent, sober class. I'm speaking of society men—gentlemen I may call them. I don't know much of the others. The majority of us are members of literary institutions, and some of us have saved money. There is great improvement since I first knew bedstead-makers, in point of temperance. There used to be hard drinking and less working. In 1810, when we met for society purposes, our allowance of fourpence a night per man that had to attend was drunk in an hour; now it's not consumed in the course of the meeting. Several of us are housekeepers, and can support our wives and families comfortably. I don't think one of the wives of the members of our society work in any way but for the family. I have brought up seven children well, and now five are working at other trades, and two girls at home. Very few good hands now earn less than 30s. a week, and some 8s. or 9s. more. I do that, and I've been very rarely out of work. There is no importation of French bedsteads now; there used to be, but they didn't stand. When I first made bedsteads, tents, four-posters, and half-testers were the run; now half-testers and tents are never asked for. Then came the Waterloo bed, which turns up with a curtain over it. The French bedstead next came in, with and without canopies. The Arabian bed is the present fashion. It resembles a half-tester. The iron-work has interfered greatly with my trade. I remember when there were no iron bedsteads at all; now —— sends out 60 or 70 in some weeks. The iron bedsteads came into more general use about ten years ago. People fancy they're free of vermin, but I have had to take some to pieces, and have found them full of bugs in the lath and sacking parts. We've no grievances—not a bit of them. I think workmen themselves might remedy some of their grievances. They should be united, and they shouldn't encourage low-priced shops of any kind by buying things there. I pay 12s. a pair for my shoes, and one of my sons tells me it's foolish to do so, but the shoemaker has as good a right to a good week's earnings as I have, and to encourage slop work is to help on our own trouble."

I shall now conclude with the following statement, which I received from an elderly man, the second member, in point of seniority, of the present Cabinet-makers' Society of the eastern district of London. My informant is a freeman of the Ancient Joiners' Company of the City:—

"I went apprentice to a cabinet-maker," he said, "my friends paying £50 premium with me, a sum which very few can pay now. That was in 1812. Trade was then in full swing. There was a general war in Europe, and men and subsidies were required to keep up the armies. When peace came, in 1815, and large armies came to be disbanded, the men naturally sought employment at the trades they were taken from. Then trade came to a stand still. To meet the declining markets, employers began to reduce wages; the corn-laws were passed, so that no great reduction in the price of provision took place. Workmen found they could not get so remunerative a price for their labour, and a great many commenced masters on their own account. Trade not improving caused further competition, so that by the time my term of apprenticeship expired, in 1819, I found the price of work reduced from 20 to 30 per cent. From that period to the present, fashion and style have been continually altering; while those alterations have generally thrown more work into *jobs*, with no proper remunerating pay for the same. Understand at the East-end there is no regular or fixed price to work for—the jobs are invariably what is called 'lump'—little day-work employ, with few exceptions. From the above circumstances men have been induced, and especially those who do not belong to the society, to confine themselves to one line of work—taking apprentices and employing youngsters from the country, who are not proficient workmen. Timber-yards now carry on a profitable business by retailing small lots, so that a man can purchase stuff for a job in the same way one can for a pair of shoes—say, for a chest of drawers, the top ends, fronts, sides, &c., &c. So with a table, and other furniture. These articles are hawked from Bethnal-green, Curtain-road, and along Holborn, Fleet-street, taking the west route to Hammersmith and its vicinity, of a Saturday, the wood having been in the timber-yard the Saturday previous." [Here my informant gave an account of the system of hawking to the "slaughter" houses similar to what I have given, and to the injury they inflicted upon the masters in the honourable trade, as well as upon the men. He continued.] "As for me, I have before now been driven, in a slack time, to purchase material to make up a job; and in some instances I have not been able to realise the price of a day's work, say 5s., above the cost of materials, though upwards of a week has been consumed in manufacturing the article—the consequences being short fare, scanty clothing, a selling and pledging of all the necessary articles of home, neglect of children's education, and, should a longer continuance of want of employment have ensued, every vestige of home must have been swept away. The question seems to me, what are the remedies to be applied to this state of things? An attempt to regulate the price of labour, to legislate for supply and demand, would be to disturb an hornets' nest. Still the general impression of the working classes is, that if a properly constituted Labour Board was established by the Legislature, empowering employers and men to agree to a fair remunerating price of labour in their respective trades, great good would arise. The working classes, it is true, are not themselves free from blame, for they have yet a great power to ensure many advantages, if they would but unite for the best purposes."

In my next Letter I shall give an account of the better-paid fancy cabinet-makers, the carvers, the buhl-cutters, the marqueterie-workers, &c., and I shall then pass on to describe the slop-trade in connection with these different branches of art.

The Morning Chronicle, Thursday, August 1, 1850.

We have to acknowledge the receipt of 5s. from "An Artisan," towards redeeming the Poor Carpenter's tools from pawn, mentioned in the Letter of July 25.

LABOUR AND THE POOR.

THE METROPOLITAN DISTRICTS.

[FROM OUR SPECIAL CORRESPONDENT.]

OF THE FANCY CABINET-MAKERS OF LONDON.

LETTER LXIV.

The "art and mystery" of cabinet-making consists of two main branches—"general," and "fancy" cabinet work. The general cabinet-makers, as I have before stated, are employed upon all the large work, such as the manufacture of tables, cheffoniers, bookcases, wardrobes, sideboards, chairs, sofas, couches, and bedsteads. The fancy cabinet-makers, on the other hand, are the "small workers" of the trade, manufacturing the lighter articles, such as desks, dressing-cases, work-tables and boxes, cribbage and chess boards, tea-caddies and tea-chests, &c. In my last Letter I gave a description of the condition and earnings of the "general cabinet-makers," working at the best shops for the best prices. In the present Letter I purpose treating of the other branch of the art—namely, the "fancy" part of it, or rather that portion of the fancy cabinet-workers who belong to the "honourable" trade; reserving till my next communication all account of the cheap or slop work, in connection with this and the "general" branch of cabinet-making.

In almost all trades there are two broadly distinguished classes of workmen, known as "society" and "non-society" men; that is to say, a certain portion (usually about one-tenth of the whole) of the operatives belong to a "society" for upholding the standard rate of wages, as well as supporting their unemployed members. These society-men constitute what may be termed the aristocracy of the trade. They are not only for the most part the more intelligent and respectable of the craft, but by far the more skilful workmen. They are stanch upholders of their order, and the sturdiest of sticklers for what they believe to be their rights. To give them their due, however, if they will not allow their employers to wrong any of their body, they also will not permit any of their body to wrong their employers. In the general cabinet-makers' trade, for instance, if a society man overdraws his account with his master, the members make a point of seeing the extra money refunded; so, in the tailors' societies, the members are answerable for the due execution of the work by any of their association. The wages, moreover, which they are bound to uphold, have generally been agreed upon by a committee composed of an equal number of operatives and employers, and in some cases the price-book in which the rate of pay for the making of the different articles belonging to the trade is fixed, has been got up at an expense of several thousand pounds. Further, the sums which they contribute to the support of their members out of work amount to many hundreds in the course of the year.

The wages of "society men," therefore, are regulated by *custom;* those of the non-society men, however, are determined solely by *competition.* It is the competitive men who are invariably the cheap workers, and the prey of the slopsellers of every trade. Of the latter class belonging to the cabinet-making trade I shall speak in my next communication. For the present I purpose confining my remarks to the condition and earnings of the society-men employed at the fancy branch of the business.

Let me, however, first give a description of the several kinds of work pertaining to the craft. Of fancy cabinet-makers there are two classes, viz., those engaged in the manufacture of the cases or exteriors, and those employed upon the fitting up or interiors of the different articles produced in the trade. Those employed upon the exteriors are makers of dressing-cases, writing-desks, work-boxes and tables, jewel, glove, card, gun, and pistol-cases; cribbage, chess, and backgammon-boards; tea-caddies and tea-chests (the difference being that the "chest" contains a glass for sugar, while the "caddy" does not). Those employed upon the interiors of the above articles are the "pine-worker," who makes the partitions of work-boxes, &c.; the fitter-up, who arranges the compartment of dressing-cases; and the liner, who covers the several parts of the interiors with coloured paper, silk or satin, as the case may be. Contrary to what I have remarked of the "general" trade, the employers of the fancy cabinet-makers require the operatives to confine themselves as much as possible to one especial branch; that is to say, the desk-maker is expected to make only desks—the dressing-case only dressing-cases—and so through all the divisions. I was told that the "scamping," or low-priced, masters encouraged this close division of labour, as they thought it made the men more dependent. A man employed on low terms at desk-making was, for instance, unwilling to leave that for dressing-case making, at which, perhaps, his hand "was out;" and so, to avoid a change, he would submit to reduction upon reduction in his wages. All concurred in asserting, that fancy cabinet work is becoming more and more "scampish" every year—the exception of "honourable" employers in it being one in forty. Thus we have another instance of the privations and degradations which working men are called upon to endure, not for the production of the necessaries of life, the articles which the poor and even the pauper must eat and wear, but for the manufacture of *cheap luxuries*—of wares demanded not by necessity, but as a matter of taste, of mere convenience, or mere parade. "If we are fairly paid," said a fancy cabinet-maker to me, "we work all the better, but now quantity is the object with the greater part of us instead of quality. Twenty years ago I had 6d. an inch for the making of a 20-inch desk of solid mahogany—that's 10s. for the entire article; now I've 2s. 3d. for the same thing. Smaller desks, with four brass caps and four brass corners to them, *did* average to us—large and small—6s. each for wages; now they average to us 1s. large and small, and 1s. extra if inlaid with brass. But prices—that is, masters' prices—have not at all lowered in proportion to the lessening of our wages. Let ladies be told that we've had for making 12-inch work-boxes, with plate and 'scutcheon, 3s. 6d. and 4s. a-piece twenty years ago—beautiful wood, rosewood or any fancy thing, and beautiful work, such as a man might feel pride in when he thought it would go into a good lady's hands—and now for such work-boxes 5s. a dozen is paid, 5d. a piece, but they're given out in dozens; 7d. a piece, or 7s. a dozen, for better work. Many are half starving in making work-boxes and desks for ladies, and can't help themselves." This man spoke with bitter indignation as to the state of his trade.

Desk makers and the other branches of the fancy cabinet trade are further divided into "solids" and "veneers," and the handicraftsman working at the one is unable to work so quickly or well at the other, though he does it when required. The "solid" work is the nicer art. The payment for such work has, however, fallen in a more rapid ratio than almost in any other trade. "I don't understand about per cents." was said to me, "but this I do know, the prices I get have, within these 20 years, fallen from 4s. to 5d., I might say 4½d., take it at the outside 5d." Another man calculated that twenty-six years ago the wages were from 300 to 400 per cent. better than they are at present. Where they formerly got 15s. they now receive but 5s., or even 4s. Among this class, as among others, I found unanimity in one complaint—that while wages were so much reduced, while all kinds of provisions were much lower in price, the rent of their rooms had increased rather than diminished. I speak of men in "society," be it remembered; the state of the non-society men is still worse. I find, moreover, that masters pretty generally have raised the wages of their men 3d. a dozen within these two months. The other divisions of the craft are those of the "pine-worker" and the "fitter-up." The pine-worker is the man who makes the interior of ladies' work-boxes, the divisions for thread, &c. He is, for inferior work, one of the worst paid of all. For the mere labour which, 15 years ago in some cases, and 20 or 25 years ago in all, brought him 2s. 6d., he now receives 6d., and he must, moreover, find the material, which (with glue and glass paper) reduces his 6d. to 4d., and sometimes even to 3d. His tools, new and for repairs, may cost him 6d. a week more. Among these men 12s. is considered a good and full week's work, and frequently they are unemployed. Many pine-workers are, however, continually at work on their own account, without having any definite order, and the work so accumulated is sold to the hawkers to complete the boxes, or is ready in case of a hurried demand. The pine-worker's family sometimes cover the interiors with paper or silk—and sometimes the masters employ their own workwomen or girls to do so.

The "fitter up" makes the interior of the dressing-case, as the pine worker does that of the workbox. The fitter-up usually does nothing else. For the interior of a dressing-case, which, as an average "regulation" in a 12-inch case, must contain partitions for four razors—a pair of boot hooks—two, and sometimes three, places for shaving powders or soaps—a shaving brush—a hair brush—a clothes brush—one, two, or three scent bottles (and gentlemen's dressing-cases now-a-days have generally as many divisions for scent bottles as ladies'), and "a looking glass for the head"—for this work the fitter-up, even of the better class—a "society man"—receives 6d.; but that 6d. is subject to the same deductions as I have recorded in the case of the pine-worker. The "casemaker," as the artisan who makes the exterior case is called, receives 10s. a dozen, and despite the "fitters-up" being less skilled labourers, they not unfrequently earn more than the casemakers.

Women are employed in fancy cabinet work as "liners." They affix the paper, or other linings, to work-boxes, and are invariably em-

          Labour and the Poor Volume IV.

ployed in that department of labour. They do the same usually with dressing-cases, but far less frequently with jewel-cases; "for," said a workman, "jewel-cases generally require greater care and nicety in the lining, and so men do them." The wives and daughters of the workmen are usually the parties thus employed, and concurrent testimony proves the young women thus employed to be virtuous and prudent, with very few exceptions. Of all the branches of the fancy cabinet maker's work, wages for the making of jewel cases have fallen the least. This work requires a very nice admeasurement, an accurate eye, and great tastefulness in the workman, especially when the case is made in "angles;" that is, not to present a flat, but a projecting and receding exterior. The fall within fifteen years has been from twenty to thirty per cent.; but some masters have reduced the wages 200 per cent. for inferior work, and on that the operative and his family may starve while making jewel-cases.

A great quantity of French fancy cabinet-work is imported into London. Of this, however, the better class of workmen made no complaint, as the French work is undersold, sometimes as much as thirty and even fifty per cent., by the London slop work. I found, among the men, moreover, a universal opinion, that French fancy cabinet-work, if more tasteful, or rather—for that was the word used—more "showy" than English work, was less solid, and altogether not so well made; it not very unfrequently dropped asunder, I was told, so that ladies were getting tired of it.

The fancy cabinet-makers are, I am informed, far less political than they used to be. The working singly, and in their own rooms, as is nearly universal with them now, has rendered them more unsocial than they were, and less disposed for the interchange of good offices with their fellow-workmen, as well as less regardful of their position and their rights as skilled labourers. "Politics, sir," said one man, in answer to my inquiry, "what's politics to me, compared to getting my dinner—and what's getting my dinner, compared to getting food for my children?"

The amusements of the cabinet-makers, I was told by one of the older workmen, used to be principally the play. Some were very fond of going to the Polytechnic Institution. "Now, however," he said, "few comparatively can afford the 1s., or 6d. that's wanted, and they go to penny concerts, and get to think that 'Sam Hall,' or some nigger thing is very prime indeed. In my own case I've seen Liston play *Paul Pry*, and Farren play the *Colonel*, and Mrs. Glover the *House-*

keeper. I think that was the cast at the start, but I'm not quite sure. I went to see it, sir, at least eight times at my own expense. Latterly I've been to the play only once these three years, and then I had an order." Card-playing, dominoes, and games that are carried on without bodily exertion, seem now to be the chief recreations of the fancy cabinet-makers. The fancy cabinet trade has of late years almost entirely sunk into low prices and inferior workmanship. There are still five or six West-end masters who give good wages—six times as much as I have detailed—but none of the masters employ more than two or three hands, and for these hands there is not, at the fancy cabinet trade, half employment, so they become general workmen.

A complete set of fancy cabinetmaker's tools, which they find themselves, is worth £10. The tools of the pine-workers and fitters-up are worth from 40s. to 50s.

Before proceeding to give the subjoined statement of a desk-maker, I premise that "solid" desks are made out of a plank of mahogany, as it comes from the sawyer, or of whatever wood is the material required. This plank the deskmaker has to plane and to cut to his purpose. He has generally the material for twelve desks given to him at once. If the manufacture be "veneers" the same rule is observed, and the journeyman then receives a quantity of deal commensurate to the veneer. The journeyman executes the ink range, or the portion devoted to holding ink bottles, pens, pencils, wafers, &c., and indeed every portion of the work in a desk, excepting the "lining" or covering of the "flaps," or sloping portion prepared for writing. This "lining" is done by females, and their average payment is 15d. a dozen. Desks now are generally "lap-dovetailed;" that is, the side edges of the wood are made to lap over the adjoining portion of the desk.

The person from whom I received the following narrative was an elderly man, and a workman of great intelligence. He resided in a poor and crowded neighbourhood. His wife was a laundress, and there was a comfortable air of cleanliness in their rooms. I give this man's statement fully, as it contains much that has been repeated to me by others in different branches:—

"I've known the London fancy cabinet trade," he said, "for forty-five years, as that's the time when I was apprenticed in London. My father was a button-maker in Birmingham, and gave a premium of fifty guineas with me. But he failed, and came to London, and was for some time a clerk with Rundell and Bridge, the great jewellers. My master was a tyrannical master; but he certainly made a workman of me and of all his apprentices. I don't recollect how many he had. I think that now even a little master treats his apprentices middling well; for if he don't they turn sulky, and he can hardly afford their being sulky, as he depends on them for work and profit, such as it is. I got work in a good shop immediately after I was out of my time. No good hand need, then, be a week out of work. Masters clamoured for a good man. I have made £3 3s. a week, and one week I made £3 15s. For twenty years after that I didn't know what it was to want a job. I once during that time had three letters altogether in my pocket from Mr. Middleton, the great fancy cabinet-maker—you may have heard of Middleton's pencils, for he was the first in that line too—pressing an engagement upon me. Then I prided myself (and so did my mates) that I was a fancy cabinet-maker. I felt myself a gentleman, and we all held up our heads like gentlemen. I was very fond at that time of reading all that Charles Lamb wrote, and all that Leigh Hunt wrote. As to reading now, why, if we have a quarter of cheese or butter, I get hold of the paper it's brought in, and read it every word. I can't afford a taste for reading if it's to be paid for. I got married twenty-five years ago, and could live very comfortably then without my wife having to work to help me. We had two houses towards the West-end, and let them out furnished. But twenty years ago, or less, I resisted reductions in our wages, and fought against them. I fought against them for 3¾ years, and things went wrong—uncommon wrong—and I had to sacrifice everything to meet arrears of rent and taxes, and I was seized at last; for it wanted a weekly lift through a man's earnings to keep all prosperous. I've done all sorts of work in my time, but I'm now making desks—'ladies' school,' or 'writing'—of mahogany, rosewood, and satin-wood. Those are the principal; though every now and then another fancy wood is used. Walnut sawn solid makes a beautiful desk or box. I think walnut's coming into fashion again for that work. Twenty years ago I made 35s. at the least a week the year through. My family then, and for five, six, or seven, or more years after that time, had the treat of smelling a real good tasty Sunday dinner of beef, or pork, or mutton, as it came hot from the baker's, steaming over the potatoes. And after smelling it we had the treat of eating it, with a drop of beer to wash it down. On week days, too, we had the same pretty regular. I've had six children. Now we have still the smell and the taste of a Sunday meat dinner, but there it stops. We have no such dinners for week days. I'm forced now-a-days to work on Sundays too, and almost every Sunday. People may talk as they like about Sunday labour; I know all about it; but an empty cupboard is stronger than everything. If I have the chance I may make 15s. a week at present prices. I work, as we mainly do, at my own bench, in my own place, and find my own tools, glue, glass-paper, candles, and et ceteras; so that my 15s. a week sometimes falls down to 12s. clear. I work for masters, but not always, that find their own materials; but a great many of us have to find material and all. When our work's taken in, if the key breaks, the foreman—and the foreman is often the master's very convenient tool—fines a man 2d., or he may take back the work, and make it good, if he's found the material—that's called 'stopping.' Locks for the low-priced works are paltry, infamous things. Good locks used to be put to good work; they cost 10d. and 1s. for inferior, and averaged 2s. for better, and from 5s. to 7s. for desks and boxes, where security was wanted. Now locks costs 2d. and 2½d.—slop things, that's no safeguard. What was reckoned, and indeed was, inferior box-locks, was 6d., and is now 1½d. Work's huddled together any how. How it'll all end with me is a poser. I suppose in the workhouse. I almost always worked at piece-work, and don't object to it when wages are fair; indeed, piece-work is better for a good hand, and he's more independent. If a man was on by day he would be expected to do so much work a week, and that would come to about the same thing. In 1825 or 1826 I had 4s. for making a lady's workbox if it was ordered to be first-rate, as the customer was very particular; 3s. 6d. was the regular wages, and I could make ten or eleven, or, in long days, twelve, in a week. Candlelight isn't well adapted for our trade; and when a man works in his own room, as I've mostly done, and as has been and is the custom in our trade, he don't think of gas. Cheap provisions is a great blessing. No one knows what we suffered in '47, when bread was 11d. to 1s.; and when it was at the highest our wages were reduced. When I was first a journeyman I had 10s. for making a 20 inch desk, and it fell to 8s., and 7s., and 6s., and by littles and littles down to what it is now, 4s.; and it's pretty well two days' work to make it properly, but it ain't made properly nineteen times out of twenty. It can't be done at the money. Perhaps a scamping hand might make five such things in a week, or six if he worked on Sundays, and if he was kept regularly at it, but he never is, or very seldom. In my young days an inferior hand couldn't get work in London; now he has a better chance. I think that machinery has been a benefit to us: it increases the material for our work. If there wasn't so much veneering there wouldn't be so much fancy cabinet-work. To show how wages have fallen, I'll mention this. A month back I walked through the Lowther-arcade, and saw fancy boxes, made of different kinds of wood, marked 2s. 6d., and I've had twenty years ago—aye, and fifteen years ago, but not so often—3s. for the more making of them, and found nothing at all. The material couldn't cost less than 1s. or from that to 1s. 6d. altogether. Such boxes are plastered together by boys—or most likely by girls, if a man has sharpish girls in his family, and works at his own bench. Hawkers have sold such boxes so that they didn't get 1½d. a piece for making them. The French goods, in my opinion, don't harm us now; they did at one time. I fancy that little masters sprung up twenty years ago, and have gone on increasing. How many of them there are I don't know; Lord knows there's too many. I'm satisfied that a scamping hand will do his work in one quarter of the time that a good hand will. I can't scamp. A man must be brought up to it to do it."

Work-boxes, whether solid or veneered, are made after the same plan as desks; the "pine-worker's" portion of the labour being always done independently of the case-making. The lining, as I said before, is the work of women and girls.

The work-box maker whom I saw gave me a statement not dissimilar to that of the desk-maker. Like him, he was an old man, had been regularly apprenticed to the trade, and had passed his youth in comfort and respectability. He got married when he was between forty and fifty, and after that the expense of a family, together with the falling off in the wages of his business, exhausted whatever he had accumulated, and he was reduced to poverty. He told me he thought of trying the country, the neighbourhood of Bath, for employment, as there he had friends. He is still known as a first-rate workman. He is slow, I was told, but firm and solid. He would rather trundle a barrow, he said, at Covent Garden—if he could get one to trundle— than do what he was doing. For every 35s. that he earned in a week twenty years ago—and he had on rare occasions, and working night and day, earned 63s.—he now earned from 9s. to 12s., and had a wife and five children to support. He couldn't adapt himself to the demands of the scamping masters, and so, as he must work slow and well, he wasn't for their turn.

Dressing-cases are made after the same mode as work-boxes. The material is given out by the employer and prepared by the workmen. Nine out of every ten dressing-cases made at present are veneered.

Three-fourths of the veneers are now rosewood; mahogany being less and less used. Some dressing-cases are made of deal and covered with ornamental leather, but these belong to the department of "the pine-worker." The interior is made by "the fitter-up," and the furniture, the bottles, brushes, &c., are added by "the shopkeeper," as the cutler, toyman, perfumer, silversmith, or whatever tradesman supplies the case to the customer, is called. From one of the most respectable workmen in the trade (as I was assured) I had the following statement. I found him at work in what is generally the under-ground kitchen of a small house, but which, with him, was altogether devoted to the purposes of a workshop:—

"I have been ten years in the trade, and am a 'society man.' I think if our society were more numerous it would be far better both for masters and men. These cases here are twelve inches. They have twelve brass corner-hoops and four brass caps. I get 3s. a piece for making them. No doubt, at a first-rate West-end shop, I should have 9s., or 10s. a piece for the work, but in those shops it's odd jobs only that way, and under employers such as mine we have a quantity in at one time, and so can keep at work regularly. I was not apprenticed, but served five years to the trade under an agreement, which is the same thing. Sometimes the master or foreman affixes the fitter's-up work himself—indeed generally so; sometimes it's sent to us to have that done. By working long hours I can make eight of these boxes a week. For average hours, say ten hours a day, I can make 20s. a week at my work, but against that there's the wear and tear of tools, which I find myself; there's the expense of glue and glass-paper, and so the 20s. is about 18s. clear. I make also common dressing-cases, which have no brass corners or caps. They are 1s. a piece. A good hand is expected to be able to make two dozen of them in a week, but he won't make more money at them than at the better ones. There's all the more glue, &c., used. We send our work home unvarnished. A French polisher does the varnishing."

The making of tea-chests and tea-caddies does not differ from the making of dressing-cases; but the whole work is done by one man. The earnings are in the same ratio. There is no subordinate branch of fitters-up. The 20-inch chests are 5s. in a middling, and 7s. in a good shop for wages, and as low as 3s. 6d. among the worst-paid workmen, and out of this, too, deductions for glue, &c., have to be made.

A young man gave me the following account. As with other branches, the pine-worker saws, planes, and in all respects prepares the material as it is given out to him by the master:—

"I served seven years' apprenticeship as a fitter-up of dressing-cases, and most in my line do the same. We most of us serve apprenticeships. I served with a little master, for he was so then, but he is now a large master. I was an in-door apprentice, and had no fault to find with my usage. I now do journey-work, and have done so for six or seven years. The material is given to us by our employers; it is always clean pine, and we have it in 'leaf stuff,' that is the whole or half the length of the tree from which it is cut. It is cut at the veneer mills, 4 or 5-cut we call it; that is, 4 or 5 cuts to the inch in thickness. We are paid by the dozen. The largest size I have made in dressing-cases is 20 inches in length, and in that may be a dozen partitions. By hard work and long hours, a man may earn 20s. a week at fitting-up—that's of the best description of work. Trade's uncertain. I'm not to call busy above six months in the year—the spring and summer parts. After that I have only about half or three-quarters work in the week, and sometimes none at all. 14s. a dozen is the price for fitting-up a dozen 20 inch desks, and other sizes in proportion. I've nothing at all to complain of. I'm not a married man, and have only myself to care for."

A pine-worker for a better-class shop gave me information almost identical as to prices and employment.

The "liners," a class of which I have previously spoken, are, with the exception of those employed in the "getting up" of jewel cases, invariably women. To execute the work tastefully and skilfully, and with an economy of material, no little tuition and no little skill is necessary. From a respectable young woman, residing in a good house, with a large garden in front, who, I was informed, was the best in the trade, I had the following information:—

"I was brought up to the business, and I think every person, to do the work well, ought to be. I now live here with my sister. My friends were in the line. The work of the better class is usually given out to the liners at their own houses, as it is now generally to me. It is my business to cut it so as to fit it precisely to the parts of the work required to be lined. I have in this way every kind of coloured paper given to me for lining, as well as all colours and qualities in silks, satins, and velvets. I use both paste and gum, but each must be of the best and most delicate kind. I do not work by any regular scale of prices, so I cannot give prices. I only do the best work, and for houses where I am known. I take or send the work in when completed, and receive what the master thinks proper. By my own labour I can make from 15s. to 20s. every week. I have sometimes to employ an assistant. I had rather not state anything more; indeed I don't know anything more that I have to state. I have understood that many women in my line are wretchedly paid and wretchedly off, but of their earnings or their characters I know nothing personally."

Such is an account of the earnings of those working at the better-paid branches of the Fancy Cabinet-trade. There are, however, several descriptions of work, belonging both to the general and fancy trade, that still remain to be described. These are the Marqueterie-workers, the Buhl-cutters, and the Wood-carvers—each of these having, like the other branches, its skilled and slop-labourers. I shall for the present merely give an account of the more skilful and better-paid workmen belonging to these arts.

The beautiful art of *Marqueterie*, which had fallen somewhat into disuse in this country, experienced a revival ten or twelve years ago. Marqueterie is the inlaying of coloured woods, so as to present a group of flowers, or any object, in their proper forms and appropriate hues. It is generally used for the adornment of furniture, such as ladies' work-tables and loo tables, but it is sometimes—though very rarely in this country—applied to the internal decoration of a house. There is an inlaid floor in Buckingham Palace, executed by order of George IV.; but the workmanship, I am informed, is inferior to that of the present day, as, at the time the floor was inlaid, there were not three thoroughly good artificers in marqueterie in England. The woods used in this art are holly, pear-tree, and sycamore, which are all fine-grained, and take the dye readily; for the wood used is all dyed, and always worked from veneers. Four veneers are held firmly together in a frame, and the outer veneer has been marked, after a drawing, to the pattern to be cut. The workman in cutting uses saws made out of the hardest-tempered, thinnest, and narrowest watch-springs; the saw is attached to a slender frame, and forms what may be described as the string of a bow, and this fine saw, which is made by the workman himself, is directed according to the pattern marked until the shape required is cut out. No cavity can be seen where the saw has done its work, so fine and delicate is the process. Thus four portions are cut at one operation. By the old system each veneer was dyed *before* it was sawn, and so there was a uniformity of colour, which made a group of flowers, for instance, look flat, hard, and unnatural. About four or five years ago, however, Mr. Bayles, who lately received, at the hands of Prince Albert, the prize awarded by the Society of Arts for the finest specimen of marqueterie, introduced a decided improvement. Mr. Bayles dyes the woods *after* they have been cut, and by his peculiar art gives them the great advantage of "shading." For his dyes he resorts both to boiling and scorching the wood. When the respective portions of the pattern are cut out, they are fitted together and fixed to the furniture. The making of the furniture, apart from the marqueterie, is the work of the cabinet-maker, who now uses walnut for the material of the table, or whatever be the furniture, more frequently than any other wood; as the flowing and delicate shades of walnut blend best with the hues of the marqueterie.

Of the English workmen in this art there are now in London upwards of 100, of whom eight or nine are pronounced highly accomplished artists, the others being for the most part those engaged in the mechanical portion of the art. The divisions in the trade are the designer, cutter, dyer, and putter-together. The departments of the designer and dyer require the largest amount of skill. Twenty-five years ago the marqueterie workers could earn 30s. a-day, and be employed, if they chose, the year through. Now the best hands earn 7s. and 8s. a-day, the employment being all by the day, and the work is more uncertain—nine months in the year, or somewhat less than nine, being the average of employment. The marqueterie workers find their own tools, which are chiefly their saws. They have no society, but are steady men, and pretty well informed. I was told that they might, as a body, advantageously interest themselves more in the progress of the fine arts, were it but to the same extent as the wood carvers. The mode of acquiring a knowledge of the trade is by apprenticeship, it being at least twelve months before a boy can be of any use with his saw. The great decline in the wages of the men has been in the last two years, when their wages fell in some cases about one half, having gradually fallen from the 30s. a day of 25 years ago. The decline was owing to the great influx of foreigners practising this art who hurried over from France and Germany on the breaking out of the revolutions, and who continue to arrive still. The prices of marqueterie work fell at once about 100 per cent. from the competition, and the English masters were compelled to reduce wages. The foreigners now employed in marqueterie in London are about double the number of the English. They are not considered superior, and rarely equal, workmen to the English, as they do not excel in "effect." As to whether the work of the Englishman or the foreigner may be the more durable, there is hardly a means of judging; for, as was observed to me, "no man can expect to outlive a marqueterie table." The impression is, however, that the English work is the best adapted for durability.

The habits of the foreigners, I am told, are sober and penurious. They manifest little care for what an English artisan frequently prides himself upon—"a respectable appearance;" and, indeed, show no great regard for the comforts or decencies of life. "Ten or twelve of them," I was told by a person (an Englishman) familiar with their habits, "master and men, all pig together, sleeping where they work."

A very intelligent man, in a very comfortable abode, gave me the following account:—

"I've been a buhl-cutter for fourteen years, and served a seven years' apprenticeship to it, and then became a little master on my own account. There are very few journeymen among us; we are mostly little masters. There are two kinds of buhl cutting, 'plain' and 'French ornament.' The plain is mother of pearl laid on to the veneer; the 'French ornament' is brass and green shell (foreign snail shell) greatly variegated. The brass is cut first and fitted into the wood, and then the brass is cut to admit the green shell, and cut by myself or my fellows in the trade. It is an art demanding the utmost nicety. I work almost entirely by my eye, but the slopworkers make a sad mess of it. The buhl worker then introduces a wire scroll into the pattern, and a few little brass pips (tacks). When finished, I clean it off with a 'toothing iron' and a file. When it's so cleaned off, it's sent to the cabinet-maker, and he must be a first-rate workman for the French ornament work. Then it's sent back to me to engrave. There are not above 20 good buhl-cutters in London, and none anywhere else. Of an inferior sort there may be 100. The pearl-worker prepares the material for us, grinding it down to a uniform charge by the job. I could once earn £1 a day, but now I can only earn £2 a week. The slop-fellows get my good patterns, and I form my own patterns and we all do, and they imitate our patterns. I adopt a pattern now and then from any tasteful engraving I see, or anything in my way. My tools are all very small and niggling, and will cost altogether about £5. The chief tool for size is called 'a neddy' with the shops, which is something like a saddler's or boot-closer's clams, but we do not hold it between our legs—we sit astride on the frame, and so go to work with our saws. Another of our principal tools is a frame-saw. I defy anybody to learn our business without great practice. It's a business always changing, and always demanding some new exercise of skill. When my work has been fitted into the dressing-case, or whatever it may be, the cabinet-maker completes the article, and then it is sent back to be 'engraved up,'—generally crests, cyphers, and coats of arms. We have no scale of prices, and no society. Jobbing is generally 9d. an hour, because master must have a profit after mine, but I've little jobbing. The first worker in buhl in this country was a German—I forget his name—between twenty and thirty years ago. He did well, but would not communicate his secret. A man he employed found out his secret, and improved upon it, and so the art grew. The best buhl-cutter after that is now in Birmingham, and very poor. His style is altogether superseded."

The *carvers of wood*, for cabinet-making and other purposes, are divided into the carvers of hard and white woods. The carving of the hard woods, such as oak, walnut, mahogany, and rosewood, now comprises the most skilled portion of the art. At one period, and indeed up to the time when George IV. (then Regent) renewed many of the ornaments of Windsor Castle, under the direction of Sir J. Wyattville, the carving of the white woods was the most skilled. The white woods carved are chiefly pine and lime tree. The white-wood carver, until within the last fifty years, executed the work for the gilder's purposes, such as picture and mirror frames, but now such labour is entirely superseded by the use of composition ornaments and machine-cut mouldings. There are still some very tasteful and elegant artificers in white-wood carving, and in the Grinling Gibbons' style—game, fruits, and trophies being so carved in lime. The art reached its perfection in the hands of Grinling Gibbons. I am assured, however, on the best authority, that many carvings have been sold as Gibbons's which were far more modern than his era. Mowatt, a Frenchman, exhibited great skill in the flowers he executed at Windsor Castle for George IV., and may be considered to rank next to Gibbons. Mowatt is less bold in style, more conventional, but remarkable for delicacy and finish. [These opinions, it is right I should state, were what I heard expressed by a working man.] Hardwood carving is now chiefly required for furniture, such as mahogany sideboards, &c., also for church work—oak being then the material on which the artificer's skill is exerted. The styles most popular now for churches are the Norman-Gothic, and the early English. Very little of the mediæval style is at present, or has been lately, demanded from the wood-carvers. The most recent style introduced is the Italian, "which is becoming," I was told, "the most fashionable for churches, though introduced less than five years ago." Until the revival of this art, which is within these twenty years, the styles followed were the Roman and Louis Quatorze. Then sprung up a demand for the Elizabethan and *renaissance* (Italian) styles, and the demand has progressed, and very superior skill has been elicited. I heard this revival of a taste for the wood-carver's beautiful and enduring art attributed, among other causes, to the establishment of the Schools of Design in Somerset-house. Until then there was, I was told, really no artistic education for the young wood-carver. The opening of Hampton-court, &c., to the public, I was assured by a practical man in the trade, with great powers and means of observation, had tended to create and foster this taste. The Houses of Parliament, too, at one time gave employment to eighty wood carvers, and another impetus was thus given to the progress of the trade, but the eighty are now reduced to twenty. They are paid from 36s. to £2 a week. The grotesque figures of animals in the Gothic church-carvings are accounted the most difficult portion of the art. Figure-carving is also the "high art" of furniture woodwork, and is demanded most for sideboards, but not to any very great extent. The figures so carved are chimeræ, fruits, flowers, "strap-work" (inter-lacing bands), and foliage. The rate of wages in this business ranges from 30s. to £3 a week; 36s. being about the average earnings of the operative when at work. His employment, however, is very uncertain, being greatly dependent on the outlay of the wealthier classes in taste-ful furniture and decorative embellishments. Within the knowledge of my informant, the trade suffered greatly after the panic of 1826, and after every subsequent panic. "The passing of the Reform Bill," said a tradesman of the first class to me, "depressed wood-carving to a great degree, as many members of the aristocracy became alarmed, and put a check on their accustomed patronage of art." Even now the trade, I am informed, has hardly recovered from the depressing ef-fects of the panic of '47, many excellent workmen being unemployed. The wood-carvers of the best class number from 250 to 300. Those of an inferior and underpaid description, residing chiefly in Moor-fields, the Curtain-road, and Bethnal-green, are about as numerous. These men are wretchedly paid for so skilled a kind of labour, some not earning 15s. a week. They work in their own rooms, or have a bench and sleep under it. The West-end carvers used to be altogether em-ployed on the cabinet-maker's premises—an arrangement, however, now becoming less prevalent. Machinery has not affected the purely artistic portion of the carver's business, but it has been applied (six such machines are now in use at the new Houses of Parliament) to "rough out" the carving. The men of the best class are paid both by the piece and the day. If by day, a good workman receives 6s. and 7s., and can generally earn about that by piece work. They have a society (to which employers are admissible), but it is only for the obtaining of casts and books required for the artificers' advancement in their calling. There is no benefit society, nor any which at all deals with the regulation of wages. The wood-carvers are now a remarkably well conducted class. Some have saved money, and others have insured their lives. "I don't know," said one of them, "an habitual drunkard in my trade, but I only speak of the West-end workmen, as I'm acquainted with none else; but I fear that, except in the very highest departments of furniture work, they will be driven down by Moorfields competition, and then they may take to drink." About twenty-five years ago nearly all the best workmen (most of them Scotchmen) were hard drinkers. At that time the body was not a third, perhaps not more than a quarter, so numerous as it is now, and the men easily earned £4 a week. The majority, or a very large proportion, of wood-carvers are now countrymen, the best "Gothic" carvers coming from Norwich, Lincoln, and other cathedral towns. There are no foreigners among these operatives. The restoration of York Cathedral did little for the art, as, at the time of Jonathan Martin's incendiarism, a great deal of the carved wood work was sent to be executed in Holland for cheapness. Apprenticeship is the mode by which the young wood-carver is taught his business in London, and generally by apprenticeship to small masters. An average fee is £15 out of doors, and £40 or £50 if in doors. Country apprentices usually, as it is called, "try London," and many of them remain. For two years a boy is almost useless as an assistant in the carving. The wood-carvers find their own tools. They are almost entirely gouges, with which the artificer scoops out the wood to the pattern, drawing, or model spread before him on his bench. A good set of tools is worth £5, and the wear and tear of them will not amount to 1s. a week. There are no recognised subdivisions in this trade; but if an artificer manifests peculiar skill in any one department, he is frequently employed in that department—as in the carving of Gothic figures, for instance. This, done by piece, ensures the highest amount of remuneration. There is no scale of prices; merely an understanding or an arrangement as to the amount between master and man. The regulation, however, as to employment in one particular branch, is dependent on an employer's discretion. The same workmen are employed on side-boards as are employed on fonts and pulpits.

LABOUR AND THE POOR.

———◆———

THE METROPOLITAN DISTRICTS.

[FROM OUR SPECIAL CORRESPONDENT.]

OF THE SLOP CABINET TRADE.

Letter LXV.

The Cabinet Makers, socially as well as commercially considered, consist, like all other operatives, of two distinct classes; that is to say, of "society" and "non-society men," or, in the language of political economy, of those whose wages are regulated by *custom*, and those whose earnings are determined by *competition*. The former class numbers between six and seven hundred of the trade, and the latter between four and five thousand. As a general rule, I may remark that I find the "society men" of every trade comprise about one-tenth of the whole. Hence it follows, that if the non-society men are neither so skilful nor so well conducted as the others, at least they are quite as important a body, from the fact that they constitute the main portion of the trade. The transition from the one class to the other is, however, in most cases, of a very disheartening character. The difference between the tailor at the West-end, working for the better shops at the better prices, and the poor wretch slaving at "starvation wages" for the sweaters and slop-shops at the East-end, has already been pointed out. The same marked contrast was also shown to exist between the society and non-society boot and shoemakers. The Carpenters and Joiners told the same story. There we found society men renting houses of their own—some paying as much as £70 a year—and the non-society men overworked and underpaid, so that a few weeks' sickness reduced them to absolute pauperism. Nor, I regret to say, can any other tale be told of the Cabinet Makers—except it be that the competitive men in this trade are even in a worse position than in any other. I have already portrayed to the reader the difference between the homes of the two classes—the comfort and well-furnished abodes of the one, and the squalor and bare walls of the other. But those who wish to be impressed with the social advantages of a fairly-paid class of mechanics should attend a meeting of the Wood-carvers' Society. On the first floor of a small private house in Tottenham-street, Tottenham-court-road, is, so to speak, the museum of the working men belonging to this branch of the Cabinet Makers. The walls of the back room are hung round with plaster casts of some of the choicest specimens of the arts, and in the front room the table is strewn with volumes of valuable prints and drawings in connection with the craft. Round this table are ranged the members of the society—some forty or fifty were there on the night of my attendance, discussing the affairs of the trade. Among the collection of books may be found "The Architectural Ornaments and Decorations of Cottingham," "The Gothic Ornaments of Pugin," "Tatham's Greek Relics," "Raphael's Pilaster Ornaments of the Vatican," "Le Pautre's Designs," and "Baptiste's Collection of Flowers" (large size)—while among the casts are articles of the same choice description. The objects of this society are, in the words of the preface to the printed catalogue, "To enable wood-carvers to co-operate for the advancement of their art, and by forming a collection of books, prints, and drawings, to afford them facilities for self-improvement, also by the diffusion of information among its members, to assist them in the exercise of their art, as well as to enable them to obtain employment." The society does not interfere in the regulation of wages in any other way than by the diffusion of information on the subject, so that "both employers and employed may, by becoming members, promote their own and each other's interests." The collection is now much enlarged, and, with the additions which have been made to it, offers aid to the members which in many cases is invaluable. As a means of facilitating the use of this collection, the opportunities of borrowing from it have been made as general as possible. The meetings of the society are held at a place where attendance is unaccompanied by expense; and "they are therefore," says the preface, "free from all objection on account of inducements to exceed the time required for business." All this appears to be in the best possible taste, and the attention of the society being still directed to its improvement, assuredly gives the members, as they say, "good reason to hope that it will become one of which the wood-carver may be proud, as affording valuable assistance both in the design and execution of any style of wood-carving." In the whole course of my investigations I have never experienced more gratification than I did on the evening of my visit to this society. The members all gave evidence, both in manner and appearance, of the refining character of their craft; and it was indeed a hearty relief from the scenes of squalor, misery, dirt, vice, ignorance, and discontent with which these inquiries too frequently bring one into connection, to find oneself surrounded with an atmosphere of beauty, refinement, comfort, intelligence, and ease.

The public generally are deplorably misinformed as to the character and purpose of Trade Societies. The common impression is that they are combinations of working men, instituted and maintained solely with the view of exacting an exorbitant rate of wages from their employers, and that they are necessarily connected with "strikes," and with sundry other savage and silly means of attaining this object. It is my duty, however, to make known that the rate of wages which such societies are instituted to uphold has, with but few exceptions, been agreed upon at a conference of both masters and men, and that in almost every case I find the members as strongly opposed to "strikes," as a means of upholding them, as the public themselves. But at all events the maintenance of the standard rate of wages is not the *sole* object of such societies—the majority of them being organised as much for the support of the sick and aged as for the regulation of the price of labour; and even in those societies whose efforts are confined to the latter purpose alone, a considerable sum is subscribed annually for the subsistence of their members when out of work. The General Cabinet Makers, I have already shown, have contributed towards this object as much as £1,000 per annum for many years past. It is not generally known how largely the community is indebted to the Trade and Friendly societies of the working classes dispersed throughout the kingdom, or how much expense the public is saved by such means in the matter of poor-rates alone.

According to the last Government Returns, there are at present in England, Scotland, and Ireland, upwards of 33,000 such societies, 14,000 of which are enrolled, and 8,000 unenrolled—the remaining 11,000 being secret associations, such as the Odd-Fellows, Foresters, Druids, Old Friends, and Rechabites. The number of members belonging to these 33,000 societies is more than three millions; the gross annual income of the entire associations is £4,980,000; and their accumulated capital—£11,360,000. The working people of this country, and, I believe, of this country alone, contribute therefore to the support of their own poor nearly five millions of money every year, which is some thousands of pounds more than was dispensed in parochial relief throughout England and Wales in 1848. Hence it may be truly said that the benefits conferred by the Trade and Friendly societies of the working classes are not limited to the individuals receiving them, but are participated by every ratepayer in the kingdom; for, were there no such institutions, the poor-rates must necessarily be doubled.

I have been thus explicit on the subject of Trade Societies in general, because I know there exists in the public mind a strong prejudice against such institutions, and because it is the fact of belonging to some such society which invariably distinguishes the better class of workmen from the worse. The competitive men, or cheap workers, seldom or never are members of any association, either "enrolled" or "unenrolled;" the consequence is, that, when out of work, or disabled from sickness or old age, they are left to the parish to support. It is the slop-workers of the different trades—the cheap men, or non-society hands—who constitute the great mass of paupers in this country. And here lies the main social distinction between the workmen who belong to society, and those who do not—the one maintain their own poor, the others are left to the mercy of the parish. The wages of the competitive men are cut down to a bare subsistence, so that, being unable to save anything from their earnings, a few days' incapacity from labour drives them to the workhouse for relief. In the matter of machinery, not only is the cost of working the engine but the wear and tear of the machine considered as a necessary part of the expense of production. With the human machine, however, it is different—slop wages being sufficient to defray only the cost of keeping it at work, but not to compensate for the wear and tear of it. Under the allowance system of the old poor-law, wages, it is well known, were reduced far below subsistence point, and the workmen were left to seek parish relief for the remainder; and so, in the slop part of every trade, the under-paid workmen, when sick or aged, are handed over to the State to support.

As an instance of the truth of the above remarks, I subjoin the following statement which has been furnished to me by the Chairmakers' Society concerning their outgoings:—

Average number of members, 110.

Paid to unemployed members from 1841–1850	£1,256 10 0
Ditto for insurance of tools	211 10 0
Ditto loss of time by fire	19 2 8
Ditto funerals of members	120 15 0
Ditto collections for sick	60 4 0

"The objects which the London chairmakers have in view by associating in a Trade Society," says the written statement from which the above account is extracted, "is to insure, as near as possible, one uniform price for the work they execute, so that the employer shall have a guarantee in making his calculations that he will not be charged more or less than his neighbours, who employ the same class of men; to assist their members in obtaining employment, and a just remuneration for the work they perform; to insure their tools against fire; to provide for their funerals in the event of death; and to relieve their members when unemployed or in sickness;—the latter being effected by paying persons to collect voluntary subscriptions for invalid members (such subscriptions producing on an average £5 in each case). The members have, moreover, other modes of assisting each other when in difficulties."

I may as well here subjoin the statement I have received from this society, concerning the circumstances affecting their business:—

"Our trade," say they, in a written communication to me, "has suffered very materially from a change which took place about thirty years ago in the system of work. We were at that time chiefly employed by what we term 'Trade-working masters,' who supplied the upholsterers with the frames of chairs and sofas; but since then we have obtained our work directly from the sellers. At first the change was rather beneficial than otherwise. The employer and his salesman, however, have now, in the greater number of instances, no knowledge of the manufacturing part of the business, and this is very detrimental to our interest, owing to their being unacquainted with the value of the labour part of the articles we make. Moreover the salesman sends all the orders he can out of doors to be made by the middleman, though the customer is led to believe that the work is executed on the premises; whereas only a portion of it is made at home, and that chiefly the odd and out of the way work, because the sending of such work out of doors would not answer the end of cheapness. The middleman, who executes the work away from the premises, subdivides the labour to such an extent that he is enabled to get the articles made much cheaper, as well as to employ both unskilful workmen and apprentices. Placed in the position where the employer gets the credit of paying us the legitimate price for our labour, it would appear that we have no cause of complaint; but owing to the system of things before stated, as well as to the number of linendrapers, carpetmakers, and others who have recently entered the trade, without having any practical knowledge of the business, together with the casualty of our employment, our social position has become scarcely any better, or so good, as that of the unskilful or the dissipated workmen; while from the many demands of our fellow-operatives upon us in the shape of pecuniary assistance, we have a severe struggle to maintain anything like a respectable footing in the community. The principal source of regret with us is, that the public have no knowledge of the quality of the articles they buy. The sellers, too, from their want of practical acquaintance with the manufacturing part of the business, have likewise an injurious effect upon our interests, instead of second-ing our efforts to keep up a creditable position in society.

"The subjoined is the amount of the capital of our society at the present time:—

Property in the Funds	£300
Out at use	175
Other available property in the shape of Price- books, &c.*	200
	£675 "

* " The Price-books are our exclusive right as well as copyright, we selling them to masters, journey-men, and the trade, and deriving a profit there-from. "

Such, then, is the state of the society men belonging to the Cab-inet Makers' trade. These, as I before said, constitute that portion of the workmen whose wages are regulated by custom, and it now only remains for me to set forth the state of those whose earnings are determined by competition. Here we shall find that the wages a few years since were from three to four hundred per cent. better than they are at present—20s. having formerly been the price paid for making that for which the operatives now receive only 5s., and this notwith-standing that the number of hands in the London trade from 1831 to 1841 declined 33 per cent. relatively to the rest of the population. Nor can it be said that this extraordinary depreciation in the value of the cabinet-maker's labour has arisen from any proportionate de-crease in the quantity of work to be done. The number of houses built in the metropolis has of late been considerably on the increase. Since 1839 there have been 200 miles of new streets formed in London— no less than 6,405 new dwellings having been erected annually since that time; and as it is but fair to assume that the majority of these new houses must have required new furniture, it is clear that it is im-possible to account for the decline in the wages of the trade in ques-tion upon the assumption of an equal decline in the quantity of work.

How, then, are we to explain the fact, that while the hands have decreased 33 per cent. and work increased at a considerable rate, wages a few years ago were 300 per cent. better than they are at present? The solution of the problem will be found in the extraordinary increase that has taken place within the last twenty years of what are called "garret masters" in the cabinet trade. These garret masters are a class of small "trade-working masters," supplying both capital and labour. They are in manufacture what "the peasant proprietors" are in agriculture—their own employers and their own workmen. There is, however, this one marked distinction between the two classes—the garret master cannot, like the peasant proprietor, *eat* what he produces; the consequence is that he is obliged to convert each article into food immediately he manufactures it, no matter what the state of the market may be. The capital of the garret master being generally sufficient to find him in materials for the manufacture of only one article at a time, and his savings being but barely enough for his subsistence while he is engaged in putting those materials together, he is compelled, the moment the work is completed, to part with it for whatever he can get. He cannot afford to keep it even a day, for to do so is generally to remain a day unfed. Hence, if the market be at all slack, he has to force a sale by offering his goods at the lowest possible price. What wonder, then, that the necessities of such a class of individuals should have created a special race of employers, known by the significant name of "slaughter-house men"—or that these, being aware of the inability of the "garret masters" to hold out against any offer, no matter how slight a remuneration it affords for their labour, should continually lower and lower their prices until the entire body of the competitive portion of the cabinet trade is sunk in utter destitution and misery. Moreover, it is well known how strong is the stimulus among peasant proprietors, or, indeed, any class working for themselves, to extra production. So it is, indeed, with the garret masters; their industry is almost incessant, and hence a greater quantity of work is turned out by them, and continually forced into the market, than there would otherwise be. What though there be a brisk and a slack season in the cabinet-maker's trade as in the majority of others—slack or brisk, the garret masters must produce the same excessive quantity of goods. In the hope of extricating himself from his overwhelming poverty he toils on, producing more and more—and yet the more he produces the more hopeless does his position become; for the greater the stock that he thrusts into the market, the lower does the price of his labour fall, until at last he and his whole family work for less than half what he himself could earn a few years back by his own unaided labour.

Another cause of the necessity of the garret master to part with his goods as soon as made, is the large size of the articles he manufactures, and the consequent cost of conveying them from slaughterhouse to slaughterhouse till a purchaser be found. For this purpose a van is frequently hired; and the consequence is that he cannot hold out against the "slaughterer's" offer, even for an hour, without increasing the expense of carriage, and so virtually reducing his gains. This is so well known at the slaughter-houses, that if a man, after seeking in vain for a fair remuneration for his work, is goaded by his necessities to call at a shop a second time to accept a price that he had previously refused, he seldom obtains what was first offered him. Sometimes, when he has been ground down to the lowest possible sum, he is paid late on a Saturday night with a cheque, and forced to give "the firm" a liberal discount for cashing it.

For a more detailed account, however, of the iniquities practised upon this class of operatives, I refer the reader to the statements given below. It will be there seen that all the modes by which work can be produced cheap are in full operation. The labour of apprentices and children is the prevailing means of production. I heard of one small trade working master, who had as many as eleven apprentices at work for him; and wherever the operative is blessed with a family, they all work, even from six years old; for it is generally in the worst paid trades that the labour of children is valuable, and hence a premium is given for the over population of a business that is already too fully stocked with hands. The employment of any undue number of apprentices—a system which I find is invariably adopted in those trades where the remuneration has fallen below the standard of men's labour—also tends to increase the very excess of hands from which the trade is suffering; and thus it is that the lower wages become, the lower still they are reduced. There are very few—some told me there were none, but there are a few—who work as journeymen for "little masters;" but these men become little masters in their turn, or they must starve in idleness, for their employment is precarious. There is among the East-end cabinet makers no society, no benefit or sick fund, and very little communion between the different classes. The chair-maker knows nothing of the table maker next door, and cannot tell whether others in his calling thrive better or worse than he does. These men have no time for social intercommunication. The struggle to live absorbs all their energies, and confines all their aspirations to that one endeavour. Their labour is devoted, with the rarest exceptions, to the "slaughter-houses," "linen-drapers," "polsterers," or "warehouses." By all these names I heard the shopkeepers who deal in furniture of all kinds, as well as drapery-goods, designated. These shopkeepers pay the lowest possible prices, and in order to insure a bare livelihood under them, the cabinet-makers must work very rapidly. This necessity has led the men to labour only at one branch, at which an artisan becomes expert; but he can do little or nothing else, and that again makes him more dependent on the warehouses. The loo table maker only makes loo tables; the cheffonier maker, only cheffoniers. The men find their own material, and hawk the article when completed to the different warehouses. Even a wet Saturday is a disadvantage to the poor artizan, for his goods become either damaged, or lose their freshness of appearance if they get wet, and the man is unwilling to subject them to a further wetting by exposing them still further to the weather, so that often enough, rather than take his goods back or hawk them to another warehouse, the poor fellow accepts the first warehouseman's paltry offer. "One Saturday afternoon, sir," said a respectable artizan to me, "I happened to hear a slaughter-house keeper say, 'I hope to God it'll rain hard to-night, that'll put £20 into my pocket.'" The necessity of raising money on a Saturday night, to buy materials on Monday morning for the next week's toil, is often an irresistible motive for accepting the very worst offer, if it be but barely the price of the material.

These men work in their own rooms in Spitalfields and Bethnalgreen, and sometimes two or three men in different branches occupy one apartment and work together there. They are a sober class of men, but seem so perfectly subdued by circumstances that they cannot, or do not, struggle against the system, which several of them told me they knew was undoing them.

This remarkable monopoly and subdivision of labour was brought about gradually. The warehouses I have described began to flourish about twenty years since, and fifteen years ago they increased, and have increased rapidly since. The proprietors of these places purchased ready-made furniture of any one, and in large or small quantities; and men out of work eagerly seized the opportunity to employ their time in making goods for them, and so the system grew gradually to what it is now. "There's another thing, sir," said a man to me; "many a man didn't like the restraint of a shop, and didn't like the master or the foreman, and to work on his own account was the very thing that pleased him, so such a one would try his hand for the slaughter-houses. They've found it out since, that they have."

The subdivisions of this trade I need not give: they are as numerous as the articles of the cabinet-maker's calling.

I have mentioned that the "black" houses, or "linendrapers," at the West-end of London were principally supplied from the East-end. In the neighbourhood of Tottenham-court-road and Oxford-street, for instance, most of my readers will have had their attention attracted by the dust-covered appearance of some poor worker in wood carrying along his skeleton of an easy chair, or a sofa, or a couch, or his two or three office or parlour chairs, to dispose of in some shop; while, occasionally, two persons may be seen staggering and sweating beneath the heavier load of a large chest of drawers, or even a wardrobe. Often, too, a carter has to be employed for the same purpose—the man getting sixpence an hour for this service, while the charge for the horse is 1s.; so that for every hour this sale-seeking has to be continued the cost is 1s. 6d., and thus even but two hours will exhaust the very fullest value of a long day's labour to this class of workmen, and four or six hours the earnings of two or three days. From a furniture carter of this description I received some most shocking details of the miseries of having to "busk" it, as this taking about goods for sale is called by those in the trade.

From a pale feeble-looking man whom I met on a Saturday evening at the West-end, carrying a mahogany cheffonier, I had the following statement:—

"I have dragged this cheffonier with me," he said, "from Spitalfields, and have been told to call again in two hours (it was then half-past seven). I am too tired to drag it to another linendraper's, and, indeed, I shouldn't have so good a chance there, for if we go late the manager considers we've been at other places; and he'll say, 'you needn't bring me what others has refused.' I was brought up as a general hand at ——; but was never in society, which is a great disadvantage. I feel that now. I used to make my 25s. to 28s. a week six or seven years back; but then I fell out of employ, and worked at chair-making for a slaughter house, and so got into the system, and now I can't get out of it, at least I don't know how to set about it. I have no time to look about me, as, if I'm idle, I can't get bread for my family. I have a wife and two children; they're too young to do anything, but I can't afford to send them to school, except every now and then, 1d. or 2d. a week, and so they may learn to read perhaps. The anxiety I suffer is not to be told. I've nothing left to pawn now, and if I don't sell this cheffonier I must take it back, and go back to a house bare of everything, except perhaps 3s. or 2s. 6d. my wife may have earned by ruining her health for a tailor's sweater, and 1s. 6d. of that must go for rent. I ought to have £2 for this cheffonier, for it's superior mahogany to the run of such things, but I ask only 35s., and perhaps may be bid 28s. and get 30s., and it may be sold perhaps by the linendraper for £3 3s. or £3 10s. Of course we're obliged to work in the slightest manner possible, but good or bad, there's the same fault found with the article. I have already lost 3½ hours, and there's my wife anxiously looking for my return to buy bread and a bit of beast's head for to-morrow—it's hard to go without a bit of meat on Sundays—and indeed I must sell, at whatever price, it don't matter, and that the linendraper depends upon."

An elderly man whom I found at work with his four sons, all grown up, or nearly so, in a good sized room, gave me the following account:—

"I've been 45 years a cabinet-maker, and indeed was born one, as my father before me was one, but I was put to learn my trade with my uncle. I've worked all those years in London, except nine that I was abroad. I was away in his Majesty's service. You see I had a taste for a roving life, so when I'd been two years more at the trade I ran away, and got service on board the Redwing, sloop of war. That was easy enough done in them days. I didn't much like the service. There was lots of flogging. I got my liberty at nine years' end, and I was pretty well sobered by that time. I went back to work at my own business, and as I'd been more used to table making than anything else I stuck to that, and got employment chiefly in making Pembroke tables, doing other work now and then, but I had relations in the trade, and so did better than I could otherways. At that time I had 9s. a piece for 'Pembrokes,' and found nothing but tools. All the material was given me, and 3d. was allowed for glue. I could make by working hard six a week—I make them at my own place. 20 years ago things continued good; there was no slaughter-houses then that I know'd of. I worked only for regular cabinet-makers, or cabinet-brokers. The 'polsterers (Upholsterers) too, then did little or nothing beyond fitting up bed hangings and curtains, and such like. Now they go for everything. Perhaps it's 15 years ago when things began to decline. I still work at

Pembrokes and must work from six to eight and later to get 18s. for my labour, where I did get 54s. in a week—that's just a third. I could in the old times give my children good schooling and good meals, and all right every way. Now children has to be put to work very young. I have four sons working for me. I never had any 'prentices; I never had any journeymen either; indeed you can't get any but some inferior hands not worth 10s. a week. I pay my eldest son 15s. or 16s. a week, because he's married and lives away from me. The others I don't pay anything regular to, but I keep them and find them all they want. Altogether we do pretty well, but I couldn't do so well if I hadn't my family at work. They've never made anything but Pembrokes. I know it's a bad plan. I know it's bringing them up to knock under to the slaughterhouses, but I can't help it. They couldn't live on anything else when I'm gone. I was very badly off till one and a half or on to two years back, when I came into possession of a little money, and that kept me from sinking, as I could buy materials better, and, bless you, the slaughterers soon found that out, and didn't try it on with me so much when I wasn't so depending on 'em. Oh, they're a bad crew. Now, I may take six Pembroke tables of solid mahogany—all mahogany—to a slaughterer's in ——, and ask 18s. a-piece for them, and at that price I couldn't make more than 18s. a week at them, and work long hours every day, without losing time in hawking. Well, the slaughterer will offer 12s.—that's his standing price. He knows they're not bread and water to a man at that, but what does *he* care? He depends upon a man's being hard up. Why, before I got my bit of a rise, I've waited at his door two or three hours, and then had a blackguard price offered me, and was sometimes forced to take it. We can't pawn our goods now; they won't take them. He keeps men waiting just to get things at his own price; they keep open late on purpose to catch us. Now look you here, sir, as to a Pembroke for 12s. I find all the material, everything, myself, same as others—in course solid mahogany. The material costs 9s. or 10s., and a man working hard may make three a week. Now, how's he to live honestly if he must sell at 12s. a table?"

Such is the statement of what may be called "the family worker" of the garret-masters. I now subjoin a statement of another garret-master—a maker of loo tables—who was endeavouring to make a living by means of a number of apprentices:—

"I'm now 41," he said, "and for the last ten or twelve years have been working for a linen-draper, who keeps a slaughterhouse. Before that I was in a good shop, Mr. D——'s, and was a general hand, as we are in the fair trade. I have often made my 50s. a week on good work of any kind—tables, drawers, or cheffoniers. Now, with three apprentices to help me, I may make 25s. Work grew slack, and rather than do nothing, as I'd saved a little money, I made loo tables, and sold them to a linen-draper, a dozen years back or so; and so somehow I got into the trade. For tables that eighteen years ago I had in a good shop 30s. for making, now 5s. is paid, but that's only in a slaughterer's own factory when he has one. Of course it's every way inferior, shockingly scamped, rubbish. I've been told oft enough by a linen-draper, 'Make an inferior article, so as it's cheap. If it comes to pieces in a month, what's that to you or me?' Now, a 4-foot 'loo' is an average, and if for profit and labour, and it's near two days' work, I put on 7s., I'm bid 5s. less. I've been bid less than the stuff, and have on occasions been forced to take it. That was four years ago, and I then found I couldn't possibly live by my own work, and I had a wife and four children to keep. So I got some apprentices. I have now three, and two of them are stiff fellows of 18, and can do a deal of work. I pay them 5s., 7s., and 9s. a-piece a week, and they live at their homes. I'm obliged to do that to live myself, but it's not what I call a fair system—certainly not, but then I was so drove down. For a 4-foot 'loo' I have only £1, though the materials cost from 11s. to 13s., and it's about two days' work. There's not a doubt of it that the linen-drapers have brought bad work into the market, and have swamped the good. They were just gamblers in the trade when they began, but now they go on by system. For in their own shops a very inferior quality, both in stuff, substance, and workmanship is used to what was used eight or ten years back. For work that ten or twelve years ago I had £3 5s. to £3 10s. from them I have now 30s. Of course it's inferior in quality in proportion, but it doesn't pay me half as well. I know that men like me are cutting one another's throats by competition. Fourteen years ago we ought to have made a stand against this system; but then we must live."

A *drawer maker*, a young man working in the same room as a furniture tassel turner, gave me the following information:—

"I served my time to a drawer maker, a small master (he had nine apprentices), and I then started as a small master myself. I make only drawers or wardrobes, or anything in the drawer line, but I can take a turn at tables, but it don't suit out of one's own line. I make drawers, and hawk them to the slaughterhouses. I can make 12s. a week with luck, and by cutting away hard. I've been six years this way, and can't get a penny ahead. This drawers that I'm at work on now is a 3ft. 6in. It's a cheap deal for japanning. I must first go and buy my stuff at the timber-yard, and it'll cost me 10s. 6d., and it'll take me two days to make it, and I'll ask 16s. 6d. for it at a slaughterhouse, and can hardly get it if I lose half a day over it. I'm always bid less than I ask at a slaughterer's, and I have been offered less than the price of the stuff, and that the slaughterers knew well enough, and I have been forced to take it. I've wanted many a meal's victuals. When I've had to sell for less than the stuff cost, I had to begin next week on a smaller article, say a wash-hand stand, or any little thing with drawers, and, as I may, raise money to get drawer stuff again. For journeywork at drawer making for a little master a man may get 5s. or 5s. 6d. for a 3ft. 6in., or two days' labour. But it's so seldom a journeyman's wanted by a little master, that a journeyman, if he can work at all, must be a little master himself, like me, and hawk like me. A veneered mahogany chest of drawers, 3ft. 6in., sides and top and all veneered, will cost me 20s. for material, or 18s. for inferior stuff, and it's good 2½ days' work, and I can only get 30s. for it at a slaughterer's, and sometimes only 25s. If it rains while I'm on the busk (hawking) I can't get so much by 5s., for wet spoils the appearance of the article. I've known slaughterhouse men beg and pray for a wet Saturday. I'm married, but as yet have no family. My wife works for a slop tailor, and may make 3s. 6d. a week."

A pale young man, working in a room with two others, but in different branches, gave me the following account:—

"I have been two years making looking-glass frames. Before that I was in the general cabinet line, but took to this when I was out of work. I make frames only. The slaughter-houses put in the glasses themselves. If I had other work I couldn't afford to lose time by going from one to another that I wasn't so quick at. I make all sizes of frames, from nine-sevens to twenty-four-eighteens (9 inches by 7, and 24 inches by 18). Nine-sevens is most in demand, and the slaughter-houses give 10s. 6d. a dozen for them; two years back they gave 15s. All sizes has fallen 3s. to 4s. a dozen. I find all the material; it's mahogany veneered over deal. There's only five or six slaughter-houses in my way; but I serve the Italians or Jews, and they serve the slaughter-houses. There's no foreigners employed as I'm employed; it's not foreign competition as harms us, it's home. I always ask more than I mean to take, for I'm always bid less than a fair price, and so we haggle on to a bargain. The best weeks I have had I cleared 25s.; but in slack times, when I can hardly sell at all, only 12s. Carrying the goods for sale is such a loss of time. Things are very bad now, but I must go on making, and get a customer when trade's brisker, if I can. Glass has rose 1s. a foot, and that's made a slack in the trade, for my trade depends greatly on the glass trade. Things get worse and worse. I know of no women employed in my trade, and no apprentices. We are all little masters."

A hale-looking elderly man, with a good open countenance, who was working in a decent garret in Hoxton, gave me information concerning his trade as a *Wood-carver:*—

"I've known the trade as a worker at it," he said, "for 49 years— I'm now turned 60. I served my time with my father, and gave him £2 a week to be my own master the last year of my apprenticeship, but he was to keep and clothe me. That year I made almost every week £2 5s. When I was my own master I made from 40s. to 50s. a week, at not very hard work, the year through—7s. a day was then a regular thing, and more for better hands. Twenty years back things got worse. I have worked both at Gothic and other things, but 15 years or so back I could not work as I once could for the West-end; so I came here, and am now chiefly on chair carving, and earn from 12s. to 18s. a week—just as there's a call for my work. They can't work at the East-end as they can at the West. It's like a blackguard trying to be a gentleman. So here I'm a topper. We have no scale of prices—men grasp at anything they can get—and no society. When I'm past work I've only the parish to look to. I did belong to a benefit club, but it failed. I now get one meat dinner where I did get six. I can't make out how it's all come to pass. I'm no politician, and I never was. If I could be a gatekeeper or anything that way, at 15s. a week, wouldn't I give up my tools?"

I shall now proceed to the other branch of the trade. The remarks I have made concerning the wretched social condition and earnings of the fancy cabinet makers who are "in society," apply even more strongly to the *non-society men.* The society men are to be found chiefly in Clerkenwell—the non-society men in Spitalfields and Bethnal-green. With these unfortunate workmen there is yet a lower deep. The under-paid men of Clerkenwell work generally "to order," if the payment be never so inadequate. But the still more underpaid men of Spitalfields work almost universally on speculation. They supply the "slaughter-houses," as they designate the large warehouses at the East-end, where every kind of fancy cabinet work is sold, alike for the supply of the retail dealers in town, and in all parts of the United Kingdom (many of these warehousemen sending out travellers), and for exportation. The proprietors of these establishments very rarely give an order, and if they do (as is shown in a narrative I have given), it is hardly an advantage to the makers. The Spitalfields Cabinet-maker finds his own material, which he usually purchases of the great cabinet-makers or the pianoforte-makers, being the veneers which are the refuse of their work. The deal required can be "picked up," as it was worded to me, "at any shop." The poor fellow thus loses time in finding out the cheapest marts; and, if the wood be deficient in quality, the article is pretty certain of rejection at a warehouse. The supply of the East-end warehousemen is derived from "little masters"—men who work at their own abodes, and have the assistance of their wives and children. It is very rarely that they, or their equally underpaid fellows in the general cabinet trade, employ an active journeyman. Almost every man in the trade works on his own account, finds his own material, and goes "on the busk to the slaughter-houses"—that is, hawks his goods to the warehouses for the chance of a customer. There are, however, a few journeymen to be engaged, but as they are generally little masters as well as journeymen, they know that their services are required only upon an emergency, and they demand a payment which is considered equivalent to their employer's earnings. When at the busiest they demand 15s. a week. The old and the sickly, however, are glad to be employed as journeymen at the barest remuneration—at piece-work labour which may leave them 5s. or 6s. a week. "This is how it is," said a tea-caddy maker to me; "I don't like to put on a hextra hand ven the varehouses is brisk, because they may turn on me any time and say, 'Not vanted, not at all,' just as I've taken in my goods and expects sale and pay. If I don't sell, I can't pay my journeymen, and that the slaughter 'ouses knows, and so they pulls up stiff and von't buy if there's a notion it's a try on in a brisk time."

I found these fancy cabinet-makers certainly an uninformed class, but patient, temperate, and resigned. Some few could neither read nor write, and their families were growing up as uninformed as the parents. The hawking from door to door of workboxes made by some of the men themselves, their wives assisting them with hawking, was far commoner than it is now, but it is still practised to a small extent.

An elderly man, with a heavy careworn look, whom I found at work with his wife and family, gave me the following information concerning his occupation as *a little master*. He was then engaged in making tea-caddies, his wife and daughter being engaged in "lining" work-boxes for the husband's next employment. They resided in a large room, a few steps underground, in a poor part of Spitalfields. It was very light, from large windows both back and front, and was very clean. A large bed stood in the centre, and what few tables and chairs there were were old and mean, while the highly-polished rosewood tea-caddies, which were placed on a bare deal table, showed in startling contrast with all the worn furniture around. The wife was well-spoken and well-looking; and the daughter, who was also well-looking, had that almost painful look of precocity which characterises those whose childhood is one of toil:—

"I have been upwards of 40 years a fancy cabinet-maker," the man said, "making tea-caddies and everything in the line. When I first worked on my own account I could earn £3 a week. I worked for the trade then, for men in the toy, or small furniture, or cabinet line only. There was no slaughter-shops in those days. And good times continued till about 21 years ago, or not so much. I can't tell exactly, but it was when the slaughter-houses came up. Before that, on a Saturday night, I could bring home, after getting my money, a new dress for my wife, for I was just married then, and something new for the children when they came, and a good joint for Sunday. Such a thing as a mechanic's wife doing needlework for any but her own family wasn't heard of then, as far as I know. There was no slop needlewomen in the wives of my trade. It's different now. They must work some way or other. Me and my father before me, for he brought me up to the business, used to supply honourable tradesmen at a fair price, finding our own material; all the family of us is in the trade, but there was good times then. This part didn't then swarm with slaughter-houses, as it does now. I think there's fifty at this end of the town. I have to work harder than ever. Sometimes I don't know how to lie down of a night to rest best, from tiredness. The slaughtermen give less and less. My wife and family help me, or I couldn't live. I have only one daughter now at home, and she and my wife line the work-boxes as you see. I have to carry out my goods now, and have for 15 years or more hawked to the slaughter-houses. I carried them out on a sort of certainty, or to order, before that. I carry them out complete, or I needn't carry them out at all. I've now been on tea-caddies, 12-

inch, with raised tops. The materials—rosewood veneers, deal, locks, hinges, glue, and polish—cost me £1 for a dozen. I must work hard and very long hours, 13 or more a day, to make two dozen a week, and for them I only get at the warehouse 28s. a dozen, if I can sell them there. That's 16s. a week for labour. Sometimes I'm forced to take 25s.—that's 10s. a week for labour. Sometimes I bring them back unsold. Workboxes is no better pay, though my wife and daughter line them. If I get an order—and that's very seldom, not once a year—for a number of tea-caddies, I must take them in at a certain time, because they're mostly for shipping, and so I must have some help. But I can't get a journeyman to help me unless I can show him he'll make 15s. a week, because he knows I just want him for a turn, and can't do without him, and so the profit goes off. Old men can't work quick enough. They may be employed when there's no particular hurry. If I'm not to time with a shipping order, it's thrown on my hands. The slaughter-house men will often say to my asking 28s. for a dozen caddies, 'Oh, we don't want them; and we can get better at 25s.; but we don't mind giving you that.' Many a time, when trade's been very slack, I've had 20s. offered, or 19s., which is less than the stuff cost. They knew that, but say they must make their harvest. And they know well enough that we have no society, and no benefit fund, and nothing to look to but the workhouse. I have to buy my materials at the great cabinet-makers and at the pianoforte-makers, such as is over in their work—the odds and ends. If any of the veneer's flawed the slaughterer won't have it—it's flung on my hands, as many an article is, for pretended faults. No man on my earnings, which is 15s. some weeks, and 10s. others, and less sometimes, can bring up a family as a family ought to be brought up. Many a time I've had to pawn goods that I couldn't sell on a Saturday night to rise a Sunday's dinner." "Yes, indeed," interposed the wife, "look you here, sir; here's forty or fifty duplicates (producing them) of goods in pawn. If ever we shall get them out, Lord above knows." "Yes, sir," said the man, taking up a ticket, "and look at this. Here you see the pawnbroker has lent me 2s. 6d. on this box. It's such as is sold in cheap shops at 5s. 6d. Well, after walking my feet off, I couldn't get more than 24s. a dozen offered at a slaughter-house. That's 2s. a piece, and I got 2s. 6d. at a pawn-shop. And here's another; it was the largest size, and the pawnbroker lent 5s. 6d. on it; more than I could get offered at a slaughter-house; though in Lowther Arcade, such an one will be marked 22s. 6d., just with the addition of a glass basin, which costs only 1s. wholesale. I haven't any apprentices; it wouldn't suit me, because I haven't any sure sale for my goods. The men that has apprentices is either slaughterers, or people they keep going."

This man sent his daughter to show me a house I had next to call at, but had not been able to ascertain the number. She was quick, but told me she could neither read nor write. She couldn't spare time to learn if she could be taught for nothing. She was eleven, and worked at the lining, and could work, she thought, as well as her mother. She had been thus working since she was six years old.

I called on an old couple to whom I was referred as to one of the few parties employed in working for the men who supplied the warehouses. The man's appearance was gaunt and wretched. He had been long unshorn, and his light blue eyes had that dull half-glazed look which is common to the old when spirit-broken and ill-fed. His room—a small garret in Spitalfields, for which he paid 1s. 3d. a week—was bare of furniture, except his workbench and two chairs, which were occupied by his wife, who was at work lining the boxes her husband was making. A blanket rolled up was the poor couple's bed. The wife was ten years younger than her husband. She was very poorly clad, in an old rusty black gown, tattered here and there, but she did not look very feeble.

"I am 63," the man said—and he looked 80—"and was apprenticed in my youth to the fancy cabinet trade. I could make £4 4s. a week at it, by working long hours, when I was out of my time, forty-two years back. I have worked chiefly on workboxes. I didn't save money—I was foolish, but it was a hard living, and hard drinking time. I'm sorry for it now. Thirty years ago things weren't quite so good, but still very good, and so they was twenty years back. But since the slaughter-houses came in men like me has been starving—starving as we makes good work for rich people. Why here, sir, for a rosewood workbox, like this, which I shall get 6d. for making, I used to give a brother of mine 6s. 6d. for making twenty years ago. I've been paid 22s. 6d. twenty years ago for what I now get 2s. 6d. for. The man who employs me now works for a slaughter-house, and he must grind me down, or he couldn't serve a slaughter-house cheap enough. He finds materials, and I find tools and glue, and I have 6s. a dozen for making these boxes, and I can only make a dozen a week, and the glue and other odds and ends for them costs me 6d. a dozen. That, with 9d. or 10d. a week, or 1s., that my wife may make, as she helps me in lining, is all we have to live on. We live entirely on tea and bread and butter, when we can get butter. Never any change—tea, and nothing else, all day; never a bit of meat on a Sunday. As for beer, I haven't spent 4s. on it these last four years. When I'm not at work for a little master I get stuff of one, and make a few boxes on my own account, and carry them out to be sold. I have often to go three or four miles with them; for there's a house near Tottenham-court-road that will take a few from me generally out of charity. When I'm past work, or can't meet with any, there's nothing but the workhouse for me."

The Morning Chronicle, Thursday, August 15, 1850.

To the EDITOR of the MORNING CHRONICLE.

Sir—As your next Letter on "Labour and the Poor," in reference to the cabinet-making trade, will doubtless give many more important facts, allow me to give you a few lines of truth, in case such have not already been supplied to you.

I presume that the practice of houses in dealing with poor artisans will be fully exposed, as the mode of "grinding down" these poor men (and women too) is so disgraceful.

It is the habit of many of these poor industrious people to wait humbly for hours at the houses of these "slop capitalists," thus making their loss still greater than the already wretchedly diminished price given for the goods, which, although not of the first quality, yield an enormous profit to the purchasers, who in many instances arrogate to themselves much conscientiousness, but by their conduct appear to have entirely forgotten those precious words, "Blessed is he who considereth the poor."

I hope your information on this part of the subject is complete, as there are the most bitter oppressions exercised in this way that the human imagination can conceive, and this too frequently by houses of whom better things might be expected. I could detail (from personal observation) much of this, but if you think any extract from this worth your introduction in the next letter, it may perhaps reach the eye and soften the heart of some of the covetous ones who need improvement in this particular.

I am, sir, your obedient servant,

London, Aug. 12.   VERITAS.

The Morning Chronicle, Tuesday, August 20, 1850.

FRIENDLY ASSOCIATION OF LONDON COSTERMONGERS.

A "supper and ball," the first of a series of projected entertainments in aid of the funds of this institution, took place yesterday evening at the City Working Man's Hall, 26, Golden-lane, Barbican. The plan of the originators of these *soirées* appeared manifold in its design, and, so far, seems likely to be successful in its issue. They propose to make their gatherings sufficiently attractive to draw the costermongers from the public-house, to afford them elsewhere amusements at once innocent and elevating, yet not above their capacity of enjoyment; and, last not least, to divert the profits which now flow into the till of the publican to the treasury of the costermongers' own Provident Association. The attendance yesterday, notwithstanding intoxicating liquors were altogether prohibited, was very numerous. About a hundred men and women were present at the supper, and others arrived before the commencement of the ball. Mr. Henry Mayhew occupied the chair.

The supply of edibles was liberal in quantity as well as unexceptionable in quality, whilst the trifling deficiency in the serving, which might have been detected by the fastidious, only tended to illustrate the doctrine which the speakers were assembled to teach—that the working classes must, if they wanted helping, always be ready first to help themselves. Huge joints of beef, mutton, and veal were before them; it was their own fault if they did not get their share. Grace was said by the Rev. Mr. Larken, who is one of the committee of the association. Then, like Milton's angels, "down they sat, and to their viands fell, nor seemingly, but with the keen despatch of real hunger." Mr. Mayhew, though chairman, prudently left the carving to a "vice," whose office was no sinecure. At last, however, there appeared a visible diminution in the joints, and a perceptible decrease in the appetites of their consumers, to whom pudding, of which there was plenty, evidently became a subject of philosophic contempt and indifference. The conversational hiatus, usually occurring during the removal of the cloth, was admirably filled up by a Polish refugee, who sang the "Marseillaise" with great spirit amongst the choruses of the audience; and so began the lighter pleasures of the evening. The supper, it must be mentioned, went off most happily, its conviviality being just sufficient to remove restraint, without encouraging the slightest indecorum. Short speeches, characteristic songs, and animated dances came next in order. Several costermongers and working men, amongst whom were Messrs. Salmon, Leno, and Osborne, advocated "sentiments," which appeared to be teetotal toasts, and were as follows:—"The people: May they accomplish their permanent elevation by their mild and persevering efforts for self-improvement." "The Friendly Association of London Costermongers: May they be successful in their praiseworthy attempts to improve the condition of themselves and their families." "Henry Mayhew and the other gen-

tlemen who have so nobly come forward to assist the costermongers:
May they have all the reward they seek, namely, in the consciousness
of having done something to assist their suffering brethren."

A list of subscriptions was also announced. It included donations
from Lord Dudley Coutts Stuart, M.P., Earl Stanhope, Mr. Bright,
M.P., Mr. Evelyn, M.P., Sir Benjamin Hall, M.P., Mr. Wyld, M.P.,
Mr. Charles Knight, Mr. Charles Cochrane, &c.

Mothers, wives, and sweethearts had honoured the proceedings
with their attendance; so, of course, the "ball" part of the entertain-
ment was not forgotten. Between the speeches and the songs came
always an interlude for the ladies, consisting of dances sufficiently ob-
solete to look altogether original. Resuscitated hornpipes, jigs, and
country dances of the last century were gone through with a spirit
which made up for the want of grace in the performers, whose happiness grew so infectious that at last the platform was deserted by its oc-
cupants, who were soon seen whirling, like every one else, in the body
of the hall. The only incident which marred the evening's enjoyment
was the entry at a late hour of two noisy and drunken fellows, styling themselves costermongers, who claimed the right of interrupting
the proceedings, and were for some time permitted to obstruct their
fellows. Not content, however, with talking, they began to swear,
when a young man got up, and asked, in great indignation, whether
such language was to be allowed before the sisters, wives, and sweethearts of those who composed the meeting? Mr. George Cruikshank,
who was among the number of the visitors, also spoke, and, declaring
himself a tee-totaller of three years' and-a-half standing, attributed
the behaviour of the intruders to their evident intoxication, and took
occasion to make a few appropriate remarks on the use of stimulating
liquors. The disturbers were ultimately expelled, and peace restored.
Ginger-beer being the strongest drink allowed in the house, this incident was one for which the meeting was in no way responsible. On
the contrary, the general tone of the conversation, and style of the
deportment of all present, went to prove most forcibly that it is nothing but the want of better amusements which now drives the poorer
classes into pleasures at once expensive and degrading.

The evening went off most pleasantly, and with the utmost propriety. The funds of the institution were by its means increased; and
this experiment having proved successful, "suppers and balls" may be
expected in many other parts of the metropolis.

LABOUR AND THE POOR.

THE METROPOLITAN DISTRICTS.

[FROM OUR SPECIAL CORRESPONDENT.]

OF THE "GARRET MASTERS" OF THE CABINET TRADE.

Letter LXVI.

The decline which has taken place within the last 20 years in the wages of the operative Cabinet-makers of London is so enormous, and, moreover, it seems so opposed to the principles of political economy, that it becomes of the highest importance, in an inquiry like the present, to trace out the circumstances to which this special depreciation is to be attributed. It has been before shown that the number of hands belonging to the London cabinet trade decreased, between 1831 and 1841, 33 per cent. in comparison with the rest of the metropolitan population; and that, notwithstanding this falling off, the workmen's wages in 1831 were at least four hundred per cent. better than they are at present—20s. having formerly been paid for the making of articles for which now only 5s. is given. To impress this fact, however, the more strongly upon the reader's mind, I will here cite a few of the many instances of depreciation that have come to my knowledge. "Twenty years ago," said a workman in the fancy cabinet line, "I had 6d. an inch for the making of 20-inch desks of solid mahogany—that's 10s. for the entire article; now I get 2s. 3d. for the same thing. Smaller desks used to average to us 6s. each for wages— now they don't bring us more than 1s. Ladies' 12-inch workboxes twenty years ago were 3s. 6d. and 4s. a piece making, now they are 5d. for the commoner sort, and 7d. for those with better work." "I don't understand per cents.," said another workman, "but this I *do* know, the prices that I get have within these 20 years fallen from 4s. to 5d., and in some cases to 4½d."

Here, then, we find that wages in the competitive portion of the cabinet trade—that is, among the "*non-society* hands" (the wages of the "*society*" men, I have before explained, are regulated, or rather *fixed*, by custom), were twenty years ago 400 per cent. better in some cases, and in others no less than 900 per cent. higher, than they are at present; and this while the number of workmen has decreased as much as one-third relatively to the rest of the population. How, then, is this extraordinary diminution in the price of labour to be accounted for? Certainly not on the natural assumption that the quantity of work has declined in a still greater proportion than the number of hands to do it; for it has also been proved that the number of new houses built annually in the metropolis, and therefore the quantity of new furniture required, has of late years increased very considerably.

In the Cabinet Trade, then, we find a collocation of circumstances at variance with that law of supply and demand by which many suppose that the rate of wages is invariably determined. "Wages," it is said, "depend upon the demand and supply of labour," and it is commonly assumed that they cannot be affected by anything else. That they *are*, however, subject to other influences, the history of the cabinet trade for the last twenty years is a most convincing proof; for there we find that, while the quantity of work, or, in other words, the demand for labour has increased, and the supply decreased, wages—instead of rising—have suffered a heavy decline. By what means, then, is this reduction in the price of labour to be explained? What other circumstance is there, affecting the remuneration for work, of which economists have usually omitted to take cognizance? The answer is, that wages depend as much on the distribution of labour as on the demand and supply of it. Assuming a certain quantity of work to be done, the amount of remuneration coming to each of the workmen engaged must, of course, be regulated, not only by the number of hands, but by the proportion of labour done by them respectively; that is to say, if there be work enough to employ the whole of the operatives for sixty hours a week, and if two-thirds of the hands are supplied with sufficient to occupy them for ninety hours in the same space of time, then one-third of the trade must be thrown wholly out of employment; thus proving that there may be surplus labour without any increase of the population. It may therefore be safely asserted that any system of labour which tends to make the members of a craft produce a greater quantity of work than usual, tends at the same time to overpopulate the trade as certainly as an increase of workmen. This law may be summed up briefly in the expression that *over-work makes under-pay.*

Hence the next point in the inquiry is as to the means by which the productiveness of operatives is capable of being extended. There are many modes of effecting this; some of these have been long known to students of political economy, while others have been made public for the first time in these letters. Under the former class are included the division and co-operation of labour, as well as the "large system of production;" and to the latter belongs the "strapping system," by which men are made to get through four times as much work as usual, and which I described in Letter LXI. But the more effectual means of increasing the productiveness of labourers is found to consist, not in any system of supervision, however cogent—nor in any limitation of the operations performed by the workpeople to the smallest possible number—nor in the apportionment of the different parts of the work to the different capabilities of the operatives; but in connecting the workman's interest directly with his labour, that is to say, by making the amount of his earnings depend upon the quantity of work done by him. This is ordinarily effected in manufacture by means of what is called piece-work. "Almost all who work by the day, or for a fixed salary, that is to say, those who labour for the gain of others, not for their own, have," it has been well remarked, "no interest in doing more than the smallest quantity of work that will pass as a fulfilment of the mere terms of their engagement. Owing to the insufficient interest which day labourers have in the result of their labour, there is a natural tendency in such labour to be extremely inefficient—a tendency only to be overcome by vigilant superintendence (such as is carried on under the strapping system among the joiners) on the part of the persons who *are* interested in the result. The 'master's eye' is notoriously the only security to be relied on. But superintend them as you will, day labourers are so much inferior to those who work by the piece, that, as was before said, the latter system is practised in all industrial occupations where the work admits of being put out in definite portions, without involving the necessity of too troublesome a surveillance to guard against inferiority (or scamping) in the execution." But if the labourer at piece work is made to produce a greater quantity than at day work, and this solely by connecting his own interest with that of his employer, how much more largely must the productiveness of workmen be increased when labouring wholly on their own account. Accordingly it has been invariably found that whenever the operative unites in himself the double function of capitalist and labourer, making up his own materials or working on his own property, his productiveness, single-handed, is considerably greater than can be attained even under the large system of production where all the arts and appliances of which extensive capital can avail itself are brought into operation.

Of the industry of working masters or trading operatives in manufactures there are as yet no authentic accounts; we have, however, ample records concerning the indefatigability of their agricultural counterparts—the peasant proprietors of Tuscany, Switzerland, Germany, and other countries where the labourers are the owners of the soil they cultivate. "In walking anywhere in the neighbourhood of Zurich," says Inglis, in his work on Switzerland, the south of France, and the Pyrenees, "one is struck with the extraordinary industry of the inhabitants ... When I used to open my casement between four and five in the morning to look out upon the lake and the distant Alps, I saw the labourer in the fields; and when I returned from an evening walk long after sunset—as late, perhaps, as half-past eight—there was the labourer mowing his grass or tying up his vines." The same state of things exists among the French peasantry, under the same circumstances. "The industry of the small proprietors," says Arthur Young, in his "Travels in France," "was so conspicuous and so meritorious, that no commendation would be too great for it. It was sufficient to prove that property in land is of all others the most active instigator to severe and incessant labour." If then this principle of working for oneself has been found to increase the industry, and consequently the productiveness, of labourers to such an extent in agriculture, it is but natural that it should be attended with the same results in manufactures, and that we should find the "small masters," like the "peasant proprietors," toiling longer and working quicker than labourers serving others rather than themselves. But there is an important distinction to be drawn between the produce of the "peasant proprietor" and that of the "small master." Toil as diligently as the little farmer may, since he cultivates the soil not for profit, but as a means of subsistence, and his produce contributes *directly* to his support, it follows that his comforts must be increased by his extra production, or, in other words, that the more he labours the more food he obtains. The small master, however, producing what he cannot eat, must carry his goods to market and exchange them for articles of consumption; hence, by overtoil, he lowers the market against himself, that is to say, the more *he* labours the *less* food he ultimately obtains; and this is true the more especially of the artificers of those articles the demand for which is limited, and the lowering of the price of which, therefore, by any extra supply, is not necessarily attended with any increased desire for it on the part of the community. Whether there will be a greater permanent supply of a commodity after its production has been cheapened, depends on the question whether or not a greater quantity is wanted at the reduced value. "But there are many articles," says Mr. De Quincey, "for which the market is absolutely and merely limited by a pre-existing system to which those articles are attached as subordinate parts or members." The demand for cabinet work, for example, must invariably be regulated by the quantity of new houses built in the kingdom. It is impossible to find a sale for more tables and chairs, sofas and cheffoniers, than there are rooms to hold them. Hence it is evident that in a trade where the supply cannot be extended beyond a certain limit, any circumstances tending to stimulate the labourer to further production cannot but tend at the same time to deprive others of work, or else so to increase the supply beyond the power of disposing of it, that the harder the workmen slave the less they will get for their labour.

But not only is it true that overwork makes underpay, but the converse of the proposition is equally true, that underpay makes overwork—that is to say, it is true of those trades where the system of piece-work or small mastership admits of the operative doing the utmost amount of work that he is able to accomplish; for the workman in such cases seldom or never thinks of reducing his expenditure to his income, but rather of increasing his labour, so as still to bring his income, by extra production, up to his expenditure. This brings us to another important distinction which it is necessary to make between the peasant proprietor and the small master. The little farmer cannot increase his produce by devoting a less amount of labour to each of the articles—that is to say, he cannot scamp his work without diminishing his future stock. There is no cheating nature by palming off inferior workmanship as equal to the most skilful. Agriculture has at least one great advantage over manufacture—it is impossible to have any slop-work in it. A given quantity of labour must be used to obtain a given amount of produce. None of the details can be omitted without a diminution of the result—"scamp" the ploughing, and there will be a smaller crop. It is the same with the employment of bad materials as with slovenly labour: use inferior seed or manure, and the produce is decreased, not only in quality, but in quantity too. In manufactures, however, the result is very different. There, one of the principal means of increasing the productions of a particular trade, and of the cabinet trade especially, is by decreasing the amount of work in each article; indeed, it is one of the necessary consequences of all *interested* labour, such as piecework and small mastership, where the operative's earnings depend upon the quantity of articles made by him rather than the time he has been employed upon them, that it necessarily leads to "scamp work"—that is to say, to the omission of all such details as can be left out without the inferiority of the workmanship being detected. Hence, in such cases all kinds of schemes and impositions are resorted to to make the unskilled labour appear equal to the skilled, and thus the market is glutted with slop productions till the honourable part of the trade, both workmen and employers, are ultimately obliged to resort to the same tricks as the rest. We find that, as the wages of a trade descend, so do the labourers extend their hours of work to the utmost possible limits—they not only toil earlier and later than before, but the Sunday becomes a work-day like the rest (amongst the sweaters of the tailoring trade Sunday labour, as I have shown, is almost universal); and when the hours of work are carried to the extreme of human industry, then more is sought to be done in a given space of time, either by the employment of the members of their own family, or apprentices, upon the inferior portion of the work, or else by "scamping it." "My employer," I was told by a journeyman tailor working for a large West-end show shop, "reduces my wages one-third, and the consequence is, I put in two stitches where I used to give three." "I must work from six to eight and later," said a Pembroke table-maker to me, "to get 18s. now for my labour where I used to get 54s. a week—that's just a third. I could in the old times give my children good schooling and good meals. Now children have to be put to work very young. I have four sons working for me at present." Not only, therefore, does any stimulus to extra production make overwork, and overwork make underpay, but underpay, by becoming an additional provocative to increased industry, again gives rise in its turn to overwork—so that, the wages of a trade once reduced, there appears to be no means of predicting to what point they shall ultimately descend.

Let us now seek to apply these principles to the reduction of prices which has lately obtained among the competitive portion of the cabinet trade. In the first place it should be observed that almost every craft suffers from some system of labour peculiar to itself. The wages of a few, for instance, are found to be depressed below subsistence point, because their labour is brought into competition with that of paupers and criminals, whose subsistence is supplied them by the State. Others, again, do not obtain a fair living price for their work because, as in the case of the needleworkers and other domestic manufacturers, their livelihood is supposed to be provided for them by the husband or father, and hence the remuneration is viewed rather as an aid to the family income than as an absolute means of support. The ballast-heavers and lumpers again were found not to be suffering so much from the depression of wages, as from a compulsory system of drinking for the benefit of their employer—the publican. The evil of the tailors' trade, on the other hand, was the sweating or middleman system, by which one operative traded on the toil of another. The carpenters and joiners were labouring under a similar grievance, viz., the letting and sub-letting of work. The sawyers had been deprived of employment by the introduction of machinery. The bane of the dock labourers was the uncertainty of their work—their living being at the mercy of the winds to such an extent that an easterly breeze prevailing for a week was sufficient to deprive thousands of their bread. The street sellers, on the other hand (numbering 20,000), were often reduced to starvation by a few days' continuous rain; and now we find the cabinetmakers, like the boot and shoemakers, depressed by the increase of "small masters"—that is to say, by a class of workmen possessed of just sufficient capital to buy their own materials, and to support themselves while making them up. I purpose, therefore, inquiring more minutely than I have yet done into the history of this order of operatives—the motives for their passing from the state of *employés* into that of "masters," as well as the facilities for their so doing—their usual time of labour, together with the quantity of work they do, and the quality of it—the nature of the "helps" they employ when they require extra hands—their dependence in sickness and old age—the time lost in finding purchasers for their goods—and lastly, the effect they have had, and are likely still to have, upon the more honourable part of the trade.

First, then, as to the history of "small," or, as they are frequently called, "garret masters" in the cabinet trade.

Little masters, both in the general and fancy cabinet trade, are now, strictly speaking, the men who purchase the material of the articles they manufacture, and who avail themselves of their own labour, that of their families, not unfrequently that of apprentices, and, very rarely, that of journeymen. In fact, they unite in their own persons the two functions of employer and employed, as they provide their own materials, set themselves to work, and execute the work by their own exertions, with the occasional aids I have mentioned. They work on speculation, carrying their goods, when made, to the "slaughter-houses" for sale. This mode of business was hardly known until about twenty years ago. Prior to that time a little master was a man of limited means, having a front shop for the display of his goods, and a contiguous workshop for their manufacture. He worked usually "to order," and was an employer; but in most cases he worked himself along with those he employed, and in all cases prepared or "cut out" the stuff which his journeymen made into furniture, on his own premises. He employed from two to five journeymen, having the greater number when trade was brisk. These journeymen were non-society men, but they were paid tolerable wages, and always, as now, by the piece, earning from 20s. to 35s. a week; the wages were generally 15 per cent. lower than those of society men. Inferior work was not then the common practice of the little masters. They sold their goods at from 15 to 25 per cent. lower than the great houses. There are still some of these little masters in the cabinet trade, but since the establishment of the warehouses some fifteen years back they have dwindled away to one-fiftieth of their number. Some of them, when business fell off, "worked journeywork" for the better houses; some of the younger men among them emigrated, and some are now working for the "slaughter-houses."

There were also, twenty years ago, a numerous body of tradesmen, who were employers, though not salesmen to the general public, known as "*Trade Working Masters.*" These men, of whom there are still a few, confined their business solely to "supplying the trade." They supplied the greater establishments, where there were "show rooms," with a cheaper article than the proprietors of those greater establishments might be able to have had manufactured on their own premises. They worked not on speculation, but "to order," and were themselves employers; some employed at a busy time from twenty to forty hands, all working on their premises, which were merely adapted for making, and not for selling or "showing" furniture. There are still such "trade working masters," the extent of their business not being a quarter what it was; neither do they now generally adhere to the practice of having men to work on their premises, but they give out the material, which the journeymen make up at their own abodes.

A trade working master, now carrying on that business in the fancy cabinet line, told me that he was about withdrawing himself from it. He worked to order, and always kept a supply of goods for "stock," from which either town or country tradesmen could select whatever they required. He paid fair wages, and dealt only in good articles. Now, however, he assures me that it is impossible to compete with the warehousemen, who purchase of the garret or little masters, and avail themselves of those poor men's necessities. And so my informant is relinquishing the business, as he says it is "not fit for honest men—it is now only fit for scamps and scamping masters."

"About twenty years ago," said an experienced man to me, "I dare say the small masters formed about a quarter of the trade. The slacker trade becomes, the more the small masters increase; that's because they can't get other work to do, and so, rather than starve, they begin to get a little stuff of their own, and make up things for themselves, and sell them as best they can. Anything's better than standing idle and starving, you know. The great increase of the small masters was when trade became so dead. When was it that we used to have to go about so with our things? About five years since wasn't it?" said he, appealing to one of his sons, who was at work in the same room with him. "Yes, father," replied the lad; "just after the railway bubble; nobody wanted anything at all then." The old man continued to say, "The greater part of the men that couldn't get employed at the regular shops then turned to making up things on their own account, and now I should say there's at least one-half working for themselves. About twelve years ago masters wanted to cut the men down, and many of the hands, rather than put up with it, took to making up for theirselves. Whenever there's a decrease of wages there's always an increase of small masters; for it's not until men can't live comfortable by their labour that they take to making things on their own account."

Such, then, is the history of this class of workmen in the Cabinet Trade. Concerning the motives for men to become small masters, I had the following statement from one of the most intelligent workmen belonging to the craft:—

"One of the inducements," he said, "for men to take to making up for themselves is to get a living when thrown out of work until they can hear of something better. If they could get into regular journeywork there a'n't one man as wouldn't prefer it—it would pay them a deal better. Another of the reasons for the men turning small masters is the little capital that it requires for them to start themselves. If a man has got his tools he can begin as a master-man with a couple of shillings. If he goes in for making large tables, then from 30s. to 35s. will do him, and it's the small bit of money it takes to start with in our line that brings many into the trade, who wouldn't be there if more tin was wanted to begin upon. Many works for themselves, because nobody else won't employ them, their work is so bad. Many weavers has took to our business of late. That's quite common now—their own's so bad; and some that used to hawk hearthstones about is turned Pembroke table-makers. The slaughterers don't care what kind of work it is, so long as it's cheap. A table's a table, they say, and that's all we want. Another reason for men turning little masters is because employment's more certain like that way; a man can't be turned off easily, you see, when he works for himself. Again, some men may prefer being small masters because they are more independent like; when they're working for themselves, they can begin working when they please, and knock off whenever they like. But the principal reason is, because there an't enough work at the regular shops to employ them all. The slaughterers have cut down their prices so low that there ain't no work to be had at the better houses, so men must go on making up for the 'butchers' (slaughterers) or starve. Those masters as really would assist the men couldn't do it, because they're dead beat out of the field by the slaughter-houses. There was a large house lately as used to employ sixty men at fair living wages was broke up owing to the master going to the Cape of Good Hope, and then the whole of the men was turned adrift. Well, what was to be done? Some was lucky enough to get into a job, but a good part was obligated to buy a bit of stuff for themselves, and to set to working on their own account. Half a loaf you know is better than no bread at all, and nobody knows that so well as the slaughterers."

I now come to the amount of capital required for an operative Cabinet-maker to begin business on his own account.

To show the readiness with which any youth "out of his time," as it is called, can start in trade as a garret cabinet-master, I have learned the following particulars:—The lad, when not living with his friends, usually occupies a garret, and in this he constructs a rude bench out of old materials, which may cost him 2s. If he be penniless when he ceases to be an apprentice, and can get no work as a journeyman, which is nearly always the case for reasons I have before stated, he assists another garret master to make a bedstead perhaps, and the established garret master carries two bedsteads instead of one to the slaughter house. The lad's share of the proceeds may be about 5s., and out of that, if his needs will permit him, he buys the materials for a small clothes-horse, or any trifling article, and so proceeds by degrees. Many men, to "start themselves," as it is called, have endured, I am informed, something very like starvation most patiently. The tools are generally collected by degrees, and often in the last year of apprenticeship, out of the boy's earnings. They are seldom bought "first hand," but at the marine store shops, or at the second-hand furniture broker's, in such places as the New Cut. The purchaser grinds and sharpens them up at any friendly workman's, where he can meet with the loan of a grindstone, and puts new handles to them himself, out of pieces of waste wood; 10s., or even 5s., thus invested has started a man with tools; while 20s. has accomplished it in what was considered "good style." Old chisels may be bought from 1d., 1½d., 2d., to 5d.; planing irons from 1d. or 1½d. to 3d.; hammer heads from 1d. to 3d.; saws, from 1s. to 2s. 6d., and rules and the other tools equally low. In some cases the friends of the boy, if they are not poverty-stricken, advance him 40s. to 50s. to begin with, and he must then shift for himself. When a bench and tools have been attained, the young master buys such material as his means afford, and sets himself to work. If he has a few shillings to spare, he makes himself a sort of bedstead, and buys a rug and a sheet or a little bedding. If he has not the means to do so, he sleeps on shavings stuffed into an old sack. In some few cases, he hires a bench alongside some other garret-master, but the arrangement of two or three men occupying one room for their labour is more frequent when the garrets where the men sleep are required for their wives' labour in any distinct business, or when the articles the men make are too cumbrous, like wardrobes, to be carried easily down the narrow stairs.

A timber-merchant, part of whose business consists in selling material to little masters, gave me two instances, within his own knowledge, of journeymen "beginning to manufacture on their own account."

A fancy cabinet-maker had 3s. 6d. at his command. With this he purchased material for a desk as follows:—

	s.	d.
3 ft. of solid five-eighths mahogany	1	0
2 ft. of solid three-eighths cedar, for bottom, &c.		6
Mahogany top		3
Bead cedar, for interior		6
Lining		4
Lock and key (no wards to lock)		2
Hinges		1
Glue and sprigs		1½
Lining		4
	3	3½

The making of the desk occupied four hours, as the man bestowed extra pains upon it, and he sold it to a slaughterer for 3s. 6d. He then broke his fast on bread and water, bought material for a second desk, and went to work again, and so he proceeds now; toiling and half-starving, and struggling to get 20s. ahead of the world to buy more wood at one time, and not pause so often in his work. "Perhaps," said my informant, "he'll marry, as the most of the small masters do, some foolish servant of all-work who has saved £3 or £4, and that will be his capital."

Another general cabinet-maker commenced business on 30s., a part of which he thus expended in the material for a 4-foot chest of drawers:—

	s.	d.
Three feet six inches of cedar for ends	4	0
Sets of mahogany veneers for three big and two little drawers	2	4
Drawer sweep (deal to veneer the front upon)	2	6
Veneer for top	1	3
Extras (any cheap wood) for inside of drawers, partitioning, &c.	5	0
Five locks	1	8
Eight knobs, 1s., glue, sprigs, &c.	1	4
Set of four turned feet, beech stained	1	6
	19	7

For the article, when completed, he received 25s., toiling at it for 27 or 28 hours. The tradesman from whom I derived this information, and who was familiar with every branch of the trade, calculated that three-fifths of the working cabinet makers of London make for the warehouses—in other words, that there are three thousand small masters in the trade. The most moderate computation was that the number so employed exceed one half of the entire body of the five thousand metropolitan journeymen.

The next point in this inquiry is concerning the industry and productiveness of this class of workmen. Of over-work, as regards excessive labour, and of over-production from scamped workmanship, I heard the following accounts, which different operatives, both in the general and fancy cabinet trade, concurred in giving; while some represented the labour as of longer duration by at least an hour, and some by two hours, a day than I have stated.

The labour of the men who depend entirely on the slaughter-houses for the purchase of their articles, with all the disadvantages that I described in a former letter, is usually seven days a week the year through. That is, seven days—for Sunday work is all but universal—each of 13 hours, or 91 hours in all; while the established hours of labour in the "honourable trade" are six days of the week, each of 10 hours, or 60 hours in all. Thus 50 per cent. is added to the extent of the production of low-priced cabinet work merely from "over hours;" but in some cases I heard of 15 hours for seven days in the week, or 105 hours in all. The exceptions to this continuous toil are from one hour to three hours once or twice in the week, when the workman is engaged in purchasing his material of a timber merchant, who sells it in small quantities, and from six to eight hours when he is employed in conveying his goods to a warehouse, or from warehouse to warehouse, for sale.

Concerning the hours of labour, I had the following minute particulars from a garret-master who was a chairmaker:—

"I work from six every morning to nine at night; some work till ten. My breakfast at eight stops me for ten minutes. I can breakfast in less time, but it's a rest; my dinner takes me say twenty minutes at the outside, and my tea, eight minutes. All the rest of the time I'm slaving at my bench. How many minutes rest is that, sir? Thirty-eight; well, say three quarters of an hour, and that allows a few sucks at a pipe when I rest; but I can smoke and work too. I have only one room to work and eat in, or I should lose more time. Altogether I labour 14¼ hours every day, and I must work on Sundays—at least forty Sundays in the year. One may as well work as sit fretting. But on Sundays I only work till it's dusk, or till five or six in summer. When it's dusk I take a walk. I'm not well dressed enough for a Sunday walk when it's light, and I can't wear my apron on that day very well to hide patches. But there's eight hours that I reckon I take up every week, one with another, in dancing about to the slaughterers. I'm satisfied that I work very nearly 100 hours a week the year through; deducting the time taken up by the slaughterers, and buying stuff—say eight hours a week—it gives more than 90 hours a week for my work, and there's hundreds labour as hard as I do, just for a crust."

This excessive toil, however, is but one element of over-production. "Scamping," adds at least 200 per cent. to the productions of the cabinet-maker's trade. I have ascertained several cases of this overwork from scamping, and adduce two. A very quick hand, a little master, working, as he called it, "at a slaughtering pace," for a warehouse, made 60 plain writing-desks in a week of 90 hours, while a first-rate workman, also a quick hand, made 18 in a week of 70 hours. The scamping hand said he must work at the rate he did to make 14s. a week from a slaughter house; and so used to such style of work had he become, that, though a few years back he did West-end work in the best style, he could not now make eighteen desks in a week, if compelled to finish them in the style of excellence displayed in the work of the journeyman employed for the honourable trade. Perhaps, he added, he couldn't make them in that style at all. The frequent use of rosewood veneers in the fancy cabinet, and their occasional use in the general cabinet trade gives, I was told, great facilities for scamping. If in his haste the scamping hand injure the veneer, or if it has been originally faulty, he takes a mixture of gum shellac and "colour" (colour being a composition of Venetian red and lamp black), which he has ready by him, rubs it over the damaged part, smooths it with a slightly-heated iron, and so blends it with the colour of the rosewood that the warehouseman does not detect the flaw. Indeed, I was told that very few warehousemen are "judges" of the furniture they bought, and they only require it to look well enough for sale to the public, who knew even less than themselves. In the general cabinet trade I found the same ratio of "scamping," compared with the products of skilled labour in the honourable trade. A good workman made a four-foot mahogany chest of drawers in five days, working the regular hours, and receiving at piece-work price 35s. A scamping hand made five of the same size in a week, and had time to carry them for sale to the warehouses, wait for their purchase or refusal, and buy material. But for the necessity of doing this the scamping hand could have made seven in the 91 hours of his week, of course in a very inferior manner. "They would hold together for a time," I was assured, "and that was all; but the slaughterer cared only to have them viewly and cheap." These two cases exceed the average, and I have cited them to show what *can* be done under the scamping system.

I now come to show how this "scamp work" is executed—that is to say, by what helps or assistants, when such are employed. As in all trades where lowness of wages is the rule, the apprentice system prevails among the cheap cabinet workers. It prevails, however, among the garret masters, by very many of them having one, two, three, or four apprentices, and so the number of boys thus employed through the whole trade is considerable. This refers principally to the general cabinet trade. In the fancy trade the number is greater, as the boys' labour is more readily available; but in this trade the greatest number of apprentices is employed by such warehousemen as are manufacturers, as some at the East-end are—or rather by the men that they constantly keep at work. Of these men, one has now eight and another fourteen boys in his service—some apprenticed, some merely "engaged" and dischargeable at pleasure. A sharp boy, thus apprenticed, in six or eight months becomes "handy;" but four out of five of the workmen thus brought up can do nothing well but their own particular branch, and that only well as far as celerity in production is considered.

In some cases the master takes boys without a fee, and the boy then lives with his parents or friends. For the first two years such an apprentice receives nothing; he is merely instructed. After that he receives half what he earns at piece-work prices. It is these boys who are put to make, or as a master of the better class distinguished it to me, not to *make* but to put together, ladies' workboxes at 5d. a piece, the boy receiving 2½d. a box. "Such boxes," said another workman, "are nailed together; there's no dove-tailing, nothing of what I call *work* or workmanship, as you say about them, but the deal's nailed together, and the veneer's dabbed on, and if the deal's covered, why the thing passes. The worst of it is that people don't understand either good work or good wood. Polish them up and they look well. Besides, and that's another bad thing—for it encourages bad work—there's no stress on a lady's work box, as on a chair or a sofa, and so bad work lasts far too long, though not half so long as good; in solids especially, if not in veneers."

But the usual assistants of the small masters are their own children. Upon this subject I received the following extraordinary statement:—

"The most on us has got large families. We put the children to work as soon as we can. My little girl began about six, but about eight or nine is the usual age." "Ah, poor little things," said the wife, "they are obliged to begin the very minute they can use their fingers at all. The most of the cabinet-makers of the East-end have from five to six in family, and they are generally all at work for them. The small masters mostly marry when they are turned of twenty. You see our trade's come to such a pass that unless a man has children to help him he can't live at all. I've worked more than a month together, and the longest night's rest I've had has been an hour and a quarter—aye, and I've been up three nights a week besides. I've had my children lying ill, and been obliged to wait on them into the bargain. You see, we couldn't live if it wasn't for the labour of our children, though it makes 'em, poor little things, old people long afore they're growed up. I leave you to judge how we're to live by our labour," said the man. "Just look here," he continued, producing a rosewood tea caddy. It was French polished, lined with tinfoil, and with lock and key. "Now, what do you think we get for that, materials, labour, and all? Why, 16d.; and out of that there's only 4d. for the labour. My wife and daughter polishes and lines them, and I make them, and all we get is fourpence, and we have to walk perhaps miles to sell them for that." "Why I stood at this bench," said the wife, "with my child, only 10 years of age, from four o'clock on Friday morning till ten minutes past seven in the evening, without a bit to eat or drink. I never sat down a minute from the time I began till I finished my work, and then I went out to sell what I had done. I walked all the way from here (Shoreditch) down to the Lowther Arcade, to get rid of the articles." Here she burst out in a violent flood of tears, saying, "Oh, sir, it *is* hard to be obliged to labour from morning till night as we do—all of us, little ones and all—and yet not to be able to live by it either." "Why, there's Mr. ——, the warehouseman, in ——" the husband went on, "offered me £6 a gross for the making of these very caddies, as I showed just now, and that would have left me only 1½d. a dozen for my labour. Why, such men won't let poor people remain honest. And you see, the worst of it is this here—children's labour is of such value now in our trade that there's more brought into the business every year, so that it's really for all the world like breeding slaves. Without my children I don't know how we should be able to get along. There's that little thing," said the man, pointing to the girl of ten years of age before alluded to, as she sat at the edge of the bed, "why, she works regularly every day from six in the morning till ten at night. She never goes to school; we can't spare her. There's schools enough about here for a penny a week, but we could not afford to keep her without working. If I'd ten more children I should be obligated to employ them all the same way. And there's hundreds and thousands of children now slaving at the business. There's the M——'s; they've a family of eight, and the youngest to the oldest of them all works at the bench; and the oldest ain't fourteen, I'm sure. Of the two thousand five hundred small masters in the cabinet line, you may safely say that two thousand of them, at the very least, has from five to six in family, and that's upwards of 12,000 children that's been put to the trade since the prices has come down. Twenty years ago I don't think there was a young child at work in our business, and I'm sure there isn't now a small master whose whole family doesn't assist him. But what I want to know is, what's to become of the 12,000 children when they're grow'd up, and come regular into the trade? Here are all my young ones growing up without being taught anything but a business that I know they must starve at."

In answer to my inquiry as to what dependence he had in case of sickness? "Oh, bless you," he said, "there's nothing but the parish for us. I did belong to a benefit society about four year ago, but I couldn't keep up my payments any longer. I was in the society above five-and-twenty year, and then was obliged to leave it after all. I don't know of one as belongs to any friendly society, and I don't think there is a man as can afford it in our trade now. They must all go to the workhouse when they're sick or old."

From a man who, with his wife and young child, occupied rather a decent room in Spitalfields, I had the following statement as to his mode of living. He was a fancy cabinetmaker:—

"I get up always at six, summer and winter. I wake natural at that hour, if I'm ever so tired when I go to bed and sleep ever so dead. If it's summer I go to work in the daylight at six; if it's winter by candle-light. My wife gets up an hour after me. Indeed she can't well sleep in the room I'm working in. (We've only one room.) She makes the fire and boils the kettle, and gets breakfast ready at eight. It's coffee and bread and butter. I may take ten minutes to it, sometimes only five. She has dinner ready at one, and that's coffee and bread and butter three days at least in the week, and that's finished in ten minutes too. Then I've tea, not coffee, for a change about five, and I go to bed at ten without any supper—except on Sundays—after sixteen hours' labour, just with a few breaks, as I've told you. Most people in my way, who are as badly off as I am, work on Sundays. All that I know do, but *I* don't. I haven't strength for it after sixteen hours' work a day for six days, and so I rest on Sunday, and stay in bed till twelve or after. When we haven't coffee for dinner we have a bit of cheap fish—mackerel at 1½d. or 1d. a piece, or soles at 2d. a pair, and a potato with it. Sometimes they're almost as cheap as coffee for dinner. For breakfast for me, my wife, and a child five years old, coffee, half an ounce, costs ½d.; bread and butter, 3½d.—1d. butter, and 2½d. bread. Dinner the same, but an ounce of coffee instead of half an ounce as at breakfast; so that's 4½d., and about the same if it's fish, or 1d. or 1½d. more, but there isn't as much fish as we could eat. Tea's ½d. more than breakfast. No supper, and to bed at ten. On Sundays we have mostly half a bullock's head, which costs 10d. to 1s. We have it boiled, with an onion and a potato to it; or when we're hard up we have it without either for dinner, and warm it for supper. There's none left for Monday sometimes, and never much. I don't taste beer above once a month, if that. In winter, fire and candlelight cost me 3s. to 4s. a week for some weeks, or 4s. 6d. a week when there's a fog, for my place isn't very light, and I'm forced to burn candles all day long then, and I must have a bit of fire all times for my glue-pot. There *have* been times—but things are cheaper now, though work's not so brisk—when we've had no butter to our bread, and hardly a crumb of sugar to our coffee. My rent is 1s. 10d. a week, and my own sticks. It costs at least 7s. to keep us, and that's 8s. 10d. altogether. I don't earn more than 12s. a week the year through, so that the extra fire and candle in the winter takes it every farthing, and more; and then we're forced to go without butter. There's 3s. 2d., say, left in summer time for clothing, and all that; but I haven't bought a new thing that way since I got married seven years back. My wife earns, perhaps, 2s. a week at charing, but her health's bad. I work for a slaughterer; not one in particular, but one is my principal customer. I began as a little master when I'd been a fortnight out of my time. My mother lent me 20s. She's middling off, and in service. I'd picked up tools before. Then my wife had saved on to £5 in service, which furnished the room, with what I made myself. I think most of us marry servants that have saved a trifle. A good many have, I know. My little girl's too young to do anything now, but she must work at lining with her mother when she's old enough. Children soon grow to be useful, that's one good thing. She goes to a Sunday school at present, and is learning to read."

To show the time consumed—or, as the men universally call it, "lost"—in the conveyance of the goods to the warehouses, I am able to give the following particulars. There can be no doubt, as I have stated, that more than one-half of the working cabinet-makers in London work for the supply of the warehouses; but that I may not over-estimate the number, I will say one-half. The least duration of time expended by these men in their commerce with the "slaughter-houses" is an average of eight hours weekly per man. But this is not all. At least one-fourth of their number expend 2s. 6d. each in the hire of carts and trucks for the conveyance of the heavier articles to the warehouses. Sometimes, when the bulk of the articles admits of it, trucks or barrows are used, the charge for which is 2d. an hour. But lighter articles of furniture are carried on the shoulder. "Why, sir," said one man to me, "I have sometimes carried as much as three-quarters of a hundred weight on my shoulder, and have taken that weight as far as Knightsbridge and Pimlico and back again, and then not sold it. I have then been obliged to take it out again the next day in a different direction, as far as Woolwich, and have took what I could get for it, or else go without victuals. I find about Thursday to be the best day, and the most profitable, as I can generally get more on a Thursday for an article than on a Saturday or Monday, because if you call on Saturday they think you are hard up for Sunday's dinner, and if you take it on Monday they think you are hard up for rent, and so they play upon you, and, besides, they think you couldn't get rid of it on Saturday. The usual rounds we take for the sale of our articles are Moorfields, Tottenham-court-road, Oxford-street, Edgeware-road, Knightsbridge, Pimlico, and other parts of the West-end." Another party informed me that he has had to call no less than seven or eight times for his money after he had "sold his goods to a butcher," and then only got about half of what was coming to him. At these slaughterhouses, I was informed, "the butchers occasionally pay part cash and part by check, due in two months. But when we get outside, their clerks meet us to know if we have any checks to cash, for which they charge 3d. in the pound."

Concerning the employment of a carter I had the following account from one of the body:—

"I am a tradesman—a corn-chandler—and having a horse and cart I am in the habit of doing little jobs for persons in this neighbourhood (Hoxton). I never let out to hire. I am often employed by the numerous small cabinet manufacturers in this locality, to take their work out with them, on what is called the 'buz,' *i.e.* (the hawk). The goods I am employed to carry out consist of loo tables, cheffoniers, Pembroke tables, oak chairs, and other large articles of cabinet work, and for this I charge on the average 1s. per hour. Whether the goods are sold or not my charge is the same. Sometimes I am paid after the articles are sold, and sometimes I have to trust. There are no particular days in the week for the sale of the articles, but mostly Saturdays. There are dozens employed in the same line as myself. I generally start about nine or ten o'clock in the morning, calling first at several houses in Tottenham-court-road, then to Oxford-street, Wardour-street, Knightsbridge, and often back again with the whole lot to ———'s, where the articles are left and sold for what the slaughterer likes to give. In case of rain I cover the goods. Sometimes the articles are sold directly, and sometimes in five or six hours. The longest time I have known it to take to dispose of the goods is seven hours in one day and five the next. It is no uncommon occurrence for a poor working man to stand an hour, two, or three at a slaughter-house door before the master butcher will condescend to give him an answer." In answer to my inquiry where do they get their meals while out selling, the reply was, "Why they starve till the goods are sold."

I have before alluded to the utter destitution of the cheap workers belonging to the cabinet trade, and I now subjoin the statement of a man whom I found last winter in the Asylum for the Houseless Poor:—

"I have been out of work about a twelvemonth, as near as I can reckon. When I was in work I was sometimes at piece work and sometimes at day work. When I first joined the trade (I never served my time—my brother learnt me) there was plenty of work to do. For this last twelvemonth I have not been able to get anything to do—not at my own trade. I have made up one dozen of mahogany chairs on my own account. The wood and labour of them cost me £1 5s. I had to pay for a man to do the carving and sweeping of them, and I had to give £1 for the wood. I could get it much cheaper now; but then I didn't know anything about the old broken 'ship' wood that is now used for furniture. The chairs I made I had to sell at a sacrifice. I was a week making them, and got only £2 for the dozen when they were done. By right I should have had at least 50s. for them, and that would have left 25s. for my week's work, but as it was I had only 15s.

clear money, and I have worked at them much harder than is usual in the trade. There are two large houses in London that are making large fortunes in this manner. About a fortnight after I found out that I couldn't possibly get a living at this work, and as I didn't feel inclined to make the fortunes of the large houses by starving myself, I gave up working at chair making on my own account. I then made a few clothes-horses. I kept at that for about six months. I hawked them in the streets, but I was half-starved by it. Some days I sold them, and some I was without taking a penny. I never in one day got rid of more than half a dozen, and they brought 3s.; out of which there was the wood and the other materials to pay for, and they would be 1s. 6d. at least. If I could get rid of two or three in a day, I thought I did pretty well, and my profit upon these was about 9d.—not more. At last I became so reduced by the work, that I was not able to buy any more wood, and the week after that I was forced to quit my lodging. I owed three weeks' rent, at 1s. 6d. a week, and was turned out in consequence. I had no things for them to seize—they had all gone long before. Then I was thrown upon the streets. I had no friends (my brothers are both out of the country), and no home. I was sleeping about anywhere I could. I used to go and sit at the coffee houses where I knew my mates were in the habit of going, and they would give me a bit of something to eat and make a collection to pay for a bed for me. At last this even began to fail me, my mates could do no more for me. Then I applied to some of the unions, but they refused to admit me into the casual ward on account of my not being a traveller. I was a whole week walking about in the streets without ever lying to rest. I used to go to Billingsgate to get a nap for a few minutes, and then I used to have a doze now and then on a door step and under the railway arches. All this time I had scarcely any food at all—not even bread. At last I was fairly worn out, and being in the neighbourhood I applied at St. Luke's, and told them I was starving. They said they could do nothing for me, and advised me to apply at the Houseless Poor Asylum. I did so, and was admitted directly. I have been four nights in the Asylum already, and I don't know what I shall do when I leave. My tools are all gone—they are sold; and I have no money to buy new ones. There are hundreds in the trade like me, walking about the streets with nothing to do, and no place to put their heads in."

I shall now conclude this letter with the following statement as to the effects produced by the slop cabinet business upon the honourable part of the trade. I derived my information from Mr. ——, one of the principal masters at the West-end, and who has the highest character for consideration for his men. Since the establishment of slaughter-houses—"and aptly, indeed," said my informant, "from my know-ledge of their effects upon the workmen, have they been named—the demand for articles of the best cabinet work, in the manufacture of which the costliest woods and the most skilled labour London can supply are required, has diminished upwards of 25 per cent. The de-mand, moreover, continues still to diminish gradually. The result is obvious. Only three men are now employed in this trade, in lieu of four, as formerly, and the men displaced may swell the lists of the un-derpaid, and even of the slop workers. The expense incurred by some of the leading masters in the honourable trade is considerable, and for objects the designs of which inferior masters pirate from us. The designs for new styles of furniture add from five to ten per cent. to the cost of the more elaborate articles that we manufacture. The first time any of these novel designs comes to the hammer by the 'sale of a gentleman's effects,' they are certain of piracy, and so the pattern descends to the slaughter-houses. These great houses are frequently offered prices, and by very wealthy persons, which are an insult to a tradesman anxious to pay a fair price to his workmen. For instance for an 8 ft. mahogany book case, after a new design, and made in the very best style of art, the material being the choicest, and everything about in admirable keeping, the price is 50 guineas. 'O, dear,' some rich customer will say, 'Fifty guineas! I'll give you twenty, or, indeed, I'll give you twenty-five!'" [I afterwards heard from a journeyman that this would be the cost of the labour alone.] The gentleman I saw spoke highly of the intelligence and good conduct of the men em-ployed, only society men being at work on his premises. He feared that the slop-trade, if not checked, would more and more swamp the honourable trade.

LABOUR AND THE POOR.

THE METROPOLITAN DISTRICTS.

[FROM OUR SPECIAL CORRESPONDENT.]

OF THE TURNERS OF LONDON.

Letter LXVII.

In the present Letter I shall speak of the earnings and condition of the London Turners.

The number of turners in Great Britain at the time of taking the last census was 7,159; of these, 5,925 were resident in England; 1,042 in Scotland, 147 in Wales, and 45 in the British Isles. Out of the 7,159, 5,941 were males and 83 females of 20 years of age and upwards; while of those under 20 years, 1,113 were males and 22 females. Whether the female turners belonged to the operative or trading class the Government returns do not afford us any information. I find, however, that females have often been known to work at the trade.

This was the number of hands in the business in 1841. In 1831 the number of male turners of twenty years of age and upwards was 5,905. In England, the hands had decreased no less than 218 during ten years between 1831 and 1841; whereas in Scotland they had increased 197, and in Wales 22. Whether the wages of the turners rose in the English counties where the decrease took place, I have, as I said before, no means of ascertaining. It is clear, however, that according to the mere law of supply and demand, the price paid to the operatives for their labour should have increased precisely in the same ratio as the hands decreased—provided, of course, that the quantity of work to be done, or, in other words, the demand for the turners' labour, remained the same.

As regards the Metropolis, however, I have been at considerable pains in collecting information both as to the amount of work and the prices paid for it between 1831 and 1841; so that the public may have another instance, in addition to that of the cabinet trade, that the wages of a trade may, under particular circumstances, decline, while the supply of hands is decreasing, and the demand for their labour is increasing.

The number of turners of twenty years of age and upwards who were resident in London in 1841 amounted to 1,320; in 1831, however, there had been 150 more hands in the metropolis—that is to say, according to the census of that date, the London turners of the same age amounted to 1,470. Here, then, was a decrease in the number of hands, very nearly equal to 10 per cent.; so that, allowing the quantity of work to have remained stationary during that time, wages ought to have risen 10 per cent. from 1831 to 1841. But, strange to say, the quantity of work actually increased—for it was during that period that it became the fashion to have several articles, such as door-knobs, curtain poles and rings, &c., made of wood which had before then been manufactured of brass—and yet, notwithstanding this augmentation of the ordinary amount of turning work, and the decrease in the quantity of hands in the trade, wages were 400 per cent. better in 1831 than they were in 1841.

The turners themselves, it will be seen, attribute the decline in their wages to the same cause as that in the cabinet trade—viz., to the competition of the small masters in reducing the prices of the articles they produce. I shall now proceed to describe the different varieties of the operatives, and then to give the statements of the most intelligent individuals belonging to each of these varieties.

The trade of a turner has many ramifications. In the first place, as regards the materials used, there are general turners, hard wood and ivory turners (the hard woods being principally lignum vitæ, ebony, cocoa tree, saffron and rosewood). Then, as regards the articles made, there are tassel and fringe mould turners, cotton bobbin, lace bobbin, toy, plumber's, and oval turners. Brush turning is also a distinct branch. Of toy turning, I may premise, I gave an account in my Letter concerning the toy makers.

The work of the general turner consists principally in making articles required by joiners, chairmakers, cabinetmakers, and upholsterers; such as door knobs, stair banisters and newels (the upright pillar supporting the scroll of the stair hand-rail), which are most required for building purposes, and are usually turned out of deal. For cabinetmakers the general turner makes bed posts, table legs and pillars, drawer knobs, cornice ends, and different kinds of beadings, all kinds of wood being employed for these purposes, though mahogany is the principal. "Legs" are turned for the chairmakers, either for sofas, chairs, or stools. The upholsterer's demands on the turner's skill are often identical with those of the cabinetmaker. The hard wood and ivory turner forms all the toys made of ivory, as well as chessmen, which they afterwards carve; they are also the artificers of billiard balls, pestles, twine boxes, skittle balls, and of similar articles made of the harder kinds of timber. The tassel and fringe turner is employed entirely for the upholsterers, who use the productions of their skill for the drapery with which our bed and window hangings are decorated. The last mentioned class of turners all use soft woods, principally alder, lime, and chestnut. The cotton bobbin, toy, and lace bobbin turners are occupied in the respective callings indicated by their appellations. The cotton bobbin and toy turners use soft woods, but the lace bobbins are made of hard woods, being polished, and sometimes highly ornamented. This is a trade, however, which is fast declining, as these bobbins are only used for lace made by hand, and they are hardly made at all in London now. At one time lace bobbin turning was a very prosperous occupation. The plumber's turner forms suckers and buckets for pumps, dressers (a kind of mallet with which the lead is "flatted"), wedges, mallets, and moulds for casting lead; beech, elm, ash, box, hornbeam, and alder being used for these purposes. Brush turners are employed in making the different kinds of broom heads, and on the stems of painter's brushes, all made of alder, or some equally soft wood, but principally of alder.

Steam turning is applied more or less to all the descriptions of labour I have specified. Steam machinery was first applied to turning in the metropolis about twenty-five years ago. It was in use in the manufacturing districts, however, some ten years before it was introduced into the London trade. Its use is still far more prevalent in the great manufacturing towns of the provinces than here. "I remember," said a well-informed man to me, "that when I was a boy in the business, the notion of turning by steam was laughed at, and a man who thought it could be done was reckoned fit to *turn* into Bedlam. That's 35 years ago; but the trade has found it out since, and severely." Steam is, however, only used now as the motive power, for a man must still be employed to "turn." Steam power, however, enables a man to do twice the ordinary quantity of work, and with less fatigue.

The trade of a turner is carried on by means of a crank, a wheel, and a collar-and-mandrel. The wheel is turned by the pressure of the foot (either the right or left, though the left is more generally used, as the body is thereby steadier). The big wheel turned by hand is now very rarely used, and only when the wheel usually employed and kept in motion by the turner himself is not of sufficient power; an assistant then turns the big wheel. The tool for cutting is held in both hands, but worked by the right hand. The wood to be turned is fixed to a spike chuck, with contrivances to affix it of any length. It is set revolving by the wheel and the apparatus attached to it. The wood is first "roughed" with the gouge as near as possible to the shape required before it is submitted to the chisel. The workman in turning applies his chisel (as a general rule) on a rest (which slides along the top of his bench), holding it in an oblique direction as it cuts the wood being turned. The same form of chisels and gouges as those now employed has been used within the memory of the oldest man in the trade. After this it is glass-papered, and so finished as regards the turner's craft. Polishing or painting is the business of the tradesman who requires the article. About fifty years ago the pole-lathe, which is worked without a wheel, was in general use. It is now confined to only one or two branches of the trade. With the pole-lathe the workman, by means of a treadle, can give the work a turn forward or backward. The pole, which is placed above his head, sinks or rises to the pressure of the treadle, so that the work is done by a series of cuts, with an interval of time between each, instead of one continued revolution. The pole-lathe is still used in the country, especially in Buckinghamshire, where "rapparee" (painted bed-room) chairs are principally turned out of the beech, which is plentiful there; it is used too in some parts of Yorkshire. The London flute-makers and the bobbin-turners still use the pole-lathe. The wheel-lathe has been in common use for forty years.

The general turner's part of the business is considered to demand the greatest exercise of skill. He has frequently to work from drawings, and to work to great nicety, especially in new patterns for bed-pillars and table-legs; and an experienced cabinet-maker or an upholsterer will soon detect any irregularity in the turner's work, or any deviation from the pattern. Toy turning is not considered so nice an art, and the turning of drawer knobs is about the easiest of all descriptions of turned work; on them, and on ball feet for plain tables, boys are generally instructed. Boys, however, are of little use at turning until they have had a year and a half or two years' practice. "I myself never knew a woman employed in turning," said a workman to me, "except one, and her husband used sometimes to make her turn the big wheel, as a punishment for drunkenness. There have been a few females who have 'turned' in London, however, and more in the country." They all belonged to the turner's family.

The ivory and hard woods, however, are "turned" by a different method, and different tools are used from those of the general turner. The commonest implements of the hard wood and ivory turners are the firmer (a kind of chisel), the round-mouthed tool, the point tool, and the screaver or parting tool. The firmer is used to accomplish the finishing work, and is equivalent to the chisel of the general turner. The round-mouth tool is used as a gouge, and the others are applied to effect the openings or elevations on the pattern. If the article turned in ivory be large, it is frequently made of separate portions, the slender part being screwed firmly to the more bulky, as in letter stamps, and by this screwing material is saved. All ivory is turned by "scraping," the tool being applied horizontally to the work, while wood is turned by "cutting." The trade distinction is, that the ivory is "under-handed" work, and wood turning "over-handed." Hard woods are turned like ivory. Metal turning is more under-handed than ivory or hard wood turning, the turner applying his shoulder to the tool to keep it on the rest. In hard woods and metals, as in ivory, "scraping" is the process observed. It is impossible to lay hold of the metal, I am told, unless the tool be applied below the centre. As a rule, the application of the tool in general turning is above the centre—in metal turning below it—while in ivory and hardwood turning it is held even with it.

All the wares which the turner's craft is now called upon to form are paid for by the piece (they have, however, neither a price nor a log book), as far as the operative is concerned, in the regular establishments where men, and not merely boys, are at work. Some of the smaller articles, such as tassel moulds, are, however, paid for by the day, and the diurnal mode of payment is the rule also for very heavy work of the more skilled description, and for that the payment is 6d. an hour, but in the best shops only; 20 years ago it was 8d. The "East-end boys," or "the cut-and-run men" (as I heard them indifferently styled), who are the slop turners, give, however, only about 1½d. for every 4d. paid by the honourable trade. The men thus underpaid are to be found in the Curtain-road, Spitalfields, Bethnal-green. The reduction in the prices paid by the honourable trade is very considerable in some articles, and the rate is unchanged in one only. The reduction is the greatest in drawer knobs; 36s. a gross was paid for turning them 30 years ago; now 7s. 6d. is paid for the same work, and even a lower amount. The decline was about 14 years ago, when the prices fell at once from 33s. to 7s. 6d., and since they have dropped to 2s. 9d. at the East-end of the town. Bed-posts are reduced two-thirds; what were 7s. 6d. are now 2s. 6d., the fall having been gradual within these 12 years. A workman who brought me the accounts of his earnings for several years past showed me that in 1836 he was paid 2s. 6d. a dozen for deal columns with two pins, and now he gets only 1s. 6d. for the same articles. Chair and sofa legs alone maintain the old prices to the workman. An intelligent operative said to me:—

"I date the *very good* prices from 35 years ago, when a man could earn £3 or £4 a week. I've earned £1 a day myself occasionally, and it was a shocking day when I couldn't earn a crown; and I date the *fair* prices, when we could earn 35s. or 40s. a week regularly, from 8 to 12 years ago. Now, for the very same kind of work, and working the same hours, and the same every way, on the average I can't touch 20s. a week, tho' I may make 18s. and 19s."

I here subjoin a copy of his earnings for the last year:—

"1849.

	£	s.	d.			£	s.	d.
1st week	0	3	7	30		1	5	0
2 and 3	0	10	7	31		1	1	4
4	1	6	0	32		1	10	0
5	1	2	6	33		1	4	6
6	1	8	6½	34		1	4	5
7	0	10	9	35		1	6	0
8	0	19	6	36		1	2	10
9	0	5	7½	37		0	19	0
10	0	8	6	38		1	0	0
11	0	4	8	39 and 40		1	5	0
12	0	9	6	41		1	2	6
13, 14, and 15	0	4	1	42		1	0	0
16	0	7	7½	43		1	0	0
17 and 18	1	0	0	44		0	3	9
19	1	5	0	45		1	10	0
20	1	12	9	46		1	5	0
21	1	2	6	47		1	3	8
22	1	10	4	48		0	17	0
23	1	1	5	49		1	3	0
24	1	4	0	50		1	10	0
25	1	7	6	51		1	10	0
26	1	10	0	52		0	17	0
27 and 28	2	3	3½					
29	1	10	0	Total	£48	8	3

"Average of the above earnings per week, 18s. 7¼d. My books show that's been my earnings for these last four years; and as I've kept an account of my earnings I can prove the same as the 'very good' and the 'fair' prices. Now, sir, there's door furniture, for 'turning' which six years ago I had 21s. a dozen sets (a single set is two large knobs, with brasses, two roses, bolt knob and rose, 2 escutcheons, and covers). These dozen sets the London trade now get supplied from Birmingham for less than 15s., the material included. Six years ago I was paid 21s. for my labour alone. The Birmingham man for the same work gets about 4s. Our earnings were 400 per cent. better on most things, and the reduction has fallen principally on the man, and not much on the master."

The fall, I am informed, was going on gradually, if not rapidly, from 1831 to 1841. During that period a change, before alluded to, took place in the fashions of the cabinetmakers' trade. Many ornamental portions of furniture, such as door and drawer knobs, the rings for cornices, and other articles, were then made of wood in the place of brass, which went entirely into disuse. Thus there was a greater amount of work than usual to be done, and fewer hands to do it, and yet wages declined. Among the working turners there is at present no society, nor has there been any since 1844. The last was broken up in that year through a disagreement among the members, as to whether or not little masters should be admitted "into society." There are now no houses of call, or "labour markets," so to speak, for the London turners. One was opened by the last society, but there were only two calls made from it. There are among turners, moreover, no superannuation, sick, or benefit funds, and in case of permanent sickness, or in old age—for only a few of the turners are saving men, and one told me that not above a dozen of them were so—there is nothing but the parish or the workhouse for them to fly to for maintenance. This class has been very burdensome, I am told, to the parish of St. Giles. I regret to add I am unable to show statistically to what extent; for, strange to say, and much to our national disgrace, there are as yet no returns as to the trades or occupations of those receiving parish relief. In case of an accident to a turner, a collection is now made among his brethren, a petition being carried round, and a praiseworthy liberality is not unfrequently manifested by the operatives of this class towards their suffering brethren. One man who had the misfortune to break his arm lately received 55s. by this mode. The same process is observed for the burial of any working turner. The operatives in this trade are nearly all married, the very young being the only exceptions. Some of their wives work for the slop tailors, under whose employ 7d.

a day (less by the expense of thread, candle, &c.), is considered good earnings. The best class of workmen average about 18s. a week wages, nearly the whole being payments for piece work. (In the country the payment is almost always by the day.) The very inferior workmen, the East-enders, earn, it appears, from 3s. to 5s. a week less than the West-end men. Among the turners at the East-end there are few journeymen; they are nearly all little masters, and do their work in the hastiest and roughest manner, so as to gain payment for the largest possible quantity. They dispose of this work to the little masters in the cabinet trade and to the ironmongers. They or their wives hawk ball feet and small knobs, and feet of all kinds, to cabinet makers as well as to their own trade. They are subject to the usual distress of the under-paid classes, being kept waiting (the women more especially) before receiving any decisive answer until a Saturday night is almost spent, and the necessity of having *something* for a Sunday dinner allows a customer to purchase upon his own most niggardly terms.

Men out of work, or "on tramp" from one part of the country to another, can now only gain employment by calling at the turners' shops. There is no arrangement for the assistance of a man "on tramp," but if he be known and in distress there is usually, in the different shops that he may call at, a gathering among the men at work for him. Some men give 4d. each—some smaller sums—when they think him a deserving object. Nothing was allowed to men on tramp when the society was in existence.

The turners are instructed in their craft principally by means of apprenticeship. Some masters take a great many apprentices, and some of the little masters, whether they have the means of employing boys or not, make a traffic, I am assured, in apprentice premiums, being always on the look-out for boys apprenticed by parishes or public institutions. The object of such masters is to secure the fees; and instances have been known where a man has run off, leaving his apprentices behind him with their trade but half-taught to them, and the world before them. The apprentice system, indeed, appears to be one of the crying evils of all trades, and especially the underpaid ones. It is common for masters in the turning trade to have four or five apprentices at one time. The indoor apprentices, after payment of the premium, which has varied from £5 to £40, receive for their labour their board and lodging, but not their clothing or washing, nor the support during sickness. The plan of taking apprentices by the little masters has the injurious effect of throwing into the labour market a continued series of little-skilled workmen, brought up in the midst of poverty and hardship, and often with no aspirations to rise into a better condition. "Ill-treatment and half starvation," said a turner to me, "is more often these lads' lot than anything else. I've seen as much, both in town and country." I find, too, that gentlemen's servants not unfrequently become turners. I heard it attributed to some of them having acquired a taste for such work by having served masters who were amateur turners, of whom among the wealthier classes there are many. "Some of the first gentry, I assure you, sir," said a master, "are fond of a turn at the lathe, and some of them are very good hands, especially the late Lord Y——. He was excellent, and so is the present Lord ——, and Mr. G. T——, the rich banker in ——." In King's College there are about 25 lathes for the amusement and tuition of the pupils, many of whom are very efficient and tasteful workmen, especially some young Egyptians. Some of the gentlemen's servants pay a premium (one paid £20) to be instructed in turning, three years being devoted to that purpose; and they received a small sum per week at first, 5s. or thereabouts for the first year, and then the amount of their labour. It is supposed that there are now in London thirty turners who have been gentlemen's servants, some of whom are now masters.

There are not among the turners the brisk and slack seasons so prejudicial to the interests of the journeymen in other trades. The turner's work is one of tolerable regularity. There have been no strikes in London for forty years, and they are very unfrequent in the country. I heard no complaints from the men as to the prevalence of steam power being applied to their work. Their chief objection to machinery was, that, but for steam, there would be employment for half as many more turners as are now in existence.

The general hours of the London turners are from six in the morning till seven in the evening, less by the two hours for meals; but these hours are little regarded, as piece-work is the usual mode of employment, and that leads to an irregularity as respects hours, for if the work be completed it is no matter at what time. This system thus leads to unpunctuality, and thence frequently to idleness.

I met a few intelligent men among the turners, but intelligence is not the characteristic of the great mass of them. The poverty of the little masters tempts them, as I have stated, to take numbers of apprentices, who in their turn become little masters, and boys reared as I have described cannot be expected to attain tastes beyond such as can be gratified in the tap-room or the skittle-ground. Their ordin-ary amusements are skittles, cards ("all fives" being their usual game), and dominoes, played in the tap-rooms for beer. Nor is there any distinction between the journeyman and the little master, except that the journeyman may be better off. Drunkenness is far less common among them than it used to be, but that I found to be mainly attrib-uted to the scantiness of their means. "Most turners in small wares," said a fringe turner to me, "amuse themselves in the public-houses near where they work. I amuse myself with reading the papers or anything when I have a little spare time; but the Spitalonians (Spit-alfields men) are rare fellows for skittles, cards, and dominoes, and, badly as they're off, numbers of them don't work on a Monday. I like a game at knock-'em-downs (skittles) now and then myself. It's good exercise, and good for trade, as skittles is turners' work, but I hate cards without it be a hand at cribbage, and cribbage is a cut above the Spitalonians."

A highly intelligent man gave me an account of what he knew of the state of his calling:—

"I have known the trade upwards of forty years; and as soon as I was out of my apprenticeship, I could make £2 to £2 10s. a week on the average the year through. Some made more. I know one man who made £2 in one day, in turning 'pateras' for billiard tables, but that was an exception. Pateras were 6s. a gross then; they're now 3s. 6d. Wages have been falling gradually these last twenty years. They fell long before provisions did. Now there's hardly a job we do, but there's a reduction or an attempt at it. 'If you won't do it,' the masters say, 'there's plenty will.' 'Well, then,' I say, 'you'd better get them; I'll take no less;' for I know, you see, sir, that I'm a skilful hand, and that makes a man independent. I turn bed-posts, table and chair legs, and everything required in the furniture line, door knobs, and all those sort of things included. I average the year through 18s. a week, or hardly that; and them's the best earnings in the trade, excepting the turners employed by the best cabinet-makers, who have their own lathes and turners, and employ the men on their own premises. There may be seven cabinet-makers who do this, and their men may average from 32s. to 36s. a week. The reduction in the wages paid to us since I have known the trade, amounts to between one-third and two-thirds of what we formerly received, and there are still attempts to lower our wages further. We feel the want of a society, but it's no use to raise one, as the men won't stick to it, and on the whole, the main body of us turners are not so intelligent as other mechanics. Our work is noisy, too, and no talk can be carried on, as in a tailor's shop, by which men can pick up a little politics or knowledge. We are now like the bundle of sticks after it was opened, and masters know that, and know we have nothing to fall back upon, and they treat us accordingly. I am married, but have no family, and have the good fortune to have a careful wife, and a comfortable bit of home, but that can only be done by my being abstemious, for I often suffer from sickness, and that brings such a heavy expense that I can't save anything."

In connection with the general branch of the turning trade, there is engaged for the larger work a "turn-wheel" (or man to drive the lathe by means of "the big wheel"). This man is usually paid by time, 3d. per hour being the ordinary rate of remuneration. Those hired for this service are frequently old soldiers, but blind men are generally preferred to all others. The reason of this is, I am told, because men who are not deprived of their sight do not turn the wheel at one uniform speed. Their mind, to use the words of my informant, is wandering away from their labour, owing to their attention being taken off by surrounding objects. The blind man, however, like the blind horse in the mill, does his work without any alteration in his velocity. Formerly there used to be many blind men thus employed in the turning trade, and these were mostly soldiers who had lost their sight in Egypt. There were likewise many blind sailors gaining a livelihood in this manner. Now, owing to the use of steam power for the heavier work, there are no regular "turn-wheels" belonging to the business.

I am indebted for the following information concerning hard wood and ivory-turning, to a man to whom I was referred as a skilful and tasteful workman:—

"I have known the London *hard wood and ivory turning* trade," he said, "upwards of twenty-one years. I believe that there are now about 200 working men in my business. We have no society, nor superannuation fund, nor any provision of the kind. In sickness or distress each man must shift for himself. We all work by piece. There is no printed or acknowledged list of prices. Masters and men understand, or agree, what should be paid for work, according to the character and scale of prices of the shop. I have worked at all branches of the business, and twelve years ago I could make, and did make, 12s. a day. Now-a-days an average workman can make 30s. a week in a good shop all the year through, for one season is about as good as another. The turning of chessmen in ivory is from £1 to £2 journeymen's wages, according to the size and quality. Wood chessmen, ebony and box, are, as a fair average price, 3s. 6d. the set, but they're not to compare, in form or work, with ivory. We turn—in ivory and hard wood, ebony, rosewood, satinwood, or any wood—pincushions, door handles, bell-pulls, small boxes, and a good deal of work for carriages, such as the door handles. All flat work in ivory is done by hand, not by the lathe. [My informant then showed and explained to me the mode of working, which I have already described.] I have had advantages besides regular work. I have given gentlemen lessons in turning. Many gentlemen, and some peers, are very good ivory turners. I gave lessons to a gentleman who had the lathe and all the turning tools and apparatus that old George III. used to work with. It cost £500 at a sale. I have seen some of the old King's turning, and it was very fair. With industry he might have made 40s. or 50s. a week as a hardwood and ivory turner. A first-rater at that time, when times and wages were good, would earn twice as much or somewhere on to it. The King's lathe and all connected with it was the best and the most beautiful I have seen. No women work at my trade. I ought to have told you before, that ivory turners, when they have skill enough, are employed to carve the chessmen—though that has nothing to do with the turning. Perhaps, to make a handsome knight, or a good castle is the most difficult. Billiard balls are all made of ivory. We get 2s. the set for turning them in good shops, 1s. in inferior shops, and they're done for 6d. by the 'master-men,' as we call the low-priced men, or what you call the slop-workers. The billiard ball must of course be perfectly circular, and we form it mainly by the eye, so that ours is really a nice art. Any little unevenness is regulated afterwards by 'papering,' that is by rubbing it down with glass-paper; but I can do it without papering. The ivory is first sawn, and by a very fine saw, to the size wanted. It is then roughed with the gouge, towards the shape required. Then, if it's for a good shop, it's laid by for nine months; for if it's worked wet— and ivory's like wood that way—it will cast (warp) or crack. I have known billiard balls made out of green stuff in ivory, go an eighth of an inch longer one way than another. But the 'master-men,' the cheap fellows, work it green, and so can do it cheaper. They don't care whether their work stands true or not—not they. We don't call the 'master-men's' work 'slop,' we call it 'bad' work. These men's work is very inferior. It's hard to say to what degree they undersell a good master, for every shop has, perhaps, a different scale of prices. Say they work for one half the money, and with less than half the skill and pains. They hawk their goods to the toy and fancy shops, and to private houses. They take lots of apprentices, who grow as well into master-men. I know one man who has six, and another who has fourteen of these apprentices, and the fourteen man has got most of them from the workhouse. The Lord knows how they're treated. These master-men are very poor. They live chiefly in Clerkenwell and Bethnal-green. I don't suppose they earn more than 15s. a week, indeed not that the year through. These men expose the better masters to a very unfair competition. The foreign trade doesn't affect us much. One of our lathes costs from £4 to £5, and our tools may cost from £150 to £200; perhaps there is more than 200 of them of all kinds and substances, of firmers and the others. I'm speaking of the very best and handsomest sort of tools; such as gentlemen have; and it was this as made George III.'s lathe and kit so valuable. In our trade, however, the master finds tools (and they may generally cost half what I've mentioned), and the journeyman, if he's not a master-man as well, always works on the premises. The understanding is, that when new tools are wanted the master finds the material, and the journeyman makes the tool. The wear and tear of them isn't 6d. a week. We turn bones as well as hard woods and ivory, but ivory's our main business. Leg-of-beef and shin bones are turned into surgical instruments, such as syringes; calf shin-bones are turned into common chessmen, but they have a scrubby look with them. When an article's turned, it's polished off with putty-powder, or something of the kind. Some are dyed after they're turned. There's two men in London who do nothing but dye our work, and they must make £3 to £4 a week. They say they have secrets, but I dare say it's just chemistry. The demand for chessmen has increased in my time. There is half as many more required now as when I first knew the trade. The ivory we work is African, Siam, and East Indian, or Ceylon. The Ceylon is the finest grain, but the Siam is the largest."

A man long familiar with the trade gave me an account of his experience as a *plumber's turner:*—

"I have known the trade 28 years in town and country, and have worked the last nineteen years in London. At first I was a general turner, and I am now a plumber's." [He described the nature of his work as I have given it previously.] "Ours is all piece-work, except a few new models, and that's day-work; but it's very unfrequent. I could earn 8s. or 9s. a day 15 years ago, or rather more in winter, when I first was a plumber's turner in London; then it was my own fault if I stood still a single day, but I had to work very long hours for it, sometimes from 5 to 8 or 9 at night. Now, tho' there's no quicker hand in London, I must work harder to make 5s. than I did to make 9s. Wages have been so reduced, and the fall is on all the things made by plumber's turners alike—they are all of one sort of work. I have earned 10s. a day in making plumber's dressers. I had 3s. 6d. a dozen for them, and now it's 2s. 3d. There are now many things in my way, such as buckets and sockets, and plumber's tools in general, hawked about the streets for less than I have received for my labour on them. These cheap things are badly made; there's neither good workmanship nor good stuff in them, but they supplant better things." [I had from this man the same account of the want of a society as from the general turner.] "My wife does not go out to work, but then we have no family, or she must. I can still keep a pretty comfortable home, as I average 12s. a week the year through. My wife and I used to go to the play now and then six or eight years ago, and to Hampton Court sometimes, but, cheap as those things are, it's out of the question with us at present. There's other things to think of—a decent sort of an appearance and a tidyish room, and it's only by being careful and steady that we can manage even that."

A pale but keen-looking man gave me the following account of *tassel and fringe mould turning:*—

"I have known the London trade from my childhood, and my ancestors have been engaged in it 100 years back, though not all that time in London. When I first knew the trade, twenty-three years ago, it was very prosperous. A good hand would then earn 36s. a week by piece-work at fringe moulds; and now, for the same amount of work, he wouldn't earn a third of that, not more than 10s., if as much. We were paid by the piece then as now, for 'fringes' so much the gross. Tassel-mould turning is the best part of the trade. These moulds are used for upholsterers' hangings, either for the drapery of beds or windows, for bell pulls, blinds, pulpit cushions, and similar things. There's numbers made for what's known as 'pulpit cushions,' but only a small part of them's used for parson's pulpit cushions; they're used for sofa cushions and such like. Trade was better when tassels were the fashion for the hammer-cloths of gentlemen's carriages, and indeed almost all our work is still for 'the nobs,' and yet it's most badly paid. We turn the wooden moulds in the usual way, treading and standing on one leg all day long, and the upholsterers' work-women cover these moulds with silk, velvet, worsted, or whatever's wanted.

They're very badly paid. The fringe moulds are made for the same purposes as the tassel. The tassel is a plain mould and the fringe is rounded. We generally do tassels—and tassels only—by day-work, a good shop gives 25s. a week day-work (30s. to a very extraordinary hand), and inferior shops 20s. An average workman will do four gross a day of the easiest style of tassels, and short of a gross of the most difficult. It depends upon the pattern. The largest sizes are not the most difficult. It was all piece-work when first I knew the trade, but tassels hadn't come in then. I first worked on tassels ten years ago, and they'd come in a few years before that, perhaps. The wages haven't varied. We make about as many tassels as fringes; one tallies with the other. In turning fringes, we have, for 'short pipes' 9d. the gross; they are 9d. up to 3½ inches, and they rise at the rate of a half-penny and a penny a gross through the different sizes, the highest being 4s. a gross for twelve inches, and 6s. for fourteen inches. Work night and day—and the men do so nearly—and they make from 15s. to 20s. a week. These prices are a third of what they were twenty years ago, and they have kept falling gradually. I consider the fall is chiefly owing to so many small masters underselling each other, and eating one another up. When a lad's out of his apprenticeship, if he can only raise the expense of a lathe (and you can get a second-hand one for £1—a good new lathe is worth £5), and can raise the tools required, which may be bought for another £1, these, with a bundle of wood, is all the stock in trade wanted for a start; and then the upholsterers and the cabinet-makers and the trade all know they have needy men to deal with, and make their bargains accordingly. The goods are hawked from shop to shop, and the customers put on the screw, and the little masters are left very little, hardly enough to pay just for their labour. I am a journeyman, but very few fringe turners employ journeymen, as their work is chiefly done by apprentices. I average 20s. a week. Among the apprentices a great many are parish boys, with whom a premium is given—I don't know what exactly. I know one who had several parish apprentices—it was for the sake of cheaper workpeople, not for the sake of the fees. The apprentices are bound for seven years generally, and must be kept all that time by the master. The little masters are drinking men frequently, and very poor. If anything happens to them there's nothing but the parish. Most of them have large families, and they live and work all in one room. The button-turners are amongst the worst off, but some button-turners are tassel-turners also, in which case they may take an apprentice. If they are only button-turners, I think an apprentice is almost beyond them. They live a good deal about Spitalfields. I can't say the turners I speak of are ever out of work, as they're little masters, and set themselves to work. But it's only raking up an existence, it's not a living; not to be called one. As for myself, I'm not very partial to the turning business, only I'm among friends who are in it. I may cut it soon, as I have before now. Altogether I think I have worked eight years at other things, for I'm an independent sort of a man. Nobody whatever shall put upon me; a word, and I'm off. I've worked at repairing guns, and at shoemaking. I picked up the skill somehow by seeing others, and being quick. [Another turner told me that he was his own tailor.] I did tidy that way. But my main employ when away from my own trade—and I was never apprenticed to it, but was taught by my relations—was in having the care of steam-engines in factories. I've made 27s. and 30s. a week that way. I've had the care of a steam-engine at a great brewer's, so you perceive I can make a shift many ways."

A man with a delicate look, and a stoop (not uncommon in his business, as the turners lean over their labour all day long), gave me the following statement concerning bobbin-turning:—

"I am *a bobbin turner*, and may say I was born one, as I was born in Spitalfields, and have been in the trade all my life, and my father is 79, and has been in the trade since he was nine years of age. About 25 years ago my trade was good. I could live comfortably, and could have kept a wife and family comfortably. I wasn't married then, but I did marry 20 years ago, and at that time I had every prospect of keeping a wife and family well. It's a hard thing on working men like me, sir, that we marry when we find ourselves in a pretty good business, and of course we can't see why it should fall off, and then it does fall off, from no fault of ours, and so we are left to trouble and distress. It's a hard thing, sir; steam has taken away a great part of my labour, but how could I tell that? And yet I've often heard it said, that poor men shouldn't marry because trade was so bad. I have now a wife and seven children. I turn nothing but bobbins; that is a branch by itself. I turn cotton, lace, worsted, and silk bobbins. I work with the pole. The bobbins are made out of a solid piece of wood, always the trunk of the alder tree. The master supplies solid logs of wood, varying in length, which we cut into six or seven substances lengthways. We then cut these substances to the length required for the bobbins, and split them with a knife and mallet to the right thickness. The alder we use is grown chiefly in Kent and Berkshire. 'Reading staves' are the best in my trade. I am paid by the piece. 25 years ago I was paid 6s. a gross, journey-work, for silk bobbins, and could make five gross a week. I was paid 30s. a gross for large cotton bobbins, and could make a gross and a half a week; but for that work I had to find the material, which cost me from 12s. to 14s. Lace-bobbins were 8s. a gross, and I could make 4 gross a week. At that time, sir, I averaged 30s. a week. 20 years ago I could make about the same, but 17 years ago the fall began. Steam first began it. Silk bobbins first fell 6d. a gross, and the others in proportion. Our wages have kept falling and falling ever since, until last year we had 3s. For silks and for cottons and laces there's no demand; they're all country work, made mostly at Leicester, where wood's cheap, and steam power 10d. a day. They make cotton and lace bobbins, and find their own material, at one quarter the price we used to get. When I last worked on cotton bobbins, about 18 months ago, I had 8s. for the gross, and it's horse's work; they're too heavy for the foot, and with slaving like a horse or a slave, I could only make 12s. a week; but that was for the labour. The fall was gradual, from 30s. a week to 8s. I am now occupied only on silk bobbins, and last year they were 3s. a gross, and we then said one to another, 'They can't be lower anyhow,' but this year they are lower, only 2s. 9d., and as my master knows I'm a poor man with a large family (seven children), he's on the look out to reduce me to 2s. 6d., and I haven't full work at 2s. 9d. I can make five gross a week, but don't average more than four, that's 11s. Out of that I have to keep a wife and six children; one of my girls is in service. My wife works for a slop tailor, and makes 2s. 6d. a week by very hard work, and finds her own thread, too. One of my sons earns 3s. a week at glass-blowing, he's grown up, but he's a cripple, and does it by night work; he can do nothing else. My other children are under nine years of age. My rent is 2s. 3d. a week for one room unfurnished. In that room I have to work, and in it my wife has to work, and we have to cook in it, but it's very little cooking does for us, though we have to keep a fire to heat the irons for pressing my wife's tailoring work. She works for a sweater, and is now making postmen's waistcoats at 6d. a piece. We have all to sleep in the same room, which is a goodish size. If I could afford it two rooms would be a great good to me. We live on bread and butter and tea, three times a day. That for breakfast at half-past seven, the same again between twelve and one, and the same again about seven at night. We may taste meat once in every four or five Sundays, mostly this time of the year" (this was said a few weeks ago), "for when the weather's so hot butchers are glad to get rid of meat at any price when they find it's a-going, and really it's not fit to eat. As for clothing, the children have oft enough to go without it, and so should I, if I hadn't an old thing given me by people my wife has nursed. I've never heard any particular reason for the reduction of our wages. Now the master weavers say that they can't afford the present wages, silk is so dear. The silk is wound ready for the weaver's use round the bobbins we turn. A great many in my trade have to live as I live. There's at least forty as badly off as I am in Spitalfields. I should have told you that I drink a great deal of water, and I really think that does me harm, for it's bad water, as one cock serves all the premises. I'm so weak in the evening I can hardly stand. My children play about in the court when it's fine, and when it's wet in the room. A girl of nine jobs and cleans about the house, or my wife could do no work at all. I have two children at a Ragged School. I can't afford to send them to any better place. They seem to like it very well. They are continually thinking of the loaf and bun they get at Christmas; last year they had a loaf and a twopenny pie; they often talk about that. All the families of the men situated as I am, live like mine. The little masters are a great cut-up to our business by underselling the better masters. I can't say that I know any drunkards among the journeymen in my trade. We've given over caring about politics since the time of the union, and then we didn't understand it. We are quiet men, and submit quietly to what we suffer. I can read and write, as I dare say most of us can. We have no fund, and no society, and never had. I see no prospect of better times, not at all; and if provisions were dearer, we might go to the parish, as we've done before, and in old age a man like me must come to the workhouse, and that's a sorrowful thought. A penny or a halfpenny a loaf makes a great difference to me; it does, indeed, sir—a very great difference, for bread's our great expense. It's dear eating, after all, is bread and butter for a family— there's no strength in it."

Another man in this trade told me that he was eighty or there-abouts, and had been married fifty-two years, and that he could still work at his trade, but could only make from 5s. to 6s. a week. He had never worked at anything but bobbins, and until within these nineteen or twenty years he could earn about 25s. a week. He could not work so well or so fast as he could a few years ago, he said, "but the fall in the prices is my great hindrance." "Yes," said his wife, "and if we ask a little help from the parish, they say, 'O, you can come into the house;' but then you see, sir, we should be parted, and that's a hard thing after being together above fifty years."

A *button mould trimmer*, living in a wretched room, told me that his trade was "sinking out." He made the button moulds which were covered with silk, and used for ladies dresses. He had, some years ago, he hardly knew how many, 4d. and 4½d. for what he had now 1½d. and 2d. a gross, and very little work he could get now even at those prices. He made 4s., 5s., or 6s. a week now, and 10s., 12s., or 14s. formerly.

I saw several of these humbler workmen, and found their rooms bare of furniture, but generally clean. The pride of the artisan to have "something to call a home," still exists.

Concerning the "little masters," I had the following information. There were very few little master turners in the general branch of the trade before 1823. The operative turners were, prior to that time, generally journeymen working for the respectable master turners, who were then four times as numerous as now. Each of these masters employed from three to half a dozen men on their premises, having very rarely more than one or two apprentices. The wages of the journeymen ranged from £5 to £2, the average earnings being between 50s. and 60s. per week. After the year 1823 the cabinet makers by whom the master turners were employed, finding that they could not get their work done owing to the drinking habits of the journeymen turners, determined on reducing the prices paid to the masters, on the plea that they gave too much money to their men; and no sooner were the masters' prices reduced than they lowered the wages of the men. The journeymen, however, knowing that it was the custom of the masters to charge one-third as profit upon the amount paid to the journeymen for their labour, determined not to submit to the reduction, and accordingly several started in business for themselves. These journeymen then solicited the custom of the cabinet makers who had employed their former masters, offering to do their work at a lower rate. The more respectable masters, finding themselves undersold by the journeymen who had left their employ, then went to work to reduce the prices of the men that still remained with them, and thus sought to get their work back again from the cabinet makers. This further reduction, however, caused more journeymen still to leave their masters' employ, and to start in business for themselves, seeking to obtain work at a lower rate still. And thus matters have been going on to the present time—journeymen trying to cut under the masters, and the masters, partly in self defence and partly in revenge, trying to cut down the wages of the men.

There are now, I am told, four principal reasons for turners becoming little masters. First, says my informant, the men are generally so fond of drink that a large master won't employ them. Then they commence business themselves, and work for little master cabinet makers. Another cause is, that it takes but a few pounds to commence operations on their own account. A third reason is, because they don't like to be under the control of an employer. And the fourth, because, when working for themselves, they can begin when they like, and leave off and have "a spree" when they please.

The little masters in the turning trade work the same long hours as the garret-masters in the cabinet trade. When a man begins for himself he gets a boy to tread the lathe, clean up the articles with sand-paper, and chop up the wood ready for turning. I heard of no boys working at a lathe who are less than twelve years of age. "You see, sir," I was told, "the work is so heavy that it requires a strong boy to do it."

The East-end turners generally, I was informed, labour at the lathe from six o'clock in the morning till eleven and twelve at night, being 18 hours' work per day, or 108 hours per week. They allow themselves two hours for their meals. It takes them, upon an average, two hours more every day fetching and carrying their work home. Some of the East-end men work on Sundays, and not a few either, said my informant. "Sometimes I have worked hard," said one man, "from six one morning till four the next, and scarcely had any time to take my meals in the bargain. I have been almost suffocated with the dust flying down my throat after working so many hours upon such heavy work too, and sweating so much. It makes a man drink where he would not. It is generally considered that about nine-tenths of the turners are little masters. In fact, nearly the whole of the general turners are little masters, and one-quarter of these hire the lathes they use, for which they pay from 2s. to 2s. 6d. per week. The little master turners seldom or never work upon their own materials. It costs about £3 to set up in the business in a little way. A lathe (second-hand) costs £2, and tools £1."

The little masters, I am informed, spend at least 4s. per week in beer; and almost all agree in ascribing the impoverishment of the trade to the drinking habits of the men. The Metropolitan Police returns, however, show the turners to be the least criminal in this respect, and, indeed, in all others, of the whole of the artisans that I have yet treated of. Striking the average of those taken into custody for drunkenness during the last ten years, the ratios have been as follows:—sailors, 1 drunkard in every 13; labourers, 1 in every 31; carpenters and joiners, 1 in every 59; sawyers and tailors, 1 in every 63; weavers, 1 in every 75; carvers and gilders, 1 in every 89; shoemakers, 1 in 91; coachmakers, 1 in 106; and turners and cabinet-makers, 1 in every 580 of the entire body. The turners and cabinet-makers are also the least criminal; that is to say, there have been the least relative number of them taken into custody during the last ten years for manslaughter, rape, common assaults, and simple larceny.

LABOUR AND THE POOR.

THE METROPOLITAN DISTRICTS.

[FROM OUR SPECIAL CORRESPONDENT.]

OF THE SHIP AND BOAT BUILDERS.

LETTER LXVIII.

According to the last census the number of "Ship-builders, Carpenters, and Wrights" (terms between which it is not easy to distinguish, the builder, carpenter, and wright being, according to my informants, one and the same individual), were in 1841 20,424 throughout Great Britain. Of these 17,498 were resident in England and Wales, and 2,926 in Scotland. The number located in the Metropolis—with whom I have more particularly to deal—was then 2,309. Since that period the number appears to have increased nearly one-fifth, for, according to the best-informed persons in connection with the trade, the following may be taken as a correct estimate of the hands belonging to the different branches of the business at the present time:—

	Society Men.	Non-society Men.	Total number of Society and Non-society Men.
Shipwrights	1,500	500	2,000
„ Joiners ..	110	230	340
Mast and Block makers	110	140	250
Boat-builders	30	80	110
Barge-builders	—	150	150
	1,750	1,100	2,850

The building of a ship may be not inaptly compared to that of a house, as I have described it in my former Letters. The modeller executes the plans of the architect. The shipwright is the carpenter. The ship-joiner's department of the work is not very dissimilar in its character to that of his namesake ashore; while the labour of the mast and block makers, of the boat-builders, and the sail-makers, may roughly typify that of the cabinet-makers and upholsterers, and other furnishers and finishers of our dwellings.

It is not my intention fully to describe the whole process of the important art of ship-building, nor would the limits of a newspaper admit of such description. To show the divisions of the trade, however, and so to render the statements I give more clear and intelligible, I will very briefly explain the process as it was described to me by working men, to whom I was referred as being the most skilful and intelligent. Three classes of workmen are employed in the construction of a vessel, before it is "ready for rigging." These are the *ship-wrights*, the *ship-joiners*, and the *caulkers*. The work (as regards the mechanical labour employed) commences with the shipwright; and he and the ship-joiner make the whole "carcass" from "keel to gunal" (gunwale); the joiner's work being confined principally to the formation of the cabins. Drafts and plans are given out by the foreman for the guidance of all the operatives. The shipwright begins with the keel, which is always made of elm—sometimes American, but chiefly English, timber being used. They then "put in the floors;" which are the timbers that constitute the bottom of the vessel and float upon the water. These "floors" consist of first, second, and third "futtocks" (fuddocks), the form of which I described in my letter on ship-timber sawing, and they are made so as to give, when put together by the skill of the workman, the form, the bend, and sweep of the hull. The perfect construction of this portion of the vessel is the high art of the shipwright. "Top-timber" is then placed above the floors for the purpose of binding and strengthening them by an interior as well as an exterior connection, and when that is done—English oak being used as the material—the ship is said to be "in frame." She—for I found the feminine appellative applied, no matter in what stage the vessel might be—is then "standed;" that is, pieces of timber, five and six inches square, are affixed fore and aft, as a temporary hold or binding to the timbers, so that they may "set" properly, for which a month is sometimes allowed. After this the ship is in a state to be "skinned," or planked, the wrights commencing with "the wale," or continuation of the bottom; and thus they work on to the completion of the "up sides" which surmount the upper deck.

Thus far outside work alone has been spoken of. After this the inside portion is begun; but sometimes the outside and inside works are carried on simultaneously. The inside work is generally commenced at the lower deck clamp—the clamp being the part which holds and supports the beams. The lower deck beams are "crossed," or adjusted, in a way not unlike the adjustment of the girders and joists of a house; and the same labour is completed as regards the middle and upper decks (supposing the vessel to be 1000 tons), but the planking is "left to the last to give the ship air." If a smaller vessel be built, the same method is practised. The next stage is to form "the poop," which comprises the outer portion, or carcass, of the captain's, officers', and passengers' apartments; and then that of the forecastles, or sleeping places of the crew. The beams, of English or African oak—English oak and sometimes teak having been used for all the previous portions—are then laid across, to form the quarter-deck, and the decks are afterwards "planked." The planks are of Dantzic fir, and are laid in a way very similar to that practised in flooring a room, but the shipwright must lay his planks with a nice adjustment to the curved and sweeping outline of the ship; while the outline to which the house joiner has to work in the floors is generally straight.

The ship-joiner, when the work is advanced as I have detailed, is required to ply *his* avocation. He makes and fits up the whole of the interior accommodation of the ship, such as the cabins for the officers and passengers, and the forecastles. Deal, which is afterwards painted, is the wood generally used for the cabins of merchant vessels; but when the fitting-up is in a superior style, handsome mahogany or maple gives a richness and elegance of appearance to the interior of the ship. I was told by an experienced person that the costly furniture and fitting-up of a cabin greatly reassured any timid passenger to whom sea voyaging was new, and who felt nervous and apprehensive before the hour of sailing. Such a passenger—a lady especially—I was assured, seemed to feel, and had not unfrequently expressed an opinion, that the owners of the ship were confident there was no danger of its being wrecked, or they would not have expended so large a sum in mere adornment. The saloon of a steamer, or the equivalent "cuddy" of a passengers sailing vessel of the first class, is often fitted up with mirrors, sofas, and expensive wainscotting, in a style that is known as the "gorgeous." The ship-joiner makes also the sideboards, the sofas, and every article of furniture which is fixed or stationary in the vessel, and so he must be able to work as a cabinet-maker as well as a joiner. On the very rare occasions on which the ship-joiner is required to work by the day his wages are 5s. 6d.; on piece-work, however, he earns somewhat more.

The caulkers are employed solely in "caulking" the vessel, the process required to ensure her proper floating. They drive a caulking-iron (not unlike a blunt square chisel) into the ship's seams, and then "horse it up;" that is, fill the interstice with oakum, driven in as close and tight as possible with a tool called "a horse." The surface is then pitched over, and the pitch is afterwards scraped and painted. But "caulkers," according to the divisions of artizans which I have here adopted, belong to a different class, and cannot be included among the workers in wood.

In the principal, and, indeed, in nearly all the ship-building yards, the men work by contract—a system which has been pursued for the last fifty years at the least. A shipwright contracts to do all the wright's work, or a portion of it, and employs men under him. In these cases no day-work is performed; all is done by the piece. In some yards, however, there is occasional day-work, and the payment for it is 6s. and 7s. a day. I am assured, moreover, that on piece work, in a good establishment, good workmen earn an equivalent amount at least, as the proprietors will not allow them to be ground down to swell the profits of the contractors. Nor, in the best yards of which I am now writing, are there any middlemen (beyond the contractor), or any sub-letting. The same system is pursued in the departments of the joiner and the caulker. Under the best management, however, and with all the checks adopted against abuse, the system of contract leads to the following grievance. Each contractor can employ his own men, or "mates" as they are termed, and of course he gives the preference to his own friends and relatives, who may be young men, while wrights or joiners who have spent half a life time in working, "off and on," for the same firm, may stand by idle. In case of a discharge from one of her Majesty's dockyards, "the hands," as it was worded to me, "make for London, for river-work," and cause somewhat of a glut of ship-building operatives. Many of the men thus discharged may be friends and relatives of a contractor, and men who have superannuated pensions from Government are "put on" over the heads of workmen to whom long employment in an establishment has given what they not unreasonably consider a sort of prescriptive right of engagement. These cases are, I understand, exceptional, and in the ship-builders' yards, which may well be called of the "honourable trade," the contractor must not, and does not, use his power to employ under-paid workmen. Skilled labour is indispensable for employment. The only complaint of which I heard was that an undue preference was shown.

The shipwrights and all the mechanics employed in ship-building find their own tools. The wright's tools are not costly. The principal are the axe, adze, maul, mallet, saw, and chisel. A complete set is not worth more than 50s., and some work with tools of the value of 25s., carrying them all in a bag. The joiner's tools, which are similar to those of his brother operative on shore, are worth, in their fullest completeness, £20. I heard of one ship-joiner whose tools, along with the handsome mahogany chests in which they were contained, were worth £80; £10 may be the average value of the tools that a ship-joiner possesses. A caulker's tools, however, cost only a few shillings.

The hours of labour are from six in the morning in summer, and from daylight in winter, until six at night, or until dusk. Out of this term of labour half an hour is allowed for breakfast, half an hour for luncheon, an hour for dinner, and half an hour for tea; so that the entire term of labour is at the utmost nine hours and a half.

There is no especial subdivision among any of the classes that I have spoken of, and they are employed alike in building steamers and every kind of sailing vessel. The contractor, or the foreman, who has the general overlooking and direction, will take care that a workman is employed on the work in which he is the most skilled, but no department of the labour must be strange to him. Some of the joiners, who may be less efficient than their fellows, are often "put to embossing"— that is to say, they work after the shipwrights, in planing the sides of the vessel, and in putting the ornaments to the head, side, and stern. When a joiner, even of the very best order, has completed the particular work given to him, he also—if no "job" that is more suitable to him be ready—is put to embossing, until other work can be given to him. The calling of the shipwright is exclusively his own. No house-carpenter can undertake—or rather would, in a good yard, be allowed to undertake—the execution of the shipwright's work. But the case is different with the joiner. A clever house-joiner readily becomes a clever ship-joiner, and is occasionally so employed by a befriending contractor. The ship-joiner in like manner can work as a house-joiner, and did so before the house-joining sank into its present condition—a condition which I have fully depicted in my letters on the subject. Among the ship-joiners—I must still be understood to speak of the honourable trade—there are no "improvers," no "strapping," indeed none of the more serious grievances by which his less fortunate brother operative ashore is afflicted.

The work of the ship-builders is very hard, and demands not merely the customary skill and quickness of the handicraftsman, but great manual strength; they must either carry heavy beams or wood-work from the workshops to the ship, or else they must convey ponderous timbers complete to the workshop for affixing in the ship, and with these they must ascend and descend the ladders. In the course of my inquiry the weather was very sultry, and the men suffered greatly by having to work in the broiling sun; for in many parts of the labour on the ship itself they could have no shelter. The work is always carried on in the "dry dock," where the vessel is being built, or in the workshops adjacent, where everything is made (such as doors, furniture, &c.) that is susceptible of admeasurement, and then taken to the ship to be "fitted." In the winter the men suffer much from exposure to the cold. In rainy weather they are employed as much as possible in the workshops, or under cover.

The caulkers' work is especially hard, so much so that they do not toil later than three in the afternoon. The greater fatigue of the caulkers is attributable to their having to caulk in all positions of the body—recumbent or half-recumbent. When the bottom of the ship, for instance, is caulked, the men have hardly room to stand. Accidents are not unfrequent among shipwrights, who work on "stages" (equivalent to the scaffolding of a house) lashed to the ships' sides. A short time before my visit to one of the yards, one of the chains of a stage holding four men broke, and they all were suddenly precipitated some twenty feet to the ground; all were hurt—one seriously—though no lives were lost. A fall of this kind is the more dangerous as the men work with sharp tools.

In point of intelligence, the ship-builders must be ranked high—quite as high as their fellow-labourers of the best class (I now allude to none other) ashore. One shipwright, however, thought that many of his fellows did not avail themselves so freely as they might of the munificent means for the education of children which an eminent shipbuilder has so generously provided—I allude to Mr. Green. I was assured, notwithstanding, that every shipbuilder, not an "emigration" or "a lath and plaster man," or a "boiler-maker"—terms that I shall presently explain—could, at the very least, read and write.

The shipbuilders are, I found, great politicians. It is customary, during their half hour's luncheon at eleven o'clock, for one man to read the newspaper aloud in the public-house parlour; a discussion almost invariably follows, and is often enough resumed in the evening. The men for the most part go home to their dinners. The earnings of the shipwrights of the best class are, while at work, from 40s. to 50s. a week; and those of the joiners and caulkers from 10 to 15 per cent. less; but it must be borne in mind that the average employment of the general body does not exceed nine months in the year. The majority of the shipbuilders are married men with families, residing chiefly in Poplar and the adjacent parts. Some whom I called upon had very comfortable homes, and in their apartments there was no lack of books—a very fair test, it may be said, of the intelligence and prudence of a working man. Not a few of the shipbuilders have brought up their sons to their own calling, or to some other branch of ship-building, or else to a sea-faring life. Within these twenty years the shipbuilders generally were hard drinkers—now, I am assured, there are 50 steady men to 1 tippler.

In some yards the workmen are paid once a fortnight, the money being disbursed to them out of the counting-house on a Friday evening, the payment being for all that was due up to the previous Tuesday night. In other yards they are paid at four p.m. on the Saturday. I was informed that it is common enough for a shipbuilder, with his wife and children, to enjoy his Saturday evening in some suburban excursion. Payment in public-houses, or anything approximating to the truck system, is unknown.

The average time now occupied before a ship of 1,000 tons can be built and launched is twelve months; but on an emergency an 800 ton ship has been commenced and launched in four months. Formerly, I was assured, ships were kept so long on the stocks for "seasoning"—especially the East India Company's large vessels—that the dry rot appeared in their timbers before planking. "Now," said my informant, "that's only the case in her Majesty's dockyards."

In the course of my inquiries, I heard the better class of shipbuilders speak of a description of work known in the trade by the very expressive title of "emigration work"—by which was meant the building of a vessel "just for a passage out." The men thus employed were either unskilful, or not respectable, but the demand for such vessels has now almost ceased—old vessels alone being fitted up for emigrants. "There's Mr. ——," I was told, "picks out old ships and prepares them, and sends them out. He supplies emigration companies." Another class of ships I heard described as "lath and plaster" ships. "They are thrown together," I was told—another informant said "blown together—in the north of England; made cheap, of Quebec oak and inferior stuff, and inferior work; the timber ain't squared, it's sided together with the sap in it, and so it'll shrink and warp." I was told, however, that some ships are built in a northern port, almost equal to those built in London.

The shipbuilders in London are—as regards the majority—natives of the metropolis. The others are principally Scotchmen, and west of England men, with a small proportion of north countrymen, and a very small proportion of Irishmen. In one large yard there was but one Irishman. All whom I saw, no matter from what part of the country, spoke of the London-built ships, in the good yards, as being the best in the world.

There are two other classes of operatives connected with ship-building, to whom I need only allude, as my present inquiry is confined to the workers in wood—viz., the workers in iron. These are the ship's smiths (called blacksmiths in the trade), who make the bolts, knees, and other iron work of the ship, and who are a highly respectable class; as well as the iron shipwrights, or men employed in constructing the iron steam-boats. Between these last-mentioned workers in ship iron and the workers in ship wood, there is no cordiality. The iron workers are called "boiler-makers" by the regular shipwrights, who describe them as an inferior class to themselves, made up from all descriptions of workers in iron, and including many boys and unskilled labourers.

The first process usually observed in ship-building is the preparation of the model, showing the form and proportions of the vessel to be built. In large establishments a modeller is employed by the ship builders, and his services are confined to them alone. For the purposes of general trade this profession is very limited; only one name appears in the Post-office Directory as a *ship modeller*. This gentleman employs only the members of his own family in the business, and his calling seems so far hereditary that it has been pursued by his family from the time of his grandfather. A draft is first pencilled, and by that the modeller works. Until about twenty years ago one draft served from generation to generation for one particular kind of vessel. Now, a draft and model are prepared expressly for every ship. The art of modelling requires not only the exercise of the most patient and minute nicety, but a thorough knowledge of ship-building in all its ramifications. The artist, too, must give the precise form of the vessel, as well as every separate portion, called "sections," for the guidance of the builder. Moreover the model is sometimes "rigged," and the masts, blocks, &c., are shown according "to scale;" and further the tonnage of the ship to be built must be expressed by the admeasurement of it.

Ships are now registered according to the new plan of admeasurement (established about ten years ago). The great difference between the two systems is that the new is inside, and the old outside, measurement. To ascertain the tonnage by the new mode, the middle (or medium) length of the vessel inside, from stem to stern, is taken; also the depth amidships, one-sixth of the depth forward and one-sixth aft; the breadth, one-third from the deck amidships, and one-third from the bottom; the same forward and aft; and these respective admeasurements are then multiplied together, decimally, and when divided by 3,500 the result gives the "register tonnage." To show the tonnage by the old mode, the outside length "between the perpendiculars" (or from stem to stern) was ascertained; also the measurement of two-fifths of the main beam (which gives the length of the keel for tonnage); and these results being multiplied by the breadth, and by half the breadth of the vessel, and then divided by 94, gave the builder's measurement. I am informed that, notwithstanding every precaution, the tonnage measurement of a ship is hardly ever correct. Ships are "cramped," as it is called by the builder; that is, the proportions of the parts where the admeasurement takes place are so managed that the result shall, for purposes of registry, &c., be as favourable as possible to the shipowner.

The modeller works to any scale required. For a small yacht or schooner an inch to a foot has been worked; for a large ship, an inch to 20 feet. The woods he uses are the finest firs, holly, mahogany, box, and ebony. The pulleys and all the tackle for a full-rigged model are made of bone or any hard wood. Sometimes the model shows only what may be styled the exterior of the vessel, the holds and cabins being left to the discretion or the instructions of the builder. Sometimes every portion, down to the minutest part, is expressed. A model can, moreover, be taken to pieces, when made for that purpose, and all the component parts of the important process of shipbuilding are thus displayed individually. To show the labour and nicety required for such a model, I may mention that one of a West Indiaman, 350 tons burden, was made for a learned judge now on the bench, and when taken to pieces, the parts numbered 651. My informant attributed much of the greater care and attention now given to the production of ships' models to the improvements introduced by the Yacht Club, the members having frequently required models, both for experimental and practical purposes.

Another, and an important department of the ship-modeller's business, and one subjected to severe examination, is to prepare the models of vessels for the Admiralty and law courts, to illustrate collisions; and thus to show, as far as possible, by the nature and locality of the damage, if the vessels were on the right or wrong tacks, according to the regulations of the Admiralty and the Corporation of the Trinity House, and sometimes to demonstrate the extent of damage sustained.

A *ship-joiner*, whom I found in a very comfortable room with his wife and family, gave me the following account:—

"My father was in the business, and I was brought up to it by a friend of his. That's often reckoned a better way, as fathers are too severe or too indulgent. I was regularly apprenticed, and have never worked anywhere but in London, except once. I have always worked under the contractors, and have made my 33s., 36s., and 38s. a week when at work, according to the piece work—it's all piece work—that I get through. There is no fixed price—so much for the job, whatever it may be—and I've done all parts, I think. There's an understanding as to the pay. We know that we can make our living out of it. I may work rather more than nine months in the year altogether. In a good yard, after a ship is finished, there may be a slack of two or three months before we are wanted on a new ship. We are not kept going regularly at any one yard—only as long as a ship's in hand. We look out at all the yards. I'm a society man, and wish everybody was. I earn as much now as I did twelve or thirteen years back, when I first worked as a journeyman, and as provisions are cheaper I'm better off, or I could not give my children—there's three of them—good schooling as I do. I don't know that I can do better than bring up my boy—the others are girls—to my own trade, if he grows up sharp and strong; it's no use without. I know of no grievances that we have. I worked, not long since, in the joinering of an iron ship. There's more joinering in them than in wood ships, as there's a lining of wood to back the iron work. I don't mix with the 'boiler-makers.' I seldom stir out of a night, as I'm generally well tired after my day's work. I live near my work, and take every meal at home, except my luncheon, and that's a draught of beer, and sometimes a crust with it and a crumb of cheese, that I now and then put in my pocket."

The *carving of the figure-heads* of vessels is a distinct branch of the business of ship-building. In some yards this carving, as at present pursued, partakes more and more of the characteristics of a fine art, and in all it is less rude than it was. The monstrosities, the merely grim and grotesque, which delighted the seamen of the past age, are now almost entirely things of the past. In the figure-heads of the meanest vessels now built, some observance of truth and nature is displayed. The figure-head is ordered of the carver for the general trade (the greater builders usually comprising that department as well as others in their own establishments). Sometimes he works from a drawing— rarely from a model. A carver upon whom I called, had a spacious workshop in the corner of a large garden, immediately behind his dwelling-house, which was near the Thames. Ranged alongside the wall, at the top of the garden, were a row of colossal and semi-colossal figure-heads, exceedingly grim and dusty, and seeming singularly out of place, for they loomed down, with their unmistakeable seafaring look, upon the white and orange lilies, the many-tinted sweet peas and carnations, and the red and white roses. The figures were all of elm, and each had a preliminary coat of paint of a dull brick colour, to prevent the wood from cracking, so that their uniformity of hue added to the curious effect that they presented. It was easy enough to recognise the features, or rather the approximation to the features, of the Queen, Prince Albert, and the Duke of Wellington; though there were several countenances which looked familiar enough, and yet puzzled the memory as to whose effigy was represented. Some figure-heads were robed, and starred, and coronetted, and some had the plain coats of the present day. With these were mingled female forms, some with braided hair, others with very rigid ringlets, carved out of the solid wood. I ascertained that it would have been idle in- deed to speculate on the "likeness" of most of these figures, as they are ready for an emergency. Sometimes a "head" is demanded in a hurry—the name of the vessel not being determined upon until she is in an advanced stage of completion. Then the well-known effigies are ready; while the plain are available, with the least delay, for the "Williams" or "Georges" of the smaller merchant ships, and the dec- orated and coronetted for any given peer or potentate that may be popular for the time being; or else, with the addition of painting and gilding, and a little alteration at the hands of the carver, the general figures are ready to be converted into any given individual whose popularity attracts the shipowner's attention, or whose patronage ensures his regard. The female figures are in like manner convertible into any "Jane" or "Ann," or into the allegorical "Justice," "Peace," "Concord," or "Commerce," according as they are wanted at "the shortest notice."

Along the wall of the workshop were the same array of effigies, while in one corner, amidst heaped up timber, was a covered figure in a sitting position, which was much more elaborately worked than the others. A cornucopia rested on its left arm, while the right hand grasped a snake, the head of which had been broken off, and lay close by. The carving of the thick curly hair was minute, and showed great painstaking. This, I found, was at one time a choice ornament of the Lord Mayor's state barge, and represented "Africa." An opposite figure, allegorical of another quarter of the world, I was told, became rotten and had to be removed from the barge, and "Africa" was removed at the same time, or she would have appeared isolated. When deposited in its present place the figure was gilt, but a great part of the gilding having been rubbed or fallen off, its new owner had it painted all over to resemble the others.

Figure-heads are generally made of elm; a few, however, are of fir, a material demanded by some builders from its cheapness. The largest English elms are used by the ship-carvers; the figure-heads are worked out of the solid trunk, except the arm, if it be extended in the act of pointing, as it often is. An arm, or a telescope, or any projecting portion, is then jointed or "limbed" to the trunk. The ship-carvers make the cat-heads, for which elm is used; and until within these eight or ten years, they carved the ornaments required for the cabins, and the scrolls, or twisted snakes, or roses, thistles, or shamrocks that were sometimes demanded for the adornment of the ship's hull; but this department of their trade is now superseded, composition ornaments being almost universally in use.

The ship-carvers in the general trade are a small body of men, numbering only 5 masters, 15 journeymen, and 4 apprentices—all, I was told, London men. The work is by day, 6s. being the established day's wage. The employment of the men is tolerably regular. They have no society, and no benefit or sick funds among them. They all live near the river, and three-fourths of them on the Surrey side. Their character and habits in no respect differ from those of the shipwrights.

The price of an average-sized elm figure-head, exclusive of any cost in painting or gilding, is from £6 to £7 10s.—more sometimes, according to the work required. A figure-head of the more elaborate style is about a fortnight's work for one man. The men find their own tools, which are worth, in their completeness, £5 or £6. The tools are axes, saws, chisels, and gouges, but principally gouges. Among them are no slop-workers, and I heard of no grievances; but more than one workman expressed some apprehension of the proceedings of two men who were in the habit of frequenting the docks, and offering to get repairs to figure-heads executed below the established and fair prices. Of these men, mention is made in the following narrative, and the fact was confirmed by others:—

A muscular, hearty, and hale-looking young man, whom I found at work in a shop, presenting many of the characteristics of one I have more particularly described, but not the same, gave me the following information:—

"I was apprenticed to Mr. ——, and have never left London. My father was connected with ship-building, and so put me to this branch. I'm unmarried, and live with my friends. I have nothing to complain of in the way of business, as I have pretty good employment. We all drink beer—some of us, perhaps, too much, but nothing compared to other trades. Ours is hard work, but we don't drink much at work. Look you here, sir, this log of ellum, with just the sides taken off by the sawyers, to make it square, has to be made into a 'head'—into a foreign nobleman or prince—I don't remember his name, but it's a queer one. To do that is heavy lifting and hard work. None of these fellows here (pointing to the figures), is the proper size, hardly big enough, or I could easily gouge this one now into a lord. We first axe the log into a rough shape, a sort of outline, and then finish it with chisels and gouges. I sometimes work from a drawing, but mostly out of my own head, and direct myself by my eye. We have nothing to do with painting or gilding the heads. They're sent home in their own woods just with a coat of paint over them, to save them from cracking. Yes, you're right, sir, that head will do for the Queen; but if a Queen isn't wanted, and it's the proper size, I can soon make her into any other female. Or she might do for a 'Mary Anne,' without altering; certainly she might. The way the hair's carved is the Queen's style, and has been in fashion these eight or ten years. Ringlets ain't easy; particularly cork-screw ringlets, as they're called. The watch-chain and seals to a gentleman ain't easy, as you have to bring out that part and cut away from it. The same with buttons and stars. Perhaps we aren't as good at legs as at other carving. We generally carve only to the knee. The shipwrights place our work on the ship's knee caps. We have no slop-workers among us; but there are two men who keeps a look out at the docks for broken heads, or heads damaged any way, and offer to repair them cheap. They're not workers themselves, but they get hold of any drunken carpenter, or any ship carver that happens to be hard up and out of work, and put them to the job at low prices. But the thing don't satisfy, and they do very little; still, it's a break in upon us. I make from 24s. to 30s. a week the year through, oftener nearer 30s. than 24s. I make 36s. at full work."

The builders of ships' boats are a distinct body, as are the builders of wherries for racing or other aquatic amusements; and the general boat-builder constructs skiffs, lug-boats, lighters, and barges. These divisions, however, are not very precisely observed, for almost every master will undertake the building of any description of boat.

Six boats are the complement of a ship of 1,000 tons—the long boat, two cutters, gig, jolly boat, and life boat. The "long boat" is used for the lading and discharging of the cargo, and for the rescue of the crew when the vessel is in danger of being wrecked. The "cutters" are principally employed for communication with the shore when the ship is on a foreign station, or is moored out at sea. The "jolly boat" is made available for any temporary or unimportant service, and is more in use than any other boat—while the "gig" is the captain's boat. A merchant vessel of 350 tons carries four boats. Of these, the life boat must, by a recent Act, be one; the long boat is usually another; and the remaining two boats are provided according to the discretion of the captain, as he may judge that the nature of his service and the character of the ports or shores to which he is bound may require. Smaller ships have two or three boats.

The other boats are those used for carrying on the traffic of the river; for the conveyance of "fares," as persons who "take a boat" are styled by the watermen; or for the recreation of those who are fond of "boating," wherries being now almost entirely in the hands of amateurs. The "lug boat" is a large roomy boat adapted for the conveyance of luggage to and from a ship; the "lighter" is made to fulfil the same purposes as regards cargo; the barge is useful for general purposes, but principally for the conveyance of coal or any heavy material. The "skiff" is the boat with a round stem and a square stern, that the watermen now ply with. The "wherry" is the long, narrow boat, the character of which I have already indicated.

The first process in boat-building is the formation of the keel, which is of American elm or oak, and must be of good, long-grained, tough wood. The "timbers" (ribs) are next placed together, having been prepared to the proper sizes and shapes by the sawyers; they are "moulded," or fitted one to another, on the same principle as in ship-building. This done, the carcass of the boat is formed. Oak, elm, and (though rarely) fir are the materials of these carcasses—the majority being made of English elm. The carcass is then "skinned;" that is, the "streaks" (pronounced strakes), or exterior timbers, are placed to complete the work. For ships' boats the streaks are of mahogany or "wainscot" (as the Baltic oak is called in boat-building), or fir, which is the cheapest, and makes the lightest but the least durable vessel. The streaks of skiffs, wherries, lighters, and lug-boats are of English oak, as are those of the barges, with an occasional exception, where fir is so employed.

The London boat-builders are not now a numerous class—numbering only about 120, independently of the builders of wherries, who are not more than 35. Three-fourths of these operatives are London men; the majority of the others being from Deal and the north of England, especially from Whitby. They are a sober and far from ignorant class. "I really don't know one drunkard among us," said one of them to me, "and I think we can all read and write; but we are a downcast lot to what we were once." Another man, whose information I found corroborated, said, "I think the men in my trade are steady and domestic. Most of us have wives and families. I don't know a gambler among us, and there's only a few youngsters that care for a hand at cards. Generally of a Saturday night, if we've had a middling week in the yard, we pay 6d. a piece, and enjoy ourselves quietly over our beer or ale, or whatever we like, and our pipes, and our talk, and when the money's out we go away."

The boat-builders work by contract and by day; the contract or piece-work system greatly predominating. The payment by day, of ten hours' labour, is 5s. 6d. An operative contracts with a master to build a boat complete, which he does by his unassisted labour, or if it be a large-sized boat, or demanded in a hurry, two men undertake it. The employer finds all the material, and the work is carried on in his "yard," as the boat-building establishments are always called. The operatives engaged in this business have a list of prices agreed upon in concurrence with their masters in 1824, but now little regarded. The boat-builders have a society, but it is only for providing members' funerals, and for relief during sickness. They have no provisions for the regulation of wages, so that, according to the "honourable" or "screwing" character of the employer, there is a difference in the rate paid of 6d., 9d., and even 1s. a foot. The observance of the prices of 1824 is rendered (nominally) a dead letter by the following method:—In the case of a gig of the first class 5s. a foot is the amount on the list of prices, and 5s. a foot is still paid; but in 1824, there were only nine streaks worked where there are now thirteen, and so, in a gig of the largest size, twenty feet being an average length, there is almost a week's extra work, and at the same rate of remuneration to the artificer. And thus through all the grades of boat-building. Nor is this all. Payment for "extras," such as a "shifting wash-streak," or board over the gunwale, was allowed to the workman, but that, with some others, has been gradually "knocked off." There are, however, still a few exceptions to this under-payment.

The boat-builders are not affected by the introduction of unskilled labour. Want of regular employment and uncertainty of remuneration are their principal grievances. The average work of those best employed is for about nine months in the year, realising 33s. a week during that time, or 22s. a week for the twelve. This uncertainty or irregularity of employment is a great evil to the working-men. "If we lives casual," said one man to me, "we grows careless."

The boat-builder finds his own tools, a complete set of which is worth from £3 to £4. Many manage to work, however, with tools worth not more than 25s. I am assured that their tools are now seldom pledged. A boat-builder will suffer a great deal before he resorts to the pawnbroker with his tools; some of them knowing, from woful experience, how difficult is the redemption of a pledge to a man whose employment is irregular. They seldom reside very near their place of work, but are scattered about wherever lodgings may be most economical. They are paid every Saturday night, nine o'clock being the very latest hour in the worst yards. They have no grievances as to payment in public-houses, or enthralment to a publican connected with a master or foreman.

The business is generally learned by apprenticeship to a master. Twenty-five or thirty years ago £50 was not an unfrequent premium for an out-door apprentice; now premiums are never given, but a youth's labour is paid at a mere nominal rate, or not paid at all, for one year or eighteen months, and this is considered equivalent to a premium. Each master has his own scale of wages to his apprentice.

In the last year of the apprenticeship, when the lad is often as good as a journeyman, and can be employed while the men are idle, the rate is usually 15s. The apprentices taken, however, are not so numerous as to be complained of by the journeymen.

I now give two statements from working boat-builders. The first is that of a highly intelligent man who has had great experience, and has observed many changes in his trade. For these changes he gave what he considered the causes, expressing himself with terseness and propriety. Many grievances also are specified; the depression of the trade is accounted for, according to the best of my informant's judgment, and a further account of the habits and social condition of the boat-builders is detailed or intimated:—

"My trade," he said, "is greatly depressed to what it was. When I was out of my apprenticeship, thirty-three years ago, there was twice the employment for boat-builders that there is now. At that time I think boat-builders were doubly as numerous as at present, as well as having double the employment. I consider the change owing to the many railways and steamboats now in operation. When the Scotch steamers came up, between twenty and thirty years ago, the Scotch smacks plying to London and back were soon run off that coast, and the same with other coasts. These smacks were always knocking their boats to pieces, and wanting new ones, or wanting repairs. They had to get the boats out to get alongside the wharfs, but now the steamer goes right up alongside, and hardly ever wants boats, and can hang them up as in a parlour. Then the jetties and piers do away with the use of boats. At Ryde now, and in many a foreign part, the steamer goes right up to the pier, and the boats come home without a scratch. Before the piers came up, passengers, and luggage, and cargo, used to be landed in boats. Of course there's fewer wanted at present. I could and did earn 50s. a week the year through, thirty years back. At that time boat-builders were far better situated in having comfortable homes, and in being able to educate and provide for old age, or for families, than at present. There are more and cheaper schools now, certainly, but look at the difference of 50s. a week the year through, and 22s. or 23s., which I take to be the present average for those in the best work. I'm satisfied that boat-builders are an intelligent set now, but I think there was more intelligence among us in my young days. There's not much drinking among us at present, and there was less then. Indeed, the less a man earns, and the more he's out of work, the more he's tempted to drink. He's driven to drink by poverty and oppression. He's often afraid to face his home. We were far better treated, too, by our employers formerly. Now, we're bullied and sworn at by many a master, 'till a man's blood boils. We're exposed to degrading words, that lower a man. Not that all masters are such; for there's Mr. F——, I worked for him a few months back, and there's no under-working or under-paying there; it's a good yard, I wish to God there were plenty such; and there's your money early on a Saturday evening, and all proper treatment. With the cutting masters, however, a poor man has no check. If he says anything he gets abused. And now I'll tell you, sir, of a crying evil, and if it was necessary I'd get, in two hours from this time and place, twenty honest men's signatures to prove that I state nothing but the fact. It's a crying evil that captains and owners will go up and down the river and buy old rotten boats, and have them painted up to look viewy. Emigrants' ships are surveyed, to be sure, but the survey of the boats is often nominal. Why, how often do we read of an emigrant ship having been in distress in a storm, and how her long-boat was launched and was stove in in no time, and how numbers of poor fellows' lives were lost? And why was the boat stove so soon? Just because she was 'nail-sick.' What do I mean by nail-sick, sir? Why, it's our word when the nails have rusted asunder in the old rotten wood, and so when there's a stress on the boat, and she gets a hard blow, why, she goes slap to pieces. She was all rottenness, paint, and putty, at start. There ought to be an officer to survey every boat, and attend to nothing else, and who wouldn't be humbugged with paint. Owners and captains won't give anything like a fair price for necessary repairs. If a man asks £1, though that may be only a reasonable price, they'll say, 'A pound, pooh! The ship's carpenter shall do it;' and then perhaps, and very frequently too, it's not done at all. When the act of Parliament, three or four years ago, required every ship to carry a life-boat, it caused good work for us, because shipowners did provide life-boats at that time. Now, when they're wanted, owners and captains go up and down the river, and pick up any old rubbishing thing, and fit it for one. When it's trimmed up it looks very well. But, if any one were to go on board a ship that didn't belong to a good owner—some little shifty owner's ship—and if he would just try with a small knife under the bilge of the boat, why many's the time it'll go through it as if it was through a wafer. Or they'll find, perhaps, six or seven coats of paint, after a little scraping, for the paint holds the streaks together until there's stress and danger; so that when there is, down she goes with, may be, many a fine fellow in her."

Another boat-builder, employed at present in the building of ships' boats, gave me the following statement. He resided in a crowded neighbourhood, not far from the river-side. His room was small and dark, but fully furnished, and a few numbers of a cheap periodical lay on the table. He was a grave good-looking man:—

"I have been a boat-builder fourteen or fifteen years," he said, "and served an apprenticeship in London. My father was a waterman, and I wish he had brought me up to some better business; but they say no businesses are as good as they were once. He's been dead some years. There's no reduction in the wages paid me since I was out of my time, but I must do more work for less money. [He then made a statement as to streaks, &c., similar to what I have given.] I lived with my mother until she died, four or five years back, and all I'd saved went to bury her. I don't think I could very well afford to keep a wife, though it's very lonesome having nobody to care about one. No doubt I could get a wife, but to keep her is another thing. I shouldn't like two to be in poverty instead of one, and I wouldn't like any decent girl I might marry to have to do work for the sweaters, to help us to make both ends meet when work's scarce. Some have to do it, though, to my knowing; and don't the girls find out the difference between that and being in good service, as some of them have been! I'm not employed— and very few of us are—three-quarters of my time; and, take the year through, I don't earn more than a guinea a week. I may be hard at work this month and have nothing to do for the next fortnight, but go from yard to yard and be told I'm not wanted. Now, suppose I've 21s. a week, and I'm a single man. I pay 2s. a week for this room, with a recess there for my bed. They're my own sticks. Then say 8d. a week for my washing, as I can't bear to be dirty. Well, then, I often work a good way off, and must live out. I can potter on cheaper at home. My breakfast, at the very lowest, is 3½d., and that's only 1½d. for half a pint of coffee, penny loaf, and penny butter. Properly, for a working man, it should be 7d.—pint of coffee, 3d., penny loaf, and penny butter, and 2d. for a rasher; but say 3½d. When one's hard at work one requires some refreshment before dinner time, and you can't have anything cheaper than half a pint of beer—a pint's not too much; the half pint's a penny. Then for dinner, half a pound of steak is 3½d.; if you get it cheaper it's tough and grisly, and no good. I get it cooked for nothing at a public-house if I take a pint of beer with it, and that's

2d., and a penny for potatoes, and a halfpenny for bread; altogether the lowest for a decent dinner, anything like satisfying, is 7d. Tea is a halfpenny more than breakfast; for it's tea instead of coffee, you see, sir. Then there's a pint of beer, and a penn'orth of cheese and a penn'orth of bread for supper, that's 4d. I know there's plenty of working men who go without supper; but I'm hearty myself, and feel I want it. That's 1s. 7½d. for a day's keep, and a boat-builder's is hard work, and we require good support. Seven times 1s. 7½d.—and indeed Sunday should be reckoned more, for if I have a good dinner off a joint with my landlord and his family, as I have every now and then, I pay him 1s.—but, say 7 times 1s. 7½d. that's how much?—11s. 4½d. Well, then, there is my club money, and I pay 3d. a week for papers; and I go to chapel on a Sunday pretty regular, and there's often a collection, and I can't pass the plate without my 3d., and, indeed, I oughtn't; and I sometimes get a letter from a brother, a mason, I have in Australia, and I sometimes write to him: and besides there's 4d. a week for tobacco, at the very least, as a pipe's a sort of company to a lone man; and for such like things we can't say less than 2s. a week; indeed not less than 2s. 6d. Now, sir, what's that altogether? [I told him 16s. 6½d.] Then there's 4s. 6d. a week, he continued, left for clothes, and for any new tool I may want, and for everything else; and I couldn't keep a wife, let alone a family, on that." [He seemed to enter with great zest into these explanations.] "Besides, this is the most favourable way to put it; for when I have a good week's work, and make 33s. or 34s., or as much as 36s., I want more support, and my living costs me more, though I keep it as square as I can for a rainy day or a slack time. If I ask for work, and say I'm quick at clinch boats (ship's boats), a master will say, 'Now here's a long boat I want building, how much will you do it for? Don't tell me about prices, I can't get my price, and if you won't come down a peg, another will.' If I ask £4, he'll bid £3 3s., and will bargain, perhaps, for £3 10s., and it's from eight to ten days' work. I can't very well pass an offer, as I may not very soon have another. I have worked ten months and more in Mr. ——'s yard; but that was only once. I know men and families live on 12s. a week. It's not living, though; it's only tea and bread and butter, or no butter. There can't be any strength in that."

The making of oars and sculls is a distinct branch from boat-building. The *oars* are used when two men row the boat; the *sculls* when one man is so employed. I need not further describe articles so well known. The oars are made of ash; the sculls of fir. The scull-

makers, as they are generally called, make oars and sculls indiscriminately, unless a master chooses to employ them entirely on one branch,
which is a rare occurrence. These operatives are about twice as numerous as the boat-builders. This seems an anomaly, but it was accounted
for to me thus:—Whilst a boat is in use many pairs of oars or sculls
are lost or broken. When broken they can seldom be repaired, as no
jointing, lashing, or dovetailing will sustain the pressure of the water.
It is not unusual, too, for a ship to carry out at the least duplicate
pairs of oars; sometimes more than that. The oars thus carried out,
if the ship be bound to a warmer climate, must be of well-seasoned
ash, or they will warp; and an oar that is not "true" is difficult of management, and the cause of excessive fatigue. The amateurs, who row
their own wherries, are excellent supporters of the oar makers, as they
are not unapt to lose or break their oars. Some of the river clubmen,
however, I was told by a scull maker, were among the best of rowers,
and would make capital watermen. This was not said scoffingly, but
in the way of commendation. Then it must be remembered that to
some wherries there are six pairs of oars, and to many boats two pairs.
The scull-makers work by the piece, so much the pair. In their habits
and social characteristics they do not differ from the boat-builders.

LABOUR AND THE POOR.

THE METROPOLITAN DISTRICTS.

[FROM OUR SPECIAL CORRESPONDENT.]

OF THE LONDON COOPERS.

LETTER LXIX.

I now come to describe the numbers, state, and earnings of the Coopers of London. In 1841 there were 18,379 persons belonging to this trade in Great Britain, 13,550 of whom were resident in England, 3,825 in Scotland, 812 in Wales, and 192 in the British Isles. As regards the age and sex of these, 16,012 of the number located in Great Britain, of twenty years and upwards were males, and 121 females, while of those under that age, 320 were males and 55 females.

Such was the number belonging to the trade at the time of taking the last census. In 1831 the coopers were more numerous in some counties and less numerous in others. By referring to the Occupation Abstracts for the two last decennial periods, we find that the greatest increase amongst the coopers of twenty years of age and upwards, over and above the increase of the population of the same age, occurred in the following counties, in the proportions below stated. The county in which the greatest increase took place was Lanark, where the trade was augmented 50 per cent. more than the cotemporaneous increase of the population. In Stafford the increase was 38 per cent. above that of all other classes in the same county. Kinross showed an augmentation equal to 32 per cent. Bucks and Flintshire each 31 per cent., Durham 30 per cent., Lancaster 29 per cent., and Forfar 21 per cent., over and above the other inhabitants of those districts. The counties in which the greatest decrease occurred were the following:—In Carnarvon (taking into consideration the increase of all other classes in the same locality) the coopers diminished, from 1831-41, as much as 49 per cent., in York city and Ansty 40 per cent., in Brecon 39 per cent., in Renfrew 37 per cent., in Ayr 33 per cent., in Roxburgh and Selkirk each 30 per cent., in Hertford, Denbigh, and Merioneth each 29 per cent., and in the North Riding of Yorkshire 27 per cent. The number of coopers in all England increased 3 per cent. over and above the population generally, whereas in Wales there was a decrease of 12 per cent., and in Scotland an increase of 37 per cent. In the whole of Great Britain, however, the coopers, in comparison with the rest of the population, decreased one per cent. In the metropolis, with which we are here more particularly concerned, there was an increase of 13 per cent. over and above all other classes. The number of London coopers at the time of taking the last census was as follows:—Twenty years of age and upwards—males, 3,098; females, 22. And under twenty years of age—males, 369; making together a total of 3,489. Considering the trade to have increased since that period at the same rate as formerly, there must be very nearly 4,000 coopers at present located in London. Of this number about 300 may be said to be employers (the "Post-office Directory" gives the names of 291 coopers in business for themselves), so that it would appear that the Metropolitan Operative Coopers amount to somewhere about 3,700.

The trade of the cooper is divided into wet, dry, white, and general coopers. The wet (or tight) cooper makes every kind of vessel used for the reception of liquids—such as wines, spirits, beer, vinegar, oil, and water. The dry cooper, on the other hand, makes the casks used to contain dry goods—such as sugar, bottled wines, cement, linens, biscuits, and for dry packages generally. The white cooper forms tubs, pails, churns, and similar articles; while the block, or general cooper, is practised in all of these branches.

The wet, or tight, work, is that which requires the greatest exercise of skill in the cooper's art. Oak is the material which the "wet cooper" forms into the wine, spirit, beer, vinegar, or water cask. Five kinds of oak are used—Quebec, Virginia, Dantzic, Hamburg, and English. For vessels to contain spirits or any liquid not liable to fermentation, Quebec and Virginia oak is used, Quebec being the best on account of the closeness of its grain. The other three kinds of oak are of a more porous and more durable quality, and are used for the manufacture of beer casks, or whenever fermentation is likely to ensue. English oak is by far the best and hardest, and requires in its working such an exertion of strength and skill, that the cooper receives about 30 per cent. higher wages for making an English oak barrel than for any other. For molasses hogsheads a very porous American timber, called "reed" or "red," oak, is employed. This oak expands, or, as is technically said, "gives" to the treacle; and yet even with this quality there must be two vent holes by the bung-hole to allow the molasses to work through, and to admit air, so as to check fermentation, or the cask would assuredly burst. Molasses cannot be contained in a tight cask. These hogsheads, however, are now seldom made in this country; they are usually sent from the United States to the West India islands.

The manufacture of wine casks in this country is but an inconsiderable portion of the cooper's trade. All foreign wines are imported in casks made in the country whence the importation has taken place. In the French, Spanish, and Portuguese vineyards the cooper's establishment occupies an important position. Madeira, however, is an exception to the rule, that island supplying no timber altogether suitable for wine casks, which are consequently sent out ready made from this country; sometimes, however, Quebec oak staves are exported, and put together by Portuguese coopers at the Madeira vineyards. The Spanish sherry "butts" and the Portuguese port "pipes" are good specimens of the cooper's art; they are as well made by native workmen as they could be in London, little advanced as the people of the Peninsula may be in industrial arts or manufactures. The port pipes are of a peculiar form, being narrower at the ends and higher at the "bouge" (the bulge, or centre) than any other casks; they are made of a native oak, resembling English, but more open in the veins, less knotty and more easily worked, and the staves are not sawn, but hewn. The sherry butts are wider than the port pipes, and have less "bouge." The Portuguese cooper is a superior workman to the Spanish. The French brandy casks are well made, and their wine casks are of indifferent workmanship. Rum puncheons, molasses hogsheads, sugar hogsheads, and tierces (the tierce being a smaller hogshead) used to be sent out in great quantities from this country. They were, and, to a small extent, are, exported "in packs;" that is complete, with the exception of the hooping, which is done in Jamaica or whatever island has the consignment. Changes in the tariff, however, opened this trade to the Americans, and it is now almost monopolized by them; as they have the advantage of cheap timber close at hand, and can undersell the English tradesman. The Canadas, although possessing equal advantages as regards timber, send very few puncheons or hogsheads to the West Indies. At one period 500 working coopers were engaged in London solely in the West Indian trade, while now there are not 60. The cooper's goods which are at present exported to these colonies are sent out chiefly as packages, containing soot or some dry article, and thus a double purpose is subserved. The loss of the West India trade is a source of great regret to the London coopers, as it supplied them with a regular and lucrative winter employment. Oil casks are made both in London and Sydney, but the London trade, as regards the oil from the whale fisheries, is very inconsiderable to what it was formerly. American whale oil (now admitted free of duty) is brought over in American-built casks; these casks are often used for the re-exportation of oils, or for the home trade, and are frequently made smaller for that purpose.

Coarse oak, beech, and ash, are woods greatly in use by the dry coopers. The huge currant butts are made in the Ionian Islands, Zante, Cephalonia, Patras, &c., whence the currants are brought. They are made very roughly and in an unworkmanlike way, the material being a coarse oak. The Smyrna raisins are brought in barrels, made by the Turks, also of rude workmanship. The rice barrels are made in Carolina, and are very badly made of pine wood, clove the reverse way to the grain; on these, slave labour is not unfrequently employed. The tallow casks are made in Russia, and are very fairly put together as requires skill; they are of fir.

The principal material used by the white cooper in the country is ash, but any straight-grained wood, provided it be of the hardness of ash, answers the purpose equally well. In London, however, the ends of oak staves sawn off by the cooper who makes the "large work," are used by the white cooper. This branch of the trade is the worst paid of all, owing to causes which I shall hereafter explain.

The wet cooper's work is very laborious, and requires practice and a quick and accurate eye; for it is by the eye that the cooper chiefly works. His eye, indeed, may be said to be his sole guide; he derives no help from the rule or the square, measurement being only resorted to for obtaining the due lengths of the staves prior to a commence-ment. The first process observed in making a wet or tight cask is to "list" the staves as they come from the saw yard or the pile. To "list" is to shape the staves with the axe, so as to render them suitable for "jointing," the ends being made somewhat narrower than the middle. "Backing" is next performed; that is, the stave is more minutely and carefully formed to the shape required by means of a two-handled "drawing knife," which the cooper holds with both hands, and "backs" or draws towards him so as to cut the stave rapidly, guided by a skilled and practised eye. "Jointing" is the next, and nicest stage, constitut-ing, so to speak, the "high art" of this very nice craft. To joint is to prepare the sides of the staves in such a manner that they shall not only fit closely, but be adapted to ensure the perfect form of the cask, both as regards bouge and curvature. One stave is adjusted to another simply by fitting, that is to say, by the nicest adjustment, as there is no groove nor any such means of connecting the staves one with another. Nor is this all. The cask, when completed, must not only prevent the oozing of a single drop of the subtlest fluid, but must be made to contain a certain quantity; it must hold so many gallons and no more; and when we find that, to effect this, the artificer's eye is the chief guide and surety, the cooper's art—or, as it is called in ancient records, the "mystery"—certainly appears to partake far more of skilled labour than is usually supposed. The staves being thus "jointed" or prepared, are fitted one to another round a block; a "head hoop" afterwards encircling them, and holding them all in one round. "Truss hoops" are then applied, which are strong wooden hoops, holding the staves firmly together until the iron hoops can be affixed. Before affixing the iron hoops, however, a fire made of chips and shavings lighted in a cresset, or small iron grate, is placed within the staves, so as to make them tough by warming the sap, and thus get them to bend without cracking. To this "firing" the closest attention must be given, for if it be prolonged beyond the exact time, the staves are rendered brittle instead of tough. As soon as the cask is sufficiently fired, an "overrunner" is put round the staves; this overrunner is a very strong wooden hoop, and is driven down by the cooper's "trussing adze," the upper part of the cask being first bent close together. The lower ends of the staves distend, through the action of the heat, but the overrunner is driven gradually down to the "bouge;" to effect this in large and strong work the cooper calls out "Truss, oh!" and immediately two or three of his fellows come to his aid, and drive the overrunner down so as to compress the staves sufficiently and reduce the distention. The cask is then prepared with tools called "chimes," used for "sloping" the ends of the staves, and grooves are made for fitting in the heads; this being done, the hoops are affixed, and the cask is then complete. All "wet" casks are made in the same way, and are iron-bound as a rule; vinegar casks, however, are an exception, for they are bound with "twigged hoops," that is to say with hoops twisted round with twigs, the hoops being of hazel, and the twigs, or overlapping part, of willow.

Regarding the skill displayed in cooperage, Mr. Cox says:— "Some few coopers there are who are exceedingly ingenious and skilful in giving a high degree of finish to their work when making model casks. One especially we may mention, whose name is Shaw, now an aged man, formerly employed for many years in the docks as a wine cooper, who is known to the whole trade as a most exquisite workman. His model casks are made of mahogany, and hooped with silver and cane hoops, the latter bound with silver wire. Two of such casks have recently been presented by Mr. Capel, of Tower-street, to the Coopers' Company, and are intended to ornament their hall. No cabinet work can be more highly finished than these casks; and when it is remembered that these beautifully-formed and finished models have been, in common with all other casks, made entirely by the accuracy of eye and by the perfect judgment of the workman, without measurement, square, or model to work by, they certainly present a striking illustration of what may be done by patience, care, and a diligent cultivation of the natural faculties of man."

Some of the technical terms of the trade are curious enough. To smooth the head of a barrel is called "smuggling;" and it creates no little surprise for a person to hear, on his first visit to a cooper's yard, directions given to the workmen to be "careful about that smuggling." If a cask when finished does not stand perfectly firm, that is to say, if it be at all lop-sided or top-heavy, it is called "a lord."

The dry cooper's work is carried on in the same way as that of the wet; but it is a less nice art, as so perfect an exactitude of adjustment is not required.

"White work," says Mr. Cox, "is chiefly distinguished from other kinds of work by the form of the articles that are made, and the manner in which they are finished off. The form of white work is *splay*, instead of *bouge;* or, to drop the technical terms, white work is all of the same form as a pail, small at one end and large at the other, while casks are small at both ends and large in the middle."

At the docks the trade of the cooper is still further classified into wine, block, oil, dry, and molasses coopers. The explanations I have already given show the nature of these further sub-divisions; the block cooper, who has not hitherto been mentioned, is the general cooper. It must, however, be borne in mind that the block cooper deals, as a general rule, with *full* casks only. At the St. Katherine's Dock there are employed about twenty "permanent," with a usual addition of from thirty to forty "preferable" hands, and all of them must be experienced coopers. Those employed at dry work are paid by the day, receiving 4s. 2d. per diem; while the wet coopers work by the piece, and average about 4s. 8d. a day. In the summer season, which is the busiest, about fifty more hands are employed; but in the slack season, only two or three extra hands are taken on. The additional men are known as "ticket men," in contradistinction to the "permanent" men. They have tickets duly numbered, and among them are the distinctions of "preferable" and "extra" men. They are employed by rotation (the preferable having the first turns), and if a vacancy occur among the "permanent" men, a preferable man is appointed to fill it, and an "extra" man thus becomes a preferable. The "extras" are appointed by the head of the department, and the men so appointed must be good workmen and of good character. This, however, is the system adopted concerning all labourers at these admirably conducted docks. The labour of the coopers at the docks depends upon the consignment of goods, and they average, according to the nature of the year's business, from six to nine months labour in the year; the "extra" men obtaining, of course, the lower amount, the "preferable" the higher, and the "permanent" men being employed the year through. Among the permanent men are the "bond" coopers. They have the charge of all the casks of wine, or spirits, or whatever the wet casks may contain bonded in the dock. The bond cooper must report any deficiency he may find in the contents of a cask. It is common enough, I am assured, for sailors to "tap" a wine or spirit cask during the voyage, but all such pilfering is made good before the cask is deposited in the vault of a dock. The deficiency then occurring is through leakage or the bursting of a hoop. The acid of the wine not unfrequently rots the hoop; "it eats it right through, sir," I was told. There are four bond coopers at each of the three wine vaults, and at this dock "preferable" hands do the same work as the permanent bond coopers when the state of dock business requires it. It is also in the department of the bond cooper to draw samples of wines and to wait upon and supply those who have orders for "tasting." "I have seen," said a highly respectable dock cooper to me, "very temperate gentlemen—aye, and ladies, too—very queer indeed after tasting wines at our dock. In the atmosphere of the vault the wine goes down *so* mildly; but it is served in very big wine glasses, so that when the 'tasters' get into the open air, their heads go round like whirligigs." The permanent men in the wet department have all 28s. a week. The dry coopers have 25s. The casual hands, or the ticket men, are paid by the piece as regards the wines, as a rule, and earn from 3s. to 4s. 10d. a day, according to the demand for their services, averaging on the week something near the payment of the dry cooper. The prices paid for piece work are 8d. for trimming both ends of sherry butts or port pipes, or 4d. an end; port or sherry hogsheads are 5d. each; the quarter wine casks are 2d. and 2½d.; brandy puncheons are 3d. an end, or 6d. the cask; brandy pieces (the next size) are 4d. the cask, and the quarters 3d. These things comprise the whole of the piece work. The most efficient hands at coopering on piece work who are at the St. Katharine's Dock, limit their earnings, by an understanding among themselves, to a certain sum a day, to enable them to assist older and slower hands to a better day's earnings. "In my opinion," said a gentleman familiar with the matter to me, "this very praiseworthy arrangement does away with much of the inequality, and therefore the mischief, of piece work."

The dock cooper is the repairer, re-adjuster, or re-fitter of the full casks unshipped at the dock. This labour requires no little practice and no little skill. The re-adjustment of the "wet" goods seldom extends beyond the refitting and renewing of the hoops, but with "dry" goods it is different. After a stormy voyage, sugar casks, for instance, are landed in all possible shapes. Some have been compared to an old hat which had just been subjected to the operation known as "bonneting;" they are crushed into irregular flatness. Some are rudely triangular, others are as rudely quadrangular; indeed, they present every shape except their original rotundity. Yet these "crippled nondescripts," as Mr. Cox calls them, are restored to a proper form by the dry cooper, and without loss of the sugar. This is done by the renewing or re-adjusting of the hoops, and by inserting new staves in the room of those that are bent or broken. The dock coopers, then, are principally employed in the charge and repairs of the casks. But some of the good and experienced hands selected from the body of dock coopers do occasionally make casks, and that chiefly by reducing larger casks that have been damaged into smaller dimensions.

I had the pleasure of hearing very high commendations of the management of the St. Katharine's Docks from all the coopers I saw; and the most respectful and even in some instances grateful mention of Sir John Hall and Mr. Tomlins, for their attention to the well-being of the working men generally. I wish I could say the same for the superintendents of the London Docks. The St. Katharine's Dock coopers have no superannuation or burial funds. They have what is called "the gift," to which it is optional to belong. This "gift" has generally from 20 to 30 members, and each contributes 6d. a week to a sick member. The dock coopers are, on the whole, intelligent men—sober men they must be, as drunkenness is certain dismissal.

Their hours of labour are from eight to four, only a quarter of an hour being allowed for luncheon, which is of course the men's dinner. At that meal a pint of beer is allowed to each working cooper, and that is all he can drink during his work at the dock, for each man is searched upon entering, and is not allowed to leave the dock until the regular hour. I heard also many acknowledgments (from the working men) of the system of gradation and advancement—as respects the "permanent," and "preferable," and "ticket" men—working well, and being an incentive to good conduct.

In the London Docks, there are 50 working coopers permanently employed at day-work, for which they receive 28s. a week, and generally 20 first-class and 150 second-class recommended men, who earn at piece-work about 27s. a week. Here the coopers' work is done chiefly by contract; and such has been the practice for a considerable time. But the coopers were not materially injured by it until about twelve months ago. The contractors are men who have been well recommended to the company, and are, therefore, equivalent to the preferable workmen of the most respectable docks. The contractors usually consist of a gang of seven or eight men, who work together, without any foreman over them, and share all alike. They contract with the company to make all the casks in a particular ship, sound, and fit for housing. The prices at present paid to the contractors by the company are, for sugar hogsheads, 4d. each; molasses puncheons, 4d.; coffee tierces, 3d.; barrels, 1½d. Formerly the Company paid to the contractors for sugar hogsheads and molasses puncheons 1s. each, coffee tierces and barrels not being done then by contract. In the course of last year, a gang of seven (casual) men took a contract of the Company to make all casks and barrels, fit for housing, at the low prices above mentioned, to the injury of the recommended men, seventeen of whom remained idle from December to March, owing to the contractors monopolizing all the trade. The recommended men then made known their grievances to the superintendent, which ended in the company granting them the privilege of taking contracts at the same prices as the other parties, to which the recommended men agreed. They then formed themselves into two gangs, one of eight men and the other of seven. The contractors are not paid till they have done working the ship, though if the men stand in need of a little money—as is sometimes the case—and have a portion of their work done and housed, the company will advance them a few pounds, according to the quantity of work executed. The hours of labour among the contractors are the same as with the other men, viz., from eight till four, but I am told that the men at contract work do treble the amount of work they would do if employed by the Company in the regular manner. The contracting coopers earn, upon an average, £2 per week during the brisk season, but during the slack very little more than one-third of that amount. Under the contract system the men work very hard. "Indeed," said one, "it is downright slavery, and brings old age upon a man before he is in his prime." Sometimes only a portion of the gang of contractors is employed in "working a ship," then the remainder of the gang are engaged upon some other coopering work. "I have known (said my informant) a ship of 600 tons burden worked out by four men in five days; whereas, if the men had been employed by the company in the regular way, it would have taken 16 men a week to do the same amount of work." The average amount received for working a ship of 600 tons burden by the contractors is about £13, but if the men were employed in the regular way by the company, at 4s. 9d. per day, their wages would come to about £20.

I have before pointed out the evils of the contract system, and shown how it always is found to flourish in those docks where the least regard is evinced for the working men. This contract system, I am assured on excellent authority, makes the men so contracting hurry recklessly through their work, careless of what property is destroyed, so that they can complete their undertaking and hurry to another job, as they get the same remuneration whether the ship be "worked out" in a week or in two days. "No one who hasn't seen it would credit the destruction of property," said an experienced London Dock man to me. "I have seen it, and have been sometimes a party, and forced to be a party, to the destruction. Both the merchant's property and the Company's material, such as hoops, staves, and nails, are consumed needlessly in the hurry of the contract work. The worst lot of coopers generally go to this work; many of them are men that have been turned out of the other docks. I'm sure of that. Much as I hate an Union house, I would rather be in one than work on such contracts at the London Docks." This refers only to dry goods. The wine-cooper's trade used also to be done by contract at this dock, but it is now done by piece work. The employment of the wine-coopers is left to the discretion of the principal wine-cooper, who, I am assured, exercises a wise and honourable discretion in this particular. There are at the London Docks no such regulations as at the St. Katharine's Docks as regards "permanent" men, &c. The wet coopers are paid for this piece work less than at the St. Katharine's Docks; in brandy pieces a farthing an end less, and other work in proportion. The established men working at the London Docks, of whatever calling, are enrolled in a benefit society under the direction of the company.

When a cooper is employed permanently by the company, from 4d. to 6d. a week (according to his age) is stopped out of his wages, and when he reaches sixty years of age he is superannuated, and receives 10s. a week for the remainder of his life. If, however, the man be guilty of the least misdemeanour, he is immediately discharged, whereupon all the money he has previously paid in to the superannuation fund is forfeited. One man, who had been in the company's service upwards of twelve years, was found intoxicated, and he was instantly cashiered. The consequence was, that he lost all the money he had contributed to the superannuation fund during that time, or upwards of £40. I am told that many instances of this kind occur. "Indeed (said my informant) such circumstances are a pleasure to the company, as they are benefited thereby."

At the West India Dock the classification and the payment are nearly the same as at the St. Katharine's Dock. Indeed, the same "ticket-men" ply alternately, or rather as the state of business requires, at the St. Katharine's and the West India Docks. The number and pay of the coopers employed at this dock are as follows:—

Ten permanent working coopers, day-pay, 4s. 6d. Forty first-class, who are subject to be out of work by slackness of business, but during the past year (1849) the business admitted of their being constantly employed, and it has been the same this year up to the present time; these are partly employed at day-pay, and part at piece-work. The pay per day is 4s. 6d.; the piece-work averages 5s. There is also a "preferable" second-class of coopers (sixty-four), who have a preference of employment over the "extra coopers;" but they are frequently unemployed at the dock—day pay, 4s.

These are the only docks (with insignificant exceptions) in which coopers are employed.

The journeymen coopers in the general trade are paid almost entirely by the piece. The distinctions of work which I have noticed are becoming less and less regarded; general hands, or men practised, however superficially, in all branches, are more sought after than they were. The work for the brewers is still, however, kept distinct. At a great brewery, inferior cooperage is detected in a moment. In the very best shops—which, however, are now exceptional establishments—the men can earn, by working long hours, £2 a week. The average earnings in the honourable trade are from 26s. to 30s. the year through, when fully employed, at twelve hours a day, deducting two hours for meals; and the majority are so employed nine months in the year, and perhaps one-tenth of the whole body are so employed for twelve months. The summer is the brisk and the winter the slack season, and in winter very many are out of employment. There is nothing to class precisely as slop work in the cooper's trade, for every "wet" cooper's work is tested. The cask is "quarter filled" with boiling water; this generates a powerful steam which will ooze through any slight flaw in the work (which the journeyman must then make good), or even through a worm hole, or any petty defect in the timber. Thus slop work is not so easy among coopers as in some trades. "Our work, sir," said a man to me, using a professional joke, "*must* hold water." Even in the lowest priced yards the foreman closely tests and examines both the wet and dry work, and nothing bad passes, lest it should be sent back from the purchaser. There is not among them even a technical term for under-paying or slop employers. In all shops, wages have been reduced. Twenty years ago a cooper on the best work could earn £3 where he now earns £2, and the fall in inferior work is greater still. The society men's prices are regulated by themselves, and printed. A rum puncheon made of "single imported" staves, is now 3s. 6d.; and within ten years was 3s. 10d. and 4s., and yet that is the article which has declined the least. Oil butts have fallen from 15 to 20 per cent. in journeymen's wages in the last seven years, and all other goods in proportion. The coopers find their own tools, a kit for a general workman being worth £12. These tools are the axe, adze, backing, heading, hollow and drawing knives, jiggers, crows, and saws. The wear and tear of his tools costs the workman 1s. a week. The masters find the jointers (tools for striking and fixing the joints of the staves). The wages of non-society men are from 15 to 20 per cent. less than in the honourable trade, but the price of the material used for casks and tubs varies little, so that this per centage in the lowering of wages does not enable the slop master greatly to undersell the honourable trade.

As a body the coopers are an intelligent class of mechanics. I met among them some superior men, and heard of several who had saved a little money. Hard drinking, I regret to say, though not drunkenness, prevails among the majority of the men employed in large cooperages. "I seldom see them drunk," said one cooper to me, "and I think it's not in the drink to intoxicate some of the seasoned hands." This addiction to continuous drinking, rather than to drunkenness—and the coopers drink principally beer—was accounted for to me by their work being very laborious, while the heat is often so great that they acquire a distaste for solids during the hours of labour, and stay the cravings of the appetite with draughts of beer. In a shop where "large work" is made, and where the timber is the stoutest and the fire the hottest, a moderate drinking cooper, as he is accounted, drinks two pots of beer a day; some will drink three pots and upwards, but in such circumstances two pots is the average drinking. The most moderate coopers, I am told, expend not less, on the average, than 4s. a week on beer. The coopers become prematurely old, suffering greatly from pains in the chest and across the back, attributable to their bending over their hot work. "A cooper at large work is an old man, sir, at forty," said one of them to me; "his physical energies then are nearly exhausted."

Coopers are generally fond of manly exercises, such as cricket. There are very few skittle-players among them. Cards are played sometimes in the public-house on Saturday night, but not generally. "Had the coopers a taste for cards, it would be very easy to introduce them into the workshops," said one of them to me, "by making a card table on a barrel head. Often for days together a master never enters a shop, and the foreman, when he has given a man the stuff, leaves him almost entirely to himself." The theatre and the public gardens, I am told, are, however, the principal recreations of the coopers.

The coopers are mostly married men, living in unfurnished lodgings (generally two rooms), at about 4s. a week rent. They usually reside as near to their work as possible; consequently the majority are to be found in Whitechapel, where the largest sugar-houses are situate; whilst some of the men, for the same reason, are located in St. George-in-the-East. A few have houses at £25 a year rent, letting off part of them, but this is the exception rather than the rule. The operatives have generally from two to five or six in family, and only some of the children are put to school. "I don't consider," said an intelligent member of the trade to me, "that coopers' children are properly looked after, or that they are as well educated as they ought to be. I believe that it is owing to the drinking habits of our trade that the men's families are neglected as they are; perhaps another reason for this is, because during the slack season it takes all the men can earn to procure even food for their families. Upon an average in the slack season, which lasts about four months in the year, I think the coopers' earnings are not above 10s. a week. In the brisk, however, they make about 30s. a week; and I have no doubt it is this great fluctuation in their incomes that makes the men less provident and less attentive to their homes than they otherwise would be. I think the majority of the operative coopers' wives take in slop-work, and many of their daughters do so. This has been the custom as long as I can remember. Some of the wives were formerly employed in winding silk for the Spitalfields weavers; but now that's all knocked on the head. The cause of the coopers' wives taking to slop-work is partly owing to the slackness of the trade at certain times and partly to their living in the neighbourhood of the slopsellers. Lately there has been a great reformation in the drinking habits of the men. There are two causes for this, in my opinion. One is the closing of the public-houses at twelve o'clock on Saturday night, and not allowing them to be opened until after church time on Sunday; and the other is the cheapness of railway travelling, so that the men are induced to go a little way into the country on a Sunday, instead of wasting their money and ruining their health in taverns." The usual time of labour among the coopers is from six in the morning till eight o'clock at night (fourteen hours a day). This is generally considered in the trade to be two hours too much, and is looked upon as a great evil, it being considered one of the principal reasons why so many are out of employment. The hours of labour, however, have always been the same. The coopers are not very partial to piecework, though this is their usual mode of payment. They consider it makes men do more work than they ought, and thus deprives others of their fair share of employment. They are never employed at day work in shops, but I am assured that they would prefer this mode of working to all others. Most of the coopers are London men, having served their time in the metropolis. About half, I am told, are the sons of former workmen.

The coopers in large establishments work in lofty brick sheds, with large open frontages; these are usually well ventilated, which indeed is indispensable, on account of the fires, where there is the slightest regard for the health and comfort of the workmen. They work singly, each man being engaged on his own cask. When it is finished, it is rolled into an adjacent yard, and there awaits the testing or inspection of the foreman or master.

Nearly all the working coopers can read and write, and some are educated men. Their moral standard is quite equal to that of the generality of trades. They were described to me as rough but manly. Some years ago, "strikes" were common among the coopers, and tended to promote idleness and foster the love for drink; but within the last twenty years strikes have been few and partial, and the men are now opposed to them as to a bad policy.

If any disagreement arises between master and men, the president of one of the societies to be presently mentioned, waits upon the master in a friendly manner, nor in one solitary instance has there been a failure, the grievance being always amicably settled.

The trade of a cooper is usually acquired by an apprenticeship of seven years. The little masters take very many apprentices, and take them for the fees, but they have very few from the parishes. Some of them get a premium with their apprentices of from £10 to £20, and in some instances keep the boy, finding him board and lodging for one or two years, allowing him one-third of the regular wages when he has completed a piece of work, which he is seldom able to do in less than three years' training. For the last two years of his apprenticeship, he has two-thirds of the regular wages of the trade. This system unquestionably tends to increase the number of hands willing to work for inferior wages, and so to perpetuate inferior handicraftsmen.

The Coopers have four societies in connection with their trade. One is the Parent Society and the other three are Branches. The branch societies are called the "Local Trade Societies." The Parent Society is termed the "Philanthropic," and is held at the Tower Shades, Tower-hill. The local trade societies are designated the "Hand-in-Hand"—the "Brewhouse Coopers" and the "Runlett Coopers." The first of these is held at the Old Commodore, Montague-street, Whitechapel; the second at the Queen's Head, Blackfriars; and the last at the Eight Bells, Bermondsey.

The White Coopers have no trade society, but many of them are connected with Friendly Benefit Societies of various kinds.

The following table will show the number of society men and non-society men in the Cooper's trade, exclusive of the white and the dock coopers:—

	In Society.	Out of Society.	Total of Society and Non-Society men in each Branch.
Philanthropic Coopers	460	...	460
Hand-in-Hand „	100	70	170
Brewhouse „	70	70	140
Runlett „	60	40	100
	690	180	870

The objects of the trades societies in connection with the coopers are twofold—first, for the purposes of trade; secondly, for philanthropic objects.

The trade purposes consist of the upholding of such prices as the operatives consider a just remuneration for their work, and of the maintenance of their members when out of employ; while the philanthropic objects are the support of their aged and helpless members, and the allowance of a certain sum at the death of a member or a member's wife. These objects are carried out by assembling at their society houses weekly, monthly, and half-yearly, and contributing a portion of their weekly earnings in aid of the funds. The affairs of each society are placed in the hands of a president, secretary, two auditors, four stewards, and six committee-men. If an individual wishes to become a member, he is proposed at one of the monthly meeting nights, and admitted by a show of hands on the following night of meeting.

The society houses are not houses of call, but simply "trade societies." However, when any of the members are out of work, they make it known to the president, who, being acquainted with the trade generally, can tell whether there are any fresh hands wanted; and, if there be an opening, the president sends such individuals as are qualified to undertake the job. The non-society men call at the various cooperages and solicit employment.

The amount of contribution varies with the "society." The members of the parent society contribute a per centage of their earnings—one forty-eighth part, or a farthing in every shilling they obtain by their labour; those belonging to the branch societies pay 1s. per month. The "benefits" of the societies are 6s. per week to the unemployed members during the season of slackness, £5 at the death of a member, and £3 at the death of a member's wife. There is a superannuation fund in connection with the parent society, from which an aged or infirm member is allowed 3s. per week. There are at present seven members in receipt of this fund. The wages of the white coopers have been reduced full two-thirds within the last twelve years, and this, I am informed, is mainly owing to the Irish under-working the rest of the trade. Machinery has not in the least affected the coopers' art, as at present, to use the words of the operatives, "it cannot touch it." The coopers having no connection with country societies, they entirely discountenance all relief of tramps; they are firmly persuaded, they say, that it merely fosters idleness and vagabondism. The coopers' trade, like other trades, ebbs and flows. Their brisk season continues generally from May to Christmas, and is then slack from Christmas to May. During the slack time the unemployed coopers repair to the different docks, where they generally obtain two or three days' work during the week. As to the cause of these fluctuations in trade, the coopers cannot assign any particular reason. The present season has been the best that they have realised for many years past, there having been a great quantity of new work required.

A tall spare man, looking much older than he represented himself (a common case among coopers), whom I found in a comfortable home, gave me the following account of his earnings as a wet cooper:—

"I have worked in London about seventeen years as apprentice and journeyman, and am now thirty-one. I lived at home during my apprenticeship, but my master was a relation of my father's, and they were very friendly, so my apprenticeship is not just a sample of what others may be. It was an understanding between the two. I have always worked for the best shops, and so I suppose I may reckon myself a good workman; but for all that I found great difficulty in learning the business when a boy. It was five years, or thereabouts, before I could 'joint' tolerably; and to know how to grind the tools well and quickly, is not an easy thing to learn, and many coopers who have mastered it don't like to let others see them grinding. Ours is hard and difficult work. There's no help with tools or colours for a cooper to regulate his work, or hide the faults of it. He must depend upon his eye. I have been always very fortunate in getting work, and that has allowed me to get a little on in the world. I think I have averaged from 30s. to 32s. a week for five years past, and rather more before that, though then I seldom worked on a Monday, as it was very little the custom of that shop. I consider it impossible to work without beer, but I very seldom care to taste it when I'm not at work; the heat and smoke causes such thirst when at work. There is still a good deal of drunkenness among the men certainly, but I think the journeymen have greatly improved of late in their habits. They are more temperate and more saving, perhaps more intelligent than was the case. They have become so gradually, I think, and within these eight or ten years. I am paid good wages, and work all the year through. My health is now pretty good, but many in my trade suffer greatly. When I first began I had bilious headaches, and flying pains about my back. We have so much stooping, you see, and perspire a good deal, some of us—it's not often you see a working cooper very fat—and go heated into cold air; and those things affect our health. I am a society man. I know of no grievances to complain of in the shops I have worked in. I can keep a wife comfortably, but I haven't been long married. I dare say my beer, when at work, doesn't cost me less than 3s. 6d. a week, and I'm one of the moderate ones. In many places a block cooper, or general hand, has a better chance of employment, than a man who wants to confine himself to one branch. In the great shops, especially for brewer's work, there's still a proper division of labour observed. I work by the piece, but I think if we were put on by day work, masters would be better served, for a man would take more time. To be sure a master might have *rather* less work done, but then a man not up to the average quantity of work in a day wouldn't often get regular employment, and so it might be all the same that way. I fancy, however, some men prefer piece work. It doesn't tie them so to time—they think they are more independent at it than at day work."

Concerning the dry-coopers, I had the subjoined statement from one of the most intelligent of the body. He was a society man:—

"I am a dry-cooper," he said; "I have been twenty years in the trade. I served my time in the country, and ever since that I have been in London, in the 'dry' branch. I have always belonged to a society. The rate of wages was much better when I first came to London than it is now, but the quantity of work was much about the same. The men were paid by the piece, as at present. The decline in our wages has been in these ways. In the first place, we used to have what was called beer-money—that is a penny on every shilling that we earned was paid to us extra. This was termed 'beer money,' though it was part and parcel of our wages. Among the 'new (or brewers') coopers' there was always a cask on tap for the men to go to; but among 'the dry coopers' it was usual to pay in money only. At the time of the Income-tax Bill being brought in by Sir Robert Peel, the employers took off the beer money so as to meet the new tax. Since that time, cement casks have been reduced from 1s. to 10d., and bottle-porter casks have been lowered also, but I can't exactly state how much. Twenty years ago, I could earn five shillings a week more than I can now, working the same hours. After Christmas, my work is always very slack for three or four months. During that time I am employed on an average about four days a week, and so I think are most of the dry coopers. It was always the same as long as I can remember. About this time is, and always has been, our busiest time, in consequence of the ships going out to the West Indies, and the 'dry'—or, more properly speaking, 'the molasses-coopers' are busiest then. The main dependence of the dry coopers, however, is the sugar refiners' work. A large sugar house will keep eight men fully employed in the season, which lasts about six months in the year. There are about ten or twelve such large sugar houses in London. Altogether, I should say there are from 80 to 100 dry coopers in London employed in this way. I think a dry cooper's average earnings are about 24s. a week all the year round. Mine, perhaps, may be a little more than that; but then I am not a fair criterion, for I am considered a very quick hand. Most of our men would be glad to give up piece work, and take a constant situation at day work for 24s. a week. In the slack season we have nothing to depend upon but the sugar-house work, such as making puncheons for treacle, and casks for sugar. The small masters have already had a very injurious effect upon the dry branch of the trade, and I have no doubt they will injure us still more. To them only is to be attributed the decrease of our wages in the cement and bottle-porter cask work. The small masters cannot interfere with our sugar work, or our West India work; they have neither premises nor capital sufficient. They can only manage the small work—such as can be done in cellars and small premises."

The "slop" part of the coopering trade consists in what are called "cutting shops," and the "small trade-working masters." But these are confined solely to the "dry and white work." The cutting shops usually employ non-society men, with a number of apprentices, and are enabled to undersell the more honourable tradesmen by this cheaper labour. Many of these cutting masters are engaged in the manufacture of one article alone, and I was informed of one such master who had a number of hands continually engaged in converting old American flour barrels into bottled-porter casks, at 1d. a piece. One of the small employers whom I visited, lived at the corner of a low, dirty street. His premises were entered by means of what was literally a hole in the wooden wall, on which swung a small door. In the interior of his shop were heaped hoops, staves, and all the requirements of the coopers' trade. In an inner room, four men were at work. "I make only colour kegs," he said, "and have been in the trade many years. My men work by the piece, and the best and quickest hands make from 32s. to 33s. a week. Inferior hands get from 22s. to 25s. I used to employ fourteen hands, where I now employ half that number. Nearly all colour kegs, more than nineteen-twentieths of those made, are for exportation. For the home trade, a colourman will make the same casks go backwards and forwards fifty times. There used to be 800 hands employed in the wood keg trade for colourmen; now there is not half that quantity. The falling off is owing to the demand for sheet iron kegs, made under Brown's patent by steam machinery. They now make from 300,000 to 400,000 iron kegs every year, and have done so for five or six years past. They are much neater casks than the wooden to look at. I don't know about their durability, but that's little looked to in the export trade. I make every kind of style, kegs from two to twelve quarts; all those used for colours, white lead, &c. A two-quart sells at 6d., a twelve-quart at 14d. The iron are 20 to 30 per cent. higher. It's not the hawkers that have injured the trade of masters like myself; it's only the introduction of iron kegs."

A man working for another small employer (after many praises of his master's keeping on men, when he merely worked on speculation to supply the colour factories) told me that he earned 24s. a week. His hours of labour were from seven in the morning till ten at night. "We shall all come to be mere labourers soon," he said.

Another man, working for a small master, was a smoke-dried old man, apparently between 70 and 80. He had served under Admiral Duncan, and was concerned in the mutiny at the Nore. He could only make 4s. a week. Besides this he had a pension of 1s. a day.

The small employers in the neighbourhood of St. George's-in-the-East now number about thirty or forty, whereas a few years back I am credibly informed there were from 100 to 120 located in that neighbourhood. The little trade-working masters consist principally of the casual hands working as coopers at the docks. There appear to be two or three reasons for the dock coopers taking to make up small articles on their own account. One is, the early hour at which their labour at the docks ceases, so that a man, if in any way industrious, on returning home in the early part of the evening usually sets to work for himself, and makes up in his over-time tubs, pails, or kegs, which he either sells to the country hawkers, or his wife carries them round town for sale to the houses or shops. Another reason why the journeymen coopers become small trade-working masters, is owing to the uncertainty of all kinds of dock labour. Of this I have before spoken at considerable length. The "extra coopers," therefore, when not wanted at the docks, employ their spare time in manufacturing small articles on speculation, for which, as in the cabinet trade, they are obliged to find a market as soon as made, whether there be a demand for them or not. The third and principal reason is the small capital required for journeymen coopers to begin labouring for themselves in the white branch of the trade, as well as upon the smaller articles appertaining to dry work. The majority of the small masters are Irishmen, living in the neighbourhood of the docks; one of these, whom I saw, resided in a court at the back of Rosemary-lane. In the centre of this place stood clothes-props supporting lines laden with yellow-looking shirts and brown blankets, which swung backwards and forwards in the wind. Seated on the stones outside of each of the doors, were small groups of fuzzy-haired Irishwomen, all engaged in chopping wood and talking to one another across the court. The working cooper himself was a good-looking intelligent man, with the handsome grey eye and long sweeping lash peculiar to the natives of the Emerald Isle. He was very proud of the neatness of his sitting-room, and took me upstairs expressly to show it to me. It was decorated with portraits of Mitchell, Meagher, and Father Moore, together with a picture of the Siege of Limerick dedicated to the women of Ireland. Down stairs, amid the shavings, lay a copy of the *Nation* newspaper, in which my informant told me there was "some sublime poethry."

"I am a small master," he said, "though I don't know exactly that you can call me so rightly—I don't employ any one. You can put me down a manufacturer, if you please. I make up things on my own account. I have been at coopering now I dare say 26 years. I was about 14 when I first went to it. It was in Ireland I learnt the trade. I used to be engaged in my own unfortunate counthry making provision casks, but now that trade's entirely done away with. I came over here—let me see—fourteen years last May. Then I got my name on at the West India Dock as an extra cooper, and I have worked there in succession every year since. I got a number, and have kept at it all along. After working in the docks, if I don't feel too much fatigued, I do a bit of work for myself when I get home at night; or if I have an order for my customers that requires speed, then I stop here and work at it altogether. You see I am not obligated to go to work at the docks unless I please. I should say that, take it the year through, I am employed at the docks about three months out of the twelve. After October, the season is looked upon to be over, and it begins again about April. I don't always go to work after coming from the docks; but the most of the small masters works after their dock labour. When I work at home, I begin about seven and keep on till about nine at night, that's fourteen hours. One small master I know begins often at four or five in the morning. You see it all depends upon the industrial habits of men. If you're at work for an employer, you must leave off at a certain hour, but if you're your own master, you can work all night, if you've a fancy. I've often worked all night myself. I feel more pleasure doing a bit for myself here by candlelight than if I was wandering about the streets. I sell the goods I make to hawkers, and they make a living of it by hawking them to the public and to shops. I am in the habit of making oval tubs of different sizes—that's the principal branch that I'm employed in. Other small masters are engaged in making flour kegs, colour kegs, oyster barrels, mustard kegs—but that's all dry work. The small masters never do any large work. Some of the small masters will take round a sample of their work to a colour or mustard factory, or to a merchant, and so get an order; and many make up goods on speculation, and then take them round to sell. As simple a trade as oyster barrels is, still there's hundreds made up on speculation, and taken round to be sold. I've made them up myself. A man does this because he can't get other employment. May be there'll be a slackage at the docks, and a man will rather do that than be idle and starve. If he's out of work, he can make a dozen of oyster barrels for three shillings. The material will only cost him that much. It would take him a day to make them, and when he had done them, perhaps his wife, or may be his daughters, if he have any, will take them out to sell—to Billingsgate Market, may be. At oyster barrels the men frequently work all night, and some of them on the Sunday as well. Seventeen years ago, oyster barrels were nine shillings a dozen, and now they're four shillings and sixpence— that will show you how such work knocks up a trade. Many of the small masters lives about here, some in ground cellars, cobbling up old tubs and what not, to get a crust."

LABOUR AND THE POOR.

THE METROPOLITAN DISTRICTS.

[FROM OUR SPECIAL CORRESPONDENT.]

OF THE TRANSIT OF GREAT BRITAIN AND THE METROPOLIS.

Letter LXX.

As the entire transit system of Great Britain—with all its railroads, turnpike roads, canals, and navigable rivers—converges on London, I propose to make it the subject of the following letter, by way of introduction to my inquiry into the condition of the metropolitan labourers connected therewith:—

"There is a very great amount of labour employed," says Mr. Stewart Mill, "not only in bringing a product into existence, but in rendering it, when in existence, accessible to those for whose use it is intended. Many important classes of labourers find their sole employment in some function of this kind. There is the whole class of carriers, by land or water—waggoners, bargemen, sailors, wharfmen, porters, railway establishments, and the like." "Good roads," continues the same eminent authority, "are equivalent to good tools, and railways and canals are virtually a diminution of the cost of production of all things sent to market by them."

In order to give the public as comprehensive an idea of this subject as possible, and to show its vastness and importance to the community, I shall, before entering upon the details of that part of it which more immediately concerns me, viz., the transit from and to different parts of the metropolis, and the condition and earnings of the people connected therewith—I shall, I say, furnish an account of the extent of the external and internal transit of this country generally. Of the provisions for the internal transit, I shall speak in due course, first treating of the grand medium for carrying on the traffic of Great Britain with the world, and showing how within the capital of an island, which is a mere speck on the map of the earth, is centered, and originated, planned, and executed, so vast a portion of the trade of all nations. I shall confine my observations to the latest returns and the latest results.

The number of vessels belonging to the United Kingdom was in 1848 nearly 25,000, having an aggregate burden of upwards of 3,000,000 tons, and being manned by 180,000 hands. To give the reader, however, a more vivid idea of the magnitude of the "mercantile marine" of this kingdom, it may be safely asserted that, in order to accommodate the whole of our merchant vessels, a dock of 15,000 square acres would be necessary, or, in other words, there would be required to float them an extent of water sufficient to cover four times the area of the city of London, while the whole population of Birmingham would be needed to man them. But, besides the 20,000 and odd British vessels, with their 180,000 men, that are thus engaged in conveying the treasures of other lands to our own, there are upwards of 13,000 foreign vessels—manned by 100,000 hands—that annually visit the shores of this country.

Of the steam-vessels belonging to the United Kingdom, in 1848, there were 1,100. Their aggregate length was 125,283 feet, their aggregate breadth 19,748 feet, their aggregate tonnage 255,371, and their aggregate of horse-power 92,862. It may be added that they are collectively of such dimensions that, by placing them stem to stern, one after the other, they would reach to a distance of 23½ miles, or form one continuous line from Dover to Calais; while, by placing them abreast, or alongside each other, they would occupy a space of upwards of 3½ miles wide.

According to the calculations of Mr. G. F. Young, the eminent ship-builder, the entire value of the vessels belonging to the mercantile marine of the British empire is upwards of thirty-eight million pounds sterling; the annual cost of the provisions and wages of the seamen employed in navigating them, £9,500,000. The sum annually expended in the building and outfitting of new ships, as well as the repairing of the old ones, is £10,500,000; while the amount annually received for freight is £28,500,000.

The value of the merchandise thus imported or exported has still to be set forth. By this we learn not only the vast extent of the international trade of Great Britain, but the immense amount of property entrusted annually to the merchant seamen. It would perhaps hardly be credited that the value of the articles which our mercantile marine is engaged in transporting to and from the shores of this kingdom, amounts to upwards of one hundred of millions of pounds sterling.

Such, then, is the extent of the external transit of this country. There is scarcely a corner of the earth that is not visited by our vessels, and the special gifts and benefits conferred upon the most distant countries thus diffused and shared among even the humblest members of our own. To show the connection of the metropolis with this vast amount of trade, involving so many industrial interests, I shall conclude with stating that the returns prove that one-fourth of the entire maritime commerce of this country is carried on at the port of London.

As a sad contrast, however, to all this splendour, I may here add, that the annual loss of property in British shipping wrecked or foundered at sea, may be assumed as amounting to nearly *three millions of pounds sterling* per annum. The annual loss of life occasioned by the wreck or foundering of British vessels may be fairly estimated at not less than *one thousand souls in each year;* so that it would appear that the annual loss by shipwreck amongst the vessels belonging to the United Kingdom is, on an average, one ship in every 42; and the annual loss of property engaged therein, £1 in every £42; while the average number of sailors drowned amounts to 1 in every 203 persons engaged in navigation.

I now come to speak of the means by which the vast amount of wealth thus brought to our shores is distributed throughout the country. I have already said that there are three different modes of internal communication—(1), To convey the several articles coastwise from one port to another; (2), to carry them inland from town to town; and (3), to remove them from and to the different parts of the same town. I shall deal first with the communication along the coast.

In 1849 the coasting vessels employed in the intercourse between Great Britain and Ireland made upwards of 26,000 voyages, and the gross burden of the vessels thus engaged amounted to more than 3,500,000 tons. The "coasters" engaged in the carrying trade between the different ports of Great Britain, in 1849, made no less than 255,000 voyages, and possessed collectively a capacity for carrying upwards of 20,000,000 tons of goods. Of the steam-vessels employed coastwise in the United Kingdom, the number that entered inwards, including their repeated voyages, was 17,800, having an aggregate burden of upwards of 4,000,000 tons, while 14,500 and odd steam-vessels, of not quite the same amount of tonnage, were cleared outwards. This expresses the entire amount of the coasting trade in connection with the several ports of Great Britain. London, as I have before showed, has four times the number of sailing vessels, and ten times the amount of tonnage, over and above any port in the kingdom; whilst of steam-impelled coasting vessels, it has but little more than one-third, compared with Liverpool.

The next branch of my subject that presents itself in due order, is the means by which the goods thus brought to the several ports of the kingdom are carried to the interior of the country. There are two means of effecting this—that is to say, either by land or water carriage. Land carriage consists of transit by rail and transit by turnpike-roads; the water carriage, of transit by canals and navigable rivers. I shall begin with the first-mentioned of these, namely, turnpike-roads, and then proceed in due order to the others.

The *turnpike-roads* of England present a perfect net-work of communication, connecting town with town, and hamlet with hamlet. It was only within the present century, however, that these important means of increasing commerce and civilization were constructed according to scientific data. Before that, portions of what were known as the "great coaching roads" were repaired with more than usual care; but until Mr. McAdam's system was generally adopted, about 35 years back, all were more or less defective. It would be wearisome were I to add to the number of familiar instances of the difficulties and dilatoriness of travelling in the old days; of the way in which the ancient "heavy coaches" were merged in the "fast light coaches," which, in their turn, have yielded to the greater speed of the railways.

In 1818, according to the Government Report on the Turnpike roads and the Railways of England and Wales, there existed:

	Miles.
In England and Wales, paved streets and turnpike-roads to the extent of	19,725
Other public highways	95,104
Total	114,829

Other Parliamentary returns show that in 1829 the length of only the turnpike roads in England and Wales was 20,875 miles, or upwards of 1,000 miles more than they (together with the paved streets) extended to ten years before. In 1839 the length of the turnpike roads and paved streets throughout England and Wales amounted to 22,534 miles, while "all other highways" were 96,991 miles long, making in all 119,527 miles of road. By this it appears that, in the course of twenty years, upwards of 4,500 miles of highway had been added to the resources of the country. As these are the latest returns on the subject, and it is probable that, owing to the establishment of railways, there has been no great addition since that period to the aggregate extent of mileage above given, it may be as well to set forth the manner in which these facilities for intercommunication were distributed among the different parts of the country at that time. The counties containing the greatest length of turnpike roads, according to their size, were Derby, Worcester, Flint, Gloucester, Somerset, Monmouth, Stafford, Hereford, Southampton, &c., which severally contained one mile of turnpike road to about each thousand statute acres—the average for the entire country being nearly double that amount of acres to each mile of road. Those counties, on the other hand, which contained the shortest length of turnpike roads in relation to their size, were Anglesey (in which there was only five miles of road to 173,000 statute acres, being in the proportion of one mile to 34,688 acres), then Westmoreland, Suffolk, Essex, Norfolk, Pembroke, and Cumberland. The counties containing the greatest length of paved streets at the above period were, first, Middlesex, where there was one mile of street to every 774 acres; second Suffolk, third Lancaster, fourth Warwick, fifth Surrey, and sixth Chester. The average number of acres to each mile of paved street was 12,734, and in the districts above specified the number of acres to the mile ranged from 3,600 to 6,900. Those counties, on the contrary, which contained the shortest length of streets were Radnor and Anglesey, in which there were no paved streets whatever; Brecon, which has only one mile; and Carnarvon, only two; whereas Middlesex, the county of the capital, has as many as 232 miles of streets extending through it. The cost of the repairs of the roads and streets in the different counties is equally curious. In Merioneth the rate of the expenditure is 12s. 11¾d. per mile; in Montgomery, £1 14s. 2½d.; in Radnor, £1 18s. 1d.; Brecon, £2 6s. 6½d.; Carnarvon, £2 10s. 1¾d.; Anglesey, £3 8s.; Cardigan, £3 3s. 0½d.; whereas in Middlesex the cost amounts to no less than £87 1s. 6½d. per mile; in Lancashire, the next most expensive county, it is £32 2s. 6d.; in the West Riding of Yorkshire it comes to £23 4s. 3d., and in Surrey, the other metropolitan county, to £19 1s. 1½d.— the average for the whole country being £10 12s. 1½d. per mile, or £1,267,848 for the maintenance of 119,527 miles of public highway throughout England and Wales.

These roads were used for a three-fold purpose—the conveyance of passengers, letters, and goods. The passengers, letters, and parcels were conveyed chiefly by the mail and stage coaches; the goods, by waggons and vans. Of the number of *passengers* who travelled by the mail and stage coaches, no return was ever made. I am indebted, however, to Mr. Porter for the following calculation, as to the number of stage-coach travellers, before their vehicles (to adopt their own mode of expression) were "run off the road" by the steam-engine:—

> "In order to obtain some approximation to the extent of travelling by means of stage coaches in England, a careful calculation has been made upon the whole of the returns to the Stamp-office, and the licenses for which coaches were in operation, at the end of the year 1834. The method followed in making the calculation has been to ascertain the performance of each vehicle, supposing that performance to have been equal to the full amount of the permission conveyed by the license, reducing the power so given to a number equal to the number of miles which one passenger might be conveyed in the course of the year. For example:—A coach is licensed to convey fifteen passengers daily from London to Birmingham, a distance of 112 miles. In order to ascertain the possible performance of this carriage during the year, if the number of miles is multiplied by the number of journeys, and that product multiplied again by the number of passengers, we shall obtain, as an element, a number equal to the number of miles along which one person might have been conveyed, viz., $112 \times 365 \times 15 = 613{,}200$. In this case the number of miles travelled is 40,880, along which distance fifteen persons might have been carried during the year; but, for the simplification of the calculation, the further calculation is made, which shows that amount of travelling to be equal to the conveyance of one person through the distance of 613,200 miles. Upon making this calculation for the whole number of stage-coaches that possessed licenses at the end of the year 1834 it appears that the means of conveyance thus provided for travelling were equivalent to the conveyance during the year of one person for the distance of 597,159,420 miles, or more than six times between the earth and the sun. Observation has shown that the degree in which the public avail themselves of the accommodation thus provided is in the proportion of nine to fifteen, or three-fifths of its utmost extent. Following this proportion, the sum of all the travelling by stage-coaches in Great Britain may be represented by 358,295,652 miles. ... We shall probably go to the utmost extent in assuming that not more than two millions of persons travel in that manner. ... It affords a good measure of the relative importance of the metropolis to the remainder of the country, that of the above number of 597,159,420, the large proportion of 409,052,644 is the product of stage-coaches which are licensed to run from London to various parts of the kingdom."

In this calculation, the stage-coach travelling of Ireland is not included; nor is that of Scotland, when confined to that kingdom, but when part of the communication is with England, it is included. Of course only public conveyances are spoken of; all the travelling in private carriages, or post-chaises, or hired gigs, was additional.

The number of stage coachmen and guards returned is the following, there being no returns later than 1843:—In 1839 they were 2,619 in number; 1840, 2,507; 1841, 2,239; 1842, 2,107; 1843, 146.

The expenditure on account of these roads, in 1841, amounted to £1,551,000; the revenue derived from them, for the same year, having been £1,574,000.

A great change has been induced in the character of the turnpike-roads of England. The liveliness imparted to many of the lines of road by the scarlet coats of the drivers and guards, and by the sound of the guard's bugle, as it announced to all the idlers of the country place that "the London coach was coming in"—these things exist no longer. Now, on very few portions of the 1,448 miles of turnpike-road in Yorkshire, or the 840 of Gloucestershire, is a stage coach and four to be seen; and the great "coaching inns" by the way-side, where the tribe of ostlers and helpers "changed horses" with a facility almost marvellous, have become farm-houses, or mere way-side taverns.

The greatest rate of speed attained by any of the mail coaches, was eleven miles an hour, "including stoppages;" that is, eleven miles, notwithstanding the delay incurred in changing horses, which was the work of from one minute to three, depending upon whether any passenger was "taken up" or "set down" at that *stage* (the word "station" is peculiar to railways). If there was merely a change of horses, about a minute was consumed. The horses were not unfrequently unsuccessful racehorses, and they were generally of "good blood." Some would run daily on the same stages eight and ten years. About 10⅝ miles was an average rate for the mail, and 8½ to 9 miles for the stage-coaches. They often advertised ten miles an hour; but that was only an advertisement.

So rapid, so systematic, and so commended was the style of stage-coach travelling, that some of the great coach proprietors dreaded little from the competitive results of railway travelling. One of these proprietors, on the "great north road" used to say, "Railways are just a bounce; all speculation; people will find it out in time, and there'll be more coaching than ever. Railways can never answer."

So punctual, too, were these carriages, that one gentleman used to say he set his watch by the Glasgow mail as "she passed his door" by the roadside at three minutes to ten.

Nor is it only in the discontinuance of stage-coaches that the "roads" of the kingdom have experienced a change in character. Until the prevalence of railways, "posting" was common. A wealthy person travelled to London in his own carriage, which was drawn by four horses, almost as quickly as by the mail. The horses were changed at the several stages, the ostler's cry of "first turn out!" summoning the stable-men and the postillions, with a readiness second only to that in the case of the passengers' coaches. The horses, however, were ridden by postillions in red or light blue jackets with white buttons, light-coloured breeches, and brown top boots, instead of being driven four-in-hand. This was the aristocratic style of travelling, and its indulgence was costly. For a pair of good horses, 1s. 6d. a mile was an average charge, and 3d. a mile had to be given in the compulsory gratuities of those days to the postillion; 3s. a mile was the charge for four horses, but sometimes rather less. Thus, supposing that 500 noblemen and gentlemen "posted" to London on the opening of Parliament—each, as was common, with two carriages and four, and each posting 200 miles, the aggregate expenditure, without any sum for meals or for beds, and to "sleep on the road" was common when ladies were travelling—would be £35,000; and to this add 5 per cent. for the turnpike tolls, and the whole cost would be £36,750—an average of £73 10s. for each nobleman and gentleman with his family, and the customary members of his household. The calculation refers merely to a portion of the members of the two Houses of Legislature, and is unquestionably within the mark, for though many travelled shorter distances and by cheaper modes, many travelled 400 miles, and with more carriages than three. No "lady" condescended to enter a stage coach at the period concerning which I write. As the same expense was incurred in returning to the castle, hall, park, abbey, wood, or manor, the annual outlay for this one purpose of merely a fraction of the posters to London, was £73,500. It might not be extravagant to assert that more than five times this outlay was annually incurred, including "pairs" and "fours," or a total of £367,500. This mode of travelling, I believe, is now almost wholly extinct, if, indeed, it be not impossible, since there are no horses now kept on the roads for the purpose. I have been informed that the late Duke of Northumberland, who died in 1847, was the last, or one of the last, who, in dislike or dread of railways, regularly "posted" to and from Alnwick Castle to London.

The next branch of the transit by land appertains to the conveyance of persons and goods per rail. The *Railways of the United Kingdom*, open, in course of construction, or authorised to be constructed, extend over upwards of 12,000 miles, or four times the distance across the Atlantic. The following is the latest return on the subject, in a report printed by order of the House of Commons, the 22d of March last:—

	Miles.	chains.	Persons employed.
Total length of railway open on 30th June, 1849, and persons employed thereon	5,447	10¾	55,968
Total length of railway in course of construction on 30th June, 1849, and persons employed thereon	1,504	20½	} 103,816
Total length of railway neither open nor in course of construction on 30th June, 1849	5,132	38¾	
Total length of railway authorised to be used for the conveyance of passengers on 30th June, 1849, and the total number of persons employed thereon	12,083	70	159,784

There are now upwards of 6,000 miles of railroad in actual operation in the three kingdoms, 549 miles having been opened in the course of the half-year following the date of the above return. At that date 111 lines of railroad were open for traffic, irrespective of their several branches; 266 railways, including branches, were in the course of construction, and 393 railways and branches were authorised to be constructed, but had not been commenced.

The growth of railways was slow and not gradual. They were unknown as modes of public conveyance before the present century; but roads on a similar principle, irrespective of steam, were in use in the Northumberland and Durham collieries somewhere about the year 1700. The "iron rail" now in use was unknown, wood being the material, and a small cart, or a series of small carts, was dragged through this mechanical means of easier transit by a pony or a horse, to any given point where the coal was to be deposited. In the lead-mines of the North Riding of Yorkshire, the same system was adopted, the more rapidly, and with the less fatigue, to convey the ore to the mouth of the mine. Some of these "tramways," as they are called, were and are a mile and more in length; and visitors, who penetrate into the very bowels of the mine, are conveyed by those tramways in carts, drawn generally by a pony and driven by a boy (who has to duck his head every here and there to avoid concussion) into the galleries and open spaces where the miners are at work.

In the year 1801, the first act of Parliament authorising the construction of a railway was passed. This was the Surrey, between Wandsworth and Croydon, nine miles in length, and constructed at a cost, in round numbers, of £60,000. In the following twenty years, sixteen such acts were passed, authorising the construction of 124¾ miles of railway, the cost of which was £971,232, or upwards of £7,500 a mile. In 1822 no such act was passed. In 1823, Parliament authorised the construction of the Stockton and Darlington, and on that short railway, originated and completed in a great measure through the exertions of the wealthy Quakers of the neighbourhood, and opened on the 27th of December, 1825, was the first use of steam power, as the means of propulsion and locomotion on a railway. It was some little time before this that grave senators and learned journalists laughed to scorn Mr. Stephenson's assertion that steam "could be made to do 20 miles an hour" on a railway. In the following ten years 30 railway bills were passed by the Legislature, and among these, in 1826, was the "Liverpool and Manchester," which was opened on the 16th September, 1830, an opening rendered as lamentable as it is memorable by the death of Mr. Huskisson. In 1834, seven railway bills were passed; ten in 1835; twenty-six in 1836; eleven in 1837; one in 1838; three in 1839; none in any year till 1843, and then only one, the Northampton and Peterborough, which extends along 44½ miles, and cost £429,409, was authorised. The mass of the other railways have been constructed or authorised, or the acts of Parliament authorizing their construction have been shelved, all since the close of 1843. I find no official returns of the dates of the several enactments.

The following statement, in averages of four years, shows the amount of the sums which Parliament authorized the various companies to raise, from 1822 to 1845. Upwards of one-half of the amount of the aggregate sum expended in 1822-6 was expended on the Manchester and Liverpool Railway, £1,832,375. The cost of the Stockton and Darlington, £450,000, is also included:—

Average of four Years.

From	1822	to	1825	inclusive,	£451,465
„	1826	„	1829	. . . . . .	816,846
„	1830	„	1833	. . . . . .	2,157,136
„	1834	„	1837	. . . . . .	10,880,431
„	1838	„	1841	. . . . . .	3,614,428
„	1842	„	1845	. . . . . .	20,895,128

Of these years, 1845 presents the era when the rage for railway speculation was most strongly manifested, as in that year the Legislature sanctioned the raising, by new railway companies, of no less than £59,613,536—more than the imperial taxes levied in the United Kingdom; while in 1844 the amount so sanctioned was £14,793,994. The total sum to be raised for railway purposes for the last 20 years of the above dates was £153,455,837, with a yearly average of £7,672,792. For the four years preceding the yearly average was but £112,866.

The Parliamentary expenses attending the incorporation of 16 of the principal railways were, £683,498; or an average, per railway, of £42,718. It will be seen from the following table that the greatest amount thus expended was on the incorporation of the Great Western. On that undertaking an outlay not much short of £90,000 was incurred before a foot of sod could be raised by the spade of the "navvy."

Birmingham and Gloucester	£22,618	London and Birmingham	£72,868
Bristol and Gloucester	25,589	London and South-Western	41,467
Bristol and Exeter . .	18,592	Manchester and Leeds	49,166
Eastern Counties . . .	39,171	Midland Counties . . .	28,776
Great Western	89,197	North Midland	41,349
Great North of England	20,526	Northern and Eastern	74,166
Grand Junction	22,757	Sheffield, Ashton, and Manchester . . .	31,473
Glasgow, Paisley, and Greenock	23,481	South-Eastern	82,292

It must be borne in mind that these large sums were all for parliamentary expenses alone, and were merely the disbursements of the railway proprietors whose applications to Parliament were successful. Probably as large an amount was expended in opposition to the several bills, and in the fruitless advocacy of rival companies. Thus above a million and a quarter of pounds sterling was but a *preliminary* outlay.

Of the railway lines, the construction of the Great Western, 117½ miles in length, was the most costly, entailing an expenditure of nearly *eight millions;* the London and Birmingham, 112½ miles, cost £6,073,114; the South-Eastern, 66 miles, £4,306,478; the Manchester and Leeds, 53 miles, £3,372,240; the Eastern Counties, 51 miles, £2,821,790; the Glasgow, Paisley, Kilmarnock, and Ayr, 57½ miles, £1,071,263, an amount exceeded by the outlay on only the 3½ miles of the London and Blackwall, which was first opened, and which cost £1,078,851. I ought to mention that the length in miles is that first opened to the public in these respective lines, and first authorized by parliamentary enactments. "Junctions," "continuations," and the blending of companies, have been subsequent measures, entailing, of course, proportionate outlay. The length of line of the Great Western, for instance, with its immediate branches, open on the 30th June, 1849, was 225 miles; that of the South-Eastern, 144 miles; and that of the Eastern Counties, 309 miles. It is stated in Mr. Knight's "British Almanack" for the current year, that "The London and North-Western is almost the only company which has maintained in 1849 the same dividend even as in the preceding year—viz., 7 per cent. The Great Western, the Midland, the Lancashire and Yorkshire, the York and Newcastle, the York and North Midland, the Eastern Counties, the South-Eastern, the South-Western, Brighton, the Manchester and Lincolnshire—all have suffered a decided diminution of dividend. These ten great companies, whose works up to the present time have cost over *one hundred millions sterling,* have on an average declared, for the half year ending in the summer of 1849, a dividend on the regular non-guaranteed shares between 3 and 4 per cent. per annum. The remaining companies, about 60 in number, can hardly have reached an average of 2 per cent. per annum in the same half year."

The following Table gives the latest returns of railway traffic from 1845. Previous to that date no such returns were published in Parliamentary Papers:—

COMPARATIVE STATEMENT OF THE TRAFFIC ON ALL THE RAILWAYS IN THE UNITED KINGDOM FOR THE FIVE YEARS ENDING JUNE 30, 1845, 1846, 1847, 1848, 1849; TOGETHER WITH THE LENGTH OF RAILWAY OPEN ON DECEMBER 31 AND JUNE 30 IN EACH YEAR.

—	Length Open on June 30 in each Year.	Total Number of Passengers.	Total Receipts from Passengers.			Receipts from Goods, Cattle, Parcels, Mails, &c.			Total Receipts.		
Year ending	MILES.		£	s.	d.	£	s.	d.	£	s.	d.
June 30, 1845	2343	33,791,253	3,976,341	0	0	2,233,373	0	0	6,209,714	0	0
„ 1846	2765	43,790,983	4,725,215	11	$8\frac{1}{2}$	2,840,353	16	$6\frac{1}{4}$	7,565,569	8	$2\frac{3}{4}$
„ 1847	3603	51,352,163	5,148,002	5	$0\frac{1}{2}$	3,362,883	19	$6\frac{3}{4}$	8,510,886	4	$7\frac{1}{4}$
„ 1848	4478	57,965,070	5,720,382	9	$1\frac{3}{4}$	4,213,169	14	$5\frac{1}{2}$	9,933,552	3	$7\frac{1}{4}$
„ 1849	5447	60,398,159	6,105,975	7	$7\frac{3}{4}$	5,094,925	18	11	11,200,901	6	$6\frac{3}{4}$

This official table shows a conveyance for the year ending June, 1849, of 60,398,159 passengers. It may be as well to mention that every distinct trip constitutes a passenger. Thus a gentleman travelling from and returning to Greenwich daily figures in the return as 730 passengers. Of the number of individuals who travel in the United Kingdom I have no information. Thousands of the labouring classes travel very rarely, perhaps not more than on some holiday trip in the course of a twelvemonth. But assuming every one to travel, and the population to be 30,000,000, then we have two railway trips made by every man, woman, and child in the kingdom every year.

There are no data from which to deduce a precisely accurate calculation of the number of miles travelled by the 60,398,159 passengers who availed themselves of railway facilities in the year cited. Official lists show that 78 railways comprise the extent of mileage given, but these railways vary in extent. The shortest of them open for the conveyance of passengers is the Belfast and County Down, which is only four miles 35 chains in length, and the number of passengers travelling on it 81,441. The Midland and the London and North-Western, on the other hand, are respectively 465 and 477 miles in length, and then their complement of passengers severally of 2,252,984 and 2,750,541½. The average length of the 78 railways is 70 miles; but as the stream of travel flows more fully from intermediate station to station along the course of the line, than from its one extremity to its other, it may be reasonable to compute that each individual passenger has travelled one-fourth of that distance, or 17½ miles. A calculation confirmed by the amount paid by each individual, which is something short of 2s., or rather more than 1¼d. a mile.

Thus we may conclude that each passenger has journeyed 17½ miles, and that the grand aggregate of travel by all the railway passengers of the kingdom will be 1,052,327,632½ miles, or near upon eleven times the distance between the earth and the sun, every year.

The Government returns present some curious results. The passengers by the second-class carriages have been more numerous every year than those by any other class, and for the year last "returned" were more than three times the number of those who indulged in the comforts of first-class vehicles. Notwithstanding nearly 1,000 new miles of railway were opened for the public transit and traffic between June, 1848-49, still the number of first-class passengers decreased no fewer than 112,000 and odd, while those who resorted to the humbler accommodation of the second-class increased upwards of 1,700,000. The numerical majority of the second-class passengers over the first were, in the

Year ending June, 1845 8,851,662
       „   „   1846 10,770,712
       „   „   1847 12,126,574
       „   „   1848 14,499,730
       „   „   1849 16,313,760

These figures afford some criterion as to the class or character of the travelling millions who are the great supporters of the railways.

The official table presents another curious characteristic. The originators of railways, prior to the era of the opening of the Manchester and Liverpool, depended for their dividends far more upon the profits they might receive in the capacity of "common carriers," upon the conveyance of manufactured goods, minerals, or merchandise, than upon the transit of passengers. It was the property in canals, and in "heavy carriage," that would be depreciated, it was believed, rather than that in the stage-coaches. Even on the Manchester and Liverpool, the projectors did not expect to realise more than £20,000 a year by the conveyance of passengers. The result shows the fallacy of these computations, as the receipts for passengers for the year ending June, 1849, exceeded the receipts from "cattle, goods, parcels, and mails," by £1,011,050. In districts, however, which are at once agricultural and mineral, the amount realised from passengers falls short of that derived from other sources. Two instances will suffice to show this. The Stockton and Darlington is in immediate connection with the district where the famous "short-horn" cattle were first bred by Mr. Collins, and where they are still bred in high perfection by eminent agriculturists. It is in connection, moreover, with the coal and lead mining districts of South Durham and North Yorkshire, the produce being conveyed to Stockton to be shipped. For the last year the receipts from passengers were £8,000 and odd, while for the conveyance of cattle, coals, &c., no less than £62,000 were paid. From their passengers the Taff Vale, including the Aberdare Railway Company, derived, for the same period, in round numbers, an income of £6,500, and from their "goods" conveyance £45,941. In neither instance, did the "passengers" pay one-seventh as much as the "goods."

I now present the reader with two "summaries" from returns made to Parliament. The first relates to the number and description of persons employed on railways in the United Kingdom; and the second to the number and character of railway accidents.

Concerning the individuals employed upon the railways, the following is the latest official information:—

	Secretaries and Managers.	Trea-surers.	Engi-neers.	Superin-tendents.	Store-keepers.	Account-ants and Cashiers.	Inspec-tors and Time-keepers.	Station Masters.	Draughts-men.	Clerks.	Fore-men.
Total Number of per-sons employed upon Railways Open for Traffic on the 30th June, 1849	156	32	107	314	120	138	490	1,300	103	4,021	709
Total Number of per-sons employed upon Railways not Open for Traffic on the 30th June, 1849 ...	142	7	269	419	182	144	821	...	153	421	1,421
Total Number and Description of per-sons employed on all Railways (Open and Unopen), autho-rized to be used for the Conveyance of Passengers	298	39	376	733	302	282	1,311	1,300	256	4,442	2,130

	Engine Drivers.	Assistant Engine Drivers and Firemen.	Guards and Breaksmen.	Switchmen.	Gatekeepers.	Policemen or Watchmen.	Porters and Messengers.	Platelayers.	Artificers.	Labourers.	Miscellaneous Employment.	Total.
Total Number of persons employed upon Railways Open for Traffic on the 30th June, 1849	1,839	1,871	1,631	1,540	1,361	1,508	8,238	5,508	10,809	14,029	144	55,968
Total Number of persons employed upon Railways not Open for Traffic on the 30th June, 1849 ...	...	...	...	...	...	481	118	...	16,144	83,052	42	103,816
Total Number and Description of persons employed on all Railways (Open and Unopen), authorized to be used for the Conveyance of Passengers	1,839	1,871	1,631	1,540	1,361	1,989	8,356	5,508	26,953	97,081	186	159,784

Of the railways in full operation, the London and North-Western employs the greatest number of persons, in its long and branching extent of 477 miles 35¼ chains, with 153 stations. The total number employed is 6,743, and they are thus classified:—

Secretaries or managers .	8	Assistant drivers, or firemen	318
Engineers	5	Guards or breaksmen .	207
Superintendents	40	Artificers	1,891
Storekeepers	8	Switchmen	363
Accountants or cashiers .	4	Gatekeepers	76
Inspectors or timekeepers	83	Policemen or watchmen	241
Draughtsmen	11	Porters or messengers .	1,456
Clerks	775	Plate-layers	14
Foreman	130	Labourers	30
Engine drivers	334		

On the Midland there were employed 4,898 persons; on the Lancashire and Yorkshire, 3,971; Great Western, 2,997; Eastern Counties, 2,939; Caledonian, 2,409; York, Newcastle, and Berwick, 2,731; London and South-Western, 2,118; London, Brighton, and South Coast, 2,053; York and North Midland, 1,614; North British, 1,535; and South-Eastern, 1,527. Then the 12 leading companies retain permanently in their service 35,735 men, supplying the means of maintenance—reckoning a family of 3 supported by each man employed—to 122,940 individuals. Pursuing the same calculation, as 159,784 men were employed on all the railways, "open and unopen," we may conclude that 739,136 individuals were dependent, more or less, upon railway traffic for their subsistence.

The other summary to which I have alluded is one derived from a return which the House of Commons ordered to be printed on the 8th of April last. It is relative to the Railway Accidents that occurred in the United Kingdom during the half-year ending the 31st of December, 1849, and supplies the following analysis:—

"54 passengers injured from causes beyond their own control.

"11 passengers killed, and 10 injured, owing to their own misconduct or want of caution.

"2 servants of companies or of contractors killed, and 3 injured from causes beyond their own control.

"62 servants of companies or of contractors killed, and 37 injured, owing to their own misconduct or want of caution.

"28 trespassers and other persons, neither passengers nor servants of the company, killed, and 7 injured by improperly crossing or standing on the railway.

"1 child killed, and 1 injured by an engine running off the rails and entering a house.

"Suicide 2.

"Total, 106 killed, and 112 injured.

"The number of passengers conveyed during the half-year amounted to 34,924,469."

The greatest number of accidents was on the Lancashire and Yorkshire. 2,793,764 passengers were conveyed in the term specified, and 17 individuals were killed, and 24 injured. On the York, Newcastle, and Berwick, 15 were killed and 6 injured; 1,613,123 passengers having been conveyed. On the Midland, 2,658,903 having been the number of passengers, 9 persons were killed and 7 injured. On the Great Western, conveying 1,220,507½ passengers, 2 individuals were killed and 1 injured. On the London and Blackwall, with 1,200,514 passengers, there was 1 man killed and 16 injured. The London and Greenwich supplied the means of locomotion to 1,126,237 persons, and none were killed and none were injured. These deaths on the railway, for the half-year cited above, are in the proportion of 106 to 34,924,469, or 1 person killed to every 329,476, and the 106 killed include 2 suicides and the deaths of 28 trespassers and others. The total number of persons who suffered from accidents was 218, which is in the proportion of 1 accident to every 160,203 persons travelling; and when the injuries arising from this mode of conveyance are contrasted with the loss of life by shipwreck, which as before stated, amounts to one in every 203 individuals, the comparative safety of railway over marine travelling must appear most extraordinary. Mr. Porter's calculation as to the number of stage coach travellers (which I cite under that head) shows that my estimates are far from extravagant.

The next part of my subject is the "water carriage" carried on by means of canals and rivers. The means of inland navigation in England and Wales are computed to comprise more than 4,000 miles in admeasurement, and of these 2,200 miles are in *navigable canals*, and 1,800 in *navigable rivers*. In Ireland such modes of communication extend about 500 miles, and in Scotland about 350. As railways have been the growth of the present half century, so did canals owe their increase, if not their establishment in England, to the half century preceding, from 1750 to 1800; three-fourths of those now in existence having been established during that period. Previously to the works perfected by the Duke of Bridgewater, and his famous and self-taught engineer, James Brindley, the efforts made to improve our means of water transit were mainly confined to attempts to improve the navigation of rivers. These attempts were not attended with any great success. The current of the river was often too impetuous to be restrained in the artificial channels prepared for the desired improvements, and the forms and depths of the channels were gradually changed by the current, so that labour and expense were very heavily and continuously entailed. "Difficulties in the way of river navigation," says Mr. McCulloch, "seem to have suggested the expediency of abandoning the channels of most rivers, and of digging parallel to them artificial channels, in which the water may be kept at the proper level by means of locks. The act passed by the Legislature in 1755 for improving the navigation of Sankey Brook, on the Mersey, gave rise to a lateral canal of this description, about 11¼ miles in length, which deserves to be mentioned as the earliest effort of the sort in England. But before this canal had been completed, the Duke of Bridgewater and James Brindley had conceived a plan of canalization, independent altogether of natural channels, and intended to afford the greatest facilities to commerce, by carrying canals across rivers and through mountains, wherever it was practicable to construct them."

The difficulties which Brindley overcame, were considered insurmountable until he *did* overcome them. In the construction of a canal from Worsley to Manchester, it was necessary to cross the river Irwell, where it is navigable at Barton. Brindley proposed to accomplish this by carrying an aqueduct 39 feet above the surface of the Irwell. This was considered so extravagant a proposition that there was a pause, and a gentleman eminent for engineering knowledge was consulted. He treated Brindley's scheme as the scheme of a visionary, declaring that he had often heard of castles in the air, but never before heard where one was to be erected. The Duke, however, had confidence in his engineer; and a successful, serviceable, and profitable aqueduct, instead of a castle, in the air was the speedy and successful result. The success of Brindley's plans, and the spirited munificence of the Duke of Bridgewater—who, that he might have ample means to complete his projects, at one time confined his mere personal expenses to £400 a year—laid the foundations of the large fortunes now enjoyed by the Duke of Sutherland and his brother the Earl of Ellesmere.

The canals which have been commenced and completed in the United Kingdom, since the year 1800, are 30 in number, and extend 582¾ miles in length.

Mr. McCulloch gives a list of British canals, with the numbers of shareholders in the proprietary of each, the amount and cost of shares, and the price on the 27th of June, 1843. The Erewash, with 231 shares, each £100, returned a dividend of £40, each share being then worth £675. The Loughborough, with only seventy £100 shares, the average cost of each share having been £142 17s., had a dividend of £80, and a selling price per share of £1,400. The Stroudwater, with 200 shares of £150, returned a dividend of £24, with a price in the market of £490. On the other hand, the £50 shares of the Crinan were then selling at £2. The £50 shares of the North Walsham and Dillon were of the same almost nominal value in the market; and the shares of the Thames and Medway, with an average cost of £30 4s. 3d., were worth but £1. Of the cost expended in the construction of the canals of England, I have no means of giving a precise account, but the following calculation seems sufficiently accurate for my present purpose. I find that, in round numbers, the 250,000 shares of the 40 principal canals averaged an expenditure of £100 per share, the result would be £25,000,000, and perhaps we may estimate the canals of the United Kingdom to have cost £35,000,000, or one-tenth as much as the railways.

The foregoing inquiries present the following gigantic results:— There are employed in the yearly transit of Great Britain with the world and with her own shores, 33,672 sailing vessels, and 1,110 steam vessels, employing 236,000 seamen. Calculating the value of each ship and cargo, as the value has been estimated before Parliament, at £5,000, we have an aggregate value—sailing vessels, steamers, and their cargoes included—of £173,910,000. Further, supposing that the yearly wages of the seamen, including officers, was £20 per head, the amount paid in wages would be £4,720,000.

The railways now in operation in the United Kingdom extend 6,000 miles, the cost of their construction (paid and to be paid) having been estimated at upwards of £350,000,000. Last year they supplied the means of rapid travel to above 63 millions of passengers, who traversed above a billion of miles. Their receipts for the year approached 11¼ millions of money, and nearly three quarters of a million of persons are dependent upon them for subsistence.

The turnpike and other roads of Great Britain alone (independently of Ireland) present a surface 120,000 miles in length, for the various purposes of interchange, commerce, and recreation. They are maintained by the yearly expenditure of a million and a half.

For similar purposes the navigable canals and rivers of Great Britain and Ireland furnish an extent of 4,850 miles, formed at a cost of probably £35,000,000. Adding all these together, we have of turnpike roads, railways, and canals no less than 130,000 and odd miles formed, at an aggregate cost of upwards of £386,000,000. If we add to this the £54,250,000 capital expended in the mercantile marine, we have the gross total of more than 440 millions of money sunk in the transit of the country. If the number of miles traversed by the natives of this country in the course of the year by sea, road, rail, river, and canal were summed up, it would reach to a distance greater than to the remotest planet yet discovered.

LABOUR AND THE POOR.

THE METROPOLITAN DISTRICTS.

[FROM OUR SPECIAL CORRESPONDENT.]

OF THE LONDON OMNIBUS DRIVERS AND CONDUCTORS.

LETTER LXXI.

The subject of omnibus conveyance is one to the importance of which the aspect of every thoroughfare in London bears witness. Yet the dweller in the Strand, or even in a greater thoroughfare, Cheapside, can only form a partial notion of the magnitude of this mode of transit, for he has but a partial view of it; he sees, as it were, only one of its details.

The routes of the several omnibuses are manifold. Widely apart as are their starting points, it will be seen how their courses tend to common centres, and how generally what may be called the great trunk lines of the streets are resorted to.

The principal routes lie north and south, east and west, through the central parts of London, to and from the extreme suburbs. The majority of them commence running at nine in the morning, and continue till twelve at night, succeeding each other during the busy parts of the day every five minutes. Most of them have two charges— 3d. for part of the distance, and 6d. for the whole distance.

The omnibuses proceeding on the *Northern* and *Southern* routes are principally the following:—

The Atlases run from the Eyre Arms, St. John's-wood, by way of Baker-street, Oxford-street, Regent-street, Charing-cross, Westminster-bridge and road, and past the Elephant and Castle, by the Walworth-road, to Camberwell-gate. Some turn off from "the Elephant" (as all the omnibus people call it), and go down the New Kent-road to the Dover Railway Station; while others run the same route, but to and from the Nightingale, Lisson-grove, instead of the Eyre Arms. The Waterloos journey from the York and Albany, Regent's-park, by way of Albany-street, Portland-road,

Regent-street, and so over Waterloo-bridge, by the Waterloo, London, and Walworth roads, to Camberwell-gate. The Waterloo Association have also a branch to Holloway, *viâ* the Camden Villas. There are likewise others which run from the terminus of the South Western Railway, in the Waterloo-road, *viâ* Stamford-street, to the railway termini on the Surrey side of London-bridge, and thence to that of the Eastern Counties, in Shoreditch.

The Hungerford-markets pursue the route from Camden-town along Tottenham-court-road, &c., to Hungerford, and many run from this spot to Paddington.

The Kentish-towns run from the Eastern Counties station, and from Whitechapel to Kentish-town, by way of Tottenham-court-road, &c.

The Hampsteads observe the like course to Camden-town, and then run straight on to Hampstead.

The King's-crosses run from Kennington-gate, by the Blackfriars-road and bridge, Fleet-street, Chancery-lane, Gray's-inn-lane, and the New-road, to Euston-square, while some go on to Camden-town.

The Great Northerns, the latest route started, travel from the railway terminus, Maiden-lane, King's-cross, to the Bank and the railway stations, both in the City and across the Thames; also to Paddington, and some to Kennington.

The "Favourites'" route is from Westminster Abbey along the Strand, Chancery-lane, Gray's-inn-lane, and Coldbath-fields, to the Angel, Islington, and thence to Holloway; while some of them run down Fleet-street, and so past the General Post-office, and thence by the City-road to the Angel, and to Holloway. The Favourites also run from Holloway to the Bank.

The Islington and Kenningtons' line is from Barnsbury Park, by the Post-office and Blackfriars-bridge, to Kennington-gate.

The Camberwells go from Gracechurch-street, over London-bridge to Camberwell; while a very few start from the West-end of the town, and some two or three from Fleet-street; the former crossing Westminster, and the latter Blackfriars-bridge; while some Nelsons run from Oxford-street to Camberwell, or to Brixton.

The Brixton and Claphams go, some from the Regent-circus, Oxford-street, by way of Regent-street, over Westminster-bridge, and some from Gracechurch-street, over London-bridge to Brixton or Clapham, as the case may be.

The Paragons observe the same route; and some of these conveyances go over Blackfriars-bridge, to Brixton.

The Carshaltons follow the track of the Mitchams, Tootings, and Claphams, and go over London-bridge to the Bank.

Within the last few days some penny omnibuses have commenced running from the London-bridge Railway Station to the Bank.

Those omnibuses pursuing the *Eastern and Western Routes* are as follows:—

The Paddingtons run from the Royal Oak, Westbourne-green, and from the Pine Apple-gate, by way of Oxford-street and Holborn, to the Bank, the London-bridge, Eastern Counties, or Blackwall Railway termini; while some reach the same destination by the route of the New-road, City-road, and Finsbury. These routes are also pursued by the vehicles lettered "New-road Conveyance Association," "Paddington Conveyance Association," and "London Conveyance Company," while some of the vehicles belonging to the same proprietors run to Notting-hill, and some have branches to St. John's-wood and elsewhere.

The Wellingtons and the Marlboroughs pursue the same track as the Paddingtons, but some of them diverge to St. John's-wood.

The Kensall-greens go from the Regent-circus, Oxford-street, to the Cemetery.

The course of the Bayswaters is from Bayswater *viâ* Oxford street, Regent-street, and the Strand, to the Bank.

The Bayswater and Kensingtons run from the Bank, *viâ* Finsbury, and then by the City-road and New-road, down Portland-road, and by Oxford-street and Piccadilly, to Bayswater and Kensington.

The Hammersmith and Kensingtons convey their passengers from Hammersmith, by way of Kensington, Knightsbridge, Piccadilly, &c., to the Bank.

The Richmond and Hampton Courts from St. Paul's Churchyard to the two places indicated.

The Putney and Bromptons run from Putney-bridge, *viâ* Brompton, &c., to the Bank and the London-bridge Railway Station.

The Chelseas proceed from the Man in the Moon to the Bank, Mile-end-road, and City Railway stations.

The Chelsea and Islingtons observe the route from Sloane-square to the Angel, Islington, travelling along Piccadilly, Regent-street, Portland-road, and the New-road.

The Royal Blues go from Pimlico, *viâ* Grosvenor-place, Piccadilly, the Strand, &c., to the Blackwall Railway.

The direction of the Pimlicos is through Westminster, Whitehall, Strand, &c., to Whitechapel.

The Marquess of Westminsters follow the route from the Vauxhall-road, *viâ* Millbank, Westminster Abbey, the Strand, &c., to the Bank.

The Deptfords go from Gracechurch-street and over London-bridge, and some from Charing-cross over Westminster-bridge to Deptford.

The route of the Nelsons is from Charing-cross, over Westminster-bridge, and by the New and Old Kent-roads to Deptford, Greenwich, and Woolwich; some go from Gracechurch-street over London-bridge.

The Shoreditches pursue the direction of Chelsea, Piccadilly, the Strand, &c., to Shoreditch, their starting place being Battersea-bridge.

The Hackneys and Claptons run from Oxford-street to Clapton-square.

Barber's run from the Bank, and some from Oxford-street to Clapton.

The Blackwalls run some from Sloane-street to the Docks; and the Bow and Stratfords from different parts of the West-end to their respective destinations.

I have enumerated these several conveyances from the information of persons connected with the trade, using the terms *they* used, which better distinguish the respective routes than the names lettered on the carriages, which would but puzzle the reader, the principal appellation giving no indication of the destination of the omnibus.

The routes above specified are pursued by a series of vehicles belonging to one company or to one firm, or one individual, the number of their vehicles varying from twelve to fifty. *One* omnibus, however, continues to run from the Bank to Finchley, and one from the Angel to Hampton Court.

The total number of omnibuses traversing the streets of London is about 3,000, paying duty (including mileage), averaging £9 per month each, or £324,000 per annum. The number of conductors and drivers is about 7,000 (including 1,000 "odd men," a term that will be explained hereafter), paying annually 5s. each for their licenses, or £1,750 collectively. The receipts of each vehicle vary from £2 to

£4 per day; estimating the whole 3,000 at £3, it follows that the entire sum expended annually in omnibus hire by the people of London amounts to no less than £3,285,000, which is more than 30s. a head for every man, woman, and child in the metropolis. The average journey, as regards length, of each omnibus is six miles, and that distance is, in some cases, travelled twelve times a day by each omnibus, or, as it is called, "six there and six back." Some perform the journey only ten times a day (each omnibus), and some, but a minority, a less number of times. Now, taking the average as between forty-five and fifty miles a day travelled by each omnibus, and that I am assured on the best authority is within the mark, while sixty miles a day might exceed it, and computing the omnibuses running daily at 3,000, we find "a travel," as it was worded to me, of upwards of 140,000 miles daily, or a yearly "travel" of more than 50,000,000 of miles; an extent that almost defies a parallel in any distances popularly familiar. And that this estimate in no way exceeds the truth is proved by the sum annually paid to the Excise for "mileage," which, as was before stated, amounts on an average to £9 each "buss" per month, or collectively to £324,000 per annum, and this, at 1½d. per mile (the rate of duty charged), gives 51,840,000 miles as the distance travelled by the entire number of omnibuses every year.

On each of its journeys, experienced persons have assured me an omnibus carries on the average fifteen persons. Nearly all are licensed to carry twenty-two (thirteen inside and nine out), and that number perhaps is sometimes exceeded, while fifteen is a fair computation; for as every omnibus has now the two fares of 3d. and 6d., or as "bus-men" call them, "long-uns and short-uns," there are two sets of passengers, and the number of fifteen through the whole distance on each journey of the omnibus, is, as I have said, a fair computation, for sometimes the vehicle is almost empty, as a set off to its being crammed at other times. This computation shows the daily "travel," reckoning ten journeys a day, of 450,000 passengers. Thus we might be led to believe that about one-fourth of the entire population of the metropolis and its suburbs—men, women, and children; the inmates of hospitals, gaols, and workhouses; paupers, peers and their families, all included—were daily travelling in omnibuses. But it must be borne in mind that as most omnibus travellers use that convenient mode of conveyance at least twice a day, we may compute the number of individuals at 225,000, or, allowing three journeys as an average daily travel, at 150,000. Calculating the payment of each passenger at

4½d., and so allowing for the set-off of the "short-uns" to the "long-uns," we have a daily receipt for omnibus fares of £8,439; a weekly receipt of £58,073, and a yearly receipt of £2,903,650; which it will be seen is several thousands less than the former estimate; so that it may be safely assumed that at least three millions of money is annually expended in omnibus fares in London.

The extent of individual travel performed by some of the omnibus drivers is enormous. One man told me that he had driven "his bus" 72 miles (12 stages of six miles) every day for six years, with the exception of twelve miles less every second Sunday, so that this man had driven in six years 179,568 miles.

This vast extent of omnibus transit has been the growth of 20 years, as it was not until the 4th July, 1829, that Mr. Shillibeer—now the proprietor of the patent mourning coaches—started the first omnibus. Some works of authority, as books of reference, have represented that Mr. Shillibeer's first omnibus ran from Charing-cross to Greenwich, and that the charge for outside and inside places was the same. Such was not the case. The first omnibus, or rather the first pair of those vehicles—for Mr. Shillibeer started two—ran from the Bank to the Yorkshire Stingo. Neither could the charge out and in be the same, as there were then no outside passengers. Mr. Shillibeer was a naval officer, and in his youth stepped from a midshipman's duties into the business of a coach-builder, he learning that business from the late Mr. Hatchet, of Long-acre. Mr. Shillibeer then established himself in business in Paris as a builder of English carriages, a demand for which had sprung up after the Peace, when the current of English travel was directed strongly to France. In this speculation Mr. Shillibeer was eminently successful. He built carriages for Prince Polignac and others of the most influential men under the dynasty of the elder branch of the Bourbons, and had a bazaar for the sale of his vehicles. He was thus occupied in Paris, in 1819, when M. Lafitte first started the omnibuses which are now so common and so well-managed in the French capital. Lafitte was the banker (afterwards the Minister) of Louis Philippe, and the most active man in establishing the Messageries Royales. Five or six years after the omnibuses had been successfully introduced into Paris, Mr. Shillibeer was employed by M. Lafitte to build two in a superior style. In executing this order Mr. Shillibeer thought that so comfortable and economical a mode of conveyance might be advantageously introduced into London. He accordingly disposed of his Parisian establishment and came to London, and started his omnibus as I have narrated. In order that the introduction might have every chance of success, and have the full *prestige* of respectability, Mr. Shillibeer brought over with him from Paris two youths, both the sons of British naval officers, and these young gentlemen were for a few weeks his "conductors." They were smartly dressed in "blue cloth and togs," to use the words of my informant, after the fashion of Lafitte's conductors, each dress costing £5. Their addressing any foreign passenger in French, and the French style of the affair, gave rise to an opinion that Mr. Shillibeer was a Frenchman, and that the English were indebted to a foreigner for the improvement of their vehicular transit; whereas Mr. Shillibeer had served in the British navy, and was born in Tottenham-court-road. His speculation was particularly, and at once, successful. His two vehicles carried each twenty-two, and were filled every journey. The form was that of the present omnibus, but larger and roomier, as the twenty-two were all accommodated inside, no one being on the outside but the driver. Three horses, yoked abreast, were used to draw these carriages. There were for many days until the novelty wore off crowds assembled to see the omnibuses start, and many ladies and gentlemen took their places in them to the Yorkshire Stingo in order that they might have the pleasure of riding back again. The fare was 1s. for the whole and 6d. for half the distance, and each omnibus made twelve journeys to and fro every day. Thus Mr. Shillibeer established a diversity of fares, regulated by distance; a regulation which was afterwards, in a great measure, abandoned by omnibus proprietors, and then re-established on our present 3d. and 6d. payments, the "long-uns" and the "short-uns." Mr. Shillibeer's receipts were £100 a week. At first he provided a few books, chiefly magazines, for the perusal of his customers; but this peripatetic library was discontinued, for the customers—I give the words of my informant—"boned the books." When the young gentlemen conductors retired from their posts they were succeeded by persons hired by Mr. Shillibeer and liberally paid, who were attired in a sort of velvet livery. Many weeks had not elapsed before Mr. Shillibeer found a falling off in his receipts, although he ascertained that there was no falling off in the public support of his omnibuses. He obtained information, however, that the persons in his employ robbed him of at least £20 a week, retaining that sum out of the receipts of the two omnibuses, and that they had boasted of their cleverness and their lucrative situations at a champagne supper at the Yorkshire Stingo! This necessitated a change, which Mr. Shillibeer effected in his men, but without prosecuting the offenders, and still it seemed that defalcations continued. That they continued was soon shown, and in "a striking manner," as it was called. As an experiment Mr. Shillibeer expended £300 in the construction of a machine, fitted to the steps of an omnibus, which should record the number of passengers, as they trod on a plate in entering and leaving the vehicle, arranged on a similar principle to the tell-tales in use on our toll bridges. The inventor, Mr. ——, now of Woolwich, himself "worked" the omnibus containing it for a fortnight, and it supplied a correct index of the number of passengers; but at the fortnight's end, one evening after dark, the inventor was hustled aside while waiting at the Yorkshire Stingo, and in a minute or two the machine was smashed, by some unknown men, with sledge hammers. Mr. Shillibeer then had recourse to the use of such clocks as were used in the French omnibuses as a check. It was publicly notified that it was the business of the conductor to move the hand of the clock a given distance when a passenger entered the vehicle; but this plan did not avail. It is common in France for a passenger to inform the proprietor of any neglect on the part of his servant, but Mr. Shillibeer never received any such intimation in London.

In the mean time Mr. Shillibeer's success continued, for he insured punctuality and civility, and the cheapness, cleanliness, and smartness of his omnibuses were in most advantageous contrast with the high charges, dirt, dinginess, and the rudeness of the drivers of many of the "short stages." The short stage proprietors were loud in their railings against what they were pleased to describe as a French innovation. In the course of from six to nine months Mr. Shillibeer had twelve omnibuses at work. The new omnibuses ran from the Bank to Paddington, but by the route of Holborn and Oxford-street as well as by Finsbury and the New-road. Mr. Shillibeer feels convinced that had he started fifty omnibuses, instead of two, in the first instance, a fortune might have been realised. In 1831-2 his omnibuses became general in the great street thoroughfares, and, as the short stages were run off the road, the proprietors started omnibuses in opposition to Mr. Shillibeer. The first omnibuses, however, started after Mr. Shillibeer's were not in opposition. They were the *Caledonians*, and were the property of Mr. Shillibeer's brother-in-law. The third started, which were two-horse vehicles, were foolishly enough called "Les Dames Blanches," but as the name gave rise to much low wit in equivoques, it was abandoned. The original omnibuses were called

Shillibeers, from the name of their originator on the panels, and the name is still prevalent on those conveyances in New York, which affords us another proof that not in his own country is a benefactor honoured, until perhaps his death makes honour as little worth as an epitaph.

The opposition omnibuses, however, continued to increase as more and more short stages were abandoned, and one oppositionist called his omnibuses *Shillibeers*, so that the real and the sham *Shillibeers* were known in the streets. The opposition became fiercer. The "busses," as they came to be called in a year or two, crossed each other or raced, or drove their poles recklessly into the back of one another; and accidents, and squabbles, and loitering grew so frequent, and the time of the police magistrates was so much occupied with "omnibus business," that in 1832 the matter was mentioned in Parliament as a nuisance requiring a remedy; and in 1833 a bill was brought in by the Government, and passed, for the "Regulation of omnibuses (as well as other conveyances) in and near the metropolis." Two sessions after, Mr. Alderman Wood brought in a bill for the *better* regulation of omnibuses, which was also passed, and one of the provisions of the bill was that the drivers and conductors of omnibuses should be licensed. The office of Registrar of Licenses was promised by a noble lord in office to Mr. Shillibeer (as I am informed on good authority), but the appointment was given to the present Commissioner of the City Police, and the office next to the principal was offered to Mr. Shillibeer, which that gentleman declined to accept. The reason assigned for not appointing him to the registrarship was, that he was connected with omnibuses. At the beginning of 1834 Mr. Shillibeer abandoned his metropolitan trade, and commenced running omnibuses from London to Greenwich and Woolwich, employing 20 carriages and 120 horses; but the increase of steamers and the opening of the Greenwich railway in 1835 affected this trade so materially that Mr. Shillibeer fell into arrear with his payments to the Stamp-office, and seizures of his property, and re-seizures after money was paid, entailed such heavy expenses, and such a hinderance to Mr. Shillibeer's business, that his failure ensued.

I have been thus somewhat full in my details of Mr. Shillibeer's career, as his procedures are in truth the history of the transit of the metropolis as regards omnibuses. I conclude this portion of the subject with the following extracts from a parliamentary paper, "Supplement to the Votes and Proceedings, Veneris 7° die Julii, 1843," containing the "petition of George Shillibeer."

"That, in 1840, after several years of incessant application, the Lords of the Treasury caused Mr. Gordon, their then financial secretary, to inquire into your petitioner's case, and so fully satisfied was that gentleman with the hardship and cruel wrongs which the department of Stamps and Taxes had inflicted upon your petitioner, that he (Mr. Gordon) promised, on behalf of the Lords of the Treasury, early redress should be granted to your petitioner, either by a Government appointment adequate to the loss he had sustained, or pecuniary compensation for the injustice which, upon a thorough investigation of the facts, Mr. Gordon assured your petitioner he had fully established to the satisfaction of the Lords of the Treasury.

"That in proof of the sincerity of Mr. Gordon, he, in his then official capacity of Secretary to the said Lords of her Majesty's Treasury, applied in April, 1841, to the then heads of two Government departments, viz., the Marquess of Normanby and the Right Hon. Henry Labouchere, to appoint your petitioner 'Inspector-General of Public Carriages,' or some appointment in the railway department at the Board of Trade; but these applications being unsuccessful, Mr. Gordon applied for and obtained for your petitioner the promise of one of the twenty-five appointments of Receiver-General of County Courts (testimonials of your petitioner's fitness being at the Treasury), the bill for establishing which was then in progress through Parliament.

"That, shortly after your petitioner's claims had been admitted, and redress promised by the Lords of the Treasury, Mr. Gordon resigned his situation of secretary, and on the 6th May, 1841, your petitioner again saw Mr. Gordon, who assured your petitioner that but for the fact of the Miscellaneous Estimates being made up and passed for that year, your petitioner's name should have been placed in them for a grant of five thousand pounds, further observing that your petitioner's was a case of very great hardship and injustice, and assuring your petitioner that he (Mr. Gordon) would not quit the Treasury without stating to his successor that your petitioner's case was one of peculiar severity, and deserved immediate attention and redress."

And so the matter remains virtually.

I will now give the regulations and statistics of the French omnibuses, which I am enabled to do through the kindness of a gentleman to whom I am indebted for much valuable information.

As the regulations of the French public conveyances (*des voitures faisant le transport en commun*) are generally considered to have worked admirably well, I present a digest of them. The earlier enactments provide for the numbering of these conveyances, and for the licensing of all connected with them.

The laws which provide the regulations are of the following dates. I enumerate them to show how closely the French Government has attended to the management of hired vehicles:—Dec. 14, 1789; Aug. 14, 1790; 9 Vendemaire, An. VI. (Sept. 30, 1797); 11 Frimaire, An. VII. (Dec. 1, 1798); 12 Messidor, An. VIII. (July 1, 1800); 3 Brumaire, An. IX. (Oct. 29, 1800); Dec. 30, 1818; July 22, 1829; Aug. 1, 1829; March 29, 1836; Sept. 15, 1838; and Jan. 5, 1846. The 471st, 474th, 479th, and 484th articles of the Penal Code also relate to this subject.

The principal regulations now in force are the following:—

The proprietors of all public conveyances (for hire) shall be numbered, licensed, and find such security as shall be satisfactory to the authorities. Every proprietor, before he can change the locality of his establishment, is bound to give 48 hours' notice of his intention of removal. The sale of such establishments can only be effected by undertakers (*entrepreneurs*), duly authorised for the purpose; and the privilege of the undertaker is not transferable, either wholly or partially, without the sanction of the authorities. The proprietors cannot employ any conductors, drivers, or porters, but such as have a license or permit (*permis de conduire, &c.*); neither can a master retain or transfer any such permit if the holder of it have left his service; it must be given up within twenty-four hours to the prefecture (office) of police, and the date of the man's entry upon and leaving such his employ must be inscribed by his late master on the back of the document. Proprietors must keep a register of the names and abodes of their drivers and conductors, their numbers as entered in the books of the prefecture; also a daily entry of the number of the vehicle in use, as engraved on the plates affixed to it, and a record of the conduct of the men to whom it has been entrusted. No proprietor to be allowed to employ a driver or conductor whose permit, through ill-conduct or any cause, has been withdrawn. In case of the contravention of this regulation by any one, the plying (*la circulation*) of his carriage is to be stopped, either temporarily or definitively. No carriage shall be entrusted to either driver or conductor if either be in a state of evident uncleanliness (*mal propreté*). No horse known to be vicious, diseased, or incapable of work is to be employed.

The conductors are to maintain order in their vehicles, and to ob-serve that the passengers place themselves so as not to incommode one another. They are not to exceed the number of persons they are authorized to convey, which number must be notified in the interior and on the exterior of the omnibus. They are also forbidden to admit individuals who may be drunk, or clad in a manner to disgust or annoy the other passengers; neither must they admit dogs, or suffer persons who may sing, drink, or smoke to remain in the carriages; neither must they carry parcels which, from their size, or the nature of their contents, may incommode the passengers. Conductors must not give the coachman the word to go on until each passenger leaving the omnibus shall have quitted the footstep, or until each passenger entering the omnibus shall have been seated; every person so entering is to be asked where he wishes to be set down. All property left in the omnibus to be conveyed to the prefecture of police. It is, moreover, the conductor's business to light the carriage-lamps after night-fall.

The drivers (*cochers*), before they can be allowed "to exercise their profession," must produce testimonials as to their possessing the necessary skill. They are not to gallop their horses under any circumstances whatever. They are required, moreover, to drive slow, or at a walk (*au pas*) in the markets, and in the narrow streets where only two carriages can pass abreast, at the descent of the bridges, and in all parts of the public ways where there may be a stoppage or a rapid slope. Wherever the width of the streets permits it, the omnibus must be driven at least three feet from the houses where there is no footpath (*trottoir*), and where there is a footpath two feet from it. They must as much as possible, keep the wheels of their vehicle out of the gutters.

No driver or conductor can exercise his profession under the age of eighteen, and before being authorised to do so he must show that his morals and trustworthiness are such as to justify his appointment. (The ordonnance then provides for the licensing, at the cost of 70c., of these officers, by the police, in the way I have already described.) They are not permitted to smoke while at their work, nor to take off their coats, even during the sultriest weather. The stops of the omnibus are to take place on the right hand side of the street; but if there be any hindrance, then on the left.

The foregoing regulations (the infractions of which are punishable through the ordinary tribunals) do not materially differ from those of our own country, though they may be more stringently enforced. The other provisions, however, are materially different. The French Government fixes the amount of fare, prescribes the precise route to be observed, and the time to be kept, and limits the number of omni-buses. On the 12th of August, 1846, there were 387 in number run-ning along thirty-six lines, which are classed under the head of twelve routes (*entreprises*), in the following order:—

Routes.	No. of Lines.	No. of Car-riages.	Nos. accord-ing to the Licenses.
1. Omnibus-Orléanaises, and Diligentes ...	13	151	1 to 151
2. Dames-réunies	3	29	152 to 180
3. Tricycles	1	11	181 to 191
4. Favorites	4	47	192 to 238
5. Béarnaises	2	19	239 to 257
6. Citadines	2	13	258 to 270
7. Batignolles-gazelles .	2	19	271 to 289
8. Hirondelles	2	30	290 to 319
9. Parisiennes	3	33	320 to 352
10. Constantines	1	12	353 to 364
11. Excellentes	2	15	365 to 379
12. Gauloises	1	8	380 to 387
	36	387	

In order to prevent the inconvenience of too rigidly defined routes, a system of intercommunication has been established. At a given point (*bureau des correspondances*) a passenger may always be trans-ferred to another omnibus, the conductor giving him a free ticket, and so may reach his destination, or the nearest point to it, from any of the starting places. This system now, but very partially, prevails on some of the London lines.

The number conveyed by a Parisian omnibus is fixed at sixteen; each vehicle is to be drawn by two horses, and is to unite "all the conditions of solidity, commodiousness, and elegance, that may be desirable." In order to ensure these conditions, the French Govern-ment directs in what manner every omnibus shall be built. Those built prior to the promulgation of the ordonnance (Aug. 12th, 1846) regulating the construction of these vehicles, are still allowed to be "in circulation," but after the 1st January, 1852, no omnibus not construc-ted in exact accordance with the details laid down, will be allowed "to circulate." The height of the omnibus is fixed, as well as the length and the width; the circumference of the wheels, the adjustment of the springs, the hanging of the body, the formation of the ventilators, the lining and cushioning of the interior, the dimensions of the footsteps, and the disposition of the lamps, which are three in number.

The arrangements, where a footpath is not known in the streets of Paris, and a gutter is in existence, are tolerably significant of distinctions between the streets of the French and English capitals.

I shall now pass to the consideration of the English vehicles as they are at present conducted.

The "labourers" immediately connected with the trade in omnibuses are the proprietors, drivers, conductors, and timekeepers. Those less immediately, but still in connection with the trade, are the "odd men" and the horsekeepers.

The earlier history of omnibus proprietors presents but a series of struggles and ruinous lawsuits, one proprietor with another, until many were ruined, and then several opposing companies or individuals coalesced, or agreed; and these proprietaries now present a united, and, I believe, a prosperous body. They possess, in reality, a monopoly in omnibus conveyance; but I am assured that it would not be easy under any other plan to serve the public better. All the proprietors of omnibuses may be said to be "in union," as they act systematically, and by arrangement, one proprietary with another. Their profits are, of course, apportioned, like those of other joint-stock companies, according to the number of shares held by individual members. On each route one member of the proprietary is appointed "director" by his co-proprietors. The directory may be classed as the "executive department" of the body. The director can displace a driver on a week's notice; but by some directors who pride themselves on dealing summarily, it seems that the week's notice is now and then dispensed with. The conductor he can displace at a day's notice. The "odd men" sometimes supply the places of the officials so discharged, until a meeting of the proprietary, held monthly for the most part, when new officers are appointed, there being always an abundance of applicants, who send or carry in testimonials of their fitness from persons known to the proprietors or known to reside on the line of the route. The director may, indeed, appoint either driver or conductor, at his discretion, if he see good reason to do so; the driver, however, is generally appointed and paid by the proprietor, while the conductor is more particularly the servant of the association. The proprietaries have so far a monopoly of the road that they allow no new omnibuses to be started upon it. If a speculator should be bold enough to start new conveyances, the pre-existing proprietaries put a greater number of conveyances on the route, so that none are well filled, and one of the old proprietaries' vehicles immediately precedes the omnibus of the speculator, and another immediately follows it, and thus three vehicles are on the ground which may yield only customers for one; hence, as the whole number on the route has been largely increased, not one omnibus is well filled, and the speculator must in all probability be ruined, while the associated proprietors suffer but a temporary loss. So well is this now understood, that no one seems to think of embarking his money in the omnibus trade unless he "buys his times"—that is to say, unless he arranges by purchase—and a "new man" will often pay £400 or £500 for his "times"—to have the privilege of running his vehicles on a given route and at given periods—in other words, for the privilege of becoming a recognised proprietor.

The proprietors pay their servants fairly, as a general rule, while, as an universal rule, they rigidly exact sobriety, punctuality, and cleanliness. Their great difficulty, all of them concur in stating, is to ensure honesty. Every proprietor insists upon the excessive difficulty of trusting men with uncounted money, if the men feel there is no efficient check to ensure to their employers a knowledge of the exact amount of their daily receipts. Several plans have been resorted to in order to obtain the desired check; Mr. Shillibeer's I have already given. One plan now in practice is to engage a well-dressed woman, sometimes accompanied by a child, and she travels by the omnibus, and immediately on leaving it fills up a paper for the proprietor, showing the number of insides and outs, of long and short fares. This method, however, does not ensure a thorough accuracy. It is difficult for a woman, who must take such a place in the vehicle as she can get, to ascertain the precise number of outsides, or their respective fares. So difficult, that I am assured such a person has returned a *smaller* number than was actually conveyed. One gentleman, who was formerly an omnibus proprietor, told me he employed a "lady-like," and as he believed, trusty woman, as a "check;" but by some means, the conductors found out the calling of the "lady-like" woman, treated her, and she made very favourable returns for the conductors. Another lady was observed by a conductor, who bears an excellent character, and who mentioned the circumstance to me, to carry a small bag, from which, whenever a passenger got out, she drew, not very deftly it would seem, a bean, and placed it in one glove, as ladies carry their sixpences for the fare, or a pea, and placed it in the other. This process the conductor felt assured was "a check;" that the beans indicated the "long-uns," and the peas the "short-uns;" so when the unhappy woman desired to be put down at the bottom of Cheapside, in a wintry evening, he contrived to "land her" in the very thickest of the mud, handing her out with great politeness. I may here observe, before I enter upon the subject, that the men who have maintained a character for integrity regard the "checks" with great bitterness, as they naturally feel more annoyed at being suspected than men who may be dishonestly inclined. Another conductor once found a small memorandum book in his omnibus, in which were regularly entered "longs" and "shorts."

One proprietor told me that he had once employed religious men as conductors, but, said he, "they grew into thieves. A methodist parson engaged one of his sons to me—it's a good while ago—and was quite indignant that I ever made any question about the young man's honesty, as he was strictly and religiously brought up; but he turned out one of the worst of the whole batch of them." One check resorted to, as a conductor informed me, was found out by them. A lady entered the omnibus carrying a brown paper parcel, loosely tied, and making a tare on the edge of the paper for every "short" passenger, and a deeper tare for every "long." This difficulty in finding a check where an indefinite amount of money passes through a man's hands— and I am by no means disposed to undervalue the difficulty—has led to a summary course of procedure, not unattended by serious evils. It appears that men are now discharged suddenly, at a moment's notice, and with no reason assigned. If a reason be demanded, the answer is, "You are not wanted any longer." Probably the discharge is on account of the man's honesty being suspected; but whether the suspicion be well founded or unfounded, the consequences are equally serious to the individual discharged; for it is a rule observed by the proprietaries not to employ any man discharged from another line. He will not be employed, I am assured, if he can produce a good character; and even if the "bus he worked" had been discontinued, as no longer required on that route. New men, who are considered unconnected with all versed in omnibus tricks are appointed, and this course, it was intimated to me very strongly, was agreeable to the proprietors for two reasons—as widely extending their patronage, and as always placing at their command a large body of unemployed men, whose services can at any time be called into requisition at reduced wages, should "slop drivers" be desirable. It is next to impossible, I was further assured, for a man discharged from an omnibus to obtain other employ. If the director goes so far as to admit that he has nothing to allege against the man's character, he will yet give no reason for his discharge, and an inquirer naturally imputes the withholding of a reason to the mercy of the director.

The driver is paid by the week. His remuneration is 34s. a week on most of the lines. On others he receives 21s. and "his box," that is, the allowance of a fare each journey, for a seat outside if a seat be so occupied. In fine weather this box plan is more remunerative to the driver than the fixed payment of 34s., but in wet weather he may receive nothing from the box; the average the year through being about 34s. a week, or perhaps rather more, as on some days, in sultry weather, he may make 6s., "if the bus do twelve journeys," from his box.

The omnibus drivers have been butchers, farmers, horsebreakers, cheesemongers, old stage coachmen, broken down gentlemen, turf-men, gentlemen's servants, grooms, and a very small sprinkling of mechanics. Nearly all can read and write, the exception being de-scribed to me as a singularity, but there are such exceptions, and all must have produced good characters before their appointment. The majority of them are married men with families, their residences be-ing in all parts, and on both sides of the Thames. I did not hear of any of the wives of coachmen in regular employ working for the slop tailors, "We can keep our wives too respectable for that," one of them said in answer to my inquiry. Their children, too, are gener-ally sent to school, frequently to the national schools. Their work is exceedingly hard, their lives being almost literally spent on the coach-box. The most of them must enter "the yard" at a quarter to eight in the morning, and must see that the horses and the carriage are in a proper condition for work, and at half-past eight they start on their long day's labour. They perform, I speak of the most frequented lines, twelve journeys during the day, and are so engaged until a quarter past eleven at night. Some are on their box till past midnight. Dur-ing these hours of labour they have twelve "stops," half of ten, and half of fifteen minutes duration. They generally breakfast at home—or at a coffee-shop, if unmarried men—before they start, and dine at the inn where the omnibus almost invariably "stops," at one or other of its destinations. If the driver be distant from his home at his din-ner hour, or be unmarried, he arranges to dine at the public-house; if near, his wife or one of his children brings him his dinner in a covered basin, some of them being provided with hot water plates to keep the contents properly warm, and this is usually eaten at the public-house

with a pint of beer for the accompanying beverage. The relish with
which a man who has been employed several hours in the open air enjoys his dinner can easily be understood, but if his dinner is brought
to him on one of his shorter stops, he often hears the cry before he
has concluded the meal, "Time's up," and he carries the remains of his
repast to be consumed at his next resting-place. His tea, if brought
to him by his family, he often drinks within the omnibus, if there be
an opportunity. Some carry their dinners with them, and eat them
cold. All these men live "well," that is, they have sufficient dinners of
animal food every day, with beer. They are strong and healthy men,
for their calling requires both strength and health. Each driver (as
well as the time-keeper and conductor), is licensed at a yearly cost to
him of 5s. From a driver I had the following statement:—

"I have been a driver fourteen years. I was brought up as a builder,
but had friends that was using horses, and I sometimes assisted them
in driving and grooming, when I was out of work. I got to like that
sort of work, and thought it would be better than my own business, if
I could get to be connected with a bus; and I had friends, and first got
employed as a time-keeper; but I've been a driver for fourteen years.
I'm now paid by the week, and not by the box. It's a fair payment, but
we must live well. It's hard work is mine, for I never have any rest but
a few minutes, except every other Sunday, and then only two hours,
that's the time of a journey there and back. If I was to ask leave to
go to church, and then go to work again, I know what answer there
would be, 'You can go to church as often as you like, and we can get
a man who doesn't want to go there.' The cattle I drive are equal to
gentlemen's carriage horses. One I've driven five years, and I believe
she was worked five years before I drove her. It's very hard work for
the horses, but I don't know that they're overworked in busses. The
starting, after stopping, is the hardest work for them, it's such a terrible strain. I've felt for the poor things on a wet night, with a bus full
of big people. I think that it's a pity that anybody uses a bearing-rein.
There's not many uses it now. It bears up a horse's head, and he can
only go on pulling, pulling up a hill one way. Take off his bearing
rein, and he'll relieve the strain on him, by bearing down his head,
and flinging his weight on the collar to help his pull. If a man had
to carry a weight up a hill on his back, how would he like to have his
head tied back? Perhaps you may have noticed Mr. ——'s horses pull
the bus up Holborn-hill; they're tightly borne up; but then they're
very fine animals, fat and fine; there's no such cattle, perhaps, in a

London bus—least ways there's none better; and they're borne up for show. Now a gib horse won't go in a bearing rein, and will without it; I've seen that myself, so what can be the use of it? It's just teasing the poor things for a sort of fashion. I must keep exact time at every place where a timekeeper's stationed. Not a minute's excused. There's a fine for the least delay. I can't say that it's often levied, but still we're liable to it. If I've been blocked, I must make up for the block by galloping, and if I'm seen to gallop, and anybody tells our people, I'm called over the coals. I must drive as quick with a thunder-rain pelting in my face, and the roads in a muddle, and the horses starting—I can't call it shying, I have 'em too well in hand—at every flash; just as quick as if it was a fine hard road and fine weather. It's not easy to drive a bus; but I can drive, and must drive to an inch; yes, sir, to half an inch. I know if I can get my horses' heads through a space, I can get my splinter-bar through. I drive by my pole, making it my centre. If I keep it fair in the centre, a carriage must follow, unless it's slippery weather, and then there's no calculating. I saw the first bus start in 1829. I heard the first bus called a 'Punch and Judy carriage,' 'cause you could see the people inside within a frame. The shape was about the same as it is now, but bigger and heavier. A bus changes horses four or five times a day, according to the distance. There's no cruelty to the horses—not a bit; it wouldn't be allowed. I fancy that buses now pay the proprietors well. The duty was 2½d. a mile, and now it's 1½d. Some companies save 12 guineas a week by the doing away of toll-gates. The 'stablishing the threepennies, the short-uns, has put money in their pockets. I'm an unmarried man. A bus driver never has time to look out for a wife. Every horse in our stables has one day's rest in every four, but it's no rest for the driver."

The conductor, who is vulgarly known as the "cad," stands on a small projection at the end of the omnibus, and it is his office to admit and "set down" every passenger, and to receive the amount of fare, for which amount he is of course responsible to his employers. He is paid 4s. a day, which he is allowed to stop out of the moneys he receives. He fills up a way-bill each journey with the number of passengers. I find that nearly all classes have given a quota of their numbers to the list of conductors. Among them are grocers, drapers, shopmen, barmen, printers, tailors, shoemakers, clerks, joiners, saddlers, coach-builders, porters, town travellers, carriers, and fishmongers. Unlike the drivers, the majority of the conductors are unmarried men, but perhaps only a mere majority. As a matter of necessity every conductor must be able to read and write. They are discharged more frequently than the drivers, but they require good characters before their appointment. From one of them, a very intelligent man, I had the following statement:—

"I am 35 or 36, and have been a conductor for six years. Before that I was a lawyer's clerk, and then a picture dealer, but didn't get on tho' I maintained a good character. I'm a conductor now, but I wouldn't be very long behind a bus if it wasn't for necessity. It's hard to get anything else to do that you can keep a wife and family on, for people won't have you from off a bus. The worst part of my business is its uncertainty. I may be discharged any day, and not know for what. If I did, and I was accused unjustly, I might bring my action, but it's merely 'You're not wanted.' I think I've done better as a conductor in hot weather or fine weather than in wet. Tho' I've got a good journey when it's come on showery as people was starting for or starting from the City. I had one master, who when his bus came in full in the wet, used to say, 'This is prime; them's God Almighty's customers; he sent *them*.' I've heard him say so many a time. We get far more ladies and children too on a fine day; they go more a shopping then, and of an evening they go more to public places. I pay over my money every night. It runs from 40s. to £4 4s., or a little more on extraordinary occasions. I have taken more money since the short-uns were established. One day before that I took only 18s. There's three riders and more now where there was two formerly at the higher fair. I never get to a public place—whether it's a chapel or a play house—unless indeed I get a holiday, and that is not once in two years. I've asked for a day's holiday and been refused. I was told I might take a week's holiday, if I liked, or as long as I lived. I'm quite ignorant of what's passing in the world, my time's so taken up. We only know what's going on from hearing people talk in the bus. I never care to read the paper now, though I used to like it. If I have two minutes to spare I'd rather take a nap than anything else. We know no more politics than the backwoodsmen of America, because we haven't time to care about it. I've fallen asleep on my step as the bus was going on, and have almost fallen off. I have often to put up with insolence from vulgar fellows that think it fun to chaff a cad, as they call it. There's no help for it. Our masters won't listen to complaints. If we're not satisfied we can go. Conductors are a sober set of men. We must be sober. It takes every farthing of our wages to live well enough and keep a wife and family. I never knew but one teetotaller on the road. He's gone off it now, and he looked as if he was going off altogether. The other day a teetotaller on the bus saw me take a drink of beer, and he began to talk to me about its being wrong, but I drove him mad with argument, and the passengers took part with me. I live one-and-a-half mile off the place I start from. In summer I sometimes breakfast before I start. In winter I never see my three children only as they're in bed, and I never hear their voices, if they don't wake up early. If they cry at night it don't disturb me, I sleep so heavy after fifteen hours' work out in the air. My wife doesn't do anything but mind the family, and that's plenty to do with young children. My business is so uncertain. Why I knew a conductor who found he had paid 6d. short; he had left it in a corner of his pocket, and he handed it over next morning, and was discharged for that. He was reckoned a fool. They say the sharper the man the better the bus-man. There's a great deal in understanding the business, in keeping a sharp look out for people's hailing, and in working the time properly. If the conductor's slow, the driver can't get along; and if the driver isn't up to the mark, the conductor's bothered. I've always kept time except once, and that was in such a fog that I had to walk by the horses' heads with a link, and could hardly see my hand that held the link, and after all I lost my bus, but it was all safe and right in the end. We're licensed now in Scotland-yard. They're far civiller there than in Lancaster-place. I hope, too, they'll be more particular in granting licences. They used to grant them day after day, and, I believe, made no inquiry. It'll be better now. I've never been fined; if I had, I should have to pay it out of my own pocket. If you plead guilty, it's 5s.; if not, and it's very hard to prove that you did display your badge properly if the City policeman—there's one always on the look out for us—swears you didn't, and summons you for that; so if you plead not guilty because you wern't guilty, you may pay £1. I don't know of the checks now, but I know there are such people. A man was discharged the other day because he was accused of having returned three out of thirteen short. He offered to make oath that he was correct, but it was of no use; he went."

Another class employed in the omnibus trade are the time-keepers. On some routes there are five of these men, on others four. The time-keeper's duty is to start the omnibus at the exact moment appointed by the proprietors, and to report any delay or irregularity in the arrival of the vehicle. His hours are the same as those of the drivers and conductors, but as he is stationary, his work is not so fatiguing. His remuneration is generally 21s. a week, but on some stations more. He must never leave the spot. A time-keeper on Kennington-common has 28s. a week. He is employed sixteen hours daily, and has a sort of box, to shelter him from the weather when it is foul. He has to keep time for forty omnibuses. The men who may be seen in the great thoroughfares, noting every omnibus that passes, are not time-keepers; they are employed by Government that no omnibus may run on the line without paying the duty.

A time-keeper made the following statement to me:—

"I was a grocer's assistant, but was out of place, and had a friend who got me a time-keeper's office. I have 21s. a week. Mine's not hard work, but it's very tiring. You hardly ever have a moment to call your own. If we only had our Sundays, like other working men, it would be a grand relief. It would be very easy to get an odd man to work every other Sunday, but masters care nothing about Sundays. Some buses do stop running from 11 to 1, but plenty keep running. Sometimes I am so tired of a night that I dare hardly sit down, for fear I should fall asleep and lose my own time, and that would be to lose my place. I think time-keepers continue longer in their places than the others. We have nothing to do with money taking. I'm a single man, and get all my meals at the —— Inn. I dress my own dinner in the tap-room. I have my tea brought to me from a coffee-shop. I can't be said to have any home, just a bed to sleep in, as I'm never ten minutes awake in the house where I lodge."

The odd men are, as their name imports, the men who are employed occasionally, or, as they term it, "get odd jobs." These form a considerable portion of the unemployed. If a driver be ill, or absent to attend a summons, or on any temporary occasion, the odd man is called upon to do the work. For this the odd man receives 10d. a journey to and fro. One of them gave me the following account:—

"I was brought up to a stable life, and had to shift for myself when I was 17, as my parents died then. It's nine years ago. For two or three years, till this few months, I drove a bus. I was discharged with a week's notice, and don't know for what—it's no use asking for a reason—I wasn't wanted. I've been put to my shifts since then, and almost everything's pledged that could be pledged. I had a decent stock of clothes, but they're all at my uncle's. Last week I earned 3s. 4d., the week before 1s. 8d., but this week I shall do better—say 5s. I have to pay 1s. 6d. a week for my garret. I'm a single man, and have nothing but a bed left in it now. I did live in a better place. If I didn't get a bite and sup now and then with some of my old mates, I think I couldn't live at all. Mine's a wretched life, and a very bad trade."

LABOUR AND THE POOR.

THE METROPOLITAN DISTRICTS.

[FROM OUR SPECIAL CORRESPONDENT.]

OF THE LONDON HACKNEY COACH AND CABMEN.

LETTER LXXII.

In my last letter I described the earnings and condition of the drivers and conductors of the London omnibusses, and I now proceed, in due order, to treat of the Metropolitan Hackney-coach and Cabmen. In official language an omnibus is a "metropolitan stage carriage," and a "cab" a "metropolitan hackney" one; the legal distinction being that the stage carriages pursue a given route, and the passengers are mixed, while the fare is fixed by the proprietor; whereas the hackney carriage plies for hire at an appointed "stand," carries no one but the party hiring it, and the fare for so doing is regulated by law. It is an offence for the omnibus to stand still and ply for hire, whereas the driver of the cab is liable to be punished if he ply for hire while his vehicle is moving.

According to the Occupation Abstract of 1841, the number of "Coachmen, coach-guards, and post-boys" in Great Britain at that time was 14,469, of whom 13,013 were located in England, 1,123 in Scotland, 295 in Wales, and only 138 in the whole of the British Isles. The returns for the metropolis were as follows:—

<pre>
Coach, cab, and omnibus owners   650
Coachmen, coach, and omnibus-guards, and post-boys 5,428
Grooms and Ostlers 2,780
Horse-dealers and trainers   246
                                                                   ─────
         Total   9,104
</pre>

In 1831, the number of "coach-owners, drivers, grooms, &c.," was only 1,322; and the "horse-dealers, stable, hackney-coach, or fly keepers," 655, or 2,047 in all; so that, assuming these returns to be correct, it follows that this class must have increased 7,027, or more than quadrupled itself in ten years.

The returns since the above-mentioned periods, however, show a still more rapid extension of the class. For these I am again indebted to the courtesy of the Commissioners of Police, for whose consideration and assistance I have again to tender my warmest thanks.

A Return of the Number of Persons licensed as Hackney Drivers, Stage Drivers, Conductors, and Watermen, from the Year 1843 to 1850.

Year.	Hackney Drivers.	Stage Drivers.	Con-ductors.	Water-men.	Total.
1843	4,627	1,740	1,854	371	8,592
1844	4,927	1,833	1,961	390	9,111
1845	5,199	1,825	1,930	363	9,317
1846	5,356	1,865	2,051	354	9,626
1847	5,109	1,830	2,009	342	9,290
1848	5,231	1,736	2,017	352	9,336
1849	5,487	1,731	2,026	375	9,619
1850*	5,114	1,463	1,484	352	8,413
Totals	41,050	14,023	15,332	2,899	73,304

* From 1st May to 4th September, inclusive.

By this it will be seen that the drivers and conductors of the metropolitan stage and hackney carriages were in 1849 no less than 9,619, whereas in 1841, including coachmen of all kinds, guards, and post-boys, there were only 5,428 in the metropolis; so that within the last ten years the class, at the very least, must have more than doubled itself.

I shall now proceed to give an account of the rise and progress of the London hackney cabs, as well as the decline and fall of the London hackney coaches.

Nearly all the writers on the subject state that hackney coaches were first established in London in 1625; that they were not then stationed in the streets, but at the principal inns; and that their number grew to be considerable after the Restoration. There seems to be no doubt that these conveyances were first kept at the inns, and sent out when required—as post-chaises were, and are still, in country towns. It may very well be doubted, however, whether the year 1625 has been correctly fixed upon as that in which hackney carriages were established in London. It is so asserted in Macpherson's "Annals of Commerce," who follows Anderson's "History of Commerce," but it is thus loosely and vaguely stated:—"Our historiographers of the city of London relate that it was in this year (1625) that hackney coaches first began to ply in London streets, or rather at the inns, to be called for as they are wanted; and they were, at this time, only twenty in number." *One* of the City "historiographers," however, if so he may be called, makes a very different statement. John Taylor, the waterman and the water poet, says in 1623 (two years before the era usually assigned)—"I do not inveigh against any *coaches* that belong to persons of worth and quality, but only against the caterpillar swarm of *hirelings*. They have undone my poor trade, whereof I am a member; and though I look for no reformation, yet I expect the benefit of an old proverb, 'Give the losers leave to speak.' ... This infernal swarm of trade-spillers (hackney coachmen) have so overrun the land that we can get no living upon the water; for I dare truly affirm that every day in any term, especially if the court be at Whitehall, they do rob us of our livings, and carry 560 fares daily from us."

Of the establishment of hackney coach "stands," we have a more precise account. The Rev. Mr. Garrard, writing to Lord Strafford in 1638, says—"Here is one Captain Baily, he hath been a sea captain, but now lives on land, about this city, where he tries experiments. He hath erected, according to his ability, some four hackney coaches, put his men in livery, and appointed them to stand at the May-pole, in the Strand, giving them instructions at what rates to carry men into several parts of the town, where all day they may be had. Other hackney-men seeing this way, they flocked to the same place, and perform the journeys at the same rate. So that sometimes there is twenty of them together, which disperse up and down, that they and others are to be had everywhere, as watermen are to be had at the water-side. Everybody is much pleased with it." The site of the May-pole that once "o'er-looked the Strand," is now occupied by St. Mary's Church.

There were after this many regulations passed for the better management of hackney coaches. In 1652 their number was ordered to be limited to 200; in 1654, to 300; in 1661, to 400; in 1694, to 700. These limitations, however, seem to have been but little regarded. Garrard, writing in 1638, says—"Here is a proclamation coming forth about the reformation of hackney coaches, and ordering of other coaches about London. One thousand nine hundred was the number of hackney coaches of London, base lean jades, unworthy to be seen in so brave a city, or to stand about a King's court." As within the last twenty-seven years, when cabs and omnibuses were unknown, the number of hackney carriages was strictly limited to 1,200, it seems little likely that nearly two centuries earlier there should have been so many as 1,900. It is probable that "glass" and "hackney coaches" had been confounded somehow in the enumeration.

It was not until the ninth year of Queen Anne's reign that an act was passed appointing commissioners for the licensing and superintending of hackney coachmen. Prior to that they seem to have been regulated and licensed by the magistracy. The act of Anne authorized the number of hackney coaches to be increased to 800, but not until the expiration of the then licenses in 1715. In 1771 there was again an additional number of hackney coach licenses granted—1,000; which was made 1,200 in 1799. In the last-mentioned year a duty was for the first time placed on hired carriages of all descriptions. It was at first 5s. a week, but that sum was not long after raised to 10s. a week, to be paid in advance, while the license was raised from £2 10s. to £5. The duties upon all hackney carriages is still maintained at the advanced rate.

The hackney carriages, when their number became considerable after the Restoration, were necessarily small, though drawn by two horses. The narrowness of the streets before the great fire, and the wretched condition of the pavement, rendered the use of large and commodious vehicles impossible. D'Avenant says of hackney carriages, "They are uneasily hung, and so narrow, that I took them for sedans on wheels." The hackney coachman then rode one of his horses, postilion-fashion; but when the streets were widened, he drove from his seat on the box. In the latter days of London hackney coaches they were large enough without being commodious. They were nearly all noblemen's and gentlemen's disused family-coaches which had been handed over to the coach-maker when a new carriage was made. But it was not long that these coaches retained the comfort and cleanliness that might distinguish them when first introduced unto the stand. The horses were, as in the Rev. Mr. Garrard's time, sorry jades, sometimes cripples, and the harness looked as frail as the carriages. The exceptions to this description were few, for the hackney coachmen possessed a monopoly, and thought it unchangeable. They were of the same class of men—nearly all gentlemen's servants, or their sons. The obtaining of a license for a hackney coach was generally done through interest. It was one way in which many peers and members of Parliament provided for any favourite servant, or for the servant of a friend. These "patrons"—whether peers or commoners—were not uncommonly called "lords;" a man was said to be sure of a license if he had "a great lord for his friend."

The "takings" of the London hackney coachmen, as I have ascertained from some who were members of the body, were £10 10s. a week the year through, the months of May, June, and July being the best, when their earnings were from £15 to £18 a week. Out of this three horses had to be maintained. During the war times the quality of oats which are now 18s. a quarter were 60s., while hay and the other articles of the horse's consumption were proportionately dear. The expense of repairs to the coach or harness was but trifling, as they were generally done by the hackneyman himself, or by some hanger-on at the public-houses frequented by the fraternity.

Of the personal expenditure of hackney-coachmen when "out for the day," I had the following statement from one of them:—"We spent regular 7s. a day when we was out. It was before coffee-shops and new fangled ways came in as the regular thing that I'm speaking of: breakfast 1s., good tea and good bread and butter, as much as you liked, always with a glass of rum in the last cup, for the 'lacing' of it. Always rum, gin weren't so much run after then. Dinner was 1s. 6d.; a cut off some good joint; beer was included at some places and not at others. Any extras to follow was extras to pay. Two glasses of rum and water after dinner, one shilling; pipes found, and most of us carried our own baccy boxes. Tea same as breakfast, and 'laced' ditto. Supper the same as dinner, or 6d. less, and the rest to make up the 7s. went for odd glasses of ale, or stout, or 'short'—but 'short' (neat spirits) was far less drunk then than now—when we was waiting, or to treat a friend, or such like. We did some good in those days, sir. Take day and night, and 1,200 of us was out, and perhaps every man spent his 7s., and that's 1,200 times 7s." Following out this calculation we have £420 per day (and night), £2,940 a week, and £152,880 a year for hackney-coachmen's personal expenses merely as regards their board.

The old hackney coachmen seem to have been a self-indulgent, improvident, rather than a vicious class; neither do they seem to have been a drunken class. They acted as ignorant men would naturally act who found themselves in the enjoyment of a good income, with the protection of a legal monopoly. They had the sole right of conveyance within the bills of mortality, and as that important district comprised all the places of public resort and contained the great mass of the population, they may be said to have had a monopoly of the metropolis. Even when the cabs were first established these men exhibited no fear of their earnings being affected. "But," said an intelligent man, who had been a hackney coachman in his younger days, and who managed to avoid the general ruin of his brethren, "but when the cabs got to be 100, then they found it out. The cabs was all in gentlemen's hands at first; I know that; some of them was government clerks too; they had their foremen, to be sure, but they was the real proprietors, the gentlemen was; *they* got the licenses. Well, it's easy to understand how 100 cabs was earning money fast, and people couldn't get them fast enough, and how some hundreds of hackney coachmen was waiting and starving, till the trade was thrown open, and then the hackney coachmen was clean beat down. They fell off by degrees. I'm sure I hardly know what became of most of them, but I do know that a many of them died in the workhouses. They hadn't nothing afore-hand. They dropped away gradual. You see they weren't allowed to transfer their plates and licenses to a cab, or they'd have done it—plenty would. They were a far better set of men than there's on the cabs now. There was none of your fancy men, that's in with women of the town, among the old hackney coachmen. If you remember what they was, sir, you'll say they hadn't the cut of it."

The hackney coachmen drove very deliberately, rarely exceeding five, and still more rarely achieving six miles an hour, unless incited by the hope or the promise of an extra fare. These men resided very commonly in mews, and many of them, I am assured, had comfortable homes, and were hospitable fellows in their way, smoking their pipes with one another when "off the stones," treating their poorer neighbours to a glass, and talking over the price of oats, hay, and horses, as well as the product of the past season, or the promise of the next. The majority of them could neither read nor write, or very imperfectly, and as is not uncommon with uninformed men who have thriven tolerably well without education, they cared little about providing education for their children. Politics they cared nothing about, but they prided themselves on being "John Bull Englishmen." For public amusements they seemed to have cared nothing. "Our business," said one of them, "was with the outside of playhouses. I never saw a play in my life."

As my informant said:—"They dropped away gradual." Eight or ten years ago a few old men, with old horses and old coaches, might be seen at street stands, but each year saw their numbers reduced, and now there is not one; that is to say not one in the streets, though there are four hackney coaches at the railway stations.

One of the old fraternity of hackney-coachmen, who had, since the decline of his class, prospered by devoting his exertions to another department of business, gave me the following account:—

"My father," said he, "was a hackney coachman before me, and gave me what was then reckoned a good education. I could write middling and could read the newspaper. I've driven my father's coach for him when I was fourteen. When I was old enough, seventeen I think I was, I had a hackney coach and horses of my own, provided for me by my father, and so was started in the world. The first time I plied with my own coach was when Sir Francis Burdett was sent to the Tower from his house in Piccadilly. Sir Francis was all the go then. I heard a hackney coachman say he 'would be glad to drive him for nothing.' The hackney coachmen didn't like Pitt. I've heard my father and his mates say many a time 'D—n Pitt;' that was for doubling of the duty on hackney coaches. Ah, the old times was the racketty times! I've often laughed and said that I could say what perhaps nobody, or almost nobody in England, can say now, that I'd been driven by a king. He grew to be a king afterwards, George IV. One night, you see, sir, I was called off the stand, and told to take up at the British Coffee-house, in Cockspur-street. I was a lad then, and when I pulled up at the door, the waiter ran out and said, 'You jump down, and get inside; the Prince is a-going to drive hisself.' I didn't much like the notion on it, but I didn't exactly know what to do, and was getting off my seat to see if the waiter had put anything inside, for he let down the glass, and just as I was getting down, and had my foot on the wheel, out came the Prince of Wales and four or five rattle-brained fellows like himself. I think Major Hanger was one, but I had hardly time to see them, for the Prince gripped me by the ancle and the waistband of my breeches, and lifted me off the wheel, and flung me right into the coach, through the window, and it was open as happened luckily. I was little then; but he must have been a strong man. He didn't seem so *very* drunk either. The Prince wasn't such a bad driver. Indeed, he drove very well for a prince, but he didn't take the corners or the crossings careful enough for a regular Jarvey. Well, sir, the Prince drove that night to a house in King-street, St. James's. There was another gentleman on the box with him. It was a gaming-house he went to *that* night; but I have driven him to other sorts of houses in that there neighbourhood. He hadn't no pride to such as me, hadn't the Prince of Wales. Then one season I used to drive Lord Barrymore in his rounds to the brothels, twice or thrice a week sometimes. He used always to take his own wine with him. After waiting till near daylight, or till daylight, I've carried my lord, girls and all—fine dressed-up madams—to Billingsgate, and there I've left them to breakfast at some queer place, or to 'slang' with the fishwives. What times them was, to be sure! One night I drove Lord Barrymore to Mother Cummins's, in Lisle-street, and when she saw who it was she swore out of the window that she wouldn't let him in; he and some such racketty fellows had broken so many things the last time they was there, and had disgraced her, as she called it, to the neighbourhood. So my lord said, 'Knock at the door, Tiger, and knock till they open it.' He knocked and knocked, till every drop of water in the house was emptied over us out of the windows, but my lord didn't like to be beaten, so he stayed and stayed, but Mother Cummins wouldn't give way, and at last he went home. A wet Opera night was the chance for us, when Madame—I forget her name— Catalani?—yes, I think that was it—was performing. Many a time I've heard it sung out, 'A guinea to Portman-square,' and I've had it myself. At the time I'm speaking of, hackney coachmen took 30s. a day all the year round. Why, I myself have taken £16 and £18 a week through May, June, and July. But then you see, sir, we had a monopoly. It was in the old Tory times. Our number was limited to 1,200. And no stage-carriage could then take up or set down on the stones, not within the bills as it was called—that's the bills of mortality, three miles round the Royal Exchange, if I remember right. It's a monopoly that shouldn't have been allowed, I know that, but there was grand earnings under it; no glass coaches could take people to the play then. Glass coaches is what's now called flies. They couldn't set down in the mortality. It was fine and imprisonment to do it. We hadn't such good horses in our coaches then as is now in the streets, sartainly not. It was war time, and horses was bought up for the cavalry, and it's the want of demand of horses for the army, and for the mails and stages arter'ards, that's the reason of such good horses being in the busses and cabs. We drove always noblemen or gentlemen's old carriages— 'family coaches' they was sometimes called. There was mostly arms and coronets on them. We got them of the coachmakers in Long- acre, who took the noblemen's old carriages when they made new. The Duke of —— complained once, that his old carriage, with his arms painted beautiful on the panels, was plying in the streets at 1s. a mile—his arms ought not to be degraded that way, he said—so the coachmaker had the coach new painted. When the cabs first came in, we didn't think much about it; we thought—that is, the most of us did—that things was to go on in the old way for ever; but it was found out in time—that it was. When the clarences, the cabs that carry four, came in, they cooked the hackney coaches in no time."

For the introduction of hackney *cabriolets* (a word which it now seems almost pedantic to use) we are indebted—as for the introduction of the omnibuses—to the example of the Parisians. In 1813 there were 1,150 *cabriolets de place* upon the hackney stands of Paris; in 1823, ten years later, there were twelve upon the hackney stands of London! Long before 1823 many efforts were made to introduce a lighter hackney vehicle, cheaper, and drawn by only one horse, into the streets of London; but the "vested rights" of the hackney coachmen were an obstacle. Messrs. Bradshaw and Rotch, however, did manage, in 1823, to obtain licenses for twelve cabriolets, starting them at 8d. a mile, the hackney coach fare being 1s. The number was subsequently increased to 50, and then to 100, and in less than nine years after the first cab plied in the streets of London all restrictions as to their number were abolished.

The form of cab first in use was that of a hooded chaise, the leather head or hood being raised or lowered at pleasure. In wet, windy weather, however, it was found, when raised, to present so great a resistance to the progress of the horse, that the head was abandoned. In these cabs the driver sat inside, the vehicle being made large enough to hold two persons and the cabman. The next kind had a detached seat for the driver, alongside his fare. On the third sort the driver occupied the roof, the door opening at the back. These were called "back-door cabs." The "covered cab," carrying two inside, with the driver on a box in front, was next introduced, and it was a safer conveyance, having four wheels, the preceding cabs having had but two. The clarences, carrying four inside, came next; and almost at the same time with them, the Hansoms, which are always called "Showfulls" by the cabmen. "Showfull," in slang language, means "counterfeit;" and the Showfull cabs are an infringement on Hansom's patent. There are now no cabs in use but the two last mentioned. A clarence, built in the best manner, costs from £40 to £50; a good horse to draw it is worth £18 to £20; and the harness, £4 10s. to £5. This is the fair price of the carriage and harness when new, and from a good shop. But secondhand cabs and harness are sold and re-sold, and are repaired or fitted up by jobbing coach-builders. Nearly all the greater cab proprietors employ a coach-builder on their premises. A cab horse has been purchased in Smithfield for 40s.

Some of the cabmen have their own horse and vehicle, while others, and the great majority, rent a cab and horse from a proprietor, and pay him so much a day or night, having for their remuneration all they can obtain over the amount of rent. The rent required by the most respectable masters is 14s. in the season; out of the season the best masters expect the driver to bring home about 9s. a day. For this sum two good horses are found to each cab. Some of the cab proprietors, especially a class known as "contractors," or "Westminster masters," of whom a large number are Jews, make the men hiring their cabs "sign" for 16s. a day in the season, and 12s. out of it. This system is called "signing," instead of "agreeing," or any similar term, because the 6th and 7th Vict. provides that no sum shall be recovered from drivers "on account of the earnings of any hackney carriage, unless under an agreement in writing, *signed* in presence of a competent witness." The steadiest and most trusty men in the cab-driving trade, however, refuse to sign for a stipulated sum, as in case of their not earning so much they may be compelled, summarily, and with the penalties of fine and imprisonment, to pay that stipulated sum. I am informed, by a highly respectable cab-proprietor, that in the season 12s. 6d. a day would be a fair sum to "sign" for, and 9s., or even less, out of the season. In this my informant cannot be mistaken, for he has had practical experience of cab-driving, he himself often driving on an emergency. There are plenty, however, who will sign for 16s., and the consequence of this branch of the contract system is, that the men so contracting resort to any means to make their guinea. They drive swell mobsmen, they are connected with women of the town, they pick up and prey upon drunken fellows, in collusion with these women, and resort to any knavery to make up the necessary sum. On this subject I give below the statement of an experienced proprietor.

Among the present cab-drivers are to be found, as I learned from trustworthy persons, quondam greengrocers, costermongers, jewellers, clerks, broken-down gentlemen, especially turf gentlemen, carpenters, joiners, saddlers, coach-builders, grooms, stable-helpers, footmen, shopkeepers, pickpockets, swellmobsmen, housebreakers, innkeepers, musicians, musical-instrument makers, ostlers, some good scholars, a good number of broken-down pawnbrokers, several ex-policemen, drapers' assistants, barmen, scene-shifters, one baronet, and, as one of my informants expressed it, "such an uncommon

Joseph Powell - a London Cabman

sight of folks, that it would be uncommon hard to say wot they wos." Of the truth of all the callings specified as having contributed to swell the numbers of the cabmen there can be no doubt, but I am not so sure of "*the* baronet." I was told his name, but I met with no one who could positively say that he knew Sir V—— C—— as a cab driver. This baronet seems a tradition among them. Others tell me the party alluded to is merely nicknamed the baron, owing to his being a person of good birth, and having had a college education. The "flashiest cabman," as he is termed, is the son of a fashionable master tailor. He is known among cab drivers as the "Numpareil," and drives one of the Hansom cabs. I am informed, on excellent authority, a tenth, or to speak beyond the possibility of cavil, a twelfth of the whole number of cab drivers are "fancy men." These fellows are known in the cab trade by a very gross appellation. They are the men who live with women of the town, and are supported wholly or partially on the wages of the women's prostitution.

These are the fellows who for the most part are ready to pay the highest price for the hire of their cabs. One swellmobsman, I was told, had risen from "signing" for cabs to become a cab proprietor, but was now a prisoner in France for picking pockets.

The worse class of cabmen, which, as I have before said, are but a twelfth of the whole, live in Granby-street, St. Andrew's-place, and similar localities off the Waterloo-road; in Union-street, Pearl-row, &c., off the Borough-road; in Prince's-street and others off the London-road; in some unpaved streets that stretch from the New Kent-road towards Lock's-fields; in the worst parts of Westminster; in the vicinity of Drury-lane, Whitechapel, and of Lisson-grove, and wherever low depravity flourishes. "To get on a cab," I was told—and that is the regular phrase—"is the ambition of more loose fellows than for anything else, as it's reckoned both an idle life and an exciting one." Whetstone-park is full of cabmen, but not wholly, of the "fancy man" class. The better sort of cabmen usually reside in the neighbourhood of the cab-proprietors' yards, which are in all directions. Some of the best of these men are, or rather have been, mechanics, and have left a sedentary employment, which affected their health, for the open air of the cab business. Others of the best description have been con-nected with country inns, but the majority of them are London men. They are most of them married, and bringing up families decently on earnings of from 15s. to 25s. a week. Some few of their wives work with their needles for the tailors.

Some of the cab yards are situated in what were old inn yards, or the stable yards attached to great houses, when great houses flourished in parts of the town that are now accounted vulgar. One of those I saw is a very curious place. I was informed that the yard was once Oliver Cromwell's stable yard; it is now a receptacle for cabs. There are two long ranges of wooden erections, black with age, each carriage-house opening with large folding doors, fastened in front with pad-locks, bolts, and hasps. In the old carriage-houses are the modern cabs, and mixed with them are superannuated cabs, and the disjointed or worn-out bodies and wheels of cabs. Above one range of the buildings—the red-tiled roofs of which project a yard and more beyond the exterior—are apartments occupied by the stable people and others. Nasturtiums, with their light green leaves and bright orange flowers, are trained along wire trellis-work in front of the windows, and presented a striking contrast to the dinginess around.

Of cab drivers there are several classes according to the times at which they are employed. These are known in the trade by the names of the "long-day man," "the morning man," the "long-night man," and "the short-night man," and the "bucks." The long-day man is the driver who is supposed to be driving his cab the whole day. He usually "fetches his cab out" between nine and ten in the morning, and returns at four or five, or even at seven or eight the next morning; indeed it is no matter at what hour he comes in so long as he brings the money that he signs for. The long-day men are mostly employed for the contractors, though some of the respectable masters work their cabs with long-day men, but then they leave the yard between eight and nine, and are expected to return between twelve and one. These drivers, when working for the contractors, sign for 16s. a day in the season, as before stated, and 12s. out of the season; and when employed by the respectable masters they are expected to bring home 14s. or 9s., according to the season of the year. The long-day men are the parties who mostly employ the "bucks," or unlicensed drivers. They are mostly out with their cabs from sixteen to twenty hours, so that their work becomes more than they can constantly endure, and they are consequently glad to avail themselves of the services of a buck for some hours at the end of the day or rather night. The morning man generally goes out about seven in the morning and returns to the yard at six in the evening. Those who contract, sign to bring home from 10s. to 11s. per day in the season, and 7s. for the rest of the year, while those working for the better class of masters are expected to give the proprietor 8s. a day, and 5s. or 6s. according to the time of the year. The morning man has only one horse found him, whereas the long-day man has two, and returns to the yard to change horses between three and six in the afternoon. The long-night man goes out at six in the evening and returns at ten in the morning. He signs, when working for contractors, for 7s. or 8s. per night at the best time of the year, and 5s. or 6s. at the bad. The rent required by the good masters differs scarcely from these sums. He has only one horse found him. The short-night man fetches the cab out at six in the evening, and returns with it at six in the morning, bringing with him 6s. in the season, and 4s. or 5s. out of it. The contractors employ scarcely any short-night men, while the better masters have but few long-day or long-night men working for them. It is only such persons as the Westminster masters who like the horses or the men to be out so many hours together, and they, as my informant said, "Don't care what becomes of either, so long as the day's money is brought to them." The bucks are unlicensed cab-drivers, who are employed by those who have a license to take charge of the cab while the regular drivers are at their meals or enjoying themselves. These bucks are principally cabmen who have been deprived of their license through bad conduct, and who now pick up a living by "rubbing up" (that is, polishing the brass of the cabs) on the rank, and "going out buck," as it is called among the men. They usually loiter about the watering-houses (the public-houses) of the cab-stands and pass most of their time in the tap-rooms. They are mostly of intemperate habits, being generally "confirmed sots." Very few of them are married men. They have been fancy men in their prime, but, to use the words of one of the craft, "got turned up." They seldom sleep in a bed. Some few have a bedroom in some obscure part of the town, but the most of them loll about and doze in the tap-rooms by day and sleep in the cabs by night. When the watering-house closes they resort to the night coffee-shops and pass the time there till they are wanted as bucks. When they take a job for a man they have no regular agree-ment with the driver; but the rule is that they shall do the best they can. If they take 2s., they give the driver one, and keep the other for themselves. If 1s. 6d., they usually keep only 6d. The Westminster men have generally got their regular "bucks," and these mostly take to the cab with the second horse, and do all the night work. At three or four in the morning they meet the driver at some appointed stand or watering place. Burleigh-street, in the Strand, or Palace-yard, are the favourite places of rendezvous of the Westminster men, and then they hand over to the long-day man "the stuff," as they call it. The regular driver has no check upon these men, but, unless they do well, they never employ them again. For "rubbing up" the cabs on the stand, these bucks usually get 6d. in the season, and for this they are expected to dishclout the whole of the panels, clean the glasses, and polish the harness and brasses—the cab driver having to do these things himself, or else to pay for it. Some of the bucks in the season will make from 2s. to 2s. 6d. a day by rubbing up alone, and it is diffi-cult to say what they make by driving. They are the most extortionate of all cab drivers. For a shilling fare they will generally demand two, and for a three shilling fare they will get five or six, according to the character of the party driven. Having no licenses, they do not care what they charge. If the number of the cab is taken, and the regu-lar driver of it summoned, the party overcharged is unable to swear that the regular driver was the individual who defrauded him, and so the case is dismissed. It is supposed that the bucks make quite as much money as the drivers, for they are not at all particular as to how they get their money. The great majority—indeed, ninety-nine out of a hundred—have been in prison, and many more than once, and they consequently do not mind about re-visiting gaol. It is calculated that there are at least 800 or 1,000 "bucks" hanging about the Lon-don cab-stands, and these are mostly regular thieves. If they catch any person asleep or drunk in a cab they are sure to have a dive into his pockets, nor are they particular if the party belong to their own class, for I am assured that they steal from one another while dozing in the cabs or tap-rooms. Very few of the respectable masters work their cabs at night, and those who do so resort to it merely because they have not stable room for the whole of their horses and vehicles at the same time. Some of the cab-drivers are the owners of the vehicles they drive. It is supposed that out of the five thousand drivers in Lon-don at least two thousand, or very nearly half, are small masters, and they are among the most respectable of the men on the ranks. Of the other half of the cab-drivers about 1,500 are long-day men, and about 150 long-night men (there are only a few yards, and they are princip-ally at Islington that employ long-night men). Of the morning men, and the short-night men, there are, as near as I can learn, about 500 belonging to each class, in addition to the small masters.

The *waterman* is an important officer at the cab stand. He is, in-deed, "the master of the rank." At some of the larger stands, such as that at the Birmingham Railway terminus, there are four water-men, two being always "on duty," day and night, fifteen hours by day, and nine by night; the day watermen becoming the night watermen the following week. On the smaller stands two men do this work, changing their day and night labour in the same way. The watermen must see that there is no "fouling" in the rank; that is, no straggling or crowding, but that each cab maintains its proper place. He is also bound to keep the best order he can among the cabmen, and to restrain any ill-usage of the horses. The waterman's remuneration consists in the receipt of 1d. from every cabman who joins his rank, for which the cabman is supplied with water for his horse, and ½d. from every cabman who is hired off the rank. There are now 350 odd watermen, and they must be known as trusty men; a rigid inquiry being instituted, and unexceptionable references demanded before an appointment to the office takes place. At some stands the supply of water costs these officers £4 a year; at others, the trustees of the water-works, or the parishes supply it gratuitously. All the watermen, I am informed on good authority, have been connected at one time with the trade as cab-drivers or owners, and are now the best class, as a whole, connected with the working part of it. They must all be able to read and write, for, as one of them said to me, "We're expected to understand acts of Parliament." They are generally strong, big-boned, red-faced men, civil and honest; married, with very few exceptions, and bringing up families. They are great readers of newspapers, and in these they devote themselves first of all to the police reports. One of this body said:—

"I have been a good many years a waterman, but was brought up a coach-builder in a London firm. I then got into the cab trade, and am now a waterman. I make my 24s. a week the year through; but there's stands to my knowledge where the watermen doesn't make more than half as much—and that for a man that's expected to be respectable. He can give his children a good schooling, can't he, sir, on 12s. a week, and the best of keep to be sure? Why, with my comings-in it's a hard fight for me to do as much. I have eight children, sir. I pay £16 a year for three tidy rooms in a mews—that's rather more than 6s. a week; but I have the carriage place below, and that brings me in a little. Six of my children don't earn ½d. now. My eldest daughter, she's seventeen, earns 6d. a day from a slop tailor. I hate to see her work; work, work away, poor lass! but it's a help, and it gets them bits of clothes. Another boy earns 6d. a day with a coach builder, and lives with me. Another daughter would try her hand at shirt-making, and got work from a shirtmaker near Tabernacle-square, and in four-and-a-half days she made five bodies, and they came to 1s. 10½d., and out of that she had to pay 7½d. for her thread and that, and so there was 1s. 3d. for her hard work; but they gave satisfaction, her employer said, as if that was a grand comfort to her mother and me. But I soon put a stop to that. I said, 'Come, come; I'll keep you at home and manage somehow, or anyhow, rather than you shall pull your eyes out of your head for 3½d. a day, and less; so it's no more shirts.' Why, sir, the last time bread was dear—1847 was it? I paid 19s. and 20s. a week for bread. It's now about half what it was then—rather more, though. But there's one thing's a grand thing for poor men, and that's such prime and such cheap fish. The railways have done that. In Tottenham-court-road my wife can buy good soles as many pairs for 6d. of a night, this time a year, as would have been 3s. 6d. before railways. That's a great luxury for a poor man like me, that's fonder of fish than meat. They're a queer set we have to do with in the ranks. The 'pounceys' (the class I have alluded to as 'fancy men,' called 'pounceys' by my present informant) are far the worst—they sometimes try to bilk me, and it's always hard to get your dues from 'contractors'—that's the men what sign for heavy figures. Credit them once, and you're never paid—never. None signs for so much as the pounceys. They'd sign for 18s. Why, if a pouncey's girl, or a girl he knows, seems 'in luck,' as they call it, that's if she picks up a gentleman, partic'lar if he's drunk, the pouncey—I've seen it many a time—jumps out of the ranks, for he keeps a look out for the spoil, and he drives to her. It's the pounceys, too, that mostly go gagging, where the girls walk. It's such a set we have to deal with! Only yesterday an out-and-out pouncey called me such names, about nothing. Why, it's shocking for any female that may be passing. Aye, and of a busy night, in the market (Haymarket), when it's an opera night and a play night, the gentlemen's coachmen's as bad for bad language as the cabmen, and some gentlemen's very clever in that sort of language too. It's not as it was in Lord ——'s days. Swells now think as much of 1s. as they did of 20s. then. But there's some swells left still. One young swell brings four quarts of gin out of a public-house in a pail, and the cabmen must drink it out of pint pots. He's quite master of bad language, if they don't drink fairly. Another swell gets a gallon of gin always from Carter's, and cabmen must drink it out of quart pots, no other way. It makes some of them mad drunk, and makes them drive like mad, for they might be half drunk to begin with. Thank God, no man can say he's seen me incapable from liquor for four-and-twenty years. There's no racketier place in the world than the 'Market. Houses open all night, and people going there after Vauxhall and them places. After a masquerade at Vauxhall, I've seen cabmen drinking with lords and gentlemen—but such lords gets fewer—and cockney Tars that was handy with their fists, wanting to fight Highlanders that wasn't, and the girls in all sorts of dresses, here, and there, and everywhere among them, the paint off and their dresses torn. Sometimes cabmen assaults us; my mate's been twice whipped lately. I haven't, because I know how to humour their liquor. I give them fair play, and more than that, perhaps, as I get my living out of them. Any customer can pick his own cab, but if I'm told to call one, or none's picked, the first on the rank, that's the rule, gets the fare. I take my meals at a coffee-shop, and my mate takes a turn for me when I'm at dinner, and so do I for him. My coffee-shop cuts up 150 lbs. of meat a day, chiefly for cabmen. A dinner is 6½d. without beer; meat 4d., bread 1d., vegetables 1d., and waiter ½d. At least, I give him ½d. At ——'s public-house I can dine capitally for 8½d., and that includes a pint of beer. On Sundays there's a dessert of puddings, and then it's 1s. A waterman's birth, when it's one of the best, isn't so good, I fancy, as a 'privileged cabman's.'"

I shall now conclude with some statements of sundry evils connected with the cab business, and some suggestions for their rectification.

One cab proprietor, after expressing his opinion that the new police arrangements for the regulation of the trade would be a decided improvement, suggested it would be an excellent plan to make policemen of the watermen, for then he said the "cabmen-thieves" would be reluctant to approach the ranks. He also gave me the following statement of what he considered would be further improvements. "I think," he said, "it would do well for those in the cab trade if licenses were made £10 instead of £5, with a regulation that £5 should be returned to any one on bringing his plates in previous to leaving the trade, and so not wanting his license any longer. This would, I believe, be a check to any illegal transfer, as men wouldn't be so ready to hand over their plates to other parties when they disposed of their cabs, if they were sure of £5 in a regular and legal way. I would also (he said) reduce the duty from 10s. a week to 5s., and that would allow cabs to ply for 6d. a mile. As everything is cheaper, I wonder people don't want cheaper cabs. Busses don't at all answer the purpose; for if it's a wet day, almost every one has to walk some way to his 'bus, and some way to the house he's going to—Sunday visitors particularly, and *they* like wet the least of all. Now, if cabs ran at 6d., they could take a man and his wife and two children, and more, two miles for 1s., or four miles for 2s.; about what the 'busses would charge four persons for those distances, and the persons could go from door to door as cheap, or if not quite so cheap they'd save it in not having their clothes spoiled by the weather, and go far more comfortably than in a 'bus full of wet people and dripping umbrellas. I know most cabmen don't like to hear of this plan, and why? Because, by the present system, they reckon upon getting 1s. a mile, and they almost always do get it for an 8d. fare, and for longer distances, oft enough; but it wouldn't be so easy to overcharge when there's a fixed coin a mile for the fare. It would be one, two, three, four, five, or as many sixpences as miles. Now it's 1s. 4d. for two miles, and that's 1s. 6d.; 1s. 8d. for over two miles, and that means 2s.; of course cabmen don't carry change unless for an even sum; 2s. 4d. for over three miles and a half, and that's 2s. 6d., if not 3s., and so on. The odd coppers make cabmen like the present way."

I now give a statement concerning "foul plates" and informers. It may, however, be necessary to state, first, that every cab proprietor must be licensed at a cost to him of £5; and that he must affix a plate, with his number, &c., to his cab, to show that he is duly licensed; while every driver and waterman is licensed at a cost to each of 5s. a year, and is bound to wear a metal ticket showing his number. The law then provides, that in case of *unavoidable necessity*—which must be proved to the satisfaction of the magistrate—a proprietor may be allowed to employ an unlicensed person for twenty-four hours. With this exception, every unlicensed person acting as driver, and every licensed person lending his license, or permitting any other person to use or wear his ticket, is to be fined £5. The same provision applies to any proprietor "lending his license," but with a penalty of £10. I now give the statement:—

"You see, sir, if a man wants to dispose of his cab why he must dispose of it *as a cab*. Well, if it ain't answered for him he'll get somebody or other willing to try it on. And the new hand will say, 'I'll give you so much and work your plates for you,' and so he does when a bargain's made. Well, this thing's gone on till there's 1,000 or 1,200 foul plates in the trade, and then Government says, 'What a lot of foul plates! there must be a check to this.' And a nice check they found.

Mister —— (continued my informant, laying a peculiar emphasis on the Mister), the informer, was set to work, and he soon ferretted out the foul plates, and there was a few summonses about them at first, but it's managed different now. Suppose I had a foul plate in my place here, tho' in course I wouldn't, but suppose I had. *Mister* —— would drop in some day and look about him, and say little or nothing, but it's known what he's up to. In a day or two comes *Mister* —— No. 2; he's *Mister* —— No. 1's friend, and he'll look about, and say, 'O, Mr. ——, I see you've got so and so; it's a foul plate, I'll call on you for 2s. in a day or two.' He calls sure enough, and he calls for the same money, perhaps, every three months. Some pays him 5s. a year regular, and if he only gets that on 1,000 plates, he makes a good living of it; only £250 a year, £5 a week; that's all. In course *Mister* —— No. 1 has nothing to do with *Mister* —— No. 2—not he. It's always *Mister* —— No. 2 what's paid, and never *Mister* —— No. 1; but if *Mister* —— No. 2 ain't paid then *Mister* —— No. 1 looks in, and lets you know there may be a hearing about the foul plate, and so he goes on."

This same Mister —— No. 1, I am informed by another cab proprietor, is employed by the Excise to "see after the duty," which has to be paid every month. Should the proprietor be behind with the 10s. per week, the informer is furnished with a warrant for the month's money, and this he requires a fee of from 10s. to £1 (according to the circumstances of the proprietor) to hold over for a short time. It is difficult to estimate how many fees are obtained in this way every month, but I am assured that they must amount to something considerable in the course of the year.

It is proper that I should add that my informants, in this and other matters, refer to the systems with which they had been long familiar. The new regulations have been so recently in force that the cab proprietors say that they cannot as yet calculate on their working, but it is believed that they will be beneficial. An experienced man complained to me that the clashing of the magistrates' decisions, especially when the police are mixed up with the complaints against cabmen, is an evil. My informant also pointed out a clause in the 2d and 3d Victoria, cap. 71, enacting that magistrates should meet once a quarter, each furnishing a report of his proceedings as respects the "Act for Regulating the Police Courts in the Metropolis." Such a meeting, and a comparison of the reports, might tend to an uniformity in decisions; but the clause, I am told is a dead letter, no such meeting taking place.

Another cab proprietor said it would be a great improvement if an authorised officer of the police, or a Government officer, had the fixing of plates on carriages, together with the inspection and superintendence of them afterwards. These plates, it was further suggested to me, should be metallic seals, and easily perceptible inside or out. Some of the cab proprietors complain of the stands in Oxford-street (the best in all London, they say) being removed to out-of-the-way places.

Among the matters I heard complained of, that of "privileged cabs" was much dwelt upon. These are the cabs which are "privileged" to stand within a railway terminus, waiting to be hired on the arrival of the trains. For this privilege 2s. a week is paid by the cabmen to some of the railway companies, and as much as 5s. a week to others. The cabmen complain of this as a monopoly established to their disadvantage, and with no benefit to the public, but merely to the railway companies, for there are cab-stands adjacent to all the railway stations, at which the public would be supplied with conveyances in the ordinary way. The horses in the cabs at the railway stations are, I am informed, among the hardest worked of any in London, the following case being put to me:—"Suppose a man takes a fare of four persons and heavy luggage from the Great Western terminus to Mile-end, which is near upon seven miles, he must then hurry back again all the way, because he plies only at the railway. Now, if he didn't, he would go to the nighest cab-stand, and his horse would be far sooner relieved. Then perhaps he gets another fare to Finsbury, and must hurry back again; and then another below Brompton, and he may live at Whitechapel, and have to go home there after all, so that his poor horse gets 'bashed' to bits."

Another cab proprietor furnished me with the following statement in writing of his personal experience and observation concerning the working of the 23d clause in the Hackney Carriage Act, or that concerning the "signing" before alluded to:—"A master is in want of drivers. A, B, and C apply. The only questions asked are 'Are you a driver? Where is your license? Well, here sign this paper. My money is so much.' In very few large establishments is more caution used as to the real character of the driver than this, the effect of which is that a *man with a really good character has no better claim to employment than one of the worst.* Then, as to the feeling of a man who has placed himself under such a contract—'I *must* get my money,' he says, 'I will do anything to obtain it, and as a gaol hangs over my head, what matters about my breaking the law,' and so every unfair trick is resorted to; and the means used are 'gagging,' that is to say, driving about and loitering in the thoroughfares for jobs. It is known that some men very seldom put on the ranks at all. Some masters have told their drivers not to go on the stand, as they well know that the money is not to be obtained by what is termed 'ranking it.' Now the effect of this is, that the thoroughfares are troubled with empty cabs. It has also this effect: it causes great cruelty and over-driving to horses. And drivers, under such circumstances, frequently agree to go for very much less than the fare, and then, as they term it, 'take it out,' by insulting and bullying their customers. It may be said that the law in force is sufficient to counteract this; but it may not be known that a great many protection clubs exist, by contributions from cab-men, and which clubs are in fact premiums for breaking the law, for by them a man is borne harmless of the consequences of being fined. Now, these clubs exist sometimes at public-houses, but in many cases in the proprietors' yards; the proprietors themselves being treasurers, and so becoming agents to induce their servants to infringe the law for the purpose of obtaining for themselves a large return. The moral consequence of all this is, that men being dealt with, and made to suffer as criminals—that is to say, being sent to gaol to experience the same treatment, the same indignity as convicted felons, and all this for what they after all believe to be a debt, a simple contract between man and man; the consequence I repeat is, that the driver having 'served his time,' as it is called, in prison, returns to the trade a degraded character, and a far worse man. Be it observed also, that the fact of a driver having been in prison is no barrier to his being employed again if he will but 'sign'—*that's* the test."

I have now but to add a comparative statement of the criminality of the London coach and cab-men, in relation to that of other callings.

The metropolitan criminal returns show us that crime amongst this class has been upon the decline since 1840. In that year the number taken into custody by the London police was 1,319, from which time, until 1843, there was a gradual decrease, when the number of coach and cab-men taken into custody was 820. After this the numbers fluctuated slightly, till, in 1848, there were 972 individuals arrested for various infractions of the law.

For the chief offences given in the police returns I find, upon taking the average for the last ten years, that the criminality of the London coach and cab-men stand as follows:—For murder there has been annually 1 individual in every 29,710 of their body taken into custody; for manslaughter, 1 in every 2,829; for rape, 1 in 8,488; for common assaults, 1 in 40; for simple larceny, 1 in 92; for wilful damage, 1 in 285; for uttering counterfeit coin, &c., 1 in 612; for drunkenness, 1 in 46; for vagrancy, 1 in 278; for the whole of the offences mentioned in the returns, 1 in every 5 of their number. On comparing these results with the criminality of other classes, we arrive at the following conclusions:—The tendency of the metropolitan coach and cab-men for "murder" is less than that of the weavers (who appear to have the greatest propensity of all classes to commit this crime), as well as sailors (who are the next criminal in this respect), and labourers, sawyers, and carpenters. On the other hand, however, the coach and cab-men would seem to be more inclined to this species of atrocity than the turners, coachmakers, shoemakers, and tailors, the latter, according to the metropolitan police returns for the last ten years, being the least murderous of all classes. For manslaughter they have, however, a stronger predisposition than any other class that I have yet estimated. The average crime in this respect for ten years is one in 20,000 individuals of the entire population of London; whereas the average for the same period among the London coach and cab-men has been as high as one in every 2,800 of their trade. In rape, they rank less criminal than the labourers, carpenters, and weavers, but still much higher than the general average, and considerably above the tailors, sawyers, turners, tailors, shoemakers, or coachmakers. In the matters of common assaults, they stand the highest of all—the labourers being more pugnacious than any of the other classes, and the coach and cab-men considerably more pugnacious even than they. Their honesty seems, nevertheless, to be greater than common report gives them credit for; they being, according to the same returns, less disposed to commit simple larceny than either labourers, sailors, or weavers, though far more dishonest than the generality of the London population. Nor are they so intemperate as, from the nature of their calling, we should be led to imagine. The sailors (who seem to be the most drunken of all trades, there being 1 in every 13 of that body arrested for this offence), and the labourers (who come next), are both much more addicted to intoxication than the coach and cab-men, although the latter class appear to be nearly twice as intemperate as the rest of the people, the decennial average being 1 drunkard in every 81 of the entire residents of the metropolis, and 1 in every 46 of the London coach and cabmen. Hence it may be said that the great vices of the class at present under consideration are a tendency to manslaughter and assault. The cause of this predisposition to "violence against the person" on the part of the London coach and cab-men I leave others to explain.

LABOUR AND THE POOR.

THE METROPOLITAN DISTRICTS.

[FROM OUR SPECIAL CORRESPONDENT.]

OF THE LONDON CARMEN AND PORTERS.

Letter LXXIII.

In the two preceding letters I have dealt with the social condition of the conductors and drivers of the London omnibuses and cabs, and I now, in due order, proceed to treat of the number, state, and income, of the men connected with the "job" and "glass coaches," as well as the "flies," for the conveyance of persons, and the waggons, carts, vans, drays, &c., for the conveyance of goods from one part of the metropolis to another; also of the porters engaged in conveyance by hand, &c.

The "metropolitan carriages" engaged in the conveyance of passengers are of two classes—ticketed and unticketed; that is to say, those that ply for passengers in the public streets carry a plate inscribed with a certain number, by which the drivers and owners of them may be readily known; whereas those that do not ply in public, but are let out at certain yards or stables, have no badge affixed to them, and are in many cases scarcely distinguishable from private vehicles. The ticketed carriages include the stage and hackney coaches, or, in modern parlance, the "busses" and "cabs" of London. The unticketed carriages, on the other hand, comprise the "glass coaches" and "flies," that for a small premium may be converted into one's "own carriage" for the time being. But, besides these, there is another large class of hired conveyances, such as the "job carriages," which differ from the glass coaches principally in the length of time for which they are engaged. The term of lease for the glass coach rarely exceeds a day, while "the fly" is often taken by the hour; the job carriage, however, is more commonly engaged by the month, and not unfrequently by the year. Hence the latter class of conveyances may be said to partake of the attributes of both public and private carriages. They are public, in so far as they are let to hire for a certain term, and private inasmuch as they are often used by the same party, and by them only, for several years.

The tradesmen who supply carriage horses (and occasionally carriages) by the day, week, month, or year to all requiring such temporary or continuous accommodations, are termed job-masters; of whom, according to the "Post-office Directory," there are 154 located in London—51 being also cab proprietors, and 28 the owners of omnibuses. They boast, and doubtlessly with perfect truth, that in their stables are the major part of the finest carriage horses in the world. The powerful animals which are seen to dash proudly along the streets, a pair of them drawing a large carriage with the most manifest ease, are, in nine cases out of ten, not the property of the nobleman whose silver crest may adorn the glittering harness, but of the job-master. One of those masters has now 400 horses, some of which are worth 120 guineas, and the average value is not less than £60 per horse, or £24,000 in all. The premises of some of the job-masters are remarkable for their extent, their ventilation, and their scrupulous cleanliness. All those "in a large way of business" have establishments in the country as well as in town, and at the latter are received the horses that are lame, that require rest, or that are "turned out to grass." The young horses that are brought up from the country fairs, or have been purchased of the country breeders (for job-masters, or their agents, attend at Horncastle, Northallerton, and all the great horse fairs in Yorkshire and Lincolnshire), are generally conducted, in the first instance, to the country establishment of the town-master, which may be at Barnet, or any place of a like distance. These agents have what is called "the pick of the market," not unfrequently visiting the premises of the country horse-dealer, and there completing purchases without subjecting the farmer (for country horse-dealers and breeders are nearly all farmers) to the trouble and expense of sending his "cattle" to the fair; and it is thus that the London dealers secure the best stock in the kingdom. Until within twenty or thirty years ago, some of the wealthier of the nobility or gentry, as I have previously intimated, would vie with each other, during the London season, in the display of their most perfect "Cleveland bays," or other description of carriage horses. The animals were at that period "walked" to London under the care of the coachman and his subordinates, "the family" travelling "post" to town. Such a procedure is now never resorted to. Very few noblemen at present bring their carriage-horses to town, even if within a short railway distance; they nearly all job (as it is invariably called), that is, they hire carriage-horses by the month at from twenty to thirty guineas a pair, the job-master keeping the animals, by sending the due quantity of provender to his customer's premises; for the job horses are usually kept on a wealthier customer's own premises, and are groomed by his own servants. "Why, sir," said a job-master to me, "everybody jobs now. A few bishops do, and lords and dukes, and judges. Lord D—— jobs, and lots of parsons and physicians—yes, lots, sir. The royal family job—all, but the Queen herself. The Duchess of K—— jobs. The late Duke of C—— jobbed, and no doubt the present duke will. The Queen Dowager jobbed regularly. It's a cheaper and better plan for those that must have good horses and handsome carriages. I dare say all the gentlemen in the Albany job, for I know a many that do. By jobbing, rich people can always secure the best horses in the world." I may add, that any of the masters of whom I have spoken will job a carriage, duly emblazoned (if ordered to provide one); he will job harness, too, with the proper armorial bearings about it, and job coachmen and grooms as well. For the use of a first-class carriage 80 guineas a year is paid. A brougham, with one horse and a driver, is jobbed at 16s. a day. But these vehicles are usually supplied by jobbing coachmasters; but the jobbing in carriages is not so common as in horses, gentlemen preferring to have their own chariots or broughams, while the jobbing in servants is confined principally to bachelors, or gentlemen keeping no "establishments."

The job trade, I am assured, has increased five-fold since the general establishment of railways. In this trade there is no "slop" supply. Even the smaller masters supply horses worth the money, for to furnish bad horses would be at once to lose custom. "Gentlemen are too good judges of horse-flesh," a small job-master said to me, "to put up with poor cattle—even tho' they may wear slop coats themselves, and rig their servants out in slop liveries. Nothing shows a gentleman more than his horse; and they can't get first-rate horses in the country as they can in London, because they're bought up for the metropolis."

The men employed in the job-masters' yards do not live in the yards, except a few of the higher servants, to whom can be entrusted the care of the premises, and of the costly animals kept there. Nearly all the men in those yards have been brought up as grooms, and must, in stable phraseology, "know a horse well." None of them in the better yards receive less than 20s. a week in wages, nor will any master permit his horses to be abused in any manner. Cruelty to a horse is certain dismissal if detected, and is now, I am glad to be informed on good authority, very rare. I may here mention the rather amusing reply of an old rough groom, out of place, to my remark, that Mr. —— would not allow any of his horses to be in any way abused:—"*Abused!*" said my respondent, confining the meaning of the word to one signification, "Abused, you mayn't as much as swear at them." Another rough spoken person, who was for a time a foreman to a job-master, told me that he had never, or rarely, any difficulty in making a bargain with gentlemen who were judges of horses, but, said he, "ladies who set up for judges are desperate hard to please, and talk dreadful nonsense. What do *they* know about the points of a horse? But, of all of 'em, a —— is the worst to please in a horse or a carriage—she is the very devil, sir."

The people employed by the job-masters are strong, healthy-looking men, with no lack of grey hairs—always a good sign—among them. Their amusements, I am told, are confined to an odd visit to the play, more especially to Astley's, and to skittle-playing. These enjoyments, however, are rare, as the groom cannot leave his labour for a day, and then return to it, as a mechanic may. Horses must be tended day and night, Sunday and workday; so that it is only "by leave" that they can enjoy any recreation. Nearly all of them, however, take great interest in horse-races, steeple-chases, and trotting matches; many of them dabble in the Derby and St. Leger lotteries, and some "make a book," risking from two or three half-crowns to £5, and sometimes more than they can pay. These parties, however, belong as much to the class of servants as they do to the labourers engaged in the transit of the metropolis.

I am informed that each of the 150 job-masters resident in London may be said to employ six or seven men in their yards or stables—some having at least double that number in their service, and others again only two or three; the latter, however, is the exception rather than the rule. According to this estimate there must be from 900 to 1,000 individuals engaged in the job business of London. This number is made up of stablemen, washers, ostlers, job coachmen, and glass coachmen, or fly-men, besides a few grooms for the job cabriolets. The *Stableman* attends only to the horses in the stables, and gets 2s. 6d. a day, or 17s. 6d. a week standing wages. The *Washer* has from 18s. to £1 a week, and is employed to clean the carriages only in the best yards; for those of a second-rate character the stableman washes the carriages himself. The *Ostler* attends to the yard, and

Interior of Astley's Amphitheatre in 1843

seldom or never works in the stables. He answers all the rings at the yard bell, and takes the horses and gigs, &c., round to the door. He is as it were the foreman or superintendent of the establishment. He usually receives £1 1s. a week standing wages at the best yards, while at those of a lower character only 15s. is given. The *Job-coachman* is distinct from the glass-coachman or fly-man. "He often goes away from the yard on a job," to use the words of my informant, "for three or six months at a stretch." He is paid by the job-master, and gets 30s. a week standing wages. He has to drive and attend to his horses in the stable. The *Glass-coachman* or *Fly-man* goes out merely by the day or by the hour. He gets 9s. a week from the job-master, and whatever the customers think proper to give him. Some persons give 6d. an hour to the glass-coachman, and others 5s. a day for a pair of horses, and from 3s. to 3s. 6d. a day for one horse. A "glass coach," it may be as well to observe, is a carriage and pair hired by the day, and a "fly" a one-horse carriage, hired in a similar manner. The job-coachman and the glass-coachman have for the most part been gentlemen's servants, and have come to the yard while seeking for another situation. They are mostly married men, having generally wedded either the house-maid, nurse, or cook, in some families in which they have lived. "The lady's-maid," to quote from my informant, "is a touch above them. The cooks are in general the coachmen's favourite in regard of getting a little bit of lunch out of her." The job-coachman's is usually a much better berth than that of the glass-coachman or fly-man. The gentlefolks who engage the "glass coaches" and "flies" are, I am told, very near, and the "flies" still nearer than the "glass coaches." The "fly people," as the customers were termed to me, generally live about Gower-street and Burton-crescent, Woburn-place, Tavistock-square, Upper Baker-street, and other "shabby genteel" districts. The great majority of the persons using flies, however, live in the suburbs, and are mostly citizens and lawyers. The chief occasions for the engagement of a fly are visits to the theatre, opera, or parties at night, or else when the wives of the above-named gentry are going out shopping, and then the directions I am told are generally to draw two or three doors away from the shop, so that the shopmen may not see them drive up in a carriage and charge accordingly. A number of flies are engaged to carry the religious gentry in the suburbs to Exeter Hall during the May meetings; and it is they, I am assured, who are celebrated for overcrowding the vehicles. "Bless you!" said one man whom I saw, "them folks never think there can be too many behind a hoss—six is nothing for them, and it is them who is the meanest of all to the coachman, for he never by no chance receives a glass at their door." The great treat of the glass coachmen or fly men, however, is a wedding—then they mostly look for 5s., "but," said my informant, "brides and bridegrooms is getting so stingy, that now they seldom gets more than three." Formerly, I am assured, they used to get a glass of wine to drink the health of the happy pair, but now the wine has declined to gin, "and even this," said one man to me, "we has to bow and scrape for before we gets it out of many on 'em." There is but little call for glass-coaches, compared with flies, now. Since the introduction of the broughams and clarences, the glass-coaches have been almost all put on one side, and they are now seldom used for anything but taking a party with a quantity of luggage from the suburbs to the railway. They were continued at weddings till a short time back, but now the people don't like them. "They have got out of date," said a flyman; "besides a clarence or brougham—even with a pair of horses—is one-third cheaper." There are no glass coaches now kept in the yards; if they are wanted they are hired at the coach-makers. Take one job-master with another, I am informed that they keep on an average six flies each, so that the total number of hack clarences and broughams in the metropolis may be said to be near upon one thousand. Post-boys are almost entirely discontinued. The majority of them, I am told, have become cabmen. The number of job-horses kept for chance work in the metropolis may be estimated at about 1,000, in addition to the cab and omnibus horses, many of which frequently go out in flies. One lady omnibus proprietor at Islington keeps, I am told, a large number of flies, and so do many of the large cab proprietors.

According to the Government returns, the total number of carriages throughout Great Britain in 1848 was 149,000 and odd, which is in the proportion of 1 carriage to every 33 males of the entire population above twenty years of age. Of these carriages upwards of 97,000 were charged with duty, and yielded a revenue of more than £434,000, while 52,000 were exempt from taxation. Those charged with duty consisted of 67,000 four-wheeled carriages (of which 26,000 were private conveyances and 41,000 let to hire), and 30,000 two-wheeled carriages, of which 24,500 were for private use, and 5,500 for the use of the public.

The 41,000 four-wheeled carriages, let to hire, were subdivided, in round numbers, as follows:—

Four-wheeled carriages let to hire without horses	500
Pony phaetons, &c., drawn by a pair	2,000
Broughams, flies, &c., drawn by one horse	30,000
Hearses	1,700
Post-chaises	5,550
Carriers conveyances	1,250
	41,000

Of the 52,000 carriages exempt from taxation there was the following distribution:—

Private pony phaetons	7,000
Ditto pony chaises	4,500
Chaise carts	39,000
Conveyances for paupers and criminals	1,500
	52,000

The owners of four-wheeled private carriages were, it appears from the same returns, 20,739; of whom

16,349 persons kept 1 carriage	58 persons kept 5 carriages
3,685 „ 2 „	19 „ 6 „
495 „ 3 „	6 „ 7 „
116 „ 4 „	11 „ 8 and upwards

Now the total number of persons returned as of independent means at the time of taking the last census was 500,000 and odd; of these, very nearly 490,000 were 20 years of age and upwards. Hence it would appear that only 1 person in every 23 of those who are independent keep their carriage.

Such are the statistics of the carriages, both public and private, of Great Britain. What proportion of the vehicles above enumerated belong to the metropolis I have no means of ascertaining with any accuracy.

The number of horses throughout the country is equally curious. In 1847 there were no less than 800,000 horses in Great Britain, which is in the proportion of five horses to each carriage, and of one horse to every six males of the entire population of 20 years of age and upwards. Of these 800,000 horses upwards of 320,000 were charged with duty, while nearly 500,000 were exempt from it. Among the 320,000 horses charged with duty were comprised—

Private riding and carriage horses	143,000
Draft horses used in trade	147,000
Ponies	22,000
Butchers' horses	4,750
Job horses	1,750
Racehorses	1,500
	320,000

The horses not charged with duty were, in round numbers, as under—

<pre>
Horses used in husbandry 330,500
Horses belonging to small farmers 61,000
Horses belonging to poor clergymen   1,250
Horses belonging to poor traders 10,500
Horses belonging to volunteers 13,000
Horses used in untaxed carriages 15,000
Horses used by waggoners for their own riding   2,000
Horses used by bailiffs, shepherds, &c., ditto ..   1,600
Horses used by masters,   ditto   3,700
Horses used by market gardeners   2,000
Horses used in conveying paupers and criminals   250
Horses kept for sale   7,000
Horses kept for breeding   4,500
Colts not used 16,000
Post horses   8,500
Stage-coach horses   9,600
London hackney-coach horses   3,600
                                            ____
                                             490,000
</pre>

The owners of the 140,000 private riding and carriage horses were 100,000 in number, and of these—

<pre>
78,335 persons kept......1 | 107 persons kept... 10 to 12
17,358   „   ......2 | 54   „   ... 13 to 16
 4,080   „   ......3 | 6   „ 17
 1,624   „   ......4 | 8   „ 18
   622   „   ......5 | 6   „ 19
   380   „   ......6 | 67   „ 20
   328   „   .. 7 to 8 | and upwards
    81   „   ......9 |
</pre>

From this it would appear that two persons in every seven of those who are of independent means keep a riding or carriage horse.

The increase and decrease in the number of carriages and horses within the last ten years is a remarkable sign of the times. Since 1840 the number of all kinds of horses throughout Great Britain has decreased 43,000. But while some have declined, others have increased in number. Of private riding and carriage horses (where one only is kept) there has been a decrease of 12,000, and of ponies 700. Stage-coach horses have declined 4,000; post horses, 2,500; horses used in husbandry, 57,000; breeding mares, 1,300; colts, 7,000; and horses kept for sale, 500. The London hackney-coach horses, on the other hand, have increased in the same space of time no less than 2,000, and so have the draught horses used in trade to the extent of 17,000; while those kept by small farmers are 13,000 more, and the race-horses 400 more than they were in 1840.

Of carriages, those having two wheels, and drawn by one horse (gigs, &c.), have decreased 15,000, and the post-chaises 700, whereas the four-wheel carriages, drawn by one horse, and let to hire (Broughams, Clarences, &c.) have increased 6,000, the pony phaetons 3,000, pony chaises 2,000, and the chaise carts 19,000.

The total revenue derived from the transit of this country, by means of carriages and horses, amounted in 1848 to upwards of £1,190,000. This sum is made up of the following items:—

```
Duty on  carriages ...............  £434,334
     „       horses ................   395,041
     „       horses let to hire ........   155,721
     „       stage carriages ..........    96,218
     „       hackney carriages ........    28,926
Licenses to  let horses to hire ......     6,968
     „       „  stage coaches ........     9,606
     „       „  hackney carriages .....      435
                                        ──────────
                                        £1,190,249
```

From the foregoing accounts, then, it would appear that the number of carriages and horses for the use of the public throughout Great Britain, two years ago, was as follows:—

```
Job carriages .....................      500
 „  Broughams, Clarences, flies, &c.,
    (drawn by one horse) ...........  30,000
 „  Pony phaetons and pair .........   2,000
 „  Post chaises ...................   5,500
                                      ────────
    Total carriages let to hire ........  38,000

Job horses .....................   1,750
Post horses ......................   8,500
Stage coach horses ...............   9,600
London hackney-coach horses ......   3,600
                                      ────────
    Total horses for public carriages  23,450
```

The next part of the subject that presents itself is the conveyance of goods from one part of the metropolis to another. This, as I have before said, is chiefly effected by vans, waggons, carts, drays, &c. It has already been shown that the number of carriers' waggons throughout Great Britain, in 1848, was 1,250, while the carriers' carts were no less than 1,700 odd, or very nearly 3,000 in all. This was 800 more than they were in 1840. Of the number of horses engaged in the "carrying trade," or rather that particular branch of it which concerns the removal of goods, there are no returns, unless it be that there were 2,000 horses under 13 hands high ridden by the waggoners of this kingdom.

The number of carriers, carters, and waggoners throughout Great Britain at the time of taking the last census was 34,296, of whom 25,411 were located in England, 7,802 in Scotland, 940 in Wales, and 143 in the British Isles. Of the 34,296 carriers, carters, and waggoners throughout Great Britain, in 1841, 30,972 were males of 20 years of age and upwards, while in 1831 the number was only 18,859, or upwards of 10,000 less; so that between these two periods the trade must have increased at the rate of 1,000 per annum at least. I am informed, however, that the next returns will show quite as large a decrease in the trade, owing to the conveyance of goods having been mainly transferred from the road to the rail since the last-mentioned period. The number of carriers, carters, and waggoners engaged in the metropolis in 1841 was 3,899, of whom 3,667 were males of 20 years of age and upwards. In 1831 there were but 871 individuals of the same age pursuing the same occupation; and I am assured, that owing to the increased facilities for the conveyance of goods from the country to London, that the trade has increased at even a greater rate since the last enumeration of the people. The London carriers, carters, and waggoners, may safely be said to be now nearer eight than four thousand in number.

The London carmen are of two kinds, public and private. The private carmen approximate so closely to the character of servants, that I purpose dealing at present more particularly with the public conveyors of goods from one part of the metropolis to another. The Metropolitan public master carmen are 207 in number, of whom 15 are licensed to ply on the stands in the City. The carmen here enumerated must be considered more in the light of the owners of vans and other vehicles for the removal of goods than working men. It is true that some drive their own vehicles, but many are large proprietors and belong to the class of employers rather than operatives.

I shall begin my account of the London carmen with those appertaining to the unlicensed class, or those not resident in the City. The modern spring van is, as it were, the landau or travelling carriage of the working classes. These carriages came into general use between twenty and thirty years ago, but were then chiefly employed by the great carriers for the more rapid delivery of the lightest bales of goods, especially of drapery and glass goods, and of parcels. They came into more general use for the removal of furniture in 1830, or thereabouts, and in a year or two after were fitted up for the conveyance of pleasure parties. The van is usually painted yellow, but some are a light-brown or a dark-blue picked out with red. They are fourteen feet in length on the average, and 4½ feet in breadth, and usually made so as by the adjustment of the shafts to be suitable for the employment of one, two, three, or four horses, the third horse, when three are used, being yoked in advance of the pair in the shafts. The seats are generally removable, and are ranged along the sides of the vehicle, across the top, and at the two corners at the "end," as the extremity of the van from the horses is called, the entrance being at the end, usually by means of iron steps, and through a kind of gate, which is secured by a strong latch. The driver sits on a box in front, and on some vans seems perched fearfully high. A wooden frame work surmounts the body of the carriage, and over it is spread an awning, sometimes of strong chintz-patterned, sometimes of plain whitey-brown, calico, the side-portions being made to draw like curtains, so as to admit the air and exclude the sun and rain, at pleasure. If there be a man in attendance besides the driver, he usually sits at the end of the vehicle close to the gate, or rides on the step, or on a projection fixed behind. A new van costs from £50 to £80. The average price of a good van-horse is from £16 to £18. The harness, new and good, costs £5 to £5 10s. for two horses. The furniture van of the latter end of the week is the pleasure van of the Sunday, Monday, and Tuesday, those being the days devoted to excursions, unless in the case of a club or society making their "annual excursion," and then any day of the week is selected except Sunday; but Sunday, on the whole, is the principal day. The removal of the seats and of the apparatus for the awning converts the "pleasure" into the "furniture" van. The uses to which the same vehicle is put are thus many a time sadly in contrast. On the Saturday the van may have been used to convey to the broker's or the auctioneer's the furniture "seized" in some wretched man's dwelling, leaving behind bare walls and a wailing family—and on the Sunday it rings with the merriment of pleasure-seekers, who loudly proclaim that they have left their cares behind them.

The owners usually, perhaps I might say always, unite some other calling along with the business of van-proprietorship. They are for the most part greengrocers, hay and corn dealers, brokers, beer-shop keepers, chandlers, rag and bottle-shop keepers, or dairymen. Five-sixths of them, however, are greengrocers, or connected with that trade. It is not unusual for these persons to announce, that besides their immediate calling of a greengrocer they keep a furniture van, go pleasure excursions, beat carpets (if in the suburbs), and attend evening parties. Many of them have been gentlemen's servants. They are nearly all married men or widowers, with families, and are as a body not unprosperous. Their tastes are unexpensive, though some drink pretty freely, and their early rising necessitates early going to bed, so there is little evening expenditure. I am told that their chief enjoyments are a visit to Astley's, and to the neighbouring horse-races. Their enjoyment of the turf, however, is generally made conducive to their profits, as they convey vans full to Hampton, Egham, and Epsom races. A few van-men, however, go rather further in turf business, and "bet a little," but these, I am assured, are the exceptions. The excursions are more frequently to Hampton-court than to any other place. The other favourite resorts are High Beech, Epping Forest, and Rye House, Hertfordshire. Windsor is but occasionally visited, and the shorter distances such as Richmond, are hardly ever visited in pleasure vans; indeed the superior cheapness of the railway or the steamboat has confined the pleasure excursions I am speaking of to the longer distances, and to places not so easily accessible by other means.

The vans will hold from 20 to 30 grown persons. "20, you see, sir," I was told, "is a very comfortable number, not reckoning a few little 'uns over; but 30, oh, 30's quite the other way." The usual charge per head for a "comfortable" conveyance to Hampton Court and back, including all charges connected with the conveyance, is 2s., "children going for nothing, unless they're too big for knees, and then sometimes half price." Instead of 2s., perhaps the weekly payment speculator receives 2s. 6d. or 2s. 3d., and if he can engage a low priced van, he may clear 9d. or 1s. a head, or about £1 in all. On this subject, and on that of "underselling," as it was described to me, I give the statement of a very intelligent man, a prosperous van proprietor, who had the excellent characteristic of being proud of the kindly treatment, good feeding, and continued care of his horses, which are among the best employed in vans.

The behaviour of these excursionists is, from the concurrent testimony of the many van proprietors and drivers whom I saw, most exemplary, and perhaps I shall best show this by at once giving the following statement from a very trustworthy man:—

"I have been in the van trade for twenty years, and have gone excursions for sixteen years. Hampton Court has the call for excursions in vans, because of free trade in the Palace. There's nothing to pay for admission. A party makes up an excursion, and one of them bargains with me, say for £2. It shouldn't be a farthing less with such cattle as mine, and everything in agreement with it. Since I've known the trade vans have increased greatly. I should say there's five now where there was one sixteen years ago, and more. There's a recommendable and a respectable behaviour among those that goes excursions. I have known some bother from drunkenness when excursions first came up, fifteen years back or so, but nothing much to talk about. It's not your drinkers that go excursions. But now on an excursion there's hardly ever any drunkenness, or, if there is, it's through the accident of a bad stomach, or something that way. The excursionists generally carry a fiddler with them—sometimes a trumpeter, or else some of them is master of an instrument—as they goes down. They generally sings, too. Such songs as 'There's a good time coming,' and 'The Brave old Oak.' Sometimes a nigger thing, but not so often. They carry always, I think, their own eatables and drinkables, and they takes them on the grass very often. Last Whit-Monday I counted fifty vans at Hampton, and didn't see anybody drunk there. I reckoned them early-ish, and perhaps ten came after, at least, and every van would have twenty and more. [Sixty vans would, at this moderate computation, convey 1,200 persons.] They walk through the Palace at Hampton, and sometimes dance on the grass after that; but not for long. It soon tires, dancing on the grass. A school often goes, or a club, or a society, or any party. I generally do Hampton Court in three hours, with two horses. I reckon it's fourteen miles, or near that, from my place. If I go to High Beech, there's the swings for the young ones, and the other merry-makings. At Rye House it's country enjoyment, mere looking about the real country. The Derby Day's a great van day. I'm sure I couldn't guess to one hundred, nor perhaps to twice that, how many pleasure vans go to the Derby. It's extra charge, £3 10s. for the van to Epsom and back. It's a long distance, but the Derby has a wonderful draw. I've taken all sorts of excursions, but it's working-people that's our great support. They often smoke as they come back; tho' it's against my rules. They often takes a barrel of beer with them."

It is not easy to ascertain the number of vans used for pleasure excursions, but the following is the best information to be obtained on the subject. There is not more than one-sixth of the green-grocers who have their own vans; some keep two vans and carts, beside two or three trucks; others, three vans and carts and trucks. These vans, carts, and trucks are principally used in the private transaction of their business. Sometimes they are employed in the removal of furniture. The number of vans employed in the metropolis is as follows:—

<pre>
Those kept by green-grocers about ...   450
By others for excursions 1,000
                                       ──────
         Total 1,450
</pre>

The season for excursion trips commences on Whit Monday, and continues till the latter end of September.

TABLE SHOWING THE AVERAGE NUMBER OF PLEASURE-VANS HIRED EACH WEEK THROUGHOUT THE SEASON, AND THE DECREASE SINCE RAILWAY EXCURSIONS.

	Before the Railway Excursion-trips.	Since the Railway Excursion-trips.
Hampton Court—Sunday ...	50	10
Monday ...	80	30
Tuesday ...	20	10
Rye House, weekly	35	12
High Beech	40	20
Total	225	82

From this it appears that, before the railway-trips, there were 225 pleasure excursions by vans every week during five months in the year, or 4,500 such excursions in the course of the twelve months, and only 1,640 since that time. This is exclusive of those to Epsom races, at which there were nearly 200 more.

When employed in the removal of furniture, the average weight carried by these vans is about two tons, and they usually obtain about two loads on an average per week. The party engaged to take charge of the van is generally a man employed by the owner, in the capacity of a servant. The average weekly salary of these servants is about 18s. Some van proprietors will employ one man, and some as many as nine or ten. These men look after the horses and stables of their employers. A van proprietor takes out a post-horse licence, which is 7s. 6d. a year; and for excursions he is also obliged to take out a stage-carriage licence for each van that goes out with pleasure parties. Such licence costs £3 3s. per year, and, beside this, they have to pay to the Excise 1½d. per mile for each excursion they take. The van horses number about three to each van, so that for the whole 1,450 vans as many as 4,350 horses are kept.

Calculating the pleasure excursions by van in the course of the year at from 1,500 to 2,000, and that 20 persons is the complement carried on each occasion, we have a pleasure excursion party of between 30,000 and 40,000 persons annually; and supposing that each excursionist spends 3s. 6d., the sum spent every year by the working classes in pleasure excursions by spring vans alone will amount to very nearly £7,000.

The above account relates only to the conveyance of persons by means of the London vans. Concerning the removal of goods by the same means, I obtained the following information from the most trustworthy and experienced members of the trade:—The charge for the use of spring vans for the conveyance of furniture and other damageable commodities, is 1s. 6d. an hour when one man is employed, assisting in packing, unpacking, conveying the furniture into the place of its destination, and sometimes helping to fix it. If two men are employed in this labour, 2s. an hour is the charge. If the furniture be conveyed a considerable distance, the carman's employer may, at his option, pay 6d. a mile instead of 1s. 6d. an hour, but the engagement by the hour ensues in nine instances out of ten.

The conveyance of people on pleasure excursions, and the removal of furniture, constitute the principal business of the west-end and suburb carmen. The City carmen, however, constitute a distinct class. They are the licensed carmen, and none others are allowed by the City authorities to "take up" in the precincts of the city of London, though any one can "put down" therein; that is to say, the unlicensed carmen may convey a houseful of furniture from the Strand to Fleet-street, but he may not legally carry an empty box from Fleet-street to the Strand. The city carmen, as I have said, must be licensed, and the law sanctions the following rates of payment for carriage:—

"By order of Quarter Sessions, held at Guildhall, Midsummer, 49th Geo. III.—All goods, wares, and merchandises whatsoever, weighing 14 cwt. or under, shall be deemed half a load, and from 14 cwt. to 26 cwt. shall be deemed a load; from any part of the city of London the rates for carrying thereof shall be as follow:—For any within and to the extension of half a mile, for half a load or under, 2s. 7d.; above half a load and not exceeding a load, 4s. 2d.; from half a mile to a mile, for half a load or under, 3s. 4d.; for above half a load and not exceeding a load, 5s. 2d.; a mile to one mile and a half, for half a load or under, 4s. 2d.; for above half a load and not exceeding a load, 5s. 11d., and so on, according to distance."

The other distances and weights are in relative proportion.

These regulations, however, are altogether disregarded, as are those which limit the cartage for hire within the City, to the carmen licensed by the City, who must be freemen of the Carmen's Company, the only company in London whose members are all of the trade incorporated. Instead of the prices I have cited, the matter is now one of bargain. Average charges are 1s. 6d. an hour for vans, and 1s. for carts, or 4s. and 4s. 6d. per ton from the West India Docks to any part of the City, and in like proportion from the other docks and localities. The infringers of the City carmen's privileges are sometimes called "pirates;" but within these three or four years no strenuous attempts have been made to check them. One carman told me that he had complained to the City Chamberlain, who told him to punish the offenders, but as it was left to individual efforts, nothing was done, and the privileges, except as regards "standings," are almost or altogether a dead letter. Fourteen years ago it cost £100 to become free of the Carmen's Company; ten years ago it cost £32 odd; and within these five years the cost has been reduced to £11. The carmen who resort to the stands pay 5s. yearly for that privilege. The others are not required to do so, but every year they have to register the names of their servants, with a bond of security, who are employed "on goods under bond," and it is customary on these occasions to give the toll-keeper 5s., which is equivalent to a renewal of license. Until ten years ago there were only 400 of these conveyances licensed in the City. The figures, called "carroons," ran from 1 to 400, and were sold by their possessors, on a disposal of their property and privilege, as if freehold property, being worth about £100 a carroon. No compensation was accorded when the restriction as to numbers was abolished. The principal standings are in Coleman-street, Bread-street, Bishopsgate-street, Dowgate-hill, Thames-street, and St. Mary Axe. The charges do not differ from those I have given, but some of the employers of these carmen drive very hard bargains. A car of the best build costs £60 to £70. The best horses cost £40, the average price being £20 at the least. The wages of the carmen's servants vary from 16s. to 21s. a week under the best masters, and from 12s. to 14s. under the inferior. These men are for the most part from the country.

I now approach the only remaining part of this subject, viz., the conveyance of goods and communications by means of the porters, messengers, and errand boys of the metropolis. The number of individuals belonging to this class throughout Great Britain, in 1841, amounted to 27,552, of whom 24,092 were located in England, 3,296 in Scotland, 113 in Wales, and 51 in the British Isles. Of the 27,500 porters, messengers, and errand boys in Great Britain, very nearly one-fifth, or 4,965, were lads under 20 years of age. The number of individuals engaged in the same occupation in the metropolis was, in 1841, no less than 13,103, or very nearly half the entire number of porters, &c., throughout Great Britain. Of this number, 2,726, or more than a fifth of the class, may be considered to represent the errand boys, these being lads under twenty years of age.

In the present letter, however, I purpose dealing solely with the *public* porters of the metropolis. Those belonging to *private* individuals appear to partake (as I said of the carmen's assistants) more of the character of servants paid out of the profits of the trade than labourers whose wages form an integrant portion of the prime cost of a commodity.

The metropolitan porters are, like the carmen, of two classes—the ticketted and unticketted. I shall begin with the former.

The privileged *porters* of the city of London were at one period, and until within these thirty years, a numerous, important, and tolerably prosperous class. Prescriptive right and the laws and by-laws of the corporation of the city of London have given to them the sole privilege of porterage of every description, provided it be carried on in the precincts of the City. The only exception to this exclusive right is that any freeman may employ his own servants in the porterage of his own goods, and even that has been disputed. The first mention of the privileged porters is in the early part of the sixteenth century.

It is almost impossible to classify the especial functions of the different classes of porters; for they seem to have become especial functions through custom and prescriptive right, and they are not defined precisely in any legislative or municipal enactment. Even at the present time what constitutes the business of a fellowship porter, what of a ticket porter, and on what an unprivileged porter (known as a "foreigner," because a non-freeman), may be employed, are matters of dispute.

A reference to City enactments, and the aid of a highly intelligent member of the fraternity of ticket-porters, enable me to give the following account, which is the more interesting as it relates to a class of labourers whose numbers, with the exception of the fellowship porters, have been limited since 1838, and who must necessarily die out from want of renewal. In the earliest Common Council enactment (June 27, 1606), on the subject of porterage, the distinctions given, or rather intimated incidentally, are, "Tackle-house porter, porter-packer of the gooddes of English merchants, streete porter, or porter to the packer for the said citye for straungers goodes." As regards the term ticket-porter, not mentioned in this enumeration, I have to observe that *all* porters are necessarily ticket-porters, which means that they can produce a ticket or a document, showing that they are duly qualified, and have been "admytted and allowed to use the feate of a porter" by being freemen of the City and members of a porters' company or fellowship. In some of the older City documents, tackle and ticket-porters are mentioned as if constituting one class, and they did constitute one class when their labour was contemporary, as it largely was. In 1712 they are mentioned or indicated as one body, although the first clause of the Common Council enactment sets out that "several controversies and quarrels have lately arisen between the tackle-house porters and the ticket-porters, touching the labour or work to them respectively belonging, notwithstanding the several acts of this court heretofore made." As these acts were vague and contradictory, the controversies were a natural consequence.

The tackle-porters were employed in the weighing of goods for any purpose of shipping duty, or sale, which was formerly carried on in public in the City. But there was a City officer known as the master weigher, styled "Mr. Weigher" in the old acts, and the profits of the weighings thus carried on publicly in the City went to the hospitals. In 1607 it was enacted (I give the old orthography with its many contractions) "that no pson or psons usinge the feate of a porter, or being a forreynor, inholder, wharfenger, or keye-keeper, where any merchauntes gooddes are to bee landed, or laidd, or such like, shall at any tyme after the making and publishinge of this Acte, have, keepe, or use within the said Citie or Libties thereof, any manner, triangle with beames, scales and weightes, or any other balance in any sorte, to weighe any the gooddes, wares, or merchandizes, of any merchante or merchants, pson, or psons whatsoever, within the said Cytie or Libties thereof, whereby the proffytte cominge and growinge to the hospitalls of the said Cytie, by weighinge at the yron beames, or at the great beame at the weigh-house, or the proffyttes of the Mr. Weigher and porters of the same weigh-house may in any wise bee impeached, hindered, or diminished." This privilege of "weighinge" fell gradually into disuetude, but there is no record of the precise periods. However, a vestige of it still remains, as I shall show in my account of the markets, as it properly comes under that head. There were 24 tackle porters appointed, each of the 12 great City companies appointing two. These 12 companies are the Mercers, Grocers, Drapers, Fishmongers, Goldsmiths, Skinners, Merchant Tailors, Haberdashers, Salters, Ironmongers, Vintners, and Cloth-workers. The 24 appointed porters were known, it appears, as "Maister Porters;" but as it was impossible that they could do all the work required, they called to them the aid of "fellowes," freemen of the city, and members of their society, who in time seem to have been known simply as ticket-porters. If a sufficiency of these fellows, or ticket-porters could not be made available on any emergency, the "Maisters" could employ any "Forein porter not free of this cyttie, using the feate of a porter-packer of the goods of English merchants, or the feate of a streete porter at the tyme of the making of this acte (1607), and which at this present is commorante in the same cytie, or suburbes thereof, charged with familye or being a single man, bringing a good certificate in the wryting, under the handes of the churchwardens of the parish where he is resident, or other substantiall neighbours, to the nomber of fower, of his good conversacon and demeanor." This employment, however, was not to be to the prejudice of the privileged porters, and that the employment of foreigners was resorted to jealously, and only through actual necessity, is sufficiently shown by the whole tenor of the enactments on the subject. The very act which I have just cited as permitting the employment of foreigners, contains a complaint in its preamble that the toleration of these men caused many "of badd and lewde condicon daylie to resorte from the most parte of this realme to the said cyttie, suburbs, and places adjoininge procuring themselves small habytacons, namely, one chamber-roome for a poore forreyner and his familye, in a small cottage with some other as poore as himself, to the great increase and pestringe of this cyttie with poor people; many of them provinge shifters, lyvinge by cozeninge, stealinge, and imbeazellinge of men's goods as opportunity may serve them." A somewhat curious precedent, as regards the character of the dwellings being in "one chamber-roome," &c., for the abodes of the workmen for the slop tailors and others, in our day, as I have shown in my previous letters.

The "ticket-porters" in 1646 are described as "three thousand persons and upwards," which sufficiently shows their importance; and in 1712 a common council enactment provides that they "shall have and enjoy the work or labour of unshipping, landing, carrying, and housing of pitch, tar, soap, ashes, clapboards, wainscot, fir-poles, masts, deals, oars, chests, tables, flax and hemp, brought hither from Dantzic, Melvyn, or any other part or place of the countries commonly called the east countries." Also of the imports from Ireland, from "any of the plantations belonging to Great Britain, and of all manner of coast goods (except lead)." The tackle-house porters were, by the same enactment, to "have and enjoy the work and labour of the shipping, and all goods imported and belonging to the South Sea Company, or to the Company of Merchants trading to the East Indies, and of all other goods and merchandizes coming from other ports not before mentioned." The functions of the tackle-house and ticket porters are by this regulation in 1712 made identical as to labour, with merely the distinction as to the place from which the goods were received; and as the number of tackle-house porters was, properly, 24, with them must be included, I presume, all such ticket-porters as acted with them. There are still tackle-house porters, but not to the full number, nor is it likely that they will be renewed in case of death. "The tackle-house porters that are still in existence," I was told, "are gentlemen. One is a wharfinger, and claims and enjoys the monopoly of labour on his own wharf. The tackle-house porters, or most of them, were labourers within these twenty years." The tackle-house and ticket porters still enjoy, by law, the right "to man the work," wherever porterage is required; or, in other words, to execute the labour themselves, or to engage men to do it, no matter whether the work relate to shipping, to the markets, or to mere street porterage, such as the conveyance of parcels for hire by men's labour. The number of the ticket porters was, twenty years ago, about 600. At that time, to become free of the company which has no hall, but assembles at Guildhall, cost upwards of £40; but soon after, this expense was reduced to £6 3s. 4d. By a resolution of the Common Council, no new ticket porters have been appointed since 1838. Previously to becoming a ticket porter, a man must have taken up his freedom, no matter in what company, and must produce certificates of good character, and security of two freemen householders of good credit, each in £100, so that the owner of any articles entrusted to the ticket porter may be indemnified in case they were lost. The ticket porters are not the mere labourers people generally imagine they are, but are, or were, for their number does not now exceed 100, decayed tradesmen, who resorted to this means of livelihood when others had failed. They are also the sons of ticket porters. Any freeman of the City, by becoming a member of the Tackle-house and Ticket Porters' Company, was entitled to act as a ticket porter. They are still recognized at the markets and the wharfs, but their privileges are constantly, and more and more infringed. From a highly intelligent man of their body I had the following statement:—

"It may be true, or it may not, that ticket-porters are not wanted now; but fifteen or sixteen years ago a committee of the Common Council—the market committee, I believe, it was—resolved that the ticket-porters ought to be upheld, and that £50 should be awarded to us, but we never got it; it was stopped by some after resolution. Put it this way, sir. To get bread for myself and my children I became a ticket-porter, having incurred great expense in taking up my freedom and all that. Well, for this expense I enjoyed certain privileges, and enjoy them still to some extent, but that's only because I'm well known, and have had great experience in porterage, and quickness at it is as much art as strength. But supposing that railways have changed the whole business of the times, are the privileges I have secured with my own money, and under the sanction of all the old laws of the City, to be taken from me? If the privileges, tho' they may not be many, of the rich City companies are not to be touched, why are mine? Every day they are infringed. A railway waggon, for instance, carries a load of meat to Newgate-market. Ticket-porters have the undoubted right to unload the meat and carry it to its place of sale, but the railway servants do that, though only freemen employ their own servants in porterage, and that only with their own goods, or goods they are concerned in. I fancy that railway companies are not freemen, and don't carry their own property to market for sale. If we complain to the authorities, we are recommended to take the law of the offenders, but we can only take it of the person committing the actual offence; and so we may sue a beggar, whom his employers may send down their line, an hour after, to Hull, or Halifax, as the saying is. If we are of no further use, don't sacrifice, but compensate us, and let us make the best of it; though we are, none of us, so young as we were; some are very old, and none are under 40, because no new members have been made for some years. If a man's house be a hindrance to public business, he must be paid a proper price for it before it can be removed, and so ought we. The Palace Court people were compensated, and ought not we who work hard for an honest living, and have bought the right to work in our portering according to the laws of the City, that secure the goldsmiths in their right of assaying, and all the rich companies, in possession of their lands and possessions, and so it ought to be with our labour."

The Porter-packers have been unknown in the business of the City for some years, their avocation "in the packinge and shippinge of straungers' gooddes," having barely survived the expiring of the East India Company's charter in 1834.

The Street-porters, the men who occupy, or rather did occupy, for they are not now always to be found there, standing about the principal business parts of the City, are of course ticket-porters, and by law have the exclusive right of all porterage, by hire from "aliens or foreigners" in the streets (a freeman may employ his own servant), even to the carrying of a parcel, of the burden of which any one may wish to relieve himself. They usually, but not always, wear white aprons, and display their tickets or badges. They do not confine themselves to the streets, but resort to the wharfs in the fruit or any busy season, and to the meat and fish markets, whenever they think there is the chance of a job, and the preference, as is not unfrequently the case, likely to fall to them, for they are known to be trusty and experienced men. This transition of labour from one place to another renders it impossible to give the number of ticket-porters working in any particular locality.

The Fellowship Porters seem to have sprung into existence in consequence of the misunderstandings of the tackle and ticket porters, and in this way: Fellowships, or gangs of porters, were confined, or confined themselves, to the porterage of coal, corn, malt, and, indeed, all grain, salt, fruit, and wet fish (conceded to them after many disputes by the ticket porters in Billingsgate), and their privileges are not infringed to any such extent as those of the ticket porters. I shall speak of them more particularly when I deal with the different trades where their labour is in demand.

The payments to ticket porters were settled in 1799.

"To or from any of the quays, wharfs, stairs, lanes, or alleys at the water-side, between the Tower and London-bridge, to any part of Lower Thames-street, Beer-lane, Water-lane, Harp-lane, St. Dunstan's-hill, St. Mary-hill, Love-lane, Botolph-lane, Pudding-lane, and Fish-street-hill—

"For any load or parcel, by knot or hand,

Not exceeding $\frac{1}{2}$ cwt.	0s.	4d.
„ 1 „	0s.	6d.
„ $1\frac{1}{2}$ „	0s.	9d.
„ 2 „	1s.	0d.

"For the like weights, and not exceeding Poplar, Bow Church, Bishop Bonner's farm, Kingsland-turnpike, Highbury-place, (old) Pancras church, Portman-square, Grosvenor-square, Hyde Park-corner, Buckingham-gate, Westminster Infirmary, Tothill-fields Bridewell, Stratton-ground, Horseferry, Vauxhall, Walworth-turnpike, and places of the like distance—

Not exceeding $\frac{1}{2}$ cwt.	2s.	9d.
„ 1 „	3s.	3d.
„ $1\frac{1}{2}$ „	3s.	9d.
„ 2 „	5s.	0d. "

I cite these regulations to show the distances to which porters were sent half a century ago, and the charges. The charges, however, were not always paid, as the persons employing parties often made bargains with them, and some twenty years ago the legalised charges were reduced 1d. in every 3d. The street porters complain that any one may now, or at all events does now, ply for hire in the City, and may get higher prices than them.

All ticket porters pay 8s. yearly toward the funds of their society, which is termed quarterage. Out of this a few small pensions are granted to old women, the widows of ticket porters.

The difference of the functions of the ticket and fellowship porters seems to be this—that the ticket porters carry dry goods, or those classed by weight or bulk; the fellowship porters carry measured goods.

The Morning Chronicle, Saturday, October 12, 1850.

A CASE OF REAL DISTRESS.

To the EDITOR of the MORNING CHRONICLE.

Sir—I hope the following will be an apology sufficient to ask you to insert this letter in *The Morning Chronicle*, being a case of the deepest distress. As you are always ready to assist the afflicted and distressed, your assistance is asked on behalf of a distressed young widow, named Sarah Hill, 11, Henrietta-street, Manchester-square. Her husband died on the 15th of the present month, after a brief but severe illness, leaving her with four young children, whose ages are nine years, six years, four years, and two years, and on the eve of her confinement of the fifth child. The aid of the benevolent is most respectfully solicited on behalf of the distressed, but deserving widow, and the fatherless children, who are now entirely thrown on the world without any known means of support.

I am, sir, your obedient servant,

Clement's-inn, Sept. 27.　　　　　　　　HUMANITAS.

[We have inquired into the circumstances of this poor woman's case, and can vouch for the accuracy of the statements made by Humanitas. We have to acknowledge the receipt of 2s. 6d. worth of postage stamps, for her relief, from O. M., of T——.]

The Morning Chronicle, Tuesday, October 15, 1850.

THE LEICESTER-SQUARE SOUP KITCHEN.

To the EDITOR of the MORNING CHRONICLE.

Sir—I cannot but feel assured from your past kindness you will be good enough to grant insertion to the accompanying letter, which I received last Friday evening from the teacher of a ragged school near Oxford-street.

From the painful and shocking nature of its contents I felt it my duty to see the writer, who has this morning assured me that her narration is much within the limits of misery and suffering referred to.

I am anxious that the letter should be published, as it may tend to remove many erroneous impressions which, unfortunately, too generally exist, in the minds of the wealthy and the benevolent, that the poor at this season do not endure privations and distress; and further, that the resident poor can obtain all necessary relief at the parish work-house.

I must request your permission that the name of the writer and the ragged school may be omitted, and beg simply to remark that so urgent an appeal to our kitchen, under such harrowing circumstances, will not be made in vain.

I remain, sir, your obedient servant,

Monday, Oct. 14.   CHARLES COCHRANE.

"Ragged School, Oct. 11.

"Sir—The ladies of our committee have begged me to make an application to you for soup and bread, if your committee can possibly supply the school with some, as our poor children are in very great need of nourishment; they have greatly missed what you so kindly sent previously to our closing school for the holidays.

"There has been a great deal of sickness among the poor children, and a large number have died, many, I quite believe, from want of nourishment, for, being almost starved, they sink under any attack of sickness, having no stamina to resist disease. Four and five have been carried out of a house at the same time to be buried. One poor woman told me that the soup had been a great blessing to her, as it was a good meal for her child, which she was not able to provide him with, and from the time it was discontinued he had begun to droop. Two were buried on Tuesday who had only been ill a few hours.

"I feel assured that any one who could see the joyful countenances of the children when they see the soup would know that there is no deception in them.

"The ladies are now all out of town, but the secretary, I believe, wrote to you, but I fear her letter must have miscarried. One lady begged that I would ask if we could be supplied by paying one-half, and what the expense would be. I should be much obliged by an answer which I can forward to her. Lady —— told me she intended asking the other ladies to unite with her in subscribing for a supply in the winter; but they really need it now, for many are not in a state of physical strength to receive instruction from want of food.

I remain, yours very respectfully,

"To C. Cochrane, Esq."   "—— Teacher.

The Morning Chronicle, Wednesday, October 16, 1850.

A CASE OF REAL DISTRESS.

To the EDITOR of the MORNING CHRONICLE.

Sir—Seeing a case of distress in your paper, referring to Sarah Hill, of No. 11, Henrietta-street, Manchester-square, I beg to inform you that I called on the poor woman, and found her very ill in bed, having been confined about a fortnight, and had the misfortune to lose her baby. Her husband having died but a very short time previously, leaving her with four helpless children, this poor creature has been thrown into the greatest distress and misery. I gave her a trifle, and wish it had been in my power to have given her more. I hope this will meet the eye of a humane and charitable community, as a greater case of distress seldom occurs.

Sir, by inserting this you will oblige,

A CONSTANT READER.

Portugal-street, Grosvenor-square, Oct. 15.

LABOUR AND THE POOR.

THE METROPOLITAN DISTRICTS.

[FROM OUR SPECIAL CORRESPONDENT.]

OF THE LONDON WATERMEN, LIGHTERMEN, AND STEAM-BOATMEN.

Letter LXXIV.

Of all great capitals London has least the appearance of antiquity, and the Thames has a peculiarly modern aspect. It is no longer "the silent highway," for its silence is continually broken by the clatter of steam-boats. This change has materially affected the position and diminished the number of the London watermen, whose condition and earnings form the subject of the present letter.

The character of the transit on the river has, moreover, undergone a great change, apart from the alteration wrought by the use of steam power. Until the more general use of coaches, in the reign of Charles II., the Thames supplied the only mode of conveyance, except horseback, by which men could avoid the fatigue of walking; and that it was made largely available all our older London chroniclers show. From the termination of the Wars of the Roses until the latter end of the seventeenth century—for about 200 years—all the magnates of the metropolis, the King, the members of the royal family, the great officers of State, the Archbishop of Canterbury, the noblemen whose mansions had sprung up amidst trees and gardens on the north bank of the Thames, the Lord Mayor, the City authorities, the City companies, and the Inns of Court, all kept their "own" or their "state" barges, rowed by their own servants, attired in their respective liveries. In addition to the river conveyances of these functionaries, private boats or barges were maintained by all whose wealth permitted, or whose convenience required, their use, in the same way as carriages and horses are kept by them in our day. The Thames, too, was then the principal arena for the display of pageants. These pageants, however, are now reduced to one—the Lord Mayor's show. The remaining state barges are but a few, viz., the Queen's, the Lord

Mayor's, and such as are maintained by the City companies, and even some of these are rotting to decay.

Mr. Charles Knight says, in his "London," "In the time of Elizabeth and the First James, and onward to very recent days, the north bank of the Thames was studded with the palaces of the nobles; and each palace had its landing-place, and its private retinue of barges and wherries; and many a freight of the brave and beautiful has been borne, amidst song and merriment, from house to house, to join the masque and the dance; and many a wily statesman, muffled in his cloak, has glided along unseen in his boat to some dark conference with his ambitious neighbour. Upon the river itself, busy as it was, fleets of swans were ever sailing; and they ventured unmolested into that channel which is now narrowed by vessels from every region. Paulus Jovius, who died in 1552, describing the Thames, says: 'This river abounds in swans, swimming in flocks; the sight of whom, and their noise, are vastly agreeable to the fleets that meet them in their course.'" The only relic of the palatial "landing-places" above alluded to which is now to be seen is the fine arch, or water-gate, the work of Inigo Jones, at the foot of Buckingham-street. This was an adornment of the landing-place from "York-house," once the town abode of the archbishops of that see, but afterwards the property of George Villiers, Duke of Buckingham. In front of this gate, or nearly so, the Hungerford steamboat piers are now stationed; and in place of stately barges, directed by half a dozen robust oarsmen in gorgeous liveries, approaching the palace, or lying silently in wait there, we have halfpenny, penny, twopenny, and other steamboats, hissing, spluttering, panting, and smoking.

Moreover, in addition to the state and private barges of the older times, there were multitudes of boats and watermen always "on hire." Stow, who was born in 1525, and died in the fulness of 80 years of age, says that in his time 40,000 watermen were employed on the Thames. This, however, is a manifest exaggeration, when we consider the population of London at that time; still it is an over-estimation common to old chroniclers, by whom precise statistical knowledge was unattainable. That Stow represents the number of these men at 40,000, shows plainly that they were very numerous; and one proof of their great number, down to the middle of the last century, is, that until 100 years ago the cities of London and Westminster had but one bridge— the old London Bridge—which was commenced in 1176, completed in 31 years, and after standing 625 years, was pulled down in 1832.

The want of bridges to keep pace with the increase of the population caused the establishment of numerous ferries. It has been computed that in 1760 the ferries across the Thames, taking in its course from Richmond to Greenwich, were 25 times as numerous as they are at present. Westminster-bridge was not finished until 1750, Blackfriars was built in 1769, Battersea in 1771, Vauxhall in 1816, Waterloo in 1817, Southwark in 1819, the present London-bridge in 1831, and Hungerford in 1844.

The character of the Thames watermen in the last century was what might have been expected from slightly informed, or uninformed, and not unprosperous men. They were hospitable and "hearty" one to another, and to their neighbours on shore; civil to such "fares" as were civil to them—especially if they hoped for an extra sixpence; but often saucy, abusive, and even sarcastic. Their interchange of abuse one with another, as they rowed on the Thames, down to the commencement of the present century, if not later, was remarkable for its "slang." In this sort of contest their "fares" not unfrequently joined; and even Dr. Johnson, when on the river, exercised his powers of objurgation to overwhelm some astonished Londoner in a passing boat.

During the greater part of the last century the Thames watermen were employed in a service now unknown to them. They were the carriers, when the tide and the weather availed, of the garden stuff and the fruits grown in the neighbourhood of the river, from Woolwich and Hampton to the London markets. The green and firmly-packed pyramids of cabbages that now load the waggons, were then piled in boats; and it was the same with fruit. One of the most picturesque sights Sir Richard Steele ever enjoyed was when he encountered, at the early dawn of a summer's day, "a fleet of Richmond gardeners," of which "ten sail of apricock-boats" formed a prominent and fragrant part. Turnpike roads and railways have superseded this mode of conveyance, which could only be made available when the tide served.

The observances on the Thames customary in the olden time still continue, though on a very reduced scale. The Queen has her watermen, but they have only been employed as the rowers of her barge twice since her accession to the throne—once when her Majesty and Prince Albert visited the Thames Tunnel, and again when Prince Albert took water at Whitehall, and was rowed to the City to open the Coal Exchange. Besides the Queen's watermen, there are still extant the dukes' and lords' watermen, the Lord Mayor's, and the City companies', as well as those belonging to the Admiralty. The above constitute what are called the privileged watermen, having certain rights and emoluments appertaining to them which do not fall to the lot of the class generally.

The Queen's Watermen are now only eighteen in number. They have no payment except when actually employed, and then they have 10s. for such employment. They have, however, a suit of clothes—a red jacket, with the royal arms on the buttons, and dark trowsers—presented to them once every two years. They have also the privileges of the servants of the household, such as exemption from taxes, &c. Most of them are proprietors of lighters, and are prosperous men.

The privileges of the retainers of the nobles in the Stuart days linger still among the *Lords' and Dukes' Watermen*, but only as a mere shadow of a fading substance. There are five or six men now who wear a kind of livery. I heard of no particular fashion in this livery being observed, either now or within the memory of the watermen. Their only privilege is, that they are free from impressment. In the war time these men were more than twenty-five times as numerous as they are at present; in fact, they are dying out, and the last "dukes'" and the last "lords'" privileged watermen are now, as I was told, "on their last legs."

The *Lord Mayor's Watermen* are still undiminished in number, the complement being thirty-six. Of these eight are water bailiffs, who in any procession row in a boat before the Lord Mayor's state barge. The other twenty-eight are the rowers of the chief magistrate's barge on his aquatic excursions. They are all free from impressment, and are supplied with a red jacket and dark trowsers every two years, the City arms being on the buttons.

One of these men told me that he had been a Lord Mayor's man for some years, and made about eight journeys a year, swan-hopping and such like, the show being, as he said, a regular thing; 10s. a voyage was paid each man. It was "jolly work," my informant stated, sometimes, when swan-hopping, though it depended on the Lord Mayor for the time being whether it was jolly or not. He had heard say that, in the old times, the Lord Mayor's barge men had spiced wine regularly when out. But now sometimes, they had no wine of any sort, but when a Lord Mayor pleased, and he did not always please. My informant was a lighterman as well as a Lord Mayor's waterman, and was doing well.

Among other "privileged classes" are the hog-grubbers (as they are called by the other watermen), but their number is now only four. These hog-grubbers ply only at the Pelican-stairs. They have been old sailors in the Navy, and are licensed by the Trinity-house; no apprenticeship or freedom of the Watermen's Company in that case being necessary. "There was from forty to fifty of them, sir," said a waterman to me, "when I was a lad, and I'm now fifty-three, and fine old fellows they were. But they're all going to nothing now."

The *Admiralty Watermen* are another privileged class. They have a suit of clothes once every two years—a dark blue jacket and trowsers, with an anchor on the buttons. They also wear badges, and are exempt from impressment. Their business is to row the officials of the Admiralty when they visit Deptford on Trinity Monday, and on all occasions of business or recreation. They are now about eighteen in number. They receive no salary, but are paid per voyage at the same rate as the Lord Mayor's watermen. There was also a class known as the "navy watermen," who enjoyed the same privileges as the others, but they are now extinct. Such of the City companies as retain their barges have also their own watermen, whose services are rarely put into requisition above twice a year. The Stationers' Company have lately relinquished keeping their barge.

The present number of Thames watermen (privileged and unprivileged) is, I am informed, by an officer of the Watermen's Hall, about 1,600. The Occupation Abstract of 1841 gives the number of London "boat, barge, and watermen," as 1,654. The men themselves have very loose notions as to their number. One man computed it to me at 12,000; another at 14,000. This is evidently a traditional computation, handed down from the days when watermen were in greater requisition. To entitle any one to ply for hire on the river, or to "work about" for payment, it is provided by the laws of the City that he shall have "duly and truly" served a seven years' apprenticeship to a licensed waterman, and shall have "taken up his freedom" at Watermen's-hall. I heard many complaints of this regulation being infringed. There were now, I was told, about 120 men employed by the Custom-house and in the Thames police, who were not free watermen. "There's a good many from Rochester way, sir," one waterman said, "and down that way. They've got in thro' the interest of members of Parliament and such like, while there's so many free watermen, that's gone to the expense of taking up their freedom, just starving. But we are going to see about it, and it's high time. Either give us back the money we've paid for our rights, or let us have our proper rights. That's what I say. Why, only yesterday, there was two accidents on the river, tho' no lives were lost. Both was owing to unlicensed men."

"It's neither this not that," said one old waterman to me, alluding to the decrease in their number and their earnings, "people may talk as they like about what's been the ruin of us—it's nothing but new London-bridge. When my old father heard that the old bridge was to come down, 'Bill,' says he, 'it'll be up with the watermen in no time.' If the old bridge had stood, how would all these steamers have shot her? Some of them could never have got through at all. At some tides it was so hard to shoot London-bridge (to go clear through the arches) that people wouldn't trust themselves to any but watermen. Now any fool may manage. London-bridge, sir, depend on it, has ruined us."

The places where the watermen now ply, are—on the Middlesex shore, beginning from London-bridge down the river—Somers Quay, Upper Custom-house Quay, Lower Custom-house Quay, Tower Stairs, Irongate Stairs, St. Katharine's, Aldermen's Stairs, Hermitage Stairs, Union Stairs, Wapping Old Stairs, Wapping New Stairs, Execution Dock, Wapping Dock, New Crane Stairs, Shadwell Dock Stairs, King James's Stairs, Cold Stairs, Stone Stairs, Hanover Stairs, Duke's Shore, Limehouse Hole, Chalk Stones, Mast House and Horseferry. On the Surrey side, beginning from Greenwich—are Greenwich, Lower Water Gate, Upper Water Gate, George's Stairs, Deptford Stairs, Dog and Duck Stairs, Cuckold's Point, Horseferry-road, Globe Stairs, King and Queen's Stairs, Surrey-canal Stairs, Hanover-row, Church Stairs, Rotherhithe Stairs, Prince's Stairs, Cherry Garden, Fountain High Stairs, East-lane, Mill Stairs, Horse and Groom New Stairs, George's Stairs, Horse and Groom Old Stairs, Pickle Herring Stairs, Battle-bridge Stairs, and London-bridge Stairs.

Above London-bridge, the Watermen's Stairs or stations on the Middlesex shore, are London-bridge, Allhallows, Southwark-bridge, Paul's Wharf, Blackfriars, Fox-under-the-Hill, Adelphi, Hungerford, Whitehall Stairs, Westminster-bridge, Horseferry, Vauxhall, and Hammersmith. On the opposite shore are London-bridge, Horse-shoe-alley, Bankside, Southwark-bridge, Blackfriars, Hodges, Waterloo-bridge, Westminster-bridge, Stangate Stairs, Lambeth Stairs, Vauxhall-bridge, Nine Elms, and the Red House, Battersea. Beyond, at Putney, and on both sides of the river, up to Richmond, boats are to be had on hire, but the watermen who "work" them are known to their London brethren as "up-country watermen"—men who do not regularly ply for hire, not being in regular attendance at the river side; but these "up-country men" are duly licensed. They convey passengers or luggage, or packages of any kind adapted to the burden of a boat of a light draught of water, when called upon, their boats being chained to piles driven into the river's edge. These men occasionally work in the market gardens, or undertake any job within their power; and though they are civil and honest, they are but partially employed, either on or off the river, and are very poor. Sometimes, when no better employment is in prospect, they stand at the toll bridges of Putney, Hammersmith, or Kew, and offer to carry passengers across for the price of the toll. Since the prevalence of steam-packets, as a means of locomotion along the Thames, the "stairs" (if so they may be called) above-bridge are for the most part almost nominal stations for the watermen. At London-bridge Stairs (Middlesex side) there now lie but three boats, while, before the steam era—or rather before the removal of the old London-bridge—ten times that number of boats were to be "hailed" there. At Waterloo and Southwark-bridges a man stands near the toll-gate offering a water conveyance no dearer than the toll, but it is hopeless to make this proposition when the tide is low, and these men, I am assured, hardly make 8d. a day when offering this futile opposition. The most frequented of the stairs above-bridge by the watermen is at the Red House, Battersea, where there are many visitors to witness or take part in shooting matches, or for dinner or pic-nic parties.

Down the river the Greenwich stairs are the most numerously stocked with boats. At this time about thirty boats are now to be engaged there, but the business of the watermen is not one-twentieth so much to convey passengers as to board any sailing vessels beating up for London, and to inquire, with an offer of their services (many of them being pilots), if they can be of any use, either aboard or ashore.

The number of "stairs" which may be considered as the recognized stations of watermen plying for hire, are, as I have shown by the fore-going enumeration, 75. The watermen plying at these places average, I am told by the best-informed men, seven to a "stairs." This gives 525 men and boats, but that, however, as we shall presently see, presents no criterion of the actual number of persons authorized to act as wa-termen.

Near the stairs below-bridge the watermen stand looking out for customers, or they sit on an adjacent form, protected from the weather, some smoking and some dozing. They are weather-beaten, strong-looking men, and most of them of, or above, the middle age. Those who are not "privileged"—and many of the privileged work in the same way as the unprivileged—wear all kinds of dresses, but generally in the nature of a sailor's garb—a strong pilot jacket and thick canvas trowsers. The present race of watermen have, I am assured, lost the sauciness (with occasional smartness) that distinguished their predecessors. They are mostly patient, plodding men, enduring poverty heroically, and shrinking far more than many other classes from any application for parish relief. "There is not a more independent lot that way in London," said a waterman to me, "and God knows it isn't for want of all the claims which being poor can give us that we don't apply to the workhouse." Some, however, are obliged to spend their old age, when incapable of labour, in the union. Half, or more than one-half of the Thames watermen, I am credibly informed, can read and write. They used to drink quantities of beer, but now, from the stress of altered circumstances, they are generally temperate men. The watermen are nearly all married, and have families. Some of their wives work for the slop tailors. They all reside in the small streets near the river, usually in single rooms, rented at from 1s. 6d. to 2s. a week. At least three-fourths of the watermen have apprentices, and they nearly all are sons or relatives of the watermen. For this I heard two reasons assigned. One was that lads whose childhood was passed among boats and on the water contracted a taste for a waterman's life, and were unwilling to be apprenticed to any other calling. The other reason was, that the poverty of the watermen compelled them to bring up their sons in this manner, as the readiest mode of "giving them a trade," and many thus apprenticed become seamen in the merchant service and occasionally in the Royal Navy, or get employment as working lightermen, or on board the river steamers.

At each "stairs" there is what is called a "turnway and causeway club," to which the men contribute each 2s. per quarter. One of the regulations of these clubs is, that the oldest men have the first "turn" on Monday, and the next oldest on Tuesday, and so on through the several days of the week until Saturday, which is the apprentices' day. The fund raised by the 2s. subscription is for keeping the causeway clean and in repair. There is also a society in connection with the whole body of watermen, called the "Protection Society," to proceed against any parties who infringe upon their privileges. To this society they pay 1d. per week each. The Greenwich watermen are engaged generally as pilots to colliers and other small craft.

From one of the watermen plying near the Tower I had the following statement:—

"I've been a waterman eight-and-twenty years. I served my seven years duly and truly to my father. I had nothing but my keep and clothes, and that's the regular custom. We must serve seven years to be free of the river. It's the same now in an apprenticeship. No pay; and some masters will neither wash, nor clothe, nor mend a boy; and all that ought to be done by the master, by rights. Times and masters is harder than ever. After my time was out I went to sea, and was pretty lucky in my voyages. I was at sea in the merchant service five year. When I came back I bought a boat. My father helped me to start as a waterman on the Thames. The boat cost me 20 guineas: it would carry eight fares. It cost £2 15s. to be made an apprentice, and about £4 to have a license to start for myself. In my father's time— from what I know when I was his apprentice, and what I've heard him say—a waterman's was a jolly life. He earned 15s. to 18s. a day, and spent it accordingly. When I first started for myself, 28 years ago, I made 12s. to 14s. a day—more than I make in a week now; but that was before steamers. Many of us watermen saved money then, but now we're starving. These good times lasted for me nine or ten years, and in the middle of the good times I got married. I was justified: my earnings was good. But steamers came in, and we were wrecked. My father was in the River Fencibles, which was a body of men that agreed to volunteer to serve on board ships that went on convoys in the war times. The watermen was bound to supply so many men for that and for the fleet. I can't call to mind the year, but the full number wasn't supplied, and there was a press. Some of my neighbours, watermen now, was of the press-gang. When the press was on there was a terrible to do, and all sorts of shifts among the watermen. The young ones ran away to their mothers, and kept in hiding. I was too young then—I was an apprentice, too—to be pressed. But a lieutenant once put his hand on my poll, and said, 'My fine red-headed fellow, you'll be the very man for me when you're old enough.' Mine's a very bad trade. I make from 10s. to 12s. a week, and that's all my wife and me has to live on. I've no children, thank the Lord for it; for I see that several of the watermen's children run about without shoes or stockings. On Monday I earned 1s. 9d., on Tuesday 1s. 7d., on Wednesday—which was a very wet day—1s., and yesterday (Thursday) 1s. 6d., and up to this day (Friday noon) I've earned nothing as yet. We work Sundays and all. My expenses when I'm out isn't much. My wife puts me up a bit of meat, or bacon and bread, if we have any in the house, and if I've earned anything I eat it with half a pint of beer, or a pint at times. Ours is hard work, and we require support, if we can only get it. If I bring no meat with me to the stairs, I bring some bread, and get half a pint of coffee with it, which is 1d. We have to slave hard in some weathers when we're at work, and indeed we're always either slaving or sitting quite idle. Our principal customers are people that want to go across in a hurry. At night—and we take night work, two and two, about two dozen of us, in turn—we have double fares. There's very few country visitors take boats now to see the sights about the river. The swell of the steamers frightens them. Last Friday a lady and gentleman engaged me for 2s. to go to the Thames Tunnel, but a steamer passed, and the lady said, 'Oh, look what a surf. I don't like to venture,' and so she wouldn't, and I sat five hours after that before I'd earned a farthing. I remember the first steamer in the river. It was from Gravesend, I think. It was good for us men at first, as the passengers came ashore in boats. There was no steam-piers then, but now the big foreign steamers can come alongside, and ladies and cattle and all can step ashore on platforms. The good times is over, and we are ready now to snap at one another for 3d., when once we didn't care about 1s. We're beaten by engines and steamings that nobody can well understand, and wheels."

"Rare John Taylor, the water poet," in the days of James I. and Charles I., with whose name I found most of the watermen familiar (at least they had heard of him), complained of the decay of his trade as a waterman, inasmuch as in his latter days "every Gill Turntripe, Mistress Tumkins, Madame Policot, my Lady Trash, Froth the tapster, Bill the tailor, Lavender the broker, Whiff the tobacco-seller, with their companion trulls, must be coached." He complained that wheeled conveyances ashore, although they made "the casements shatter, tatter, and clatter," were preferred to boats, and were the ruin of the watermen; and it is somewhat remarkable that the watermen of our day complain of the same detriment from wheeled conveyances on the water.

The *Lightermen and Bargemen* are also licensed watermen. The London watermen rarely apply the term "bargemen" to any persons working on the river; they confine the appellation to those who work in the barges in the canals, and who need not be free of the river, though some of them are so, and many of them seamen or old men-of-war's-men. The river "lightermen" (as the watermen style them all, no matter what the craft) are, however, so far a distinct class that they convey goods only, and not passengers; while the watermen convey only passengers, or such light goods as passengers may take with them in the way of luggage. The lighters are the large boats used to carry the goods which form the cargo to the vessels in the river or the docks, or from the vessels to the shore. The barge is a kind of larger lighter, built deeper and stronger, and is confined principally to the convey-ance of coal. Two men are generally employed in the management of a barge. The lighters are adapted for the conveyance of corn, timber, stone, groceries, and general merchandise; and the several vessels are usually confined to such purposes—a corn-lighter being seldom used, for instance, to carry sugar. The lighters and barges in present use are built to carry from 6 to 120 tons, the greater weight being that of the huge coal-barges. A lighter carrying fourteen tons of merchandise costs when new £120, and this is an average size and price. Some of these lighters are the property of the men who "drive" them, and who are a prosperous class compared with the poor watermen. The lighter-men cannot be said to ply for hire in the way of the watermen, but they are always what they call "on the look-out." If a vessel arrives, some of them go on board and offer their services to the captain, in case he be concerned in having his cargo transported ashore; or they ascertain to what merchant or grocer goods may be consigned, and apply to them for employment in lighterage, unless they know that some particular lighterman is regularly employed by the consignee. There are no settled charges; each tradesman has his regular scale, or drives his own bargains for lighterage as he does for the supply of any other commodity. I heard no complaints of underselling among the lightermen; but the men who "drive their own boats themselves" sometimes submit to very hard bargains. Laden lighters, I was told on all hands, ought not "in anything like weather," to be worked by fewer than two men, but the hard bargains I have spoken of induce some working lightermen to attempt feats beyond their strength, in "driving" a laden lighter unassisted. Sometimes the watermen have to "put off" to render assistance when they see a lighter unmanage-able. Lighters can only proceed with the tide, and are often moored in the middle of the river, waiting the turn of the tide; more especially when their load consists of heavy articles. The lighters, when not employed, are moored alongshore, often close to a watermen's stairs. Most master lightermen have offices by the water-side, and all have places where "they may always be heard of." Many lightermen are capitalists, and employ a number of hands. The London Post-office Directory gives the names of 175 master lightermen. If a ship has to be laden or unladen in a hurry, one of them is usually employed, and he sets a series of lighters "on the job," so that there is no cessation in the work. Most lightermen are occasionally employers, sometimes engaging watermen to assist them; sometimes hiring a lighter, in addition to their own, from some other lighterman. A man employed occasionally by one of the greater masters made the following statement:—

"I work for Mr. ——, and drive a lighter that cost above £100, mostly at merchandise. I have 28s. a week, and 2s. extra every night when there's night-work. I should be right well off if that lasted all the year through, but it don't. On a Saturday night, when we've waited for our money till ten or eleven perhaps, master will say, 'I have nothing for you on Monday, but you can look in.' He'll say that to a dozen of us, and we may not have a job till the week's half over, or not one at all. That's the mischief of our trade. I haven't means to get a lighter of my own, though I can't say I'm badly off, and I'm a single man; and if I had a lighter I've no connection. There's very few of the great lightermen that one has a regular berth under. I suppose I make 14s. or 15s. a week the year through, lumping it all like."

The lightermen who are employed in the conveyance of goods chargeable with duty are licensed by the Excise-office, as a check against the conveyance of contraband articles. Both the proprietors of the lighter and the persons he employs must be licensed for this conveyance, the cost being 5s. yearly. A licensed man thus employed casually by the master lightermen is known as "a jobber," and has 6s. a day. The average payment of the regular labourers of the lightermen is 25s. a week, but some employers whom I heard warmly extolled as "the old masters," give 30s. a week. In addition to these 25s. or 30s., as the case may be, night-work ensures 2s. or 2s. 6d. extra. Thus the permanent labourers under the lightermen appear to be fairly paid.

The master lightermen, as I said before, are, according to the "Post-office Directory," 175 in number. I am told that the number may be taken (as the "Directory" gives only those who have offices) at 200 at the least, and that of this number one-half employ, on an average, ten men, while the other half employ on an average, one man each. The proprietors of the lighters who average ten hands in their employ cannot be reckoned among men working on the river, except perhaps one-fourth of their number; but of the other class all work themselves. The annual number of actual labourers in this department of metropolitan industry will thus be 125 proprietors to 1,100 non-proprietors, or 1,225 in all, driving 1,100 lighters at the least. The bargemen, who are also employed when convenience requires as lightermen, are 400 or 500, driving more than half that number of barges, but in these are not included many coal barges, which are the property of the coal merchants having wharfs. The number of London boat bargemen and lightermen given in the Occupation Abstract of 1841 was 1,503; which, allowing for the increase of population, will be found to differ but slightly from the numbers above given.

The lightermen differ little in character from the watermen, and only as far as their better circumstances have influenced them. They have comfortable homes. I speak of the working lightermen, who are also proprietors, and can all, with very few exceptions, read and write. They all reside near the river, and generally near the docks, and the great majority of them live on the Middlesex side. They are a sober class of men, both the working masters and the men they employ. "A drunken lighterman," I was told, "would hardly be trusted twice."

The watermen and lightermen are licensed by the Bye-Laws of the City, passed for the regulation of the "Freemen of the Company of Master, Wardens, and commonalty of Watermen and Lightermen of the River Thames, their widows and apprentices," to row or work "boats, vessels, and other craft" in all parts of the river, from New Windsor, Berks, to Yantlet Creek (below Gravesend), Kent, and in "all docks, canals, creeks, and harbours of or out of the said river, so far as the tide flows therein." A rule of the Corporation, in 1836, specifies the construction and dimensions of the boats to be built after that date for the use of the watermen. A wherry, to carry eight persons, was to be 20½ ft. in length of keel, 4½ ft. breadth in the midships, and of the burden of 21 cwt. A skiff, to carry four persons, was to be 14 ft. length of keel, 5 ft. breadth in the midships, and of 1 ton burden. The necessity of improved construction in the watermen's boats, since the introduction of steamers caused swells on the river, was strongly insisted upon by several of the witnesses before Parliament, who produced plans for improved craft, but the poverty of the watermen has made the regulations of the authorities all but a dead letter. These river labourers are unable to procure new boats, and they patch up the old craft.

The census of 1841 gives the following result as to the number of those employed in boat work in the metropolis:—

<pre>
Boat and bargemen, and women 2,516
     „   „   lightermen .. 1,503
     „   „   watermen ... 1,654
                                            ──────
                                            5,673
</pre>

The "boat and bargemen, and women," thus enumerated, are, I presume, those employed on the canals which centre in the metropolis—so that, deducting these from the 5,673 labourers above given, we have 3,157, the total number of boat, bargemen, lightermen, and watermen belonging to the Thames.

I have now to speak of the last great change in river transit—the introduction of *steam navigation* on the Thames. The first steam-boat used in river navigation, or indeed in any navigation, was one built and launched by Fulton, on the river Hudson, New York, in 1807. It was not until eleven years later, or in 1818, that the first English river steam-boat challenged the notice of the citizens as she commenced her voyage on the Thames, running daily from the Dundee Arms, Wapping, to Gravesend and back. She was called Margery, and was the property of a company who started her as an experiment. She was about the burden of the present Gravesend steamers, but she did not possess covered paddle wheels, being propelled by uncovered wheels (which were at the time compared to ducks' feet) projecting from the extremity of the stern. The splashing made by the strokes of the wheels was extreme, and afforded a subject for all the ridicule and wit the watermen were masters of. Occasionally, too, the steamer came into contact with a barge, or other craft, and broke one or more of her "duck feet," which might cause a delay of "an hour or so (as it was worded to me) before a jury duck-foot could be fitted, and perhaps before another mile was done there was another break and another stoppage." These delays, which would now be intolerable, were less regarded at that period, when the average duration of a voyage from Wapping to Gravesend, by the Margery, was about five hours and a half—while at present, with favouring wind and tide, the distance from London-bridge to Gravesend, thirty-one miles by water, is done in less than an hour and a half. The fares by the first river steamer were

3s. for the best, and 2s. 6d. for the fore cabin. Sailing packets at that time ran from the Dundee Arms to Gravesend, the fare being 1s. 6d., and these vessels were sometimes a day, and sometimes a day and a half, in accomplishing the distance. The first river steam-boat, after running less than three months of the summer, was abandoned as a failure. A favourite nickname given by the watermen and the river-side idlers to the unfortunate Margery, was the "Yankee Torpedo." About that time there had been an explosion of an American steamer, named the Torpedo, with loss of life, and the epithet doubtless had an influence in deterring the timid from venturing on a voyage down the Thames in so dangerous a vessel. The construction of the Margery was, moreover, greatly inferior to the steamers of the present day, as when she "shot off" her steam, she frequently shot off boiling water along with it. One waterman told me that he had his right hand so scalded by the hot water, as he was near the Margery in his boat, that it was disabled for a week.

In the following summer another steamer was started by another company, the "Old Thames." The Old Thames had paddle wheels, as in the present build, and her speed was better by about one mile in ten than that of her predecessor, and her success was greater. She ran the same route and at the same prices until the Majestic, the third river steamer, was started in the same year by a rival company, and the fares were reduced to 2s. 6d. and 2s. The Majestic ran from the Tower to Gravesend. At this time, and twenty years after, the watermen had to convey passengers in boats to and from the steamers (as one of the watermen has stated in the narrative I have given); this was an additional source of employment to them, and led to frequent quarrels among them, as to their "turn" in conveying passengers and luggage; and these quarrels led to frequent complaints from the captains of the steamers, owing to their passengers being subject to annoyances and occasional extortions from the watermen. In 1820, two smaller boats, the Favourite and the Sons of Commerce, were started, and the distance was accomplished in half the time. It was not until 1830, however, that steam navigation became at all general above-bridge.

The increase of the river steam-boats from 1820 is evinced by the following table:—

Years.	No. of River Steamers.	No. of Voyages.
1820	4	227
1830	20	2,344
1835	43	8,843

Thus we have an increase, in the ten years from 1820 to 1830, of 16 steamers, and in the five years from 1830 to 1835 of 23 over the number employed in 1830, and of 39 over the number of 1820. In the last 30 years, that is, from 1820 to 1850, there has been an increase of 65 steamers.

The time occupied by the river steamboats in executing their voyages evinces the change in their management quite as fully as the increase of their numbers. In 1820, four boats performed 227 voyages, or, presuming that they ran at that period 26 weeks in the year, 56¾ voyages, or about two a week each. In 1830, following the same calculation, 20 steamers accomplished 2,344 voyages, being 117, or between four and five voyages a week each. In 1835, 43 steamers made 8,843 voyages, being 205 voyages each, or about eight a week. During this time some of the steamers going the longer distances, such as Richmond, Gravesend, &c., ran only one, two, or three days in the week, which accounts for the paucity of voyages compared with the number of vessels.

The following Table shows the number of river-steamers running during the season of 1850, above and below bridge, with their routes, the daily trips of each boat, with its average number of passengers each run, the expenditure in fares, and the average amount of money spent in the transit of persons up and down the river weekly, and throughout the season:—

Companies.	Number of boats running.	Daily trips of each up and down the river.	Average number of passengers each run.	Fares of each boat.	Weekly expenditure in this transit.	Average amount paid during the season in transit by river steamers.
Above Bridge.						
Citizen, to Chelsea …	12	12	50	2d. to 7d.	£840 0 0	£21,840 0 0
Echo, Kew and Richmond ..	2	4	50	6d. to 9d.	87 10 0	2,275 0 0
Eclipse, ditto …	1	2	50	6d. to 9d.	21 17 6	568 15 0
Iron boats, ditto …	15	8	60	2d. to 7d.	945 0 0	24,570 0 0
Locomotive, ditto and Hampton Court …	1	2	50	6d. to 1s. 3d.	30 12 6	796 5 0
Vivid, three times a week to Richmond …	1	2	50	6d. to 9d.	5 12 6	146 5 0
Ant and Bee, Adelaide-pier .	3	30	60	½d.	78 15 0	2,047 10 0
Westminster, Westminster-bridge …	5	24	60	1d.	175 0 0	4,550 0 0
Below Bridge.						
Dryad to Gravesend, Sheerness, and Southend …	1	2	100	6d. to 3s.	105 0 0	2,730 0 0
Diamond …	5	4	400	6d. to 3s.	4,200 0 0	109,200 0 0
Sons of the Thames …	3	4	100	6d. to 3s.	630 0 0	16,380 0 0
Emmet, to Gravesend …	1	2	100	6d.	35 0 0	910 0 0
Waterman, to Woolwich and Greenwich …	8	12	80	4d. to 6d.	1,120 0 0	29,120 0 0
Woolwich …	11	12	80	4d. to 6d.	1,540 0 0	40,040 0 0
	69	120	1,280		£9,814 7 6	£255,173 15 0

In 1820, only 227 voyages were accomplished during the season of twenty-six weeks; in 1850 upwards of half that number of voyages were accomplished *daily* during a similar term, and in that term the river steam-boats conveyed 27,955,200 passengers. The amount expended in this mode of transit exceeds a quarter of a million sterling, or upwards of half-a-crown a-head for the entire metropolitan population.

The consequences of the increase of steam navigation commanded the attention of Parliament in the year 1831, when voluminous evidence was taken before a committee of the House of Commons, but no legislative enactments followed; the management of the steam traffic, as well as that of all other river traffic, being left in the hands of the Navigation Committee of the Corporation of London, of the composition of which body I have already spoken. "Collisions have taken place," said Sir John Hall in 1836; "barges, craft, and boats have been swamped, and valuable property destroyed, from the crowded and narrow state of the passage through the pool, and human life has, in some instances, also fallen a sacrifice from such collisions, and in others from the effects of the undulation of the water produced by the action of the paddle-wheels of steam-boats, circumstances which have been aggravated by the unnecessary velocity with which some of those vessels have been occasionally propelled." The returns laid before Parliament show three deaths in 1834 attributable to steam craft. In 1835 the number of deaths from the same causes was no less than ten. In all these cases inquests were held. In 1834 the number of deaths from all causes, whether of accident or suicide, on the river, as investigated by the coroner, was 54; the deaths caused by steam-boats being one-eighteenth of that number; while in 1835 the deaths from all causes were 41, the steam-boats having occasioned loss of life to nearly one-fourth of that number.

To obviate the danger and risk to boats, it was suggested to the committee that the steamers should not be propelled beyond a certain rate, and that an "indicator" should be placed on board, which, by recording the number of revolutions of the paddle-wheels should show the speed of the steam-vessel, while excessive speed, when thus detected, was to entail punishment. It was shown, however, that the number of times the wheels revolve affords no criterion of the speed of the vessel, as regards the space traversed in a given period. Her speed is affected by depth of water, weight of cargo, number of passengers; by her superior or inferior construction and handling, and most especially by her going with or against the tide; while in all these circumstances of varying speed, as regards rates of progress, the revolutions of the paddle-wheels might, in every fifteen minutes, vary little in number. The tide moves, ebb and flow, on the average, three miles an hour. Mr. Rowland, the present harbour-master, has said, touching the proper speed of steam-vessels on the river:—"Four miles an hour through the water with the tide and seven against the tide would give ample speed for the steam-boats; an opportunity would thus be afforded of travelling over the ground against the tide at the rate of about four miles an hour, and with the tide they would positively pass over the ground at the rate of about seven miles." The rate at which the better class of river steamers progress, when fairly in motion, is now from eight to nine miles an hour.

Although no legislative enactments for the better regulation of the river steam navigation took place after the report of the committee, accidents, from the cause referred to, are now unfrequent. In the present year, I am informed, there has been no loss of life on the Thames, occasioned by steam-boats. This is attributable to a better and clearer "water-way" being kept, and to a greater efficiency on the part of the captains and helmsmen of the river steam-fleet.

It is common for people proceeding from London-bridge to Gravesend, to exclaim about the "crowds of shipping!" The fact is, however, that notwithstanding the great increase in the commerce and traffic of the capital, the Thames is less crowded with shipping than it was at the beginning of the century. Mr. Banyon, clerk to the Watermen's Company, in his evidence before a committee of the House of Commons, described himself as a "practical man 22 years before 1811." He says—"There is a wonderful difference since my time. I was on the river *previous to any docks being made*, when *all the trade of the country* was lying out in the river. ... The river was then so crowded that the tiers used to overlap one another, and we used to be obliged to bring up, so as to prevent getting athwart hawse." I mention this fact to show that, without the relief afforded by the docks, steam navigation below bridge would be utterly impracticable.

The average tonnage of a steam-vessel of a build adapted to run between London and Greenwich or Woolwich is 70 or 80 tons; one adapted to run to Gravesend, or beyond, is about 180 tons; and those merely suitable for plying between London-bridge and Westminster, 40 or 50 tons. What is the number of persons, per ton, which may safely be entrusted to the conveyance of steam boats, authorities are not agreed upon. Mr. W. Cunningham, the captain of a Woolwich steamer, represented it to the committee as four or five to the ton, though he admits that five to the ton inconvenienced the passengers by crowding them. The tonnage of Mr. Cunningham's vessel was 77; his average number of passengers, "on extreme freights," was 200; yet he once carried 500 persons, though, by his own admission, 385 would be a crowding.

The changes wrought in the appearance of the river, and in the condition of the watermen, by the introduction of steamers, have been rapid and marked. Not only since the steam era have new boats and new companies gradually made their appearance, but new piers have sprung up in the course of the Thames from Gravesend to Richmond. Of these piers, that at Hungerford is the most remarkable, as it is erected fairly in the river; and on a fine summer's day, when filled with well-dressed persons, waiting "for their boat," it has a very animated appearance. A long-wooden frame-work, which rises into a kind of staircase at high water, and is a sloping platform at low water, connects the pier with Hungerford-bridge. At Southwark and Vauxhall bridges the piers are constructed on the abutments of an arch, and a staircase conducts the passenger to the bridge. The steam-boat piers from London-bridge "up" on the north side of the river, are—three at London-bridge, one at Southwark-bridge, at Paul's Wharf (Blackfriars), Temple, Arundel-street, Waterloo-bridge, Fox under the Hill, George-street, Adelphi, Hungerford, Pimlico, Cadogan Pier, Chelsea, Battersea-bridge, Hammersmith, and Kew. On the other side are two at Richmond, one at Putney, Red House, Battersea, Nine Elms, Lambeth, Westminster Bridge, and London Bridge. Below bridge, on the Middlesex side, the piers are—the Tunnel, Limehouse Hole, Brunswick, North Woolwich, and Purfleet. On the Surrey side there are two piers at Gravesend, one at Rosherville, Erith, Woolwich, East Greenwich, Greenwich, and the Commercial Dock, Rotherhithe.

The piermen at the pier belonging to the Gravesend Diamond Company (the oldest company now flourishing, as it was started in June, 1828), and to others of similar character, are seven in number; at Hungerford, however, there are eleven piermen; and taking the steam-boat piers altogether, it may be safely said there are four men to each on an average, or 168 men to 42 such piers. The piermen are of three classes as regards rates of remuneration. The piermaster, who is the general superintendent of the station, has 35s. a week, the others have 25s. and 21s. These men are not confined to any one duty; as the man who takes the tickets from the passengers one day may assist merely in mooring, or in "touting," the next, though a good touter is not often changed. The colour of the tickets is changed daily, unless a colour has "run out," in which case another colour must be substituted until a supply can be obtained. The majority of the piermen have been watermen or seamen, or in some way connected with river work. They are, for the most part, married men, supporting families in the best manner that their means will admit. From a gentleman connected with a steam packet company I had the pleasure of hearing a very good character of these men, while by the men themselves I was informed that they were, as a body, fairly treated, never being dismissed without reasons assigned and due inquiry. The directors of such vessels as are in the hands of companies meet weekly, and, among their general business, they then investigate any complaints by or against the men, who are sometimes suspended as a punishment, though such cases are unfrequent.

All the men employed on board the river steamers are free watermen, excepting those working in the engine room. In the winter some of them return to the avocation of watermen, hiring a boat by the month, or week, if they do not possess, as many do, boats of their own. In the course of my inquiries among the merchant seamen, I heard not a few contemptuous opinions expressed of the men on board the river craft. There is no doubt, however, that the captain of a river steamer, who is also the pilot, must have a quick and correct eye, to direct his vessel out of the crowd of others about London-bridge, for instance, without collision. The helmsman is frequently the mate of the steamer—sometimes, but rarely, one of the crew; while sometimes the captain himself relieves the mate at the helm, and then the mate undertakes the piloting of the vessel. During the season, when a steam-boat is "made safe" for the night, one of the crew usually sleeps on board to protect what property may be kept there, and to guard against fire. The crew go on board about two hours before the vessel starts, to clean her thoroughly; the engineer and his people must be in attendance about that time, to get the steam up; and the captain about half an hour or an hour before the boat leaves her mooring, to see that everything is in order.

The river steamers generally commence running on Good Friday or Easter Monday, and continue until the 1st of October, or a little later, if the weather be fine, as during the present season. Each steamer carries a captain, a mate, and three men as crew, with an engineer, a stoker, and call boy—or eight hands altogether on board.

The number daily at work on the river steamers is thus 552; so that, including the piermen, the clerks, and the "odd men," between 700 and 800 persons are employed in the steam navigation of the Thames. Calculating each voyage to average 6 miles, the extent of steam navigation on the Thames, performed daily in the season, is no less than 8,280 miles. The captains receive from £2 to £3 per week; the mates from 30s. to 35s.; the crew, 25s. each; the call boy, 7s.; the engineer from £2 to £3; and the stokers, 30s.

The class of travellers by these steam-boats is mixed. The wealthier not unfrequently use them for their excursions up or down the river; but the great support of the boats is from the middle and working class, more especially such of the working class as are enabled to afford the expense of a Sunday excursion on the river, and such of the middle class (including the artisans) as reside in the suburbs, and proceed by this means of conveyance to their accustomed places of business. In all or nearly all the larger steamers a band of music adds to the enjoyment of the passengers, but with this the directors of the vessels have nothing to do beyond giving their consent to the gratuitous conveyance of the musicians, who go upon speculation, their remuneration being what they can collect from the passengers.

The Morning Chronicle, Thursday, October 17, 1850.

A CASE OF REAL DISTRESS.

To the EDITOR of the MORNING CHRONICLE.

A lady encloses 10s. for the "Case of Real Distress" of the widow in Henrietta-street, Cavendish-square, mentioned in *The Morning Chronicle*, and attested by an inhabitant of Portugal-street, Grosvenor-square.

Oct. 16.

We have also to acknowledge the receipt of 20s., from W. C. H. for the same party.

The Morning Chronicle, Saturday, October 19, 1850.

"A Case of Real Distress."—We have to acknowledge the receipt of a cheque for 2*l.* from "J. N.," and a Post-office order for 1*l.* from "I. U.," for Sarah Hill, of 11, Henrietta-street, Manchester-square, the poor widow with four young children, and who has just passed through her confinement with a fifth (dead), since the death of her husband.

The Morning Chronicle, Tuesday, October 22, 1850.

"A CASE OF REAL DISTRESS."

We have to acknowledge the receipt of a Post-office order for 1*l.* from "P." at Bradford; and 10s. in postage stamps from "R. B.," for Sarah Hill, of 11, Henrietta-street, Manchester-square, the poor widow with four young children, who, since the recent loss of her husband, has been confined with a fifth child, that survived its birth but a few days.

To the EDITOR of the MORNING CHRONICLE.

Sir—Will you be good enough to give one sovereign for the benefit of the starving children at the ragged school mentioned in Mr. Charles Cochrane's letter in your paper last week; half a sovereign to the poor widow left with several children, and on the eve of her confinement with another, whose case was reported in a letter signed (I think) "Humanitas," which appeared in *The Morning Chronicle* a fortnight since; and half a sovereign to a poor groom's wife out of place, who was confined of three children at a birth some time since? If you will also acknowledge the receipt of this letter, and the enclosed, you will greatly oblige,

Sir, your obedient servant,

Oct. 20, 1850. G. H. F.

[Two sovereigns were enclosed in the above.]

The Morning Chronicle, Wednesday, October 23, 1850.

The Leicester-square Soup Kitchen.—His Royal Highness the Duke of Cambridge presided yesterday at a committee meeting of the Leicester-square Soup Kitchen and Hospice, when a most comprehensive plan for preventing destitution and mendicancy in the metropolis was considered and adopted. The details of the project, which is both simple and inexpensive, are not to transpire until a public meeting shall have been convened, and this is expected to take place at the Egyptian Hall in the Mansion-house. In the meantime the Leicester-square Soup Kitchen and Hospice are to be re-opened on Nov. 1, and in consequence of the unusual amount of physical suffering endured by the children of the unemployed poor, it is intended to make a great effort to give food gratuitously to the ragged schools of the metropolis.

LABOUR AND THE POOR.

THE METROPOLITAN DISTRICTS.

[FROM OUR SPECIAL CORRESPONDENT.]

THE LONDON DRESSMAKERS AND MILLINERS.

LETTER LXXV.

The working *dressmakers* and *milliners* of London are, as a body, composed of a more mixed class of the community than are the members of any other calling. Among them are the daughters of clergymen, of military and naval officers, and of surgeons, farmers, and tradesmen of every description. The great majority of these dressmakers—fully three-fourths of them—have been reared in the country. The number of dressmakers and milliners in London, at the time of taking the last census (1841), was 20,780. Of this number 17,183 were females of twenty years of age and upwards, and 3,480 under that age. The remaining 117 were males, 10 of whom were below twenty years of age.

The business of dressmaking is carried on by two classes—the dressmaker and the milliner. The dressmaker's work is confined to the making of ladies' dresses, including every kind of outwardly-worn gown or robe. The milliner's work is confined to making caps, bonnets, scarfs, and all outward attire worn by ladies other than the gown; the bonnets, however, which tax the skill of the milliner, are what are best known as "made bonnets"—such as are constructed of velvet, satin, silk, muslin, or any other textile fabric. Straw bonnet-making is carried on by a distinct class, and in separate establishments. The milliner, however, often *trims* a straw bonnet, affixing the ribbons, flowers, or other adornments. When the business is sufficiently large, one or more millinery hands are commonly kept solely to bonnet-making, those best skilled in that art being of course selected; but every efficient milliner so employed is expected to be expert also at cap-making, and at all the other branches of the trade. The milliner is accounted a more skilled labourer than the dressmaker.

Of milliners and dressmakers there are, as in most other trades of the present day, two distinct classes—viz., the adequately and the poorly paid, or, in other words, those belonging to the "honourable," and those belonging to the "dishonourable" or "slop" part of the trade. I shall confine my present letter to an exposition of the earnings and condition of the former class.

The division of labour which I have pointed out is closely observed in all large establishments, though in some only millinery work is done, and in others only dressmaking; but in the majority of the London houses the two branches are carried on together. The workers employed consist of apprentices, improvers, assistants (including day workers), third hands, second hands, and first hands. Each department has a *first hand*, whose business it is to wait upon the customers, receive orders, take measures, cut out the material (unless a second hand or another first hand be so employed in a very large establishment), and give it out to the workwomen to be made. The young women who attend in the show-room, to display the silks, velvets, laces, &c., and to dispose of any ready-made articles, such as gloves, bonnets, scarfs, collars, &c., are called the *showwomen*, in establishments known as "private houses"—that is houses without shops—and *saleswomen* in houses to which shops are attached. This is the case in both French and English houses. Each department has also a *second hand* or *superintendent*, who works along with the others, directs or superintends their labour, and instructs the improvers and apprentices. She is responsible for the proper execution of the work, and for the due exertion of industry on the part of all employed. A *third hand* is employed in a similar way.

The *assistants* are hired workwomen, employed on the premises in some cases, and when so employed sleeping there, and in most cases boarding with their employers. Some are engaged by the month, or the quarter, or the year; others by the week or the season. Their "busy time" is during the fashionable season, or about six months out of the twelve, from February to July. A week or two before and after Christmas is also a busy time in many houses, and in others six weeks before Christmas for the winter fashions, and three or four weeks after it.

The *improvers* are a very numerous class. When a girl has completed her apprenticeship or other term of engagement in a country town, or even in Edinburgh, or Dublin, she comes to London *to improve*. If she has an intention of establishing herself in business in the town where her parents and friends reside, she and they feel that it would be hopeless to attain the "patronage" of the neighbouring ladies unless she have the *prestige* of having been trained to the perfect exercise of London taste and skill—a *prestige* which must be duly maintained, when in business, by at least one annual visit to London "for the fashions." The improver is engaged for a given period (generally for two years) and is almost always boarded in the house of her employer, who, not unfrequently, receives a premium with her, while the improver receives no remuneration for her labour. She is there not to be paid, but to be improved. The premiums with improvers vary from £10 to £50.

The *apprentice* is the young girl placed with a dressmaker to be instructed in all the "art and mystery" of the calling. If she be lodged and boarded in the house, as is frequently the case, a premium is paid with her. If she remain with her friends, lodging with them, and going home also to her meals, no premium is given, while her labour is considered merely equivalent to her tuition, and she consequently receives no payment for what she does. The term of apprenticeship is from two to five years, and the premium from £10 to £50; sometimes, however, but rarely, it is even higher. In addition to these varieties of workwomen, but connected more particularly with the dressmakers, are the *day-workers*—a class of assistants hired, as their name expresses, by the day, in contradistinction to those who are engaged by the month or year.

To all these regulations there are exceptions in some establishments, but the arrangements and the disposition of the work which I have described are the general rule.

The principal dressmaking and millinery establishments are at the West-end, in the two Grosvenor-streets, Bond-street, St. James's-street, Oxford-street, Piccadilly, and some of the streets off Piccadilly, and off Hanover and Grosvenor squares. The very first-rate houses, with the exception of two or three, are all kept by French women. These are principally in the neighbourhood of Hanover-square. Some of the English houses, however, rank as high as the French. But English women, I am informed, are never made first hands in these large and first-rate houses, as the customers prefer the French. And even the second and third-rate houses get French first hands if they can. The French, I am further informed, are paid extravagant yearly sums. "Mdme. ——," said one of my informants, "has a young lady to superintend the whole establishment, and she has a salary of £200 a year." In these great establishments, I may repeat, the first hands, numbering from eight to eleven, are all French—while the second hands number not more than six, half of whom may be French, and the other half English; and there may be about five or six more third hands or assistants, living in the house, and all English, and as many apprentices and improvers as can be got. In the season, from fifty to sixty, and even more, day-workers are employed. The regular hands who live in the house are kept all the year, with the exception of a month's holiday in the autumn; but the day-workers are all sent away after the summer season, when there is no more work for them until the winter season returns. In the generality of the best houses, the rooms are large and airy, and the young people are well treated. Each first hand has a room to herself, and the others sleep in a large apartment, in which are about half a dozen beds, and in these sleep twelve young people. They rise about seven, and all, with the exception of the mistress or the young person who may be the superintendent, breakfast together, a first hand presiding. The superintendent takes her meals with the proprietress of the establishment. Some, but only some, have meat suppers, others have bread and cheese. "This meal takes place," said a milliner to me, "at ten, after which (if it is not in the season) the young ladies do not sit down to work again, and they can generally go out and take a walk until midnight, if they choose, but at which time they are expected to be home. If, however, they do not return till the morning, no questions are asked, in some establishments, provided they are in the work-room at the proper time." The ages of the second and third hands are from 18 to 25 among the English; a few, however, are older still; among the French 30 is the usual age. I was told that the young women at the first houses can usually number up some eight or nine who have died at the establishment. One of the first houses has acquired a reputation for not over-working their young people, as they always make them leave off at five in the evening; but then, I am informed, they compel them to begin at six.

"In Madame ———'s house," said a lady familiar with the place, and with many others of equal fashion, "the young people are all obliged to be very decorous, as Madame is very strict herself. They work, however, extremely hard there; the rooms are very close and confined, twelve persons sleeping in one room only twenty feet square. In all the large houses everything is sacrificed to work in the season." But the proprietors of several of the establishments think nothing of the morals of those under their care. On Sunday those who have friends in London go to pass the day with them, and those who stay at home, if there be no work to do (though there frequently is in the season), never think of going to church, but lounge about the whole time. Some will allow them to remain in bed all day, which many do, and read cheap publications of a low character. A lady asked them in one house lately why they did not go to church or say their prayers? They said they had not time to pray in the morning, and they were too tired at night. One of them said, "When I was in the country I was taught to say my prayers and to go regularly to church; and when I came here at first I did so, but I soon got into the ways of the others." I have found those young persons generally ignorant of any kind of literature except the penny publications. They can most of them write legibly, but that is all. "I was alone," said a lady to me, "one Sunday with a young person about 20. She was reading one of the penny romances. I said to her, 'If you will not read anything more suitable for Sunday than a novel, why don't you get a good and instructive one? You have got to the 82d number of that, and it has cost you 82 pence. And for 24 pence you could have got one of Sir Walter Scott's works.' And this was her answer—'What, is he a great writer?' I replied," continued my informant, "that he was." "Dear me!" she said, "and selling his books for 2s. I dare say, poor thing, he is starving in some garret, as I'm told all great writers do." "On another day," said the lady to me, "an advertising cart bearing a placard, announcing in large letters Shakspeare's house to be sold, passed the window of a work-room. The young ladies actually asked one another who he was: I said he was a great poet. One wanted to know if he was the author of 'Don Juan.' Another wondered why he was going to let his house; whether he was getting poor, or going to take a larger one. And this was in one of the very highest and most fashionable houses in London."

I now subjoin the account given by a lady concerning the internal economy of some of the first-rate milliners' establishments at the West-end. I give it as it was furnished to me in writing:—

"A first-rate house of business, conducted by a dressmaker and milliner of the highest fashion, is always a very large house, more like a mansion for a nobleman than a milliner's establishment. In some there is nothing to indicate that they are places of business, except a plate on the door with the names of the proprietors engraved thereon; while others have two or three splendid plate-glass windows—each window consisting of one pane—with a brass bar outside, across which a lace vest or an embroidered collar or handkerchief is hung, to show the business carried on within. These large houses are not only milliners and dressmakers, but they supply every kind of ladies' wearing apparel, with the exception of shoes. A lady goes to order perhaps her wedding *trousseau*, or a train for the Queen's Drawing-room, or her morning and evening dresses. She alights from her carriage. The hall-door is opened by the footman of the establishment, and she is ushered through a splendid hall, and up a broad stone staircase, covered with an elegant Brussels carpet, to the first landing place, where she is met by the mistress of the establishment, who bows her into what is called the 'premier magasin,' or 'first show-room.' Then comes a French lady, dressed in a silk dress, with short sleeves, and a very small lace cap, with long streamers of ribbon that fall over her shoulders down to her feet. She walks before the lady to a counter, and places a chair for her. These French ladies are styled 'magasinières,' or 'showroom-women.' There are generally five or six of these showroom-women kept in a first-rate establishment. The first showroom is about 130 feet long, and 60 feet wide. In every other panel there is a looking-glass from the floor to the ceiling, set in a handsome carved gilt frame. The floor is covered with a very expensive carpet of a rich pattern, sometimes of a violet and amber colour. The window-curtains are of rich dark green velvet. In different parts of the room there are counters of polished ebony, elegantly ornamented with gilding. The lady customer is then shown an assortment of magnificent silks and velvets. She looks them all over, tries the shades in different lights, asks the Frenchwoman which is most becoming by daylight, and which most becoming by candlelight. After a considerable deliberation, she selects one or two dresses of whatever colour she may want. She is then asked if she will walk into the other rooms, which are as magnificent as the first; in these are displayed shawls and mantles of the first style of fashion, and of the most expensive material. In another apartment are laces and linens of every kind. The visitor is still accompanied by the French lady in short sleeves and long ribbons, bowing as before. As they walk through the showrooms, the lady is generally tempted by the superior style or work of the articles displayed there to order a great many things that she wants, and a great many that she does not want. In these large houses there are two or three gentlemen kept as clerks, who attend to the books, and occasionally assist in the showroom. They leave at seven in the evening. When the lady visitor has been bowed out to her carriage, and has driven off from the establishment, the showroom-woman measures off a certain quantity of silk or velvet (whichever it may be), sends for the first hand dressmaker, and gives her the order to make the dress. After this, as soon as convenient to the lady, the first hand goes to take her measure. For this purpose a one-horse Brougham, with a servant in livery, is brought to the door, and the first hand goes in it to measure the lady for her dress. When she returns she gives it out to another first hand, who takes it up into the work-room and cuts it out. The work-room is nearly as large as the first show-room, with a fireplace at each end. Three large deal tables run down the middle, with a gas-pipe over them, and there are as many chairs as the room will hold, all filled with young ladies working at the tables. These young ladies are generally short. If there is a tall one amongst them she is usually an 'improver,' and has grown up before she learned her business. Very few of them can be called pretty, for if their features are well formed, they are so thin and pale-looking that their appearance is not very prepossessing. The first hand comes in with the dress, and throws it down on the first table she comes to. The young ladies look up to see what is the matter. At last one ventures to ask, 'Who is it for?' 'Oh,' the first hand answers, 'it's for Lady or Mrs. So-and-so, and she wants it to-morrow morning.' 'To-morrow morning,' cry half-a-dozen voices, 'how is it possible, when we have so many other dresses to do? Why, she has kept us up three nights this week already.' 'Well, it's of no use,' replies the first hand, 'she must have it; so we must all sit up to-night again.'

"Shortly afterwards one of the porters comes to the door, and says, 'Please Miss —— have you got any skirts? Mrs. ——'s boy has called to know if you have any.' 'Yes, wait a minute, I have one,' and gives him the skirt of the dress. He takes it down, and in an obscure corner of the hall stands Mrs. ——'s boy, a ragged dirty little creature, about seven years old. 'Here,' says the porter, 'take this to your mother, and tell her if she doesn't get it done by nine o'clock to-morrow morning she will get no more work from this house.' 'I shall be sure to tell her, sir,' the boy replies, taking the skirt. He goes his way with the magnificent Genoa velvet under his arm, and walks slowly along until he comes to a dirty narrow street, in the neighbourhood of Carnaby Market, Golden-square. He stops at a house, pushes open the door, for it has no fastening, and mounts to the top of the house. On the landing-place there are washing-tubs and slop-pails full of dirty water, saucepans, frying-pans, and old stumps of brooms. He makes his way through these with the 'velvet skirt,' and enters a room to the left; there being four families living on this story. The garret he enters is a sort of triangular-shaped room, about twelve feet square; the window is near the ceiling. In one corner of the apartment there is a small skeleton stove; in the opposite corner stands an old broken bedstead, and in one an old rickety chair. In the middle of the room is a deal table, and around this are seated seven women, dirty, thinly clad, with pale and hollow countenances, weak red-looking eyes, and lean emaciated frames. The one working at the head of the table is Mrs. ——, the boy's mother. Her husband is dead; she is about the middle age. She rises and takes the skirt from the boy, and demands of him when it is wanted. He answers that it is to go home at nine. 'Nine in the morning!' she exclaims. 'Why I have got six from the City to go home at eight.' 'How do you know,' inquires one of the workpeople, 'that it is the lady's fault? I dare say the lady who this dress is for knows nothing about how it is made. She pays a very high price to the French people whom you have it from.'

"I must now return to the work-room at the dressmaker's where the bodies and sleeves of the lady's dresses are made. A few minutes after the porter goes away with the skirt a bell rings, on hearing which the first hand gets up to go down to tea, and all the others follow her. All who are employed in the house take their meals together. In the class of houses I speak of there is a superintendent at the head of the table, and in others the mistress of the establishment serves at the meals. When there is a superintendent, the mistress does not appear. The tea consists of bread and butter and tea of very good quality, and all can have as much as they wish. After tea they go up to work again until ten o'clock, when they go down to supper, and partake of cold meat, cheese, and table ale. They then go up to work again, and work probably until four the next morning. Perhaps one of them may faint, and ask if she may leave off and go to bed, as she feels too ill to continue working. The first hand says that it is quite impossible, as, if she did allow her to go to bed, the work could not be done. So the poor creature sits down to work again. At four in the morning they leave off, and retire to rest. The first hand has a small room to herself, very nicely furnished. The room in which the young ladies sleep is at the top of the house—about fifty feet long and forty wide, but no carpet on the floor, and neither drawers nor wardrobes. The young people keep their things in the boxes they bring with them. There are two or three dressing-tables with looking-glasses and a few chairs. There are eight beds in it, and two sleep in each bed. At half-past seven the young ladies are obliged to assemble to breakfast. They have tea and bread and butter of very good quality, and as much as they wish to eat. They go up to the workroom at eight; and at ten the lady's dress is finished. The first hand tries it on one of the young ladies, and looks it well all over to see that there is no fault. It is then packed up in a wicker basket lined with oilskin, and one of the porters (of whom there are generally four or five kept in the large houses) is called up, and the dress is given him to take home. The brougham is then called out, and the first-hand, who went to take the measure, goes again to try on the dress. Perhaps the customer is not easy to please, and requires all sorts of needless alterations, in which case the dress is altered, and, of course, will not do then— having fitted before. It is sometimes altered again and again, until it is comparatively spoiled. In some cases, to my knowledge, dresses are not altered at all, but are kept a day or two, and then sent back, when they are frequently found to fit beautifully. At one, the young ladies dine on roast or boiled meat, with bread and potatoes; the meat is of the best kind.

"In a large house they keep five or six showroom-women, six or seven first hands, and from fifteen to twenty young people as second and third hands. The first hands have from £40 to £100 a-year, and the others from £12 to £20, and their board and lodging. Besides these, they employ in the season from sixty to eighty day-workers. These large and very fashionable houses seldom take more than four apprentices and two or three improvers, as they do not take them for the sake of the premium, like others. In some of the large houses there are eight or ten domestic servants."

I shall now add first the opinion of a highly-respectable lady, who had herself been an employer, and then the statements of the several classes of workwomen themselves concerning their earnings and condition:—

"They are generally considered too dressy," she said, "and I think they are so; but it must be recollected that they can only indulge in their finery one day in the week, namely, Sunday. Then, certainly, their stiff skirts outdo our very customers, whom they rub against at church. I am sorry for this, because censorious people, who may not know the earnings of some of these young people, *will* be censorious about it. But then, again, they are so constantly among dresses, and hear so much about dress, that we can hardly wonder they think more of that than of anything else. There are many of them, I am sure, who would not go to church if they were not handsomely dressed. I think the plainer-looking girls are the dressiest, and dress in the worst taste."

From a first hand in one of the best houses I had the following statement:—

"I have been five or six years a first hand in dressmaking in different houses. In my recollection there has been an improvement in the treatment of young women in the superior houses. The hours are not so long as they were, and more time is given for meals, and far better meals. I cannot say that the sleeping rooms are better ventilated than they were, but they are less crowded. Where there might be eight, there are now six. I attribute this improvement a good deal to the Association. I have nothing to do with it myself, so I speak impartially. In a bad case, the manager will call on the proprietor and expostulate, or, perhaps, some member of the committee will call, and that has a great effect. The prices and profits of the business are not what they were. I have known great shabbiness practised by great people, even on a wedding occasion; and yet they wanted everything in the best style. I have waited upon very many ladies, and have generally, but not always, been politely treated; but some ladies, both young and old and middle aged, are so very hard to please about dress, that it is very trying to the temper. I had £35, board and lodging, the first year I was a first hand, and £40 the second. I have never had less than £40. Many working dressmakers, and more milliners with good earnings, might save money than do so. I can hardly tell how some spend it, when they are so little out."

A *second hand*, a milliner, gave me a similar account as to better hours, &c. She was the daughter of a small tradesman, and had been apprentice and assistant before she was second hand. "I have more trouble," she said, "in teaching the improvers than the apprentices, especially the improvers from the country, who have not been well taught there—it is so difficult to get them out of their country ways. Some of them are intended for ladies' maids, and have friends in town who are pretty well off, and perhaps they have paid a premium, and so they are hard to manage. They will give themselves airs. I have known improvers, I dare say twenty at least, who used to work longer hours in country towns, such as Bath, than they did in London, except on particular occasions. I think few milliners save money. They are better paid than dressmakers, perhaps by one-sixth. Last season, really good milliners were not to be had in sufficient numbers. I have £24 a year, with board and lodging, and shall have an advance next season. Sundays I spend at home, but a dinner is provided in the house, though it is seldom any one is there to eat it. We all go to our friends."

From an *improver* and an *apprentice*, both in superior houses, I had statements of sufficient kind treatment and good meals, with fair hours of labour generally. The improver, who was from the country, and had paid a premium of £15 for two years' "improvement," had merely board and lodging. The apprentice, with whom a premium of £25 was given for three years, had also board and lodging.

A day-worker stated to me that her business was greatly affected by the system of taking improvers, as they did the work for nothing beyond board and lodging, which must otherwise be paid for. As much as 1s. 6d. a day and her tea is sometimes given to the day-worker, but this is a rare occurrence. The usual payment under the best employers is 1s. a day and tea. The hours are from eight to eight, or nine to eight—indeed the hours vary—but the day-workers at least *expect*, if they do not always *receive*, overpay for overhours. One young woman, a day-worker, who lived with her mother, a poor widow, told me that she earned 7s. a week eight or nine months of the year, and not 1s. 6d. a week the three or four months she was not at her usual day-work. "There are," she said, "several respectable tradesmen who get daywork for their daughters, and who like that way of employing them better than in situations as assistants, because their girls then sleep at home, and earn nice pocket-money or dress-money by day work. That, again, is a disadvantage to a young person like me who depends on her needle for her living. The most of our day-workers are from twenty to thirty, some from fifteen to twenty, and a few between thirty and forty; but I know of no old woman who is a day-worker in the superior trade. You must be quick and have good sight. You never, or very seldom, see a milliner or dressmaker wear glasses, unless she's quite young and does it to preserve her sight, or because she thinks she looks better in them, or unless she's a first hand and is independent and doesn't care. I have gone from my work to my mother's at all hours of the night, as I always endeavour to work overhours if I can, and I never was insulted in the streets. I have heard, and a very good thing it is, that if any young person is insulted by any bad drunken fellow in the street, the police-inspectors, if she tells them she is a dressmaker going home from her work, and they are satisfied she is so, are instructed to call a cab and send her home in it, and the Association pays the expense."—[I ascertained that this was the case].

Concerning late hours I had the following statement from a trustworthy source:—

"I was *second hand* at Mrs. ——'s. I had £20 a year, or at that rate for as long as I stayed, and board and lodging. In the busy time I worked, and so did six others of us, to twelve at night, and then had to get up again at four the next morning, and work again till twelve. This happened four times a week, or eight or nine times in the season, as nearly as I can recollect. We had only ten minutes or a quarter of an hour allowed for any meal—even for dinner. The rest of the time was spent at work. I have dozed over my work and have wakened from a sort of dream with a start, and have felt quite cold, though the room was hot from the gas lights. If I complained, or if any of the others complained, we were told 'Oh, it's only for an occasion; it's a sudden order, and we can't get hands in a moment;' but the sudden orders came very often. My health suffered very much. My back ached from long sitting, I had flying and severe pains in my chest and sick headaches, and no appetite. I have sat working for twenty hours two or three or four days in a week. When business was slack we worked from eight to eight, or nine; or from nine to eight, or seven, or six. In the busy time six hands certainly did work enough for nine. We cannot, even if we wished, put in inferior work, for we are told often enough that ladies are good judges of work, and their maids are better, and good work they must have. It can only be the wish to make money by any means that makes employers over-work young persons. Improvers work the same hours; but apprentices don't. They are too young. It would kill them. I have often walked home, about a mile and a half off, on a Saturday night at twelve o'clock; we never work later, nor on Sundays, and I could hardly walk so far. It was only over-work that I suffered from. Often on a Sunday I could not eat the nice dinner at home, though I went home only once a week, and my mother got alarmed, and the doctor said I must either give up my place or go into a consumption. The dread of such a thing is shocking. So I gave up my situation, and have enjoyed some rest and country air, and now I am quite well."

Concerning diet, also, I was informed in several quarters that there was a great improvement within these four or five years, but that there are still many instances of very insufficient diet being given.

The Dressmaker's Workroom, at the West-end of London

From a dressmaker, filling a responsible situation in a fashionable house I had the following statement:—

"The quality of the meat we have is good, but the quantity is sadly deficient. I have sometimes to send out for a mutton chop and get the cook to dress it, in addition to my dinner, though my appetite is delicate. This is always the case if I have to carve, as I have sometimes, for really I feel for the young persons who are so poorly fed, and I leave hardly a bit for myself. For breakfast we have poor tea (I sometimes put some of my own in the pot to make it palatable), and bread and butter, and not enough of either. For dinner, at one, nineteen of us will sit down to dine off a leg or a shoulder of mutton that weighed 7, or 8, or 9 lbs. before it was put down to be roasted; for we have roast meat oftener than boiled. I don't know what it loses in cooking. If it's pork, however, that is generally boiled. Along with it we have vegetables in quite insufficient quantities, when vegetables are cheaper than potatoes, and potatoes when they are cheaper than vegetables. For pudding, or with the joint if we choose, we have plain boiled rice—nothing with it. The mistress is generally present and pretends to make her dinner with us, eating the least of all, and leaving a little in her plate, and always saying what beautiful meat it is. Sometimes, but very seldom, it has been tainted; but that was the butcher's fault, or the cook's. I have really felt for hearty girls coming from the country. They look on the little joint and the number at table, quite frightened. In time they lose their appetites. I have known girls with good appetites spend almost their whole salaries in buying little things that they could eat, and say that they must do it or be famished. Tea is the same as breakfast. For supper we have each a small slice of bread and a small bit of cheese—the two may cost a halfpenny—and a glass of table beer. I can't eat cheese, so I may eat dry bread. The beer is very good when it's fresh, but it gets partly or quite sour before we've got through the barrel; but we must drink it through before another can be bought. There is a dinner on Sunday, but only odds and ends, to deter anybody from having a Sunday's dinner, for we are asked every Saturday night if any one dines at home on Sunday. In our house nearly all are improvers or apprentices, which makes bad diet worse, when such young girls have to put up with it."

It is not so often the custom now as it was eight or nine years ago, I am informed, for the dressmaking houses not to provide a Sunday's dinner. Those who are mean enough to wish to escape the cost make it a disagreeable meal, rather than refuse it. "It is only very lately, however, within these six or eight months," said a married lady to me, "that a first-rate house I was connected with had no Sunday dinners. The country improvers and apprentices, if they have no friends in town, must pass the day as they best could. I have seen two of them sitting in the park on a Sunday afternoon, and as they were smart and good-looking you may be sure, sir, there were gentlemen to accost them. The principals took no interest in what they did. The girls had no comfort at home, and wandered in the streets or the park."

Day-workers were unknown as a systematic part of the business of dressmaking until the latter part of the year 1844. As this mode of employment was called into existence by the exertions of the "Association for the Aid and Benefit of Dressmakers and Milliners," before alluded to, it is necessary that I should give an account of the institution.

In 1841, Parliament instituted the "Children's Employment Commission," for which a mass of evidence, showing the then state of the "London dressmakers and milliners," was collected by Mr. R. D. Grainger. The evils of long hours, insufficient food, and ill-ventilated working and sleeping apartments, which were then exposed, called public attention to the matter, and the society in question was established in March 1843, chiefly through the exertions of a committee of ladies. The objects of the Association are:—

"1. To induce the principals of dressmaking and millinery establishments to limit the hours of actual work to 12 per diem, and to abolish working on Sundays. 2. To promote improved ventilation. 3. To aid in obviating the evils connected with the present system, by inducing ladies to allow sufficient time for the execution of orders. 4. To afford pecuniary assistance to deserving young persons in temporary distress. 5. To afford to such young persons as require it early and effective medical advice, change of air, and other assistance in sickness."

The report for the year ending March 25, 1850, says:—

"When the effort to reduce the inordinate hours of work formerly prevailing in the dressmaking and millinery business was first made by this Association, it was immediately perceived that the only effectual method of securing this object, without injuriously interfering with the occupation itself, would be to introduce a system of registration, by means of which it was confidently anticipated that any presumed necessity for overtaxing the powers of the young women, especially during the busy season of the year, would be entirely obviated, inasmuch as the principals, by applying at the office, might, without delay, be provided with any number of extra assistants, according to the emergency. That this expectation was well founded has been amply confirmed by the experience of several years. The number of young persons registered in the books of the Association has, until last year, steadily continued to increase. The numbers registered by the Association in the year 1844 was 309; 1845, 899; 1846, 930; 1847, 1,217; 1848, 1,273; 1849, 1,331; 1850, 1,161: Total, 7,120. In the last year, no less than 1,161 young persons have been registered at the office free of cost, of whom 488 were provided with permanent situations; the remainder being, for the most part, employed as 'day-workers.' It is a circumstance highly creditable to the character of these young women, and at the same time illustrative of the judicious superintendence of the manager, Miss Newton, that in no single instance has any complaint been made by principals of misconduct on the part of those recommended through the office."

A strict inquiry is made into the characters of all who apply to have their names registered; the manager addressing the following queries to the applicant's last employer:—

"How long was M———— in your employ? In what capacity? Was she quick in her work? Was she neat in her work? What work does she most excel in? Was her general conduct to your satisfaction? How long is it since she left you? Do you consider her capable of undertaking the situation of a ———" [milliner or dressmaker, as the case may be].

If the applicant to the Association seek to be registered as a day-worker, the same inquiries are addressed to her last employer, with the addition, "Do you consider I may recommend her as a day-worker to dressmakers?" In the millinery department of the business, I may add, the system of day-workers is unknown—it is confined to dressmaking.

The young women who place their names on the books of the Association are not subjected to any cost, while a Provident Fund forms a part of the provisions of the institution, and any dressmaker who chooses to pay 5s. is entitled to advice and medicine, from eminent physicians and surgeons, employed and paid by the society, the remuneration of those gentlemen being all but nominal.

In my next letter I purpose dealing with the slop part of the milliners' trade.

The Morning Chronicle, Wednesday, October 30, 1850.

LEICESTER-SQUARE SOUP KITCHEN AND HOSPICE.

At a numerous MEETING of the VICE-PRESIDENTS and COMMITTEE, held on the 22d instant,

His Royal Highness the Duke of CAMBRIDGE in the chair,

"It was unanimously resolved, on account of the great distress usually existing among the unemployed poor at this season of the year, that the soup kitchen be re-opened on the 1st of November next, and that a great effort be made to supply food gratuitously to the ragged schools all over the metropolis."

The Committee earnestly invite the attention of the benevolent supporters of this institution to the following account of its operations, feeling assured that the timely relief afforded has not only been the means of removing much suffering and privation, but also of preventing many acts of lawlessness which too frequently attend on unappeased hunger.

They confidently trust, as the funds are exhausted, and their "labour of love" must be re-commenced entirely at their own risk, the friends of the poor will cheerfully and generously assist in lessening their future pecuniary liabilities.

Relieved in the kitchen, with soup and bread, 476,118 persons. Lodged in the Hospice, with supper and breakfast, 16,964. Provisions supplied to eleven ragged schools,* 1,192 quartern loaves, 2,192 gallons of soup. Free registry for domestics, 102 males, 135 females, provided with situations. Free lavatories, cabinets, &c., 227,371 accommodated with a plentiful supply of water, soap, and towels, always at command.

The Committee earnestly request the nobility, gentry, and tradespeople to send to the registry whenever they require servants, as every pains are taken to inquire into their characters. The free registry is open daily, domestics being assisted without any charge whatever.

Donations and subscriptions thankfully received by Messrs. Ransom and Co., No. 1, Pall-mall East; by Messrs. Hatchard, Piccadilly; Mr. Nisbet, Berners-street; and by the Collector, Mr. John Smart, 40, Leicester-square.

* "Feed my lambs."—John xxi. 15.

"It is not the will of your Father which is in heaven, that one of these little ones should perish."—Matthew xviii. 14.

LABOUR AND THE POOR.

◆

THE METROPOLITAN DISTRICTS.

[FROM OUR SPECIAL CORRESPONDENT.]

OF THE LONDON DRESSMAKERS AND MILLINERS.

Letter LXXVI.

Of the twenty thousand "young ladies" working as Milliners and Dressmakers in the metropolis it is difficult to say how many belong to the "honourable" part of the trade—that is to say, to the better paid and better fed portion of it. The only means of arriving at any conclusion on this point is by consulting the registry of that most admirable institution, the Dressmakers' and Milliners' Association. There are upwards of 7,500 names entered on the books of that establishment; of these, 1,500, I am informed, are employed in the country, the remaining 6,000 being engaged by the better class of milliners and dressmakers in London. As the Association supplies "hands" only to the more respectable houses, we may assume that there are upwards of ten thousand young women working for the "dishonourable," or slop part of the trade.

The Milliners and Dressmakers constitute a peculiar class of workpeople—a part of the remuneration for their labour being paid in kind rather than money. Those who are engaged by the year, like domestic servants, not only receive wages, but are generally boarded and lodged in the house of their employers; while the dayworkers, or those who receive a daily salary, are supplied with their tea. Hence it is evident that those establishments which seek to undersell or compete with their neighbours by reducing the price of the labour of their workpeople, may do so as well by supplying them with a less quantity or inferior quality of food, or by providing them with worse lodging than is usual in the trade, as by diminishing the amount of their salary. Moreover they may attain the same end by extending the ordinary hours of labour, and so making a small number of hands do the work of many. Such, I find, are the common expedients resorted to for reducing the ordinary remuneration of the operative milliners and dressmakers. In few houses is the amount of money paid to the workpeople directly reduced—but the young women are either badly fed, badly lodged, or over-worked. These practices, however, I am credibly informed, are much less usual than they were a few years back; an improvement which is mainly, if not wholly, owing to the praiseworthy exertions of the Association.

The employers of the operative dressmakers are divisible into two distinct classes—according as they have or have not the skirts of the dresses made on the premises. The more fashionable houses always put out the skirts, and of these houses there are again two kinds—"first" and "second" rates, as they are usually termed in the trade. A first-rate house is one where Court dresses are made, and which works for the ladies of the nobility rather than the gentry. In a second-rate house, Court dresses are but seldom furnished, the customers belonging to the middle rather than the upper classes. Those houses where the skirts are made at home seldom work for "gentlefolks," but are supported by the wives of tradesmen and mechanics. These are termed third and fourth rate houses, and they are distinguished from one another by the circumstance that in a third-rate "establishment" more silk dresses than cotton ones are made, whereas in the fourth-rate house it is the reverse.

But these constitute what are called the private milliners, where no show is made. Besides these there are the shops in which the goods are displayed and ticketed in the windows. These are divided into the West and East end "show-shops." The first class of these establishments is at the West-end, in Regent-street; the second class in Oxford-street, Edgeware and Tottenham-court Roads; and the third class in Cranbourne-street. At the East-end, the first-class milliner shops are situate on Ludgate-hill and St. Paul's-churchyard; and the second-class in Whitechapel and the Commercial-road. In addition to these, there are, at both ends of the town, a still lower class—the bonnet-shape shops, where ladies can have their own materials made up. Then there are the drapers' shops, most of which have now milliners and dressmakers continually at work on the premises. In the better class of shops in Regent-street and Waterloo-place as many as twenty or thirty hands are constantly employed. The first-rate shops all put out their skirts and mantles, whereas the second-rate, like the inferior private establishments, do a great quantity of this work on the premises. Further there are the cap and drawn-bonnet warehouses, where the articles are produced wholesale, there being now a large export trade carried on in drawn bonnets, a considerable number of which are sent off every year to Canada, Australia, and the British settlements. Then, again, there are the skirt and mantle-makers, or rather middlemen, who take them out by hundreds from the linendrapers; and, lastly, the wardrobe shops, where ladies' old dresses are purchased, and either re-made, or mended, as may be needed.

Such appears to be a full description of the several varieties of employers in the millinery and dressmaking trade. The different classes of operatives I described in my last Letter:—they are first-hands, second-hands, assistants, improvers, apprentices, and day-workers—all of whom, with the exception of those last named, are generally engaged by the year, and boarded and lodged in the house of their employer.

I shall now proceed to give an account of the condition and earnings of such of the classes as still remain undescribed. The first instance I shall give is one that was described to me as follows:—

"The place where the business was carried on was an ordinary-sized brick house. Mrs. —— had the upper part of it. The shop was let off to a business of another kind. She paid £120 per year for her part. She kept only one first-hand (as she attended to the business herself), from six to eight second-hands or assistants, and twenty day-workers. She advertised every year for improvers and apprentices, and took as many as she could get. At the time I was there she had six improvers and five apprentices. She had one female servant and a very small boy (a page), dressed in a tight green suit, with a great many buttons. Two rooms on the first floor, communicating by folding-doors, were fitted up as a show-room. They were furnished with a green and red carpet, of very bright hue, some chairs, a couch, and a large swing looking-glass. A loo table in the middle of the room was covered with a very showy cloth. Several wooden stands were in different parts of the room, with various articles of ladies' wearing apparel upon them. There were three windows in front, ornamented with a gilt pole, to which were attached long white muslin curtains. When a lady calls to order or buy a dress, she is shown into this room by the small boy in buttons, and the first-hand or mistress is called down to wait upon her. In these houses the ladies can find their own materials. The room above that was Mrs. ——'s bed and sitting room. Her three children slept in the back room on the same floor. Mrs. —— often spoke of her husband. She said he was a 'traveller,' but he never came home. On the third floor were the bed-rooms for the 'young ladies.' There were six bedsteads in the front room, and three in the back; there were two dressing-tables, two looking-glasses, and two washstands in the front room, and one in the back. The apprentices had to bring up the water to the bed-rooms and make the beds. In the front kitchen they all had their meals. The clothes of the family were dried and ironed in it, and besides this, the servant slept, and all the cooking was done there. The washing was done in the back kitchen. The workroom was a third room on the first floor; a long narrow room with a very low ceiling, and two small windows; the gas was laid on, and a pipe ran across the room over the table at which the young people sat to work. When the gas was lighted, it was almost impossible to breathe. They began work at eight in the morning, and worked until eleven or twelve at night. This was not always because ladies wanted their things in a hurry, but because Mrs. —— wanted to make as much profit as possible. We all breakfasted together in the kitchen at half-past seven. The mistress did not rise so early. The one servant prepared the breakfast. We each had a mug of very weak tea (about half a pint), and a round of bread and butter. If any ventured to ask for more the servant was so long preparing it, and looked so black, that they became ashamed. Then we worked until one, when we went down to dinner, and the mistress of the house dined with us. There was generally a joint of meat, potatoes, and a pudding (plain suet, or batter, or suet with a few currants in it). The meat was so under-done that it was almost impossible to eat it. On Saturday there was what was called a giblet pie. It was made out of all the odds and ends that were left through the week. Mrs. —— always left a small piece of meat on her plate; she used to say that she thought it very vulgar to eat up every bit; and of course the others did the same. Mrs. —— used to cut a small portion of meat for each, and it was quite understood that no more was to be asked for. After this we then had each a piece of pudding. If any of the young ladies passed their plate for more, Mrs. —— would not refuse, but she would make some remark that would prevent them from doing so again. Occasionally, in going for a reference, they ask what kind of an appetite the young woman has.

"We had tea at five; the same as breakfast; and at ten a little bread and cheese for supper. Mrs. —— was constantly changing her hands; they always went away in a few weeks, from bad health. On Sunday the apprentices mend their clothes, as they have no time in the week. There is no sitting room for the young people in houses like these. In no house are they allowed in the workroom when not at work, and of course they can't go into the kitchen. The only place they have to sit in is the wretched bed rooms at the top of the house. Sometimes on a Sunday, those who had no friends to go home to, and were not obliged to work, would not rise all day, but keep in bed ('To rest themselves' as they said, 'for the next week.') When the mistress was busy we worked all day on Sunday, and two or three nights a week. The first hands in these houses are paid £24 or £26 per year; the others get from £8 to £18 per year. The customers the second-rate dressmakers work for are not so aristocratic and fashionable as the first-rate houses."

The third-rate houses, as I said before, are those that work for the wives of rich tradespeople and the second sort of gentry, professionals, &c. They are very like the second-rate houses, only in a smaller way of business.

I had the following account of a third-rate house in one of the best parts of the suburbs:—

"Mrs. —— was in another way of business, but connected with ladies' dress. Her husband was a humble man working at his business, but Mrs. —— had lofty ideas, and what was earned was not sufficient to keep up her gentility; so she thought she would combine the dress-making with her former business, and she advertised in the newspapers for apprentices and improvers, stating the extraordinary comforts they would have at her house. Although she had then only a small parlour, her advertisement was answered by people in a distant part of the country, who were tempted by the lowness of her terms, and she got four apprentices at £20 premium each, and three improvers at £10; so that she received £110, and with that she took the other part of the house, and furnished it. She then had home the apprentices and improvers. There were but four rooms in the house, and she made the most of them. The parlour in which she had been accustomed to live she made the dining-room, and a small room over that, at the back of the house, was converted into the work room; and over that was the bed room, in which the young people were to sleep. Mrs. —— had a large family, and in this room slept her six daughters—the four apprentices, the three improvers, and the first-hand, who has to teach them—Mrs. —— and none of her family knowing anything of the business. The other room was that of Mr. and Mrs. ——. She engaged a person as first-hand, and got a very good business. As the apprentices and improvers leave her she gets others, and makes quite a living by the premiums she gets; and if their parents complain that they have not learnt anything, she says that it was owing to their stupidity. The first-hand she had died not very long ago, and she sent to the Association for one, and she was referred to a young lady who was going to leave the situation she was in. I had better let her tell the story herself, as I heard it.

"Mrs. —— came to Mrs. —— where I was living, and I agreed to go for £18 a year. Mrs. —— went up stairs to give her my reference, and Mrs. —— said, 'I am quite satisfied, but I am afraid she does not look strong, and I am pestered out of my life by all my young people going home ill.' Mrs. —— said I could but try, and I did try. I promised to go on the following Monday. I arrived there about nine in the evening. I had been occupied all day, and had had nothing to eat since breakfast. Mrs. —— met me at the door of her shop, and took me up stairs to the work-room. 'Do you want any supper?' she said, 'we have all done.' It was asked in such a tone that it was impossible to say yes—so I went faint and weary to bed that night. I never saw such a desolate-looking place. There was not the sign of a smile on one of their countenances. The bed-room was deplorable. Six or seven old ricketty bedsteads, and one washstand, with two dirty broken basins. When we got up in the morning there was such pulling and dragging of one another to get at the basins; and at last it came to a fight. Mrs. —— and the Misses —— (her daughters), and the Masters —— and Mr. ——, all had a secret breakfast, and then she rang for us. When we went in they were all seated, as if they had not had anything. The breakfast was deplorable. The tea was scarcely coloured, and was sweetened with a small portion of the coarsest brown sugar, without milk. The bread was as hard as if it had been a week old; it was all cut ready for us with the least scrape of rancid butter on it. I could not eat the bread, and felt quite ill from want. I had to go out to try on a lady's dress after breakfast; so I bought myself a bun, or I should have been starved. At dinner there was a joint of meat and a plain pudding. Mr. —— carved, and he cut two bits of meat as thin as a wafer, and put them on each plate; and if any of us asked for more, Mrs. —— would say to one of her daughters, 'Do you want any more, love?' 'Oh no, mama,' would be the certain answer, 'I have had quite sufficient!' After this anybody was, of course, afraid to ask for a fresh supply. We then each had a piece of pudding. They never allowed bread at dinner, and the potatoes were of the worst kind. At five we had tea, the same as breakfast; and supper at half-past nine—a very small piece of Dutch cheese about an inch square, and a quarter of a round of bread. I did not go into work after supper, but went to the door to see if I could get a breath of air; when I heard Mrs. ——'s voice like a fury all over the house calling my name. I went to her, and she said, 'Why have you not gone to work again? this is no time to leave off.' I said, 'That I thought as it was not in the season, I need not work late.' 'And do you suppose,' she answered, 'that I am going to keep you and pay you for nothing?' We worked every night until twelve or one. The ladies were pleased with the things made for them, and told Mrs. —— so; and consequently she was very anxious for me to stay, and let me into the secret of her private dinners and breakfasts, and said I might join them if I would stay, and keep the secret from the others. But I could not stay. I never was so wretched in my life. The apprentices could not complain to their friends, as they were all from a long way off in the country."

This account applies equally well to many a third-rate house in town.

Of the *day workers* for such houses as those described I had the following account:—

"They are not considered so genteel as the others. I cannot tell why, but the others look down upon them. They work fifteen or sixteen hours a day, and their pay is nine shillings a week, that is, if they understand their business perfectly; otherwise they do not get so much. They are only employed for about three months in the summer, and three in the winter; this makes an average of 4s. 6d. a week for their earnings throughout the year, and that to provide food, fire, pay house-rent, shoes, stockings, dresses, bonnets, shawls, under-clothing, and washing; but they do not, and cannot, provide all these things with so little—it is impossible. What can they do? They sink into sin and misery for the common necessaries of life."

"There is," said one of my informants, "another class of dress-makers in London. They make for the wives and daughters of trades-people, and do the work very cheap. They employ a great many hands, from eight to ten usually, but some have as many as fifty. The most they ever pay their workpeople is from 3s. to 5s. a week. These em-ployers seldom have more than one or two rooms. I have seen a whole family—husband, wife, and three children—live in one room; sleep, cook, wash, and everything, and have ten day-workers come at nine every morning to work. There is usually a large table at the window, at which they sit to work; and at the other side of the room the family take their meals. The workpeople do not have any meals in the house.

They breakfast before they come in the morning, and go home to their dinner at one, and to their tea at five. In the morning the man and children get washed and dressed before the workpeople come, and they do not retire to rest until they are gone in the evening."

A numerous class of underpaid dressmakers (for as dressmaking it is classed) are the makers of the cloaks, or out-of-door garb of ladies, worn over their in-door attire. Whatever name fashion may give to these garments, they are known in the trade as "mantles." In the drapery shops, which are also millinery shops, at the West-end, the mantles are sometimes made on the premises. In many cases, after the demand for summer fashions has ceased, "the work girls," as a lady connected with the trade expressed it to me, "go to the mantles; for the mantle season sets in at the end of August, or the beginning of September." Of this trade, I had the following account, as regards fashionable, or semi-fashionable, establishments:—

"There is a business now carried on in London that was not thought of twenty-one or twenty-two years ago—the 'mantle making.' Silk, velvet, and cloth, are tortured into the most grotesque shapes imaginable. Some of these are styled the 'Polka,' the 'Corsair,' the 'Chesterfield,' the 'Russian Bear,' the 'Shaftesbury,' and a hundred other such unmeaning titles. We see a lady walking in a cloth mantle, with a peak behind and two peaks in front, and one for each shoulder. This is the last and most fashionable pattern. They are called 'mantles,' but they are as unlike such things as they can possibly be. Two or three of the first-rate houses in the drapery, shawl, and mantle line, send to Paris for the most fashionable patterns, and all the rest of London depend upon them. The parties employed by these houses, anxious to increase their business, when they get the new patterns to make up, go round to all the other houses and show their patterns. These houses give them a few to make to get the patterns, and then they set their own mantle-makers to make some in the same shape. Nearly all the drapers in London sell mantles. The highest employ young people on the premises to make them. There are some West-end houses who, when their young people are not sufficiently employed for their own establishments, supply the City warehouses. All the drapers employ mantle-makers, find the material, and give it to be made at extraordinarily low prices. At the West-end they paid, for a full-sized velvet mantle, lined all through with silk, very neatly quilted, trimmed with three rows of lace trimming, 4s. last year; and 3s., or any price, is paid this year, for the price given is not uniform. Some drapers, fancying that the mantle-makers got more material than was necessary, now employ a tailor on the premises to cut out all the mantles before they're given out to the makers. Others give out the stuff whatever it may be, and the mantle-makers cut them out themselves. Notwithstanding the small sums paid for making mantles, there is a great deal of money made out of them. One man takes the mantles at the prices I have named, smaller sums being given in proportion for less work. He takes them, too, in hundreds from the City warehouses at half the price. Yet he has made a fortune by it. He employs hundreds of young women, and pays them from 3s. to 7s. per week. Others make a fortune in this way by it—they take out mantles, but do not have them made up, giving them out to other parties, receiving a profit out of them. There is a Mrs. ——, at the East-end, who keeps a house and several people only to give out mantles, and they are given to those who offer to do them at the lowest price. In some cases they are given out from one middle hand to another, until they come to be made—for ladies' wear, too—by the very poorest people, sometimes not by good characters, and in the most dirty and obscure streets about Whitechapel, Shoreditch, and the Minories. Even the very lowest employ hands, and they all work together in wretched rooms, like the shirt-makers. The warehouses (continued my informant) in the City are very large establishments, in which they supply not only mantles, but everything that you can imagine. Gentlemen's clothes of every kind, ladies' and children's clothes of every kind—all sorts of fancy goods, mantles, shawls, furs &c. In those there are generally two departments for the mantles—one for silk and velvet, and another for cloth. In each there is a gentleman, who, as the head of the department, has two or three young ladies to attend, for cutting off the cloth, silk, or velvet, and giving it out to the mantle maker. Mr. —— or Mr. —— will get 100 or so to make at once, and they put them out at starvation prices, taking, of course, all responsibility on themselves, as they very well may, when they exact so much from poor women. The people who take these mantles generally live in one or two rooms. They are sometimes poor widows, sometimes the wives of men out of employ. It is not necessary that employers should understand the dressmaking business, as they can always get plenty of people to work for them who do understand it. Out of all those who make money by mantle-making in London, three-fourths are those who do not understand the business. There is a Mrs. ——, in a very large way in the mantle-making. She takes them out from the warehouses, and has them made up for a City house for 5s. a dozen—5d. a-piece—and yet she is making a fortune out of it."

Of mantle-making for the warehouses, more especially those in the City, I had the following statement:—"Hundreds of young women work at mantle-making. The season lasts about three months in the summer, and the same in winter. In the large warehouses in the City they have great quantities made to send into the country and to export. They pay for children's mantles, with quilted silk linings and trimmed with braid, 1s. to 1s. 6d., and from 1s. 9d. to 2s. 6d. for ladies' mantles. Any person who can leave a large deposit in money can get them out from the warehouses. These parties perhaps take 100 at a time. They then give them out to another party, reserving a good profit for themselves. The first party who takes them out does not ask a deposit in money; if they did they would find it difficult to obtain it, as the second parties are never in circumstances to give it. Consequently (as among the slop tailors) they get a housekeeper to give security for them. These second parties often give them out to a third, and sometimes the third even to a fourth, until the mantles pass through three or four different hands, each reserving a profit for themselves. At last the person who can make them (for many of those who take them out are unable to do so) gets them and employs women and girls to make them. Day workers at the mantle business are paid from 3s. to 7s. a week. When they are engaged they are told that their hours are from eight in the morning till nine at night; but they never get away at that time. Some have no clock, and declare it is not nine until eleven or twelve; and others ask them to stay an hour or two to oblige them; so that they generally work fifteen or sixteen hours a day. Many different classes work at this description of work; for any one who can sew a seam can work at mantle making. A great many of the respectable tradespeople allow their daughters to go out to work at this business for pocket-money, and so do the wives of working men, such as are not paid sufficient for their labour to support their wives and families. Then comes the poor young woman who has neither husband nor father, but is forced to drag out a miserable existence upon the few shillings she gets a week. It is surprising how anxiously they try to conceal their poverty, and to appear as well dressed as the others, and to look cheerful when their hearts are heavy, and to work when their hands are burning with fever from want of proper nourishment."

To show the wretched remuneration paid to mantle-makers, and its rapid reduction, I give the following statement from a mantle-maker of the skilled class, who had, in the winter of 1849-50, received from a West-end house the higher rate of remuneration mentioned:—

"I worked," she said, "for a house which does not go to the expense of purchasing the fashionable patterns, but depends upon the few who do send to Paris for them, by giving those who work for the houses having patterns from Paris mantles to make to those patterns. I applied as usual, but was informed that they could get them beautifully made for little better than half what they had been accustomed to pay for them last season, and so I was obliged to take them, as half a loaf is better than none. These houses find no difficulty in getting them done, as those persons who employ a number of young people will take them at any price. If you remonstrate with the draper, and say that it is impossible to do them at the price, the answer is, that you must pay your workpeople accordingly, which is about as much as to say—'Go into the streets, you and all you employ, and make it out that way. What do we care what you do? What is it to us so long as we make money out of you?'"

A very delicate-looking woman, apparently from 30 to 35 years of age, gave me the subjoined statement. She was a widow, but without children, and occupied a room along with another widow who had two little girls. The room was small, but instead of being bare of furniture, as is the case with many working mantle-makers, it had the uncomfortable appearance of a room littered with too much furniture, as what had constituted the furniture of two rooms was crowded into one. Connected with the room was a recess, or small apartment, for a sleeping-room. My informant said:—

"I was brought up to dressmaking, and did good work for West-end houses. I was next a lady's maid, but I married, and my husband's death brought me to poverty, and I now work for my bread with my needle. I am now on mantles for ——, in the City. When I am not on mantles I work at dressmaking, either on my own account—and I have gone out to a day's work at private houses—or for dressmakers, who put out work when they are busy. The prices are greatly fallen. For making silk or muslin dresses, with flounces or with deep tucks, for which seven years ago I had 7s. 6d., I now have 4s. I am very badly off in the dull portions of the year. My rent is 2s. a week, and I may not make at slack time 4s. or 5s. a week. I live chiefly on tea then, which certainly does not make me strong. I am now, as I told you, sir, on mantles, and I can make 12s. to 14s. a week by hard work, as I am a remarkably quick hand, and can make two and a half 'Little Duchesses' a day—but it's a long day, about 14 hours, or 15 or 16 if I don't feel very well. A Little Duchess is the simplest form of a mantle, just four pieces put properly together, back and front. The thread, &c., for a Little Duchess costs about 2d., rather under than otherwise; and it takes four hooks-and-eyes, but they are only 1d. a dozen; so that it's about 2¼d. altogether that I pay for thread, &c. I work both for a wholesale warehouse and a draper. Both pay me alike, but the draper gives me patterns to cut the mantles by, and the warehouseman sometimes requires me to find my own patterns. I sometimes have to buy them at the bazaars. At the Soho Bazaar patterns cost from 1s. 6d. to 3s. 6d. each. They are rather lower at the Pantheon. For lined and quilted mantles I had last winter 2s. 6d., and one is one-and-a-quarter or sometimes one-and-a-half day's work, and the 'thread' [by 'thread' the dressmakers mean all the things they find at their own cost] costs 6d. but this winter it's only 2d. There's no reduction, that I know of, in the charges to the purchaser. Plain work in mantles pays best, you can get on with it so. Ladies' cashmeres, which are lined and quilted, and corded with satin, three or four rows, I have 4s. 6d. for; the thread costs 8d. or 9d., and it's two days' work. The bad prices, and the bad times, sir—but the cheap provisions are really a great blessing after all—are, I am afraid, greatly our own fault. Last winter I was in Mrs. ——'s parlour about work, and a woman there in my hearing offered to make cloaks for 1s. 6d. that I had 2s. 3d. for, and so I lost the work. Perhaps she made it out by wickedness; I'm sure I don't know, but I believe such things are done. It's shocking to think what poor women suffer, and it's no wonder they're driven to the streets. God help them, they're to be pitied."

A young woman, who resided with her mother—who earned 5s. or 6s. a week, or sometimes more, in another line of business, their rent being 1s. 9d.—gave me the following account. Their room was very clean, and very light, as the window was larger than usual for a small apartment; but it may be best described as bare. The walls were cleanly white-washed, and the furniture was three chairs (one without a back), a Pembroke table, an old piece of carpet, about one and a half yard square, and a turn-up bedstead, with a small looking-glass on the top of it. The young woman was not so much unhealthy-looking as listless-looking. She said:—

"I was brought up to dress-making, by helping a relation. Last week and the week before I had 9d. a day for working on mantles with Mrs. ——, and worked from eight in the morning to ten at night, and found myself. That was for her when she was first hand (had the first take). I made only 4s. a week, because there was sometimes a stop in the work, and sometimes only half work in the week. It was for a good shop. I made 2s. at half work. If it wasn't for my mother, God knows what would become of me. I know a young woman who's making only 2s. 6d. a week for a Regent-street house on mantles."

To show at what rate a warehouse will supply the trade, I may mention that a respectable draper showed me a girl's mantle, the mere material of which (two yards of black silk) he, with all the aids of experience and ready money, could not procure for less than 3s. 4d.— and this mantle was purchaseable, made and ready for wear, at 3s. 9d., from the warehouse.

There are no statistical data to guide me to the formation of any correct knowledge as to the numbers employed in mantle, or, as it was formerly called, mantua making. A gentleman acquainted with the drapery trade favoured me with the following statement on the subject of mantle making:—

"I will take 1,000 slop workers—but I say 1,000 merely as the basis of a calculation—as being, at this moment, employed in London in the making of slop mantles. The workwomen for good shops that give them fair, or pretty fair wages, and expect good work, can make six average-sized mantles in a week, working from ten to twelve hours a day. But the slop-workers, by toiling from thirteen to sixteen hours a day, will make *nine* such sized mantles in a week. In a season of twelve weeks 1,000 workers for the slop-houses and warehouses would at this rate make 108,000 mantles, or 36,000 more than workers for the fair trade. Or, to put it in another light, these slop women, by being compelled, in order to eat, to work such over-hours as inflict lasting injury on the health, supplant by their over-work and over-hours the labour of 500 hands, working long hours enough, exercising skill, and receiving but a moderate remuneration."

There is another class of dressmakers who "go out to days' work," not to the trade, except on rare occasions, but to private houses. They make up "ladies' own materials," at the ladies' own abodes, and are employed by tradesmen's wives, and often by the wives and daughters of rich men, who are, or pique themselves on being, economists, and occasionally by the upper servants in a large establishment. These workwomen do not announce their calling either by advertisements, by signs, or by handbills. They sometimes leave cards at the houses in their neighbourhoods. One great source of their employment is, I am told, by "recommendation." "One lady, you see, sir," said a work-woman of the class to me, "is asked by a neighbour to recommend her a respectable young person, who is a good dressmaker; and so the lady recommends me, or some one she knows, and in that way we get a connection." I could not ascertain what proportion of these workwomen were married. One of their body thought they might number from one thousand to 1,500—upwards of a third being married, and pursuing their calling after marriage until, perhaps, the cares of a family prevent their so doing. Their greatest fault, I was told—and that may be the fault of but a portion of their body—was their being somewhat inordinate gossips, regaling any lady for whom they might be working with a recital of the peculiarities in housekeeping, dress, or manners, of any of her neighbours. In this, however, the employer must be more blameworthy than the employed, for the gossiping must be encouraged. The dressmakers in the superior trade speak of these "out-by-the-day" workwomen slightingly enough as regards their skill. "They are always behind the fashion," was said to me, "and some of them have such square cuts that they are enough to spoil any lady's figure." From an experienced person, a day-worker at private houses, I had the following statement:—

"I have gone out to work at dressmaking," she said, "for eight or ten years—ever since I was a girl. I live with my mother, who has been a widow a long time, and keeps a small shop, and lets part of her house furnished. I charge 1s. a day and my meals when I go out to work. I now and then have 1s. 6d. given me for a day's work, but not often. For that I work from eight to eight, or, if there's only half an hour's or an hour's work left at eight, I'm expected to stay and finish it. I seldom get anything extra for overtime. I find nothing but my own needles and my thimble. I have a good connection, and work for some large families. I have worked for ten days and more together for them. I'm sure I can hardly tell how I got my connection together. I was recommended by a kind old lady that knew my family to some of her acquaintances, after I had pleased her in making some mourning for herself, and so one has recommended me to another. I work at nothing but dresses. I carry my patterns with me. I get anything new from a friend in a West-end house, but most of my customers lay down their own notions of fashion to me, from what they've seen at parties, or at church, or from the fashion-books. Many of them are very hard to please, as they want the height of fashion out of the least possible stuff. I was glad when full sleeves went out, on that account. If I work in a small tradesman's house I have my meals with the family, and work in the regular sitting-room—the mistress or some of her daughters, if she has any, assisting me in sewing the skirts and such like. With a little help like this I can make a mousseline-de-laine dress in a day. If it was put out to a cheap dressmaker's it would be charged 3s. 6d. and something for trimmings—from 6d. to 1s., perhaps. A middling establishment might charge 5s., and a first-rate house 10s. 6d., but there's no rule for prices. In some better sort of houses I work with the servants in the area kitchen or in a bed-room, the mistress coming now and then to see how I'm getting on. They are often private houses, the master having offices or places in the City. I then have my meals with the servants, which I don't much like, as they're often rather pert. I often see sad shabbiness, and in those that are best off. I don't mean shabbiness in clothes, for they like to be well dressed, and cheaply dressed, too. There's one widow who has three grown-up daughters, and an upholstress, and I worked for them for nearly a week at a time, she at her line and I at mine, and when I first went, Mrs. —— said, 'Oh, Miss ——, we are teetotallers here.' So I said, 'Very well, ma'am, it don't matter;' but I found afterwards, from the servant, that they were only teetotallers when they had people to work for them. I'm always kindly treated where I'm well known, and one lady gives me 3d. extra to pay an omnibus home when it's bad weather, though it's only a short distance. I suppose I make 5s. a week the year through, or not quite that, besides saving expense in board. I made almost as much from the first. I sometimes carry jobs home with me, and charge them according to time."

I was afterwards informed that the average earnings of this class were not so high as those of the dressmaker who gave me the foregoing account—perhaps 10 or 15 per cent. lower, and sometimes 20 per cent. I was told, moreover, by a traveller for a wholesale drapery house, who is acquainted with the state of the trade in most parts of England, that this custom of going out to work is more common in country towns, villages, and in farm-houses, than it is in London, or in the great cities, where there are such facilities for buying all kinds of millinery, &c., ready made, and that going out to work is more frequent in the suburbs than in the business parts of the metropolis. The same gentleman is of opinion that the number going out to work in London is diminishing yearly, owing to the prevalence of slop mantle and millinery work.

There is yet, if it be possible, a worse remunerated class—the milliners at the East-end and elsewhere, who may be classed as *slop-workers*. They toil in their own bare and cheerless rooms. The staple material of the article they make is given to them (with the exceptions I shall mention) by the tradesmen who deal in those articles, but the workwoman must find her own silk, needles, &c. (found by the employer in all the other grades). She must pay rent, and provide her own fire and candle; every meal she can afford to herself or her family must be paid for out of her own means; she must lose time in going to and fro between her employer's shop and her own garret or second-floor back; she is not a member of any society; she is exposed, in short, to all the evils which the working tailors and tailoresses endure under slop-masters, and with the grievous addition to those evils, that her work is more uncertain and irregular—it is more than the tailors' work, only for the "season," and it is more affected by the caprices of fashion. These workwomen are found chiefly about Shoreditch, Hoxton, the Hackney and Kingsland roads; in Spitalfields; in the Waterloo, Borough, and Walworth roads, and the small streets connected with them; in Lisson-grove, in some of the meaner streets about Golden and Fitzroy squares, and about the Tottenham-court and Edgware roads.

The appearance of the two classes of the "superior" and "inferior" dressmakers is quite as strongly in contrast, or even more strongly, than the regulations which affect their relative positions. The West-end dressmaker (excepting when exposed to long hours or insufficient diet) is smart and dressy—fond of admiration it may be, and so making the most of any personal advantages. The "inferior" dressmaker exhibits few or none of these qualities. She is slow and heavy in her deportment; generally listless, little regardful (one of the fruits of her drudgery and poverty) of her appearance, her dress being usually a dark-coloured and hard-worn stuff or cotton gown, a threadbare shawl sometimes pinned about her, a soiled cap, a bonnet of faded black, and patched half-boots. Continual labour, and often by an inadequate light, has made her eyes dull and weak-looking; and she may be seen walking along with her hands and arms covered by her shawl, to hide, it may be, the absence of gloves. Her Sundays, when not desecrated by toiling for the adornment of the more fortunate of her sex, are usually devoted to rest; some, who are dissenters, supplying an exception; and, as was explained to me by a milliner, the mistress of a small bonnet shop, as a potent reason why Sunday should be spent indoors, "the poor thing has no Sunday dress." Perhaps more than half of these workwomen are married to mechanics or labourers, or are widows. "Many of them must be on the town," said an employer to me, "to work at the rate they do; I dare say they are."

In dressmaking there is less slopwork than in millinery. The gown is generally made to the individual order of the wearer, but bonnets, caps, or collars are made for the "stock," of the shopkeeper, who consequently "speculates" in the sale of those articles, and will speculate as cheaply and as safely as possible, as a change of fashion may, for instance, materially reduce the value of a stock of bonnets. Children's and babies' dresses are, however, among ready-made articles.

In the low-priced millinery trade the workwomen are not only indifferently paid when employed by tradesmen, and the material supplied to them, but they more and more supply their respective articles of millinery as the result of speculation. Widows' caps, cap fronts, dress caps, and fancy collars, are all made more than ever on speculation, as tradesmen now, with rare exceptions, do not supply the material for widows' caps. In the construction of these caps a "goffering" machine is used. This machine now costs about 20s. new, and from 10s. to 15s. second-hand, when little or nothing the worse for wear. It is like a small mangle, the interior (and sometimes the exterior) being made of iron, and by the turning of a handle the fabric to be "goffered" (or "crimped") is passed through the machine, and is goffered accordingly.

My readers will no doubt have noticed announcements in shop-windows of "Widows' cap hands wanted," or "Cap front hands wanted," or some similar intimation. To the uninitiated, the modest looking placard seems to make public the fact that there is employment for a certain number of workwomen, and of course at a regular wage, as their services are in demand. Such, however, is not the case. These "wanteds" are to intimate that the purveyors of caps may carry in their wares, and the placarder may, of course, buy or refuse to buy at his option. "Only do that, sir," said a competitive tradesman to me, "and you'll have a hundred of them in an hour, with all sorts of caps. Where they come from to my place I don't know, haven't a notion—don't know the address of one of them—they're nothing to me. They come with their goods in boxes, and of course I make the best bargain I can with them."

In the not very frequent cases where tradesmen give out the material for widows' caps, the charge is 3½d. to 4½d. per dozen for making. Three dozen may be readily made in a day, with the assistance of the goffering machine, and so slight is the labour of putting the goffered portions (which are the front) and the head part together, that for three dozen the cost of the thread is not 1d. I speak of the commonest kind of caps, of which a workwoman could make more than 36 a day, but that appears to be the average number made. These widows' cap-makers frequently unite with that avocation some other needlework; but as the widows' caps are often their principal employment, they are distinguished as "widows' cap-makers," whatever be their other manufacture. Those employed in making up the materials given out to them by the more respectable houses may make from 7s. to 9s. a week, but more frequently 7s. than 9s.

It is on those who work on speculation that the pressure of distress falls the heaviest. Perhaps one-half of the body of cap-makers do so work. Their lodgings are 1s. 3d. to 1s. 6d. a week for an unfurnished garret, and their principal diet is tea, morning, noon, and night; and that may be said of all classes of underpaid milliners. Among the slop cabinetmakers, as well as among other artisans, coffee, as I have shown, was frequently the principal "dish" (as I heard it called) of the three meals a day, but with female workers it is tea. I am told that the makers of widows' caps may be estimated at 250, or certainly under 300. If each of these made, as they easily can, thirty-six caps a day, and worked but the six working days of the week, their united labour would produce 9,000 widows' caps in a day, 54,000 a week, or 2,808,000 a year. But it must be borne in mind that one of these caps will not wear, on the average, above a week, as if it becomes "crumpled" or soiled, to repair or to clean it, were either process practicable, would cost more than the price of a new cap. Thus, the apparent number of widows is reduced from its alarming sum, as a year of widowhood entails the wearing of 52 caps, by all whose means enable them to do so, and thus a sufficient stock is yearly made in London for the wear of 54,000 widows during the first twelve months of their bereavement. This calculation, however, affords no criterion of the actual number of widows' cap wearers in town, as a quantity is sent to the country.

From a middle-aged woman, working in a decent apartment, but in a very poor neighbourhood, I had the following statement:—

"I was taught widows' cap making when I lived at home with my father, and did very well at it then, as there were fewer in the trade ten or twelve years back. I paid 30s. for being taught, and 30s. for a machine. I generally found my own material, but I have made it up for the shopkeepers. Now I always find material. I got married and began business in the cheap millinery line, but it didn't answer, and now my husband is in a situation, and I have gone back to my old trade. That's three or four years since. My husband has 20s. a week now, but two years or more back, when he was nearly six months with nothing to do, we suffered greatly. We had two young children, and have still, but they were ill then with hooping-cough, and we had nothing but my cap-making to depend upon, and sometimes I was not able to work. Whatever could be pawned was pawned then, and some nice things were lost. I did not clear above 5s. a week all that time, take one week with another, and out of that we must pay 2s. 6d. a week for the rent of two rooms, for we dursn't get into arrears, or we might have been turned out of doors, and we had no friends in London—mine were dead, and my husband is a countryman. That was my season of trial. Widows' cap-making is a poor trade—very poor. The cheapest book-muslin I buy is 4¾d. a yard, and it takes three-quarters of a yard to make a cap, that's threepence-half-penny-half-farthing. The thread's a mere nothing—about a farthing a dozen; but if I make four dozen caps a day, as I have done by working from seven to nine, or half-past nine, the stuff costs me 13s. 3d., or I may get it for 13s., and perhaps I can't get more than 15s. for the four dozen, or 3s. 9d. a dozen, or only 14s., or 3s. 6d. a dozen; 3s. 6d. is a common price, but mine is rather a better cap. I have had to take less than the stuff cost me, and I have had to bring my caps home unsold. I make from 5s. to 6s. a week by cap-making. I suppose I make from sixteen to eighteen dozen every week. How those that depend upon widows' caps live I can't tell—they must have other ways of getting money. I'm not often kept waiting; never at any shop that takes from me regularly; but they are beginning to grumble at my prices. Last week I heard a shopkeeper offer a customer 'a lot of job widows,' as he called them, at 2s. 9d. a dozen. The stuff would cost 3s., at least; and though they were called 'job,' they seemed in good condition enough. I don't know what things will come to. As I have a sort of connection now, I seldom go to a shop that has 'widows'-cap hands wanted'—but

I did go to one, it was so near me, and a new shop, but the shopkeeper pretended that I wanted to take him in at 3s. 9d. a dozen, as he could be served at 3s. 3d. and less. There is such competition among poor needlewomen that they'll work for what gets them only tea and dry bread."

Cap-fronts are also made on speculation, but in a less degree than widows' caps, and they are carried by the makers for sale to the shopkeepers, and to any distance if they hear of cap-front hands being wanted. The variety of forms, fashions, and adornments in caps, as well as the varying price of the material, render it impossible to give any fixed amount as that at which caps are usually sold. They are made for house caps which cover the head, and are worn without the bonnet, or bonnet caps (cap fronts as they are generally called), which are worn with the bonnet, and cover only the front part of the head. It is on these cap-fronts that the slop cap-makers are employed more than on other kinds. They are made for common wear of tulle or of blonde. Tulle varies in price from 2½d. to 10d. a yard. The best blonde used by the slop-workers is 1¼d. a yard; the inferior is three-farthings. In addition to this varying price in the material, the cap may be with or without ribbons, with or without flowers, and with or without bugles—though bugles, I learned, are now out of fashion and considered vulgar even by the poorest wearers of caps. When a cap has the addition of ribbons, &c., it is said to be "trimmed;" when without ribbons or other ornaments it is "plain." Perhaps an average retail price for a cap-front trimmed is 1s.; for one plain, half that amount.

A pale woman, with a feeble look, whom I found at work making caps, gave me the following account. Her room was a small attic, and its principal furniture was a Waterloo bed, with its decent curtain. There were also two tables, six chairs, a painted chest of drawers, and some other articles of furniture in much greater profusion than is usual in the rooms of the poor. This was accounted for by the husband being a bedstead-maker, and having made the other furniture partly himself, or having bartered bedsteads for it. She said:—

"I got married out of a place where I had saved a few pounds, between four and five years back. My mother was a milliner, working for a cheap shop; so I was taught the use of my needle for cap-making and such like, before I went to service. My husband's earnings won't keep us both. He doesn't clear 12s. a week the year through, at least not more than 12s. at his trade, and no man works harder; but then he works for what they call a slaughter-house. I have 4¼d. per dozen for making these plain fronts. I find nothing but thread, and a penny-worth will make three dozen fronts, which I can make in a day, from seven in the morning to seven or eight at night. I reckon I clear 1s. a day on whatever work I get from Messrs. ———, my present employers. I am not fully employed, but I earn 4s. a week, not less, all the year through. Our rent is 1s. 4d. a week, which is considered cheap for this room, and there is again 1s. 6d. a week for part of a room where my husband works with another man, a chair maker, as there's not room for his work here, and the landlord would object to it. These caps are what we call 'fronts and whiskers.' [The "front" was a ribbon with blonde round it, the "whisker" fully frilled blonde.] I sometimes, when I'm not on for shop, make some on my own account. They used to be called 'lappets.' They are made up plain, because some customers like to trim them themselves; but the trimming's never so well done after the cap's made; but customers such as I mean will half cover them with flowers or ribbons. It takes 2½ yards of blonde to make one of these fronts. At three-farthings a yard, that makes the stuff cost 2d. all but half a farthing; then there's thread and making, there's 2d. say for candles, and a shopkeeper will offer 2s. 6d. a dozen for them, or as low as 2s., which is the price of the stuff. They are not so well made as those I am doing now—nothing like it. I can make half as many again in the time. If a capmaker takes in plain caps a shopkeeper will say, 'They are never asked for now; only trimmed caps.' If we take in 'trimmed,' then he says, 'Plain caps are more wanted; people like to trim them themselves;' all to beat down the prices, and I don't think the public's any cheaper served. My trade would be far better if there wasn't so many respectable young women, living with their parents, who work at it for next to nothing, just for pocket-money, and because it's better than being idle, and they consider themselves too good to go to service, or too delicate to 'make place' (fill a servant's place), and so they earn 3s. or 4s. a week at cap or bonnet making. It buys them clothes perhaps. I live a good deal on tea. My husband has tea, too, three times a day, four days in the week, and sometimes with beef sausages, or a rasher, or a bit of fish with it. Always a meat dinner on Sunday, and a pint of beer, but beer at no other time. Fire at my husband's workplace and here where we live costs 2s. 6d. a week, but he only wants a fire sometimes. I can't work without one, I get so chilled if I do. If my husband fell sick and continued sick two or three weeks, or less, there's only the parish to look to. We make both ends meet as it is, and that's all. If I had any family I don't know what we should do."

There is also a large class employed in bonnet-making; on light bonnets in the spring, and on stronger bonnets in the winter. The material is generally given out to them by the warehouseman or shop-keeper in the slop trade, and is made at the workwoman's own abode. The gauze bonnets are, however, the exception to this arrangement, as they are carried in by the dozen ready-made. The bonnet-makers are now receiving 1s. 6d. and 2s. for silk drawn bonnets, according to the size. Some work on them as low as 1s. 3d. a bonnet, all sizes, but they are accounted inferior workwomen even in the slop-trade. The bonnet-maker finds her own "thread," which costs about 2d., also the "body" of the bonnet, which is made of cane, and costs 2d. or 3d.; and the "top," which costs 2d. when made of willow, and 3d. when of transparent net. A good hand will make two or three bonnets (according to size, &c.) in a day of 16 hours, or from six to ten, which are common hours of labour in this business. To make two a day is an average day's work, and when 2s. each is paid to the maker, her profit, after the payment for the "body," &c., would be 2s. 9d. Were this continued through the week, a bonnet-maker would realise 16s. 6d.; but in many instances she is employed only two days in the week, and in the winter often not at all.

The Morning Chronicle, Saturday, November 2, 1850.

THE LEICESTER-SQUARE SOUP KITCHEN AND HOSPICE.

This institution was yesterday re-opened on behalf of the resident and other unemployed poor. The number of applicants for relief was unusually great, and they appeared to belong to the better class of mechanics and gentlemen's servants. The recipients, however, included two tradesmen, who were known to be recently in comparative prosperity. One hundred gallons of soup, with a proportionate amount of bread, were distributed to the resident poor families and the ragged schools in the neighbourhood. The superintendent states that among the extremely destitute applicants were five girls—mere children—whose condition and career were fearful to contemplate; they were evidently fit objects for a female asylum. The parties seeking nightly shelter at the Hospice are represented to be very well behaved, but wretchedly poor.

LABOUR AND THE POOR.

THE METROPOLITAN DISTRICTS.

[FROM OUR SPECIAL CORRESPONDENT.]

OF THE JOURNEYMEN HATTERS OF LONDON.

Letter LXXVII.

The hat manufactories of London are to be found in the district to the left of the Blackfriars-road (as the bridge is crossed from the Middlesex side), stretching towards and beyond the Southwark-bridge-road to the High-street, Borough, and to Tooley-street. There are, moreover, no inconsiderable number of hat factories in Bermondsey. Hat making is almost entirely confined to the Surrey side of the Thames, and until within the last twenty years, or thereabouts, it was carried on chiefly in Bermondsey. In Bermondsey, however, there are still many large "hatteries;" one of them, the property of a wealthy Quaker firm, ranks among the largest in London, rarely employing, in the slackest seasons, fewer than 90 or 100 men, and sometimes as many as 300, with, of course, a proportionate number of the women who are employed in the trade. Although hat-making has experienced a migration, the tradesmen who supply the hatters with the materials of manufacture are still more thickly congregated in Bermondsey than elsewhere. These tradesmen comprise wool-staplers, hat-furriers, hat-curriers, hat-block makers, hat-druggists, hat-dyers, hat-lining makers, hat-bowstring makers, hat-trimming and buckle makers, hat calico makers, hat-box makers, hat-silk shag makers, and hat-brush makers. These several appellations indicate the character of the business carried on; only two of them require any explanation here.

The *hat furriery* business, as regards beaver skins, is now little more than a twentieth of what it was twelve years ago. The hat furriers remove the fur of the beaver, the hare, or the rabbit from the skin—which, when thus denuded, is called a pelt—and they prepare this fur for the uses of the hatter. An intelligent man calculated that from fifteen to twenty years ago, and for some years preceding, four millions of beavers were killed annually for the supply of the hat-makers of the United Kingdom.

"The earliest notice we find of beaver hats," says an eminent authority, "is an inventory of the effects of Sir John Falstoffe in 1459. Philip Stubbs, in his 'Anatomie of Abuses,' published in 1585, mentions, amongst other varieties, bever hats of 20, 30, and 40 shillings price, being fetched from beyond the seas." In subsequent reigns, and particularly during the Commonwealth, the manufacture of both beaver and felted hats must have arrived at some importance; and not only the quality, but the shape of the hat began to possess an influence in denoting the religious or political bias of the wearer—a characteristic of this article of dress which obtains, to some extent, even at the present day.

"The furs now used for hat making," writes Mr. McCulloch, "are beaver, musquash, otter, nutria, hare, and rabbit; but each of these may be subdivided into twenty different sorts or classes." The nutria, I may observe, is a species of otter. In 1787, the duty on beaver skins (undressed) was 8¼d.; in 1819, 8d.; and in 1844, 8d. on beaver skins from foreign countries, and 2d. from British possessions. The imported nutria skins were, in 1787, charged £27 10s. per cent. duty; in 1819, £20 per cent. duty; in 1844, 1s. per 100 from foreign countries, and 6d. from British possessions. The operative hatters call foreign furs generally "beaver." In 1787, the importation of felt, hair, wool, or beaver hats was prohibited; in 1819, the duty was as high as 10s. 6d. a hat; in 1842, 2s. 6d. a hat, whether from foreign countries or our colonies. The duty in 1844, on hats made of silk, silk shag laid upon felt, linen, or other material, from whatever part imported, was fixed at 3s. 6d. each.

The estimated yearly value of the hat trade (exclusive of straw hats, or cloth caps) has been stated as £3,000,000. "In 1836," says Mr. McCulloch, "53,849 dozen hats were exported, of the real or declared value of £148,282; but in 1841, the exports only amounted to 22,522 dozen, of the value of £81,583; the falling off having been principally in the exports to the West Indies and Brazil."

I was told by practical men that one beaver-skin furnished the "nap" for two hats; and three tradesmen whom I conversed with calculated, without concert, that eight millions of beaver hats were made in the three kingdoms twenty years ago, as the export trade in those hats was then very considerable. Now the importation of beaver skins is, as I have said, but a twentieth of what it was before silk hats came into demand, from twelve to fifteen years ago. The trappers and hunters had more and more difficulty to keep up the supply of beaver skins—those animals being pursued so hotly and continuously that they were exterminated in many of their most accustomed haunts, or retreated before their pursuers further into the interior of the American forests; and as the importation fell off the introduction of a new material became imperative.

The *Hat Currier* prepares the leather lining, which is made of sheep or well-grown lamb's skin. After the wool is removed the pelt is slit into two portions. The surface (to which the wool was attached) is called a skiver, and is dressed for the hat lining; the other division is usually curried as a "chamois," the common wash-leather used in cleaning plate, windows, &c., and is largely hawked.

The first process in the manufacture of silk or velvet hats—for they are identical—is "body-making." Silk and velvet hats are now the great staple of the trade. Calico, made for the purpose of silk hat body making, is steeped in a solution of gum shellac, and wrung whilst wet, after being thoroughly saturated; it is then dried on a frame. The part to form the brim and the "tip" (or crown) is subjected to the same process, the brims and tip being afterwards sewn to the body by women. When thoroughly dried, the body, &c., is put round a block, the desired shape of the hat, the ends being nicely fitted to adhere together by the application of the admixture just described; and the calico thus prepared is "ironed to make it firm." In an inferior silk hat the sewing together of the ends soon becomes apparent. The heated irons used weigh 12 and 14 lb. The application of spirits of wine, or of naphtha, and after that of an oil varnish to the body, completes the "bodymaker's" work—and the hat, in its so far advanced state, then comes into the hands of the *finisher.* The master, or foreman, gives the finisher the quantity of "silk" required. This material is a silk plush, made for the purpose, the surface being that shown in the "nap" of the hat. This silk is cut "on the bias," as that "puts it on the stretch, and it sticks better." It is damped on the under side, and so readily adheres to the prepared body—the adjoining parts of the silk, alike in the body and the brim, being "closed," in a good hat, with the utmost nicety. Any "bump," even the slightest, at this adjoinment, is bad workmanship, and the finisher may be twitted with being "fit for the fowls," or best suited to work for the slop-trade.

After this comes the *shaper's* art. He is considered the most accomplished workman, and, in the language of the trade, "puts the curl in." He forms the brim, to make it assume and retain a graceful curve, by ironing it on blocks, and adjusting it, by his eye, to the shape required. This is the last process, as far as the men's labour is concerned. The irons used by the finishers and shapers weigh about 8 lbs.; they are provided by the employer, and cost about 2d. or 3d. per lb. The women's work is then again called into exercise to affix the linings. These are of silk, of muslin, or of glazed calico, as regards the body or upper part of the hat—and of light or dark coloured, or black patent (glazed) leather attached above the interior of the brim, and coming immediately upon the head of the wearer. The "binding" of the hat and the ribbon round the brim edges is done at the same time by the workwoman. Silk hats came into use, as I have said, upwards of twenty years ago, but they were then very hard, and often unsightly, the body being of willow, instead of as now of calico. The silk (Paris) hats were first introduced at the time I have mentioned, but were then expensive—almost the price of good beaver hats, which were retailed at from 21s. to 24s. The making of the stuff or beaver hats, which were the staple of the trade until 12 years ago, is by another process, and one in some respects so different that old hands, when they could not get employment in "stuff," had almost to re-learn their craft on "silk." This they called being "whimsied." In the making of stuff hats, the body is a substance of *felt*. This felt, for good beaver hats, is made of rabbit's (always called coneys in the trade), or occasionally of hare's fur. It is separated, as far as the separation of the hairs is possible, into what may be best understood as "down," or clean down. This separation is effected by the workman very rapidly passing his bowstring gradually through this fur, and separating it so nicely that no dirt or extraneous matter of any kind be admixed. The bowstring (with its frame) used for this purpose resembles a child's bow on a large scale, and loosely strung. The felt is then worked, I might say kneaded together, by being rolled in cotton cloths. It is then boiled, and is again rolled, or kneaded, by the hands. This rolling is generally an hour and a half's work, and the stuff is this way "shrunk," so that it will not further "shrink" or warp, or lose shape in the wear. The application of the beaver's fur, or of any fur used in constructing the stuff hats, takes place next, the felt having been placed on the block. This "beaver" (as the fur is called) has been "blown" by the hat-maker, to "get the coarse hairs out of it;" and after it has been worked into a sort of pulp, by being rolled in strong hair cloths for an hour and a half or two hours, it is affixed by hand, and with hair cloths, to the hat body—the adhesion being accomplished with gum shellac, spirits of wine, and "turps" (turpentine), applied to the body. The preparation of this "nap" is really that of a fine soft loose felt, and it is so adapted for a "nap." The preparation of "turps," &c., is called a "proof," and the working hatter's labour is facilitated or obstructed by the good or bad quality of the "proof" supplied to him. The beaver hat is the "skilled" manufacture of the trade. Its "body" is formed of one substance, there being no sewing in of the tips or of the brims, as in the manufacture of silk hats. The beaver hat is moreover dyed by the class of tradesmen known as "hat dyers" after it has been made. In silk hats the dyer's work is perfected in the manufacture of the silk plush.

The *plated* hat is an inferior stuff hat—Spanish, Kent, or Shropshire wool being used for the nap, or "plate," instead of beaver's fur. A small number of plated hats are made in London; the manufacture is the most considerable in Lancashire, Cheshire, and Staffordshire.

The number of hatters and hat manufacturers in Great Britain at the time of taking the last census, was 18,012; of these, 16,635 were located in England; 447 resided in Wales; 818 in Scotland, and 82 in the British Isles. Of the whole number employed in Great Britain 14,000 were adult males, while nearly 2,000 were females of twenty years of age and upwards—the remaining 2,000 being young people of both sexes, in the proportion of three boys to one girl. The hatters and hat manufacturers of the metropolis in 1841 were 3,506 in number, of whom 2,600 were males of twenty years of age and upwards, the other 900 being composed of nearly 600 women, and upwards of 300 children. The Government returns do not admit of any comparison being made between these numbers and those of the previous census; for, in the Occupation Abstract of 1831, the hatters are mixed up with the hosiers—the workmen employed in those two trades being lumped together, and computed at 2,662 individuals—while in the Occupation Abstract of 1841, the London hatters are given by themselves as before quoted, and the hosiers are classed with the haberdashers. Nor can we separate the two last mentioned trades, for on referring to the first abstract we find that the haberdashers are there jumbled together with the linen-drapers; so that it is a matter of absolute impossibility to say whether the trade increased or not during the period above referred to. The distribution of hatters throughout England and Wales is as follows:—

England—		Salop	110
Bedford	18	Somerset	112
Berks	49	Southampton	82
Bucks	38	Stafford	710
Cambridge	32	Suffolk	67
Chester	1,811	Surrey	2,139
Cornwall	173	Sussex	52
Cumberland	299	Warwick	450
Derby	329	Westmoreland	28
Devon	215	Wilts	37
Dorset	30	Worcester	86
Durham	132	York, East Riding	114
Essex	38	„ City and Ainstey	33
Gloucester	984	„ North Riding	56
Hereford	37	„ West Riding	488
Hertford	33	Wales—	
Huntingdon	4	Anglesey	22
Kent	194	Brecon	28
Lancaster	5,546	Cardigan	117
Leicester	81	Carmarthen	98
Middlesex	1,330	Carnarvon	43
Monmouth	48	Denbigh	26
Norfolk	111	Flint	9
Northampton	48	Glamorgan	37
Northumberland	201	Merioneth	6
Nottingham	177	Montgomery	26
Oxford	49	Pembroke	30
Rutland	1	Radnor	5

From the above it appears that the greatest number of hatters are resident in Lancashire, after which comes Surrey, then Chester and Middlesex.

The hatters work by the piece, and have done so beyond the memory of the oldest members of the trade. The scale of prices I am enabled to give, through the courtesy of Mr. Holland, the secretary of the Hatters' Society. Their present average earnings are shown in the statements I have collected.

WAGES GIVEN FOR MAKING AND REPAIRING DIFFERENT KINDS OF HATS IN THE METROPOLIS DURING THE UNDER-MENTIONED YEARS.

Years.	For finishing French or English short nap, per doz.	For making gossamer bodies, per doz.	For repairing stuff bodies, per doz.
1824-26 ...	None.	None.	18s.
1834-36 ...	8s., 10s., and 14s.	9s. and 10s.	15s. and 18s.
1844-46 ...	9s., 11s., and 13s.	8s. and 9s.	8s.

The above statement represents the wages paid to society-men only, whose regulations I now subjoin:—

"RESOLUTIONS OF THE JOINT COMMITTEE OF THE STUFF-HATTERS' SOCIETY AND THE SILK-HATTERS' PROTECTIVE UNION, AS SANCTIONED BY A GENERAL CONGRESS OF EACH BODY.

"September, 1846.

"1st. We mutually agree not to work in any shop where the prices are below 9s., 11s., and 13s. per doz. for French or English short-nap silk finishing; 8s. and 9s. per doz. gossamer body-making; and 8s. per doz. for preparing stuff bodies.

"2nd. We mutually agree that in case of a strike by the members of one society, no man belonging to the other shall be allowed to go in, except when the object sought for by the men so striking would be positively injurious to the interest of the members of the other society.

"3rd. We mutually agree by every means in our power to suppress the system of out-door work, believing it to be pregnant with ruin to ourselves, and ultimately to our employers.

"4th. We mutually agree that if any man wishes to be asked for in any shop where there are none of the society employed to which he belongs, and the men of the shop refuse to ask for him, he shall get a man from the nearest shop where his own society men are employed to do so. But such man shall call down the regular short turn of the shop, who may, if he pleases, hear the man asked for, and see that nothing unfair takes place. In shops where both bodies are working, each shall ask for their own men.

"5th. We mutually agree not to stand by more than two apprentices, either in silk or stuff, who shall serve seven years.

"6th. We mutually agree to stand by each other's caulkers for contributions and other trade business.

"7th. We mutually agree not to take any important step affecting the general interests of the trade without first communicating with each other.

"8th. And in order to prevent any serious misunderstanding, and to avoid as much as possible the existence of any ill-feeling between the members of the two societies, we earnestly recommend the members of each not to give credence to idle rumours, but in all cases to apply to the committee, who will give correct information, and see that justice be done if an injury has been sustained.

"Printed by order of the joint committee.

"January, 1846."

The secretary of the Hatters' Society, in a written communication to me, says:—"The prices above-named would no doubt have been maintained if it had not been for the slop-workers, who will work at any price sooner than lose the job; as it is, we have been obliged to give way, particularly in the lower qualities."

These workmen carry on their trade in large rooms, generally well ventilated and commodious, but in some employs dirty, dark, and confined. Each workman has his own "plank," or "bench," as it is called in other trades, for certain stages of his work; but the men, when engaged in working their "proofs," stand round a large tub, or open vat, the "liquor" in it steaming freely. In summer the heat is often excessive, as in so many stages of the manufacture the workmen require fires. The men work in trowsers, flannel shirts, and slippers, or wooden clogs, their arms being bared above the elbows. Notwithstanding the exposure to heat, I am assured that the hatters' is not an unhealthy calling, as their lives are of the average duration, and men of 65 are now working efficiently in the business. These operatives used to drink great quantities of beer when at work—two pots, or even ten pints, a day being a frequent consumption by a man not accounted a "fuddler." There is now a great change in this respect, few drinking more than a pot a day whilst at work. In the larger shops, however, it is still the practice for a new comer to pay his "footing," which in this trade is called "garnish." A workman refusing to join in this conviviality is stigmatised as a "straight stick." A first-rate workman informed me that 18 or 19 years ago he regularly spent 18s. a week in drink, but at that time he earned as much as £4 in a week, and very frequently £3. The same workman told me that at the Wheatsheaf, a public-house near the Borough-market, 20 years back, the hatters used to be "dancing and footing it, and drinking, of course," all the week long, but that now there is nothing of the kind.

In the London houses from 12 to 20 journeymen are more frequently employed in the "fair" trade than any larger or smaller number. The majority of these journeymen, perhaps three-fourths of them, are countrymen, chiefly from Cornwall, Gloucestershire, and Lancashire, with a few Scotchmen, and a very few Irishmen. A great number of hats, principally of the cheaper sorts, used to be sent from the country to London until eleven or twelve years ago, when the substitution of silk hats for stuff put an end to the trade, or nearly so, as the country hat-makers were not sufficiently skilled in the new manufacture. Winterbourne and Hollands Common in Gloucestershire, and Oldham and its neighbouring villages in Lancashire, were places in which were many large hat factories, the trade being now in those localities only a tenth of what it was. "The stuff hands," I was told by a hatter, himself acquainted with the Gloucestershire factories, "went into silk, such as could work on silk and could get work; some emigrated, and some got navvy's work on the railways."

The demand for Paris hats, of which I have spoken, caused a number of hatters—one man said between 200 and 300—to come from France to England; but coarse silk hats were introduced twenty years ago. These men soon became on good terms with the English workmen, and readily instructed them in the Parisian mode of workmanship. There are now about 20 Frenchmen to every 500 Englishmen in the "fair" trade, the Frenchmen being members of "society." I heard of no foreigners in the slop or "foul" trade. The best silk plush is still imported from France; it is manufactured in Paris and Lyons. The "slop," or underpaid hat makers are known as the "foul" trade, in contradistinction to the "fair" or "honourable" trade.

The way in which a hat-maker acquires a knowledge of his craft is by apprenticeship. In the strictest branch of the "fair" trade no man is admitted as a member of "society" who has not served a seven years' apprenticeship; and no master, employing society men, can have more than two apprentices at one time besides the members of his own family whom he may choose "to put to the trade," and they must be regularly "bound." The number of apprentices is not influenced, as in the printers' and some other businesses, by the number of journeymen employed. Whether a master hatter employ one journeyman or 100, he is alike limited to two apprentices. Small as this number of apprenticeships may appear, it ensures a full supply of skilled labourers.

In the "foul" or slop trade, no regulations of the kind I have described exist. The workers in this trade are men who have served no apprenticeship, or who, from drunkenness or other causes, have not kept up their payments to the society, and have ceased to be members of it—or who have left other callings, such as that of weaving, to work as hatters; a course which is facilitated by the silk hat manufacture being a much easier or less skilled process than that of the stuff hat. I was told, indeed, that sweeps and costermongers had "turned foul hatters." These men are somewhat equivalent to the garret masters in the cabinet-making business; but with this distinction, that the hatters do not *complete* the articles of their manufacture as does the slop cabinet maker for the "slaughter-houses;" the "foul" hatter makes only "bodies." They are to be found about Brick-lane, Whitechapel, in Spitalfields, and in Lock's-fields, Walworth. They work in their own rooms—which the operatives in the fair trade never do—and have to find their own irons and material. They are thus "little masters," as they nearly all work on their own account. Sometimes two or three work together in one small garret; for the landlord of the house, wretched as it may be, will sometimes object to their working in any part but a garret, on account of the fire and smoke. Sometimes a man works by himself. "It depends upon the number of planks there is convenience for," I was told; "but it's a saving in firing when more than one works in a room." The calico, gums, &c., for the manufacture of a dozen silk bodies cost 4s. 6d. or 5s. By close application from seven in the morning to ten at night a workman can make a dozen in a day, and for these he may receive 8s., which is about the rate of wages paid for the mere making in the "honourable" trade. The slop-hands work very rapidly, taking little or no pains; they confine their labours solely to the making of silk hat bodies, as the material for the making of a beaver hat is too expensive for their means, and the skill required in its construction has not been attained by them. The bodies when completed are hawked to the trade, and the inferior workman, or "little master" as he may more properly be called, is of course exposed to the evils, delays, and hindrances which I have so often pointed out as inseparable from this mode of business. These bodies are sold to the master hatters, especially the "cutting-shops," who furnish the low-priced hats, best known as the "four-and-nines." They are sometimes finished by workmen on the premises of the purchaser, such workmen receiving a much lower remuneration than is given in the "fair" trade. Some of the bodies produced by this slop labour are, I am assured, "finished for superior work," and sold at good prices.

The "foul" hatters are many of them young men, with a smaller proportion of married men among them than is common, perhaps, among handicraftsmen. When they are married, the wives have usually some slop employment. They very rarely finish a hat, unless when they avail themselves of a practice known in the trade as "malokering." A maloker, frequently a Jew, collects old hats from door to door, and sells them to the dealers in Rosemary-lane. The slop hatter buys them of the dealer at from 1s. 6d. to 5s. a dozen. If any of the silk be tolerably good, he strips it off, and puts it upon a new body, or "congles in" the old body (as the restiffening of it is called) and sells the hat new lined, re-dyed, and "trimmed up," to the dealers in secondhand attire, or hawks it to public houses, sometimes "swopping" it for an old hat and a shilling.

I heard the number of these little masters (who were unknown in the trade ten years ago) computed at 1,000 at the present time, and their earnings at from 10s. to 12s. a week, taking the year's average. Previously to ten years back the little masters in the trade supplied the general public, or worked to order, as "out-door hands," for the greater houses. A man "taking up the trade" has generally to pay for instruction about £2, and to supply three weeks' or a month's labour gratuitously to his instructor. A working hatter told me that in a fortnight's time he could teach a quick lad how to make calico bodies for common silk hats well enough for the slop trade.

The working hatters in the honourable trade generally take some interest in politics, and are for the most part Protectionists, as they think protection would have "kept out the French hats." Indeed, I did not meet with one Free-trader. I did not hear of their being more inclined to one particular amusement than to another, but a game at cards is common with them in the public-house when the day's work is over. They are generally married men, and reside in the neighbourhoods of the hatteries. Some of their wives are employed as hat binders and liners, but none, I am informed, work at slop-work. Among the hatters I found many intelligent men, but as a body they are certainly less advanced in education than some other classes of handicraftsmen. Some of them have saved money.

The hat manufacture is confined to the distinct branches of the body makers, the finishers, the shapers, and the binders and liners— the same woman being both binder and liner. There used to be a close distinction between the "stuff" (or beaver) and the "silk" workers, but it is becoming less and less observed, so many stuff workers having "to go to silk."

From a *stuff body maker* I had the following account:—

"My father was a hatter," he said, "and I was put as an errand boy to a hat dyer, and then I learned that business; but when I was twenty, I got myself apprenticed to a hat maker whom I knew, and who paid me the journeymen's wages, by agreement, with a small deduction for himself. I did very well at this, as I had known the business pretty well before. I did so well, indeed, that I got married during my apprentice-ship. This was in the country, but near London, and I have worked in London thirteen years. I am now a stuff body maker, but can make silk bodies as well. I found it necessary to learn that, since the Paris hats came in, or I might have been out of work oft enough, there are so few beaver hats made now. I now earn 30s. and 32s. a week during the busy time, and not less than 20s. in the slack. The busy time is for six or seven months; but when there's a slack my employer divides the work among us in preference to discharging hands. We like that plan better than a smaller number being kept on at full work. I have two children, and do pretty well on my earnings. If ladies' beavers came into fashion again it would be a great thing for the trade, as, after the gentlemen's summer trade was over, they would come in. I wish they would become fashionable, and in my opinion a handsome lady looks handsomest in a beaver. When beaver bonnets were last in they were so frightfully big that I'm afraid ladies got to dislike them, but the fashion may come round again."

Another stuff body maker, in better employ, averaged 36s. a week; he did average 55s. to 60s. twenty years back.

The earnings of the *finishers* and *shapers* are higher than those of the body-makers, in the proportion of 40s. to 30s., or thereabouts; so that a clever body-maker generally aims at following one or other of those branches. From a shaper I had the following statement:—

"I served my apprenticeship in London, and have been a journeyman, off and on, in town, for twenty-two years. I could earn three guineas a week twenty years ago, and seldom earned less than £2. I saved money then, and might have saved more, but I am well satisfied as it is, and needn't have much fear when a rainy day comes. The trade is not what it was, but I make from 35s. to 40s. still in a busy time, and from 20s. to 25s. or 28s. in a slack. Hatters are an independent set of men still, but they were more so. If a master said a word that wasn't deserved, when I first knew the trade, a journeyman would put on his coat and walk out, and perhaps get work at the next shop. It's different now. The 'fouls' have become more numerous, and we are afraid of letting them into good shops, though I don't know why we should be afraid, for few of them can work well enough. None indeed can work well enough on the best stuff. There used to be far more drinking among hatters when I was a lad. I have known some of them be steady and industrious for the week, and on a Saturday night order 'a bottle of wine in a white bottle' (decanter), just for themselves. A man was almost forced to drink a lot of beer at that time in a workshop, or he would be counted a sneak. Now we do just as we like in that way. I am now a shaper in silk, but I am master of all branches of the business. There has been very little change in the fashion the brims are worn in, during my time. Not in the best work. If you see hats with odd shapes in a shop window, marked 'the slap-up,' or 'the Corinthian,' they're slop-made things generally, and don't take. Working hatters have been greatly affected in the way of their earnings from the French hats. In my opinion they've been reduced in their earnings beyond what good they get from cheap provisions. There's less employ, for one thing—as a man will make three good silk hats, and some will make four, in as short a time as he can make two good stuff hats. But we must just make the best of it."

A *finisher* gave me an account of his earnings, which were about the same as those of the shaper.

The hat-binding and lining is done entirely by women. They have no recognised scale of prices, the societies of the hatters not interfering in any manner with the remuneration of the "trimmers," as these women are usually called in the trade. Of these workwomen, whose numbers I heard calculated at 1,000, perhaps three-fourths are the wives and daughters of journeymen hatters. About a tenth, or more than a tenth, of this body of binders work on the employers' premises, and they are the best-paid of any—receiving about 4s. 6d., where a woman doing "out-door work" (as hat-binding when pursued in her own abode is termed) receives 2s. 6d. The low-priced hat-makers, who supply the cheap warehouses and the "cutting shops," pay very low wages for binding. Some of them give out several dozen hats at a time to one trimmer, at 2s. a dozen or less, and the binder undertakes to "have them in" at a fixed time. In order to be "to time" (or she would lose her work), the first contractor gives out such a quantity as she finds suitable at 1s. 6d. a dozen, and this practice is carried on to a great extent. To bind and line six hats in a day of ten hours' labour, is considered good work in the fair trade. The lining of silk, or of glazed calico, is inserted in the body or upper part of the hat; the leather lining is sewn to the foot of the brim, and the edge of the brim is bound round with ribbon.

From a highly respectable woman, whom I found at work, assisted by one of her daughters, a young girl of 17 or 18, I had the following account of hat binding, which may be taken as a correct statement of the average earnings of the out-door workwomen in the fair trade:—

"I have been a binder," she said, "for twenty years. I was brought up to it by my friends, who were in the line, and soon after I worked for myself I got married. I have worked at it ever since, except when the care of my children prevented me. I married a journeyman hatter.

He is now on three days' work a week, and earns 13s. or 14s., or a little more, in those three days. I think most hat binders marry hatters. I have earned 30s. a week fifteen or eighteen years ago, but now I must work hard indeed to earn 10s. Sometimes, when work is slack, I earn 6s. a week. Out of that I have to provide my own thread, which costs 2d. to 3d. for a dozen hats. Prices for binding have fallen gradually and gradually since the silk hats came in, and there have been more hands brought in or come in as binders. Ten years ago, or rather more, I had 6s. a dozen for binding and lining, where I now have 2s. 6d. or 3s. I once left a shop because I was paid only 4s. and 4s. 6d. a dozen, and now they are done for that shop at 2s. 6d. and 3s.—poor women undersell one another so. They go to the masters and offer to do binding at next to nothing, and so prices have fallen. I generally work ten, and sometimes thirteen hours a day. I believe it's women who have not been regularly brought up to the hat binding that undersell us. I have heard that some of them are on the streets, but I think not any who were brought up among their friends as hat-binders. They would suffer much before that, I'm satisfied. I have 3s. 6d. a dozen for binding these hats (pointing to a heap), which are the largest size; smaller sizes run 2d. or 3d. a dozen less. Most shops have some difference in their prices to trimmers. When silk hats first came in it was very hard work for the fingers—it was like sewing through a piece of board; now it's quite easy in comparison. We are forced to put up with such prices as we can get—even the best hands among us are, and there's a great difference both in neatness and quickness; for if I myself, for instance, refused to take a lower price, there's plenty will jump at it. So we injure one another, and make rich people richer. With our family my husband and I did better when wages was good and work plenty, and bread and meat dearer, than now that bread is cheap and wages and employment fallen off. With what we earn at present we couldn't have clothed and educated our children so decently as we have."

A pale and sickly-looking woman, of 35 or 40, gave me the following account. Her room was decently, but sparely, furnished. There was only a bed, three chairs, a small table, and a tea-tray, with the coloured remains of some bird upon it, over the mantel-shelf. There was no uncleanliness. My informant's statement shows the lower depth of the hat-trimming trade. She said:—

"I was brought up to the hat-trimming, but have suffered so much from ill health that, though I did well when I was younger, 10 or 12 years ago, I always lost my connection, and had to find it again. I did middling somehow, however, until two years back; an aunt helped me sometimes, but she's dead. My parents have been dead these thirteen years. Twelve years ago I earned from 18s. to 22s. a week at hat-trimming; sometimes more, and seldom, perhaps never, less than 18s., for I'm known as a good binder. Now, take the year through, I don't earn more than 5s. a week, perhaps not so much; for though I sometimes make 6s., or 6s. 6d., or even 7s. 6d. a week, some weeks I make only 4s., and for ten days this year I had nothing to do. I shall make 6s. 9d. this week, and as much next, I expect, for work wanted in a hurry. I mean 6s. 9d. over what it cost me for thread, but not for fire and candle. I have been forced to have relief from the parish. I have generally to look out for work and call at the shops or trimmers I think likeliest to have any, and I offer to work very cheap. Not long since I took four dozen to trim at 1s. 6d. and 1s. 8d. a dozen, at second hand, from Mrs. ———. I don't know exactly what she had. I did them all myself by working 18 hours a day. I must live, and I can't live if I ask fair wages, because I can't get them. I'm a very small eater, which is one thing. I live on little besides tea and bread and butter, or dripping in cold weather, when I toast the bread. My rent is 1s. 6d. I sometimes think I'll go into the workhouse, or I shan't live long. My work's uncertain, besides being badly paid. Really I do hope that things are at the worst, but I thought so long before. I can read and write, but don't know any good that's done me. If I was sick I must apply at once to Mr. ———; he's the relieving officer. If bread was any dearer, I should just die out thro' starvation, for I don't suppose I could earn more then, perhaps not so much. I sew tips and brims, as well as trim and bind. I have 1s. a dozen for tips and trims, and can do 15 or 16 in a day. I used to have 1s. 6d. a dozen."

I have already spoken of the little masters. They are divisible under two heads. Some, and for the most part elderly men, are little masters, working for the general public, or rather for a "connection" (though with no shop or even a window for display); and they employ from one to seven hands, or carry on their business by their personal labour, altogether unaided, in the slackest times. In those times they work both on their own account and on speculation; providing their own material, when speculating in their labour, and hawking their manufacture for sale to the lower priced hatmakers, or to the better hatmakers inclined to give a tolerable price—or what they account tolerable—for skilled labour. They speculate principally in silk bodies; some, however, finish the hat. From one of the better class of little masters I had this statement. My informant was an elderly man, residing in a comfortable house, and had known the trade familiarly for many years:—

"I started as a little master," he said, "about 20 years back. I supply the trade with bodies sometimes, and find my own material. Mine is very uncertain work—it's mostly a summer trade. I work for my private customers, or for the trade, on order; and I make bodies to carry out to the trade for sale on speculation. I only do the best work in bodies to carry out. I have earned £3, £3 5s., and £2 18s., when a journeyman at ——'s. If a man didn't earn his £2 a week in those days, he was reckoned not worth his plank room. That's far better than being a little master, as far as money goes, for I consider that one week with another, for all I have a connection, I only make 22s. I mightn't have started for myself, but I fell in with some overbearing masters and foremen. I've had as many as four journeymen working up stairs, and four down stairs, for me in this house; now I've only myself; but the brisk season's over. I get 10s. 6d. a dozen for my bodies, and am oft enough bid 8s. 6d., because bodies can be bought for less than that, but they're rubbish. The stuff costs me 5s. There's Mr. ——, he'll give 8s. a dozen always for the better sort of bodies, and I've gone to him sometimes in a pet, and as a last resource. Though mine are real good bodies, a master or foreman will 'star them' (crush them), pretending to examine their quality, but just to show his power—foremen are worse than masters that way—and I then have to make them over again partly. Out of six dozen I've taken into ——'s, I've had three dozen starred, and had to take them back. It was nothing but to show power. I can make a dozen of my bodies in a day and a half. A young fellow by working very long hours may make a dozen, but they're only fit for the lowest gossamers, the 'four-and-nines.' They're bad work; there's too much water used in them. There's such a difference in trade, that I could keep a wife and five children better nineteen years ago—my youngest is turned 19—than I can keep myself now. I think little masters are increasing. I used to reckon that master hatters got 12s. a hat profit on the best stuff, and that was one thing to tempt me to start for myself; but a little master can't command a trade in the best articles. I reckon there's 2s. profit a hat in silk; but at this part (Walworth), if you walk out, you'll see 500 silks to 20 stuffs. A stuff will wear two silks at least. A four-and-nine can be supplied to a shopkeeper at 3s. 6d."

The other, and by far the most numerous, class of little masters I have already described. From one of the class I received the following account. He was a pale, weak-eyed looking man, with a stoop, as if contracted by leaning over his work. When I saw him he was busy at work in the garret of an old and apparently frail house, the narrow stairs seeming to bend under the tread. The walls of his room had been recently white-washed. A penny sheet almanac was pinned over the fire-place, and was almost illegible from the smoke it was exposed to, "when the wind was in the north," the man said. The furniture was a small bed, covered by a thin but clean rug, on a heavy old frame, a table, two chairs, a stool, a hatter's plank, fitted below the small window, a kettle, a gridiron, and a few pots and pans.

"I was a weaver in the north," he said; "never mind where. I left home in a bit of a scrape, but for nothing dishonest, and so we'll say nothing about that. I was a fool, and that's a fact. I had £9 or £10 to call my own, fairly, and I came to London, as fools often do. I found I could as soon have got work at being a lawyer as at my own trade— so, as I had an acquaintance a hatter, he said to me, 'learn hatting.' I bargained with him, and wish I hadn't. I paid my friend, for learning me a bad trade, two guineas; he wanted £3, and then 50s. It's between three and four years ago, and I worked for him a month for nothing, finding myself. Before my month was up my money ran taper, and I was afeard I shouldn't have enough left to start me, but I had. I took this very room as you see me in, and gave 30s. for the sticks, just as an old cobbler, that died in that very bed, had left them. The landlady took his traps for burying him. She's really a good soul. That was £2 2s. gone; and two hat irons, one 14 lb. and the other 10 lb., cost me 2s. 9d. at a sale. They are old things. Here they are still. But they cost 3d. a pound new. I got twelve blocks at 1s. a-piece second-hand. They cost 4s. to 5s. a-piece new, and they would have been about as cheap new, for they wasn't just in the fashion; two of them in particular, and I paid 2s. a-piece to get them 'turned down' again, and put into the fashionable shape, for you must work fashionable. A plank and a table cost me 4s. 9d., second-hand of course. I paid 5s. for the calico and gums to make my first twelve bodies to begin with, and I set to work. The bigger fool for it. It took me a day and a half, or 19 hours to make the dozen—I can do it in 13 or 14 hours now—and I took them to Mr. —— for sale. I asked him 8s. 6d., as I thought he would reckon that low, and it would recommend me, for my friend got 10s. Mr. —— said 'Pooh, I can get better at 7s.,' but I got 7s. 6d.

for them; and if I had asked him 7s., he'd have said 'I can get better at 6s.' I carry on this way still. I had a bit of a demand the autumn before last for bodies, and I got a man to help me, and I made 18s. a week for four weeks, and 16s. for the next week, and the next week to that only 4s. I can't tell what made the brisk, exactly; but I thought I was doing rarely, and I took an apprentice; his parents is poor people, close by. I gave him nothing. I was to teach him his trade—there's no indenture or anything of that sort—for two months, and then he was to have half of what he brought me in; but he and his father and mother cut away after I'd had him three weeks, and I've never seen him since. I've gone on this way all along, living from hand to mouth very often. I'm not treated like a Christian by some of the shops I take my bodies to. Last winter I was often starving. I've gone out with half-a-dozen bodies in a morning, and have brought them back at night, without a farthing in my pocket: of course I couldn't break my fast. I've gone to bed to try and sleep off the hunger—gone there at four o'clock, as I had neither fire nor candle, and have kept waking every hour, a dreaming that I was eating and drinking. I suppose it was the gnawing at my stomach that caused the dream. I was three weeks in arrear for rent, too, at 18d. a week, but my landlady's very good. I hardly know what I make a week, take the year through; perhaps 6s. or 7s. a week; some weeks only 4s., some weeks 10s. or 12s., or more. I've been rather in luck these three or four last weeks as I haven't made—that is, I haven't cleared—less than 10s. 6d. a week. But if I do make 10s. at this time (October), what is it? Fire costs me 5d. a day—say for six days. I'm out the rest of the week, when I'm busiest. That's 2s. 6d.; candles is 1s. for the time I'm at work; rent's 1s. 6d., and 3d. extra to rub off an arrear that's out this week. How much is that?" 5s. 3d. "Then there's 5s. 3d. left to live on. I live mostly on coffee, three times a day, with bread and butter. If I can't afford butter, I toast the bread. I gave ½d. for this old fork to do it with. It's better that way than dry. Sometimes I have one or two, or three, fresh or salt herrings for dinner, that cost 1½d. or 2d.; or sometimes only 1d., or ½ lb. of beef sausages, that cost 2d. common, or 2½d. better; but what's ½ lb. sausages for a man like me, that, when it's wanted, gets out of his bed at daylight, and goes to his plank? That sort of living costs 7d. or 8d., or 9d. a day. Beer I very seldom taste. Tobacco 2d. for three days: it puts off the hunger. I've always worked by myself, but perhaps I could do better at working with two or three mates. Sometimes my bodies have been starred, and I've had to set to work, half starving, on a Sunday, to make them good again; but that hasn't happened lately."

From an elderly man I had the following account of his "going on tramp" 22 years ago. I give it to show what the system then was; there is comparatively little of it at present:—

"There's no doubt," he said, "that many a hatter went on tramp, and got to like the life, when he needn't have gone, if he'd looked out fairly for work. When I started from London, I needn't have gone if I hadn't liked it, if I'd exerted myself; but I wanted a change. I made for Lancashire. I had 1½d. a mile allowed then, and a bed at every 'lawful town.' Sometimes, if the society's house, which was always a public-house, was small, and full, I had half a bed—for other societies used the house, and I have slept with tailors, and curriers, and other trades on tramp. Sometimes the landlord bedded me out. It was a pleasant life enough. You saw something new every day, and the fresh air and exercise made a man as strong as a horse. I know plenty of men in different trades that wouldn't thank you for work—they liked tramping better. I got good work at Oldham, and after that came to London, or I might have become one of that sort myself. When I went to work at first, after tramping, I didn't feel quite settled for a week or so. I've seen some queer doings among tramps. One was regularly joined by a woman as soon as he left a town, and she quitted him just before he went into one, if it was a small place, though a 'lawful town,' or she might be noticed with him. She sold laces, and was no better than she should be, so tramp money went to help to keep her. A tramp's was a jolly life enough, but it's different now. But I reckon I should be very sorry to see the allowance to tramps done away with, for I think it helps to keep a man more independent, and prevents many a hand from having to work at under wages as he might be driven to do otherwise."

The result of my inquiries is certainly not favourable to the tramping system. Habits of vagabondism appear to be generally induced by it, and the civilized artisan is gradually transformed into the predatory (because non-producing) nomade. That in every well-regulated trade there should be some means of passing the surplus of indigent labourers from one town to another, no one can doubt; still I am convinced that the tramping system is not the best mode of attaining this end.

LABOUR AND THE POOR.

THE METROPOLITAN DISTRICTS.

[FROM OUR SPECIAL CORRESPONDENT.]

OF THE LONDON TANNERS, CURRIERS, &C.

Letter LXXVIII.

"The leather manufacture of Great Britain," says Mr. McCulloch, "is of very great importance, and ranks either third or fourth on the list, being inferior only in point of value and extent to those of cotton, wool, and iron—if it be not superior to the latter." As regards the metropolis, the tanned material required for this great manufacture is prepared almost exclusively in Bermondsey. A walk through the streets and roads of that district is sufficient to convince three of the senses—the sight, the smell, and the hearing—how extensive is this branch of industry. On every side are seen announcements of the carrying on of the leather trade; the peculiar smell of raw hides and skins, and of tan pits, pervades the atmosphere; and the monotonous click of the steam engines used in grinding bark assails the ear.

A cursory glance even at the signboards of Bermondsey shows that the commerce and manufacture of the district are mainly derived from the uses to which hides and skins, with their coverings of hair and wool, and their appendages of horns and hoofs, are subjected. The signboards announce, in thick profusion, dealers in bark, tanners, curriers, French tanners and curriers, leather-dressers, morocco and roan manufacturers, leather-warehousemen, leather factors, leather dyers, leather enamellers, leather sellers and cutters, hide salesmen, skin salesmen, fellmongers, tawers, parchment makers, wool factors, woolstaplers, wool warehousemen, wool dealers, wool dyers, hair and flock manufacturers, dealers in horns and hoofs, workers in horn, glue makers, size makers, and neat's-foot oil makers. To this list must be added the tradesmen who supply the different implements used by the workmen in the industrial occupations I have enumerated. Occasionally, too, is seen an announcement, not very common in London manufactures, "tan given away."

What may be styled the *architecture* of the district is that rendered necessary by the demands of its chief commerce. Long, and sometimes high, and always black wooden structures, without glass windows, but with boards that can be closed or opened to admit air at pleasure, irregularly surround a series of closely-adjacent pits, filled to the brink with a dark, chocolate-coloured, thick liquid. Running alongside the pits, or in any convenient part of the premises, are low sheds, with red-tiled roofs, but blackened with age, often covering other pits; while, high above all, towers a tall narrow chimney, throwing out thick columns of black smoke. Stacks of new bark, or of bark "spent" in the pits, and ready to be carted away for manure or other purposes—such as to spread over the street pavement that no noise may disturb the rich invalid—occupy corners of the tan "yards." In other corners is spread what appears refuse, but is really the parings, the "odds and ends," of the leather, such as are used by the glue-makers. Elsewhere are heaped horns to be disposed of to comb-makers, knife-handle makers, &c. These places are the tanneries. As regards the wooden structures of the tanneries, where leather is hung "to dry" in what may be called a series of galleries, the curriers' and leather dressers' premises present a rather close resemblance, but there is an absence of similar pits of tan. The fellmonger's trade is carried on in large "yards," partly in the open air and partly in sheds. The wool warehouses are lofty stone buildings, some of them with considerable architectural pretensions. Where, in other edifices, is seen the window, is a large door, which can be "let down" level with the floor, and through which huge bales of wool are craned to or from any of the floors. What windows there are, are small and dusty.

To the right and left of some of the principal thoroughfares, such as Bermondsey-street, run series of small streets of small houses. A few of these off-streets or alleys are trim and new; but many of them are dirty and ruinous-looking, showing broken and uncleaned windows, and with water standing on the black unpaven ground. These are the residences of working people, according as their character, habits, or means, induce a tidy or a squalid dwelling-place. The names of some streets, such as Abbey-street and Crucifix-lane, tell of the existence of an age when Bermondsey presented very different characteristics—when it was chiefly remarkable for conventual magnificence, wealth, and hospitality.

The early establishment of the tanning trade in the locality was no doubt owing to the number of tidal streams or ditches that intersect it, and supply the abundant water necessary for trade purposes. Perhaps there was formerly but one tidal stream,—the Neckinger. At the present time this and its associate streams are far less the medium of water supply to the tanners than was the case ten or twelve years ago. The proprietors of many tanneries have made the fine springs with which Bermondsey abounds more available for their business purposes, and some have expended considerable sums in the sinking of Artesian wells.

The tariff which has influenced the trade in leather has undergone several changes. In 1787 there was placed on "hides of horse, mare, gelding, buffalo, bull, cow, ox, calf, kip, swine and hog, sea cow, elephant, and eland or large deer, not tanned, tawed, curried, or in any way dressed," a duty of 9d. per hide; in 1819 the duty was raised to 10d.; in 1844 it was lowered to 6d. per cwt. "dry" from foreign countries, and 3d. per cwt. "wet;" and 2d. and 1d. respectively from British possessions. As beast hides rarely weigh a hundredweight without the horns, but vary from 56 to 112 lbs., the reduction is considerable. In dressed hides—and I may here mention that in the trade the skins of bulls, oxen, and cows are styled *hides*, those of horses *horse hides*, while those of sheep, lambs, calves, and pigs are called *skins*—in dressed or tanned hides, a still greater change has taken place in the tariff. On foreign "hides, or pieces thereof, tanned, tawed, curried, or in any way dressed," for every £100 value the duty in 1787 was 77 per cent.; in 1819, it was lowered to 75 per cent., and in 1844 to 10 per cent., from foreign countries, and 5 from British possessions. In skins, also, the reduction of duty has been commensurate with that on hides. On goat skins, raw, there was in 1787 paid a duty of 5s. 6d. per dozen; in 1819, of 2s. 10d.; and at present, and since 1844, of 3d. and 2d., according as they are from foreign or British possessions. The reduction in the duty on all dressed skins and furs is at the same rate, per £100 value, as on hides.

It may be tolerably safe to assume that the duty on the hides of sea cows did not materially benefit the revenue. In the matter of skins, also, the present tariff contains charges that cannot be largely productive, fiscally speaking, nor promote to any considerable extent the tanner's industry. I may instance the following:—

	Rates of Duty in 1844.		Duty in 1819.	Duty in 1787.
	From Foreign Countries.	From British possessions.		
	s.　d.	s.　d.	s.　d.	£　s.　d.
Fox-tails, undressed, each	0　2	0　1	20 per ct.	27 10　0 per ct.
Leopard, undressed, per skin	1　6	0　9	9　6	0　6 11
Lion, ditto	0　2	0　1	7　6	0　3　6
Ounce, ditto	0　6	0　3	6　0	0　2　9
Panther, ditto	0　2	0　1	9　6	0　5　6
Tiger, ditto	1　6	0　9	9　6	0　2　9
Wolf, undressed, per dozen skins	2　0	1　0	2s. p. skin	0　6　4 p. skin
Wolf, tawed, per skin	5　0	2　6	17　6	0　8　3
Wolverines, undressed, per skin	0　3	0　2	1　0	0　3　6

The materials used in the conversion of hides and skins into leather are also subject to proportionately lower rates of duty.

The strongest and heaviest hides from the bull, ox, or cow, are tanned for the shoemakers and for soling leather. When tanned, these hides are known in the trade as "crops" and "butts." The crop is the tanned hide, including the "shoulder" and the "belly," which are the inferior parts of the leather, and are known as the "offal." The butt is the crop reduced; it is tanned precisely in the same way as the crop, but the inferior parts are cut off after being tanned, and all the best of the leather, and only the best, is to be found in a good butt. The offal is sold to the low-priced boot and shoemakers. Of hides, and almost entirely of English hides, are made *dressing hides*, which are curried after being tanned—no currying or any analogous process being required for soling leather. The divisions of dressing hides are into common, harness, bulls', shaved, and Scotch shaved.

Horse-hides are used for purposes which ensure that there shall be no *pull* upon the leather, as there is upon the traces of a carriage or the reins of a bridle. The nature of the leather is fine-grained and brittle; it breaks when dried after a thorough wetting. The divisions are into English, German, Tartary, Russian, and Spanish; the supplies from Buenos Ayres, Monte Video, &c., being still called Spanish. Three-fourths of the supply is foreign, the English bringing the lowest prices.

     Labour and the Poor Volume IV.

The great consumption of horse leather is for the "uppers" of ladies' shoes; it constitutes the leather known in the trade as "cordovan"— a name derived from the fine leather manufactured at Cordova, in Spain, when in possession of the Moors.

The foregoing statements show the divisions in the trade respecting hides. I now come to *skins*. *Calf-skins* are English, Irish, French, Dutch, Danish, German, and Cape. They vary in weight from 20 lbs. to 120 lbs. per dozen. They are sold whole or "rounded," the "offal" being taken off in the round (and bought for inferior work) in the same way as in the soling butt. Calf leather is used almost entirely in the making of men's boots and shoes, the great exception to this being the portion worked by the bookbinders. *Seal-skins* are used for ladies' and children's shoes. They weigh from 18 lb. to 60 lb. per dozen, and are known as Blue-backs, White-coats, Small-hairs, and Large-hairs. About 5 per cent. of the supply is derived from the northern ports of Scotland and the Zetland and Orkney Isles; but the great bulk is imported from Newfoundland, British North America, Greenland, and the northern ports of the Russian empire. The supply of *Kips* is chiefly foreign. They are known as Petersburg, Cape, East India, African, German, Memel, Riga, Danish, Irish, and English. The kip is the skin of the calf, when too big and coarse to be dressed as "calf," and of small and inferior cattle when killed young. This leather is principally used by the lower-priced shoemakers, for their stronger work.

The leather trade comprises many other articles, which I shall touch upon very briefly. *Morocco*, for the purposes of ladies' shoemakers, upholsterers, and bookbinders, is dressed from goat skin; while *roan*, which is an imitation of morocco, is a sheep skin. Goat skin is also made into gentlemen's boots, when it is known as "grained leather." *Kangaroo*, ten or twelve years back, was in demand for fine boots; and so was *dog skin*, to a small extent, but they have been almost superseded by the French calf leather. *Kid skins* are prepared from the skins of the young goats; the imitation for the lower priced gloves being of *lamb skin*. *Rat skins* have been dressed for gloves. The coloured leather lining in boots and shoes is lamb skin. The use of *pig skin* is confined to the exterior parts of the best saddles. The *chamois* (or wash leathers) are of sheep skin, made when the grain or surface has been taken thinly off to supply *skivers* for hat-linings. *Basils* are dressed sheep skins; they are used for the covering of wooden trunks, and in various ways in saddlery. *Buck* and *doe leather* is made into the hunting or riding breeches of gentlemen (a trade that has greatly fallen off), and the dress breeches of grooms—also for the nether garment of the jockey when labouring professionally at the races. It is, moreover, in use for the manufacture of boots and shoes for tender feet; it is soft when new, and very durable. Tawed *white leather*—which is made by the system of "tawing," instead of "tanning," or by the application of salt or alum, or both, to the hide or skin, instead of "tan"—is now in very little demand, and is chiefly used in the manufacture of whip thongs. *Parchment* is made of sheep skins. *Buffalo skins* are dressed for soldiers' belts, and sometimes for machinery.

The number of tanners in Great Britain at the time of taking the census of 1841 was 6,601. Of these there were residing in England, 5,485; in Wales, 306; in Scotland, 775; and in the islands in the British seas, 35. Of the whole number employed in Great Britain, 5,909 were adult males, and 48 females of twenty years of age and upwards—the remaining 644 being juveniles of both sexes, in the proportion of sixteen boys to one girl. The number of tanners in the metropolis in 1841 amounted to 901; of these, 819 were males of twenty years of age and upwards, 7 adult females, and 75 boys. The increase in Great Britain, exclusive of the British Isles, in the number of tanners from the time of taking the census in 1831 to that of 1841, was, of males of twenty years of age and upwards, 326. The increase of adult males of this class in England was 413. In Wales a decrease of 38 took place; and in Scotland there was a decrease of 49. In the metropolis there was a decrease in the number of tanners of twenty years of age and upwards, to the amount of 46. The distribution of tanners throughout England and Wales was as follows:—

TANNERS.

England—			
Bedford	9	Salop	101
Berks	28	Somerset	245
Bucks	27	Southampton	126
Cambridge	9	Stafford	70
Chester	155	Suffolk	83
Cornwall	140	Surrey	877
Cumberland	104	Sussex	95
Derby	82	Warwick	105
Devon	397	Westmorland	42
Dorset	56	Wilts	72
Durham	134	Worcester	158
Essex	92	York, East Riding	144
Gloucester	129	„ City and Ainstey	14
Hereford	50	„ North Riding	101
Hertford	47	„ West Riding	355
Huntingdon	15	WALES.	
Kent	175	Anglesey	12
Lancaster	420	Brecon	11
Leicester	66	Cardigan	25
Lincoln	143	Carmarthen	33
Middlesex	126	Carnarvon	23
Monmouth	35	Denbigh	58
Norfolk	89	Flint	12
Northampton	30	Glamorgan	44
Northumberland	245	Merioneth	20
Nottingham	66	Montgomery	40
Oxford	28	Pembroke	17
Rutland	—	Radnor	11

From the above table it appears that at the time of taking the last census the greatest number of tanners were resident in Surrey—Lancashire standing next, and then Devon and the West Riding of Yorkshire.

The largest market in the metropolis connected with the leather trade is the skin market in New Weston-street, Bermondsey. Here the skins, nearly all sheep and lamb skins, are exposed for sale. An archway leads from the front of the building to an open court, the interior of which is now green with thick grass. This was intended for the hide market. Beyond it is the skin market—an oblong space, with semi-circular ends, and with four entrances. Along the high walls runs a colonnade, and the interior is paved. The flagged side space, between two columns, is called "a bay," and is let for the traffic in skins. The rent for a bay is £15 a year, at which rate forty-five bays are now let. In addition to the bays, ten "tails" are let. A tail is a space in the market let for 10s., and may be retained until the renter has sold 1,000 skins. The market days are Tuesdays, Thursdays, and Saturdays. The sellers of the skins in the market are not the butchers who have bought and slaughtered the animal, but a class of middlemen known as skin salesmen. These traders buy the skins of the butchers in all parts of the metropolis, and even as far as Gravesend, Mitcham, Richmond, and Barnet. They cart their purchases to the skin market, where the fellmongers attend to buy them. Each sheep or lamb skin is carefully examined as to the texture of the wool, before a bargain is struck. No labourers are employed in this market beyond the servants of the salesmen and of the fellmongers.

The present "London new leather market" was built in 1833 by a company, for the most part connected with the trade, at an expense of £50,000. It was hoped that the trade in hides, as well as skins, would have been carried on in the new market; but though the new locality was more convenient for the tanners, it was less convenient for the hide salesmen. The traffic in hides is now so inconsiderable in the Bermondsey skin market that it requires no further notice. The decline has been gradual. In the first year of the new market, 58,488 hides were sold; in the second year, 37,825; in the third, 34,244; in the fourth, 33,272; in the fifth, 31,166; in the sixth, 30,017; in the seventh, 27,226; while in the eighth and last year of which an account has been kept, the falling off from the numbers of the first year was upwards of 43,000, as only 15,455 hides were sold.

The hide market is at Leadenhall, in a large and nearly square open space, roofed over in parts, near the meat market. The hide market, or, as it is more usually called, the "leather market," has been held in this locality upwards of a century. The functions of hide salesmen are the same as those of skin salesmen. The market days are Mondays, Wednesdays, and Fridays. The arrangements do not differ materially from those of the skin market. The market is also one for tanned leather, as well as for hides, and a few sheep skins. The principal customers are country dealers, who visit London to make purchases. To test the quality and ascertain the substance of the soling leather, a small piece is cut from the centre of a crop or butt. It is closely examined to ascertain the texture of the grain, and applied to the nostril and the tongue to test the nature of the tannage. "For all their terrar japonicars, sir," said a working tanner to me, "a good judge will buy leather, if he wants to please good customers, that has the real smell and smack of oak bark, when it's a regular nosegay." The sellers of leather in Leadenhall-market are either the tanners, their servants, or factors employed for the purpose. The fellmonger's business is confined to sheep and lamb skins. He removes the wool from the skin or pelt, and is so far a middleman that he sells the wool to the woolstaplers, and disposes of the pelts (sometimes in the skin market) to the leather-dressers. The woolstapler, the wool warehouseman, or wool dealer—for their functions are identical—are again middlemen between the fellmonger and the manufacturer. As my present inquiry relates to the leather trade, I need not further notice these tradesmen.

With regard to the number of hides and skins which are yearly converted into leather in London, I had the following calculation from a highly respectable master butcher:—

"There is no way," he said, "of getting at the exact quantity; but I was once connected with the tanning trade, besides having had great experience as a butcher, and I think we can calculate pretty closely. We'll take the numbers of Smithfield-market, English and foreign cattle and sheep; for there is no doubt their hides and skins all go to the London leather makers. We must take a very high number, beyond an average, and for this reason. A great many sheep and other cattle are slaughtered at outside places, such as Gravesend. They are bought of the farmers in the neighbourhood, or selected from droves on their way to London. The skins of the cattle slaughtered at those places are sent to or collected by London salesmen; and this supply, and that of cattle driven direct to the butcher's premises, being bargained for without seeing Smithfield, will make up the number. Now, we'll reckon 4,000 head of cattle every week, which is really a moderate calculation. We will reckon also 33,000 sheep and lambs a week, which is not too many, considering the addition of the skins from other parts, and 300 calves a week. Of pigs I can form no calculation, for many are not skinned. That will give, if we multiply rightly, 208,000 cattle in a year, 1,716,000 sheep, and 26,600 calves from London and the neighbourhood. Then there's the foreign supply. As far as my experience and observations of the trade circulars extend, the salted hides from foreign parts more than treble the London raw hides; but say treble. For foreign and Irish calfskins, say four times the London supply. Sheepskins from abroad may be about a fifteenth of what London gives; I think not more. But the foreign goat and kid, and seal skins brought to London for the trade, must be quite as many as the new sheepskins obtained here. Horsehides may, I think, be taken—English and foreign—at 700,000 in a year. Take the kips at 150,000 a month—and that is within the mark, as last month there were arrivals of more than 133,000 East India alone, or 1,800,000 in a year; and in my opinion the total of all this, leaving out kangaroos and such like, will be as near the correct amount as can be arrived at."

My informant's calculation gives the following result in the aggregate, as to the number of English and foreign hides and skins that form the staple of the industry of the London leather-makers:—

Beast hides	832,000
Sheep and lamb skins	1,830,400
Calf ditto	133,000
Goat and kid ditto	1,716,000
Horse hides	700,000
Kips	1,800,000
Total	7,011,400

Another informant estimated horse hides at ten per cent., if not more, higher.

So many are the ramifications in the several departments of the leather trade, that it is no easy matter to draw the distinctions which it has been my custom to do. The trade, however, may be divided—waiving the fellmongers and those connected with that department—into tanners, curriers, leather-dressers, skinners, morocco and roan manufacturers, oil and white leather finishers, tawers, and parchment makers. The two last-mentioned callings constitute but a small proportion of the great leather manufacture. Of the other callings, though the subdivisions are many, the blendings are frequent. Some masters are both tanners and curriers, though in these two avocations the workmen are usually kept distinct. Other masters are curriers and leather dressers, and the parchment makers often exercise their skill in other descriptions of sheep-leather dressing.

The several workers in the preparation of leather—the curriers being an exception—are not an educated class. There need be no stronger proof of this than the fact, as I was informed by an intelligent workman from his own knowledge, that in their societies not one man in three can write his name legibly, or spell it correctly. I found a working tanner, to whom I was directed, in a public-house, reading to two of his trade, who regretted their inability to read an account of a prize fight. Among tanners, I was told, there was still a strong "hankering after a prize fight," and that some noted boxers had sprung from them—among others "Ned Turner," who was brought up as a tanner, but was afterwards a *frizer*, or a man who divided the grain of a sheep-skin for hat linings and other purposes from the flesh, to be manufactured into "chamois." The operation is now done unerringly by machinery, and the frizer's occupation is extinct. The workmen in this trade are generally married men. They reside in Bermondsey or its immediate vicinity, occupying one room at about 1s. 6d., or sometimes two rooms (according to their means) at from 2s. 6d. to 3s. a week. There is still a good deal of drinking prevalent among them, and little inclination for working on Mondays, but in both these respects there has been within these 12 years a decided improvement. The workers not *in* but *on* leather, now rarely drink more than a pot of beer a day when at work; from twelve to twenty years ago they consumed twice that quantity. On Father Mathew's visit to Bermondsey, six or seven years ago, a great number of the men in this trade took the pledge, but, with the exception of about one in 20 or 25, they have all broken it. "I took the pledge, sir," said a tanner to me, "and kept it rather more than two years. I was often teased by my mates to drink, but they got tired of that. I used to say, when I walked past Simon the Tanner, 'Simon, you'll get no more tanners out of me;' but I found, or fancied, though I don't think it was fancy, that I couldn't work so well without a reasonable allowance of beer, so I gave up teetotalling." I may explain that "Simon the Tanner" is the sign of a house of call, much frequented by the fraternity, and that a "tanner," in slang language, is sixpence. One custom still prevails—but very partially, indeed to only one-tenth, if so much, of its former prevalence—which is now known in very few trades, viz. the payment of men in public-houses. These public-houses are called "garrison" houses. The foreman makes himself responsible to the innkeeper for all the liquor drunk on the premises of the employer when the men are at work, and he deducts the amount from their wages on the Saturday night. The journeymen shrewdly suspect that there is an understanding between the foreman and the publican, and that the beer, which is 4d. a pot to the workmen, is but 3½d. to the foreman. On inquiring of a man who gave me information on this subject, if the masters approved of such a mode of payment, I was told that the master was perhaps a rich man, having his country house at some distance, and that, provided his returns were satisfactory, he left all such matters entirely to his foreman. The system seems dying out, however, and is commended by no one, not even by those workmen who are addicted to drinking.

I now give the subdivisions of the several trades I have mentioned, as detailed to me by intelligent men, with statements fully elucidating the condition of the operatives in the trade. First, of the tanners:—

The divisions in the tanning trade, in large establishments, are into the beam-men, yard (or job) men, and shed-men. The beam-man is the first hand employed on a hide, which, I will suppose, is to be tanned for soling leather. He removes the horns from the head, and in the country he removes the tail, which, however, is removed by the London butchers. In country tanneries, I may mention, the tail, with the flesh attached to it or to any part of the hide, is the perquisite of the working tanner. This perquisite is called "rumps and birrs," and in some weeks suffices to maintain a family independently of other sources; sometimes it can be sold to advantage, but only in the larger towns. In London, the tail, for which 1s. is an average price, is sold by the butcher for the making of oxtail soup. The beam-man next "sleeks" the hair off the hide, using lime to facilitate the process. He next pulls the hide out to its utmost extent, pares away any jagged particles hanging loosely to it, and puts it into a pit of pigeon's dung, which is of a very acrid nature. In this dung it remains on an average five days. The operative next "fleshes" the hide, removing all excrescences, shaving it where necessary, and preparing it in every way for the pit of oak bark tan. It is then consigned to the yardman. Under the direction of the foreman, the yardman places the hide in the tan pit. As the name imports (for I heard him also called the job-man), he is not a skilled, but he is a labourious worker. He places the hides in the pit, carries the bark in a basket, and deposits it in the pit; pumps the water in or out; "draws" the hides, using a long hooked pole, out for inspection, that it may be ascertained when they have been pitted a sufficient time. A hide weighing 70 lbs., remains in the pit for a twelvemonth. The yardman also fulfils other functions, often understood as those pertaining to an "odd man." When the hide—then, indeed, the "crop"—is ultimately drawn from the pit, it comes to the hands of the shed-man, and is "sammed." For this purpose it is hung up on an iron beam, in a drying shed, that it may drip; and, to facilitate the dripping, it is struck at intervals with a kind of stave; any protuberant part being struck, so that the leather, whilst wet, may be made as level as possible. The hanging, &c., continues two days, and then the finishing work commences. The shedman places the still wet crop on a low iron bed, and "rolls" it. The rolling is done by means of a brass roller, on which is a frame containing from seven to ten cwt.; nine cwt. being a usual weight for larger hides. This rolling levels the hide, expresses the wet from it, and so prepares it for market. Rolling is only resorted to for soling leather. The crop is not, however, fit for sale until it has been for three or four days hung in the sun, or in a heated apartment.

There are no working tanners—except perhaps some yard-men—but what are masters of all branches of the business; nor does any branch tax their ingenuity or skill very severely. It is only in some larger establishments, that the workmen are confined with strictness to the branches I have described. The payment of the tanner is both by day and by piece. The beam work averages 21s. a week, the yard work 18s. a week, and the shed work 21s. to 25s. a week; but the shed work alone, the most skilled portion of the tanner's labour, is paid by the piece, and that only in some yards. Piece prices or day prices realise about the same to the workman.

In one of the principal tanneries, the regular hours of labour—which are from six to seven in summer, and from daylight to dark in winter—have been extended an hour, gas being now used. This increase of labour has not, however, been accompanied with any increase of remuneration; so that it is a virtual decrease of wages, to the extent of more than half a day's work in a week, or of six hours. The cause assigned is the cheapness of provisions enabling men to live at less cost; but the house in question, rather than reduce the actual amount of payment, has added to the hours of work. The men resisted at first, but gave way rather than lose their employment. Another large firm has just proposed a similar measure, but the matter is as yet unsettled.

From a shedman, a strong, fresh-coloured man, I had the following statement:—

"I learned all parts of the tanning trade, and was apprenticed to my father, who had the management of a business in the country. I've known the London trade for twenty years, or thereabouts. I work in the shed now, and have for a long time. I don't remember how long. I work by the piece at present, and have from 1s. to 1s. 9d. a hide, according to size. My work's constant now, and I make about 24s. a week. I live as comfortably as a working man can, and support a wife and two children on that. I have a sort of double room, and pay 2s. 3d. a week for it, unfurnished. I could read a little once, but I've been out of practice so long that I've forgot it; but I'm very fond of hearing my wife read the paper on Sundays, as I smoke my pipe. It was capital reading about Manning and his wife, as they lived just by us, you see. My children both go to school. The work in tanning's the same, whether the hide goes into clean oak bark or terra japonica. The terra tans the offal well, but the prime parts not so well. I have no grievances to complain of in my yard, none at all; and I hope bread won't be any dearer this winter, as some say it will. It's a great good to a man like me that it's so cheap, as well as fish and meat, for I'm a hearty eater. I go home to all my meals."

Some working tanners complained that the use in tanning of terra japonica, &c., which they called "chemicals," was a serious injury in diminishing the amount of work, and consequently the number of workmen. I found, moreover, that the men all represented "chemical" tanning as producing a very inferior article to that produced by the use of bark.

The majority of the yard-men are Irishmen, and are paid by the day. Their work is laborious, and they are paid 2s. 6d. and 3s. a day. One of them told me that he was very grateful for the good earnings of 18s. a week; he had learned the tanning trade in Ireland, his master being both a farmer and tanner; and on his master's failure he could obtain no employment, and with his wife and one child came to Liverpool, and tramped to London, eight or ten years ago. "We had to live on 5d. a day, sir," he continued, "and nothing for Sundays, when we got to London, for I had odd jobs that brought me 2s. 6d. a week, for three weeks; when I was lucky enough to get work thro' a friend—and have kept it pretty regular ever since. How we lived on 2s. 6d. a week—I have now 18s.—I can hardly tell, but the poor helps the poor." This man told me he had saved a little money, and that he drank a pot of beer a day, and had to "slave," as he called it, very hard indeed. He resided in a small but not bare, and certainly not clean room, which smelt strong of fried fish, on which, he said, he lived a good deal, and never touched meat on any fast day, as they were Catholics. His wife sometimes made 1s. or 1s. 6d. by washing for a neighbour, the child being then left in the care of another neighbour at 3d. a day. There are now many tanners out of work. I saw one strong young man who had been out of work for seven months, and had tramped half the time. He was in no society, and lived principally on the little help he got from his former mates; but that was chiefly in giving him beer, or in sharing their bread and cheese with him.

He was very anxious to emigrate, as he had heard that tanners were wanted in Sydney. "But there's no way out of England for me," he said, alluding to his want of means.

The working dress of the tanners is most commonly a pair of thick corduroy or yellow canvas trowsers, dyed a deeper yellow with bark at the ends, leather leggings, a striped shirt of strong calico, a jacket of corduroy or thick coarse flannel, wooden clogs, a leather or flannel apron, and a paper cap. I was informed that, notwithstanding the constant dabbling in wet by the working tanners, rheumatism and colds were almost unknown among them. "Use," said one of my informants, "is second nature."

The London tanners have a society with three branches—the Old Union with 172 members, the Tramp Union with 50, and a branch of the Old Union, and consisting chiefly of elderly men, numbering also 50; in all 272. There are, moreover, now in London between 600 and 700 working tanners not belonging to any society. Tramps continue to be relieved by the United Tanners, or the Old Union. If the funds are under £50 a tramp is paid 10d. a day, and if accompanied by his wife, 1s. 3d.; when the funds are over £50 and under £100, 1s. a day for a single man, and 1s. 6d. for a married couple; when over £100, 1s. 2d. and 1s. 9d. a day respectively. The tramping is to average twenty miles a day, no tramping being allowed on Sundays; but what is called a "Sunday benefit," regulated as the day allowance is by the state of the funds, is granted instead. Any member tramping with a woman to whom he is not married is expelled the society. The payments by the members to support the fund are 3s. each entrance money, and 1s. 3d. per month.

Apprenticeship used to be the regular mode of acquiring a knowledge of the tanner's business, but it is now much less so—the reason given to me being that so few would now pay any premium. The apprentices are now generally the sons of the operative tanners.

The payment to the three branches generally is 3d. a week per member. The allowance to a member out of work is 6s. a week, regulated in great measure, as I was afterwards told, by the curriers, whose rules are full and clear. All the tanners' societies, except the one I have described, discourage tramping, and withhold any allowance to men on tramp in the country.

In *currying*, the men work both by the day and by the piece, but far more frequently by the piece. An operative currier is expected to know every branch of the trade, but in London his labour is generally confined to one department—viz., to shoe curriers', saddlers' curriers', or coach curriers' work.

In shoe currying, the production of fine "cordovan" demands the highest exercise of skill of any article in the trade, and a nice judgment; for no precise rule can be laid down, as to the oil, &c., to be applied, as the horse-hide varies in the fineness of the "grain," the part from which the hair has been removed, and in the substance and softness or toughness of the "flesh," or underside of the leather; and so the application of oil, "dubbing," &c., must be duly apportioned. In the currying of calf-skins and of kips there is a material difference when compared with that of cordovan, for the calf and kip skins are "coloured" (blacked) on the flesh side, instead of the grain. The "uppers" of gentlemen's shoes and the "fronts" of their boots are un-lined, and therefore the cleanest (or grain) part of the leather is made to come into contact with the stocking, which otherwise would be sooner soiled. The grain side, too, "cracks" sooner than the flesh.

In saddlers' work, the most difficult articles to curry for the tradesmen who require the very best and best-coloured leather are bridle hides, which must be at once strong and flexible. In the currying of a harness hide, which is the same process as that in currying the other leathers used in saddlery, and does not much differ from that observed by the shoe currier, the first process is to "strike out" the "hide," as the tanned leather continues to be called. To effect this, it is steeped in water, spread on a table, and "sleeked" with a "sleeker"— a wooden instrument like a flattened rolling-pin. It is thus sleeked to its utmost extent of dilation, until the water is pressed out of it. When so stretched it is affixed to iron hooks, each side being so held, and left to dry. It is then put on a "beam" and "fleshed." The beam is a sloping and upright wooden frame, of some hard firm wood, such as beech or ash; and the "flesher" is a long two-handled, somewhat blunt, knife—one edge being sharper than the other—made of fine steel. The currier thus removes whatever portions of the flesh are protuberant; and when a "thin" hide is required, the fleshing is carried on—a sharp flesher being then used—so nicely and gradually that some of the "shavings" are as thin as writing paper. "Scouring" is the next process; the grain and flesh being rubbed rapidly with pumice or other stone, so that it is "raised" on both sides, and the better adapted for the next stage, which is the application of the "dubbing," or, as it is indifferently called, "stuffing." The dubbing is an admixture of oil and tallow, which is spread alike upon the grain and flesh, to "mellow" the leather. The dubbing remains on the leather for two days, and is then "sleeked" off by the process I have described. After that the surface is "coloured," according to the purpose required; the hide is dried, and is then complete for the market. Boot-top colouring is often very difficult. "The fashion has changed in them, sir," said an old currier to me, "from a deep yellow, or yellowish brown, to a sick white, and now it's a white with a yellowish bloom to it."

A currier who had worked about eight years in London, a man of about thirty-five, gave me an account of his earnings, which, as he had been fortunate in obtaining good work, ranged from 30s. to 42s. a-week. His earnings, however, are those of the very best, the readiest (the usual word in most trades for a quick workman), and the most skilful workmen; and his statement gave me no interesting facts beyond what he mentioned of the changes in the trade as he had heard them from his father and grandfather, both curriers. The principal employment of both these men, from thirty-five to sixty years ago, was on "saddle-bag hides" (the leather for saddle-bags), which were formerly slung over the horse's back, being attached to the saddle and the saddle girths, containing the "patterns" of the commercial traveller, and the change of linen, &c., of the ordinary traveller, as he travelled on horseback. This department of the trade has now entirely, or almost entirely, disappeared. The great grievance of the superior workmen in currying is the employment, at inferior wages, of non-society men, who, in all branches of the leather trade, are called "blacks."

The curriers in society, and working for good shops, are the most intelligent of the operatives engaged in the trade I am treating of. One currier knew of none but what could read and write, and some of them were very well informed and took an interest in politics, there being as many Free-traders as Protectionists, or nearly as many among them. The abodes of the curriers are in different parts of the metropolis and of the suburbs, as the trade is not so exclusively confined to Bermondsey as that of the tanners, though Bermondsey is its head quarters. They are principally married men, occupying one or two comfortable rooms. The non-society men, on the other hand, are driven to the usual shifts of slop workmen.

The working dress of the curriers is generally very thick blue flannel trowsers and jacket, strong coarse shirts, and blue flannel aprons. As is common enough with working men of the better class whose trade necessitates the wearing of coarse and inexpensive clothing and linen all day, the curriers are rather remarkable for being well dressed and with superior linen on Sundays, or when they "dress to go out on an evening." Their boots are often of the very best.

The wages of the operative curriers were settled by agreement with their masters in 1812, and have continued unchanged. The list of prices may be called even an elaborate production—it contains such ample specifications, and descends to such minutiæ. To give anything but a condensed account of it is not possible in my limits. Under the very first head, "calf skins," there are divisions into "English," and "foreign," and into "russet," and "black," the prices being regulated by the weight of the skins consigned to the workmen to be curried. I give a specimen:—

	English.		Foreign.	
	Russet.	Black.	Russet.	Black.
	s. d.	s. d.	s. d.	s. d.
Skins under 20 lbs., per doz. ..	4 0	4 6	4 3	4 6
And so the scale proceeds to additional weights of 10 lbs. per doz. to,				
Skins 90 lbs. to 100 lbs., per doz.	8 6	9 6	9 6	10 6

"and to advance 1s. for every 10 lb. (the advance on the lighter weight being 6d. per dozen). All skins shaved on the butt with a currier's knife, 1s. per dozen. Skins rounded before tanned, under 60 lbs. per dozen, to be allowed 4 lbs. and upwards, to add 7 lb. per dozen. Skins dressed with two cheeks 6d. per dozen." Equally precise are the specifications of the journeymen's charges under the heads "kips, English and foreign," "calf butts," "kip butts," "boot legs," "seal skins," "goat skins," "French fronts," "shoe hides," "horse hides," "extra work at the option of the master," and "water-scouring." The longest enumeration of prices relates, however, to the diversified articles of leather required for the uses of the saddler, the harness maker, the army accoutrement maker, and the coachbuilder; of these prices there are 85.

The Curriers' Society also publishes a "list of employers," of all who are recognised in the "honourable," or "fair" trade. Of these there are in the City division, 33; in the Westminster inner division, 14; in the Westminster outer division, 28; in the Borough division, 46.

I have heard working men in other callings point to the curriers as a very compact and well regulated trade society, and I was assured that, so far from their employers having been injured by the operations of the society, they ranked as wealthy tradesmen, with any other class, and much higher than many other classes, and that both in town and country; while the "black" masters, or those employing non-society men, were far less prosperous, and were indeed often needy. This account was confirmed to me by a master currier of the honourable class; but his profits, he said, had fallen off from five to ten per cent. these last four or five years, owing to the demand for French leather by the first-rate bootmakers having diminished the demand for the "best (English) calf butts and legs," which formed a considerable part of his business. My informant spoke favourably of the independent spirit of his men; but what he called independence, he said, other masters might perhaps call sauciness.

The articles of the London society provide that a house suitable for the reception of the unemployed country members shall be appointed, and that "the landlord shall furnish a sufficient number of good and clean beds for their accommodation, together with a separate room or rooms for those who have wives or families with them." For this the landlord receives £31 10s. yearly. The secretary receives £1 weekly. The contribution of the members is 1s. per week, and 20 weeks must be paid before a currier is entitled to the benefits of the society. One of these benefits is the "home allowance." This is 8s. a week for thirteen weeks, to a free member, and 4s. for the next thirteen weeks, "and not to receive any more for thirteen weeks; after which, if still out of work, he may receive 4s. per week for thirteen weeks longer, and then cease. Should he be a married man, and goes upon tramp, his wife may receive the home allowance; and if single, he may have it remitted to him at any place he may appoint." This home allowance is not paid a second time, unless a member has been working and paying for twenty weeks before he claims it. Men on tramp in the country are allowed 8s. per week, with 2s. additional for a wife, and 1s. for each child under fourteen, with beds for six nights.

The instruction of the currier in his ancient art and mystery is by apprenticeship. In the "fair" or "honourable" trade an employer has, if he chooses, two apprentices and one turnover, or two turnovers and one apprentice. Among the rules regarding apprentices I find:—"N.B. No foreigner can be admitted."

The "arms" of the journeymen curriers, as they appear on the title-pages of their articles, show the appropriate supporters of a horse and an ox rampant; the shield is set off with curriers' tools, and the motto is, "United to support, but not combined to injure." The non-society hands outnumber the others. The curriers have instituted a pension or superannuation fund in connection with their society. As soon as a sum of £500 has been funded, pensions or superannuations (all life annuities) will be granted to the members considered best entitled to them.

There is also a branch of the trade differing decidedly from the currier's craft (though sometimes united with it), the *leather dressers*. They dress leather which it is not necessary to tan previously, as for the currier's manufacture—the skins being sufficiently cured for the leather dresser's purpose before he takes them in hand; as I have stated, for instance, concerning the Mogadore goat skins, &c. These workmen dress goat and kid skins for the purposes of the glovers, bootmakers, and bookbinders. The goat skins thus dressed, however, are not the leather usually known as "morocco," and used for ladies' shoes, but the "goat skin" (as the manufactured article is still called) for Wellington or button boots, and the kid for ladies' slippers. The morocco and roan manufacturers are a distinct branch, of whom I shall treat.

The leather-dressers are divided into *dressers, grounders*, and *finishers*. The dresser removes the hair from the goat or kid skin, using animal salts where the tanner uses lime, and the work is then transferred to the grounder. He removes, by scraping, all dirt or exuberance of any kind from the skin, and fits it for the finisher. So far the skins are dressed white. The finisher "colours" them, and in all the respects required, fits them for use. The highest class of leather-dressers, as regards skill, are London men, who are generally proficient only in one branch, but in that particular branch are unequalled. These workmen are paid by the piece, and by the day; but far more usually by the piece. They have a society, and when in regular work earn good wages. They all work and reside in Bermondsey. Many of them are uneducated men. From an intelligent leather-dresser, whom I found at work, I had the following account:—

"I have been a journeyman twenty years," he said, "and am a London man. I make my £2 a week regularly, and twelve years back or so did make 50s. or £3. Wages were reduced gradually, but I am very well off, and have every reason to be satisfied. I work for an excellent employer; there's not such another in all Bermondsey, I do believe. I am a finisher, and confine myself to that branch; but I have done all branches. I could earn as much, or very nearly as much, as a dresser, but not as a grounder. I was a grounder for seven or eight months, three years back, and could only make 25s. a week, working harder than I now do to make 40s. I was very glad to get out of it. I now work by piece, which I prefer. I think the men in my trade are both more temperate and more moral than they were ten or twelve years back; but when work's scarce, and pay bad, as it is with a number of grounders, one can't expect them to spare much for the education of their children." Of leather dressers in London there are about 100 in society, and twice as many "blacks."

The "United Skinners of Great Britain," of whom I need not further treat at present, have a society, but it is only for the relief of tramps. The published list shows 1,095 members in Great Britain, but of this number the cards of 36 have been "demanded for debt," and one for imposition. This imports that unless the demands of the society are satisfied, those in debt will be deprived of their privileges. In London the society has two branches, the "Horns" and the "Fox and Goose;" the one having 56, and the other 41 members; in all 97.

In the *morocco and roan* trade (a branch of leather-dressing) the subdivisions are numerous, and pretty closely observed. The name of the leather so well known as "morocco" is another indication of the ancient superiority of the Moors in the manufacture of fine leather. A great number of goat-skins are still brought from Mogadore, the principal port in the empire of Morocco.

The divisions in the trade are into the *skinner, pureman, shaver, dyer,* and *finisher.* The skinners remove the hair from the skin by the same means as I have mentioned concerning the leather dressers. The pureman then reduces the skin to the substance required, and places it "in pure," spreading on it, and working into it, pigs' or dogs' dung—dogs' dung being gathered by poor fellows in the street, and sold at 10d. or 1s. a pailfull. The skin is then placed in shumac tan, where it remains for twelve hours. It then goes to the shaver, who shaves it to a regular consistency and transfers it to the dyer, who applies the dyes demanded by the colour which the leather is to assume. The finisher's art is the next and last resorted to. He "puts the print in" by working the leather manually, so as to give it the "grained" or *creasy* appearance of morocco leather. He then rubs it with white of egg, and rolls it with a hard wooden roller on a slanting mahogany table, to "put the bloom in;" the manufacture is then complete. The finisher's part is the most skilled and the most laborious. The roans, or mock moroccos, are made by much the same process, but with far less labour, and of sheep instead of goat-skins. These operatives work by the piece. They reside in Bermondsey, and do not differ in their character, &c., from the leather dressers.

In this trade the grounders are the unskilled and under-paid workmen. In addition to the wages of society men being much lower than those of dressers or finishers, the non-society men work at their own abodes, carrying a dozen or two dozen skins to ground there, by the piece. The work is dirty, the employment irregular, and this practice of working "in-doors," as it is called, in contradistinction to working on the premises, adds to the ordinary discomforts entailed by poverty on a poor man's abode.

A finisher gave me a statement which showed his earnings to be 30s. a week, as he was in good work the year through. The brisk season, he said, in his shop, was for six months in the summer, when he earned 40s. a week, realising only half that sum in the other six months.

In this department of the leather trade, the system of little masters and of hawking prevails rather extensively. In some establishments when the slack time comes, hands are discharged, and being unable to get work elsewhere, or preferring as some do to work on their own account, wretched as is their remuneration, they start to "make for hawking." It is common enough to see a poorly-dressed man, his patched clothes partly covered by his apron, hurry along the streets with a few skins of what appears morocco leather hanging over his arm. Sometimes his wife will hawk them. This is the little master, who is hawking his wares to the cheap bookbinder, the slop shoemaker, or the warehouseman. From an old man with quite a venerable look, tall, and little bent with age, but walking feebly, I had the following account:—

"I earned 40s. a week 40 years ago, and sometimes more, but it came down to 20s. these last few years, and now I'm past work for a good shop. I might have saved money but for a deal of sickness. I live in this public-house where you see me, where I have a furnished room for 1s. a week; for my landlady's husband—she's a widow now—was a shopmate of mine. All I have to live on is 4s. a week, which I receive from the sick fund of the society. That leaves 3s. a week, or 5d. a day to live on. I can't stand it long, and shall soon be driven to the great house (Bermondsey workhouse). A week or two back I made a dozen roans, and hawked them. I'd often hawked before for another man, who kept going on making. It is a wretched trade. Then it's such a nasty thing being forced to work with your pure and your shumac in the room where you must eat and sleep. The stuff for the dozen roans cost me 6s. 3d. They were small skins, but not holey. For hawking, we buy the stuff of a master, and get it no cheaper than you or any one not in the trade could. I worked hard at those skins for two days. I asked 12s. for the lot, and after losing two days, and being treated by the Jews and the shoemakers as if I was a thief, I was forced to sell them for 8s. In good shops the labour alone would be from 6s. to 7s. 3d. It's a most wretched life is a morocco hawker's. Not that we hawk moroccos—only roans, which are mock moroccos; and sad rubbish the Jew warehousemen and cheap shoemakers buy. They care nothing for quality, only for cheapness, because they can always glaze them up to the eye."

The morocco and roan manufacturers have a society, which embraces about 50 members in London, while the number of non-society men is 100. The rules of the society do not differ from others I have cited, as in relieving tramps, &c. Their wages are about equivalent to those of the curriers.

Another calling is that of the *oil and white leather finishers*. The principal employment of these workmen—and I found intelligent men among them—is the manufacture of buck and doe leather for the breeches-makers (or the tailors who work in buckskin), and for the bootmakers. Their present wages enable them, when in work, to earn 20s. a week on the year's average. Their wages have not been reduced since the times when their manufacture was in constant wear. Indeed, I was told by an old tradesman (in a different line) that he remembered London drapers wearing buckskin breeches and top-boots when behind the counter. But though the wages have not been reduced, the extra labour now demanded by the employers entails such a greater tax upon the workman's time, that his wages are virtually reduced 50 per cent. This demand for extra labour has gone on gradually, and it seems somewhat curious that the manufacture of an article has been improved as the demand for it has diminished. Such, however, is the case. "The buck leather, which forty years ago," I was told, "was almost as harsh and hard as untanned leather, must now be as fine as velvet." A tradesman, who uses this leather in his business, gave me a similar account, adding that buck leather was now as flexible as if it had India-rubber through it, or more so, and as fine as the finest Yorkshire cloth. Some employers in this business now seek to reduce their workmen's wages, because they say they can work cheaper, as provisions are cheaper. One of the operatives told an employer that provisions were as cheap to masters as to men, and they all object to the reduction.

These workmen have a society in which are fifty members, while the non-society men are about 150. The payment to the society is 2s. 6d. a month. The rules provide that a member, who has been out of employ for six successive days, shall have 10s. from the fund; and that a member "afflicted with sickness or lameness for six successive days, shall receive the sum of 10s. per week for one month; and should he still continue sick, he shall not be allowed a further sum until another month has expired, making the sick benefit one month off and one on." On the death of a free member, his wife, heir, or nominee receives £3 from the fund, and on such occasions a payment of 1s. each is made by resident members in aid of the fund. The society discourages tramping, allowing nothing to those who resort to it.

The workmen in this trade, I am informed, do not often attain a higher age than forty. The pipe-clay and ochre dust (those materials being used in their business), being inhaled by the men, bring on pulmonary diseases.

The Morning Chronicle, Wednesday, November 20, 1850.

FEMALE EMIGRATION FUND.—Intelligence has been received by yesterday's overland mail of the safe arrival in Australia of the two ships first despatched with emigrants under the auspices of Mr. Sidney Herbert's fund. The Culloden arrived at Port Phillip on the 6th of July, and the immigrants were most favourably received by the colonists; the ladies' committee that undertook to provide for their reception expressing the utmost satisfaction at the arrival of a party so well selected and so admirably suited for a colonial career. The girls, thirty-eight in number, were landed at Melbourne on the 8th of July, and the *Melbourne Argus* of the 11th of July states that thirty-one of them had then been engaged, at wages varying from 12*l.* to 20*l.* a year. Subsequent advices state that every one of the girls had obtained excellent situations, and that if 200 of them had been sent out they would all have had good places. The ship Duke of Portland, which sailed on the 8th of April, arrived at Adelaide, all well, on the 2d day of August. The female emigrants, 65 in number, had conducted themselves with great propriety throughout the voyage. All who were destined for Adelaide were landed safely and well, and every one of them obtained eligible situations within six days. Their cleanly and healthy appearance seems to have impressed the colonists very greatly in their favour; indeed, both at Port Phillip and Melbourne this immigration appears to have given the greatest satisfaction. The *Melbourne Argus* says—"The girls appear to belong to a class of immigrants peculiarly adapted to this colony, being young, healthy, and intelligent, and apparently possessed of that happy buoyancy of mind, and hearty determination of purpose, which will enable them to act well their part in any of the many situations of usefulness which lie so invitingly before them."

LABOUR AND THE POOR.

THE METROPOLITAN DISTRICTS.

[FROM OUR SPECIAL CORRESPONDENT.]

OF THE "LIVE" MARKETS OF LONDON.

LETTER LXXIX.

I propose in my present and the next letter to show the condition of the meat markets of London, and in the two following letters I shall treat of the "fish" and the "green" markets. Fully to elucidate so important a subject as that relating to the supply of food to the metropolis, several tables have been carefully prepared to show the vast extent of business done in Newgate, Leadenhall, Whitechapel, and the other meat markets; also in Billingsgate fish market, and in Covent Garden and the other fruit and vegetable markets. In these inquiries I have been greatly aided by the courteous assistance of the authorities of the several markets.

Of all the London markets, Smithfield, the only "live" market in the metropolis, is the oldest. That the cattle market for the city of London was held in an open field beyond the walls—for London was then a city within the walls—shows that the space required was far beyond that ordinarily devoted to the markets of the country; for in the older times markets were held on Sundays and holidays in the churchyards, for the convenience of those who attended divine worship, and who congregated together on few other occasions. It was not until 1677 that the holding of fairs or markets for any purpose on Sundays was prohibited. It would be easy to draw a striking contrast between ancient and modern Smithfield—between the Smithfield of 800 years back, when it was the arena for the sports of the citizens, and the Smithfield of a later era, where in 1381 Wat Tyler, among other claims of "justice to the people," demanded that all lawyers should be beheaded, and where he was stabbed by Sir William Walworth—between the Smithfield where Edward III. held "high tourney" in honour of his mistress, Alice Piers, or the Smithfield where martyrs were burnt, and that where only cattle or horses may be maltreated. My business, however, is with Smithfield as a market, but I should hardly have done justice to the associations of the locality without these brief allusions.

Torchlight View of Smithfield, 1841

The precise period when Smithfield became a cattle market is unknown. The growth of such markets is gradual, and is little noted in rude times. Fitzstephen, however, just 700 years ago, speaks of Smithfield as a place where horses and cattle were sold. The market in Smithfield is held by prescription, the most ancient of all tenures. "This market," said Mr. Sergeant Merewether, a high authority in all matters of municipal law, before a parliamentary committee, "so far as any record goes back, is without metes, or bounds, or days, or times; but they have been all altered from time to time by the mayor and aldermen, and therefore I imagine that it is that which is common throughout England—a general grant of the privilege of a market; it is indeed a market to be held at Smithfield, because it has always been so held, and the charter of Edward III., which contains a clause prohibiting, almost in the words of the common law, any other market being erected within seven miles of the city of London, is only of importance so far as, being a charter confirmed in Parliament, it is a parliamentary recognition of the existence of a market in the city of

London, because otherwise there could not be such a provision. The next charter, which refers not to the subject of the market, but which refers to Smithfield, is the charter of the 14th Charles I., which declares and grants that the city of London shall enjoy the inner and the outer moor, as well as Smithfield, in the manner they have hitherto enjoyed it." "Smithfield," he says, "in fact is Smoothfield. I imagine it is only a description, by the Saxon term, of the ground."

The accounts which show the "sales" in Smithfield in former years are very meagre, or altogether wanting, and the returns are sometimes conflicting. From the best statistical authority, it appears that in 1732 there were sold in Smithfield 76,210 cattle and 514,700 sheep. In 1827 the cattle numbered 138,363, and the sheep 1,335,100. In the interval between 1732 and the beginning of the present century, the greatest number of cattle sold in Smithfield was in 1795—viz., 131,092, and of sheep in 1799, 834,400. In 1762 the cattle were 102,831, and the sheep 772,160—an increase of more than 20,000 cattle and more than 105,000 sheep over the preceding year, while in 1763 the numbers fell to 80,851 and 653,110 respectively. The lowest number in the period specified was in 1748—cattle 67,681. The year 1743 was the lowest as regards sheep—468,100. From 1800 to 1827 (inclusive), the greatest amount of cattle sold was in 1824, being 163,615; and of sheep in 1822—1,340,160. During the years of the war, 1808 saw the most abundant supply, both of cattle—144,082; and of sheep—1,015,280.

To show the increase in the trade I append the last Parliamentary Return, which commences from the year succeeding that I have spoken of:—

Year.	Cattle on Great Day at Christmas.	Sheep on Great Day at Christmas.	Cattle during the Year.	Sheep during the Year.
1828.....	4,823	20,540	161,600	1,438,790
1829.....	3,202	18,350	175,211	1,422,740
1830.....	4,616	20,600	177,730	1,485,850
1831.....	3,671	19,340	172,113	1,401,820
1832.....	3,643	19,230	164,190	1,329,320
1833.....	4,146	19,630	154,943	1,206,730
1834.....	4,518	20,900	174,837	1,364,470
1835.....	3,885	22,720	183,101	1,563,500
1836.....	4,286	21,150	177,334	1,343,770
1837.....	4,020	21,440	186,336	1,460,160
1838.....	4,558	22,510	199,369	1,540,280
1839.....	4,966	23,370	193,332	1,481,920
1840.....	3,348	20,430	186,955	1,527,550
1841.....	4,209	19,870	176,658	1,432,040
1842.....	4,422	24,730	191,075	1,655,370
1843.....	4,541	25,360	187,547	1,817,460
1844.....	5,633	32,640	197,837	1,804,850
1845.....	5,276	22,250	204,055	1,539,660
1846.....	5,362	23,550	213,525	1,527,220
1847.....	4,276	17,960		
1848.....	5,638	22,870		

The following, according to the experience of Mr. Hicks, is the value of the stock annually sold in Smithfield, more especially for the year 1848:—

```
  224,000 Horned Cattle, at £18 10s. each....£4,144,000
1,550,000 Sheep          at   1 18s.  „   ....  2,945,000
   27,300 Calves         at   3 15s.  „   ....    102,375
   40,000 Pigs           at   1 10s.  „   ....     60,000
                                                 ──────────
                                                 £7,251,375
```

The foreign cattle are comprised in the foregoing table. Mr. W. Shank, the collector and manager of Smithfield-market, in his evidence before the Select Committee, on the 22d May, 1849, said of the proportion of foreign cattle sold in that market, "From the 10th of May, 1847, to December, we had 31,670 foreign beasts consigned to Smithfield-market—I have not the account further back than that—and 140,560 sheep, 7,550 calves; those were all from Holland and Germany. In 1847, from the 10th of May, we had 150 beasts from Spain. In the year 1848, we had 30,681 beasts—that is a diminution from the former year, considerably—128,890 sheep, 12,927 calves, 1,034 Spanish beasts, 1,147 from France, 918 from Denmark—those are the beasts; 100 Spanish sheep, and 90 calves from France, and 258 beasts from Portugal."

	Foreign beasts.	Do. sheep.	Do. calves.
Weekly average in 1847 ...	931	4,134	222
Do. 1848 ...	590	2,478	248

The decline in the numbers continued in 1849, but the return was not prepared. Mr. Shank attributed the falling-off to the circumstance that only a lower price was obtainable.

Prior to 1842 the importation from foreign parts of all animals required for the food of man was prohibited. The present is now the rate of duty payable from foreign countries:—

		£	s.	d.			£	s.	d.
Goats	each	0	1	0	Sheep ...... each	0	3	0
Kids	„	0	1	0	Lambs ..... „	0	2	0
Oxen & bulls	„	1	0	0	Swine & hogs „	0	5	0
Cows	„	0	15	0	Pigs, sucking „	0	2	0
Calves	„	0	10	0					

The duty on these animals, when imported from British colonial possessions, is half the amount of that charged on their introduction from foreign countries. None, however, appear to have been received from British possessions. The foreign animals are generally landed at Blackwall, or the St. Katharine's Dock, from the steamers, and driven to Smithfield or the lairs.

Of the quantity of meat sent to the "dead" markets of London, I shall speak in my next Letter.

During the present century the question of the convenience or the nuisance, the benefit or the disadvantage, the sufficiency or the inadequateness, of Smithfield Cattle Market has commanded much of the attention of Parliament, and of the corporation of London. This is shown by the following return:—

"1802. A petition was presented from the corporation of London to the House of Commons, for powers to enlarge Smithfield Market.

"1803. Another petition for the same purpose.

"1805. Another petition for the same purpose.

"1806. A bill presented, 'For making certain regulations concerning Smithfield Market, in the city of London.'

"1807. Another petition presented for the same purpose.

"1808. A bill presented, 'For enlarging the market-place of Smithfield, in the city of London, for widening a part of the street called Long-lane, leading into the said market, and for making provisions for those purposes.'

"1809. A petition was presented from the corporation *for removing Smithfield Market to some place as near as might be to the city of London*, and for extending the jurisdiction of the city of London to the new market, or otherwise for enlarging the market at Smithfield, and a bill brought in.

"1810. A petition presented similar to that of last year, and a bill brought in.

"1813. A bill presented, 'For enlarging the market-place at Smithfield, in the city of London, for improving the avenues in and about the same, and for the better regulation of the said market.' This bill passed the House of Commons.

"1829. Petition from the corporation of London.

"1835. Bill brought into Parliament, 'For enlarging the market-place at Smithfield, in the city of London, and for the better regulation of the said market.'"

Since 1834 the area of Smithfield Market has been enlarged from 4½ to 6¼ acres, and at the following cost to the corporation of London:—In 1835, £6,055; 1836, £4,375; 1837, £16,777; 1838, £2,837; 1839, £427; 1847, £5,940; 1848, £1,000; total, £37,411.

In addition to the parliamentary and corporate proceedings I have alluded to there have been two select committees of the House of Commons, who, in 1847 and in 1849, inquired into the question of the removal of Smithfield-market. In 1847 no report was issued by the committee; in 1849 the committee did issue a report, the first resolution being—"That it is the opinion of this committee that the continuance of a market for the sale of live stock in Smithfield is proved by experience to be attended with serious inconvenience and objections, and that it ought to be removed." The corporation strenuously opposes the removal, and there the matter rests.

It is not my intention—and it would be in opposition to the course I have adhered to throughout the series of these Letters—to advocate any side of this question; but that it may be the better understood, and as it is one of great importance, I select some of the more remarkable parts of the evidence:—

Mr. R. Hall, linen and woollen draper, 29, St. John-street, Clerkenwell, said:—"I consider that the cattle driven up and down the street on market days deteriorates much my business. The cattle being driven furiously causes the customers, I consider, of the better class to keep out of the street on Mondays and Fridays; that draws them elsewhere, and, consequently, they go elsewhere on other days, having left the street in a very great measure. Persons are constantly rushing into the shop when cattle are being driven past my house."

Mr. Betts, brandy distiller, 7, Smithfield-bars, also stated that on a Monday his passage was often filled with ladies and persons who ran thither on being terrified by the cattle passing from the market.

Mr. J. B. Humphreys, 41, High Holborn: "Occasionally, cattle passing up Holborn are driven aside by the quantity of vehicles in the way, and will occasionally endeavour to get into the houses. Upon one occasion a bullock made its way into my establishment (a coffee-house), and terrified my customers there very much; he cleared the room of the lot of them. At the bottom of my room, which is about sixty feet long, there is a large mirror; he walked down there and took a deliberate survey of himself, turned round, and, after damaging the settles and breaking the window and door, he made his way out again."

Mr. G. Main, licensed victualler, Coppice-row: "Me and my family were at dinner last Monday; there was a great noise; the boys jumped up and ran to the door. 'Father,' they said, 'there's a mad bullock again.' I went to protect myself and my property. I saw 500 or 600 persons of the lowest description, some before the beast and some behind it; ultimately it took refuge in the passage of Mr. Irons, an ironfounder. After it had been there some period it emerged again into the street, shackled by ropes, and then there was a fine burst amongst the populace. The neighbours were compelled to put up their shutters. It is not very pleasant to live in a confined neighbourhood, and to have a mad bullock just to do as he pleases, and worse than a mad bullock—a reckless multitude that would not care what they took of yours or other people's."

It would be easy to cite other instances, as detailed to the committee, of bullocks walking into houses, sometimes committing serious damage; at others walking gravely out again. Some witnesses living near Smithfield represented that the cattle driven along the street were a constant source of danger and annoyance. Others stated that they had experienced no annoyance and no inconvenience, and that they considered the market as well managed and as properly situated as was possible. One gentleman stated that so shockingly blasphemous and bad was the language used by the drovers, as they entered or quitted Smithfield, that he was obliged to prevent the females of his family from going to the front of the house; whilst a neighbour had heard no language from the drovers, or from any parties connected with the market, of which any complaint could reasonably be made. With regard to the sanitary state of Smithfield, doctors disagreed. Dr. Burrows, one of the principal physicians of St. Bartholomew's Hospital, said—"Taking one day with another, the area of Smithfield-market is one of the purest sites in the centre of London." Mr. Lawrence, the eminent surgeon, concurred in Dr. Burrows' opinion, and considered that there was not the slightest prejudice in point of health to the surrounding neighbourhood from the existence of the market two days a week. On the other hand, Mr. R. D. Grainger said:—"I consider the market itself, to a great extent, prejudicial. A large quantity of animal matter is deposited there, and I believe there is no method of cleansing such a spot as Smithfield-market which can prevent the disengagement of noxious gases." Dr. Aldis, on being asked, "Assuming the sanitary state of the neighbourhood of Smithfield to be below the average, can you trace that inferiority of health to the influence of Smithfield market?" replied: "I think that Smithfield market contributes a portion with the slaughterhouses; they together contribute a portion of the poison."

I now give extracts on points regarded by the committee as of great importance. First, as to the treatment of the animals in the market. Mr. J. B. Clarke, a carcass butcher, made the following statement. He said, on being asked how he got at the back sheep pens—

"Sometimes parties are going up near their middle in water. On a wet morning it is just like walking into the water for a man to walk across four or five pens. When the wool of the sheep is wet the water lodges on their coats, so that when a man has to get into the back pens, he gets wet. If you want to handle a sheep you must walk up through a lot of wet sheep to get at them, and it is quite as bad as if the ground was covered with water." On being asked if there was any cruelty exercised in getting the sheep from their position, Mr. Clarke replied, "No more than what the drovers are obliged to use. They are obliged to dog them, and prick them with the goad in the stick, and pull them about any how to get them out." With regard to the bullocks and their formation into ring-droves, he said, "There is not sufficient space for them. They (the drovers) are obliged to knock them about over the head and horns to get them in the position in which they require them. There is no more cruelty, I consider, exercised than is actually necessary." On being asked by the chairman of the committee, Mr. Ormsby Gore, "what part of the head do they hit?" Mr. Clarke answered: "They are not particular to an inch; over the nose, or poke them in the eye, or anything that chances. A man cannot tell exactly where he will hit the animal; if he has got his stick up, he is as likely to poke it in the eye as hit it on the nose."

I now give the opinion of an experienced man, Mr. W. Silvester, a butcher in Chancery-lane, concerning ring-droves. "The formation of ring-droves is very cruel, and the continuing of them too is very cruel; but it cannot be avoided in that market. The drovers select from about twenty or thirty beasts that are to be in the ring-drove— three or four of the drovers what they call 'head them up,' that is, by forcing them round and round until they get their heads to the centre; and in doing that the men necessarily are obliged to use a great deal of force to get them into that situation."

Many witnesses stated that no more cruelty—some called it coercion—was exercised than was absolutely required; and that as much must be used in any market wheresoever. Others declared that no cruelty at all was displayed, and all concurred in stating that of late years there was a decided improvement in the treatment of the animals in this great market.

Concerning another important question—the deterioration in the quality of the meat, if the animal when alive has been severely coerced with blows—some witnesses stated that, from the treatment of the animals in Smithfield, they had to sacrifice pounds of meat, as bruised and useless. Others were of opinion that no market "turned out" an animal so well and so immediately fitted for the butcher as Smithfield. That it is of great consequence to protect all animals from heavy blows is shown by the following extract from the scientific and interesting evidence given by Professor Owen:—

"First, as to the arrangements for the reception of fatted animals. As these, by the fattening process, are brought into a state of plethora and fulness of blood, the weight of the body being increased by the disposition of adipose substance, which at the same time impedes the muscular actions, every such action is attended with increased exertion, producing increased action of the heart and quickened breathing, which soon passes into fever; the respiration then becomes inadequate to the complete oxygenation of the blood, which becomes dark and impure. If the over-driving take place at night, the natural season of repose, and if to this be added terror and pain, followed by prevention of rest in the posture of repose, and inability to quench the thirst excited by the fever, this morbid state is aggravated by the augmented suffering; and twenty-four hours' continuance of this state, in animals with a previously overloaded and overactive vascular system, effects a change in the quality of the muscular fibre itself, and the meat does not cut up bright (to use the butchers' expression), the cause of which is this—the blood has passed into that state of disease that the oxygen of the air does not act upon the red particles retained in the flesh, and change them to a florid hue, as it would do in the case of healthy blood. Meat in this condition is less wholesome and nourishing, and in some constitutions will produce irritation of the mucous lining of the stomach and intestines, and its continued use might lay the foundation of complaints attributed to indigestion—sometimes directly occasion diarrhœa; and in the event of the cholera-poison being in the atmosphere, such a condition of the flesh-meat would form an additional element to the chances of the inhabitants of a metropolis so supplied being attacked by that disease. The same morbid condition of the flesh-meat renders it more prone to decomposition, and more meat is thereby consumed in a state in which a certain progress of decay is added to the other unwholesomeness caused by the animal being killed in the state of fever. Meat, damaged by bruises inflicted on the living animal, is rendered similarly unwholesome, because there is a local fever going on in the part in the attempt to repair the injury during the lifetime of the animal. Bruising of dead meat may accelerate decay, but does not otherwise affect the wholesomeness of the meat. The arrangements, therefore, for the reception of the animals should ensure their not being over-driven or irritated by ill-usage, and also the opportunity of repose after any unavoidable amount of over-driving and fever before they are slaughtered."

The learned professor favoured the establishment of an abattoir system, similar to that which he considered had worked well in Paris, since its establishment in the Consulate of Napoleon, in 1803.

Another witness, Mr. W. Burness, after stating that his own observations bore out an assertion made by Dr. Johnston, in his lectures on agricultural chemistry, that the ordinary waste which the animal system sustained amounted, in an ox, to about 6 lbs. of muscle daily, continued:—"The deterioration of cattle in Smithfield I cannot estimate at less than 10s. a head upon oxen, and 5s. upon sheep. There is a loss of 10s. in value upon an ox; he is less in weight by the time he reaches the slaughter-house, compared with what he ought to be. Cattle in Smithfield are in a state of fever; perhaps the pulse of one-fourth of them is, instead of being at forty, at eighty. I know that, from feeling the pulse of some of the cattle. Sending cattle to Smithfield is injurious to the agricultural interest, taking it as a whole, to the extent of not less than from £400,000 to £500,000 yearly. Sheep are generally more excited than oxen, and suffer more during the heat of summer." Other witnesses expressed similar opinions, but intimated that, no matter where the market was, the case would be the same if cattle had to be driven through the streets. Mr. Nice, however, a veterinary surgeon, stated, concerning the cattle at Smithfield—"I find that their state of health is good; their pulse is not much excited."

No water is supplied to the animals exposed for sale in Smithfield, and concerning this non-supply there is a diversity of opinion in the evidence. Mr. W. Anderson, a grazier, and the agent of the Duke of Bedford, says—"I consider that both cattle and sheep suffer from the want of water, and ought to be allowed to have it in the market." But Mr. W. H. Billing, a Leicestershire grazier, on being asked, "Have you found any inconvenience from the want of water in Smithfield-market? It has been represented to us that the cattle suffer very much from the want of water"—replied—"No practical man who knew anything about it would have invented such an absurdity." With regard to the feeding of the cattle sold in Smithfield, it is computed that one-third of those purchased there are slaughtered on the day of purchase, and then they are not fed, or the butchers consider they will not "cut up bright." The animals not intended to be slaughtered the same day are fed on being removed from the market.

Any one is privileged to send, or personally to sell, beasts, sheep, calves, pigs, horses, or asses, in Smithfield Market. The following shows the gross produce of the market, the expenses, the tolls received, and the cost of collecting the tolls for a series of years. I reserve the two latest returns for fuller details:—

Years.	Gross Produce.			Expenses.			Tolls.			Collectors' Tolls.		
	£	s.	d.	£	s.	d.	£	s.	d.	£	s.	d.
1828	5,459	14	8	2,339	15	8	1,300	8	0	179	11	2
1829	5,440	7	5	2,724	18	1	1,185	7	10	168	14	11
1830	5,555	9	4	2,490	1	0	1,206	9	0	155	1	0
1831	5,620	9	0	3,583	8	2	1,076	17	7	155	1	0
1832	5,394	7	1	2,380	8	7	1,074	9	6	155	1	0
1833	5,209	7	1	2,368	4	3	1,110	3	4	155	1	0
1834	5,497	14	5	2,327	11	1	1,193	14	9	145	12	0
1835	5,646	16	10	1,883	0	1	1,323	16	5	155	0	1
1836	5,420	3	3	2,582	0	1	1,229	3	6	167	6	0
1837	5,557	11	7	2,407	8	6	1,306	11	0	155	1	0
1838	5,963	14	3	7,748	13	$2\frac{1}{2}$	1,355	11	11	155	1	0
1839	5,950	2	6	4,011	9	$11\frac{1}{2}$	1,331	5	8	155	1	0
1840	5,936	3	6	2,003	8	7	1,325	5	8	155	1	0
1841	5,803	4	1	1,942	0	7	1,256	1	6	157	17	0
1842	6,125	6	3	1,929	12	11	1,352	4	11	5	0	0
1843	6,050	5	1	2,180	1	9	1,413	16	7	5	0	0
1844	6,205	13	2	2,298	6	1	1,467	7	4	5	0	0
1845	6,251	18	2	1,961	7	9	1,432	9	2	5	0	0
1846	6,140	5	10	2,046	3	$5\frac{1}{2}$	1,462	13	6	5	0	0

Thus the average produce of the market for these 19 years was £6,073 16 0

Average expenses 2,789 6 8

Net average of profit £3,284 9 4

Average produce of tolls £1,356 16 0

Average of expenses 124 6 7

Net average of profit £1,231 9 5

Altogether £4,515 18s. 9d. on the yearly average. I should mention, that from 1842 to 1846 the expenses of collecting the tolls (with the trifling exceptions I have quoted) were charged in the general expenses. Toll is only levied on beasts *sold* in the market. The following two years I give with details, to show the nature of the expenditure. The amount of market charges and of toll (the freemen of the City being exempt from toll) are also shown in the account:—

AN ACCOUNT OF ALL MONEYS RECEIVED AND DISBURSED BY THE CORPORATION OF LONDON ON ACCOUNT OF SMITHFIELD MARKET (EXCLUSIVE OF ENLARGEMENT OF MARKET), FOR THE YEARS 1847, 1848, AND THE FIRST QUARTER IN 1849; SPECIFYING THE RATES OR TOLLS UPON ALL CATTLE, PIGS, CALVES, AND SHEEP BROUGHT TO AND SOLD IN THE SAID MARKET.

	Year 1847.			Year 1848.			First Quarter in 1849.		
	£	s.	d.	£	s.	d.	£	s.	d.
Sheep, calf, and pig pens, permanent pens, 1s. each, and hurdlepens, 10d. each	5,319	7	6	5,307	10	0	1,144	17	6
Ties of beasts, at 1d. each	859	4	11	864	18	11	207	9	10
Ties of calves, at 1d. each	108	1	2	120	4	8	15	8	11
Ties of horses, at 2d. each	118	7	4	107	4	6	20	11	0
Hay duty, 6d. per load, unless the property of freemen, &c., and 1d. each entry of sale	164	10	11	146	11	3	32	18	10
Straw duty, 1d. each entry of sale	5	9	4	4	2	8	0	17	0
Drovers' licences	62	19	0	70	11	0	5	2	0
Bartholomew Fair	11	13	0	10	16	0			
	6,649	13	2	6,631	19	0	1,427	5	1
EXPENSES. Taxes, repairs, expenses of management and collection	2,836	14	0	2,504	0	0	467	16	6
Net produce of Pens, &c.	3,812	19	2	4,127	19	0	959	8	7
TOLLS. Beasts sold belonging to non-freemen (20d. per score)	918	13	2	921	11	7	211	4	5
Sheep, ditto (2d. per score)	598	19	7	565	13	0	109	3	7
Horses (4d. each entry of sale)	0	16	0	0	9	0	0	3	4
Pigs (4d. per score)	30	3	9	31	2	3	4	8	11
	1,548	12	6	1,518	15	10	325	0	3
Expenses	5	5	0	5	5	0			
Net produce of tolls	1,543	7	6	1,513	10	10	325	0	3

	Year 1847.			Year 1848.		
	£	s.	d.	£	s.	d.
Pens, &c.	3,812	19	2	4,127	19	0
Tolls	1,543	7	6	1,513	10	10
Net produce of the Market ...	5,356	6	8	5,641	9	10

Smithfield Market now contains (according to official statements) room for showing 4,000 beasts, and about 30,000 small, or 20,000 large sheep. Of the number of cattle 2,750 can be tied up. When that number is exceeded, the surplus cattle are formed into ring-droves, or must be detained in some of the streets leading to the market until the sale and "drawing out" of other beasts leaves room for the new comers. For the sheep there are 1,509 pens; previously to 1828 there were but 1,186. A pen will contain 15 or 16 sheep; but when their coats have been shorn, and when they are not large-sized, 20 sheep have been stowed into a pen. To secure places for the sale of the animals, application must be made on the afternoon previous to the market, to Mr. W. Shanks, the clerk of the market—and also the collector and manager—and he or his assistant assigns the places for every drove. There are also 50 pens for pigs; but as 30 are sufficient, the surplus 20 are usually assigned for sheep. Calves can be accommodated in any quantity, as Friday is the "great calf day," and on Fridays there is never any crowding. The market-days are Monday and Friday. The supply on Mondays is generally more than three times in excess of that of Fridays.

There is also an officer whose duty it is to prevent any diseased animal being exposed for sale in Smithfield Market. He examines any animal to which his attention is directed, waiting for that purpose at the police-station, and not attending the cattle-market unless called upon by the policeman to do so. The horse-market (of which I shall speak in due course) he attends personally. A return laid before Parliament for the year 1840, and for 1845 to 1848 inclusive, gives 2 diseased beasts, 5 sheep, and 18 glandered horses, as condemned during that period. The inspector, however, stated that the return was incorrect, as from January to June, 1840 (inclusive), he had been called upon to examine 6 diseased beasts, while in August, 1847, he found 20 sheep diseased of the small pox in one pen. He was of opinion that in the 5 years specified he had reported between 20 and 30 beasts as diseased. With regard to sheep, however, he was not, as a rule, called upon above three times in two years. The number of glandered horses was correctly given. All animals returned as diseased are condemned, and handed over to the police; they are slaughtered at a knacker's yard in Cow-cross, where the flesh is boiled down under the inspection of the police.

The principal actors in the great mart of Smithfield are the beast salesmen, the sheep salesmen, the drovers, and the butchers. The salesmen, who generally undertake the sale of either cattle or sheep indiscriminately, are now about 600 in number. The drovers "take up" the sheep or cattle at any railway station, at any appointed place on the road to London, or at neighbouring farms, or at the lairs. Only licensed drovers are allowed to drive cattle of any sort to or from Smithfield "within the cities of London and Westminster, and liberties thereof, and the bills of mortality." The salesmen attend at the market to conduct the sale of the animals consigned to them, or until, if unsold, they must be driven away, as the market must be "cleared" by three in the afternoon. No animals must be driven within a shorter distance than a mile of the market after eleven, or within it until after twelve on Sunday night, for the Monday's market. The busiest period is from five to six in the morning. Some of the salesmen are cattle dealers on their own account; some few are butchers; some are salesmen to the dead markets also; some are farmers; and some land agents. Their average number for the last two years is 600. Their charges vary, but the average payment to them is 4s. per head for beasts, and 6d. to 8d. per head for sheep, lambs, calves, and pigs. Thus, if 4,000 head of cattle, and 30,000 head of sheep, &c., are sold in a week, the payment for commission to these middlemen, taking 4s. for cattle and 6d. for sheep, &c., will be £1,550, or £80,600 a year, a yearly return per individual of £134. A few graziers attend the market to dispose of their own stock, which is often superior.

The salesman does not receive the money for the stock he sells; but it is paid to a "money-taker," or Smithfield banker. Mr. J. Pocklington, who had filled that capacity for 40 years, and who seemed to look upon the attempt to remove Smithfield market as one savouring of impiety, because there "we are getting that supply directly that God has intended that we should be fed with, and at so little expense," gave the following account of his avocation. The usual charge for the money-taker's commission is 6d. per head for a beast, and 15d. per score for sheep. The money-taker remits or deals with the money as he may be instructed. Mr. Pocklington said:—

"The money-taker has to take an account for each person who sends up stock to the market; the salesman receives information either by a letter or by a drover; he then comes to the money-taker, and gives an account of the whole of what he has got under his care, and for what graziers he is to sell the stock; we then take down the names, and make out the accounts ready against the sales of the stock; and when the salesman has done selling, he comes over to inquire and to examine whether all is paid, or who has been trusted; but no one is trusted, except it is by the wish of the salesman.

"I am quite satisfied that our (the Smithfield money-takers generally) animal returns are full 6,000,000*l.* to 7,000,000*l.* a year; and I will venture to say, at eleven o'clock every Monday morning, thousands of pounds are sent down to the clearing-houses (in the City); there are at least 40,000*l.* or 50,000*l.* gone to the clearing-houses at eleven o'clock, and again at two. Now, if we are to be removed how are we to manage all these sorts of things?"

On being asked by Mr. Christopher, "Do not some of the West-end bankers deal with the clearing-houses in the City, as well as those about Smithfield?" Mr. Pocklington said—

"I do not think they do in the regular way; they may—I do not know it. The amount of money that is sent at eleven o'clock would be, in all probability, 60,000*l.* or 80,000*l.* at least. The money-takers of Smithfield do not impede business. We take light gold—we take cheques of all descriptions by householders, that are given to different butchers who have cashed their little notes and so on—we take all sorts. And then there is another thing with respect to taking cheques. A gentleman may come up from Brighton, or Margate, or different places, and buys 10 beasts, and gives us a cheque for them; we then, as cautious men, send off immediately to the bankers in the city of London. If we were three miles from London how should we do that? It would be a great impediment. It is an unfortunate thing that all this mystery of removing away Smithfield-market is one of the worst things that can happen to the city of London; for when I look at it, that it is Providence that has ordered all these sort of things to come here, not all being sent at one time, for the land does not produce that stock; what comes now, principally (June last year), is from Norfolk, and a few other sort of things from Surrey, and that way; but, sir, in the course of a month we shall have all the Northampton and the West, and all those counties, sending a very immense quantity of stock."

Mr. Pocklington said subsequently:—

"I have been at Smithfield forty years, and I have never seen business done so well and so comfortable anywhere else. Only look at the return! God bless my soul! Why I will venture to say that there is 7,000,000*l.* of money returned at Smithfield-market, and you do not hear of a single error with respect to robbery, plunder, or anything else, with respect to the whole of that. Only look at that!"

The uses of Smithfield, as a market, are not confined to the animals demanded for human food. It is also a mart for the sale of horses and of hay. The horse market commences on the Friday at three in the afternoon, at the close of the cattle-market, and continues two or three hours, or until dusk in winter. The animals sold there are generally inferior, the majority of them being spavined, lame, or blind. Some are bought by the knackers. There are, however, mixed with the inferior animals, some useful horses for cab purposes, or for the light carts driven by butchers and others, and a few good draught horses. The proportion of glandered horses I have stated. Along with the horses are sold donkeys, old harness, barrows, carts, and everything of that description required by the costermongers. This market is popularly known as "Smithfield races." In 1848 12,867 horses were exposed for sale in Smithfield, or an average of 255 each market day. The tolls, &c., chargeable on this traffic are shown in the table I have given.

Although the horses and asses shown for sale in Smithfield-market are English, I may here mention that the same tariff which removed the prohibition on the importation of foreign cattle lowered the duty on foreign horses and asses. In 1787 the duty on foreign asses was £27 10s. per cent.; in 1819 it was £3 6s. 6d.; it is now, and since 1842, from foreign countries, 2s. 6d., and from British possessions, 1s. 3d. each ass. On foreign horses the duty in 1787 was £2 4s.; in 1819, £6 13s.; and in 1842, £1 and 10s., according as they were from foreign countries or British possessions.

On Tuesdays, Thursdays, and Saturdays, Smithfield is a market for the sale of hay and straw. In 1848, 18,537 loads of hay were sold there, and 1,750 loads of straw.

"The drainage of Smithfield-market," said Dr. Hector Gavin, "is exceedingly imperfect." Dr. Edwin Lankester, however, expressed a different opinion, believing that "the district was generally well drained about there." Dr. Lankester said, with regard to the bad smells arising from the gully-holes along the valley of the Fleet Ditch:—"We are not any better off in Regent-street and Oxford-street. I believe that one part of London is as bad as another as far as drainage goes." Many medical authorities spoke of the deleterious influence of the knackers' yards, fiddle-string makers, and similar trades carried on near Smithfield.

I have next to notice the "lairs" for the animals. In these lairs the cattle are placed until it is time to drive them to the market; they are placed there also, if unsold when first offered, and are retained until the following market day. Some of the salesmen have lairs for the cattle consigned to themselves; while there are general lairs at Tottenham, Camden-town, Kennington, and elsewhere. But the great accommodation in the way of lairage is at Islington Market, which supplies eight-ninths of the metropolitan public lairage. This market was built as a speculation, by Mr. Perkins, with the intention of establishing it as a cattle market. He obtained an Act of Parliament, but not without considerable opposition, authorising it to be used for that purpose. "The property," I find stated on a plan of the market, "includes 30 dwelling-houses, taverns, market-house, and 6 public-houses; 4 banking-houses, and land nearly 30 acres in extent. Of the market there are 15 acres within the walls, which contain spacious open and covered lairs, capable of holding 8,000 cattle, and 50,000 sheep." The market was opened in March, 1836; but after continuing open a little more than seven months it proved a failure, was closed, and has not since been used as a market. The salesmen and butchers did not resort to it in any considerable number; but I find no return of the extent of the business actually transacted there. One cause assigned for the failure, and a good deal insisted upon, was that it was attributable to a combination, or rather understanding, among the salesmen. "My opinion is, (said Mr. Anderson) that the salesmen thought, if there was more room, that many gentlemen would go and sell their own beasts there. I would for one." The witnesses concurred in stating that no second live market could exist in opposition to Smithfield—a view adopted by the committee, who report that, "in accordance with the tenor of the evidence, only one great metropolitan cattle market can exist, and that, therefore, in the selection of its site regard should be had to the position of the railway termini; the place of disembarkation for Scotch, Irish, and foreign cattle; the bridges, especially Blackfriars; and to the density of the population in the neighbourhood of such site."

Each drover within the jurisdiction of the Corporation must, as I have said, be licensed, and their sticks and goads are regulated. The rules affecting this matter provide that "tickets made of iron, or other metal, be forthwith provided by the Clerk of the Smithfield-market, or such other person as shall be appointed by the Court of Aldermen." And further:—

> "That the Clerk of Smithfield-market, or such other person as aforesaid, shall, upon payment of 5s., grant to any person not under

16 years of age, who shall produce a satisfactory certificate of his good character and ability to act as a drover, a licence to drive cattle, sheep, calves, or lambs within the aforesaid limits (I have already specified these); and in every such licence shall be specified the number thereof, with the name, place of abode, and age, together with a description of the person to whom the same shall be granted; and every license shall bear date the day it is granted, and continue in force until the 1st day of July next after the date, except it shall be sooner revoked." ... "That every person duly licensed as aforesaid shall at all times during his employment wear the ticket which shall have been delivered to him, conspicuously, upon the upper and outer part of the left arm." ... "No person engaged in driving cattle, &c., shall use any stick or other instrument with a goad or point of greater length than a quarter of an inch. All sticks or other instruments used by persons engaged in driving cattle, &c., shall be stamped with such distinguishing mark as the clerk of the market shall deem expedient." ... "All cattle, sheep, calves, and lambs shall be driven on the left, or near side of the carriage way." ... "All cattle sold in the market, and known to be wild, or become so, to be secured and taken to the next public slaughter-house and there killed."

The drover may not strike any animal below the hock; there must not be more than 20 beasts or 100 sheep or lambs in one drove, and two drovers must be employed in every drove of sheep or lambs exceeding 40. No dog must be employed in driving cattle, and only one dog in the driving of any number of sheep.

In 1847, the number of licensed drovers was 902; in 1849, it had increased to 950; and at present it is about 1,000. Their division is into master and journeymen drovers. The master drovers bargain for the driving of sheep, &c., and attend in the market to see to the animals, to "draw" them when sold, divide them into the lots in which they may have been disposed of, and transfer them to the parties appointed by the purchaser to receive them. The journeymen drovers are divided into night and day drovers, and are usually engaged by the master drovers, who may be a tenth of the body. The night drovers are employed in driving the animals *to* Smithfield-market, the day men drive them *from* it. Their remuneration is by head, by score, by lot, or by job. It varies of course with the distance to be traversed, and is shown in the narratives I give. In addition to the men there are from 100 to 150 boy drovers, one-half of them without either badge or license. Of this class the men complain bitterly; they are indeed the slop labourers of Smithfield market.

The market scavengers are employed by the Corporation or by their contractors. The scavengery begins as soon as the market is cleared, and continues until the work is completed. There are also in attendance the police and the officers of the Society for the Prevention of Cruelty to Animals. Two sergeants and 18 police-men are employed in charge of Smithfield throughout the week, with an addition of four by day and two by night when the markets are held. The following return shows the nature of the police duty:—

RETURN OF COMPLAINTS MADE BY THE CITY POLICE IN CONNECTION WITH SMITHFIELD-MARKET, AGAINST DROVERS, SALESMEN, AND OTHERS, FROM 1842 TO 1848 INCLUSIVE.

	1842	1843	1844	1845	1846	1847	1848	Total
Nature of Complaint :—								
Driving sheep or cattle into the City before the prescribed hour on Sunday .	12	7	5	1	..	3	4	32
Driving more cattle in one drove than allowed	6	..	9	18	5	14	6	58
Driving more sheep in one drove than allowed	..	1	..	..	7	1	3	12
Using more than one dog in driving one drove of sheep	..	..	..	..	2	..	..	2
Cruelty to any cattle, sheep, lamb, calves, pigs, &c. ..	26	13	17	31	53	53	54	247
Not wearing metal ticket ..	25	13	11	15	58	53	32	207
Using an unstamped stick .	..	..	..	11	..	11	6	27
Using a dog to cattle	..	9	4	3	..	4	2	22
Causing an obstruction with cattle, sheep, &c.	..	..	6	5	..	..	11	22
Not renewing license	..	..	..	..	..	..	4	4
Exposing cattle unfit for human food	..	..	..	..	..	..	4	4
Not altering change of residence	..	..	..	..	3	1	..	4
Lending metal ticket to an unlicensed person	..	..	1	1	..	..	..	2
Total	69	43	53	85	128	140	125	643
How disposed of :—								
Convicted and fined	49	31	42	56	104	110	97	489
Dismissed	19	7	10	16	9	8	5	74
Not heard, withdrawn by magistrate's order, or the parties absconding	1	5	1	13	15	22	23	80

In addition to the police, two, or sometimes more, of the officers of the society I have mentioned attend Smithfield, and report any acts of cruelty they may witness to the secretary. The drovers are much more averse to the interference of these officers than that of the police.

All accounts concur in representing that within these six or eight years there has been a great improvement in the behaviour of the drovers to the animals in their care, and even in the general character of the men. "I must say," observed Mr. Pocklington, "as to the Smithfield drovers, that the manner in which the trade is now conducted, to what it was twenty years ago, is beyond conception; it is a most extraordinary thing; even the very dogs that used to be barking day and night are now learnt not to bark at all."

The journeymen drovers nearly all reside in Clerkenwell, and in the neighbourhood of Smithfield. The majority of them are married men, and generally uneducated. Most of their wives do slop or cost-ermongers' work. They reside in the narrow streets, the dirty courts and alleys, inhabited by the costermongers, and others of that class; indeed, one-half of the drovers unite costermongering pursuits with their droving, as droving occupies in general only the Sunday night or afternoon, and the Monday, and the Thursday night, and the Friday. One day-drover whom I saw resided in an alley in Clerkenwell, oc-cupying a tolerably large and very clean room, with his wife and one child. He was an intelligent-looking man. "I don't know what my parents were," he said, "but I was a boy-drover, and so got a license. I can't read or write. I'm a day drover now, but of course I do night work when I get it, for night work pays better than day. I'm 28 years old, I believe. I'm paid by the job now, as we are mostly. I have 3s. 6d. on the Monday for driving from Smithfield to the West-end, where my master has regular customers that employ him pretty constant. On the Fridays I have 2s. There's only about half the number to drive on a Friday that there is on a Monday. But my work's only chance, as sometimes my master hasn't a turn for me. I have often been in what I reckon danger from cattle, but I never got hurt. Masters are often, I thinks, unreasonable, for they discharges us when the cattle's wild and can't be managed. High-fed beasts are bad to manage, and they get so provoked, because they've perhaps never been tied up before, nor been used to handling, that a very little thing will set them off like devils. I often wonder that there's so few accidents. Mine's a bad trade, sir. The trains makes less droving wanted." "Yes, indeed," said the wife, "when we was first married, seven or eight years back, my husband has brought me home 13s. on a Monday evening, and sel-dom less than 8s. Friday was about half as good, or more than half. Ah! we was better off then, far better off, though things were dearer." "Aye," said the husband, "if things wasn't cheap we couldn't live at all.

It's all the same what I drives when I works by the job, as I've done for a long time. I don't know what my master gets for the job. More than I do, of course; but it's better working for a master drover, if you are inferior paid, 'cause work's more certain. I go a costering when I'm not droving, and make about as much at one as the other—11s. a week the two. But we've got through our stock money, from sickness, and we're hard up. My rent's 1s. 6d. a-week, and my own sticks. There's boys without a licence that injures us. People don't care breaking the law if they save 1d. or 2d. by it."

The wife, a delicate-looking woman, was at work bracemaking. She cleared 2s. a-week by hard work, but had her work "second-hand," or from a person who contracted with the tradesmen for the supply of a large stock:—"We live chiefly on bread and cheap fish, now," she said, "for 2s. a-week is all I can help my husband with. If we have a bit of meat we have it for a Sunday dinner, but I have not eaten a morsel of meat this fortnight."

A night drover, a very good-looking young man, gave me the following statement. He had just left the market when I saw him, and wore a thick corduroy jacket, a strong leather apron, and very coarse heavy shoes:—

"I am a night drover," he said, "and have all my life been a drover. I don't remember my parents. They died when I was young. I'm 18 now, and I've got a living in Smithfield with nobody to help me, and have helped a younger brother these 10 years. My name's ———. My Christian name, sir?—I don't know what you mean. I don't know what a Christian name is. No, I don't understand anything what Christianity is. I used first to mark the sheep what was sold in Smithfield with ochre. I've sometimes made 2s. 6d. on a very good market day. The ochre cost me 6d. I drove a little, as a boy, and for five years had neither badge nor stamped stick, nor anything of that sort; but here's my badge now." [The man here showed me his stick with the proper mark, but without a goad. The day drover also showed me a new one he had made and was going to get stamped, but it had a very sharp goad. Neither man had ever been "up" for cruelty; if they had been convicted of it, they said, their licenses would not have been renewed.] "Yes, sir," continued the night drover, "I can do as well without a goad, I think, as with one. I never uses no cruelty. Any drover'll tell you that people's far more particler than they was. Our dogs is very useful. They're Scotch collies mostly. A real Smithfield-bred dog of a year or two old is worth 25s. to 30s. I sold mine the other day—he was a middling dog—for 15s. I'm training another now. They're not so very easy to train. I break off a bit of their longest teeth, and file a bit off the sharpest of the others; but that isn't always wanted. That's done to take a sheep by the ear without tearing it. I don't try them with my finger to see if their teeth is too sharp or not. I have tried them on an old book-back that was of no use. I puts him in a string and pulls him along the sheep's backs, and snubs him if he barks then. A good dog only barks when he's driving. I can't either read or write. I'm not married. I have 1s. a score for driving sheep from Islington market, penning them, and minding them at Smithfield; 2s. 6d. from Tottenham; and 2s. 7d. from Chalk Farm. I have made 10s. on a Sunday night, and half that on a Thursday; but that's the top of it. I think I make 10s. a week the year through, for I'm young and strong, and can do a great deal of work. It's very seldom now any night-drover has to drive from anywhere but the lairs. Beasts is generally driven by the job. Beast driving is just about the same money as sheep. I don't know of no regular charges. It's a bargain. My best times, I thinks, is the middle of summer and the middle of winter."

A boy drover told me that his father was a costermonger, and that he helped him sometimes, but "worked" Smithfield on market days, helping the day drovers, and making 1s. or 1s. 6d. a week—sometimes, but not often, only 6d.—and sometimes nothing. But he would stick to it, he said, for he "liked drovering, as how, better nor costering; it was a freeerer sort of life." He could neither read nor write, but was a fine-looking lad of 14. He had no badge.

The Smithfield Drovers' Benevolent Society—for they have a society—was established in November, 1844. It now contains about one hundred members. At their monthly meetings in their respectable tavern there is neither drunkenness nor blasphemy among the men. The landlord of the King's Head assured me (as did others) that within his recollection of 18 years' experience as an inn-keeper, the change in the behaviour of the drovers was most remarkable, and highly to be commended—the more so, he added humorously, because they drink less, and reduce Smithfield landlords' profits. The following extract from the rules will show the nature of the society:—

> "All town and country drovers are solicited to enrol themselves as members. The payments are 2s. 1d. per month. Each member is free in twelve months from his first payment, and according to the

present state of the society will receive in sickness, per week, 12s.; death, 12*l.*; wife's death, 6*l.*; superannuated, per week, 2s. 6d.; death of a superannuated member, 6*l.* The members meet at the King's Head Tavern, Smithfield, on the first Wednesday in every month, by whom donations and subscriptions will be thankfully received."

All drovers above 18 and under 45 years of age are eligible. Super-annuation is from advanced age, blindness, or, in the opinion of two medical men, a physical incapacity to labour as a drover. Behind the King's Head are large yards and covered sheds, where the drovers re-sort after the market to wash themselves, and where they have boxes, &c., provided for the safe keeping of their ropes, &c. On my visits all were very orderly, and showed no little anxiety about cleanliness of person.

LABOUR AND THE POOR.

THE METROPOLITAN DISTRICTS.

[FROM OUR SPECIAL CORRESPONDENT.]

OF THE MEAT MARKETS.

LETTER LXXX.

I have now to deal with the dead markets, or the markets in which meat, ready for consumption, is sold. The wholesale, or carcass markets, are—Newgate, Leadenhall, and Whitechapel. In all these markets there is also a certain degree of the retail trade carried on, and in the way I shall explain. The oldest of the carcass markets is Newgate. Its area comprises a central square, 40 yards long on each side, with a wooden building in the centre, and a diversity of alleys and narrow passages. Adjoining Newgate-market is that of Mr. Tylor—its area covering 20,000 square feet. The entrances to Newgate-market are from Newgate-street (opposite Christ's Hospital), Warwick-lane, Ivy-lane, and from the labyrinth of narrow streets to the north and west of St. Paul's-churchyard.

Historical associations connected with the vicinity are not wanting. In Warwick-lane (formerly called Eldenese-lane) lived Warwick, the King-maker, in whose house, his retinue being then 600 men, there were—as if appropriately, considering the present purposes of the site—"oftentimes six oxen eaten at a breakfast."

Newgate-market is held daily, commencing at about four in the morning; the busiest days being Monday and Friday. From five to seven is the busiest period, and the wholesale business is over by nine or ten; waggons and carts fill Newgate-street in long lines from five to seven; the waggons convey the consignments from the railway stations and the wharfs. Among the remnants of the past system of carriage, I may mention that there are still two public waggons which travel direct from Clare, in Suffolk, to London. They start at nine on the Friday morning, and reach Newgate at four on the Saturday morning. Each waggon brings about three tons, chiefly of pork and veal. The carts, usually dark brown, picked out with red, are those of the purchasing butchers, or poulterers, for the conveyance of their purchases; they are sometimes called the "one-horse beef carts." The packages of meat, &c., are conveyed on men's backs or shoulders from the waggons to the premises of the salesmen; and are, when sold, conveyed in the same way to the buyers' vehicles. Newgate-market is the property of the City, excepting about a quarter of its extent, which belongs to individuals. The western end of the market is the property of Mr. Tylor. There is no express charter for the regulation of Newgate-market; but it is subject to the control of the Markets' Committee, and is superintended by a clerk, an inspector of meat (who is also the collector of rents for the Corporation), and two beadles. In addition to the regular morning business, second markets are held on the afternoons of Monday and Friday, for the convenience of those who attend Smithfield Market on the mornings of those days, and who are frequently "dead," as well as "live," purchasers. On Saturday afternoon there is a market resorted to by a class of butchers (retailers) known in the trade as "leggers," men who purchase for such localities as Bermondsey, Lambeth-walk, &c., the coarser qualities of meat, and the "clods and stickings," which are a portion of the neck and shoulders of the ox. About twelve, or an hour or two later or earlier, the wholesale "commission salesmen" weigh off the unsold meat to their assistants, who sell it by retail, on their own account. On Saturday nights the retail traffic is the greatest. Newgate-market is crowded with noisy, squabbling, straggling buyers, most of them Irish men and women, who buy small quantities, and often at very low rates, taxing sorely the patience of the sellers by coolly bidding half what they ultimately give. Mr. Tylor's part is closed at eight o'clock, a measure which one of the principal salesmen told me was attended with no inconvenience to them, and the crowd then rush across Warwick-lane, or along Newgate-street, to the adjacent market. So well known is this cheap mart, that there is not a retail butcher supplying the poor with their modicums of animal food within a mile in any direction, or within two miles in some.

Mr. Tylor's portion of this great meat mart (called College Market by the Newgate-market inspector in his evidence before the Commons' Committee on Smithfield) occupies the site of what was the Old College of Physicians. The edifice was built from Sir Christopher Wren's designs, and under his superintendence. The dome, which Garth, in his "Dispensary," pronounces "majestic to the sight," still distinguishes Warwick-lane; and the statues of Charles II., and of the Sir John Cutler who supplied Pope's instance of "want with a full purse," look down on the roofs of the butchers' shops, which are built in what was the quadrangle of the college. These shops are loftier and airier than those in Newgate-market, and better ventilated. Just before the period of my visit a subterranean communication was discovered, in the course of some repairs, between the adjoining prison of Newgate and the College, along which the bodies of criminals who had been hung were conveyed for dissection. The banqueting-hall, with its fretted roof, is now a show-shop for Mr. Tylor's braziery, and the dissecting-room is one of his workshops. A curious visitor will readily find salesmen and butchers who will unhesitatingly assert that the present purposes of the quondam college are quite as conducive to the public health as were the former.

At early morning the scene in these markets is peculiar, and peculiar to London. You walk along the narrow alleys in a perfect city of meat. The carcases of sheep, of lambs, of pigs, and of calves, and the quarters of beef, are hung, on your right hand and on your left, thickly one upon another. Meat is in some parts swinging over your head; and black, and red, and white, and parti-coloured calves' heads are spread in long rows at your feet. Here is a pile of shin bones; there are pendent great clusters of deep-coloured livers. Along the narrow alleys trot—for their walk is a trot—the blue-jacketed porters with their loads. They go straight, and as if blindly on, and the weight they carry—one of them told me he had carried 6 cwt., 8 lb. to the stone—impels them to go blindly on. The commission salesmen, or the butchers, and their customers, stand coolly by, chatting or bargaining, with the usual indifference of men to things, however remarkable, that they are accustomed to see. On a dark morning the flare of uncovered gas lights brings strongly out the red and white of the beef and mutton, and adds to the striking effect of the greatest meat market in the world.

A butchers' market was in existence in this quarter prior to the great fire of London (1666), and was then carried on in sheds in the street. The College of Physicians was devoted to its present uses about twenty-five years ago. The inspector's duties extend over it, but not those of the other officers. The statements I give contain further information descriptive of the market. The tolls are nominal. The tradesmen must be free of the City.

The business of Newgate-market, like that of Smithfield, is carried on principally through the agency of meat salesmen, or, as I heard them frequently called in the trade, *dead salesmen;* so with Leadenhall. To these dead salesmen is consigned the meat from the country, where the animal has been slaughtered and "dressed." Beef is sent in quarters, so is veal, if large; if small, the calf is sent entire; and sheep and pigs are sent both entire, in two quarters (or half sheep), in quarters or in joints. Pigs are sent entire. The commission charged per stone of 8 lbs. on beef for the whole ox is 1d.; on joints, 1½d. I may here premise that in writing of the London trade, and mentioning a stone, 8 lbs. is meant. On mutton, in joints, 1½d. per stone is the commission; or 10d. or 1s. for a dead sheep. If a sheep be consigned alive to the salesman, as it sometimes is, the charge is 14d. or 16d.; for 4d. and 6d. are the charges for slaughtering. Bullocks consigned to be slaughtered and sold, are charged 3s. 6d. per head (the slaughterer's charge), in addition to 1d. a stone commission. Calves are at 1s. 6d. or 2s. commission whole. Pigs, entire, are the same as sheep—per stone, 1d. to 1½d.

One-fourth of the beef and mutton consigned to Newgate-market (including Mr. Tylor's portion, where precisely the same system of business prevails) is from Scotland, Berwick, Dunbar, Leith, Dundee, Aberdeen, and other ports on the eastern coast. Aberdeen is the place from which the largest supply of beef is obtained; the greatest quantity of mutton is sent from Edinburgh and Leith. A small supply is also sent from Dumfries and other inland towns. Until the intimate connection of Scotland and England, by railway communication, was brought to its present state, the meat was sent almost entirely by steam-packet, but now only one-fortieth of the quantity is sent by steam-packet, compared to what was once sent. The charge per cwt. by railway from Aberdeen to London is 4s.; by steam-packet, 3s. Beef is also sent from Herts, Essex, Bucks, Beds, Suffolk, and all the neighbouring counties, but the loins are principally sent from Leicestershire and Northamptonshire, and the most of them from the county towns of those shires. The London salesmen told me that the people of these places would not go to the cost of the best joints, but lived on the "shoulders," and so London had a constant supply of choice meat. Occasionally, in the winter, choice beef is sent from the North and East Ridings of Yorkshire. The charge, by railway, from Newmarket is 1s. 9d. per cwt.; from Clare, by waggon, 2½d. per stone.

The supply of English mutton is from the same localities as that of beef, with the addition of a quantity shipped regularly from

Hull. Hind quarters of mutton are consigned from Leicester and Northampton in the same way as sirloins of beef. A small quantity of mutton is sent from Wales, but it is most usually sent direct to the retail tradesmen in fashionable quarters. The Scotch mutton is of very excellent quality.

Veal, for the London consumption, is the produce of Dorset, Wilts, and Somersetshire; with a small supply from the other western counties, and from Suffolk.

The great supply of pork is from Ireland; from Belfast, Derry, Drogheda, Dublin, Waterford, Cork, and Limerick; and from Inverness and Invergordon in Scotland; as well as some from Suffolk and the counties near to the metropolis. Dairy-fed pork is sent from Suffolk, Cambridgeshire, and other proximate counties, but is frequently sent direct to the pork-butchers. The best Irish pork, and the greatest supply, is from Waterford. The Scotch pork is much inferior to the Irish.

The system of business, as is always the case in this country at the present time where business is carried on upon a very large scale, is at once simple and rapid. This is the regular process: "We will take Aberdeen, sir," said a "dead" salesman to me, "as I receive considerable quantities of meat from there. I have a very great connection in the Scotch trade, though I never was in Scotland in my life, and I hardly know how it came to me, but it comes when you get your name up. My Aberdeen friend, whom I never saw and very likely never shall, writes to me, short and sweet, just to say, by such a train, such a consignment, arrives at such an hour, such a morning. It's brought to the market, and I employ a porter to carry it from the railway company's waggon to my shop. I have nothing to do with paying for carriage from the country or in town, that's pre-paid from Aberdeen, or arranged with the parties, and I know nothing and care nothing about it. I sell the meat, and the day of sale, or the next day, I just make out an account of weight and price received, and commission, inclose a crossed cheque on my banker, and send the letter by post, and that's all. Our cheques pass in all parts of the kingdom—Scotland, and Ireland, and all."

Another salesman, whose "connection" was chiefly English, told me that he pursued precisely the same system; and on my saying, "I presume you always remit within the week?" "The week!" he exclaimed, "if I waited a week, my consignors would think I was either dead or broke." The same salesman told me that there was a very agreeable interchange of hospitalities between the nearer consignors and their London tradesmen; the Londoner taking a holiday in the country under the hospitable care of the grazier or farmer whom he acts for; the grazier, when in town, experiencing civic hospitality in return. Concurrent testimony showed that the profit of a meat, or "dead" salesman, is about 2½ per cent. on his sale, or has been nearly that on the average for the last two years. When meat is cheap it is better for the salesman's gains, as there is a greater demand, and "I get the same commission," said a salesman, "on meat at 2s. 8d. a stone, a penny, as I did when I once sold, as I once sold it, I don't recollect the year exactly, at 6s. 3d. a stone. At that time I often got 5s. 8d., and 5s. 9d., and 5s. 10d., and sometimes 6s.; and once—I'm not speaking of prize meat—6s. 3d. Though meat's less than half the price, I don't think there's anything like half as much again bought, considering that the population increases so. I don't sell 10 per cent., perhaps not 7½, more than when meat was dearest; but there's such competition now, it's hard to say what the increase is, looking at the many ways of disposing of meat. As far as I can judge, there is not that greater, or that much greater consumption; for Smithfield returns don't show much of it, and the land don't carry so very many more beasts and sheep. But I can't well judge. I think so, and so do many that have better means of judging. The foreign supply matters nothing."

Some of the tradesmen are butchers on their own account; perhaps a third or more of them are, as well as salesmen for their country and town connection, for they have town as well as country connections, as I shall show in my account of Whitechapel-market.

The rents for the Newgate meat-shops are paid weekly, the collector calling, I was told by one of the tenants, with a most laudable punctuality. Concerning Newgate, it is hardly possible to draw an average to show the rental. One tenant averaged it at 25s. a week, another at £2; and another considered £2 too low. They range, it appears, from 10s. to £3 10s.; but there is no relative proportion in size and rent. One reason for this inequality is, that the shops which are the property of the city are let by tender. The rent is never altered; so that those who have had an advantageous "take," or whose families, partners during life and successors after death, enjoy it still, sit under easier rents than their later coming fellow traders. On Mr. Tylor's property the rents range from 12s. to 24s. weekly, for a single take; the Newgate takes may comprise what once constituted two shops.

The labourers connected with the meat-market are porters, ticketed and unticketed. The ticket-porters (a class of whom I have previously treated) are in possession of tickets, though they do not display them, which show that they are freemen of the Butchers' Company. Their number does not exceed a dozen, while the whole number of porters employed was estimated to me as sometimes being 300. The number, however, fluctuates. Men of the class of dock labourers try "for a chance" at the meat markets, when employment is scarce or altogether wanting elsewhere. According to the laws of the city the ticket porters, as freemen, are entitled to the exclusive porterage at this market, and this exclusive privilege was exercised by them for many years. When one of my informants first knew the trade twenty years ago, a ticket-porter would be engaged to carry the contents of a waggon from the street to the shops, and he, as the privileged person, employed unticketed men under him, paying them such an amount as yielded him a profit on their labour. This system continued, but with repeated infringements, until within these eight or ten years. As railway conveyances increased, and arrangements were perfected which ensured at a stated hour in the early morning, the delivery of consignments from different parts, the necessity of a more rapid and immediate command of labour was felt ("for the market," a common saying among provision salesmen, "can't wait"), and the privileges of the ticket-porters were more and more disregarded, the paucity of their numbers preventing their employment as readily as was needed. Unticketed men were employed immediately by the tradesmen four or five years ago, a privileged employ ceased, and now each porter, as it was worded to me, "is on his own head."

There is also another class, but they are more carriers than porters, who have small "beef carts," and carry meat, &c., to the customers of the market who do not "keep their own carts," at 1d. a stone for any distance within three miles. On a busy morning about a dozen of these men are in attendance.

From an old ticket porter, who did not seem to know his age with any exactitude, I had the following account. I selected him as the oldest man; but, either from failing memory or from want of intelligence, the poor man was somewhat confused in his statement, so far that I sometimes had a difficulty in understanding him. He was a middle-sized man, stooping, but not considerably, and subservient in his manner. His appearance did not indicate great feebleness, and he was decently dressed:—

"I have known the business," he said, "for 40 years, and have been for 36 a ticket porter myself, as was my father before me. I am free of the Butchers' Company, but that's thought nothing of now. It cost me between £3 or £4 to take up my freedom. I have heard my father say that when he was young he could make £4 or £5 a week at the portering, because then he had his rights, and the trade wasn't at all overdone. When I first started I had 6d. for carrying a quarter of beef, and 3d. for a sheep or such like, and men would do it under for a ticket man. I employed men. I can't tell how many I have employed in any week—perhaps six or twelve. I'm sure I don't know. I know for a long time I made £2 a week, and kept a wife, and brought up four children comfortably, and sent them to school (as I can read and write myself), and now I've only myself to keep, and can hardly keep myself. Ten or eleven years ago things was pretty good. After that they fell off and fell off, till now I don't make 9s. one week with another. I live by myself, and pay 2s. 6d. a week for an unfurnished room; but it's a good room, and I'd rather pay a little more for a good one. Mondays and Fridays are my best days. I may then make 1s. 6d., 2s., 2s. 3d., and sometimes 2s. 6d., which is a capital day. Yesterday (Monday) I made 1s. 9d., and today [I saw him about three on a Tuesday] 8d., so far. Some days I never taste meat, though I see so much of it. Aye, indeed, sir, that's true. The weights I have carried in my life time must be very great indeed."

In the question of the weight he had carried in forty years time my informant seemed to take an interest. One morning, he told me, he carried twenty prime sheep from the market to a neighbouring butcher, besides other packages; and those sheep would weigh twelve stone each. Thus the sheep alone weighed 240 stone. He had frequently carried ten quarters of beef, each 3½ cwt., or 280 stone for that porterage alone. This man now carried hampers of rabbits more than anything else, and was not able to carry very heavy burdens. I believe, and am assured by experienced men, that the statement is decidedly within the mark, if I compute that during his career this man had carried 100 stones a day for six days in the week during thirty years.

An unticketed porter, a strong active man, who "jobbed about," helping the butchers, and earning a trifle in any way, told me that he made about 10s. or 11s. a week. He had worked on a railway, and received 30s. a-week, and sometimes more, and was brought up as a labourer on a farm. He was not regular, he said, at Newgate, or any other market, but was known at most of them, and "made shift pretty middling, for it was no use fretting, and lots were worse off than he was."

Connected with the salesmen of the meat markets are a class of men known as *jobbers*, of whom there may be 100. These men are generally broken-down butchers, and many jobbers are intemperate men. They are on the look out for "bargains" in Smithfield. "A jobber," said an experienced salesman, "will buy a lot, say of bullocks, such as he thinks cheap, of a live salesman in Smithfield. They may be cattle that come in late, when the best buyers may have left, or a lot that must be sold, if money's wanted, in a falling and dull market. So he buys, and then has to find the money. Then he runs to me, or to some other dead salesman, and he says—and uncommonly polite some of them are at such times—'Mr. ——, there's a good thing to be made of a lot, and you shall have them, if you'll just oblige me with a cheque, Mr. ——, sir.' Well, either I have confidence in the jobber's judgment, or I know something of the cattle, or perhaps I'm inclined to give the poor devil a chance for a bit of a pull, if he's at low-water mark—which means he can hardly get a drop of beer—and so I hand him a cheque, crossed of course. Well, the lot comes to me, and they're slaughtered, and sold on the regular terms, just as if they were from the country, and I pay the profit, over and above commission, to the jobber; but if it's a loss, I must put up with it, for the jobber's always a man of straw. And so they live."

I may add, that I heard, incidentally, of many kindly acts done by the salesmen and butchers to their reduced brethren.

Of the nature and extent of the business transacted in Newgate-market, I had the following account from a leading tradesman there, to whose courtesy and information I am indebted. He said:—

"Of the immense business done in Newgate-market a just idea cannot be formed by the public, nor can a precise account be given by the trade. It is considered by those who have the best means of judging fairly that there is sold in this market annually as much Scotch and country-killed meat as is equal to one-third of the beasts and sheep sold in Smithfield-market in the same time. I think I shall be within the mark if I put down the quantity sold in Smithfield during the past twelve months to be 208,000 beasts, and 1,500,000 sheep and lambs, making, including pigs and calves, a money value of between seven and eight million pounds. It will follow, then, if my calculation be correct, that as there are sold in Newgate-market at least three times as many calves and pigs as are sold in Smithfield, there cannot be much less than three millions pounds worth of dead meat sold yearly in this market. Making, including Leadenhall and Whitechapel, the sum amount to upwards of twelve millions sterling for the beef, mutton, lamb, pork, and veal, that the mighty maw of the metropolis yearly consumes, and that consumption is yearly increasing. Of the buyers, we have four classes which at seasons are distinctly marked. The very earliest and most particular of these are the purveyors for the aristocratic regions of Grosvenor-square and Park-lane, which are represented by two very able amiable members from South Audley-street. Portman, Manchester, and Cavendish-squares, noble names all, are aptly represented by and served from Wigmore-street. The noble mansions of Piccadilly, May-fair, Berkeley-square, St. James's-square, and of Pall-mall, with its majestic club-houses, are most carefully and intelligently served by Air-street, Jermyn-street, Albemarle-street, Eagle-place, and Charing-cross. 'A right regal space' alone had the honour to purvey for two Sovereigns.

"These and a few others are the earliest and most particular customers as buyers of the choicest and highest priced meat. Another class, equally respectable, but having less fashionable trades, are those suburban butchers, whose customers do not daily require for their dinner parties lambs' ears and tails, sweetbreads, calves, and lambs, calves' feet by the score or hundred, ox palates, marrow-bones, and ox tails by the dozen. Their customers needing these delicacies less often, and in smaller quantities, their early attendance is of less importance. But as buyers of meat, they are as particular in selecting the very best, and no consumers are better supplied than those who dwell in the respectable suburbs of London.

"The next class are those whom we term the cutting butchers, but 'cutting' does not signify cheap or slop, as in other trades. Some of them are small buyers of dead meat, or buy only veal or pork, as they kill their beef and mutton. Some are irregular, and will sometimes buy an enormous quantity of dead meat. The largest buyers are, one from the Westminster-road and another from Somers-town. They both do an immense business, and may fairly be said to stand at the head of the chance-trade butchers of London. Amongst the most remarkable and respectable of this class is one family of many brothers, who have a great many shops in various parts of London—in fact, one in almost every poor neighbourhood. Their purchases are entirely or almost confined to mutton, fore quarters, ribs and breasts, sheeps' heads and plucks. They are also buyers of thin flanks of beef, and, I believe, to these parts they entirely confine themselves when meat is very dear. But since the reduction in the price of meat they have been regular buyers of live sheep, and so are losing the distinction they merited of being the only real *fore-quartered* family in England. With the passing away of this class arrives another, a shade lower in price, although their trades are the same in character. For, superior as are the intelligent and scientific workmen of Lambeth, or the skilful artizan and respectable clerk of St. Pancras or Marylebone, in social position to the ill-paid Spitalfields weaver, the Shoreditch cabinet-maker, or the hard-working labourers of Leather-lane and Whitecross-street, so proportionately are the prices the butchers of these poor neighbourhoods are enabled to give. With this class of the trade and a few eatinghouse keepers the business of the morning passes away."

Of some further characteristics of this market I now give an account, written for me by an experienced tradesman in the market. He put his statement in the form which best pleased him. I need hardly add that he took care, from his own intimate knowledge of the market, and from conversations with his neighbours, to confine himself strictly not *to*, but *within*, facts. The following is the account:—

"I don't know how it is, but we Newgate butchers never can succeed in impressing upon the mind of a stranger a just idea of the liberality, intelligence, and consideration of the Corporation of the City of London when viewing Newgate market. It is in vain that we assure them that the revenue derived from it is only between 3,000*l.* and 4,000*l.* a year, and for that trifling sum we have a 'Markets Committee,' which sits I scarcely know where—I don't know when; and I never yet saw anybody that knew for what; but still we are grateful, for they leave us alone. We have two beadles who perform their sometimes very heavy, and always somewhat unpleasant duties, with perfect propriety; and we of course have a collector, who also acts as inspector, with powers not strictly defined; for with some of the salesmen he is at issue, and likely to remain so, unless his duties and powers are clearly and unmistakeably defined. Besides, the corporation will put a new leg to one of its boards, or replace a broken hook on a rail, or mend a broken window, or sometimes make a vigorous effort to render the roof water-tight (alas, a vain effort), if with due respect you address yourself to the proper authority. Still our stranger is unconvinced, or ventures to remonstrate. We determine to silence him. 'Why, sir,' we exclaim with energy, 'our market was painted throughout, entirely, all over last year.' 'For the first time for twenty years,' is the cool rejoinder. Despairing of convincing, we sneeringly ask 'What do you object to? what alteration would you make? Some vast improvement, I dare say?' 'I object,' is the reply, 'to its space, to its site, to its approaches, to its disproportionate rents, to its management, to its single narrow entrance for waggons and carts, for which there is no exit provided, but by passing again down the same narrow entrance; but above all I object to the miserable meanness that has distinguished the corporation in connection with this same Newgate Market, of which you are so proud.'

"From this period the stranger became very violent, and talked very fast, and with much energy of gesticulation. However, I shall let him speak for himself; for nothing that follows do I hold myself responsible:—

"'Here, in a space utterly insufficient for the supply of a country town with 20,000 inhabitants, is sold by far the greatest part of the dead meat that supplies a meat-eating population of 2,000,000 human beings. The space is so small that it is a frequent thing that three sheep are hung upon one hook, and all other articles equally close (so close as to render it impossible that a salesman can do justice to his employer), and so accelerating the decomposition of one of the most perishable articles of human subsistence—a space so small that the trade has revenged itself by taking violent possession of the adjacent thoroughfares of Warwick and Ivy lanes, in the former of which it has annihilated the ancient College of Physicians. The wide thoroughfare of Newgate-street has not escaped—where the waggons unloading, the carts loading, the porters with their greasy loads, the execration of delayed passengers, or wearers of spoiled coats, and bruised bodies violently thrust against the houses, or into the gutters, as the cry of "backs, backs, there," meets their ears, forms a scene which I admit to be exciting, but disgraceful. Look again (pursued my strange friend) at your market on a "Scotch morning;" can anything else on this earth equal the scene of confusion which Newgate-street, Warwick-lane, Hart-street, and the narrow space between your shops then present? Immense hampers being thrown on to the pavement in Newgate-street, many of them weighing more than half a ton. The few passers by are obliged to walk on the other side, or walk in imminent danger of their lives. The lane and street so narrow that only one waggon can pass down them at the same time; the continued stoppage of Hart-street with the backing up or down of waggons and carts, the unwary drivers of which have been caught in the trap; the vexed looks of a salesman who sees an affrighted customer run from the apparent danger of a "Pickford," loaded to the first floor, the top hampers of which oscillate to the exertions of the four powerful horses to get up that horridly-paved and dangerous street (by the by, in which two or three horses fall daily), threatening with instant death any one upon whom a hamper should fall—the untiring exertions of the beadles to preserve anything like order, and enable the full waggons to unload and the empty ones to leave—the flare of a thousand gaslights—angry oaths from as many lips, rising together under the very walls of the metropolitan cathedral—must prove, if anything can, the unfitness of the site and the insufficiency of the space. Of its disproportionate rents it perhaps does not become me, as a stranger, to speak; but that there is a great disproportion you will admit.' I could not dissent. 'With all this inconvenience, some injustice, much injury to consigners, its management must be bad; and so I establish my propositions.'

"My remedy is, remove it to Smithfield, if the live market should be removed. Make a fair compensation to all holders of the houses in the market, for I know that of all the City tenants who are doing a large wholesale business, there are but two or three that have not houses in which they could and would carry on their business, even if that part of the market owned by the City were removed. Their property is valuable, and must be protected.

"Let, then, the Corporation of London, if obliged to remove the live market, determine to build upon its site a dead meat-market that shall reflect credit upon it. Let it be formed with some regard to architectural uniformity, unlike the crazy affair now known as the market, or the wigwam shed-like erections that stretch from Hart-street to Ivy-lane. Let that be the single meat-market for London. Make use of the discoveries of modern science in its ventilation—adapt it to its purpose. Convenience, adaptation, and uniformity, obtained at a moderate rental, will produce 10,000*l.* a year, and more satisfaction to the trade, and benefit the public materially."

The inspector of meat at Newgate-market has to ascertain whether the carcases are in a sound state, and to seize them if they are not. For this purpose he walks round the market and into all the shops. The respectable traders send for him when they have any doubt of the quality of the meat consigned to them. From the 19th January, 1849, to the 30th April, the inspector seized "in Newgate and College markets" 149 quarters of beef, 156 carcases of mutton, 9 calves, and 10 pigs, besides some joints of meat unenumerated. The inspector has the bad meat taken to the knackers to be boiled; he there sees it cut into pieces, put into a boiling copper, and boiled for an hour and twenty minutes. I was assured by parties who could not be in error, that it was impossible that this meat, so treated, could be used for sausages or any similar purpose. In Newgate and the adjoining market, the salesmen and butchers are about 300.

But it is not only to dead meat that the trade in Newgate-market is confined. It is a mart for butter, eggs, fowls, game, and pigeons; but in this respect its business is inferior in amount to that of Leadenhall. I am enabled through the means I have already alluded to, to present, for the first time—no previous calculation having ever been made—a detail of the fowls, game, &c., yearly disposed of in Newgate-market:—

TAME BIRDS OR POULTRY.

Domestic fowls	490,240
Ducks	147,720
Geese	113,640
Turkeys	54,936
Pigeons	98,756
	905,292

WILD BIRDS AND ANIMALS, OR GAME.

Grouse	12,000
Partridges	60,292
Pheasants	19,684
Snipe	47,000
Wild birds, unclassed (of which 5,000 were game), the consignments being mixed	26,000
Plovers	18,000
Hares	54,273
Rabbits	180,072
	417,321

Total of wild and tame birds and animals ... 1,322,613

In addition to this, for the year's traffic I must specify—

Venison	40,000	stones.
Pork	115,000	„
Sucking pigs	15,000	head.
Fresh butter	3,292,700	lb.
Eggs	950,000	

To show the extent of business yearly transacted by one firm alone, I adduce a return supplied to me by the house in question:—

<table>
<tr><td>Fresh butter, principally from Buckinghamshire, Oxfordshire, Bedfordshire, and Northamptonshire, and received within two days from the period of churning, for twelve months ....</td><td>216,060 doz., or 2,592,720 lb.</td></tr>
<tr><td>Meat, two-thirds of which is pork, for the same period ....</td><td>115,150 sts. of 8 lb.</td></tr>
<tr><td>Ducks and geese 28,532
Fowls 43,240
Turkeys 5,936
Rabbits and game 27,080
Pigeons .... 1,964</td><td>106,752</td></tr>
</table>

The courtesy of another house of high character has enabled me to give the following returns of their weekly business. The calculation is in stones of 8 lb. to the stone—a weight observed in London, and, I believe, nowhere else.

		Stones.
120 Pigs	about	920
130 Sheep	„	1,040
Hind quarters of 300 sheep	„	1,300
80 Lambs	„	360
40 Calves	„	800
10 Carcases of beef	„	800
Hind quarters of 15 beasts	„	600
Roasting beef	„	200
Sundry joints	„	150
Total number stone of meat per week ..		6,170

"The above applies," writes my informant, "to meat received nine months in the year; but in the remaining three months, say from July 1 to October 1, it may be calculated at nearly one-half less, and three-quarters of the entire quantity I receive from the country dead."

The next meat market to Newgate, as regards the extent of business, is that of Leadenhall, which is held daily. The market occupies the site of the ancient manor house of Leadenhall, which, in 1445, was converted into a granary for the City, by Simon Eyre, a draper, and Lord Mayor. In Stow's youth—he was born in 1525—it was a wool mart and warehouse. The market escaped the great fire, but at what particular period it became famous as a meat market seems not to be known. Shadwell, in 1689, mentions it as famous for "your fish and fowl;" and Gay alludes to it in his "Trivia," which was written early in the last century, as famous for "mighty beef;" while St. James's-market at that time enjoyed equal repute for veal. Leadenhall's fame for "fowl" is now greater than ever.

From a very intelligent man, whose family has been connected with Leadenhall-market for very many years, I received an account of what he believed, and showed me that he had good reason for believing, was the origination of commission salesmen there and elsewhere. It is probable that this class of tradesmen has existed about 100 years. In Leadenhall-market, there is now a portion marked off as for "country" goods. Here any one, not being a freeman—as all the salesmen, &c., must be—bringing goods, may hang them up for sale at 1d. toll per "pack." In the days when farming was extensively carried on near to London, and when facilities of public transit were slow and irregular, the neighbouring agriculturists brought their meat in their own carts to London, and sold it themselves, at Leadenhall, for instance. This entailed a great loss of time; and as these country dealers had their station in the midst of the London butchers, they gradually fell into the way of employing these butchers as their agents for sale, and so the commission trade became first established.

The tolls paid by the meat salesmen are 2s. 6d. a week each. About seven years ago they were very heavy. A highly respectable salesman told me that at that time he paid 12s. and 14s. a week as toll, and hardly knew what it was for, but the regular charge for toll was 4d. a pack. The salesmen resisted this charge, contending that the Corporation had no right to levy tolls on their own tenants, being freemen, while those who rented shops which were private property were exempt from toll. The matter was about to be submitted to the decision of a court of law, when it was compromised by the salesmen agreeing to pay 2s. 6d. each a week. The City shops are let by tender, and as in Newgate-market the rent varies considerably. Of the Leadenhall ticket porters, I have spoken in my letter on the carmen and porters.

The poultry and game market at Leadenhall is the largest in the world. It is something more than well—it is crowdedly supplied. It is not confined to poultry, though poultry (including geese, turkeys, &c.) is the staple commodity; for in one part I saw the announcement, "white rats for sale," also "gold fish," "young ravens," "hawks," "hobby hawks," "fancy dogs," "hedgehogs," and two very prominent and anti-poultryish announcements—"a pair of white foxes from Paris for sale," and "gentlemen supplied with live foxes."

On my asking a dealer in miscellaneous birds and beasts if foxes were in demand? he answered, "They might be brisker, but the season's coming on." On all sides are large and clean basket-coops, oblong shaped, full of speckled live poultry, or of stately white cocks and hens—the cocks with very scarlet combs or wattles, or with tall, dark gingery-feathered (as regards colours) game fowls, which seemed the most pacific, or at any rate to agree the best, of any congregated members of cooped poultry. In other coops, smaller and rounded, were fancy pigeons; the dark feathers of the carriers glancing with their green shades to the light; the ringdoves sleeping close together in light chocolate coloured lumps, for the form of the somnolent bird is lost; or tall poulters, with their dashed blue and white feathers, not caring to poult amidst all that throng of people. If a poultry-coop was wheeled on a truck from one part to another, the utmost care of the wheeler could not prevent the birds nearest him being flung, as the most elevated, on to the others, and forcing to themselves a place in the poultry crowd of the coop, and so driving others to the top of the elevated part, to be flung forward in their turn, amidst a great flutter and commotion, which ceased when the conveyance stopped. In the same part of the market also were, on one of my visits, owls (I am speaking of live creatures) looking sadly moped, and anything but satisfied, especially when handled and "priced" (4s. a pair was asked for them, with an assurance that owls would soon be up to 6s.); ferrets; rabbits, some of them the "real lop-eared double-smut rabbits;" dogs, being terriers, spaniels, and nondescripts, looking on with the intelligent and inquisitive expression peculiar to dogs; guinea-pigs; squirrels, gamboling in their cages; ducks, as silent as if they had never been known to "quack;" and one large live swan, which I heard a nursery-maid, who was walking about with two children, pronounce "a handsome bird, but with too long a neck." I found that there is a good trade in live swans, guinea-fowls, white, black, and grey cats of the largest size, and white rats. Attached to the wires or wicker-work of the cages of these birds or animals—and they all seemed to brook imprisonment with due philosophy—hung announcements of the wished-for sale of "five grey parrots," "All kinds of water fowls," "Gold-spangled pheasants," and "Sir John Seabright's Bantams." The supply of these "miscellaneous" is not provided for by any regular system. "They are picked up any where."

Along with the poultry market is that of game—dead grouse, blackcocks, partridges, pheasants, and hares, hanging in long rows, the birds in clusters, and the hares singly. The sale of game was first legalised in 1831. The first year of its legalisation the trade was somewhat more than a quarter what it is now. Prior to that about a tenth or a fifteenth of the first year's trade was carried on "under the rose" in Leadenhall-market. Consignments were made from poachers, the guards of the coaches being the medium of this traffic. The trade in game gradually increased, but within these five or six years the supply has been stationary.

The purveyors for the London game markets are noble lords and honourable gentlemen, who slaughter enormous quantities with their own hands, or rather guns. After a battue there is sometimes a glut in Leadenhall, as 600 extra hares may come in. The gamekeepers seem but the secondary labourers for the supply of the great game market of Leadenhall.

The supply of grouse is from the Scotch Highlands, about an eighth being sent from the Yorkshire and north of England moors. They command a ready sale generally, but on a glut the salesman has disposed of these birds quite fresh at 1s. and 1s. 3d. each. *Blackcocks* are all from Scotland; 40 or 50 a day is considered "a lot."

The principal supply of *partridges* is from Norfolk and Suffolk. In a glut they are sold at 9d. to 1s. 3d. a brace. On the day of my visit fine partridges, from a first-rate salesman, were 1s. a-piece, as "a quantity" had come in. One salesman had just sold 100 at 1s. a-piece. A few are sent irregularly from France, and French partridges have been naturalised in Suffolk.

Pheasants also are sent in greater numbers from Norfolk and Suffolk than from any other part. These two counties are the great game grounds for London, the Eastern Counties Railway being the means of conveyance. Pheasants are the only game exported to France, but not in large quantities. Pheasants are of good sale generally.

In severe winters a few *ptarmigan* are received from the north of Scotland. In a very severe winter there have been numbers sent from Norway. One salesman, a few years back, received between 9,000 and 10,000 of these birds in one day. They did not meet with a very ready sale. Some dealers bought 500 or 600 in a lot at 1s. a-piece. In hard winter Holland contributes the great stock of *wild ducks* for London tables. In Holland, Rotterdam being the shipping place, the duck decoys are objects of great care. Somewhat less than a fifth of the quantity from Holland is sent from Lincolnshire. They have been sold in a glut at 1s. a-piece. The great supply of *plovers* is also from

Holland. In severe weather they are sent from Ireland. *Larks* are the produce of Cambridgeshire, with a smaller proportion from Bedfordshire. They are of easy sale at from 6d. to 1s. 3d. a dozen, and are generally roasted for table now; at one time they were fashionable in pies. The greatest amount of *snipes* has been of late years from Ireland. *Woodcocks* are received from the same places as wild ducks, with a few from the northern counties of England. *Hares* are consigned from all parts, but more from Norfolk and Suffolk than from other counties. A few are sent from Ireland. They are of ready sale. *Rabbits* are forwarded chiefly from Norfolk, where there are very large warrens. Three-fourths of the *pigeons* sold in London are from France, Calais and Boulogne being the ports; the remaining fourth is from the counties neighbouring the metropolis.

Poultry (meaning thereby what are best known as *chickens*) are principally from Surrey, Sussex and Lincolnshire. The live poultry, the supply being not a thirtieth compared with the "dead," is mostly from Ireland. *Geese* and *ducks* are chiefly from Lincolnshire. *Turkeys* are supplied more largely from Cambridgeshire than from any other county. The next great quantum is from Norfolk. The demand for poultry increases perhaps at the rate of from 5 to 7½ per cent. yearly.

The salesman's commission—and all the Leadenhall poulterers are salesmen on commission—alike on game and poultry is 5 per cent. In the regular trade the buyers are generally the dealers in game and poultry; the cheap birds are sold principally to hawkers.

A license to deal in game costs £2 2s., and the dealer usually presents 5s. additional to the Clerk of the Arraigns. The toll on poultry and game is nominal.

The following returns, which, like the others, have been prepared for the first time, show the trade of Leadenhall Market. The butchers who have cattle consigned to them to be slaughtered for sale in this market yearly slaughter for this purpose

Oxen	832	Pigs	27,840
Sheep	23,054	Calves	2,812
Lambs	16,981		

Total head of cattle, &c. .... 70,719.

The dead meat consigned for sale to Leadenhall is principally from the counties of Essex, Herts, Cambridge, Suffolk, Norfolk, Sussex, and Devon, and from Scotland. It is to the following extent, in stones of 8 lb.:—

Beef	584,733	Pork	542,367
Mutton	946,191	Veal	398,840
Lamb	448,423		

Total, 2,920,554.

The following return shows the trade in poultry, game, &c.:—

TAME BIRDS AND DOMESTIC FOWLS.

Fowls	1,266,000	Turkeys	69,000
Geese	888,000	Pigeons	284,500
Ducks	235,000		

Total, 2,742,500.

WILD BIRDS, OR ANIMALS, OR GAME.

Grouse	45,000	Plovers	28,000
Partridges	84,500	Larks	213,000
Pheasants	43,900	Wild Birds	39,500
Teal	10,000	Hares	48,000
Widgeons	30,000	Rabbits	680,000
Snipe	60,000		

Total, 1,281,900.

Total of Birds and Animals, 4,024,400.

Besides this, the returns I have received from Leadenhall give—

| Sucking pigs | 27,400 head |
| Fresh butter | 51,720 lb. |

The joint sale of the two great markets I have treated of yields then the following aggregate:—

	Poultry, &c.	Game, &c.	Total.
Newgate	905,292	417,321	1,322,613
Leadenhall	2,742,500	1,281,900	4,024,400
	3,647,792	1,699,221	5,346,013

In addition to these numbers are those of birds the supply of which depends upon the season. Such are those of wild ducks and of woodcocks, which are abundant in severe, and hardly procurable in mild, winters. In a severe winter the supply of wild ducks may be equal to that of pheasants, of woodcocks to that of plovers.

I now give the extent of business done by one house in Leadenhall-market, as it was supplied to me in precise numbers:—

Sheep	14,496	Calves	5,411
Lambs	5,940	Quarters of beef	1,919
Pairs of quarters of mutton or half sheep	2,609	Rumps (with loins) and rumps of beef	3,965
Quarters of lamb and joints of mutton	7,453	Pigs	6,794
		Legs and loins, pork	16,871

"The above," write my informants, "is the account of meat slaughtered in the country and consigned to us for sale on commission, commencing 1st July, 1849, and ending 30th June, 1850. We had also consigned from the country, alive, to be slaughtered in London, 953 lambs, 571 sheep, and 37 calves. Also the following dead meat from Scotland:"—

Sheep	6,735	Quarters of beef	272
Lambs	2,586	Quarters of mutton	152
Pigs	244		

I proceed to the next largest market, where business is carried on both wholesale and retail—Whitechapel. To a portion of the meat here exposed for sale, may be seen attached the peculiar seal which shows that the animal was killed according to the rites to be observed by the Jews. The animal must die from its throat being cut, instead of being knocked on the head. The slaughterer of the cattle for Jewish consumption must be a Jew. The meat so prepared for use is known in the trade as "cosher." Two slaughterers are appointed by the Jewish authorities of the synagogue, and they can employ others, being Jews, as assistants. The slaughterers I saw were quiet-looking and quiet-mannered men. When the animal is slaughtered and skinned, an examiner (also appointed by the synagogue) carefully inspects the "inside." "If the lights be grown to the ribs," said my informant, who has had many years' experience in this branch of the meat trade, "or if the lungs have any disease, or if there be any disease anywhere, the meat is pronounced unfit for the food of the Jews, and is sent entire to a carcase-butcher to be sold. This, however, does not happen once in 20 times." To the parts exposed for sale, when the slaughtering has been according to the Jewish law, is attached a leaden seal, stamped in Hebrew characters with the name of the examining party sealing. In this way, as I ascertained from the slaughterers, are killed weekly, from 120 to 140 bullocks, from 400 to 500 sheep and lambs, and about 30 calves. All the parts of the animal thus slaughtered may be and are eaten by the Jews, but three-fourths of the purchase of this meat is confined, as regards the Jews, to the fore-quarters of the re-spective animals, the hind-quarters, being the choicer parts, are sent to Newgate or Leadenhall markets for sale on commission.

Whitechapel-market consists of a single row of butchers' shops, with great slaughter-houses behind them, on the south side of the High-street, extending from the Minories to Somerset-street, about 500 feet. The property belongs partly to the parish of Aldgate, partly to that of Whitechapel, and partly to private individuals. The butchers who reside at the houses connected with the shops pay an average rental of £100 per annum. There are at present residing in this market twenty-two meat salesmen and three retail butchers; the majority of the wholesale salesmen also sell by retail. This market was, when first established, about 120 years ago, known as Aldgate-market. The market days are Tuesday, Thursday, and Saturday. There are no labourers connected with the market, neither were there any officers till about fifteen months since, when the City authorities appointed an inspector of the meat. The retail purchasers are the poorer and middle classes.

The following is the return of the meat sold annually in Whitechapel-market:—

	Stones.
Pork	148,046
Mutton	107,748
Beef	70,080
Veal	73,100
Total	418,894

The supply consigned direct to Whitechapel is principally from Ross-shire, Inverness-shire, Moray-shire, and from Nairne and Cromarty. The remainder is obtained by the purchase of cattle at Smithfield, which are slaughtered at Whitechapel, for the demand there, and for Newgate and Leadenhall. Indeed, Whitechapel was described to the Select Committee on Smithfield as "the slaughter-house for Newgate-market." It is somewhat remarkable that during the prevalence of the cholera in 1832, and again last year, no person living in the market died of that disease, although the mortality was considerable in the immediate neighbourhood.

The slack season in all the wholesale markets is in August and September. Christmas and the three or four weeks subsequent are the busiest period. Mr. McCulloch, in 1842, calculates the consumption of meat, exclusive of bacon, and all salted provisions, and poultry, at 122 1-6 lb. per individual yearly. In this calculation Mr. McCulloch excludes all "dead meat" sent to London, calculating that it sufficed for the victualling of ships. Great as this consumption of animal food may be accounted, when we bear in mind how many thousands of the working poor of London rarely taste meat, or taste it but once a week, the data I have supplied for the first time shows that the consumption is now greater, and may be taken at 140 lb. yearly consumption per individual, exclusive of the consumption of tripe, beasts', sheeps', and calves' heads, hearts, livers, &c. The supply of meat to the dead markets, I may observe, is now greatly in excess of what it was when Mr. McCulloch wrote; but the tables I gave in my last letter show that the increase in the "live" market has hardly been in the same ratio as the increase of the population. It has been computed that the consumption of meat in Paris (in 1842) was 86 lb. per head; in Brussels, 89 lb.

All the wholesale markets, especially Leadenhall, are pestered with youthful pilferers, known to salesmen as "finders." The young thief prowls about with a bag, and picks up the pieces of string, &c., thrown away after the unpacking of the consignment; also pieces of offal, fat, &c., cut off in trimming the meat. On one of the mornings of my visits, a lad had "found" a new knife; but a butcher's assistant had observed him, and took the prize from the pilferer, bestowing the usual punishment—"a scruf of the neck and a kick." "The finder" is almost always let go, unless the policeman be cognisant of the offence.

The other meat markets are principally retail markets, supplied, as to three-fourths of their trade, and in some places the whole of it, from the wholesale dead markets. These places are not markets in any legal sense, but are congregations of tradesmen selling meat. Clare-market has been a meat market for about 200 years. It is mentioned in 1657 by Howell, as a "new market." It was in this market that the notorious Orator Henley preached to the butchers. What may be considered Clare-market proper, extends from the eastern extremity of Clare-street, along a narrow passage, widening at the end, towards Carey-street. In this part are only butchers' shops, but on all sides, in the neighbouring streets and alleys, are other provision shops, while street sellers occupy every available portion of the thoroughfares. This traffic may, superficially, fill a space of five acres, but

Clare-market proper hardly occupies a rood and a half. There are now in business there fifteen butchers, who supply Covent-garden, the Strand, Lincoln's-inn-fields, &c., with very excellent meat; an inferior quality being sold to the poor in the evenings. The market is held daily. Every Saturday, until past midnight, the scene in Clare-market is one of extreme bustle and business. The average rental of the shops and houses is £60 per annum.

Newport-market has been established (but has been subjected to many changes) for upwards of 120 years. It is now principally a narrow court or passage, 300 yards long and 12 wide, running between Porter and Gerard-streets, Soho. The property is that of private individuals, the rents of the houses being £50 a year as an average. There are eight wholesale and ten retail butchers in this market. The only labourers are "odd men," who are employed in carrying out meat. All classes are purchasers at this market.

Oxford-market is situated in an open space, the approaches being from Oxford-street, Portland-road, and the adjacent streets. The market-house is inclosed; a dome admitting light and air. Four paths intersect each other at right angles through the building. The market contains only shops, and is occupied by green-grocers, a poulterer, and other tradesmen, besides butchers. The area of the market-house is from two to three roods. It was built by a Duke of Portland in 1721, and is the property of the present duke. The shops average a rental of £2 10s. each per month. Here are now six retail butchers. This was the only market in which in the course of my visits I saw a fawn hanging. It had been sent to a butcher to be slaughtered. The customers are the gentry, the tradesmen, and those classes of the working men who are purchasers of animal food. The market is daily.

Brook's Market, situate between Brook-street, Leather-lane, and Holborn, covers an area of a rood. It was established one hundred years ago, and when Hatton-garden was the residence of private families of wealth it was a flourishing place, but it has now a dreary and half deserted look, as some of the sheds are unoccupied, and there is no bustle whatever. About forty years ago the butchers in Leather-lane got nearly the whole trade. There are now only three retail butchers in the market. Saturday is the only day on which there is any amount of business transacted. The principal customers are the tradesmen of the neighbourhood. The average rental of the houses is £30 a year; the sheds let from 4s. 6d. a week to £18 a year.

The place now known as St. George's-market is a portion of Oxford-street, between Southmolton, and Gilbert streets. Until about thirty years back, St. George's-market was held in a passage running from Oxford-street to Gilbert-street, a portion only of which now remains, and is still a market. It contained six butchers' shops, and more than twice the business was done in that passage—I was told by an old butcher who had himself carried on business there—than is now done by any half dozen butchers in the neighbourhood.

The meat markets of London were formerly more numerous than now. The most important of those now extinct was St. James's, which was removed for the erection of Waterloo-place.

Of the other poultry markets, that of Portman, in Church-street, Lisson-grove, is the greatest. The market covers three acres, and is the property of Lord Portman, being leased to Mr. T. Major. The staple trade here is in fruit and garden stuffs, of which I shall speak hereafter. Here, however, 16,000 head of poultry, chiefly from Hertfordshire, are sold yearly; also 1,500,000 eggs, also from Hertfordshire, and 114,000 lbs. of Devon butter.

LABOUR AND THE POOR.

—◆—

THE METROPOLITAN DISTRICTS.

[FROM OUR SPECIAL CORRESPONDENT.]

OF THE "GREEN MARKETS" OF LONDON.

LETTER LXXXI.

I now proceed to show the vastness, the regularity, and the excellence of the supply of fruit, flowers, and vegetables to the green markets of the metropolis. The markets employed, on a large and wholesale scale, for the furtherance of the important traffic I am about to describe are Covent-garden, the Borough, Spitalfields, Farringdon, and Portman. Of these the Borough market is the oldest, and Farringdon the most recent. Hungerford market, in its present state, was opened nearly seven years later than Farringdon, but as it is an old market in a new form, it cannot be classed as recent.

Covent-garden market has many associations connected with it, apart from its character as the first fruit and flower market in the world. On these associations—antiquarian, political, literary, convivial, or theatrical—it is not my intention to dwell, nor even to allude to them further than they may be useful to elucidate my subject.

Covent-garden occupies the site of the old Convent Garden of Westminster Abbey. Perhaps no other church lands, after their alienation, and after a lapse of years, have been applied to a purpose (unconnected with religion) so little alien from their original uses. Where the monks grew their comparatively rude fruits and savoury herbs—for flowers were little cultivated in those days—the choicest fruits, and the profusion of vegetables that adorn the tables of the rich, or stock those of the poor, are sold. These convent lands, after the attainder of the Protector Somerset, their first possessor from Henry VIII., were granted by Edward VI. in 1552 to John, Earl of Bedford; but it was not until two centuries later that Covent-garden market even approached to its present unrivalled celebrity.

In the old times, the principal London market was Stocks market, so called from the stocks—then a common mode of punishment in London, as it was in different parts of the country until the last generation—being placed there. This market was established by Wallis, Lord Mayor of London, in 1282, for the sale of fish and flesh. How long it was devoted to that purpose is not known, probably until the great fire in 1666. Strype, between 1690 and 1700, describes it as a place for the sale, not of fish and flesh, but of "fruits, roots, and herbs, for which it is very considerable and much resorted unto, being of note for having the choicest in their kind of all sorts, surpassing all other markets in London." Stocks market was pulled down in 1737, and afforded the site of the present Mansion-house. The market was transferred to the space which now constitutes the middle of Farringdon-street, whence in 1829 it was transferred to the present Farringdon market.

The square (or piazza) of Covent-garden is the oldest square in London. It dates from 1631, and was built at the cost of the then Earl of Bedford from the designs of Inigo Jones, but Jones's original plan was never fully carried out. It is an oblong of 500 feet by 400. The south side was occupied by the garden wall of Bedford House (the town residence of the family until 1704, when they removed to Bedford House, Bloomsbury, which was pulled down in 1800), and over this wall hung "trees most pleasant in the summer season." The square became fashionable, and persons resorted to it to sell fruit and flowers under the shelter of those trees. Thus originated the market, and its increase, notwithstanding the superiority of Stocks market, must have been somewhat rapid, as on the 12th May, 1671, Charles II. did "give and grant" unto the Earl of Bedford, "by letters patent, the right for ever to have, hold, and keep a market" in the place called the Piazza of Covent-garden, "for the buying and selling of all fruits, flowers, roots, and herbs whatsoever." Covent-garden market furnishes one of the many instances how "most poor matters point to rich ends," for Maitland, some 200 years or more back, mentions that in the magnificent square of Covent-garden, "to its great disgrace," was a fruit-market! During the infancy of Covent-garden market flourished another of the same description—that of Honey-lane, Cheapside. It was instituted after the great fire, and erected on the ground of one of the burnt churches, not rebuilt—that of Allhallows, Honey-lane. This market was abolished in 1835, and the ground is now occupied by the City of London School. Covent-garden market was brought into charge to the poor's rate in 1679, when 23 salesmen were rated at 2s. or 1s. each. The market is now rated at £4,800. From this time the progress of the market was slow until the removal of Stocks market and the opening of Westminster-bridge (in 1750) gave a great impetus to the traffic of Covent-garden. The area of the market, however, was incommodious and uncleanly, and although an act was passed in the 53d year of George III., "for regulating Covent-garden market," it was found inefficient, and the old open shed and wooden structures, with their concomitant nuisances, were swept away and the present improvements established in 1830, under the authority of 9th George IV., session 1828, Mr. Fowler being the architect.

Covent Garden

The market is now apportioned into the "yearly cart stands," "potato stands," "fruit market," "flower stands," "casual cart stands," and "yearly pitching stands," with proper footpaths and gangways. It is approached by Great Russell-street, James-street, King-street, Henrietta-street, and Southampton-street, Strand. On each side of the exterior of the market is the space for carts, waggons, and general traffic. The exterior is devoted to casual and yearly cart stands, potato stands, and (at the eastern extremity only) flower stands. Within the two exterior lines which run parallel with Long-acre and the Strand, are rows of shops, forming the outward walls of the market, beyond which the roof projects considerably. Immediately within the line parallel with Long-acre, and nearest Great Russell-street, is the fruit market, and a space of equal width and about three-fourths of the length is devoted to pitching stands. In the middle, from Great Russell-street to St. Paul's Church, which stands midway between King-street and Henrietta-street, stretches the avenue, where, in handsome shops, tastefully and temptingly arranged, are displayed the choicest native and exotic fruits and flowers, with a proportion of gold fish, silkworms, nets, labels, and anything proper for gardens. The space between the central avenue and the exterior line of shops, towards the Strand, is occupied by yearly pitching stands. At the Great Russell-street end are two conservatories above the shops.

The purpose of these several arrangements is shown in the following digest of the schedule of tolls, rents, &c., which shows, moreover, by their minute specifications, the importance and value of the market:—

"THE CASUAL CART STANDS.—Every waggon containing wholly or principally carrots, or the contents thereof pitched or exposed for sale, 1s. 6d. Every other waggon containing fruit, flowers, vegetables, roots, or herbs, 1s. Every cart containing wholly or principally carrots, 1s. Every other cart containing fruit, &c., 4d. Each stand on which any person shall place or sell any fruit, &c., such person not being the grower, nor the person by, for, or to whom the same shall be brought, 1s. per day. Each stand used or occupied otherwise, 1s. per day.

"YEARLY CART STANDS.—Each stand let, for every square foot superficial, 1s. per annum. Fruit, flowers, &c., not the growth of the holder, 1s. per waggon, 4d. per cart. Each stand used otherwise, 1s. per day.

"THE POTATO STANDS.—Each stand let, for every square foot superficial, 1s. per annum; in addition to such rent, for every sack of potatoes placed or sold, 2d.; per ton for any greater or less quantity than a sack, 1s. 2d. For potatoes placed or sold by any person, not the holder, 2d. per sack and 1s. 2d. per ton.

"THE FRUIT MARKET.—Cherries, ½d. per sieve; apples, pears, plums, apricots, peaches, nectarines, gooseberries, and currants, ½d. per sieve or bushel; strawberries, raspberries, and other fruit of that sort, for every round or head-load, 2d.; walnuts, filberts, and other nuts, ½d. per sieve, 1d. per maund, 1d. per sack; peas, beans, and French beans, ½d. per sieve, 1d. per sack; onions, ½d. per sieve or bushel; asparagus, 1d. per flat; carrots, 1s. 6d. per score dozen bunches; oranges, 4d. per chest and 2d. per box. Each stand, to the holder, not more for every square foot superficial, in addition to the tolls, than 1s. per annum. Every stand over the whole of which any covering shall extend, not more for every square foot superficial in addition to the rent before authorised than 3d. per annum (this charge applies to the other stands also). Every person using the scales ½d. per draught.

"THE YEARLY PITCHING STANDS.—Each stand, let, 1s. per annum for every square foot superficial; fruit, flowers, &c., not the growth of the holder, 1s. per waggon, 4d. per cart. For each stand used otherwise, 1s. per day.

"THE FLOWER STANDS.—For every square foot superficial, 1s. 8d. per annum. Christmas holly and other evergreens pitched, or sold in any part of the market, 3s. per waggon, 2s. per cart. Water-cresses or other spring herbs, not pitched or sold by the holder of the stand being the grower thereof, 1d. per head, load, bag, or basket. Physic herbs and dried herbs, except by the holder, 1s. per waggon, 4d. per cart. Oranges, 4d. per chest, 2d. per box. Flowers or flower-roots, by any person not the holder of the stand, 6d. per dozen."

The specifications of payment by time, as per day or per year, are rent; the others are toll. No packages can be conveyed into the market before one in the morning, nor after ten at night, at which time the market must be closed or cleared. No waggon or cart can remain on any of the stands an hour after it has been unladen. The stands are 8ft. square, and let yearly at from £5 to £10; the daily rent I have stated. The shops on the two exteriors let from 7s. 6d. to 35s. a week. The corner shops in the central avenue are £2 2s. weekly, and the others 25s. to 30s. The market is under the control of a superintendent and collector, an assistant-superintendent, an assistant-collector, three day beadles, and two night watchmen. An engineman is also employed. The market-days are Tuesday, Thursday, and Saturday, Saturday being the principal day. The retail trade is carried on every day.

On the morning of every market day, and twofold on the Saturday, carts of every description, mixed with 1 waggon for every 20 carts, line, one, two, or three deep, all the avenues to Covent-garden market. They stretch from Great Russell-street, up and down Drury-lane, down Brydges-street, Upper and North Wellington-streets; up Bow-street, into Long-acre; up James-street, into Long-acre; down King-street and New-street, to St. Martin's-lane; down Southampton-street to the skirts of the Strand; thick and crowded they stand in Henrietta-street; and stretch up and down Bedford-street. The market opens at five, or somewhat earlier, in the height of the summer. In half an hour from its opening the business is at what I heard called "high charge." Active men are seen unlading, or rather unpacking waggons, throwing about heavy hampers with an effort evidently as much the fruit—to use an appropriate word—of skill as of strength. I have frequently heard men thus employed describe it as "a way they've got," or "a knack from long practice." The men engaged in unlading are the servants (receiving generally 21s. a week) of the salesmen to whom the goods are assigned, or of the grower who brings them to market. If they labour for the salesman, a portion is at once conveyed to his premises; if for the grower, a portion is placed on his pitching stand for the examination of purchasers. As the bargaining proceeds, porters look eagerly on, offering their services. When a bargain is struck, the porter is employed to carry the hamper on his knot to the customer's vehicle (the costermongers, however, except in a hurry, are usually their own porters after a purchase), and as a porter proceeds rapidly along, trotting or half running, and never walking, he calls out the name of his employer as he reaches the street to which he has been directed, and is answered by the man in charge of the vehicle. He then delivers his burden, and trots back again to the market. All this is accomplished with far less noise and less jostle than a person who has not witnessed it would imagine. In the interior of the market, alike in fruit and vegetables, the same scene is witnessed, but as no carriages can be admitted there, the "lots" are all displayed on the ground. Every passing stranger is invited to buy. In one, two, or three hours, according to the supply and the demand, business slackens, the streets show but a straggling of market carts, and many of the salesmen and women, or rather their assistants, may be seen taking their breakfasts out of large white or yellow mugs, with a flank of bread and butter at hand. On my visits I did not see one breakfaster eat a watercress, though two or three tons weight of that "cheap and wholesome salad from the brook" might be in the market. Under the piazza, the labourers surround the many coffee stands drinking the beverage out of mugs, and biting huge bits from slices of very thick bread and butter. Women, with sheeps' trotters are standing by, soliciting the coffee-stall customers to "pick a bit" with their meal, or to do so at the public-house with their beer. On my visits the public-houses were little thronged. Business goes on still, but the crowds that stream along the intersecting passages of the market are straggling instead of being so dense and continuous that they can hardly be broken by the crowd wanting to proceed at right angles, and that crowd, when "a break" has been effected, pours along as densely and as continuously, and has to be broken in its turn. In no crowded place that I have visited was there less disorder, less noise, and less wrangling. A few Irishwomen (porteresses) may quarrel in their native Erse, but the others regard that as a thing without meaning, and not worth attention.

The early customers in this market are the costermongers, who buy singly or conjointly in large quantities (and who are quite as readily attended to, as the West-end fruiterers or greengrocers, if not more readily, as the costermongers are ready-money men), the fruiterers and greengrocers. Then as the day advances come housekeepers, cooks, and private individuals; and orders are packed up for the country. Lastly come the wealthy, who cater for their own desserts of grapes, filberts, or pine apples, or who love to purchase the vegetable dainties suited to their tastes.

The system of business is varied. Salesmen receive goods consigned to them direct, all charges of carriage by railway or from the railway station being defrayed by the arrangement of the consigner, and the salesman's commission is 5 per cent., the goods being brought to his door without any trouble to him. Growers bring their own produce to market, sell it themselves, and return to their suburban places, while others are at once salesmen, growers, and dealers. These classes are pretty equally divided, but the salesmen are the most numerous.

The labourers connected with Covent-garden market are male and female ticket-porters. No unticketed porter is allowed to ply for hire in the market, or to carry out goods from it, under penalties, but any person may carry goods made his own by purchase, as in the case of costermongers. The porter's ticket costs 1s. 6d., and as vacancies occur they are filled up by appointment from the superintendent. There are 600 male and 80 female porters. In a slack time the male porters "look out" for work at the docks or elsewhere. One tenth of the men are English, the others are all Irish. There were, until three or four years back, a few Welshmen and a few Scotchmen, but there are none now. The females are every one Irishwomen. Some, both male and female, attain a great age. The usual charge for porterage is 1d. "a turn," or load, but some will work for ½d. a turn, to the great anger and disgust of the penny hands. An Irish porter, a keen-looking and tolerably well-dressed man, whom I met in the market, and to whom I had been referred, gave me the following account:—

"Sure then, sir, it's not what it was the porthering. There's so many paupers in it, and they'll slave for a halfpenny a turn. They've come over, so many of 'em from my country—bad luck to them—that there's lots ready to work for ½d. instead of 1d. in the market, and they're slinking outside for jobs. I've never missed a morning in this market, barring the blessed days, since I came to London, just the year after the altering the market. I'd just married in Ireland, and we came over to try our luck in London, and I soon got on here. It's the thruth I'll tell you, sir. I make from 12s. to 15s. a week, from the blessed Aister Saturday to the beginning of November, and 10s. a week, taking the average, the rest o' the year. Things ain't better nor worse with me. I'd airn more once and I live chaper now. It's my counthrymen that's the ruin of me."

An old woman, whom I had some talk with, considered the improvement of the market the ruin of "porthering, for when it was less 'vanient more porthers was wanted, and now there wasn't that call for them, worse luck." She earned less, she said, since the improvement, or since five or six years after it, by one-third, making 5s. instead of 7s. 6d.

These porters, male and female, live in the courts and narrow streets about Drury-lane. One court near Great Wyld-street is full of them, and few live at any distance from the market. The court I speak of is one of those which never seem to be dry. In the drought of summer, dirty water flows or stagnates in the gutter. Barefoot children run about the court, and babies are in the care of mere children, all dirty and scantily clad. To ask a question of one of these children, of the boys especially, is to draw forth the request, "Give me a halfpenny." The women, whom you see at the windows, or at the doors, never look young, unless in mere girlhood. Dirt and foul air, and probably spare diet, make them look so prematurely old that it is difficult to guess whether one of them be 30 or 50. They live, I was told by one of them, principally on tea or coffee, bread and butter, and cheap fish. In conversing with some of them in the market, they begged importuningly, or rather those who gathered round any one singled out for conversation, begged vociferously—"Will you give *me* nothing, sir?" There was not one I saw but had her string of complaints of the hardships of the times, ill or well founded. At the time of my visits to Covent-garden, employment was slack, and certainly many of the poor women were very badly off. Some of these—perhaps a quarter, or not so many—are the wives of porters in the market. All the Irishwomen, I was assured by a gentleman familiar with the neighbourhood, and one by no means prejudiced in favour of its Irish inmates, were far more chaste in their conduct, and more decent in their language, than the same class of the English. Their very wranglings—which were neither brief nor unfrequent—were not couched in the blasphemous and abominable words hardly to be alluded to, which characterise the lowest English blackguardism; but their threats were often horrid, and their volubility, all talking together, was far beyond that of the English. I called upon an old woman, who may be called the mother of the market, as regards the porteresses. She occupied a large room, in a large house, which, from its size, the width of the stairs, the carving of the balusters, and the height of the building, showed that in the times when Covent-garden was a fashionable quarter, when court gallants revelled there in the days of Charles II., it had been one of no mean note. In its present state it holds a family—at least, so I was told—in every room. I found a woman who had the appearance of extreme age in the room to which I was directed. She was full of complaints of wretched health—evidently well-founded—and reiterated them before she even asked my business there. She was large-boned and stout, and not so untidy in her dress, though it hung loosely about her, as others I saw in the court. The room was wretched in its dirt. It had that peculiar look of discomfort given to any apartment by the want of a fender, the ashes being spread on the hearth and trampled about the floor. There was a wretched bed in one corner of the room, and in other parts were a table, two or three chairs, and some unwashed pots, while along the room was hanging yellow-looking linen to dry. The size of the room made its wretchedness more conspicuous. The old woman I saw, who seemed incapable of any labour, was the daughter of the woman I wished to see. I found the mother in the market, and found her a cheerful-looking, quiet-spoken old woman, and looking ten years younger than her own daughter. Her hair was white, her form spare, and her appearance still healthy. She had far less whine about her than some women not half her age, who were with her. Her brogue was little distinguishable. I saw the old woman afterwards and she said:—

"For nine and forty years I've been in this market, sir. For thirty-two I've been a widdur, and I've had five daughters and two sons. One daughter I have to keep now, and a sore fight we have of it. I've seen many changes here, sir, and tho' it's all better and improved times, it's worse for such as me. But I'm near the end, and I'm getting tired of my life. Oh, yes, I can carry a good weight still, glory be to God. In the old times every body wanted a porter. There was rough goings on, and often fightings in the old times, and in the 'lection times, when it was 'Burdett and liberty,' every minute; but there was better pay. Gentlemen and ladies would give a shilling then for a job sometimes, and very often a sixpence, and now they look twice at a penny, indeed they do, sir. The 'lections was often great hinders to bus'ness; and after the morning's work was over; it was often dangerous to go into the market by the church, you was so crushed. It was a very dark place in winter nights, was the market when I knew it first. There was oil lamps; but it's so long ago I almost forget; but times was far better then for the poor, or me and my children might have starved—yes, might we. I earned twice then what I can now. I can't say how long it's since, but I've been here 49 year, and 32 a widdur. I can tell you quite faithful what I make now—6d. on a bad day, and 1s. on a good, and a bad day follows a good; sometimes I make 18d. But some good people keep me a little, though I'm badly off in my old age, as I have myself to depend on. But I can't be long for this world, and what'll become of my daughter then I don't like to think of. I'm 87, as is very well known. I'm sure, sir, I'm 87, and can prove it. My best friends are ladies I wait on when they come to the market, but there's nobody in town now."

I believe that none of the wives of the porters work for slop-tailors or shirt-makers. In fact, a needle seems an unknown implement to the mass of them. They are hawkers, or out-door saleswomen of some kind, their children being left with bigger children or "wid a nabur, sure, sir." Not one in twenty, I was told, could read and write. All— at least I could hear of no exceptions—are Roman Catholics, and tolerably regular in their attendance at mass on Sundays and the great festivals of the Church—the only times some of them, I was assured, ever wash themselves. All the family's washings of clothes seem done in the one room.

Crowded as is the capital of England, and many as have been the statements of its "going out of town"—which many a statute, before the Revolution of 1688, was passed most bootlessly with an aim to check—three-fourths of its vegetable supplies may be classed as suburban, for they are grown within a radius of twelve miles from Covent-garden itself. Another eighth is grown within the radius extending to fifteen miles, and the remaining eighth comes from *the country*, or from parts more distant—even from Yorkshire. It is customary for the experience or partiality of travellers, who observe the culture of a county to specify this vale, or that plain, as the garden of the shire; but the vale of the Thames may be said literally, to be the garden of London, for within the radius of fifteen miles from Covent-garden are 200,000 acres in the hands of gardeners, all labouring for one market—London.

I now present the returns of the sales in this great Green Market. They have been prepared as were the others, and their correctness has been fully tested, and is admitted by the most experienced persons connected with the market.

The following are the returns of the yearly sales at Covent-garden, all of home grown produce:—

"Apples—360,000 bushels.

"Pears—230,000 ditto.

"Cherries—90,000 ditto.

"Plums—280,000 half-sieves, or 93,000 bushels; three half-sieves go to a bushel.

"Gooseberries—140,000 bushels.

"Currants—Red, 70,000 sieves; white, 3,800; black, 45,000, or 178,200 half-sieves; being the produce of 1,069,200 bushes, as 6 bushes on an average fill a sieve.

"Strawberries—58,000 half-sieves, or 638,000 pottles; 11 pottles go to a half-sieve.

"Raspberries—30,000 sieves, or 22,500 bushels.

"Filberts—1,000 tons.

"Walnuts—20,000 baskets, each 1¼ bushels, or 25,000 bushels.

"Cabbages—16,000 loads, 150 to 200 dozen each, or 33,600,000 cabbages.

"Turnips—10,000 loads, 150 dozen each, or 18,800,000 turnips.

"Carrots—5,000 loads, 200 doz. each, or 12,000,000 carrots.

"Onions—500,000 bushels.

"Brocoli (including cauliflowers)—1,000 loads, 150 dozen each, or 1,800,000 heads.

"Peas—135,000 sacks. A sack is two bushels.

"Beans—50,000 ditto.

"Celery—1,500,000 rolls of 12 each, or 18,000,000 heads of celery.

"Asparagus—400,000 bundles of 150 each, or 60,000,000 buds.

"Endive—150,000 scores.

"French Beans—140,000 bushels.

"Potatoes—83,000 tons.

"Watercresses—21,060 hampers, or 26,325 cwt., each hamper being 1¼ cwt."

Concerning potatoes I may add that when the supply is short, about 200 tons are sent daily from Huntingdonshire, Cambridgeshire, Norfolk, and Lincolnshire.

The Borough market is directly opposite St. Saviour's Church, near the Surrey end of London-bridge. It is covered in, and presents a rather gloomy and confused appearance, as the roofing is not so elevated as at Covent-garden, or Farringdon, and is used in many parts for lofts, so that the light is obstructed. A passage, which is a considerable thoroughfare independent of the market, runs obliquely from the exterior fronting St. Saviour's to Park-street and to Barclay and Perkins's brewery. Alleys, connected with this thoroughfare or with the streets bordering on the market, and leading to High-street, Southwark, intersect the whole of the market, which is greatly crowded. There are shops such as butchers' and public-houses on one side of the thoroughfare I have spoken of, and surrounding the market. The produce sold is the same as that of Covent-garden, except in the choicer and costlier fruits and vegetables, while that in flowers is insignificant. The retail customers are all the inhabitants of the neighbourhood; the wholesale ones are the greengrocers and costermongers, who buy in large quantities.

The Borough market was established by charter in the time of Edward VI., but at that time its contents could be packed in five carts. The market was first held in the High-street, Southwark, but as the traffic of that great thoroughfare increased, and as the market itself increased, it was found so inconvenient that in 1754 an act of Parliament was obtained for its removal to its present locality. Commissioners were appointed to carry out the provisions of the act as regards the purchase of the ground and buildings, for which they were authorized to borrow money (first £6,000, and then £2,000 additional) on the security of the tolls and rents. The property was not very valuable, as the names of the places purchased somewhat import—"To wit, a piece of ground in which is contained a spot called a triangle, abetting on a place called the Turnstile, on the backside of Three Crown-court eastward; Fowle-lane buildings in Rochester-yard, and Dirty-lane, northward; and towards Deadman's-place, eastward."

The Borough market was enlarged by an Act passed in 1829, and is about to be enlarged again. It now covers 3 acres, or 130,680 square feet, and is the property of the parish of St. Saviour. It contains about 200 stands, rented at from £1 to £30 per year. After the wholesale trade of the market is completed, which is seldom later than ten o'clock, the stands are occupied by retail sellers, at the rate of from 6d. to 1s. per day, according to their size and situation. There are from 60 to 70 in the wholesale, and about 100 in the retail business. The tolls are—on every basket of fruit, ¼d. and ½d.; boxes of fruit, ½d.; chests of oranges and lemons, 1d.; carts, 4d., &c. The tolls and regulations do not materially differ from those of Covent-garden. The occupiers of shops for general purposes pay 14s. per week; the innkeepers £30 per year. There are about nine shops and one inn on each side of the market, and over the market are about fifty lofts, used as warehouses, averaging 1s. per week. The market days are Tuesday, Thursday, and Saturday, but the market is open every day for retail sale. It is under the management of the churchwardens and overseers of St. Saviour's, and of eleven inhabitants appointed by the vestry. Half-yearly reports are published. The one published on the 25th of March last shows these receipts:—Yearly rent of houses due at Michaelmas (less income-tax), £233 12s. 3d.; ditto due at Christmas, £254 9s. 1d.; half-year's tolls (leased to Mr. Robinson), £378; half-year's rent of casual stands (leased to Mr. Palmer, jun.), £95; twenty-six weeks' rent of weekly standings (let to tradesmen and others), £418 8s. 6d.; half-year's dividends on £1,811 2s. 9d. stock in bank, £28 11s. 5d.; one year's rent of cart stand, £2 2s.

The sum of £1,157 8s., "Cash at banker's, as per last report," gives a total of £2,567 11s. 9d. By the 4th of George IV., it was enacted that, after providing for the payment of debts, &c., the rents and profits of the market "should be applied in diminution of the parochial rates," so that the chief disbursement was to the overseers, being £1,157 8s. 6d. The other payments are for gas, assessed and land taxes, pavement, water, and sewer rates; Christmas gratuities, £3 3s.; the Bishop of Rochester, one year's rent, £38 16s. 8d.; the same to the Bishop of Winchester, £5 11s. 2d.; £27 10s. for tradesmen's bills; the scavenger, two quarters cleansing, £40; beadle's salary, and sundries, £37 10s.; clerk's half-year's salary, £30; collector's half-year's salary, £10. These payments and a "balance at banker's" of £1,067 7s. 10d. balance the account. There are in this market 8 ticket-porters, who act as night watchmen.

The following returns show the business transacted in the course of the year at the Borough market. In all the returns "cauliflowers" are included under the head "brocoli."

"Cabbages—8,000 loads, 200 dozen to a load, or 19,200,000 cabbages.

"Turnips—2,000 loads, of 200 dozen each, or 4,800,000 turnips.

"Brocoli—1,576 loads, of 200 dozen each, or 3,782,400 heads of brocoli.

"Carrots—442 loads, 300 dozen each, or 1,571,200 carrots.

"Potatoes—36,000 tons.

"Peas—25,000 sacks.

"Beans—10,000 sacks.

"Currants—30,000 bushels.

"Cherries—45,000 bushels.

"Strawberries—10,000 bushels.

"Gooseberries—35,000 sieves.

"Apples—25,000 bushels.

"Pears—10,000 bushels."

This supply is derived from Surrey, Essex, and Kent, and is sent by railway from the more distant, and by cart or waggon from the nearer places of growth. At early morning the crowd is very great, sometimes so great as to render locomotion next to impossible. On a wet morning it is peculiarly uncomfortable, from the jamming together of so many people soaked with the rain on their way to the market.

Spitalfields, more than any other, is the market of the poor. It is 327 feet on the north, 349 on the south, 380 on the west, and 345 on the east. This space is covered irregularly with buildings, some of them of wood, and very dingy. Where there are no buildings, the ground, which is not remarkable for cleanliness, is occupied with stands, or heaps of baskets which are piled on all sides. Up the centre of the market runs a covered avenue with shops on both sides, somewhat after the fashion of Covent-garden, but very different in its character, as those shops which display good fruit are mixed with retail butchers, shoemakers, milliners, tailors, &c., such as supply small quantities, or low priced articles. Of these shops there are 27, letting at an average rent of 10s. weekly. The market is situated between Union-street and Lamb-street, on the north and south, and Crispin and Red-lion streets on the east and west. It is the property of Mr. Spurling, a private gentleman. The market was established by charter in the reign of Charles II. The tolls are ½d. per bushel on fruit; and ½d. per sieve on potatoes or 1s. 6d. a ton. A good portion of the supply to this market is grown on property appertaining to the Duchy of Lancaster, not many miles distant, and the consignors, it appears, claim and obtain one of the privileges of royalty, and will not pay toll. The wholesale market days are Tuesday, Thursday, and Saturday. The market is under the superintendence of a clerk and the police. Porters (unticketed) are the only labourers, and they, in rotation, act as night watchers.

One of the principal salesmen favoured me with the following communication:—

"In your letter on Spitalfields-market, you will perhaps notice that many, very many, of the things brought thereto are not subject to toll [my informant then states the privileges of the tenants of the Duchy of Lancaster]. In many of the yearly stands, only a nominal toll is taken. The classes of purchasers are—First, the shopkeepers, who come from Limehouse, Bow, Bromley (in Middlesex), Stratford, Homerton, Clapton, Hackney, Stoke Newington, Islington, Kingsland, City, Ratcliff-Highway, Mile End, Whitechapel, East Smithfield, Wapping, and Blackwall. Those (and of course from places within these radii, and adjacent thereto) from the river-side purchase largely for the shipping. Many persons, however, connected with vessels, come here and supply themselves. The second class are the costermongers, who supply all parts of London and the adjacent districts; indeed, it is only by their agency that many persons five or six miles from London, directly adjoining to market-gardens, are supplied. At times the Covent-garden, or 'Garden' people as they are called, come here to buy—also the 'Boro'. We of the 'Fields' (our technical designation) occasionally return this compliment. The supply of our market is thus derived. Many things come from Kent; our principal supply is from Essex and Middlesex. Very large supplies of fruit come from Cambridgeshire, and generally speaking all the northern and eastern counties send us a good deal of their produce. The goods on commission are generally conveyed by the Eastern Counties Railway. Vast quantities of commission goods from Middlesex and from Essex, from places not at too great a distance, are also conveyed by waggon and cart, and are unloaded in the salesman's warehouse or on his stand. The goods sold by the growers themselves come by cart and waggon; these vehicles stand in the market-place, and the goods are sold therefrom. Two of our market salesmen import largely—one of them imports vast quantities of foreign fruits. Much of this they dispose of at the waterside, and some of it comes here. The 'vast' importer will sometimes have 3,000 packages on the wharf at one time, all of which are sold and cleared away in perhaps three or four hours. I see I have run from the buyer part of the question—to conclude which let me state that the servants of many respectable persons living adjacent, many of such persons themselves, and large numbers of the labouring classes living near, are our customers. Orders, too, are often received from Manchester, Liverpool, Birmingham, Glasgow, and Edinburgh for our goods. In the course of an average season, perhaps 50,000 sacks and 5,000 sieves of peas may be sent and brought and sold here. The quantity of potatoes that our growers themselves may sell in the course of the year may be 1,500 tons. Probably from 5,000 to 6,000 loads (carts and waggons) of vegetables, principally cabbages, turnips, greens, and carrots, may be sold in this market in a year. A waggon load of good-sized cabbages is 130 dozen, of small cabbages 200. Good cabbages have been sold this season at 2d. per dozen. Little better, last season, fetched 15d. and 18d. per dozen. The average price is about 9d. 6d. or 7d. is supposed to pay the grower 20*l.* an acre."

Of the commission salesmen, or potato merchants, in this market, there are 25; of another class, who buy of the salesmen to supply the retailers, there are 15; and of retailers, 27. There are 100 stands for growers, the rents of these stands averaging £1 14s. a year. After the wholesale business of the growers is over, these stands are hired by retailers, at from 3d. to 1s. a day. There are 143 houses, inns, shops, &c., upon the outer and inner boundaries, and in the four short streets leading into the market. The houses average £35 a year—the inns more and the shops less.

The following is the business transacted in Spitalfields in a year, all home-grown:—

"Potatoes—55,000 tons.
"Peas—50,000 sacks.
"Beans—5,000 sacks.
"Cabbages—5,000 loads, 200 dozen to a load, or 12,000,000 cabbages.
"Turnips—2,000 loads, 200 dozen to a load, or 4,800,000 turnips.
"Carrots—1,000 loads, 200 dozen to a load, or 2,400,000 carrots.
"Brocoli—1,200 loads, 200 dozen to a load, or 2,880,000 heads.
"Cherries—15,000 bushels.
"Apples—250,000 bushels.
"Pears—83,000 bushels.
"Plums—45,000 bushels.
"Gooseberries—91,500 bushels.
"Currants—45,000 bushels.
"Strawberries—12,000 bushels.
"Raspberries—2,500 bushels."

It is a curious fact connected with this market, that whatever produce is sent to it from Enfield in Middlesex is subjected to neither turnpike nor market tolls; an exemption granted to Enfield because, during the Plague in 1665, vegetables and fruit were sent almost exclusively from thence—of course at the risk of the lives of all who ventured into the pest-stricken city.

Spitalfields is the great potato market, but the great stores of potatoes are on the river side, in Tooley-street; and again, but not exactly, bordering the river, in Rotherhithe (for shipping). These stores are brought by sea from Yorkshire (the best quality), Scotland, Lincolnshire, Guernsey and Jersey. From those places 1,200,000 sacks are supplied in an average season. The "water-side" potatoes are all weighed on delivery, 168 lb. constituting a sack. "Dr. Colquhoun," says Mr. McCulloch, "estimated the entire value of potatoes annually consumed in Great Britain and Ireland, at the end of the late war, at *sixteen millions* sterling. But it is needless to say that there are no materials by which to form an estimate of this sort with any pretensions to accuracy. The one in question has been suspected, like most of those put forth by the same learned person, of exaggeration; and we incline to think that had he estimated the value of the yearly produce of potatoes in the empire *at twelve millions* he would have been nearer the mark. But on a point of this sort it is not possible to speak with anything like confidence."

I have already mentioned the circumstances which led to the establishment of Farringdon market. It stands upon an area of 67,876 square feet, between Farringdon-street and Shoe-lane. It is the property of the Corporation of London. There are about 78 stands and 50 pitchings, rented by the year at £4 per stand and £2 a pitching. There are about 42 wholesale salesmen, and upwards of 50 retailers. It has been instituted about 22 years, and is chartered and incorporated. The tolls upon the various commodities are:—For every waggon, or cart, or pitching stand, 9d. per square foot; for every waggon, or its contents pitched (except potatoes), 1s. per day; every cart, or its contents pitched (except potatoes), 9d. per day; every waggon or cart stand, without a pitching stand, 1s. per day; every pitching stand, without a waggon stand, 1s. per day; potatoes, 1s. per ton; potatoes, 2d. per sack; baskets of more than a sieve, 1d. per basket; baskets of less than a sieve, ½d. per basket; oranges per chest, 4d.; boxes, 2d.; hampers of watercresses, 2d. per hamper; pitching stands under the roof, if let to tenants of opposite shops, 2s. per week; pitching stands under the roof, if not tenants of opposite shops, 5s. per week; for the use of the scales, ½d. per draught. The shops surrounding the market, which is square, more than half of them being shut up, let from 2s. to 10s. per week. These shops are occupied by general dealers, but those of the fruit salesmen average 12s. per week. The market-days are Monday, Wednesday, Friday, and Saturday. All classes are purchasers at this market. It is superintended by a clerk, beadle, and assistant. The labourers are ticketed and unticketed porters. The market is cleansed by contract. It slopes to Fleet-ditch, and is well drained. There is a sort of covered or shedded central avenue. Farringdon is the great watercress mart. In the winter, poor, shivering, half-clad boys and girls surround the dealers' stands, and buy one, two, or three handfuls. Five handfuls are 1d. These they string on neighbouring doorsteps, the snow sometimes falling on their numbed fingers.

The following are the returns of Farringdon Market for the year:—

> "Potatoes—14,000 tons.
> "Peas—7,000 sacks.
> "Beans—1,200 sacks.
> "French Beans and Scarlet Runners—3,000 bushels.
> "Cabbages—3,500 loads of 200 dozen each, or 8,400,000 cabbages.
> "Brocoli—1,300 loads, or 5,320,000 heads.
> "Turnips and Carrots—700 loads, averaging 60 dozens a load, or 504,000 turnips and carrots.
> "Onions—6,000 bushels.
> "Gooseberries—12,000 bushels.
> "Currants—5,000 bushels.
> "Cherries—12,000 bushels.
> "Plums—3,000 bushels.
> "Apples—35,000 bushels.
> "Pears—20,000 bushels.
> "Strawberries—450 bushels.
> "Watercresses—46,800 hampers, or 58,500 cwt."

There are also 60,000 flower roots sold in a year. The supply is from Middlesex, Surrey, Essex, Kent, Cambridgeshire, and Bucks. It is sent by railway, cart, and waggon.

Hungerford market was built by Sir Edward Hungerford, in 1680, and rebuilt in 1831. In Pennant's time there was "on the north side of the market-house a bust of one of the family in a large wig." It is now divided into three departments or areas. On the north, or open space, a number of omnibuses stop the entrance to the middle or grand hall, and to the south area, or fish market. The whole market stands upon an area of 52,890 square feet, and is situated opposite Charing-cross Hospital, or between the Strand and the Suspension-bridge. There are three promenades—one at the western side of the market, another on the eastern, and a third through the middle of the enclosed part. Before this enclosure (occupied by general shopkeepers), which was made four or five years ago, the *Quarterly Review* pronounced this portion of the market closely to resemble the interior of an ancient basilica. Each promenade leads to the Suspension-bridge. On the western side there are 9 butchers, 1 tripe-seller, 6 dealers in game and poultry, 2 butter shops, 1 pork, 1 milkseller, and 7 fishmongers, 1 cook shop, 1 ginger-beerseller, 2 toy shops, 1 printseller, 1 basket-maker, 1 confectioner, and 2 taverns. On the eastern side are 1 tavern, 1 hairdresser, 1 glass shop, 1 mealman, 3 potato shops, 11 fruiterers, 3 fruit and vegetable dealers, 2 greengrocers, 2 ginger-beer sellers, and 6 fishmongers. In the middle avenue there are 1 dealer in wardrobe clothes, 1 boot and shoe maker, 1 grocer, 1 hairdresser, 2 picture frame dealers, 2 milliners, 1 artist (profilist), 1 parasol and archery shop, 1 haberdasher, and 1 fishing-tackle maker; altogether, 74 shops and 3 taverns in the market, and 6 shops in the arcade leading to the market. The fishmongers, 13 in number, pay each £2 per week rent; the outside corner shops, 10s. 6d. per week; shops in the enclosed part on the east and west side, from 11s. to £1 per week; those in the grand hall, from 4s. to 8s.; and the shops with dwelling-houses attached to them, pay £60 per year. The whole of the shops are retail. This market was opened by authority of an act of Parliament in 1833. There are no tolls except for landed goods, neither is there any particular market-day. The market is superintended by a superintendent and 1 beadle. There are 10 ticket porters belonging to the company, who are employed in taking passengers' luggage to and from the cabs to the steamboats or other places. The purchasers are generally the higher classes of society, though the market is visited by all classes.

Portman market stands upon an area of 2½ acres, or 108,900 square feet; on the north and south run Huntsford-terrace and New Church-street, and on the east and west, Salisbury-street and Carlisle-street. This market is the property of Lord Portman. There are 40 stands for growers, who pay £7 10s. per year. These stands are also used by other parties, who rent them from the growers, and pay

1s. per day. There are also four wholesale and 20 retail dealers. The market was instituted in 1830 by act of Parliament. There are no tolls paid in this, as in other wholesale markets. Monday, Wednesday, and Friday are the market days. All classes of society frequent this market. A clerk is the only person who superintends it. The only class of labourers are ticket porters, of whom there are but four. The cleansing of the market is done by contract.

The returns for a year are—

> "Potatoes—6,602 tons.
> "Currants—20,000 sieves.
> "Strawberries—6,000 sieves.
> "Raspberries—4,000 sieves.
> "Cherries—15,000 sieves.
> "Apples—16,000 bushels.
> "Pears—10,000 bushels.
> "Cabbages—7,280 loads of 200 dozen each, or 16,472,000 cabbages.
> "Brocoli—1,820 loads, or 546,000 head, the supply being only for three months.
> "Turnips—40 loads of 60 dozen each weekly, for six months, or 748,800 turnips.
> "Carrots—30 loads weekly of 60 dozen each for six months, or 561,600 carrots."

To these returns must be added the sale of 12,000 bushels of oranges; also of between 300 and 400 flower roots.

Carnaby market has been abolished since 1820. It was situated at the back of Carnaby-street. Its area was 1½ acre, or 65,340 square feet. At the time of its prosperity (about 30 or 40 years ago) it belonged to Sir T. Carnaby, from whom it took its name. Since that period it fell into the hands of the Craven family, to whom it still belongs. The square upon which the market was built is now formed into shops and private residences. There are 25 houses and shops, paying a rental averaging £55 per year. Craven Chapel takes up full one-third of the space upon which the market formerly stood. The market was instituted about 150 years ago by act of Parliament.

Finsbury market stands upon an area of 14,400 square feet, and is situated at the back of Finsbury-square, between Worship and Clifton streets. It is private property, and was instituted by charter in 1822. This market flourished about two or three years after it was first opened as a wholesale market. It then began to decline, and became a retail market, but it gradually dwindled away to nothing, so that all that remains of it is the houses. These are let to various tradesmen and private individuals, some of whom sublet the rooms to other parties. The rental averages about £25 per year for each.

LABOUR AND THE POOR.

THE METROPOLITAN DISTRICTS.

[FROM OUR SPECIAL CORRESPONDENT.]

OF THE FISH-MARKETS.

LETTER LXXXII.

The next market to which I directed my attention was the great fish market of Billingsgate. The true derivation of the word Billingsgate seems to have disturbed the repose of many antiquaries. "How this gate took that name," says Stowe, "or of what antiquity the name is, I must leave uncertain, as not having read any ancient record thereof, more than that Geffrey Monmouth writeth that Belin, a King of the Britons, about 400 years before Christ's nativity, built this gate and named it Belin's gate, after his own calling; and that when he was dead, his body being burnt, the ashes, in a vessel of brass, were set upon a high pinnacle of stone over the same gate."

What more ancient record than this of "Geffrey Monmouth" the most indefatigable of London antiquaries could have desired, it is not easy to conjecture. He afterwards, however, ventures upon a much more prosaic version of the origin of the name, as probably derived from some (at the time) well-known owner of the place "happily named Beling or Biling." Until the beginning of the last century it seems to have been a custom, as recorded in "Leland's Collectanea"— "that in former times the porters that plyd at Billingsgate used civilly to entreat and desire every man that passed that way to salute a post that stood there in a vacant place." If the hapless passer-by kissed the post and gave the fraternity 6d. "they gave him a name, and chose some one of the gang to be his godfather." If he refused the salute he was by main force bumped against the post. "I believe," continues the writer, "this was done in memory of some old image that formerly stood there, perhaps of Belus or Belin."

Billingsgate cannot vie in antiquity with Smithfield; the cattle market in its present locality was far anterior to that of fish in Billingsgate. In speaking of the Fishmongers' Company, Mr. Peter Cunningham says, "Their earliest extant charter is a patent of the 37th of

Edward III.; while the acting charter of incorporation is dated 2d of James I. The London Fishmongers were divided formerly into two distinct classes, 'Stock Fishmongers' and 'Salt Fishmongers.' Then Thames-street was known as 'Stock Fishmonger-row,' and the old Fish-market of London was 'above bridge,' in what is now called Old Fish-street-hill, in the ward of Queenhithe, not as now 'below bridge' in Thames-street, in the ward of Billingsgate." In 1598, Billingsgate was a "large water-gate, port, or harborough, for ships and boats commonly arriving there with fish both fresh and salt, oranges, onions, and other fruits, and roots, wheat, rye, and grain of divers sorts for the service of the City and the parts of this realm adjoining."

Billingsgate, 1834

The uses of the "gate," in 1598, as detailed by Stowe, were in accordance with the provisions of an enactment in the first year (1558) of Elizabeth's reign, which appointed Billingsgate "an open place for the landing and bringing in of any fish, corn, salt stores, victuals, and fruit (grocery wares excepted), and to be a place of carrying forth of the same, or the like, and for no other merchandise." The subsequent enactments which, immediately or indirectly, affected the metropolitan fish market are numerous. In 10 and 11 William III., we have "an Act for making Billingsgate a free market for Sale of Fish." The 9th of Anne, c. 26, is to ensure "the better Preserving and Improvement of the Fishery within the River of Thames." The 1st George I. c. 18, is "an Act for the better preventing fresh Fish, taken by Foreigners, being imported into this kingdom, and for the Preservation of the Fry of Fish, and for the giving leave to import lobsters and turbots in foreign bottoms, and for the better preservation of salmon within several rivers in that part of this kingdom called England." The 22d of George II. provided, among other matters, for "making a free market for the sale of fish in the city of Westminster, and for preventing the forestalling and monopolising of fish." This last-mentioned act in seven years' time (29th George II., c. 39) required "an Act for explaining, amending, and rendering it more effectual." The 33d George II. repealed as much of the Act of 29th George II. as concerned "a free market for fish at Westminster, requiring fishermen to enter their fishing vessels at the office of the searcher of the Customs at Gravesend, and to regulate the sale of fish at the first hand in the fish markets in London and Westminster, and to prevent salesmen of fish buying fish to sell again on their own account." In the 2d of George III. was passed an Act, intituled, "an Act for the better supplying the cities of London and Westminster with fish, and to reduce the present exorbitant price thereof, and to protect and encourage fishermen." The 30th George III. relates to the "vesting the estate and property of the trustees of Westminster Fish Market in the Marine Society, for the purposes therein mentioned, and for discontinuing the powers of the said trustees." The 36th of the same Sovereign was passed to "authorise the sale of fish at Billingsgate by retail." Five years later came "an Act for granting bounties for taking and bringing fish to the cities of London and Westminster, and other places in the United Kingdom." The 42d George III., c. 19, was to amend the 29th George II., the said 29th George II. being itself an act to amend and explain a former act concerning "a free market for the sale of fish in the city of Westminster, and for preventing the forestalling and monopolizing of fish," &c. The 42d George III. repeals "so much of an Act made in the second year of the reign of his present Majesty, intituled 'an Act for the better supplying the cities of London and Westminster with fish, and to reduce the present exorbitant price thereof, and to protect and encourage fishermen,' as limits the number of fish to be sold by wholesale within the said city of London, and for the better regulation of the sale of fish by wholesale in the market of Billingsgate, within the said city." The 45th George III. amends a former act, "for granting bounties for taking and bringing fish to the cities of London and Westminster, and other places in the United Kingdom." The 4th of William IV. amended the enactment of 33 George II., which was "to regulate the sale and conveyance of fish at first hand." The 9th and 10th Victoria repeals all the Acts I have enumerated. This Act, as it was expressly provided, has a "short title," since it is declared sufficient to refer to it as "The Billingsgate-market Act, 1846."

This act proclaims Billingsgate "a free and open market" for the wholesale and retail sale of fish of all sorts, and in any quantity, "without any disturbance or molestation whatever." It is also enacted "that the mayor and commonalty and citizens of the city of London shall as heretofore have power, authority, jurisdiction, and control over the said market for the sale of fish, both by wholesale and retail, as they now have over the several other public markets of the said city." The act further provides that any one having the care of any description of fishing vessel passing the Nore with fish for Billingsgate-market shall pay within three days of such passing 2s. to the Collector of Customs, London. Of this payment 1s. 6d. is awarded to the Marine Society; the remaining 6d. "shall be kept and retained by and for the use of the person so receiving the said sum of 2s. per voyage."

The act legalised the following tolls to be levied on all boats, steam and other vessels, smacks, barges, lighters, or other craft laden with fish for landing or delivery at Billingsgate-market; also on all waggons, carts, machines, vans, or other conveyances, with fish for unloading or sale thereat:—

On every peter boat with river fish	0s.	6d.
„ small boat, wherry or skiff	1	0
„ hatch boat	1	6
„ great boat, smack, or vessel, laden with lobsters, mackerel, fresh herrings, sprats, or plaice	2	6
„ great boat, smack, or vessel, lighter, barge, or other craft, laden with salmon, or barrels of red and white herrings, codfish, haddocks, or any other fish not otherwise enumerated	5	0
„ lug boat, barge, smack, or vessel, not more than half laden	2	6

On every cart, machine, van, waggon, or any other
　　　description of conveyance, with fish,
　　　with not more than two horses .... 1　0
　　　with more than two horses .... 1　6
　„　　oyster boat, smack, vessel or cock, lighter, barge,
　　　or other craft, for groundage, per day, 2d.; for
　　　metage, per bushel, ½d.; and per voyage, 1s. 1d.

For many years beyond the recollection of any of the salesmen, Billingsgate might be called a free market, as any one then, as now, could convey fish there for sale without any restriction as to being a freeman of the City, &c. A few fishermen at present convey their cargoes of fish direct to Billingsgate and dispose of it themselves, but this mode of business does not amount to 1 per cent. of the general business transacted. The annoyance and hindrance to the Billingsgate tradesmen was, that the question of the supply and sale of fish was so vexed with legislation—there were so many restrictions that could not be enforced, and so many regulations that could not be observed—that the common informers reaped, for men of their stamp, an enormous harvest from the fish dealers, prior to the passing of the act of 1846. The following extract from a report of factors and others on the subject sufficiently shows the economical and judicious manner in which this act was obtained:—

> "In accomplishing these desirable objects they (a committee appointed for the management of the matter) have exercised a due regard to the funds entrusted to their care; and though the subscriptions amount to 141*l.* 10s., they have only expended, including their solicitor's bill, 78*l.* 7s. 6d., leaving a balance of 63*l.* 2s. 6d. in the hands of your treasurer, Mr. Deputy Curling, at the disposal of the subscribers. Your committee, in resigning the trust reposed in them, beg to call the early attention of the subscribers to the necessity of meeting to consider what by-laws would be suitable for the general convenience, to facilitate the sale of fish in the said market, and to solicit the corporation to adopt the same."

One of the acts I have cited relates to the "preserving" the fishery of the Thames. "Conceive an angler (says Mr. C. Knight, in his 'London,' 1841) stuck under one of the piers of Waterloo-bridge, patiently expecting to be rewarded with a salmon, or at least a barbel. Yet such things were, a century ago. There are minute regulations of the Company of Free Fishermen to be observed in the western parts of the Thames, which clearly show that the preservation of fish, even in the highway between London and Westminster, was a matter of importance; and very stringent, therefore, are the restrictions against using eelspears, and wheels, and angle-rods with more than two hooks. There is a distinct provision that fishermen were not to come nearer London-bridge than the Old Swan, on the north bank, and St. Mary Overies, on the south." I may mention that St. Mary Overies is now best known as St. Saviour's.

I have given these details of what Billingsgate was, and of what it was considered necessary to enact concerning the fishing in the metropolitan river, to indicate the difference of the present supply and system of business, now that the Thames is but the medium of carrying fish in vessels on its surface, and not, except at a distance from London, of supplying any fish from its depths. I shall first show whence the supplies are derived, and then give some information as to its extent.

The fish sent to London is divisible into "red" and "white" fish; but the red fish, as regards London, is confined to the scarcest, most valuable, and most esteemed of all fish—the salmon. Hardly any fresh water trout is sent to London, and it could not be sent, I was told, without its being deteriorated, on account of its delicacy. I was assured, also, that even the Westmoreland char—so relished by a tourist, whose appetite, however, is enhanced by keen mountain air—if brought fresh to London, would not command a sale.

The principal supply of salmon is from Scotland, and three-parts of this supply are from the "great salmon ground," so to speak, of the Tay. The remainder of the Scotch supply is from the Forth, the Clyde (which furnishes about a twenty-fifth of that from the Tay), the Dee, the Don, the Spey, the Ness, and, passing over some minor rivers, the Tweed. The salmon fishery of the Tweed was considerable. Twenty or twenty-five years ago its rental was about £15,000 a year; now it is not an eighth of that sum. The Tay—as I was informed by a gentleman who has the best means of arriving at a correct estimate—yielded salmon last season which, as far as regards Billingsgate-market, returned £15,000. The finest salmon, as regards size, sold in London, are from the Tay, and from the Linn, in Sutherlandshire. The supply of Irish salmon last season was about a tenth of that from Scotland. It is principally the fish of the Shannon, shipped from Limerick. There are also consignments from Cork, of Glyn and Lake salmon. The English supply is small—not a fiftieth of that sent to the metropolis—and is confined almost entirely to Gloucestershire and Herefordshire, to the Severn and the Wye. Salmon is also forwarded from Holland, but in the past season very little has been sent. Many fish salesmen whom I saw considered that stringent measures ought to be adopted for the better preservation of the supply of salmon, which becomes scarcer and scarcer. "All the salmon fisheries," said one tradesman to me, "are falling off. The fish can't grow any size. The reason is that they haven't rest enough for breeding; they are always at them." This year salmon was scarce and dear. The greatest quantity of Irish salmon is sent to Liverpool.

Cod is fished along the coasts of Holland, and northward to those of Norway. It is also supplied, and of very fine quality, about Christmas, from the Doggerbank, which is about 120 miles off Yarmouth. The Yorkshire coast furnishes a portion of the cod-fish sent to London, perhaps a twelfth.

"Trawl fish," being brills, turbots, halibuts, soles, plaice—indeed all flat fish—haddocks and whiting (occasionally), skate, and thornbuts (in great numbers), are derived from the same waters as cod fish; halibut being sent also from the Yorkshire coast, and soles from all the coasts within a few hours' railway communication with London. Herrings are caught (and sent to London) from all the coasts of the three kingdoms.

Mackerel are chiefly from the western counties; Plymouth, the Land's-End, and St. Ives being the places most engaged in the supply of the metropolis. No pilchards are sent from Devon or Cornwall to London; they are all used in those counties, or for exportation to Naples and other Italian cities.

Holland furnishes the London market with its chief supply of eels; they are principally shipped from Rotterdam.

John Dories are received irregularly, and in small quantities, chiefly from Torbay and its neighbouring fishing towns. "Dories" are cheap and abundant on the Galway coast, and elsewhere on the western shores of Ireland, but none are sent to London from that kingdom.

Oysters, a very great trade at Billingsgate, are the produce of the Colchester waters and of the Essex coast generally. The Milton (near Gravesend) oysters are famous. None are sent from the north of England, but "broods" are received from there, "laid down" in the Medway, and "grown" there for Billingsgate. Oysters are sent, moreover, from Jersey and Guernsey.

Lobsters are principally received from Norway; Scotland sends about half as many as Norway, and the north of England contributes a small quota. They are sent to London alive. Crabs are sent from all parts of the southern coast of England.

Shrimps are consigned from Leigh, in Essex, the great "shrimp ground," and from Boston, in Lincolnshire. They are forwarded boiled, or, in the language of the trade, "cooked," except a few from below Gravesend, which are sent alive.

Cockles and mussels are received in small quantities, and for the sufficing reason, that "they don't pay." Otherwise, great quantities might be derived from Leigh and other parts of the Essex coast. I was told, however, that mussels were coming into better demand.

The "curious" fish which are brought into Billingsgate are few. Occasionally a sturgeon is brought in; if it has been caught in the Thames, it is by law or custom the property of the Lord Mayor, but his lordship does not rigidly enforce his privileges in the matter of sturgeons. A young shark is sometimes displayed as a curiosity, and so are small dog fish and porpoises. A week or two before my visit, a large fish, called a "benetter" in the trade, and a "horse-mackerel" by the fishermen, was brought to Billingsgate. It weighed 6 cwt., and was offered for sale at £10 10s. What it was sold for my informant did not know.

Salmon—Scotch, Irish, English, and Dutch alike—are brought in boxes. Soles are brought in "pads" (hampers), which, when full, weigh about 30 lb. A "pot" is a smaller "pad," with a lid, the "pad" being "twigged" or "strawed" over. Oysters by smack are brought "in bulk" (unpacked), and by railway in sacks or any cheap packages. The same with mussels. Cockles and periwinkles are brought in sacks. Fresh herrings are delivered in bulk by boat, and are brought in tubs, or in any kind of package by railway, as are other fish sent by railway. Shrimps are packed in hampers. Mackerel is brought direct by boats in pads, and in the same manner by railway. Haddock is brought in bulk (by water), and put into baskets.

Cod is brought in hatch-boats. It is with reference to this fish alone that there is any regulation, such as is known as a "limitation of vend." The cod is brought alive, in welled smacks, and these smacks (unless there is a scarcity, which rarely happens in a fish of so abundant supply) are detained usually five days at Gravesend, waiting their turn. There is no precise rule as to the quantity to be sent up for sale, but out of 20 smacks 15 may be sent together. The codfish are taken out of their wells at Gravesend, and placed in hatch-covered boats. When taken out of the water they are stunned by a blow on the head, and when received at Billingsgate are "crimped" or sliced on the back, by the dealers in crimped cods. The Billingsgate people—all whom I questioned on the subject—averred that there is a degree of life in the fish, but no sensation, as there is not the slightest motion when the knife was applied. After it is crimped the fish is placed in water, "to bring the flake out." If there are no remains of vitality in the fish the crimping is ineffectual, as there is no opening in the surface of the cod; "it cuts stiff, like wire."

Fish, taken generally, and with the exception of salmon, is now about 50 per cent. cheaper in London than it was four years ago.

Salmon is in season from April to September. Turbot from December to the following June. Cod is in the greatest perfection in December, January, February, and again in August and December. Haddocks are always in season. Whitings are most esteemed in January, February, and March. Soles are almost always in season. The oyster season is from August to May. Lobsters are supplied all the year round, except in December or in the depth of winter. There are complaints of the indiscriminate fishing of the lobster, as tending to impair the extent of the supply, which is already much diminished, perhaps to fifty per cent., on the English coasts. Eels are in uninterrupted supply, but are the best from December to March, and again in July, August, and September. Mackerel are choicest in May, June, and July. Fresh herrings (for London consumption) in June, July, and August. These rules, however, are often more regarded by cooks than by the public. Salmon is sold, though in small quantities, when out of season, and when its colour is pink instead of a pale red brown, and its flavour inferior.

The fish sent to London for sale is consigned to the fish factors, best known as the "Billingsgate salesmen," many of them men of great wealth and influence. Their commission is five per cent. These salesmen are divided into trawl fish, salmon, codfish, herring, red herring, shrimp, lobster, and general factors. They cannot be said—excepting in the case of shrimps, and that not always—to confine their trade exclusively within the classifications I have specified; but their principal business is transacted in the different descriptions of fish which they are known to have most of at their command. Of trawl factors there are 11; of salmon, 5; of cod, 4; of fresh herrings, 8; of red herrings, 7; of lobsters, 4. These are the principal or first-class salesmen, and the smaller salesmen are about twice their number—but in shrimps five times as many. The salesmen dispose of their fish wholesale and retail, as they will sell one (uncut) of the larger fish. "I shall be happy, sir," said a leading salesman to me, "to sell you as choice a salmon as any in the market, if I can have the pleasure of seeing you at five to-morrow morning." The chief customers of the factors or salesmen are not the fishmongers, as might be supposed, but the "bummarees." I could obtain no information of the origin of this odd word. One man—I speak only of the labourers whom I questioned—said it was Irish; a second that it was Dutch; another said there always was bummarees, just as he was a "bobber," and Jack there was a "rough," and that they always were bummarees, and always would be, and he only wished he was one. One porter, more intelligent than his brethren, conjectured that it had something to do with "bum-boats," as in the old times he'd heard an old uncle say that men tried to get the start of the market in bad weather by going out in a boat and bargaining with or bribing the captain of a fishing smack for a small portion of his cargo, which they rowed with might and main either to Billingsgate or to some fishmonger's by or near the river. When a scarcity was felt, as it often was, "then you see, sir," said my informant, "the sellers of fish felt that one in the hand was worth two in the boat, and would give a good price. Perhaps them was bum-boats, and was the first bummarees." The bummarees fluctuate in number. In the busiest periods of the year, or from before Christmas to the beginning of August—"and we Billingsgate people," said a factor to me, "find *our* best season to be the West-end fashionable season"—they are most numerous, as some fishmongers then become bummarees, which class, indeed, are the speculators, or gamblers, in fish. They are classed as "keen hands," and some of them make money. They purchase the fish "in lots" (or quantities) of the salesmen, and dispose of them to the fishmongers, or, indeed, to any one. There are generally twenty bummarees custom-ers of the factors to two fishmongers. The price of fish often varies. As the supply comes in abundantly or sparely, the prices rise or fall 10 to 20 per cent. in a day. If there is a fall, of course those bummarees who are early buyers are losers, and if a rise they are gainers. They "job one to another" moreover; and "are indeed"—as a gentleman well ac-quainted with Billingsgate, and with no very favourable opinion of the bummarees, said to me—"speculators on the Fish Exchange."

As nearly as can be ascertained, one-third of the fish sold in Billingsgate is sold through the factors or the bummarees to fishmongers; one-third is sent into the country (for Billingsgate is not, and never was, a merely metropolitan market); and the remaining third is sold to the costermongers, who are often called hawkers by the salesmen. "These hawkers," said a first-class salesman to me, "are really becoming a formidable class. I find them fair fellows, but coarse and free-spoken. We are not very delicate at Billingsgate, however. I would rather deal with a costermonger than a fishmonger. The costermonger is ready money. *He* must pay; but the West-end fishmonger, and, indeed, most fishmongers, as they must give credit, must have credit, and so there's a risk to me."

The authorised labourers in this market are the fellowship porters and the ticket porters. I have previously given an account of their functions and privileges. At Billingsgate the fellowship porter has the exclusive right, by law, of carrying *from the ship* to the market, all fish, or shell fish, sold by tale (number), or by measure; thus oysters, mussels, sprats, &c., can only be portered from the water, legally, by him, and in this respect his privileges have not been infringed. One fellowship porter will in 1½ hours "clear a whiting boat." To effect this, however, he has the aid of "foreigners," as the non-freemen employed in the market are called—a name, as I have previously shown, of some antiquity.

The fellowship porter's work is known as "shoring." If the article to be shored is in bulk the fellowship porter has to find baskets. By a rule of the Markets Committee, or of the Common Council (for it appears with their authority), the fellowship porter is to receive 2d. a bushel for shoring shellfish, and other payments in proportion. The charge for "shoring" oysters, however, has been abolished. It is more usual to pay the fellowship porter so much for clearing the vessel. 8s. is a frequent payment for this labour; 10s. or 12s. is sometimes paid. The number of fellowship porters whose services are required at Billingsgate varies according to the extent of business. On the busiest days of the oyster and herring "times," 100 may be employed; on ordinary occasions not 40. Quadruple and more than quadruple the number of fellowship porters used to be employed before railway communication supplied a more rapid and certain means of transit; and not only was the larger number regularly at work, but their work was greater in extent. The conveyance of fish by water is not now one-eighth of what it was. The fellowship porters, however, even when their employment was at its height, I was told, "overdid the thing." They allowed the freedom of their company and of the

City at the cost of £5, so that many "took up" their freedom, and fellowship porterage was overstocked. Over land-sent goods they have no control. The ticket porters have the exclusive right of carrying dry fish, such as red herrings; also all dry packages, not fish, among which are classed orange and fruit boxes. Of these porters working at Billingsgate there are about 30. They charge 1½d. a pad, or box, and make a tolerable living.

There is a frequent conflict between these two classes of porters as to their rights and privileges, which do not seem to be well defined. The heaviest complaints are made by the ticket porters of alleged infringements on the part of the fellowship porters.

These porters, however, are but a portion of the Billingsgate labourers. The average daily attendance of the unprivileged porters is about 400, and they are known as "foreigners," "bobbers," and "roughs." These appellations are often enough applied indiscriminately by the men themselves, especially the word "roughs," which one of the class will apply to another, as a term of reproach, with considerable unction. The following definition, however, meets the divisions of the labour as closely, I understand, as they can be met.

The "foreigners" receive the packages which the fellowship porter brings on his head from the ship. They are employed and paid by the salesmen, or by any other party to whom the consignment may be made. Their labour is principally confined to the market and its immediate neighbourhood, and some of them have "foreigned" for one firm for forty years. The term foreigner intimates a person not a freeman of the City.

The "bobber" is a man who is sent from the market with goods to purchasers residing at a little distance. He is engaged either by the buyer or seller of the fish, &c., the buyer being often a retailer buying all descriptions of fish, and, perhaps, not in great quantities, so that a horse and cart is not required, and if the purchases were sufficient to load a cart, the crowded state of the streets causes a great delay.

The "rough" is merely the casual porter, who is on the look-out for any job, and is ready to act as a foreigner, a bobber, or an assistant to a bobber if the load be too much for one man—which, however, rarely happens, for these bobbers carry great weights. The roughs are sometimes employed in assisting to unload the railway waggons, which are now driven up to the immediate neighbourhood of the market, and are unloaded with the aid of the railway porters, or with that of any persons the parties may please to set to work. The foreigners and bobbers are usually known men; the roughs may be either known or unknown.

It is the language of the fish porters which has stocked our literature with so many allusions to "flowers of Billingsgate," &c. Pope makes "Billingsgate" one of the daughters of the goddess Dulness—hardly an appropriate maternity, for not Dulness but blackguardism is, or was, the characteristic of Billingsgate. I am assured, however, by a tradesman, who has had a long experience of the market, that there is some improvement in the porters' language, inasmuch as there is less blasphemy. The dwellings of these men are for the most part in the low streets and the lodging-houses about Whitechapel and Rosemary-lane. Others cross the river to their abodes in the Mint, the half ruinous streets near the Southwark-bridge-road, the London-road, in Kent-street, &c. Their habits are those I have so often described as characteristic of the vagrant class; for though these men's labour is confined to one locality, their constant absence from "home," if home it may be called, and their taking their meals in the open air of the market, or in the public-houses to which they resort while waiting, are attributes of vagrancy. A small proportion of them can read and write, and most of those who may be considered as the more settled class, the foreigners and bobbers, are married men. The regular foreigners and bobbers may be about a third, or more, of the whole number of porters. The hours of these people's labour, "brisker" or "slacker," are the market hours from five in the morning to five in the afternoon, and during those hours they live from home. Many of their wives hawk fish, or have "stands" for its sale, and so the pair can live, perhaps, in a sort of rude plenty, as a well-employed foreigner may earn from 15s. to 18s. a week, and perhaps his wife half as much. The employment of women to carry out fish ("fish fags") is not a twentieth of what it was 30 years ago. It is the "roughs," who may not get a job in a day, upon whom the pressure of poverty falls the hardest. I did not hear of any of the "foreigners'" wives working for the slop tailors; they aim more at open-air avocations. Between a third and a fourth of the "roughs" are Irishmen. There are among them six or seven Dutchmen and Frenchmen; a few Welshmen, a very few Scotchmen, and the rest are English. There is no fixed scale of payment for the foreigners or others; it is a matter of agreement, a bargain being generally struck "for the lot." An experienced man told me that 20 or 25 years ago, the behaviour of the porters was much more disorderly than it is now. The roughs would run against a plank along which the fellowship porter carried his load of fish, and by bumping it, perhaps cause such an unsteadiness that the porter had to drop his load, which these fellows or their comrades, costermongers perhaps, picked up at low water. They would not unfrequently pelt the privileged porters, or any one obnoxious to them, with fish, seizing the first that came to hand; and these fish were picked up by the young thieves prowling about. They are rough enough still, but a more efficient police has checked all such overt acts.

An elderly man who described himself as a foreigner, but whose appearance certainly showed the "rough," gave me the following account. He had not been shaved for a week; he wore a greasy and ragged great coat, buttoned, where it would button, over a smaller coat, more ragged still. His trowsers were coarse corduroy, and his shoes, or half boots, very brown and heavy. Of the texture of his shirt I cannot speak, as I perceived no indication of his wearing one. He had, like *Caliban*, a "very ancient and fish-like smell." This man was very garrulous. He said:—

"I've known Billingsgate-market these forty year—aye, and more than forty. I was a fishmonger's lad in Thames-street when I was a lad, but ever since I was my own man I've been a foreigner. Them was the times, master. Why, I've made £5 and £6 a week then. I've made 30s. a day—as much as I can make in some months now. Foreigners was foreigners then, but the ralleys (so this man called the railways) has dished us. They was jolly times up to eighteen year back. I got into a few shindies with the fellowship porters—there'll not be none on 'em in two year, and sarve 'em right—but I got out of trouble very soon. The fellowship porters claims everything—you may touch this, and you mustn't touch that—and if my employer didn't back me, I might touch next to nothing, and they have everything. [I cite this part of the foreigner's statement to show the feelings or prejudices by which he was actuated.] I never saved any money; it went as it came, and now it don't come. Some weeks I don't make 15s., some not 9s. I pay 1s. 3d. a week rent; it's a lodging-house, but I'm regular at it. I've only myself to keep now, and find that's not easy. There's so many savage for a turn. I don't eat much fish. I mostly buys a bit of cooked beef and eats it with bread in the public-house, and sometimes a onion. That and a pint of beer costs 5d. or 6d. I breakfast at a coffee-shop, and tea at another; it's 1d. a time for coffee if I've one cup, and 2d. if I've two. I carry my own bread and butter with me—their thins and their thicks [slices of bread and butter] is nothing to fill a man. Bread and butter is, may be, 2d. a time. Sometimes I take a piece of bread and cheese, and a pint of beer, for breakfast or tea—that's about the same money. There oughtn't to be no tax on a poor man's beer or baccy. I go to bed mostly at seven. I get 2s. a boat from a salesman I work for. I never do anything in the fish way, and never did, only sometimes a cotchel. You don't know what a cotchel is? Spell it! I don't know how to spell; how should I know? When a smack's cleared, and the oysters is measured out of bulk into bushels—they're double bushels, and there's some over the last peck, more or less—them what's over *is* a cotchel, and is the rights of the boy of the ship. I've bought cotchels of the boy for 3d., and sold them to an old woman that trades that way for 4d. or 5d. How times is changed! This morning a ralley waggon came bang up to the market, and foreigners was put on her to unload her. To be sure there was two old freemen and a fellowship on the job. There's nothing like the water trade as there was. In my day I once carried 1,600 barrels of herrings from Mr. ——'s to a ship, in one afternoon—it's no distance, certainly. This morning I earned 8d. up to half-past nine, and nothing since. There was no work. Why, master, I've seen 160 oyster vessels up in one day; there was three tier of them. I can't say how long it's since. Now if there's 15 or 16, it's all. One morning, not very long since, there was 2,000 bushels brought by ralley. Then look at the prices as was given. I've known £5 given for a barrel of oysters. I've known 22s. given for a mullet; next day they were at 1s. a piece. The times is shocking."

On inquiring of a tradesman long connected with the market, I ascertained that there was no reason whatever to question this "foreigner's" statement as to the high prices he had known given. In the depth of winter, in heavy snow-storms, or when the river was choked with ice, no supply of fish was "got up" to London, and any that might be brought thither by any piece of good luck in conveyance commanded exorbitant prices.

Billingsgate-market is situate in Lower Thames-street, from which it extends to the river, the Custom-house being on the eastern side. The area was enlarged in 1827. The property belongs to the Corporation of London, and is let out in stands at from 3s. to 15s. a week. The adjoining houses are let at from £80 to £200 a year. The fish-market is not confined to Billingsgate-market (proper), but extends to the neighbourhood. There are about 30 wholesale and 100 retail dealers. The market is held every day except Sunday. The officers, appointed by the Corporation, are a clerk of the market, an inspector, and a band of police. The inspector examines the fish, and seizes all that is unsound; but the seizures, owing to the greater facilities of transit, are not a fourth of what they were before fish was brought by railway. The fish seized is thrown into a lighter, mixed with gas tar, tarpaulined over, and conveyed away for sale as manure.

The following statement as to the extent of the business transacted at Billingsgate has been prepared in the manner I have before described. I am assured by an official gentleman connected with the market that it is as correct as it is curious:—

> "Salmon—29,000 boxes, 7 in a box, or 203,000 salmon.
> "Live Cod—400,000, averaging 10 lbs. each, or 4,000,000 lbs. of cod.
> "Barrelled Cod—15,000 barrels, 50 to a barrel, 750,000.
> "Salt Cod—1,600,000, averaging 5 lbs. each, or 8,000,000 lbs. of salt cod.
> "Fresh Haddocks—2,250 tons, 2 lbs. each, or 2,470,000 fresh haddocks.
> "Smoked Haddocks—65,000 barrels, 300 in a barrel, or 19,500,000 smoked haddocks.
> "Soles—12,000 tons, ¼ lb. each, or 97,520,000 soles.
> "Mackerel—10,500 tons, 1 lb. each, or 23,620,000 mackerel.
> "Fresh Herrings—250,000 barrels, 700 to a barrel, 3 to 1 lb., or 175,000,000 fresh herrings.
>
> "Red Herrings—100,000 barrels, 500 to a barrel, or 50,000,000 red herrings.
> "Bloaters—265,000 baskets, 150 to a basket, 4 to 1 lb., or 39,750,000 bloaters.
> "Eels—from Holland 672 tons, from England and Ireland 57 tons, 6 to 1 lb, or 9,797,760 eels.
> "Whitings—3,000 tons, 6 ozs. each, or 17,920,000 whitings.
> "Plaice—15,000 tons, 1 lb. each, or 36,600,000 plaice.
> "Turbots—2,500 tons, 2 lbs. to 16 lbs. each, 7 lbs. average, or 800,000 turbots.
> "Brills and Mullets—1,500 tons, 3 lbs. each, or 1,220,000 brills and mullets.
> "Oysters—309,935 (double) bushels, 4 pecks to a bushel, 33 dozen or 400 oysters to a peck, or 495,896,000 oysters.
> "Lobsters—1,200,000.
> "Crabs—600,000.
> "Prawns—12 tons, 120 to 1 lb., or 3,225,600 prawns.
> "Shrimps—192,295 gallons, 324 to a pint or 498,428,640 shrimps."

The great supply of the staple descriptions of fish to Billingsgate is from the fishermen of Barking, in Essex. On a visit which I paid there, in the course of my inquiries among the ballast-heavers last winter, it happened to be the first frost of any intensity or continuance in the season, and the whole population seemed astir collecting ice. Women and boys were breaking it, numbers of men were throwing or lifting it into carts, and even wheelbarrows, for all kinds of vehicles were in requisition, and some of the roads were all but impassable from the number of ice carriages of every kind. The ice was carried to the ice-houses of the fishing-smack proprietors, where it was to be reserved for the warmer seasons. It is sent out in the smacks and the fish is packed in it—such as is not brought alive—to be the better preserved. When the English winter is mild, the fishing-smack proprietors are at considerable expense in obtaining ice from Norway or other foreign countries.

There has been much legislation concerning the fisheries of the country, more especially as regards herrings, and with no very beneficial, and often with mischievous results. I have now the satisfaction of giving the following communication from Mr. J. E. Saunders, jun., of Lower Thames-street, a gentleman whose opinions on the subject are entitled to the highest consideration:—

"The history of the rise and progress of that branch of the British fisheries employed in catching live fish for the supply of the London markets, presents many changes in its mode of operations, and the improved construction of its vessels; still it has not kept pace with the improvements in agriculture or the advancement in science, and there are many valuable fishing banks around the British Isles which are yet unexplored, and in the North Sea alone upwards of twelve thousand acres of fishing ground, capable of yielding a large supply of wholesome fish-food, for the rapidly increased population of London and its environs, if means could be devised for its speedy transit to a market. The facilities of rail-roads have done much to prove this by the encouragement thus given to the boat fishermen on our coasts, who at times have forwarded by this speedy conveyance vast quantities of fish to London, though the quality is very inferior to those which are caught by our welled smacks on the Dogger and other banks off the east coast of England, and thus imported alive to the London market. Yet it is to be feared that this valuable class of deep sea fishermen must relinquish their pursuits, and this fine nursery for seamen be broken up, unless the power of steam be applied, with the patent screw-propeller, to these welled smacks, as an auxiliary to their excellent sailing qualities, so as to enable them to overcome the disadvantages under which they now labour from contrary winds or calms, and the losses they sustain from delay and dead fish, together with the expensive nature of their vessels, and the large crews they must maintain, to procure the fish alive from the open sea."

The principal articles purchased by the costermongers, the chief Billingsgate customers, for sale to the poor, are fresh and red herrings, soles, sprats, plaice, cod (when cheap), mackerel, haddocks, eels—they buy *all* the small eels in the market—mussels, whelks, periwinkles (winks), shrimps, oysters—indeed they buy *all* the oysters—and crabs (when cheap). Salmon, lobsters, and flounders, they buy only when cheap, and then they buy largely.

Fresh herrings vary in price from 1s. to 7s. the hundred of 120. They have been as low as 1s. this season, and have been retailed in the streets at twenty for 4d. Great quantities are taken into the country, where the fish has a ready sale, as the farm labourers, &c., have rarely other means of procuring them.

Red herrings vary in price from 1s. 6d. to 5s. the hundred, the actual number of 100 being given of them. The barrels contain 600 to 1,000 herrings; the barrel is sold with the fish. The half-barrel contains 300 to 500.

Bloaters vary from 4s. to 12s. the hundred of the actual number. They are always sold in pads. The Jews make "Whitechapel bloaters" cheap, but they will not keep, although they look well.

Soles vary in price, in pads containing from 3 to 4 dozen, from 1s. 6d. to 8s., according to the supply, the size, and the quality. Perhaps the cheapness of this fish, compared with the prices of a few years back, is more remarkable than that of any other. Soles are sold by the bummarees and fishmongers at Billingsgate, in dozen and half-dozen pairs, from 1s. to 6s. the dozen pairs.

Sprats are sold, when first introduced, in baskets weighing from 50 lbs. to 65 lbs., the price varying from 9s. to 12s., and then they are retailed at the shops at 2d. to 3d. the pound. They were formerly sold by the plateful, but now much more frequently by the pound, as many of the costermongers have done for some years. Soon afterwards they are brought in boats, and sold by the toss, or chuck, at 2s. 6d. the toss, which is the half bushel; they sink to 2s., 1s. 6d., and 1s.; but a bushel (two tosses) must be bought when the price is only 1s. Very large quantities of sprats are smoked, chiefly by the costermongers.

Plaice, in pads, vary in price from 1s. 6d. to 14s. A pad weighs from 30 lbs. to 40 lbs.; 5s. is an average price. The number of fish is of course dependent on their size.

Cod is bought by the single fish, or in pairs, half dozens or dozens. Lately they were bought from 1s. 6d. to 2s. 6d. the pair, weighing about 12 lbs. to 15 lbs. each fish. A good sized cod fish weighs 20 lbs. The price varies less than it did, but it still fluctuates. Two years back, one of my informants paid 10s. 6d. for a pair of cod-fish; on the following morning he bought as good fish for 2s. the pair. Codlings are sold in the same proportion, but seldom in smaller number than half dozens. Dried cod is sold in quarters (quarter of a hundred weight, or 28 lbs.) from 1d. to 2d. the lb. The consumption is very great among the Irish in London, and the principal purchasers of it at Billingsgate are Irish costermongers.

Mackerel (another fish remarkable for reduction in price and increase of supply) is sold in pads containing 60 (a half hundred), 90, or 120 fish, more or less; sometimes three or four less, but rarely more. The prices vary exceedingly, from 5s. to 20s. the sixty. When the price is down at 15s. the fishmongers purchase very little, the trade being then almost entirely in the hands of the costermongers for street sale. As small a number as 15 (called a quartern) may sometimes be bought of a Billingsgate salesman. At any time a bummaree will sell that quantity.

Haddocks (fresh) are purchased in pads, or by the dozen, varying in price from 1s. to 7s. the pad. Smoked haddocks are sold in barrels and half barrels, containing 25 to 40 dozen in a barrel. The usual price is £2 2s.; sometimes they are as low as 18s., or even 14s. The best are Scotch, but large quantities are now smoked and cured by the Jews and the London costermongers, and they are generally proclaimed "real Scotch." Codlings and a few whitings are frequently smoked in the same manner, and sold as smoked Scotch haddocks, but the flavour is much inferior. Mackerel and soles are also smoked for sale, a trade which is increasing. The bummarees sell the smoked haddocks at Billingsgate by the dozen, from 6d. to 4s. Until three years ago they were sold by the score; now they are never so sold.

Flounders are sold in small baskets, containing three dozen and upwards, from 6d. to 1s. 6d. the basket. This fish is usually sold alive. When dead the lowest price (6d.) can only be attained.

Eels are bought from the Dutch boats, only the larger fish being sold in Billingsgate-market. The average price through the year is 5s.

the draft of 20 lbs. of small eels. About one-fifth of the eels when sold by the Dutch are dead, and they are charged 2s. 6d. the draft. Seven years ago the average was 3s. 6d. per draft, and the rise in price is attributed to the great and increased demand for the cheap eel-pie shops; one man serving the pie shops will sometimes buy 50 drafts in a morning, and seldom fewer than thirty. The highest price of the best and largest eels is about 15s. the draft.

Mussels are bought by the half-peck, peck, and bushel, from 4d. to 7d. the half-peck, which contains between seven and eight quarts. They are also sold in bags at the same price in proportion.

Whelks are bought by "the measure," or half-peck of seven quarts. The price averages 14d. the measure, the year through, or twice the price of mussels. The whole supply is bought by the costermongers. They are sold too by "the wash" of four pecks. Half of those sold at Billingsgate to the costermongers are alive; the other half are "cooked" (boiled). Pickled whelks are among the delicacies of the poor.

Periwinkles are also sold by "the measure," or half-peck. The price varies from 9d. to 1s., and is generally highest on a Saturday. The trade in "winks," as this shell-fish dainty is called by its retailers in the streets, is also almost entirely in the costermongers' hands. They are also sold by the wash, and are all bought alive.

Shrimps are sold in as small a quantity as a pint, and also in quarts, half-gallons, or gallons. The regular measure is observed. The gallon (4 quarts) varies in price, for Yarmouth prawns, from 5d. to 18d. The finer qualities are from 10d. to 2s. 6d. the gallon. The wash of eight gallons is sold a little over.

Oysters can be bought by peck or bushel, varying from 10s. to 36s. the bushel, according to the quality. The bushel is about six pecks.

Crabs are sold by the half dozen, dozen, or score, at from 2s. to 10s. the dozen. They are sold also in baskets containing 8 dozen or upwards. The smaller crabs are all purchased by the little shopkeepers at from 6d. to 1s. the measure (half peck). They are retailed to children.

Lobsters can be purchased by the pair, dozen, or score, from 1s. to 2s. 6d. the pair. The small lobsters are sold at from 3s. to 12s. the score. They are all sold alive at Billingsgate, as are the crabs.

Of Salmon I have already spoken.

The other fish are disposed of after the same manner as those I have enumerated, and are subject to similar variations in price.

The Morning Chronicle, Thursday, December 12, 1850.

To the EDITOR of the MORNING CHRONICLE.

Sir—As you have in many instances kindly become the almoner of those whose attention has been directed by the letters of your Special Correspondent to cases of distress, I should feel greatly indebted to you if you could convey, in such manner as your discretion may point out, the enclosed sum of 5*l.* to the drover mentioned in your paper of Nov. 21, as not knowing what Christianity is. It is impossible to expect that a labouring man could under such circumstances give the time necessary to his instruction without the means of subsistence being supplied to him by those who pity his spiritual destitution; and it is with the view of enabling him to do so that I am desirous of transmitting through you the enclosed sum. It is probable that the case may attract the notice of some clergyman who understands that it is his duty to give to such a person the needful instruction, and who might learn from you the person so unhappily distinguished by a destitution which is much worse than the destitution of bread.

SCYPHAX.

[The man referred to by "Scyphax" has been sought out, and the 5*l.* enclosed in the above is being employed in the way desired. Does the writer wish for the address of the drover?]

The Morning Chronicle, Monday, February 17, 1851.

To the EDITOR of the MORNING CHRONICLE.

Sir—You have lately done so much for the many distressed individuals who became known to you during your researches among the London poor, that I am emboldened to bring the following case of melancholy, and, in some of its features, curiously exceptional distress under your notice and that of the public. I give a plain brief narrative, omitting names and addresses, which, however, I enclose to you separately for your satisfaction, and in order that due inquiry may be made.

Some fifteen months ago a small commission agent, with a wife and four children, determined to emigrate to Australia. He could only raise funds sufficient for his own passage, and for the purchase of the small portion of land to which he hoped soon to be able to have his wife and family conveyed. Arrived at Adelaide, he was attacked by fever, which prostrated him for upwards of three months.

The seaboard portion of the colony is of course expensive, and this unfortunate malady exhausted all the poor fellow's reserved means. He rose from his bed penniless, and was obliged to gain his daily bread by manual labour as a farm servant. In the meantime his family, of course, received no remittances from Australia, and had no means of going out. After the husband's departure, the poor woman lay in of twins. One of these has since been adopted by a relative, but she is now burdened with the support of five very young children. When her husband left her she had a respectably furnished house. Article by article has, as might be expected, gone. She is now permitted, by the charity of her landlord, to remain in the empty house until a new tenant be forthcoming—and there, early and late, she toils to support herself and her five children by the needle. The amount she can earn by working late into the night, is, of course, hardly sufficient to keep the poor family above starvation level.

Still she is not quite without resources. From the sale of her furniture, and by the kindness of friends, she has managed to raise about £25. Another sum of £20 or £25, would enable the wife and children to join their husband and father. Should they not be succoured in this time of their distress the little hoard in question must soon be dissipated, and then the workhouse stares them in the face.

A ship, sir, sails for Adelaide at the end of the month. Half the passage money is, as I have said, accumulated. Could the other half be raised by the aid of benevolent individuals, an unfortunate but deserving family would be saved from utter and absolute ruin, and holy household ties be prevented from being snapped for ever.

I am, sir, &c.,

G. M.

[Inquiry has been made into the correctness of the above statement. In all respects it is strictly and literally true; and we shall be happy to furnish names and addresses to any persons who may be disposed to inquire into the circumstances of the case.]

The Morning Chronicle, Tuesday, February 18, 1851.

We have to acknowledge the sum of two pounds (from two ladies in Middle Scotland-yard, Whitehall) for the poor woman who wishes to join her husband in Australia.

The Morning Chronicle, Wednesday, February 19, 1851.

Besides the £2, acknowledged yesterday, from two ladies in Middle Scotland-yard, the following sums have been received for this poor woman:—

The Dowager Countess and Lady Ashburnham £2   0 0
W. T.   1   0 0
O. E. 0 10 0

The Morning Chronicle, Saturday, February 22, 1851.

A HARD CASE.

To the EDITOR of the MORNING CHRONICLE.

Sir—I enclose £5 for the woman whose case appears in *The Morning Chronicle* of the 17th, in a letter by G. M.; and shall be much obliged to you to take charge of it for her.

E. C.

To the EDITOR of the MORNING CHRONICLE.

Sir—I enclose the sum of £1 for the poor woman who wishes to join her husband in Australia, mentioned in a letter on Wednesday last, the 19th inst., headed "A Hard Case," and signed "G. M." An acknowledgment in your paper will oblige,

Sir, your obedient servant,

Feb. 21.						G. H.

E. B. encloses a sovereign to the Editor of *The Morning Chronicle* for the poor woman who wishes to join her husband at Adelaide.

M. C. £2

The Morning Chronicle, Monday, February 24, 1851.

A HARD CASE.

—◆—

A Gentleman begs to enclose half-a-sovereign for the use of the poor woman mentioned in *The Morning Chronicle* of February 19, under the head of "A Hard Case," to assist her to join her husband in Australia. He will feel obliged by the Editor acknowledging it in his paper.—Feb. 22, 1851.

Further subscriptions on behalf of the poor woman wishing to join her husband in Australia:—

M. C.	£20	0
E. P., for A.	0	10
C. ——, Melton Moubray	2	0
J. R.	2	2
Lord D.	1	0

The Morning Chronicle, Tuesday, February 25, 1851.

Additional sums received on account of the poor woman wishing to join her husband in Australia:—

C. A.	£1	0	0
R. N.	0	5	0

The Morning Chronicle, Wednesday, February 26, 1851.

A HARD CASE.

—◆—

We have received the following letter from Mrs. Yates, the wife of the small commission agent, to whose case public sympathy was invited by a correspondent some days ago:—

To the EDITOR of the MORNING CHRONICLE.

Sir—Will you allow me to express my deep gratitude, in giving publicity to my case, thus preserving myself and little family from want, and enabling us, through a kind and benevolent public, to join my husband in a distant land? The contrast of our situation is indeed great, sir, through your generous interference; a few days since, sinking with fatigue, care, and anxiety—now possessed of every reasonable comfort for myself and little ones on our voyage. I shall, sir, feel still more deeply indebted if you will allow a public insertion of my thanks to those who have, in the hour of need, stepped forward to my assistance. With sincere thanks, I remain, sir, yours obediently,

E. YATES.

Feb. 25.

The following further subscriptions have been received:—

H. D. H., Sherborne, Dorset £1   0
Miss H.,   ditto 0 10

Henry Mayhew

Henry Mayhew was born in London in 1812 and came from a large family. Against his father's wishes he, along with four of his brothers, chose a literary career over the law and was subsequently disinherited.

He had an interesting start to working life, being sent to sea by his parents, but later established himself as a highly regarded dramatist, journalist and author. His reputation as a social investigative journalist grew from his extensive, admirable and compassionate original investigation into the London poor as part of *The Morning Chronicle's* "Labour and the Poor" series. His reputation was further enhanced by his own self-published "London Labour and the London Poor" voluminous series.

He co-founded *Punch* in 1841, the famous satirical magazine, and was a member of an extraordinary group of Victorian writers which included Charles Dickens and William Makepeace Thackeray. Some of Dickens' scenes are reputedly inspired by Henry Mayhew's investigations and it is for his work amongst the poor that he will be remembered as a true pioneer.

The following is a contemporary piece, written in 1856, on Henry Mayhew:—

Men of the Time, 1856.

HENRY MAYHEW.

MAYHEW, HENRY, Author, and one of the most original writers of the present day, was born in London on the 25th of November, 1812. His birth had nearly taken place in a private box of Covent Garden Theatre during a pantomime, and it is to this accident that he facetiously attributes his great love of the humorous, and his taste for dramatic literature. He was educated at Westminster, where Mr. Gilbert A'Beckett and Mr. Thomas Arnold (both magistrates now) were his schoolfellows. Twice did he run away from school—twice was he pardoned; but finding that the birch—at that time a large branch of the tree of knowledge, and the chosen instrument for inculcating in boys the spirit of forgiveness—made but little impression on his tender mind, his parents sent him to sea; it being a cherished paternal notion less than half-a-century ago that there was no school of reformation so effectual as that of the cockpit of a man-of-war. The morality of this school was such, that on the second day everything he had was stolen; and when he came back in a twelvemonth from Calcutta, so destitute was he that the very shirt he had on belonged to a "fellow-middy," who called two days afterwards to reclaim it, "as he could not spare it any longer." To complete the boy's reformation he was articled to his father, at whose office he did penance for three long subpœnaing years. He then went to Wales, changing his attention from clients to sheep; and finished his dreams and speculations amidst the goats and

mountains by coming back to London, and taking, in partnership
with Mr. Gilbert A'Beckett, the Queen's Theatre. Their joint fortune
was sixpence and two or three manuscript pieces. At that theatre he
produced the "Wandering Minstrel,"—a farce that has been acted
oftener than any other of the present day. Previous to this he had
assisted in establishing "Figaro in London," the father of "Punch,"
and the forerunner of modern satirical publications. As, several years
afterwards, in 1841, Mr. Henry Mayhew framed, built, and manned
"Punch," and was the first to launch it into popular favour, to him
belongs the credit of being the parent of the two cleverest satirical
journals that have enjoyed the greatest longevity and success in this
country. He was the first to prove in journalism that satire could be
conducted without personality, and that humour did not necessarily
consist in sneering at morality. Others have profited by the chart
which he laid down for the navigation of "Punch," and although
most of the crew that sailed with him at first still remain in the old
ship, yet he, their original commander, is no longer at the helm. A
quarrel with the proprietors made him secede from the publication,
and since that period Mr. Henry Mayhew has published works in
his own name; his reputation, if not his pocket, gaining largely by
the exchange. He has written dramas for the stage—he has engaged
in educational controversies—he has contributed to papers and
magazines innumerable—he has started a Pharaoh's host of reviews
and periodicals, all of which have been long since swallowed up in
the (un)Red Sea of literature; and in his time has known all the ups
and downs that mark, as in a "Bradshaw's Guide," the pages of a
literary man's career. In truth, the list of his works would be almost
Alexandre-Dumasian in its length; but amongst the most popular
may be enumerated "The Greatest Plague of Life, or the Adventures
of a Mistress in Search of a Good Servant;" "Whom to Marry,
and How to get Married;" and "The Image of his Father." These,
written in conjunction with his younger brother Augustus, enjoyed
an extensive popularity; and "The Greatest Plague" sold more copies
than any other serial since the days of "Pickwick." Then there were
a variety of Christmas books, such as the "Magic of Industry," and
the "Magic of Kindness;" besides innumerable almanacs and minor
publications, both comic and serious, in which he was generally aided
by the suggestive pencil of his friend, George Cruikshank. However,
the *magnum opus* of Mr. Henry Mayhew is, undoubtedly, the series
of investigations he commenced in the "Morning Chronicle," under

the title of "London Labour and the London Poor." These brought
to light, out of the garrets, and cellars, and all the dark corners of the
metropolis, where Misery is apt to crouch and hide itself, so startling
a mass of revelations, as to the struggles, privations, and heroic
sacrifices of the poorest of the working classes, that Mr. Mayhew
may be said to have discovered a new world—a new London in the
very heart of London, of which no Londoner was previously aware.
He established by himself, as it were, a Committee of Inquiry into
the state of poverty in the metropolis; and visiting the poor needlewomen, the half-starved tailors, the broken-hearted prostitutes, in
their own desolate homes, took the evidence from their trembling
lips, leaving them to tell their own tale of wretchedness in their own
piteous manner. For two years he persevered in this holy mission,
penetrating into haunts where no literary man had ever penetrated
before, relieving the unfortunate, feeding the hungry, lifting up the
fallen, and extending the hand of pity to all, even to the most abject
outcasts of society; such as philanthropy oftentimes turns away from
in sheer despair, as being almost beyond the reach of redemption.
He was the benevolent Howard of pauperism; and the awful scenes
of misery he had daily to encounter, and like a moral physician to
probe and examine, and give clinical lectures upon, whilst the poor
patient was all but dying of exhaustion, would have sickened any
other heart less sustained with the holiness of the work he was intent
upon. It was a mission of ennobling charity, such as many ministers
would be proud to have recorded in their biographies. In any other
country, Mr. Mayhew would have been assisted in his labours by the
Government; for, in truth, he was doing government work without
receiving government wages. As it is, his history of poverty is,
unfortunately, incomplete; and of the grand monument he wished to
erect as a beacon, as a lighthouse, for society, there remains at present
nothing beyond the mere foundation; a foundation that sufficiently
indicates the dangerous nature of the locality, but provides no kind
of refuge for those who may be wrecked upon it. It is to be hoped
that Mr. Henry Mayhew will one day finish the curious structure;
so that Belgravia, by looking at it after dinner, may learn now and
then how Bethnal Green lives and starves. Ever since the period that
Mr. Mayhew was obliged to abandon the grand plan on which he
was anxious to set the seal of his fame he has been engaged on various
literary works, amongst the most successful of which have been the
"Peasant-Boy Philosopher," the "Wonders of Science;" but still his

other productions, with all the glittering brightness of success upon them, appear pale when examined in the pure light of the noble work that his genius endowed, as a rich man endows a hospital, to receive the complaints and heal the wounds of the suffering poor. Mr. Henry Mayhew has had two great triumphs in his time, and triumphs gathered in totally different paths of literature,—he has been the originator both of "Punch" and "London Labour and the Poor."

Punch, Saturday, August 6, 1887.

HENRY MAYHEW.

Born, 1812. Died, 1887.

"The Mayhew Brothers." A familiar phrase
On all men's lips in *Punch's* earlier days,
Suggesting pleasant wit and genial mirth.
Green grow the grass and lightly lie the earth
Above the latest of the brilliant band!
Punch's first pages knew that skilful hand.
Henry the shrewd, and gentle Horace both
Watched o'er its birth, and helped its budding growth,
Not long, indeed, yet lovingly. Farewell!
The record of the age's course will tell
Of him whose name a double honour bore,
Comrade of *Punch*, and champion of the poor.

Index

For information on these and other titles available please visit:

DittoBooks.co.uk

www.ingramcontent.com/pod-product-compliance
Lightning Source LLC
Chambersburg PA
CBHW051537030726
47592CB00001B/10